Broadcast Writing

Consulting Editor in Journalism
Peter Sandman

Broadcast Writing

Principles and Practice

Roger L. Walters
California State University, Sacramento

McGRAW-HILL PUBLISHING COMPANY
New York   St. Louis   San Francisco   Auckland
Bogotá   Caracas   Hamburg   Lisbon   London
Madrid   Mexico   Milan   Montreal   New Delhi
Oklahoma City   Paris   San Juan   São Paulo
Singapore   Sydney   Tokyo   Toronto

PHOTO CREDITS
Cover photos, clockwise from top left: Tyrone Hall/Stock, Boston; Ken Robert Buck/The Picture Cube; Charles Harbutt/Archive; Stanley Rowin/The Picture Cube.

Figure 7.1: (left) Ed Carlin/The Picture Cube; (right) Horst Schafer/Peter Arnold. Figure 7.2: (top left) Joel Gordon; (top right) John Maher/Stock, Boston; (bottom) Elizabeth Hamlin/Stock, Boston. Figure 7.3: (left) Nancy Durrell McKenna/Photo Researchers; (right) Random House photo by Elyse Rieder. Figures 7.4 and 7.5: Joel Gordon. Figure 7.6: Random House photo by Elyse Rieder. Figure 7.7: (top) Alan Carey/The Image Works; (bottom) Frank Siteman/The Picture Cube. Figures 7.8, 7.9, 7.16, 12.2, 12.3, 12.4, and 12.5; Random House photos by Elyse Rieder.

First Edition
98765432
BROADCAST WRITING

Library of Congress Cataloging in Publication Data

Walters, Roger L.
    Broadcast writing.

    Bibliography: p.
    Includes index.
    1. Broadcasting—Authorship.   I. Title.
PN1990.9.A88W3   1987   808′.066791   87-9784
ISBN 0-07-555477-1

Text Design: Ehn Graphics, Inc.
Cover Design: Marsha Cohen

To my wife Judy, my daughter Patricia,
and to the memories of my late wife Georgia
and my mother.

Preface

This book is based on the range of experiences and writing tasks I have faced during more than fifteen years as a program producer, director, writer, and administrator in commercial and educational broadcasting, and an equal span of years teaching, among other courses, an introductory course in broadcast writing. In addition, there are the experiences, and a few of the scripts, of my students woven into the fabric of this text.

It is my firm belief that writing is a craft that can be learned, but not taught. A text can guide, point out pitfalls, suggest things to consider, and establish criteria for evaluation. But you will learn to write only through extensive practice, whether in course assignments or on the job.

Practice will be more valuable, of course, if it is accompanied by some form of feedback. If you are in a course, this feedback will come from an instructor. If you are an intern working in a professional environment, it will come from a supervisor. If you have already begun a professional career, feedback will come from more experienced colleagues.

And feedback will come from this text, which can help you in several ways. It describes principles and practices that are followed in the industry and provides reasons why those principles are important and those practices are followed. Broadcast writing does not take place in a vacuum. It is part of a larger process that involves the preparation of content for programs, and the delivery of those programs to audiences through electronic systems. The writer must have a good, broad understanding of that whole process to prepare copy successfully.

This book also sets forth criteria for good writing that you can use to evaluate your own work. It gives examples of structure, style, and content from actual broadcasts. And it relates the writer's role both to the sponsors of broadcasts and to the interests of the users of broadcasts, the audiences.

In preparing this text I have made certain assumptions. The first is that you, the reader, are interested in a career in broadcasting in which writing will be at least a portion of your job. This book will discuss the problems writers face in real world situations. It will show you how to analyze those situations to produce the best scripts.

A second assumption is that you already have a reasonable command of the English language (that is, of grammar, syntax, vocabulary, etc.). This book is not a grammar text; we do not include text or exercises that review fundamentals of language.

Features of the Text

Several features set this text apart from others in the field. The first and most obvious is its emphasis on principles. My point, on which I will elaborate in the introduction to Part 2 (''Principles'') is this: There are principles of writing for radio, TV, and cable that are peculiar to those delivery systems and to the way their audiences receive and process information. The characteristics of the media and of audience behavior, taken together, dictate broad principles writers must understand and apply if they are to be successful.

I believe these principles are not tied to any one program type or style of copy. That is, there is not one set of principles for dramatic writing and a different set for documentaries, or for news, or for interviews. Certain principles may be more important, or more obvious perhaps, in writing certain types of copy, and each type of program does have certain strengths and weaknesses. But most of the principles of good writing can, and should, be applied to most program types.

A second feature of this text is the strong relationship that has been built between writing and production. This is not a production book; it does not attempt to provide detailed instruction on the use of the facilities of broadcasting, such as microphones, cameras, or recorders. But I have tried to show how the writer's task is affected—perhaps facilitated, perhaps impeded, but always affected—by the production process. For example, different forms of continuity are required for programs that are aired live than for those that are pre-recorded. These distinctions are made throughout.

Similarly, I believe writers must understand how much their jobs are shaped by the business of broadcasting, by the demands of sponsors and the requirements of programmers and managers. I will digress frequently from the specifics of writing to place that task in the larger contexts of programming and advertising. I will also emphasize the purposes intended when programs are aired.

I likewise feel that writers need an equally clear understanding of how programs and announcements are perceived and used by audiences. Broadcast communication is incomplete and ineffective if it doesn't reach, satisfy, and even persuade audiences. Writers must know how to use the tools that accomplish those results.

My emphasis is on *process*. It is not only on what you may be expected to write, and how to do that, but also on how to analyze each task, how to apply the principles that are presented, and why. If you think about what you write, and why you write it, it will be much easier to learn to write in a creative way. This emphasis on process is also a unique feature of this text.

Plan of the Book

Chapter Organization

The book is organized into four parts and eighteen chapters. Part 1 consists of an introductory chapter, an overview of the communication process as it applies to the broadcast media. That overview establishes the relationships among the principles that will be presented in subsequent chapters. It also provides an opportunity to define terms and make distinctions that we will use throughout the remainder of the book.

Part 2—"Principles"—consists of nine chapters. It begins with a discussion of aural style. Most broadcast content, even for visual media like television, is processed by audiences through their sense of hearing. The importance of writing for the audience's ears is therefore emphasized early in the sequence.

Next I examine the relationship between writing and production. Then, since the method of production used to prepare a program has a substantial bearing on the form of scripts and on the detail that may be required in a script, there follows a chapter entitled "Script Mechanics." That chapter covers script layout and other matters such as punctuation and using abbreviations. The organization of programs and their content to attract and maintain audience attention is the subject of Chapter 5—"Program Structure."

The next two chapters examine in detail the ways in which writers manage the two senses—sound and sight—in scripts and in program production. Chapter 6—"Handling Sound"—reviews the uses of sound effects, music, and voice when used for its sound value. Chapter 7—"Handling Visuals"—presents basic principles of visual grammar.

Industry practices are then discussed in two chapters. Chapter 8 covers sponsors and their purposes. It considers how management and programming decisions affect program content and therefore the writer's role. We then reverse the perspective and examine programming and writing from the audience's point of view in Chapter 9—"Audiences and Their Expectations." The final chapter in Part 2 looks at how sponsors attempt to accomplish their purposes, with an overview of the uses of persuasion in broadcast messages.

In Part 3 the chapters are organized using, roughly, the traditional division of communication into persuasive, informational, and entertainment forms. In broadcasting, persuasive content is usually presented in the form of announcements, including commercials, public service announcements, promos, and editorials. Those are the focus of the chapter on persuasive content—Chapter 11.

Informational programs are covered in four chapters. News writing is the subject of Chapter 12, with concentration on the structure and writing of individual news stories.

Talks, interviews, and discussions, in one form or another, make up a significant portion of broadcast station schedules. The research and writing required to prepare these programs successfully are covered in Chapter 13.

Chapter 14 considers documentary programs. Documentaries have significant similarities in content, form, appeal and audience with news, with talk shows, and with dramatic programs, but there are also unique features that justify their separate consideration.

Corporate/instructional scriptwriting is discussed in Chapter 15. These are the scripts written for presentations to corporate clients or employees, to patients or to staffs of hospitals, to customers in a store considering the purchase of a major item, and so on. These scripts may be persuasive, and occasionally, entertaining, but most often they are informational, so we include them in this general group.

By far the largest number of broadcast programs have entertainment as their primary purpose, but many types of entertainment programs do not require formally written scripts. One major type of entertainment program which does require careful scripting is the drama, discussed in Chapter 16. The beginning writer is not likely to have much opportunity to write full dramatic scripts, but some emphasis is placed on the topic because the techniques of dramatic writing may be used in other program forms. For example, dramatic vignettes are a common and effective way of attracting attention within commercial announcements.

In concluding this part several other types of programs are discussed briefly in Chapter 17, including programs for women, children, and minority audiences, and musical and variety programs. The emphases are on the specific applications of structure to meet the demands of the program form and on the gratifications necessary to reach the audiences for which these programs are intended.

The final part, consisting of one final chapter, presents to the student some concerns about broadcast writing as a career. What may a writer expect from the industry he or she serves, and what will the industry expect in turn? Some ethical issues that individuals will have to face when they enter the industry professionally are also briefly raised.

Using This Book

It would be nice if all of the groups of principles presented in the chapters of Part 2 could be presented simultaneously, for all of them do interact with one another. Further, you would then be able to apply them all at once to whatever project or assignment you might have. It is not possible to do that; of necessity they must be presented in discrete chapters, and sequentially.

It is also necessary that you combine the consideration of these principles with the writing of particular types of copy. The theoretical study of the principles of good writing doesn't have much practical significance until one begins to apply those principles. Persuasive appeals have to be applied to persuasive copy—commercials or public service announcements. The principles of structure have to be considered in relation to particular types of programs that you may be preparing, be that a talk show, a drama, a documentary, or whatever. Therefore, you will need to combine readings from the genre chapters in Part 3 simultaneously with your study of the various chapters of principles.

If you are using the book as a text in an organized course, your instructor may choose to begin consideration of the principles of writing at any one of a number of entry points—not necessarily in the chapter order presented. For example, an instructor might prefer to begin by discussing aural style (Chapter 2) as it relates to the writing of news copy (Chapter 12), or perhaps to consider target audiences and persuasive appeals (Chapters 9 and 10) as those considerations affect the writing of announcements (Chapter 11).

If you are not reading this book as an assigned text, you are of course free to approach it as you choose. I suggest you skim through the chapters of Parts 1 and 2 first, so that you have some grasp of what is included there—how the various clusters of principles relate to each other and to the practical tasks of preparing copy. Then, as you attempt to write for any particular form, you can refer back to those principles you find most important to your task.

Other Features

Exercises are provided at the end of each chapter. If you are using this book as a text, some of these may be assigned by your instructor. If not, I encourage you to attempt some of them anyway. Practice is the only way you can learn to write.

Some of the exercises are intended to guide you through the process of research and decision making that must take place before actual script writing can begin. In the industry, professionals often make these judgments without conscious thought, but for beginners these exercises will help ''talk you through'' to the point where writing begins.

The remaining exercises mirror, as much as possible, the actual tasks writers face in the industry. They are also broadly described, to allow opportunity for you to seek creative solutions.

Supplementary exercises and suggested classroom activities are contained in the *Instructor's Manual*.

A list of key terms and concepts is included for each chapter. They provide a good self-test. If you can define each one and explain its significance to broadcast writing, you will know that you have a solid understanding of that chapter's contents.

Bibliographies for each chapter are placed at the back of the book. If, as is our assumption, you aspire to a career in broadcast writing, you will need a substantial personal library, for both inspiration and reference. The ''inspiration'' will be needed when you are faced with a writing task that you just can't find a good approach for. You can turn to other writers who have faced similar problems and see how they solved them. References, of course, are for checking—on style, grammar, layout, etc.

If you were to purchase all of the books listed for each chapter's bibliography it would be very expensive, and very difficult, for some are out of print. But I urge you to begin to collect for your personal library.

The *Instructor's Manual* also provides a bibliography of teaching and learning resources, examination questions, model course outlines, and some suggestions on evaluating student work.

Acknowledgments

My own career as broadcaster and educator has been influenced by three professors with whom I was fortunate to study. All three were outstanding teachers, who inspired the desire to learn in their students. They are Stanley Donner, with whom I studied at Stanford University, Harrison Summers at Ohio State University, and Kenneth Harwood, then at the University of Southern California.

Dr. Summers' ability to outline complex topics is directly reflected in several chapters of this text. The organization of Chapter 6 on program structure and the concepts of sponsorship in Chapter 8 and audience gratifications in Chapter 9 are based on materials originally presented in his courses although newer information has been added.

A number of professional broadcasters have contributed their own work or collected examples from colleagues. Their contributions are greatly appreciated. Examples of announcements were provided by Walt Shaw, KRAK, and Tom Chase, KWOD, both Sacramento, and by Frank LaRosa and Ed Goldman, who operate their own advertising and public relations businesses. The editorials are from KTXL, Sacramento, contributed by Cal Bolwinkle. Mike Koelker, with Foote, Cone and Belding/Honig San Francisco, contributed several TV photoboards.

News copy has come largely from KCRA-TV, Sacramento, collected by Steve Haskins, Executive Producer. Other items were provided by Dru Doyle at KXPR, Dick Cable at KXTV, and Don Ross at KTXL, all Sacramento.

The barter scam series in our documentary chapter is the work of Brad Willis, made available by his station, WFAA, Dallas.

The dramatic example from *Riptide* was supplied by J. Rickley Dumm, producer for that series, who also reviewed the content of the chapter on dramatic writing.

Chapter 7 ("Handling Visuals") is very largely the creation of Kent Lacin. I'm pleased to be able to preserve in that chapter the ideas Kent has presented so successfully in guest lectures for my classes.

Some of the ideas in Chapter 2 ("Aural Style") and Chapter 6 ("Handling Sound") were originally presented by Albert Crews in his book *Professional Radio Writing*. His very perceptive thoughts about the process of writing for the ear are no longer available, since his book has long been out of print, but the basic ideas are still relevant, and we've attempted to show their continued importance to contemporary broadcast writing.

The research and publications of Jay Blumler have contributed a great deal to the portion of Chapter 9 that discusses audience gratifications. Dr. Blumler has been a leader in developing methods for gratifications research, and in evaluating and synthesizing conclusions from the many studies now appearing in the literature.

The impetus for this text came originally from Roth Wilkofsky, Executive Editor for Humanities, in the College Department. During the several years it has taken to get from ideas and outlines to this final stage Roth has continued to be enthusiastic and supportive. Peter Sandman, who is the consulting editor, has likewise been very helpful throughout. In particular I value his ability to explain to me, since I am new to textbook writing and publishing, the tremendous range of decisions and options that must be considered in preparing a work for publication. One might think that having written and produced innumerable radio and TV programs it would be easy to translate those experiences to a book. Not so, and Peter has helped immeasurably.

At various stages the proposal, drafts of selected chapters, and the manuscript were reviewed by colleagues from several universities. Their comments, too, have helped to settle the final focus and scope of this text. I gratefully acknowledge the assistance of Stanley Akers, University of Akron; Norma Champion, Evangel College; Sandra R. Davis, Savannah State College; James Ettema, Northwestern University; James E. Fletcher, University of Georgia; Michael Havice, Marquette

University; Robert Jones, University of Hawaii, Monoa; Bruce Klopfenstein, Bowling Green State University; Wayne R. Oates; W. James Potter, University of Florida, Gainesville; Myron B. Shaw, State University of New York, Geneseo; David Smith, Pine Manor College; Sarah Toppins, American University; Richard Uray, University of South Carolina; and Richard Vincent, University of Hawaii, Manoa.

Finally, I wish to acknowledge substantial assistance in preparing the manuscript, often under considerable pressure of time, from Vee Carney.

Roger L. Walters
Mendocino, Calif.

Contents

Part 1

The Process of Broadcast Communication

To be successful as a broadcast writer, you will need to understand not only the principles of good writing and their application to various types of content, but also how the broadcasting industry functions. Most of this book is devoted to the first two of these requirements—writing principles and their application to the more common types of programs. We will also consider, in later chapters, the respective roles of program originators (sponsors) and of receivers (audiences). We begin, however, with the broadest perspective, an overview of the process of communication as it applies to broadcasting, and even more specifically as it applies to writers and their scripts.

Chapter 1

Broadcast Communication: An Overview

Researchers who examine the process of communication have developed various theoretical models to explain that process. We have selected from several such models in constructing a simplified statement of broadcast communication. If you are already familiar with the basic practices of the industry, then so much the better. If not, then this chapter will help set the stage.

Components of the Communication Process

Almost all communication models divide the process into these four components: (1) the *origination*, or source, of the communication, (2) the communication itself, or *message*, (3) the *channel* through which the message is communicated, and (4) the *receiver*, or audience, for the message. Three other aspects of the process often considered are: (5) the *purpose* of the message, (6) the *effect* of the message on receivers, and (7) what mechanism, if any, is available for *feedback*—communication from the receiver(s) back to the source.

In this chapter we will examine each of these seven components, with particular attention to their role in American broadcasting and their impact on writers and writing.

Origination   In most of the forms of communication with which we are familiar, messages are originated by individuals. Certainly that is true of our most common form of communication, interpersonal conversation. In contrast, broadcast messages are invariably team efforts. Further in contrast, two very different activities are involved as co-equal parts of broadcast origination. The first may be characterized as *creative origination*. It includes the work of writers, directors, producers, and all the other creative people who plan and produce the programs and announcements that make up the schedules of radio and television stations and cable systems.

The second part of origination involves the people and agencies who pay for the materials that are aired. There would be no outlet for any creative effort if there were no one willing to pay, in some form, for the costs of production and distribution. Within this category of originator, we can include advertising agencies and their clients, and the managers and programmers of stations, networks, and cable systems, among others. Later we will introduce the term *sponsorship* as the appropriate label to distinguish between this aspect of broadcast origination and the creative side.

Note too that in broadcasting the concepts of origination, message, and channel tend to overlap. A broadcast station, for example, operates a transmitter which sends its programs through the air to its audience. That transmission represents its use of a communication channel. The station will also be the originator of much of the program content which appears on the channel. And the station will be identified in the minds of listeners or viewers primarily by the content of the messages or programs its presents.

Your understanding of broadcasting will be improved by keeping clear in your mind the distinction between stations, networks, and other agencies as originators, and many of the same organizations when they serve only as channels to distribute programs originated by others.

Message

Since the bulk of this book is devoted to techniques for creating successful broadcast messages, we need say little about them here, except to point out that writers are concerned not only with the content of messages, but also with the form, or package, in which that content is delivered. If that statement seems strange to you, let us quickly point out that in many cases the broadcast writer's job does not involve original, creative work, but rather is that of re-writing from other sources—that is, reworking the *form* in which the material is to appear. For example, the content of a news program may be supplied to a station by a news service, or information on an advertiser's campaign may be provided by that client or by a salesperson. In those situations the writer's job will be to reorganize the content and re-write it into an appropriate package—a program script or announcement.

Format

We have used the word *form* as a general term to refer to matters of structure, language, vocabulary, and so on, topics we will present in several chapters of this text. Another similar word common in the industry is *format*. In radio, format describes the "sound" or "image" of a station. We may speak of a "modern, country-Western" format, or an "all-news" format, or a "contemporary" format. The words aren't always very descriptive, they tend to change with time, and they have different meanings for different persons, but they are the shorthand by which radio stations describe themselves.

For individual programs, the term *format* has a different meaning. There it refers to the sequence or pattern the program commonly follows. A news program may have a format which calls for a two-minute opening, followed by two minutes of commercials, then five minutes of international news, then more commercials. That sequence is its format.

Writers, as we will see, use *format* with yet a third meaning, to refer to the way in which the elements of script copy are laid out on the typewritten page. Usually the context will make clear which meaning of *format* is intended.

Sources of Messages

The content of broadcasting can be easily divided into two categories, announcements and programs. Announcements are further divided into commercial advertisements, public service announcements (PSAs), and promotional announcements. Programs can be categorized by their content or form, which is a difficult task, as we shall see in a later chapter, or they may be described in relation to their source.

Programs originate from one of three basic kinds of sources, although there are many variations within this structure.

Most programs are *locally originated*—that is the content of a particular broadcast has been written and otherwise prepared for the air by the one local station (or cable channel) which will deliver it to the audience. By far the bulk of radio programming is handled this way; less so in television, because the costs of local production for television are so high.

In addition to local production, or in place of it, stations can also obtain programs through two national sources of distribution—*networks* and *syndication*.

We are all familiar with the three full-service TV networks—ABC, CBS, and NBC. These same companies, and others, also operate radio networks. The distinguishing feature of networks for both TV and radio is the *simultaneous* distribution of programs to multiple stations. (Although network programs are delayed to present them at the same hour in different time zones and are sometimes recorded and delayed by individual stations for local convenience, the intent of networking is simultaneous distribution, with the timeliness and the cost-effectiveness such distribution brings.)

Networks may be established for regularly scheduled programs and series, or set up for special, one-time programs such as major sports events. Cable program services like Cable News Network, Home Box Office, The Disney Channel, and others are also networks, but instead of distributing their programs to stations, they send them to the "head-ends" of local cable systems for final delivery to subscribers.

The major networks originate some of the programs they distribute, particularly news, documentary, and public affairs programs. They also purchase program series from independent production companies—that is, they purchase the rights to distribute the series over the network to the stations affiliated with that network. Prime-time entertainment programs seen on the networks are almost all obtained from independent producers.

The other source of national program material, and an alternative to network distribution, is program *syndication*. These series, like network program series, may be seen in many markets. But unlike network programming, a syndicated series will have been sold by its syndicator separately to individual stations in each market. Then each station makes its own decision on when and how often to use the series and its programs.

Two forms of syndication exist: (1) *first-run syndication*, in which the series is originated specifically for syndicated sale. Examples include many game shows, many types of radio features, "Dance Fever," and "Donahue"; (2) *off-network syndication,* reruns of programs originally broadcast by one of the networks. These include almost every situation comedy and dramatic series that had a reasonably long life on a network. Well-known examples would be "Star Trek," "M*A*S*H," and "Barney Miller." Not only are programs syndicated, so are program segments, new stories, and features that can be used by local stations within locally produced programs.

The Parsimony Principle

Networking and syndication are two of the methods by which broadcasting's tremendous appetite for programming is satisfied. To meet the demand, which requires that every TV and radio station and every cable origination channel have some form of programming every minute that it is one the air, programmers have devised a number of ingenious strategies. One broadcast educator has given the problem and the strategies used to solve it the label "the parsimony principle":

> This basic rule of broadcasting dictates that program material must be used up as *sparingly* as possible, *repeated* as often as possible, and *shared* as widely as possible.[1]

Being parsimonious not only means that content is stretched to cover more time, but that the costs of production can be spread over more stations, more broadcasts, and larger audiences.

In addition to networking and syndication, other examples of parsimony include disk jockey formats on radio, where the use of prerecorded music, and frequent repetition of that music, reduces costs considerably; soap opera dramas, which use small casts, a limited number of different settings, and a very slow-moving script; and news programs, in which major stories may be repeated several times during a block of programming with little or no rewriting.

Channel

Traditionally we think of radio and television as the channels of electronic communication. In recent years, however, these two have been both supplemented and challenged by several additional systems that deliver programs to audiences. Most important among these additional methods of delivery is cable. But the significance of, for example, home VCRs and the potential of direct satellite-to-home channels should not be overlooked.

VCRs make it possible for individuals to record programs to play back at more convenient times. With a VCR, you can select programs aired any time during the day or night, and view them when you want. You can also fast-forward through the commercials, a practice that very much disturbs advertisers. VCRs are also used extensively to distribute feature motion pictures and original programming directly to audiences, bypassing TV stations completely.

Direct satellite-to-home distribution (known as DBS, for direct broadcast satellite) is as yet only experimental, but it too bypasses traditional TV stations. (We are not considering here those who have satellite dishes and pick up directly from the satellite those programs intended to be redistributed by stations or cable systems.) If DBS programming does become widespread, it will not need traditional networks or stations to reach audiences. Those outlets then may have to reconsider what programs they can provide to remain in competition for audiences.

The term *broadcast* obviously is inaccurate when used to describe the total range of these systems, for broadcast is legally defined as delivery by radio transmission (over the air) of programs intended for general public use. Delivery via cable, or by the coded signal of a subscription television station, is therefore not truly broadcast. Yet no better single word has been proposed to describe the increasing diversity of electronic channels, so we will continue to use the word *broadcast*.* Understand, however, that we intend to include other electronic delivery channels as well.

As a writer, you should recognize that writing for the newer media will differ somewhat from writing for traditional radio and television. One difference which is already apparent is in the number of channels available. That increase is fragmenting audiences into smaller, more narrowly defined groups. You will be expected to target scripts to these specialized audiences.

Receivers

In broadcasting, receivers mean audiences. Although as we have just noted the absolute size of individual audiences is declining as the number of choices increases, broadcast audiences, television particularly, are still the largest and most undifferentiated of those for any mass medium. And audience size, the number of people watching or listening, is still the most important determiner of success in the business. For example:

> Programs survive in network television if they are able to carve out at least a 30 percent share of the audience; usually they are cancelled if they do not. The ground rules appear bizarre to those of us who consider a book a best-seller if it sells 100,000 copies or a recording a smash hit if it sells a million. On the network level, a prime time program is a failure if it reaches only 20 million viewers—an audience that would keep an average-sized Broadway theatre filled to capacity every performance for a quarter century.[2]

While size is still the most important yardstick when considering audiences, we believe that writers must also understand a number of concepts related to audience composition and behavior, and we will consider those in a separate chapter (Chapter 9).

Purpose

This aspect of the broadcast process is directly tied to that of origination. It is the originator's purpose with which we are concerned. Throughout this book, we will emphasize that the writer's job is performed in relation to goals and purposes set by other members of the origination teams—producers, managers, advertisers. In order to be a successful writer, and we will define success as the writing of copy that accomplishes the purpose intended by the originator, you

---

*The term *telecommunications* is now being used to label all the electronic media of communication, but just as broadcast may be too narrow, telecommunications is too broad for our purposes in this book, because it includes data transfer, computer networking, and other systems that do not involve the creative writing process.

must be able to identify clearly who the originators are for each piece of copy written, and then understand precisely what they want to accomplish.

Theorists often divide communication messages into three types, based on each message's intended purpose. They classify messages as being informative, entertaining, or persuasive. Although we too will use these categories, it is our position that the basic purpose of all broadcast communication is in some way persuasive. Content is produced and presented with the intent, first, of attracting audiences. Those audiences then are susceptible to more direct, obvious forms of persuasion, such as those presented in commercial announcements.

A news broadcast, for example, is a program in which the content is primarily information, but the station's purpose in presenting that information is persuasive. It wants to attract and hold an audience. An advertiser who buys a spot in that program does so to persuade the audience to purchase its product—or do whatever else the intent of that ad may be. And despite the value of the content of that news broadcast to the viewers, the station in all likelihood would remove that program from the air, or drastically revamp it, if the audience were to fall below a certain minimum size.

Similarly, a network television situation comedy may be seen as entertainment. Certainly audiences tune in to be entertained, or to receive some similar gratification. But just as with the news program, the network wants to persuade audiences to tune in, and any advertisers who purchase participations in the program want to persuade the viewers to their purposes. That program too will be removed if it fails to attract a substantial audience.

Even for noncommercial, nonprofit forms of broadcasting such as public television and radio, and cable systems with many channels of capacity, if programs are too esoteric and fail to draw at least reasonable-sized audiences, the pressures will mount to change programming, to reach more people and broader interests. The governments, foundations, and individuals who supply the funds for the operation of these channels can be just as hardnosed about getting some results (audience) for the funds expended as any advertiser. If "Barbecueing with Ben" will draw a larger audience than the "Professional Women's Bowling Tour," and there isn't time for both, Ben will get the time.

The point we want to make is that originators who have spent money for programs and announcements expect something in return from the recipients of their messages. That something is some modification of attitude or behavior, or some action, such as the purchase of a product, a vote for a candidate, or at the very least, attention.

On the other hand, audiences are attracted to programs mainly because of the information and/or entertainment contained in them. There is a paradox here which writers must recognize: The audience's reasons for choosing programs—to be informed or entertained—are frequently different from the originator's purpose. It is the further examination of this paradox that we take up in Chapters 8 and 9.

Effect

Effect and purpose are closely related, particularly as we apply the communication model to commercial broadcasting. The commercial system would quickly collapse if there were no effect on audiences after exposure to messages—if, for example, no products were sold as a result of advertising.

We will look at this part of the process from a slightly different perspective, however. Rather than examining the effects broadcast media have on audiences, we will look at the reasons why audiences choose to be exposed to programs— that is, at what gratifications they get from their media experiences. We believe this approach, which is unique in a writing text, is much more useful for the writer who will be charged with the task of attracting and holding the attention of audiences with his or her scripts.

Feedback

For the most part, once a message has been produced and broadcast, the only choice left to the audience is that of tuning in and listening, or tuning out—take it or leave it. The familiar radio and television channels provide no opportunity for immediate feedback from the receivers to the originators of messages, and therefore no opportunity to modify that communication while it is in progress.

There are some exceptions, such as telephone talk shows. If interactive cable systems should ever become an economic reality (and there is a real question at the present time whether that will happen), immediate feedback will be possible there as well. In these cases there is an immediate influence on the content of programs, and opportunity to alter the "script," but they remain exceptions.

Delayed feedback, on the other hand, is a powerful force in the selection and content of almost all programming. Delayed feedback takes the form of *ratings*—the estimates, based on samples of TV viewers or radio listeners, of how many people were watching or listening to particular programs. Programs that do not deliver an adequate share of viewers or listeners (in the view of programmers or advertisers) will be removed from the air to be replaced by others which, it is hoped, will do a better job of attracting audiences. While broadcasters and critics alike deplore the "tyranny" of the ratings, no better system has been devised for determining the preferences of audiences or of managing the economy of broadcasting.

Conclusion

In this chapter we have introduced the process of broadcast communication, using seven components of that process which are commonly used in communication models. We considered the originators of broadcast messages, both those who are engaged in the creative process and those who support creation by paying for the programs and announcements which are aired. Broadcast messages have both content and form and, depending upon the circumstances of creation, the writer may be concerned with either or both. The channels include radio and TV stations, cable systems, and other technologies. The trend is toward not only more channels, but also greater diversity of options. The receivers, or audiences, for broadcast messages complete the four basic components that must be present for communication to take place.

Three additional aspects of the process are the purposes behind the origination of communication, its effects, and feedback.

From this brief overview, and from your general knowledge of broadcasting, having been a consumer of its programs all your life, it should come as no surprise that American broadcasting is primarily a commercial system. To be sure, there are some broadcasting stations and cable channels which are operated on a noncommercial, nonprofit basis, but these stations must operate in an environment in which they compete with commercial outlets for audiences, if not for revenue. We will therefore concentrate our examination of the industry on the implications of its commercialism. We will delay that discussion, however, until the final chapters of the next section. First we will consider principles of good writing—style, layout, structure, and the relationship between writing and production.

Exercise   Collect additional examples and data, similar to the quote on page 7, which indicate the scope of the broadcast communication process. How many people are involved, for example, in producing a network soap opera? What is the cost to an advertiser for a commercial in an NFL football game telecast? How many subscribers are there in your local cable system? These figures change with time, so follow trends as well. Then discuss how the facts and figures you have collected affect the job and, particularly, may affect the future of the broadcast writer.

Key Terms and Concepts

broadcast	origination
channel	parsimony principle
DBS	purpose
effect	ratings
feedback	receiver
format	syndication
message	first-run syndication
network	off-network syndication

Notes

1. Sydney Head, with Christopher Sterling, *Broadcasting in America,* 4th ed. (Boston: Houghton Mifflin, 1982), p. 154.
2. Les Brown, writing in the foreword to Susan Eastman, Sydney Head, and Lewis Klein, *Broadcast Programming: Strategies for Winning Television and Radio Audiences* (Belmont, CA: Wadsworth, 1981), p. xv.

Part 2

Principles

In organizing the content of this book, we have taken the position that there are principles of writing for broadcast—for radio, television, cable, and other electronic media—that are peculiar to those delivery systems and to the way audiences receive information and use their content. We believe that the characteristics of the media and of audience behavior, taken together, dictate the approaches writers must take in order to be successful in communicating their ideas.

These principles, we believe, are *not* tied to one particular type of program or style of copy. That is, there is not one set of principles for writing dramatic programs and a different set for documentaries, or news, or interviews. To be sure, certain principles may be more important, or perhaps more obvious, in writing certain types of copy, and each type of program does have its own strengths and weaknesses from a writer's point of view. But we will argue, vigorously if necessary, that most of the principles of good broadcast writing we set forth in the chapters of this section can be applied to most of the program types described in the chapters of Part 3, as well as to other types too specialized to be covered in this text.

We would find it repetitious if, for example, we were to introduce the topic of program structure in the chapter on news, then again in the one on drama, then yet again in discussing documentaries. We will consider it in each of those chapters, but with attention to the unique structural problems of each genre. Similarly, matters of script mechanics, of aural style, and of the uses of sound and visuals need not be repeated in each of the genre chapters.

Here, then, are the matters we consider sufficiently important and sufficiently universal to be classified as principles of broadcast writing.

Chapter 2

Aural Style

The unique nature of broadcast communication frequently is described as *aural* writing or *aural* style—that is, pertaining to the ear and the sense of hearing. Our emphasis on this terminology reflects our belief that in broadcasting the one critical element is the successful *reception* of the message by the audience, on its being *heard* correctly. Even with visual media such as television, the largest portion of most programs' content is presented to the audience through their ears, rather than their eyes.

Contrasts: Print, Speech, Broadcast

Consider for a moment the relationships that exist between the content of a message and its audience in three common situations—print, a public speech, and broadcast. By comparing these three we can see how broadcasting's unique characteristics shape the writing style which is most effective for radio and television.

Print Messages

The actual materials prepared for presentation through print are sequences of symbols we have come to recognize as letters, words, sentences, and paragraphs. These symbols are seen by the eyes and then given meaning in the brain of the reader. In order for the reader to interpret the symbols, he or she must know how to read. It is also necessary to know the particular language—the symbol code—in which the message is written, to know the meanings of the individual words, and to understand the significance of the sequence in which they are placed.

Once the printed communication has been prepared, its content and its style are fixed and cannot be changed, either by the writer/source or by the recipient/audience.

But while the content of the printed message has been frozen by its author, all other aspects of the reader's interaction with that message are under the reader's control. (We ignore here some rare occasions when readers must read under time restrictions, as in examinations.) The speed with which the material is read, the order in which various sections are read, the length of time spent reading, and the amount of material read before stopping are all controlled by the reader. If that person wishes to reread a sentence, paragraph, or chapter which is not clear, or which he or she simply enjoys reading again, he or she may do so. If certain words are not familiar, the reader may stop and look them up in a dictionary. When the reader loses interest or finds something else more important to do, he or she may stop and start again when it is convenient to do so.

This ability of the recipient of the message to control its reception and processing is an important difference between print and broadcast communication.

Oral Messages

The largest share of oral communication takes place in informal situations in which there is considerable dialogue among the two to several people present at the time. We will concentrate on the characteristics of the more formal public speech, where there are clearly defined roles for both speaker and audience. In this situation, the speaker usually has a prepared presentation. The content and sequence are already worked out. The talk may even have been written out word-for-word and rehearsed for timing, inflection, and style. But until the actual moment of presentation, until the actual voicing of the words, changes can still be made—either on purpose, if the speaker sees reason to modify the text, or inadvertently, by forgetting or stumbling over words.

One reason why the speaker may want to make last-minute changes is that he or she senses something in the audience—boredom, restlessness, hostility, applause—which prompts a change in content or sequence. Even though there may be no verbal communication from the audience to the speaker, there is feedback in nonverbal form. Having the audience and the source present at the same place and time permits the audience to become a modifier of the message.

The spoken message is received by the members of the audience through their ears, then relayed to their brains for interpretation, a quite different process from that used in reading. In addition, the message is delivered using a specific style, with pacing, speed, and inflection all determined by the speaker. Finally, the speaker accompanies the words with nonverbal forms of communication such as gestures, facial expressions, and movements which are visible to the audience and which supplement the verbal message.

Broadcast Messages

Broadcast shares some of the characteristics of both print and spoken messages, and has some characteristics of its own.

Like print, the messages transmitted to audiences are predetermined by the source. But in this case it is not just message content and structure that are fixed by the writers and producers; so are all aspects of delivery to its audience. The sequence, speed, pacing, and emphasis with which the message is delivered are also under the control of the producers. In this respect, broadcast differs markedly from print.

Like oral communication, the words of broadcasting are presented in spoken form. But unlike oral communication there is no two-way channel, no mechanism for feedback from recipient to source.

We can summarize broadcasting's characteristics under four headings which, taken together, set radio and television apart from other media, and which determine aural style.

1. The words used, and the sequence in which they are presented are only heard, not seen.

2. The words and sequences are presented to the audience only once. There is no provision for the listener to get a repetition of the message.

3. There is usually no mechanism for immediate feedback and therefore no opportunity for the source to modify the message during delivery.

4. Although broadcast audiences may be large in total, that large, aggregate audience is made up of many small groups or individuals at each receiving location.

Words Heard, Not Seen

It is possible to think of a few situations in television where words are printed out on the screen. The brand names of products advertised are shown as a visual reinforcement of the message. Also, rather than interrupt a program, occasionally a printed "crawl" giving program information or a news headline will be displayed on the screen without spoken accompaniment. And some television channels display written words—stock market quotations, news, weather, or teletext data, for example. But usually the visual display of words is only a reinforcement of the spoken message.

Broadcast does require that the content to be presented be put on paper in some form of script and that the script then be transformed from print into voice by the actions of announcers and actors, by the use of sound effects and music, and for television, by the insertion of pictorial material. But the script is only a transition stage in the process of communication; it is not seen by the audience.

The important point is that the verbal content of broadcast communication is received and interpreted through the listener's ear. In order to become more conscious of the characteristics of aural communication, the beginning writer should form the habit of reading his or her copy aloud. We tend to skip through the problems associated with poor aural style when reading silently. Try reading aloud the draft of a piece of copy, and it will make stylistic problems more obvious.

One-Time Presentation

Recall the difference between this characteristic and that of print. Print material may be read whenever an individual reader is ready, in whatever sequence of items that person chooses, and with whatever rereading or analysis he or she chooses. The reader controls the reception of the message and the speed and order in which its content is processed by the eye and brain.

In contrast, the originator of the broadcast message determines both the sequence of ideas and their rate of presentation. If the listener is unable to follow that sequence or keep up with that speed, for whatever reason, he or she will turn off the program or be turned off by it.

Therefore, broadcast requires especially careful attention to the sequence and pacing of materials. The recipient's only choices are to accept the message as presented, or lose that content forever. (One partial exception, which permits repeated exposure but no change in the structure of the message, is the use by individuals in an audience of a tape recorder. This option is becoming somewhat more common.)

No Feedback

There are some exceptions here too. It is now fairly common for national programs and commercials to be pretested on sample audiences. If the test audiences do not react positively to a commercial message or to the pilot program for a new dramatic series, that commercial or program can be modified before final production and presentation to the mass audience, or dropped before large costs are incurred.

In addition, there are some ways to obtain direct audience feedback to a broadcast. Telephone call-in programs, now quite common in radio, represent one way to involve an audience. Interactive cable systems, which have the capability for audiences to respond to questions asked in a program, are another. Indications are that in the future there will be more channels for audience feedback and more programming which encourages feedback, but at present these are all exceptions. For most material, the principle holds—no feedback.

A Big Audience—of Individuals

The business of broadcasting is profitable only because it is possible to reach large numbers of people, often numbering many millions, at one time and with one origination. But unlike other mass audiences, the broadcast audience is in many different locations, each isolated from the others. At best there will be only a small group of people, perhaps a family, receiving the program in one location.

In order to communicate effectively with broadcast audiences, the writer must remember to talk to them as individuals, casually and conversationally, not with the styles of oratory used for mass audiences assembled in a single location.

Clarity

The most important consequence of these unique characteristics of the broadcast message is that the writer and other persons involved in the production of scripts and programs must strive consciously to make every message clear. Since there is no way for the listener to review the content, to reread the message, to go to the dictionary to check unfamiliar words, or to respond by voice or other physical signs that he or she does not understand, the message must be clear immediately upon presentation. Anything that might interfere with the delivery and under-standing of the message must be sacrificed to clarity.

For example, a commercial may be constructed humorously, but the humor must support the persuasive message of the advertisement; it cannot mask it. A news story must present its information, which consists of events, names, dates, statistics, expert opinion, and so on, in a sequence that places new facts into the already understood fabric of the story; new names, for example, cannot be introduced without explanation of their relationship to the other persons already involved in the story.

Clarity, of course, is clarity to the listener. We can discuss clarity only as it pertains to the ear and mind of the listener, and not in relation to the words written by the writer. As a writer, you may believe that what you have written is clear and will be understood by the people in the audience. But it may not be. How can you be sure that what you have written will be clear?

You cannot be absolutely certain, but you can increase the odds in your favor by observing these two fundamental rules:

1. Know as much as possible about the audience you intend to reach with your message. We will discuss target audiences in Chapter 9. The point very simply is that certain types of people are more strongly attracted to certain types of content and styles of presentation than others. We will also consider in Chapter 9 how writers can adjust scripts to meet the interests of particular groups.

2. Write using an aural style—that is, using sentence and paragraph structures, grammatical constructions, and vocabulary which help listeners to follow and to process the content of the message. For the remainder of this chapter, we will concentrate on these principles of aural style for ensuring clarity.

Writing in an Aural Style

The single most distinguishing characteristic of the broadcast writing style, in contrast to that used for print, is that it is more informal and sounds more spontaneous. Our perceiving sense, the ear, cannot easily process the more complex, abstract, and formal style found in most printed content. That style requires more effort and attention than broadcast audience members are able, willing, or accustomed to giving. Instead, the writer should try to prepare copy that sounds as much like spontaneous speech as possible. That copy will have these characteristics. It will

1. Use *simple sentences,* and avoid complex constructions.

2. Make frequent use of *transition words and vocal cues.*

3. Maintain a *moderate pace* that is within the listener's ability to comprehend.

4. Use the *active voice.*

5. Use *contractions.*

6. Use *personal pronouns* extensively.

7. Avoid *negative constructions.*

8. Avoid the use of *homophones.*

9. Use *descriptive, connotative, forceful words.*

10. Use a more *restricted vocabulary* than is usually found in print copy.

11. Use *language correctly*.

12. Avoid *redundancies*.

Discussions and examples of the use of several of these characteristics can be found in general style manuals, for most of these are appropriate instructions for good writing in any medium. Here we will emphasize broadcast applications.

Simple Sentences

The sentences we speak are simpler than those we write, so to approximate conversational speech the writer generally should use simple constructions. It is possible to be grammatically correct and at the same time be much too complex for the listener to be able to follow a story.

One problem of particular difficulty for many beginning writers is the proper placement of modifiers within a sentence. If modifiers are placed incorrectly, the listener can easily become confused. Do not, for example, begin sentences with lengthy modifying phrases or clauses. The listener hears the modifiers first, without any reference to the main idea they are supposed to modify. Try reading these examples aloud, and you should be able to see the problem.

Now 68, silver-haired, and, with Muhammad Ali, the most identifiable of retired athletes, Joe DiMaggio is solicited regularly by writers and publishing houses to do a book. . . .

The listener cannot know who is being talked about, Joe DiMaggio, until fifteen words into the sentence. His age, hair color, and comparison with Ali have nothing to do with the main thrust of the story. Begin with "Joe DiMaggio is solicited regularly. . . ."

After practicing for 18 months on common barnyard pigs, Dr. Richard Ward, director of the liver transplant program, says that he and his team of surgeons, technicians, and nurses are ready when the first well-matched patient and donor can be identified. . . .

Again, we can't relate the "After practicing . . . on . . . pigs" to anything until after we understand that the story has to do with preparations for liver transplants. Start with the important facts, then show how the pigs tie in.

Having been a former pro football player and an athlete since my Little League days, I consider the healthy human body a gift from God and feel people should treat it right—by eating the right foods and exercising regularly. . . .

Often the best way to eliminate the opening dependent clause is just to reverse the main thought. Begin the sentence with the main clause: "I consider . . . exercising regularly. My feelings come from the fact that I have been an athlete since my Little League days and a former pro football player."

Confronted by the possibility of lawsuits for false arrest or slander, store owners have staffed their stores with more visible security agents rather than undercover agents. . . .

In this case, the sentence is not overly long or complex. It can be improved easily simply by adding: "Because they have been confronted by. . . ."

Lengthy interjections in the middle of a sentence, between the subject and the verb, also cause confusion.

Poor: The annual Pig Bowl game, which pits the Bacon Bombers from the Sacramento County Sheriff's Department against the Razorbacks from the City Police for the benefit of nine local charities, will be played this year on January 21.

Better: The annual Pig Bowl game will be played this year on January 21. As usual the two teams will come from Sacramento law enforcement agencies—the Bacon Bombers from the Sheriff's Department and the Razorbacks from the City Police. Nine local charities will benefit from the proceeds.

Poor: A computer system for fingerprints, which the San Francisco Police Department fought for years to acquire, brought about the arrest yesterday of a suspect in the fatal shooting of a Parkside District woman six years ago.

Better: A new computer system for fingerprints caught its first suspect in San Francisco yesterday. The computer identified the fingerprints of a man who has been arrested for the fatal shooting six years ago of a Parkside District woman. Police had fought for years to acquire the complex computer matching system.

Subordinate clauses and midsentence interjections should be moved to the end of the sentence they modify. Even better in many cases is to rewrite them as separate sentences, as was done in both examples above.

Generally a straightforward subject-verb-object sequence is best, but avoid constant repetition of the same pattern of sentence construction. A story with sentences of uniform brief length and with sentences phrased in precisely the same subject-verb pattern will have a "singsong" effect and rapidly bore the listener. The ear is easily distracted; it is difficult to hold its attention without changes of pace and variation.

Transition Words and Vocal Cues

Writing intended for the eye makes frequent use of punctuation marks, which are visual cues to indicate structure and emphasis. We paragraph copy to mark each stage in the development of a sequence of thought and we punctuate within sentences to clarify sentence construction. We use italics and boldface type to make certain words and ideas stand out from others.

To accomplish the same thing in aural copy, the listener is led through the structure of the material by transition words, vocal inflections, and pauses.

One group of cue or transition words relate to time sequence. They include such words as *now*, *next*, *still*, *just*, *then*, *when*, and *finally*. Also *yesterday*, *today*, *tomorrow*, *last week*, and so on. These words would be particularly helpful in constructing a news story in which a clear chronology of events is needed in order to understand the story:

In San Francisco three hostages are still being held in a downtown office building by an unidentified gunman. They have been there since three P.M. yesterday, when an attempted holdup went awry. Police have reconstructed the events this way. Just shortly before three P.M. two men entered the Crocker Bank office at Fifth and Oak. They walked up to a teller's window and demanded that money be placed in a paper sack which they held out. In the process of taking the sack from the robbers, the teller was able to trip a silent alarm, and when the men attempted to leave the bank, they found guards blocking their exit. At that time, one man pulled a gun and ordered three bank customers into an elevator, which they then took up to the top floor of the eighteen-story building. The second would-be robber evidently slipped away during the elevator ride, but one man and the hostages are still holed up in an unused office on the top floor. Negotiations between police and the gunman have been taking place, but no results have been announced.

Other transition words indicate cause and effect or similar relationships—such words as *because*, *for*, *thereby*, and *since*. Another group helps set up contrasts within a story: *however*, *on the other hand*, *but*. And there are the standard connectors: *and*, *also*, *too*, *in addition*. Be careful of these, however, as many beginning writers use connectors to make compound and complex sentences where two separate simple sentences would be better.

Changes in the vocal inflections used by announcers and actors also provide aural cues to listeners. They are particularly helpful in emphasizing certain words or phrases within a body of copy. The writer can indicate in the script where inflection is wanted by the use of standard punctuation symbols and by underlining to indicate emphasis. The actual inflection, however, has to be provided by the "voice" of the copy—the announcer or actor.

In the preceding sentence, for example, the use of quotation marks around the word "voice" would indicate to an announcer that the word should be given some special inflection which aurally sets it apart from the rest of the sentence. Another well-known example of how differences in inflection can change the meaning of copy is this line. Try reading it aloud with the different inflections noted:

- *Where* have all the flowers gone?

- Where *have* all the flowers gone?

- Where have *all* the flowers gone?

- Where have all the *flowers* gone?

- Where have all the flowers *gone*?

And this example, in which changes in emphasis add a great deal to the audience's ability to understand the writer's intent:

The President insisted that the American forces would be used for peace-keeping purposes only.

Emphasis on *President*—as opposed to some other official who might have made the same statement; emphasizes credibility of source.

Emphasis on *insisted*—makes his action the key to the sentence.

Emphasis on *American*—someone's else's forces might be used differently, but not the American forces.

Emphasis on *peacekeeping*—as opposed to, possibly, war making.

Emphasis on *only*—no other activity is proposed.

Finally, broadcast copy makes frequent use of pauses, to allow time for the listener to process the preceding information before continuing with new information. Remember, in print the reader sets his or her own pace, but that cannot be done in broadcast. The writer of broadcast copy, then, will make frequent use of the punctuation marks that indicate pauses to the announcer or actors. Commas, dashes, and ellipses will appear more frequently in broadcast copy than in print and more frequently than is called for by the strict rules of grammar. Here are two examples:

ANNCR:	(ON COLD) Building bridges from man to man . . . a whole wide world to span.
MUSIC:	CUERVA UP FOR 8–10 SECONDS, THEN UNDER
NARR:	That's the cuerva, the national dance of Chile. It's typical of a lot of South American music . . . fiery, fast, and stirring. . . . It's typical of the South American people, too . . . emotional and easily aroused. The continent to our South has always been a hotbed of emotion, and of discontent, and of uprising. . . .
MUSIC:	CUERVA UP, THEN FADE OUT UNDER NARR
NARR:	Our story involves the people of Chile, and of her neighbor Argentina. These two countries, Chile and Argentina, are very much alike in many ways. Chile is a long, thin country, shaped something like a cavalry saber. It stretches down the west coast of South America for almost three thousand miles. In the North is a vast desert, the location of large deposits of nitrates and copper ore. The central part is a wonderful valley that grows almost any crop. And the South is a wild and untouched vacationland. . . . Argentina is larger than Chile but not so long. It lies along the Southeast coast of South America. Its grasslands support large quantities of wheat and cattle. And its capital, Buenos Aires, is the largest city in South America.

The dividing line between the two countries is the rugged Andes mountains, the scene of part of today's story. Many of these peaks tower more than fifteen thousand feet in the air. And most of them are snow capped the year around.

Both Chile and Argentina were colonized by Spain in the sixteenth century. Both stayed under Spanish domination until the revolt of 1810. Then, in successful revolutions, most of the countries of Central and South America threw off the yoke of Spanish imperialism and established independent governments. Chile built her government using the United States as a model and, after a turbulent first few years, Argentina did likewise.

MUSIC: SNEAK IN OMINOUS MUSIC AND GRADUALLY INCREASE.

But despite similarities in geography, language, and background, Chile and Argentina have not always been good friends. Fifty years ago they were on the verge of war. . . .

HYDE: The recorded music industry is a 2 billion dollar a year industry . . . that's more than all professional sports and the entire film industry combined.

The music people have come out with their predictions for next year . . . and they are . . . first . . . you will have less material to select from . . . fewer artists will be recorded . . . secondly . . . you will use more recorded music because you will be forced to stay home more due to the gas crisis . . . and you will pay more for your recordings . . .

TAKE REDDY SLIDE: Helen Reddy has hit the payday jackpot in Las Vegas . . .

TAKE HYDE: Helen's just signed a million dollar deal with the M.G.M. hotel people.

TAKE DYLAN SLIDE: In an exclusive interview, Bob Dylan says he's astonished with the 92 million dollars' worth of orders for his current concert tour.

TAKE HYDE: Dylan says touring is like being in limbo . . . going from nowhere to nowhere.

TAKE GARFUNKLE SLIDE: Art Garfunkle's come out of hiding long enough to give his views on the current music scene.

TAKE HYDE: He says pop music has gone thru the standard numbers . . . creativity . . . followed by ornate exaggeration . . . followed by degenerate imitation . . . in an incredibly short period of time . . . then he went back into hiding . . .

TAKE MILLER SLIDE: Ten years of trial and error has finally paid off for Steve Miller. He's got the new #1 song on the music scene top ten.

Source: Courtesy of KCRA; Sacramento, CA.

Moderate Pace

Since in broadcast the program must be presented in a fixed sequence and at a predetermined rate, with no opportunity for the individual in the audience to adjust to either, writers and producers must use considerable care to see that materials are presented at a pace which can be handled by the members of the audience. Too many ideas, presented too rapidly, and the information will become a jumble to the listener. Too slow, and boredom settles in; the listener is ready for more information before it arrives.

The problem of too much density—too much information for the time available—can be solved in part by reducing the content, including only the most important facts within a news story, for instance, and limiting the number of persuasive concepts in a commercial. The problem can also be eased by spacing out those ideas which are presented so that the listener's ear and mind can process each idea before being hit with the next one. Transition words and pauses, already discussed, help with pacing. Two additional techniques are repetition and delay.

Repetition doesn't necessarily mean that the same words and phrases are repeated, but that a single idea is reinforced by alternative phrasings. Reread the bank holdup story (page 20). Notice the several times that the major ideas of the story—the robbery and the hostage taking—are mentioned throughout the story.

Delay is used to warn the listener that important information is about to be delivered. It also provides a buffer, a breathing space between stories or ideas. It gives the listener time to reflect, briefly, on the preceding information and then to focus attention on the upcoming story. News headlines provide warning and delay, as do some forms of news leads. Another common delay is the conversation between two news anchors prior to the presentation of the next story. This example provides transition, warning, and delay:

2 SHOT ON 1: STAN: In other capitol news, it looks like there's been a break in the deadlock over the state budget.

MARY: That's right, Stan. State employees, who have been without paychecks for over two weeks now because of the budget stalemate, may finally get paid. Today's meeting between Democratic leaders of the legislature and the governor seems to have cleared the remaining obstacles. Frank Jones has the story.

VOT—#1, Cut #2 @ 3:25 Today's meeting between Assembly Speaker. . . .

The technique is not used just in news broadcasts. In a dramatic program, when a new character enters the scene with exciting information, he or she may say:

Wow! Have I got some news! You know that old bridge down on Simpson Creek, Well, it collapsed last night and. . . .

The first statement "Wow! Have I got some news." is the delay. It says to the listener: Pay attention!

Delays are important to space out material and to recapture the attention of listeners who may have tuned out mentally on one piece of material, so that they are tuned back in for the next story or commercial.

But the pacing of a message or the spacing out of the ideas does not mean that broadcast writing can be loose or sloppy. We have mentioned that simple sentence constructions are more conversational. The same is true for shorter sentences; they more closely approach normal speech. Brevity itself is not the issue, however. What is important, especially in broadcast news and commercials where time is measured in seconds, is that the words and sentences used all contribute to the message. The writers of the best style book yet published, William Strunk and E. B. White, put it this way:

> A sentence should contain no unnecessary words, a paragraph no unnecessary sentences. . . . This requires not that the writer make all . . sentences short . . . but that every word tell.[1]

Active Voice

Broadcast style more frequently uses the active voice rather than the passive voice. The very words chosen to describe these two linguistic styles—active voice and passive voice—give a clue to their use. The active voice is more dynamic, more forceful; it makes a commercial or news copy seem more alive.

Poor: The sniper was captured by police.
Better: Police captured the sniper.

Poor: An historic agreement was signed yesterday by the Chairmen of General Motors and Toyota.
Better: The Chairmen of General Motors and Toyota signed an historic agreement yesterday.

Occasional use of the passive voice can add variety to the structure of a story and may on occasion be the best way to make a point, but it more often slows down and weakens the story's impact.

Contractions

Normal conversation uses contractions frequently and naturally. Where you would be likely to use contractions in conversation, you should use them in broadcast copy. It simply sounds more natural, more spontaneous, and more informal to say *didn't* instead of *did not*, or *we'll* instead of *we will*.

Come on down to the Saving Center this weekend.
You'll find a carload of bargains. . . .

Other common contractions you should use are these:

shouldn't for should not
won't for will not
they're for they are
haven't for have not
couldn't for could not
you're for you are
can't for cannot

aren't for are not
isn't for is not
wasn't for was not
it's for it is
they'll for they will
doesn't for does not

One occasion when you should not use a contraction is when you want emphasis. The contrast between the normal use of the contraction and the deliberate choice not to use it stands out in the copy and provides the emphasis wanted.

The coalition claims that registering hand guns will not reduce crime, but will create another costly bureaucracy.

In this example, *will not* emphasizes the negative more than *won't*. It also provides a better contrast with *will* in the second clause.

Personal Pronouns

A conversation is a conversation only if it involves two parties. In broadcast, those two parties are the individual listeners in the audience and the voice from the other end of the line—the announcer. The use of first- and second-person pronouns makes the copy sound more personal, more informal, and more conversational than if the writer used just nouns or third-person pronouns:

If *you're* having trouble finding that special gift this Christmas, *I* have some suggestions. . . .

We're going to be in for cold weather. . . .

Our utility bills will be increased drastically if the plan is approved. . . .

Most of *us* take it for granted that the sun will come up every morning, but for one man. . . .

Of course, any stylistic device can be overused, and certain types of content adapt more easily to the use of pronouns than do others, but as a general rule the attention of each individual listener will be caught more easily by a story that seems to involve that listener. The use of *you* and *we* and similar pronouns accomplishes that involvement.

However, be sure that the pronoun references are clear. A confusing antecedent in broadcast copy will throw the listener off and cause him or her to miss subsequent information. Problems similar to these incorrect examples appear frequently in the inexperienced writer's copy:

He put the vase on the mantel which had been repaired. [What was repaired, vase or mantel?]

My children had too many clothes, so I gave them away. [The children?]

The American people have elected a number of poor presidents, but Congress has generally kept them from ruining the country. [The people or the presidents?]

Negative Constructions

In general, negative statements are an obstacle to clarity. They are harder for audiences to comprehend. They are less descriptive and provide less information.

Poor: The baby ape was not breastfed by its mother.

With Jupiter's dense gravity, you could not throw a ball very far.

Schubert's first published work was not well received by the general public.

I don't know that I am certain my father did not want to show his feelings.

The first three of these constructions are vague: They provide little information. The fourth, with its multiple negatives, is confusing as well. When the mind receives negative information, it wants and tries to convert that information into positive form; the mind wants to know what is, not just what is not.

Better: The baby ape was fed a prepared formula rather than its mother's breast milk.

With Jupiter's dense gravity, you could throw a ball only three or four feet, no more.

Schubert's first published work was received hesitantly by the general public.

I wonder if my father really wanted to hide his emotions.[2]

On the other hand, *not* is appropriate as a means of expressing denial, or as a contrast:

The state will *not* have a budget today. Although the Constitution requires that the budget be completed by July first each year, legislators will *not* finish their deliberations today—nor does it look like they will reach agreement anytime soon.

But there is a danger, especially in news stories of this kind, that listeners will miss the negative word because of some distraction, and then will misinterpret the story. Repetition helps. Three negatives are used in the story above to guard against misunderstanding.

Homophones

Homophones are words that sound alike but have different meanings. They also can confuse listeners, because when a homophone is used in broadcasting, the only way the listener can tell which of the different "sound alike" words has been used is by the context.

In this chapter, we have already used one pair of homophones—*oral* and *aural*. In print they can be easily distinguished because they are spelled differently, but when heard they sound so alike that most listeners would be unable to distinguish between them.

Other groups of homophones to watch out for are *to, too,* and *two,* and *threw* and *through.* How might a listener react to these bits of copy? Try reading them aloud.

The scorekeeper gave two too many runs to the home team. Without that error, the Sox would have lost two to one.

He threw the pitcher through the picture at the pitcher.

Other homophones to avoid are these:

wait and weight	heir, air, and err
sex and sect	heel and heal
chord and cord	wear and where
wholly and holy	stationary and stationery
council and counsel	reign, rein, and rain
pier and peer	palate, pallet, and palette
symbol and cymbal	principle and principal
levy and levee	aisle and isle
pray and prey	strait and straight
bail and bale	profit and prophet
capital and capitol	serial and cereal
callus and callous	tee and tea

Although usually the context of a sentence will be sufficient to identify which word is intended, you should make it a habit to read aloud all the copy you write. If you run into a confusing homophone, rewrite.

Descriptive, Connotative, Forceful Words

A writer sensitive to words makes use of those that have high connotative value. Suggestive words will awaken associations in the mind of the listener and stir the imagination. They add color, warmth, and life to a script:

> To say "His mind quickly comprehended a problem" would convey the meaning intended, but it would be more effective to say "His mind flashed to the heart of the problem." The word "flashed" carries with it a definite connotation and a sharp visual image which not only tells the listener what happened, but also gives him the feeling of its happening. . . . It is better to say that the wind "whined and clawed at the corner of the house" than to say that the wind "was blowing." If a word can tell not only what was done but how it was done, so much the better.[3]

The use of descriptive words is particularly important in writing radio copy, where there is no visual accompaniment to the sound. Well-chosen descriptive words and phrases help the listener build a mental picture of the setting of a dramatic scene, or of an event.

Here are two brief passages of radio copy that use descriptive words effectively to build mental images. The first is an excerpt from one of Edward R. Murrow's accounts of the German bombing of London in World War II:

Up toward London we could see billows of smoke fanning out above the river and, over our heads, the British fighters climbing almost straight up, trying to intercept the bombers before they got away. It went on for two hours, and then the all-clear. We went down to a nearby pub for dinner. Children were already organizing a hunt for bits of shrapnel. Under some bushes beside the road there was a baker's cart. Two boys, sobbing, were trying to get a quivering bay mare back between the shafts. The lady who ran the pub told us that these raids were bad for the chickens, the dogs and the horses. A toothless old man of nearly seventy came in and asked for a pint of milk and bitters, confided that he had always, all his life, gone to bed at eight o'clock and found now that three pints of beer made him drowsy-like so he could sleep through any air raid.

Before eight the sirens sounded again. We went back to the haystack near the airdrome. The fires up the river had turned the moon blood-red. The smoke had drifted down until it formed a canopy over the Thames. The guns were working all around us, the bursts looking like fireflies in a Southern summer night. The Germans were sending in two or three planes at a time— sometimes only one—in relays. They would pass overhead. The guns and lights would follow them, and in about five minutes we could hear the hollow grunt of the bombs. Huge pear-shaped bursts of flame would rise up into the smoke and disappear. . . . It was like a shuttle service, the way the German planes came up the Thames, the fires acting as a flare path. Often they were above the smoke. The searchlights bored into that black roof but couldn't penetrate it. They looked like long pillars supporting a black canopy. Suddenly all the lights dashed off and a blackness fell right to the ground. It grew cold. We covered ourselves with hay. . . .

Source: Edward R. Murrow as quoted in Edward Bliss, Jr., and John M. Patterson, *Writing News for Broadcast*, 2nd ed. rev. (New York: Columbia University Press, 1978), pp. 20–21. ©1978, Columbia University Press. Reprinted by permission of the publisher.

This second example is the narrative introduction to a radio play, ''The Voice of the Fog.''

SOUND:	FOGHORN IN THE DISTANCE—AT NATURAL INTERVALS IN BACK OF—
RAY:	Have you heard the voice of the fog? As the cold white loneliness creeps in, shrouding a desolate shoreline, blotting the stars, bringing stillness to the night and hushing the wind and muffling the sad wash of the sea; until there's no motion, no sound, no reality left; nothing but you and the fog and—after a while—a strained tense listening for the voice to speak. No. No, it's not the wailing cry of a lost gull overhead, nor the foghorn's weary dirge far away, not even the dim thudding beat of your heart. It's—no, forgive me, please. Perhaps it's only to me that the fog's voice speaks. (TURN AWAY FADE)

Source: Dave Drummond, *Voice of the Fog*, an original radio play.

Short, forceful words are generally better than less emphatic ones.

POOR: He has passed away.
BETTER: He is dead.

POOR: I demand that you surrender that volume.
BETTER: Give me the book.

POOR: Assist me to arise.
BETTER: Help me up.

POOR: I hold you in high esteem.
BETTER: I like you.[4]

Aural style is also marked by words with high sound-effect value. The writer should make use of onomatopoeia, which is the use of words whose sounds suggest their sense. The words *tinkle, roar, crunch, crush, lull,* and *soothe* are onomatopoetic words. Like any other technique, onomatopoeia can be overused or badly used; used with discrimination it is an effective way to add color to narrative.

Restricted Vocabulary

The literary style can and usually does employ a much larger vocabulary than the aural style. The average person's reading vocabulary is about three times larger than his or her speaking vocabulary. A reader may recognize or be able to figure out the meaning of many words that would be lost completely if presented aurally. A reader can also look up strange words, which is a recourse not available to the listener.

The prime consideration in the choice of vocabulary is that the words used must contribute to clarity. The vocabulary should not confuse listeners. For confusion, even if it is only momentary, will cause the listener to miss a following portion of the message. The result is that he or she will be unable or unwilling to catch up to the communication and will tune out, either mentally or physically, by leaving the room, changing the channel, or turning the receiver off altogether. Therefore, the writer must choose words that will be readily recognized by listeners. That, in turn, means using a limited vocabulary for most broadcast writing, particularly if you are writing copy directed at a very broad audience, such as that for a prime-time television program. In order to reach as many of these people as possible without their turning away from the content of a program, the writer must use a straightforward, restricted vocabulary.

The structure of English is such that the setting in which a word is placed frequently gives clues to its meaning, or at least the overall sense of a message can be determined with reasonable accuracy even without knowing the meaning of every word in the statement. But the writer should not rely on this characteristic. Instead, avoid the use of "big words," when shorter, more common words will convey the same thought.

An important corollary to that principle is to avoid general, vague, abstract terms in favor of the particular word or phrase that most precisely and accurately fits the idea. The American grand master of style, William Strunk, insisted that:

If those who have studied the art of writing are in accord on any one point it is on this: the surest way to arouse and hold the attention of the reader is by being specific, definite, and concrete.

POOR: A period of unfavorable weather set in.
BETTER: It rained everyday for a week.

POOR: He showed satisfaction as he took possession of his well-earned reward.
BETTER: He grinned as he pocketed the coin.[5]

Strunk was referring to print, but the instruction is even more important for broadcast, as the writer must work within the very precise time limits of an inflexible program schedule and the scheduled time for a story is measured in terms of seconds, not minutes.

Here is a list of some "literary" or "abstract" words that in broadcast copy should be replaced by the simpler equivalent, or for which a more concrete word should usually be substituted.[6]

Avoid	Use
indignation	anger
transmit	send
remark	say
exhibit	show
require	need
lacerations	cuts
deceased	dead
attempt	try
precipitation	rain, snow
energy	gas, electricity
livestock	pigs, cows, sheep
cooking utensils	pots and pans
garment	coat
educational institution	school
petroleum	oil
sufficient	enough
residence	home
contribute	give
interrogate	question
witness	see
purchase	buy
summon	call
beverage	drink
physician	doctor
attorney	lawyer
passed away	died
terminate	end
commence	begin
endeavor	try
utilize	use

edifice	building
assemblage	crowd
consequently	so
transpire	happen
venture	try
cognizant	aware
youth	teenager
abrasion	scrape
intoxicated	drunk
visage	face
indisposed	ill, sick

Correct Language

It should not be necessary to remind writers that words should be used correctly and that grammar should be correct in all forms of writing, including broadcast, but the fact is that much too frequently words and grammar are not correct, and when they are misused the listener will be confused. We suggested in the list above, for example, that *call* was a better word to use than *summon*, but *summon* has a specific legal connotation, and it should be used if that is the meaning intended.

Good writing is marked by precision in word choice. If only one word has the precise meaning you wish to convey and if you believe your audience is familiar with that word—use it. On the other hand, if that word is *not* likely to be understood by your audience, you will have to rewrite in order to convey the meaning in a different way.

Many common words are misused by students who simply have not had enough practice using vocabulary precisely. Having, and using, a good dictionary will help you develop precision. The serious writer will also keep on hand one or more style manuals or other specialized books on language.

Redundancies

Redundancies clutter a piece of copy, reducing clarity. Among the authors who have spoken most forcefully, and at the same time entertainingly, about the correct use of the English language is Edwin Newman, who recently retired from a distinguished career as reporter and commentator for NBC News. In his book *A Civil Tongue* he provides a chapter of redundancies, including this biting excerpt:

> We no longer have rules and prospects and news but ground rules, future prospects, and newsworthy happenings. Airlines tell us to read the instructions in the seat pocket in front of us not for our safety but for our personal safety. Companies do not grow; they enjoy positive growth. The Encinitas Union School District in California announces that it will provide equal employment opportunity not merely through affirmative action but through positive affirmative action. Do new cameras obviate special lighting? They obviate the need for special lighting. Is the horse Rogue's Gambit, subject of a story in the *Washington Post,* one of a kind? No, it is uniquely one of a kind. Does Nelson Rockefeller complain of a misrepresentation by Ronald Reagan? No, he complains of a factual misrepresentation, which cancels itself. Was a woman raped? No, she had a rape experience. Shall we face reality? We can do better. We can face reality as it is.

Pillows renovated, a shop proclaims, like new. No trespassing, signs say, without permission.[7]

Special Considerations for Visual Media

We have been emphasizing those basic characteristics relating to the preparation, transmittal, and reception of broadcast content which are common to both radio and television. There is no hard copy for the recipient to process; the words are only heard; there is no opportunity for repetition; and there is no chance for feedback from recipient to source. These characteristics dictate the basic style and structure of scripts for both audio only and audiovisual media.

But there are some situations in which the addition of the visual sense calls for modifications to aural style. The addition of sight means that often the TV writer can leave out descriptive material. For example, in a radio interview it may be important that the audience have a physical description of the interviewee— age, stature, and so on. The writer or announcer must provide this. In television, the viewer can immediately perceive the physical characteristics of the person on the screen. In preparing a radio drama, the writer must describe the setting of each scene—not always in great detail because the imagination of the listener can fill in much of the scene, but with enough detail to support the plot. In television, the location of the scene can be seen—a signpost tells the name of the town being approached; a stove, pots, table, and so on indicate that another scene is in a kitchen.

Color, if important in the radio description, must be explained—written into the narrative. Generally, color is not important and the script should be written in such a way as to avoid it, but if the advertiser wants to mention the "bright blue box" of a product, you'll have to write "bright blue box." In television, the color is there on the screen for the viewers to see, and "bright blue box" in the copy is used only if the writer wants to provide additional emphasis.

Finally, if you examine the two transmission channels of television separately—that is, the sound and the picture—you will find that in most cases the sound track is reasonably independent and can stand alone, while only occasionally will the picture alone carry a clear message to the viewer. It is possible for audience members to obtain information through the aural channel while doing other tasks that require vision. It is not even necessary to be in the same room with the television set in order to get information from the sound channel. However, the viewer's full attention is required to obtain and process visual information.

This analysis of audience behavior in relation to the two channels is in no way intended to place the visual channel in a secondary position; there are many examples of the powerful impact of appropriate visual images. Almost any sporting event is more exciting to see than just to hear described; a travel program on radio pales in contrast to the visual beauty of some remote location; visual demonstration of a technique provides for better learning of how to do that task than do just words; and so on. But the point is that seldom can the picture stand alone. We are accustomed to hearing television as much as seeing it. A sound track that follows good aural style is as important to television as it is to radio.

Responding to Criticism

Critics frequently have faulted broadcast writers for using an overly simplistic style. They have argued that the dramatic scripts for prime-time television programs, which aim to reach the largest possible audiences, use language and plot structures which are insulting to the intelligence of many people. To some extent, that criticism is justified. Some writers, and some authors of writing texts, have carried the instruction "keep it simple" to extremes.

The principles of aural style given here, however, still apply in general. Clarity is still the prime objective. If the purpose of a particular program is to reach a very large audience, the writing of that program—the plot, the language, the sentence construction, and so on—must be kept sufficiently simple so that the large number and very diverse groups of people in the audience can follow and understand, and stay tuned.

Another critical argument is made about television's role as primarily an entertainment medium. These critics suggest that television has abdicated a responsibility to treat important issues in any significant fashion. Again, there is some truth to the criticism. Given the characteristics of the broadcasting process, it is difficult to present in-depth analyses of complex issues. In the electronic media, materials must be presented in a sequential fashion, and once organized into a sequence they cannot be rearranged, recalled, or examined at any length by members of the audience. These limitations do provide real constraints on the complexity of material that can be presented through these media and processed by their audiences. And one must admit that in practice the time and money necessary to prepare scripts based on complex and controversial material usually have not been provided. For the most part, the content of programs is kept to a level where audiences can listen or view with enjoyment and without effort.

But for the writer or the student who finds broadcast writing to be unchallenging, or a prostituting of his or her creative talent, there is hope. There are producers and writers in the industry who believe that the limitations of "aural style" simply provide a greater challenge to the creative use of the media and that the use of both pictorial information in motion and a creative sound track can in fact provide a better explanation of complex concepts than can print, and that therefore in-depth explanations of important and complex issues can be treated by television.

And there is a definite trend toward audience fragmentation—more channels, and more narrow, specific audiences. In these cases, writers will be permitted to use a larger vocabulary, more specialized language, and more complex ideas—so long as the target audience for the program can process the information. Maybe we can modify the basic principle just a bit to reflect the trend away from large, undifferentiated audiences. We'll say that writers should use a style and vocabulary appropriate for the audience to which the content is targeted.

Conclusion

Broadcasting is different from other forms of audio or audiovisual communication. The words used to communicate are only heard, not seen. The recipient's processing of the message is through the ear—the aural channel. These words are received at a speed and in a sequence which is predetermined by the source of the message and they are presented only once. The recipient cannot control the process of reception except to tune away from the message.

These unique characteristics of broadcasting describe a situation in which the messages prepared by the writer must be immediately clear to the recipient audience. Clarity is enhanced by using the techniques of aural style in writing broadcast scripts. The beginning writer will need to practice these techniques consciously until they become automatic.

Exercises

1. From print sources—newspapers, magazines, books, trade journals—locate five complex sentences that use long opening modifying clauses. Copy these sentences and then rewrite them for aural style, simplifying and eliminating unnecessary, confusing material.

2. Look for examples of vague, abstract language; government documents are prime sources in which to find obscure, confusing statements. Rewrite for aural style.

3. Choose a major news story from a current newspaper and rewrite it as a 90-second *radio* news story. Observe these cautions:

   a. Choose a timely story that contains enough important facts or statements for you to fill the time without padding.

   b. Your story should have a lead sentence, and the body of the story should present the information in a logical sequence. But if you have not yet covered matters of structure, or the organization of news copy (Chapters 5 and 12), don't worry; they will be taken up later.

   c. Concentrate on the principles of aural style—all those things that make broadcast writing different from writing for print media.

4. Here are just a few of the most common errors beginning writers make, presented in a form in which you can test yourself on the correct usage; answers appear in the notes for this chapter.

   (1) What was the (affect, effect) of the victory?

   (2) (Because, Since) he lied, he was expelled.

   (3) Let's go four miles (further, farther) before we make camp.

   (4) The parties entered into a(n) (verbal, oral) agreement.

   (5) The diver carried an (air, oxygen) tank to the water.

   (6) The prisoners (alluded, eluded) the guards.

   (7) Sentences with (less, fewer) words are easier to understand.

(8) The lawyer (convinced, persuaded) the jury that his client was innocent.

(9) Come and (lie, lay) down by my side.

(10) This year's corn crop will be about two million bushels (less, fewer) than last year's.

(11) Today's game was called off (due to, because of) rain.

(12) Today's game has been (canceled, postponed); it will be rescheduled for next week.

(13) The veteran outfielder was (angry, mad) because he had been released from the team.[8]

Key Terms and Concepts	active voice	onomatopoeia
	aural style	pauses
	delay	redundancy
	feedback	repetition
	homophones	transition words
	inflection	

Notes

1. William Strunk, Jr., and E. B. White, *The Elements of Style* (New York: Macmillan, 1959), p. 17.

2. Gerald J. DeMartin, "Keep Your Script From Being Tied Up in 'Nots'," *E&ITV*, August 1982, p. 65. Copyright 1982 C. S. Tepfer Publishing Company, Inc. Reprinted by permission.

3. Albert Crews, *Professional Radio Writing* (Boston: Houghton Mifflin, 1946), pp. 51–52.

4. Crews, *Professional Radio Writing*, p. 51.

5. Strunk and White, *The Elements of Style*, pp. 15–16.

6. Adapted from K. Tim Wulfemeyer, *Beginning Broadcast Newswriting* (Ames: The Iowa State University Press, 1976), pp. 8–9, and Mitchell Stephens, *Broadcast News: Radio Journalism and an Introduction to Television* (New York: Holt, Rinehart and Winston, 1980), pp. 20–21, 26.

7. Edwin Newman, *A Civil Tongue* (Indianapolis: Bobbs-Merrill, 1976), p. 160. Copyright © 1975, 1976; by Edwin Newman, used with permission of the publisher, The Bobbs-Merrill Company, Inc.

8. Adapted from Brian S. Brooks et al., *News Reporting and Writing* (New York: St. Martin's Press, 1980), p. 267. Correct usage is: (1) effect, (2) because, (3) further, (4) verbal, (5) air, (6) eluded, (7) fewer, (8) convinced, (9) lie, (10) less, (11) because of, (12) postponed, (13) angry.

Chapter 3

Writing and Production

Broadcast writing is a means to an end—the end being the completed and hopefully errorless presentation of a program or announcement. The members of the audience who listen to or watch that program do not see the written script. It is used only by the preparers of the program—by directors, announcers, actors, and control room personnel. Its function is to enable them to put the final program together as quickly, easily, and inexpensively as possible.

In this chapter we will examine briefly the relationships between continuity and production. The word *continuity*, by the way, is appropriate here, for that is the term used for any structured form of written preparatory material. A script, in contrast, is the *complete* written record of what will be (or has been) broadcast. Many programs do not use full scripts. An interview program, for example, may use a "semi-script," which consists of a scripted opening and closing, but only a series of written questions (no answers) to guide the sequence of the body of the show. A TV documentary is often assembled from "shot sheets," lists of each recorded camera shot, including the length of the shot, its basic visual content, and, if it is an interview, the essence of the comment made by the interviewee in that shot. Radio commercials too, if they are to be delivered live by an announcer, may be done ad lib from just a "fact sheet." In practice, however, the terms *continuity* and *script* often are used interchangeably. We'll use both from time to time.

Our chapter is brief. We intend to discuss production only in relation to those matters we need to consider when preparing continuity. Two later chapters— "Handling Sound" and "Handling Visuals"—also examine production matters. There our focus will be on how sound and visuals are manipulated to provide the strongest, most attractive programs for audiences.

Factors Affecting Scripting

Several factors affect the type and complexity of the continuity needed for any broadcast program. Obviously the type of program affects the form of continuity.

A dramatic program is certainly going to have different requirements from a quiz show, a recorded musical program, or a news broadcast. But those factors that most directly affect the writer are connected to the method of production used. We've identified four such factors.

1. What portion of the program will be delivered ad lib—none, some, or all? Some programs are done without much formal preparation, such as the patter delivered by a radio disc jockey. Even the disc jockey, however, will usually work from a written play list, and written descriptions of the artists and selections, which are read from the record jackets or promotional releases sent by the record manufacturer or trade publications.

One of the most famous ad lib broadcasts of all time took an unexpected and tragic twist midway in the narration. It was the narrative account of a supposedly routine docking of the passenger dirigible *Hindenburg* in 1937. Instead the announcer, Herb Morrison, had to describe to a live audience a scene of destruction and death. This excerpt, taken from the complete narration, is dramatic even in print, but it needs to be heard to get the full emotional impact.

Well here it comes, ladies and gentlemen. We're out now, outside the hangar, and what a great sight it is. A thrilling one. It's a marvelous sight coming down out of the skies, pointed directly towards us and toward the mooring mast. The mighty diesel motors just roared, the propellers biting into the air and throwing it back into a gale-like whirlpool. No wonder this great floating palace can travel through the air at such a speed with these powerful motors behind it.

Now a field that we thought active when we first arrived has turned into a moving mass of cooperative action. The landing crews have rushed to their posts and spots, and orders are being passed along and last minute preparations are being completed for the moment we have waited for so long. The ship is riding majestically toward us like some great feather, riding as though it was mighty proud of the place it's claimed in the world's aviation. The ship is no doubt bustling with activity. As we can see orders are shouted to the crew. The passengers are probably lining the windows looking down at the field ahead of us, getting a glimpse of the mooring mast. It's practically standing still now. They've dropped ropes out of the nose of the ship and it's been taken ahold of down on the field by a number of men.

It's starting to rain again; the rain had slacked up a little bit. The back motors of the ship are just holding it, just enough to keep it from—It burst into flames! Get this, Scotty; get this, Scotty! It's afire and it's crashing! It's crashing, terrible! Oh my, get out of the way, please. It's burning, bursting into flames, and it's falling on the mooring mast and all the folks between. . . .

This is terrible. This is one of the worst catastrophes in the world! There are flames, oh, four or five hundred feet into the sky. It's a terrific crash, ladies and gentlemen. The smoke and the flames now, and the frame is crashing to the ground not quite to the mooring mast. Oh, the humanity and all the passengers. . . .

I tell you. . . . I cannot talk to people and . . . If, if, oh . . . , I can't talk. Ladies and gentlemen, on this. . . . It's a mass of smoking wreckage and everybody. . . . Can hardly breathe and talk at the same. . . . I can hardly. . . .

I'm going to step inside where I cannot see it. Scotty, it's terrible. Listen, folks, I'm going to have to stop for a moment because I've lost my voice. This is the worst thing I've ever witnessed. . . .

Source: Taken from the recording of the broadcast (as reproduced in *Jack Benny Presents the Treasury of Golden Memories of Radio;* produced by Longines Symphonette Society, Larchmont, N.Y.)

Breaking stories of this sort require ad lib treatment; no time exists in which to prepare a script. But most programs, especially those which involve more than one person in their preparation, will require some form of written continuity, so that everyone involved knows what is going on.

2. Is the program live, or prerecorded, or some combination? Although a relationship exists between an ad lib and a live broadcast—the account of the *Hindenburg* crash was both—it is common for scheduled, live programs to be heavily scripted.

In the earlier days of broadcast, during the period of major network radio programs and the first years of television, when recording was inefficient and of poor quality, most programs were aired live. Now such programs, with the exception of news broadcasts, are rare. Where they exist, careful scripting and rehearsal are necessary to minimize the possibility of foulups.

Quite a few programs, among them local public affairs programs, quiz shows, and even network daytime dramas, are produced "live-to-tape," which means that they are pretaped only for convenience. A local program that airs in the early morning might be pretaped in the afternoon with guests who would be unavailable for a live broadcast, but as far as the production is concerned the program is handled as a live show, with no (or very few) retakes and as little editing as possible.

3. How much editing, if any, will be done? It's obvious from our discussion that some programs are live, others are live-to-tape, others contain some live segments mixed with prerecorded stories and commercials, and still others are totally prerecorded and heavily edited.

Most dramatic programs on television are in the last category. They are recorded one camera shot at a time, and the final sequence is assembled by people employed strictly as editors. The trend in recent years, especially in television, has been toward increased use of smaller, more compact, and more flexible production equipment. Programs that once would have been done in a studio using multiple cameras may now be produced using only a single camera on location, with a resultant heavy dependence on editing to sequence the individual shots.

4. How quickly must the program be prepared for broadcast? We've already addressed the question of timeliness; it affects all the preceding questions. An important breaking story will have to be delivered ad lib, live, and unedited to get it on the air as quickly as possible.

For most news stories, however, there is time available to record at least portions of the story, to select and edit portions of that taped material, and to prepare a script which includes both the reporter's narration, any actualities which are to be inserted, and if for TV, a description of the visual sequence. In this case a script would not be written until after the story had been researched and the information gathered, but it would be completed before the story was inserted into the final program.

Programs other than news seldom face questions of timeliness. For them, whether or not a script is prepared, and what form it takes, will be determined by the other factors previously described.

We can conclude by saying that a script, or at least an advance script, may not be needed if only one person is involved in the complete process from creative idea to on-the-air, such as a radio disc jockey, or if only one person is in charge of the gathering and the assembly of the content which will be edited into a package before being aired, such as a news reporter. But whenever precision and accuracy are needed and whenever there are groups of people involved in the preparation of the program, continuity in some form will be required.

In the next chapter we will present several of the most common methods of laying out script elements on a typewritten page.

Audio Production

Both radio and television producers and writers must be concerned with sound production. For radio, the only sense which connects listeners to a program is a continuous flow of sound. Listeners expect to hear something at all times; an interruption of only a few seconds will bring the listener to the set—to see if the power has failed, or if program transmission has been interrupted. Listeners will quickly tune to another channel or turn off the set, and probably not tune back.

In television, brief segments without sound can be tolerated, possibly a highly dramatic moment while, say, the werewolf stalks his victim. But even TV audiences expect sound almost continuously, and will attempt to adjust the set if it disappears for long. Better, usually, to accompany even the werewolf with a sound effect or eerie music.

The sounds available to the writer-producer of any program are voices, music, and sound effects. Voices, in turn, may usefully be divided into single voices, which we generally call *narration,* and multiple voices. Multiple voices may be in the form of dialogue—voices responding to each other—but other techniques can be employed. We will consider all forms of sound in detail in Chapter 6.

Sounds may be presented live—that is, created at the moment of production or broadcast—or they may be prerecorded, edited, and mixed with other sounds to form a composite track. The simplicity and convenience of tape make many alternatives possible.

**Audio
Facilities**

The equipment used to produce broadcast sound consists primarily of microphones, turntables, tape recorders, and consoles. You will find these in great variety at every station and production facility.

Figure 3.1. This microphone is mounted on a swivel arm for easy access by the operator. Since this is a radio station (KOZZ, Reno, Nevada), the size of the microphone is not a problem; it won't be seen.
Photo courtesy of Broadcast Audio Corporation

Microphones   The initial capturing of any sound is done through a microphone, which is the *transducer* that converts sound energy to electrical pulses that then can be transmitted, stored on tape or disk, and/or mixed with other signals representing other sounds.

In simple production, a single microphone may be used to collect all the sounds which can be picked up at one location. But frequently better control of the relative intensities of multiple sounds can be gained if multiple microphones are used. At a football game, if each announcer has his or her own microphone for narration, and additional microphones are used to pick up crowd sounds, bands, and so on, you should be better able to balance voices with background noise and avoid having the announcers drowned out by the yelling when a touchdown is scored.

Similarly, multiple microphones recording the various instruments in an orchestra permit the control room operator to adjust each level to get the desired balance. Frequently each microphone will be recorded on a separate track, without mixing. When that is done, any number of trial mixes can be made in order to get the best final composite.

Multiple microphones (at least two) must be used to provide stereo recordings and broadcasts, where the final two tracks differ somewhat from each other, in order to provide the binaural effect. Until recently, broadcast stereo was possible only on FM radio stations (although of course it has been available on tape and disc recordings). Now AM stations and television are rapidly converting to stereo sound as well. Most of the production necessary to achieve stereo will be handled by technicians, but writers should be concerned with ways that stereo audio can enhance their scripts.

Listeners can recognize two basic microphone characteristics or positions—on-mike and off-mike. Other effects can be accomplished by having the source of the sound, say, an actor, *fade* from on to off, or vice versa. If a sound is heard off-mike or fades off-mike, it is perceived as distant from the listener, for one of the conventions of radio is that the listener is with the microphone.

The normal position for any sound is on-mike. Unless the writer specifies a sound as off-mike, or fading, performers and technicians will assume all sounds are to presented on-mike and at normal volume. We have some examples of on- and off-mike techniques in Chapter 6.

Turntables

Turntables are used in broadcast to play back prerecorded audio discs, either music or sound effects, or occasionally complete programs. They are operated by an audio technician.

There is no question that disk recordings and turntables will continue to have a major role as a storage medium for audio material. Multiple copies of recordings can still be produced most cheaply on vinyl disks, either LPs or 45s, and the new digital compact discs (CDs), although more expensive, have extremely fine fidelity and are very easy to use. But for many purposes in broadcast, discs and turntables have been replaced by tape recorders.

Tape
Recorders

Tape is more useful than discs because of the ease of recording and the speed and convenience with which recorded material may be edited and played back. Other advantages are the portability of equipment and low costs for both recorders and tape.

Three types of machines are likely to be found in a broadcast station, each with certain advantages and limitations. Open-reel tape machines can handle long periods of uninterrupted recording or playback, often operate at higher speeds, thereby permitting greater fidelity, and can be purchased in configurations which accommodate simultaneous recording of multiple tracks. They are also most easily used for editing—that is, if one is physically editing with a blade and splicing tape.

Cassette units (like those you probably have at home) are small, and easy to use and carry. They have decent recording response for voices, but are not so good for full fidelity music recording because of slow tape speed and narrow recording track. The tapes cannot be edited easily except by rerecording the content onto another machine.

Cartridge units are most commonly used for short recordings, such as individual commercials, short audio actualities to be inserted in a news story, or individual musical selections. A cartridge can be quickly inserted into its player, will cue automatically, play, and return to its starting position so that it is ready

Figure 3.2. Every radio production studio is unique, but this layout of WIAA, Interlochen, Michigan, is typical—console in left background, reel-to-reel tape recorders in the foreground, and turntables behind the operator. Not seen are cartridge and cassette tape machines; they are in the rack at the extreme left.
Photo courtesy of Broadcast Audio Corporation

to play again. Carts can be changed quickly in their players, so two players in a control room can support an almost continuous sequence of different audio inserts.

In the next chapter the script example for radio news (page 58) has three inserted actualities. In most stations, each of these would be edited from its original recording onto a separate cart, and then at the time of broadcast be inserted into the story as called for by the script.

In some circumstances, each actuality might be placed in sequence on the same cart. The writer/reporter must be aware of the technical limitations of the facilities available to support the broadcast. With three actualities on one cart, time must be allowed in the narration for the operator or automatic cueing equipment to cue up each insert. With separate carts for each actuality and two playback units, there must be time for the operator to cue up cart number 3 on machine number 1, after cart number 1 has finished on that machine and while cart number 2 is playing on machine 2. With one player and separate carts, there must be time in the announcer's narration for the operator to take out each cart in turn, place the next in the player, and cue it.

Consoles An audio *console* is the primary control device for the various sound inputs which might be used in presenting a program. First, it permits its operator to select one or more sources from among the various microphones, turntables, tape recorders, or remote lines that may be connected to it. Second, it allows the volume level of those sources to be controlled. Third, it permits multiple sources to be mixed together, and at appropriate levels. Finally, its output can be sent to various locations—for example, to a transmitter for broadcast, to a tape recorder for storage, or fed down a cable from its location to another console at another location.

For a writer, it will be very helpful to know the limitations of consoles in those studios or remote locations where you may be producing programs. For example, you cannot write a dramatic program requiring more microphones than the console can handle.

Video Production

Television audiences expect some video information on their screens at all times. Only a brief fade to black and back up to picture is allowed when changing scenes. The images that can be used to make up television programs are practically limitless, but it is useful, for discussion at least, to classify them in a few broad categories.

1. Performers—persons seen on screen. Performers may appear in several different types of roles.

   a. Persons who are talking directly to the audience, such as news reporters, commercial announcers, lecturers, or narrators. This category of images is often called "talking heads." Talking heads are inexpensive visuals; it costs less to point a camera at a reporter than it does to tape on location, even if it is less interesting. Also, it's faster.

   b. Persons talking to each other, as in a panel discussion program or interview. Critics see this use of the medium as only slightly better than talking heads. Again the same counterarguments apply—speed and cost.

   c. Persons performing—musicians, dancers, contestants in a quiz program. In these cases the visual content does provide attraction for audiences, but that attraction will vary tremendously depending upon the type of performance. A ballet is strong visually because of its movement; a symphony is not.

   d. Persons engaged in dramatic action, with accompanying dialogue, action, and so on. Here both the content and the action provide attraction for audiences.

2. Demonstration. The demonstration of activities, processes, and events is an obvious strength of television. The writers of commercials are aware of this strength; many effective commercials use demonstration in some way. Similarly, effective corporate and instructional programs make frequent use of demonstrations. Demonstrations may or may not use people. A role-playing segment in a training tape, for example, may use persons as actors in a dramatic sketch, but the purpose of the entire sketch may be to demonstrate, say, the appropriate behavior in an office.

3. Scenics. We'll use this term very broadly to categorize a range of images in which persons and demonstrations are not the primary focus. Many programs contain scenics—for example to set the location of a dramatic program. Travelogues have a high proportion of scenic shots. News stories use them as well, on location at the scene of a news event, to show the audience what has happened and where.

4. Visuals. This term is somewhat misleading. Obviously all TV images are visuals, but the term is used in the industry to categorize all the various graphic devices used in programs and announcements—program titles (even when they contain other visual content as well), charts and graphs, credits to performers and production personnel, the lower screen identifications of guests and of actuality sources, the background pictures inserted behind a news anchor, and so on. Visuals may appear on screen by themselves or as part of a composite image containing other pictorial elements.

The only point we want to make with this very simplistic categorization is to make you aware that some picture must be on the screen at all times. Sometimes writers who are not used to writing for television become so involved in the sound of their scripts that they forget the corresponding obligation to identify some visual for each moment of broadcast as well. Using these broad categories can help remind you of basic choices to meet that requirement, at least until you develop a more sophisticated visual sense.

Sound on Television

As we have already said, for the most part the practices of sound production apply not only to radio, but equally to television. Two additional comments need to be made regarding sound on TV.

First, the pictures seen and the sound heard should be supportive of each other. In many programs, that comes naturally. In a well-written dramatic show, both dialogue and action work to advance the plot. Often a problem develops, however, in writing narration. If, for example, in an instructional program explaining a manufacturing process, the narrator says, "The key to this process is the smooth-running operation of the eccentric cam which drives the shaft," then we need to see, at that point, the eccentric cam and its shaft, not some other part of the machinery, or a wide shot of the factory, or even a talking head. If the cam is hidden in the machinery, then perhaps an animated graphic will be needed to make the point visually.

Similarly, if the news reporter is at the scene of a major fire, the reporter should not say: "The flames are leaping high above the building. Fire crews are laying hoses and attempting to get control of the situation." The picture shows the flames and fire-fighters (or should, if the camera crew is doing its job properly), and the phrase "attempting to get control" is obvious and therefore meaningless. (On the other hand, if in an interview with a fire chief you learn that the fire is uncontrollable, and they are going to have to allow it to burn itself out, that would be a fact worth reporting.)

Audio should support, amplify, and expand upon the picture, and add detail that cannot readily be seen. It should not be redundant, merely repeating what is visually obvious.

Figure 3.3. WTTV-TV, a Chicago public television station, produces programs and promos in this editing suite. Equipment includes a switcher (at left), editor and special effects system (in front of operator), videotape recorders (beyond glass wall at right), audio tape recorder (extreme right), and monitors.
Photo courtesy of Ampex Corporation

Second, for television you must consider whether narration is to be on- or off-camera. We have made indirect references throughout the preceding sections to both techniques. On-camera narration is essentially a "talking head"; the audience sees the narrator delivering lines. The immediately preceding examples, the narration accompanying the eccentric cam and the reporter at the fire, assume that the narration is off-camera, at least at that point in the program. During other portions of the program or story, the narrator may be seen as he or she speaks. In preparing scripts, make sure it is clear from the context, or by writing specific instructions, which approach is intended.

Video Facilities

Video production equipment includes cameras, tape recorders, and consoles as the major items. As with audio, these devices come with a wide range of capabilities.

Cameras

The television camera (or film camera, for either can be used to collect visual images, and it is only a technical matter to convert film images for TV) is the *visual transducer*. It converts picture information into a sequence of electrical pulses in a similar though more complex manner than that in which microphones convert sound. These pulses may then be transmitted, stored, or mixed with other sources, or some combination thereof. Chapter 7 discusses the effects upon audiences when images are sequenced in various ways. The final sections of that

Figure 3.4. Ampex founder Alexander M. Poniatoff with one of the early VR-1000 video tape recorders. The cabinets at right contained electronics for the unit.
Photo courtesy of Ampex Corporation

chapter particularly consider the effects of sequence and transition from one picture source to another.

Tape Recorders

In the past ten years or so, the advances in videotape recording have been phenomenal. Not very many years ago, the only video recorders were mammoths recording on two-inch-wide tape at fifteen inches per second tape speed from reels which were heavy and expensive. Editing was possible only with a blade, splicing tape, special solvents to "read" the patterns of magnetic particles on the tape, and magnifying glasses.

Now broadcast-quality recorders are available in a wide variety of configurations, with much reduced size and weight. A camera-recorder combination for electronic news production may easily be carried about by a reporter. Editing too is all electronic, and usually controlled by a form of computer. Video edits, and the insertion of titles and other graphics, are quickly and easily done.

The effects of miniaturization and automatic controls for both cameras and recorders have been, as we suggested earlier, to take much production out of studios to remote locations. Electronic news gathering (ENG) and electronic field production (EFP) are the current waves in production. Entire productions can

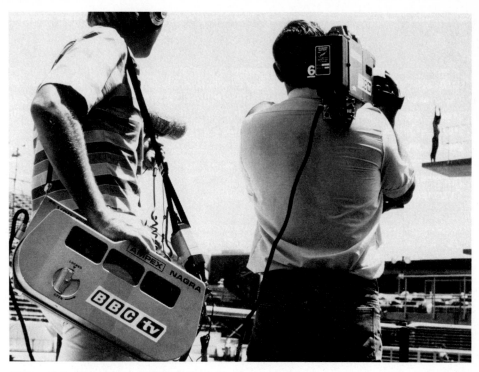

Figure 3.5. This Ampex VPR-5 portable Type C VTR illustrates how far technology has progressed in less than thirty years. Weighing in at only 15 pounds, the VPR-5 performs the same functions as the original VTR, the VR-1000. Shown here is a crew from the British Broadcast Corporation taping diving events at the 1984 Summer Olympics in Los Angeles.
Photo courtesy of Ampex Corporation.

be produced using a single camera and an episodic, shot-by-shot technique. The shots are then edited into the final program.

For writers, this approach means that it is easier to add visual variety to production. It also requires changes in writing technique. Instead of a fully prewritten script, continuity is more likely to be written after shooting the "raw" visuals onto tape. Then, while a selection is being made of those portions of the footage that will be used in the final program, the necessary narration to explain or bridge scenes will be written simultaneously. Shot sheets and other forms of notes to keep track of the visuals are more important to the documentation of these productions than would be a traditional script.

Perhaps the easiest way to understand how ENG and EFP have changed the requirements for continuity is to say that for live and live-to-tape production, scripts must be completed *prior* to production, to aid cast and crew in a successful presentation. In contrast, for ENG and EFP, continuity is more likely to be written *during* the production and editing process.

We don't mean to suggest that ENG and EFP have replaced studio production. There are advantages to studios as well, among them cost and control over such matters as lighting, sound, and weather. We do suggest that the type of production will in many cases affect the type of continuity required.

Consoles   The video control consoles at a TV station are quite sophisticated devices with which operators can select inputs, adjust levels, and create all kinds of special effects. Usually the console will be used to select a sequence of visuals from various inputs with appropriate transitions such as wipes, cuts, and fades between them. Sometimes, however, the console will be used to provide two or more simultaneous visual images, such as the inserted picture behind a news anchor, or a split screen showing both ends of a telephone conversation.

Conclusion

The written preparation, in whatever form it is put on paper, must facilitate the completed production. And the circumstances of the production, in turn, dictate the form the continuity will take and the amount of detail required.

We have further identified two trends in production which are having an impact on the writer's role in program production. One of these is the trend in audio production toward stereo reception. Writers have not been asked, until now, to consider seriously how the sound of a production might be enhanced by binaural reception.

The second, the miniaturization and automation of equipment, applies both to audio and video facilities, but is much more obvious in video. Smaller and more sophisticated cameras and tape recorders have permitted ENG and EFP techniques to be used on a scale never before possible. That style of production, in turn, has modified the requirements for scripting. A camera crew can go on location for a documentary or a news story without a script, perhaps only with the barest of notes or even just verbal instructions from a producer or reporter. They can shoot on tape three or four or even ten times as much footage as will be used for the final program and bring it back to the station. Then writers, producers, and announcers will prepare continuity, including narration and actualities, from the collected visuals. This freedom to produce ENG/EFP style has drastically changed the role of the writer and the forms of broadcast continuity.

You will be a better writer if you are also familiar with production, and in many smaller stations your job likely will involve some combination of writing and production. But you need not have had courses or practice in audio or video production in order to learn the basic principles of writing we present in this book.

Exercise   If you have had or are taking courses in radio or television production, you will have had opportunity to observe and to work with production equipment. If not, we suggest that you arrange to visit a radio and television station, or separate production facilities. Observe how the various pieces of equipment are used to get sound and picture on the air. Note what types of scripts are used in the productions you observe.

Key Terms and Concepts

ad lib
audio recorders: open-reel,
   cassette, cartridge
consoles: audio and video
continuity
dialogue
ENG and EFP
live broadcast

live-to-tape
microphone
narration
on-camera and off-camera
on-mike and off-mike
prerecorded
script: semi-script, shot sheet,
   fact sheet
talking head

Chapter 4

Script Mechanics

We can describe a broadcast script as a blueprint, or perhaps as a roadmap. Its function is to enable the production staff to prepare the program or announcement as efficiently as possible. In order to do that, all the materials that go into the script—the lines to be spoken and the instructions to cast and crew—must be clear, accurate, unambiguous, complete, and presented in a standardized form all the program "preparers" can follow.

We must be honest and point out that there is no one absolutely correct form for laying out a broadcast script. There are some general guidelines and a large body of common practice—approaches commonly accepted throughout the industry. But many supervisors have their own specific rules—the way they want it done in their newsroom or their advertising agency. When you get a job that requires writing scripts, do it the way your boss (or your instructor) wants it done. In the meantime, use the guidelines presented in this chapter.

Basic Rules for Scripting

1. All copy is typed. You cannot be sure that other people can read your writing, or even that you will be able to at any given moment, so don't take chances.

2. Use standard 8½″ by 11″ typewriter paper. Choose a paper that does not have a tendency to rattle when handled.

3. Use only one side of the paper.

4. Most scripts will require multiple copies. Make sure sufficient copies are available for all who will need one.

5. There is no universally accepted standard for the headings to be placed on a script, or for other preliminary material that may be required. Stations, networks, and advertising agencies all use forms that suit their own needs. Among the materials that appear in the heading are series title, program title, number of the program in the series, writer's, director's, and producer's names, length of program, date and time of broadcast, cast list, music list. This material may be at the top of the first

page of the script or, if it is lengthy, on a separate title page. If a separate title page is used, only a brief identifying title need appear on subsequent pages.

In general, copy should be neat—without strikeovers or deletions. Some minor corrections may be added in pencil, if necessary, but there is always a danger that pencilled changes will not be clear, and will lead to misread copy. Copy should also follow a consistent layout form.

Layout Forms for Scripts

We have a preference for using the term *layout form* to describe the arrangement on the typewritten page of the various elements that go into a script. Another word that is frequently used to describe the same thing is *format*, but, as we noted in Chapter 1, in broadcasting *format* has several different meanings. A program producer or director uses it to refer to the structural sequence of events within a program. And in radio *format* is used to describe the image or sound of a station—for example, a station may have a "Top 40" format, or a "country" format. To avoid confusion with the other meanings, we prefer to call this topic *layout form*, but frequently we will defer to standard practice and use the word *format* as well.

In this chapter we will discuss six approaches to layout, which cover the major types of copy and program content:

1. Basic radio layout, used for most radio programs that require scripts, except news.

2. Radio news layout, a simplified version of radio scripting, which provides for the easy insertion of news actualities.

3. Television split-page layout, used for most live programming. Our examples show it used for announcements.

4. Television news layout, a modification of the split-page form. Many variations are used to accommodate the different ways in which visual material may be gathered and inserted in a story.

5. Television dramatic script layout, for programs that are prerecorded and then edited on a shot-by-shot basis.

6. The storyboard, a visual layout used extensively for television commercials and in preparing slide-tape presentations.

Basic Radio Layout

Present-day radio programming is quite different from the elaborate productions of the 1930s and 1940s, which were usually broadcast live and required very detailed scripts. Much more informal programming appears on most radio stations today. A single announcer or disc jockey often broadcasts for long periods of time without any formal script—just a record library, a collection of prerecorded tape cartridges, and a microphone. Even the prerecording of commercial announcements for radio may be done by a creative producer with only a fact sheet about the product, a library of music and sound effects, and a production booth with tape recorders and turntables.

But for many radio programs and announcements, it is still necessary for a writer to assemble on the written page all the various elements that make up a complete script. Our first example is a script excerpt from a radio dramatic program. The second example is a commercial. It is also dramatic in form, and rather complex, requiring the integration of several voices with music and sound effects. Note especially how these effects—music and sound—are integrated into the scripts and how stage directions, stylistic instructions, and characterization are separated from the spoken copy.

GOLD DON'T RUST   WTR: Dan Paul Frizzelle

1	SOUND:	STREET SOUND AMBIENCE THROUGHOUT. CAR PULLS UP,
2		IDLES. WE HEAR RADIO MUSIC WHICH CUTS OFF
3		WHEN MOTOR IS TURNED OFF. CAR DOOR OPENS. DOG
4		BARKING IN BACKGROUND.
5	BUBBA:	(ON) That ain't Angel Luna polishing all those hubcaps there,
6		is it?
7	ANGEL:	(FADE ON) Que pasa, little Bubba? I ain't seen you in a year,
8		man, I figured you were dead or something.
9	SOUND:	CAR DOOR SLAMS.
10	BUBBA:	Not yet, Angel. My Uncle Ace around here somewhere?
11	ANGEL:	Where's he always, man? He's over there in his Cadillac with
12		a cooler full o'beer, staring off into space. While I do all the
13		work.
14	BUBBA:	He's got you on hubcap patrol, huh?
15	ANGEL:	Si . . . whatcha think? Is that beauty or is that beauty?
16	BUBBA:	I cain't even look, Angel . . . almost went blind when I drove
17		up.
18	ANGEL:	There must be three hundred of 'em . . . spinners, baby moon
19		. . . looks like those giant pictures of a bee's eyeball, don't it?
20	BUBBA:	Sure does. Hey, listen, I got to see the old man.
21	ANGEL:	There he is.
22	ACE:	(OFF) Hey, will ya look who's here!
23	SOUND:	FOOTSTEPS ON GRAVEL, THROUGH JUNK. DOG BARKING
24		CLOSER NOW.
25	BUBBA:	Don't jump up, Uncle Ace . . . I'd hate you to get a hernia on
26		my account.

1 2	ACE:	(FADE ON) Get in, Bubba. It's real good to see you. Help me drink some of this beer. Baby! Shut up over there!
3	SOUND:	<u>DOG QUIETS DOWN</u>
4	BUBBA:	How's the junk business treatin' you these days?
5 6	ACE:	Oh, good and bad, you know . . . your wrecked car just ain't a quality item anymore.
7	BUBBA:	I didn't know it ever was.
8 9 10	ACE:	Oh yeah . . . but everything is made outa plastic nowadays . . . one good wreck they just kinda disintegrate right there in the road. Cain't get many good parts off 'em.
11	BUBBA:	You don't look real hungry.
12 13 14	ACE:	I get by . . . I just jack up the prices on the parts I sell high enough to make a profit. (BUBBA REACTS) I'm just doing my bit to keep inflation up there in the big numbers.
15	BUBBA:	You ever thought about a different line of work?
16 17 18	ACE:	Hell, Bubba, I was in a different line of work about ever' two years most of my life . . . I just ended up here 'cause I got tired of everything else.
19	BUBBA:	Seems like it'd get old, workin' in a junkyard.
20 21 22 23	ACE:	Aw . . . I don't do no work here. That's what I pay old Angel for . . . Somethin' needs doin' I just tell Angel and he takes care of it. He's been makin' quittin' noises lately but I don't think he's gonna.
24	BUBBA:	He might, ya know.
25 26 27 28	ACE:	I ain't gonna worry a lot 'til he does it . . . then I'll have my heart attack. Til then it's a real fine thing havin' your own junkyard . . . you can pitch an empty beer can just about anywhere you want and nobody says a damn thing.
29	SOUND:	<u>EMPTY BEER CAN CLATTERS ON GROUND</u>
30	ACE:	Reach me 'nother beer outta that cooler will ya?
31	BUBBA:	Sure thing.
32	ACE:	Have one yourself f' you like.

1	BUBBA:	Thanks.

2 SOUND: CANS POPPED OPEN

3 BUBBA: Look, Ace . . . I got a problem is the reason I stopped by.

4 ACE: Yeah, you look about like your favorite sheep died. You rob a
5   bank or what?

6 BUBBA: Naw, it's worse than that. It's kinda . . . aw, what the hell,
7   you know anything about love?

8 ACE: Love, huh? Everybody knows somethin' about love. What
9   happened, Bubba, you find some or lose some?

10 BUBBA: I don't know . . . maybe both. I'm just real confused lately . . .
11   an I figured you're about the smartest guy I know.

12 ACE: That's entirely possible.

13 BUBBA: You ever been in love?

14 ACE: Course I been in love, Bubba . . . but that don't make somebody
15   an expert. You talk to your Daddy about it?

16 BUBBA: Aw, you know I cain't talk to him.

17 ACE: For what it's worth, Bubba, here's everything I know about
18   love in twenty-five words or less . . . or more. (PAUSE) One.
19   It hurts like hell. Two. It's the finest thing there is. Three. It
20   usually stops. Four. Generally when it stops it's too soon for
21   one of the folks and not soon enough for the other.

22 SOUND: DOG BEGINS TO BARK OFF-MIKE

23 ACE: Angel! Go tell Baby to put a cork in it, will you?

24 ANGEL: (FADE ON) Baby's your dog, Ace, not mine. You want me to
25   go get her put to sleep, that's one thing. Trainin' her's somethin'
     else.

27 ACE: Well I'm busy here, Angel . . . go give her a bone or somethin'.

28 ANGEL: Oh si . . . hey Bubba, you got any bones on you?

29 BUBBA: I'm fresh out.

30 ANGEL: Yeah, me too. Guess a rock'll have to do. (THROWING) Shut
31   up, dog!

1	SOUND:	ROCK HITS SHEET METAL, DOG YELPS, QUIETS.
2	ANGEL:	(FADE OFF) Works every time.
3	ACE:	Thanks a heap, Angel.
4	ANGEL:	(OFF) De nada.

Source: Courtesy of the author, Dan Paul Frizzelle.

Client: PERRY BOYS' PB 035
Media: 60 sec Radio
Date: 6/24/75

ANNCR:	Perry Boys' Smorgy Presents another "Perry Tale"
SFX:	MUSIC BOX
ANNCR:	Once upon a time . . . there lived an old woman and her son, Jack . . . a promising horticulturalist.
MOTHER:	OK son, once more . . . what did you do with the cow???
JACK:	(ENTHUSIASTIC) I traded her for a few magic beans . . . I'm gonna plant them in this pot . . . climb to the top of the beanstalk . . . and steal the hen that lays the golden eggs . . .
MOTHER:	I think I'll go lie down for a while . . .
ANNCR:	But Jack did plant the beans and a giant beanstalk grew into the sky . . .
SFX:	CRASHING WOOD
MOTHER:	OK, Mr. Green Thumb, who's gonna fix the hole in the roof???
JACK:	Later, Mom . . . I'm gonna climb to the top . . .
SFX:	STRENUOUS CLIMBING
JACK:	Wow . . . a castle . . .
SFX:	GIANT FOOTSTEPS
JACK:	And . . . Uh-Oh . . .

GIANT: (ECHO) Fee - Fi - Fo - Feel . . . I've found me a little meal . . .

JACK: Please, Mr. Giant . . . I'm so scrawny . . . You'd still be hungry . . . Let me go and I'll tell you all about Perry Boys' Smorgy . . . with over 40 delicious things to eat . . . all better tasting than me.

GIANT: Sounds good . . . race ya down the beanstalk.

SFX: BREAKING SOUND

GIANT: Yeeeeoww!

JACK: (YELLING DOWN—ECHO) . . . You win . . .

ANNCR: You'll always win when you eat at Perry Boys' Smorgy Restaurants . . . $1.99 for lunch and $2.89 for dinner . . . in Santa Cruz, Salinas . . . and Monterey at 2066 Fremont Boulevard.

Source: Courtesy of the author, Frank LaRosa.

Here, based on the examples, are important layout considerations for most radio scripts:

1. *Page layout:* Allow about one inch left margin, then leave a column which will be used to identify the source of each sound. A colon may or may not follow these items. Then leave a few spaces and begin the copy itself. All copy is double-spaced. (In this text we have not regularly followed our own rule in this regard in order to save space. Samples that have been reproduced directly from the original typed copy are double-spaced throughout, but those that have been typeset are only double-spaced between items such as speeches and music or sound cues.)

2. *Page numbering:* If the copy is more than one page long, number all pages at the top in sequence. Often the number is repeated, for example, 6-6-6-6-6, making it easier to assemble the script quickly should the pages become disarranged.

3. *Line numbering:* In complex scripts involving several characters and/or music and sound cues, the lines are numbered. The numbering aids in making corrections during rehearsals. For simple scripts, line numbering is usually omitted. Line numbers may appear at the far left of the page, as shown in the Gold Don't Rust excerpt. Or they may be placed between the "sound source" column and the copy:

   ANNCR: 1   The holiday season is in full bloom
               2   at Crystal Florist. Color your
               3   Christmas with the traditional
               4   beauty of poinsettias. Crystal
               5   Florist has a stunning selection
               6   for you to choose from.

Sometimes line numbering is continuous throughout a script. More often, line numbers, when used, are repeated on each page, again as shown in the Gold Don't Rust excerpt.

4. *Source of sound:* This column at the left of the page is used to indicate the type of sound which is to appear at that point in the script and its source—that is, some identification of the VOICE delivering the line, or of MUSIC or SOUND. If only a single voice is being used, it is frequently designated as ANNCR (for announcer) or NARR (for narrator).

   Multiple voices may be identified by the names of the characters in the drama (BUBBA, ANGEL, ACE, etc.) or if the role is too small to have a name, as MALE VOICE, FEMALE VOICE, VOICE #1, VOICE #2, and so on. However, be careful in your identifications. If you use VOICE #1 and VOICE #2 as anonymous voices in one scene of a play and then want two different voices (persons) for small parts in a later scene, use VOICE #3 and VOICE #4. If you use the identifications VOICE #1 and VOICE #2 again, the actors playing the roles might use the same vocal characterization as in the earlier scene; the audience will believe the new characters to be the same as those heard in the first scene and will become confused.

5. *Music cues:* If the cue is for MUSIC, that single word is all that is needed in the sound source column; the description of the music will appear in the body of the copy, as in these examples:

   MUSIC: LATIN THEME ON SOLO GUITAR, UP FOR 5 SEC AND FADE
   <u>   UNDER</u>

   MUSIC: <u>STINGER TO CLOSE</u>

   MUSIC: JINGLE   BELLS   INSTRUMENTAL   IN   BACKGROUND
   <u>   THROUGHOUT FOLLOWING</u>

6. *Sound cues:* Similarly, the word SOUND (some prefer SFX, for sound effects) will designate a sound cue. Its description will also appear in the body of the copy. Several SOUND cues are shown in both the Gold Don't Rust and Perry Boys examples. All material appearing in the sound source column is typed in CAPITAL letters.

7. *Script copy:* In the body of the script itself, the material to be spoken is typed in normal copy style (upper and lower case). Everything that is not spoken on the air is typed in ALL CAPITAL LETTERS: sound and music descriptions, cues, stylistic directions, and so on. Directions to the performer, which also appear in the script proper, are set off by parentheses. Music and sound cues are also underlined.

8. *Use of MORE:* If the lines of one character continue from one page to the next, the warning cue MORE MORE MORE is placed at the bottom of the page. This warning prevents the actor from assuming that a speech is completed, pausing while the page is turned, and then finding that the speech continues, because by that time the continuity and smoothness of delivery will have been broken. If another character has the first line on the following page, this cue is not used.

9. *Dividing words:* Never divide a word across a page. Try not to divide a sentence across a page, or to divide a word between lines.

**Radio News
Layout**

A radio news broadcast, particularly if it is both written and voiced by the same person, can use a more informal script. Some complication is added, however, when the actual voices of people featured in the story are inserted in the form of prerecorded *actualities*. This example shows a commonly used method for identifying actualities:

STORMS
11/10
7:30 am
doyle

Governor Deukmejian is urging Californians to take all necessary precautions for possibly severe storms again this winter. The Governor has proclaimed this week, "Winter Storm Preparedness Week" . . . already this year he has declared states of emergency in forty-four of California's fifty-eight counties. Forty-two of those have been declared major disaster areas by the President. Deukmejian says California's most destructive disasters are caused by major storms, bringing floods, mudslides and coastal erosion. Anita Garcia of the State Office of Emergency Services says there are three major steps in preparing for possibly severe winter storms:

CART:	GARCIA
TIME:	:56
OUT:	to sand bags.

In earlier Sacramento Valley geological history, frequent flooding was of major concern during heavy winter storms. But Hal Waite of the Sacramento County Office of Emergency Services says the potential for major flooding here is not nearly what it used to be:

CART:	WAITE
TIME:	:20
OUT:	kind of a basis.

Waite says the major problem posed now by winter storms in the Sacramento Valley is the way people drive in them.

CART:	WAITE
TIME:	:34
OUT:	down that line.

Source: Courtesy of KXPR; Sacramento, CA.

For radio news, these guidelines are the most important to follow:

1. Some sort of identifying *slug* is used to head the story. Practices vary; the one we have used is common. It consists of a one-word title (two at most), the date, time of broadcast, and the writer's name. Time of broadcast is particularly important with continuing stories. Over a day's time several different versions—each updated with whatever new information has become available—may be scattered around the

newsroom. The news announcer needs to know that he or she has the most recent one.

2. There is no need for a sound source column, because often only one person will read the entire newscast. If more than one person is involved, the various names may be penciled in the margin.

3. When *actualities* are used (the actual recorded voices of persons in the story), the quote has to be identified. Again, practices vary, but the style used for the three actualities in this story is common: (1) some identification of the tape cartridge on which the quote is stored (this example uses the name of the source person as the designation); (2) the time (length) of the cut; and (3) the *out cue*, the last few words of the actuality.

4. Instructions in the script on the use of *raw sound*—that is the recording of the sounds of a parade, or gunfire in a battle, or the crowd at a ball game—should be inserted into the completed script in the same way they were handled in the dramatic and commercial examples given earlier.

5. This example uses the normal pattern of upper and lowercase letters we recognize from print. Some newspersons prefer their script to be typed in *ALL CAPS*. Their preference may be the result of years of experience reading copy sent over the Associated Press or United Press International teletype wires. The wire service machines could type only uppercase letters. We believe the normal copy style is easier to read.

6. Words that are unfamiliar and may be difficult to pronounce should have a pronunciation key. Our story about California's Governor Deukmejian does not contain a phonetic spelling for his name, presumed to be familiar to California reporters. But if the story had gone out of state, a guide should have been included, as follows: "Governor Deukmejian (Dook-may-jin) is urging. . . ." A simplified phonetic spelling is inserted in parentheses immediately following the word. Both AP and UPI provide brief lists of phonetic symbols. Here is the AP list:[1]

Vowel Sounds		Consonants
a—bat, apple	oh—go, oval	g—got, beg
ah—father, arm	oo—food, two	j—job, gem
aw—raw, board	ow—scout,	k—keep, cap
ay—fate, ace	crowd	ch—chair, butcher
e, eh—bed	oy—boy, join	sh—shut, fashion
ee—feel, tea	u—curl, foot	zh—vision, mirage
i, ih—pin, middle	uh—puff	th—thin, path
y, eye—ice, time,	yoo—fume, few	kh—guttural "k"
guide		

Television Split-Page Layout

Two quite different layout forms are used in television. One evolved from radio. It uses a split-page arrangement, and is used for most live television programs including news, some commercials, and simpler programs. The other form, which comes from the motion picture industry, is used mostly for dramatic programs prerecorded on film or videotape and edited before broadcast. That form will be described in the next section.

Because television must deal simultaneously with both visual and sound elements, a split-page format is common, with the two columns labeled AUDIO and VIDEO. In practice, however, some of the visual elements, such as stage directions to the performers, tend to appear along with the spoken copy in the AUDIO column. The VIDEO column is used primarily by the director for camera cues and instructions to the technical crew. By the way, there is no agreement as to which of the two columns should be on the right or left side of the page.

Here are three examples—all announcements. There is some variation among the details of each piece of copy, because of the different video requirements in each script.

BERNIE RICHTER
TV Spot #1 "River"
August 29, 19xx (Final)

VIDEO	AUDIO	
MEDIUM SHOT—BERNIE ON LEVEE (RIVER IN BACKGROUND)	BERNIE:	I'm Bernie Richter . . . I think Butte County is a special kind of place . . . our farming is productive and our towns are prosperous . . .
DISSOLVE TO SHOTS OF:		But most importantly, our people make this the greatest place in the world to live and raise a family. . . .
FARMER ON TRACTOR IN FIELD		
DOWNTOWN SHOPPERS		They're hard-working, energetic, bill-paying people who deserve the best in the way of county government. . . .
CHILD EATING ICE CREAM		
TUBERS		
FAMILY ON BICYCLES		
FARM FAMILY AT DINNER		
STUDENTS ON CAMPUS WITH BOOKS		
CLOSEUP—BERNIE		Yet, there are some who would change our whole lifestyle to fit some misguided ideas . . .
SLIDE: RICHTER FAMILY		I think we've worked too hard to let that happen . . . Butte County is special . . .
SUPER: Paid by Citizens for Richter PO Box 1867 Chico, CA 95927	ANNCR:	Let's keep it that way. . . . Re-elect Supervisor Richter

Source: Courtesy of the writer, Frank LaRosa.

ANIMAL PROTECTION INSTITUTE
WRITER: ROESE

VIDEO	AUDIO
FADE IN L.S. OF ROOM DARK WITH SHADOWS. BABY'S CRIB IN FOREGROUND. BACK OF ROCKING ROCKER IN FRONT OF FIREPLACE IN BG. DOLLY IN SLOWLY FOR M. CU OF BACK OF ROCKER	WOMAN'S VOICE, SINGING Bye baby bunting Daddy's gone a-hunting to catch a baby rabbit's skin to wrap my baby bunting in.
DISSOLVE. FOREST SCENE. SNOWING, SNOW ON GROUND AND ON TREES. L.S. OF UNBROKEN PATH THROUGH TREES. CAMERA WALKS ALONG PATH. AT TIMES BRANCHES BRUSH PAST SCREEN	LIVE SOUND. CRUNCH OF FOOTSTEPS. NARR: (VOICE OVER) This lullaby would not give a baby sweet dreams to sleep with if she knew how daddy hunts for baby rabbit fur. Animals are trapped for their fur.
TRAPPED ANIMAL BECOMES VISIBLE IN THE DISTANCE. IT IS CENTRAL FOCUS OF CAMERA TILTED L.S. OF TRAP WITH RABBIT. TILTED M.CU OF TRAPPED RABBIT. TILTED CU. OF TRAP AND RABBIT. CU OF TRAPPED RABBIT'S FOOT	Every year thirty million animals, including fox, mink and raccoon are trapped in the United States. When the steel-jaw trap snaps shut, the animal faces a slow, agonizing death. Death from starvation, thirst, freezing or fear. (END FOOTSTEPS)
LAP DISSOLVE. CU OF RABBIT'S FACE. PAN UP TO THE TIP OF AN EAR	The lullaby is not beautiful. If it sends a chill down your back, don't throw on a fur coat to warm yourself. Please write to the Animal Protection Institute of America for information on how this cruel method of trapping can be stopped. End the use of steel-jaw traps. Wrap your baby in your arms to keep her warm.
DISSOLVE. BABY RABBITS SLEEPING NEXT TO MOTHER RABBIT. SUPER: A.P.I., BOX 220505, SACRAMENTO, CALIF. CONTRIBUTIONS ARE TAX DEDUCTIBLE. FADE OUT.	

END   END   END

Source: Reprinted by permission of Animal Protection Institute, Sacramento, CA.

SHOT No.	VIDEO	AUDIO
1	WS OF VACANT TRAIN STATION WHILE CAMERA BOOMS DOWN TO EYE LEVEL. THROUGHOUT THE BOOM A SINGLE FIGURE WALKS TOWARD THE CAMERA FROM SOME DISTANCE. THIS MAN IS THE ANNOUNCER. (THERE IS THE NATURAL SOUND OF THE MAN'S FOOTSTEPS HAVING AN ECHO QUALITY)	
		MAN: (ON CAMERA)
2	CU MAN AS HE WALKS HEAD ON TOWARDS CAMERA. AS HE WALKS THE CAMERA TRUCKS BACK TO KEEP HIM FROM COMING TOO CLOSE AND TO GIVE A FEELING OF MOVEMENT. AS THE CAMERA TRUCKS BACK VARIOUS PARTS OF THE TRAIN STATION COME INTO FOCUS IN THE BACKGROUND. THE MAN IS SOMEWHAT ELDERLY. THERE IS LITTLE DOUBT THAT HE ONCE WORKED FOR THE RAILROADS. HE IS DRESSED CASUALLY, BUT DOES NOT WEAR OVERALLS OR ANYTHING OPENLY TRITE.	Ya know, there was a time when this railroad station was full of people. People going places, places all over the country. Any more you're lucky if you can find a single soul in this entire room. Why I remember when hundreds even thousands of people would leave from here in just one day. That was when traveling by train was popular and the train was about the best way to get anywhere for a lot of folks.
	CAMERA TRUCK STOPS & THE MAN TURNS TO STEP OUT THROUGH DOORS TO THE VACANT LOADING AREA.	In fact, for many they were the only thing available. You could get a ticket over there at the window for anywhere in the good ol' US and it didn't cost an arm and a leg. Oh there was some fuss'n around with baggage and all but before long you were rock'n to sleep over the clikity clack of the rails.
	CUT	
3	OUTSIDE MAN APPROACHES CAMERA.	Yep, those were the days . . . don't reckon they'll ever come back. But the trains are back and they're better than ever. Trouble

MORE   MORE   MORE

SHOT No.	VIDEO	AUDIO
		is nobody rides them. Guess they just don't know what they're missing.
	CUT	
4	WS MAN GETS ON TRAIN AS IT PULLS OUT	ANNOUNCER: (OFF CAMERA)
	SUPER: AMTRAK LOGO	(NATURAL SOUND OF TRAIN UNDER) Next time you travel, take the train and let the good times roll.
		END

Source: Courtesy of the writer, Bernard Tagholm.

Follow these guidelines for split-page television layouts:

1. Divide your script into two parts: AUDIO and VIDEO. Instructions for things that are heard go under AUDIO; those for things that are seen go under VIDEO. One exception: Stage directions to performers generally appear on the AUDIO side, because the performers seldom pay attention to the VIDEO instructions and concentrate on the side of the page that contains their lines.

2. The basic layout is double-spaced, and audio copy is double-spaced. Video instructions, however, are single-spaced if the lines form part of the same instruction. Adjust spacing between the two columns so that audio and video are kept parallel—that is, the video instructions should come at the same point on the page as the audio they accompany. Spread out the copy whenever it begins to look cluttered. Don't try to save paper.

3. AUDIO may be handled several ways. If there is a complex sound track with numerous cues, follow the radio approach, because each source will need to be identified. Use a separate "sound source" column as in the Richter ad, or a variation, like the API script. If the audio is very simple, only a single narrator, for example, and there are no sound or music cues, the "sound source" column can be omitted.

   As with radio copy, anything that is spoken should be in upper and lower case. Anything that is *not* to be spoken should be written in ALL CAPITAL LETTERS, such as music cues, stage directions, and stylistic instructions.

4. Directions to actors or narrators within a speech should be placed at the point where they apply. Use parentheses around the direction, and type in ALL CAPS. Such directions include stage business, instructions on how a line is to be delivered, the desired mood, and so on.

   Also indicate in parentheses if the lines are to be delivered as a *voice-over*—that is, when the announcer or actor will *not* be seen speaking the lines, but will be voicing the copy over other visual material. Either of the following is acceptable:

   NARRATOR (V.O.):
   NARRATOR (OFF CAMERA):

The opposite situation, when the announcer or actor is to be seen on camera is shown in the Amtrak spot and is labeled ON CAMERA.

Identify directions for the actions by talent and stage business with the word *BIZ*. Place this identification on a line by itself, in ALL CAPS AND UNDERLINED.

> ANNCR:
>
>
>
> BIZ
> CROSSES FROM FIREPLACE TO TABLE;
> PICKS UP BOTTLE AND GLASS; POURS.
>
> When I first tasted this new. . . .

Identify other audio sources (music and sound effects), using the same layout as for radio.

5. On the VIDEO side we have used ALL CAPITAL LETTERS for all the directions, with one exception. That is for titles and other graphics when they are to be shown on the screen in lowercase. Not all stations follow this guideline; some use normal copy style in the VIDEO column.

6. Titles and captions to be displayed on the screen are "flagged" by any of several words. Some stations use FONT, others CHIRON (the brand name of the character generator used at many stations). Still others use SUPER (short for superimposition, a now old-fashioned method for inserting graphics). Following that "flag" word, write out the font information exactly as you want it to appear on the screen. Place that information at the spot in the script at which it is to appear, and also show when it is to be removed from the screen—FONT OUT.

> CHIRON: Joe Jones
>   County Supervisor
>
> TOP FONT: Recorded earlier
>
> DIAGONAL
> SUPER   SPECIAL REPORT

7. A number of common abbreviations are used, especially in video terminology, to save space and make reading easier and faster for crew members. If you are not already familiar with video production terminology, you will be after you read this text. We will use many of the basic production terms in various chapters. In the meantime, use those terms and abbreviations you understand, but most important, use descriptions that will be understood by those who have to interpret your script for the TV screen.

8. Each of the three examples we have shown was produced differently, and to some extent that is reflected in the script layout. The Richter political ad uses very simple, inexpensive, production techniques. Two visual sequences—those which show the candidate talking—were shot on location on videotape. The other visual material is slides. The audio employs two voices—the candidate and an announcer.

The API announcement used a woman's voice and a sound effect to add interest, variety and realism to the narration. Although it is written using the split-page form, it obviously requires a good deal of preproduction. The two video scenes—in the baby's room and in the forest—would be shot on film or videotape and edited. The woman's voice and the sound of the footsteps also would be preproduced on audio

Slug: Marineland   Page #1-1-1
Date: 6/23   Writer: Wilson
Length: 0:55

VIDEO	AUDIO
ON CAMERA VTR, SIL . . . :45 (STARTS 11:26 IN FROM VIDEO HEAD OF KNBC SIG.)	An eight year old Sacramento youth and his mother were among four persons injured slightly yesterday as the result of a freak accident at Marineland of the Pacific in Palos Verdes Estates. The accident occurred when Bimbo the whale smashed a porthole on the second story level of the four story tank, sending thousands of gallons of water gushing onto spectators. The force of the water carried eight year old Jack Copeland of 2038 Mission Avenue in Sacramento and 30-year-old Sonia Morales of Long Beach about fifteen feet down the corridor. The boy's mother, Mrs. Faye Copeland, and Miss Morales' sister, Amalia, were cut by broken glass. All four were treated at a nearby hospital. Their injuries were not serious. Bimbo broke the glass with his nose while he was maneuvering for a leap out of the water. He suffered a four inch cut on his snout, but it was not serious. Afterward, Bimbo and four other whales and four dolphins who shared the exhibition tank with him
DUMP TAPE	were transferred to another tank.
ON CAMERA	Marineland officials say they should have the damage repaired in a day or so.

Source: Courtesy of KCRA, Sacramento, CA.

---

tape. Then video, sound, and narration would be mixed to produce the completed spot.

The Amtrak commercial uses a simple production technique, but it depends heavily on the establishment of a mood. Therefore, there is an extensive description at the beginning of the setting and of the appearance required of the announcer.

Television News Layout

Layout for television news uses a split-page approach similar to that used for other live programs, but there are some unique characteristics, particularly in the insertion of visual material. Here are two news stories, and the opening and first story from a public affairs newsmagazine program called "DeColores."

To prepare television news copy in an acceptable layout, you should use the basic split-page form and follow the guidelines given in the preceding section, with some modifications:

1. Complexities arise in explaining the different forms of audio and video inserts so that performers and crew can integrate those inserts into the story

DECOLORES
Air: 11/15
Writer: Martinez

VIDEO	AUDIO
MS MARTINEZ	Good Morning. I'm Bob Martinez. Welcome to our program. . . . Today we'll bring you a report on the number one high school soccer team in this area. Also, a film of El Centro de Artistas Chicanos, preparing for a Christmas sale . . . Then, a talk with three representatives of the Latin American Bilingual Secretaries Association of San Joaquin. . . .
ROLL VTR PGM OPEN (SOT FULL)	And a special report on the Baja California Peninsula. All this, and more, on DeColores.
TAKE PGM OPEN	
MS MARTINEZ	El Centro de Artistas Chicanos is a group of well known Sacramento artists who literally share their talents with the community—through a series of art classes. Men, women, young, old: Everyone is invited to come and learn about a variety of art forms.
FILM/SILENT	VOICE OVER (STUDIO) El Centro has been holding these classes on Monday and Wednesday evenings for the past few months and now on display are the works of their proud students. CT FULL :08 SEC, THEN UNDER STUDIO VOICE OVER, CT UNDER If you haven't done your Christmas shopping yet, you might want to consider visiting this Christmas arts and crafts show. It starts on Thursday, and runs through Monday, December sixteenth. The hours . . . noon to six in the evening . . . at the El Centro de Artistas building at the corner of 32nd and Folsom Boulevard. You'll find only handmade works at this show—created by members of El Centro and their students from the community. CT FULL

Source: Courtesy of KCRA, Sacramento, CA.

Slug: Chichester   Page #1-1-1
Date: 9/10   Writer: Hastings
Length: 1:48

VIDEO	AUDIO
LIVE	Britain's Sir Francis Chichester is undoubtedly the world's most famous contemporary seaman. But William Willis, an American adventurer, has displayed as much daring. He has completed impressive solo voyages by raft across the Pacific . . . and he is nine years older than Chichester. Willis, a New Yorker, began a solo Trans-Atlantic crossing last Summer, but fell ill and was picked up at sea. He told news reporter Gabe Pressman he soon will set sail again.
VTR/SOT 1:29 #3 4:24 in	
	(END CUE ". . . because its in his system.")
LIVE	Willis will make his Atlantic crossing in an eleven and a half foot boat. Chichester's Gypsy Moth is 53 feet.

Source: Courtesy of KCRA, Sacramento, CA.

smoothly. The process is similar to that used for radio actualities, but more variations exist. Each of our three stories is slightly different in this regard.

The Marineland story begins with the anchor on camera, then shifts to a videotape actuality from the location of the story which is run silent and lasts 45 seconds. (The note STARTS 11:26 IN FROM VIDEO HEAD OF KNBC SIG. shows that the story is on a feed which came to KCRA from KNBC and that this video cut can be found 11 minutes and 26 seconds from the opening KNBC news signature.) The story concludes by returning to the news anchor on camera. Since the sound for this story is from a single source, it is not indicated on the script. It will be read by the anchor announcer.

The Chichester story is similar, except that the body of the story is on videotape with sound. The audio opens and closes with the anchor LIVE. The videotape insert is SOT (sound on tape). The full narration on the sound track is not included, but the end cue is given so that the director will know when to return to the studio for the anchor's tag. The videotape insert lasts 1:29 and is on reel #3 at a position 4:24 in from the beginning of the tape.

The newsmagazine program, "DeColores," contains the program opening and its first story. The story has a silent videotape segment, which is narrated (VOICE-OVER) by the anchor, and which also uses an audio cartridge of background sound to add interest and "presence" to the story.

2. We have shown these examples, as with the announcements, with the AUDIO column in normal style and the VIDEO in all caps (except for font

information). Some stations type both columns in all caps, and even use special typewriters with large typefaces, on the assumption that reporters and anchors can see the words more easily, especially when reading from a Teleprompter. Some stations reverse our pattern—all caps for AUDIO and normal style for the VIDEO column. In the industry, the decision as to which style to use will be made by the station's news director.

3. Individual stories will carry heading information (the *slug*) similar to that used for radio—a one- or two-word title, date, time, and writer's name or initials. Programs will be identified by title and date at least.

Television Dramatic Script Layout

The script form used in the motion-picture industry has quite naturally found a second home in television. Many of the dramatic programs on television are produced by the same studios and crews that produce feature motion pictures. And both feature films and television dramatic programs are produced as a series of separate camera shots. Each scene is shot individually and not usually in the order in which the scenes will be shown in the final program. After all scenes have been recorded on film or videotape, they are edited into the final presentation.

This episodic, start-and-stop type of production permits use of a layout form which is quite different from those used for radio or live television. The example here is the first pages of the shooting script for an episode of the NBC prime-time series "Riptide."

From this example, note these characteristics, which conform to more or less standard practice for scripting television dramatic programs:

1. Use a separate page or pages preceding the script itself to describe the characters, wardrobe, settings, props, and graphics needed if these descriptions are important to the production. This information should not be included in the actual script, where it clutters the layout. The amount of detail needed will vary with the program; for a continuing series much of this information will already be known to all the crew members who need to know, and need not be repeated with every script. This is the case with "Riptide." The title page will contain series title, program title, writer, producer, copyright information, dates of various revisions and other miscellany.

2. Number all pages. If the script will undergo various revisions, date the revised pages.

3. Each scene, or camera shot, is handled individually. We say scene *or* camera shot, for there are two different approaches to teleplay writing. One, called the *shot-by-shot* script, provides a separate description of the dramatic action for each camera shot. The other approach is called the *master-scene* script. It is the more common approach, and is also easier for the novice writer who may not be familiar with camera angles, distances, and movement. "Riptide" is written using the master-scene technique. The director will select the camera shots to be used within each scene (see Chapter 16 for additional comments on these differences).

4. Each scene is numbered consecutively, usually at both the left and right margins. In this "Riptide" episode several scenes which appeared in earlier drafts are now omitted; the omission is noted, but the scenes are not renumbered.

```
                           RIPTIDE


                       "PRISONER OF WAR"


                            by

                      Babs Greyhosky


              A STEPHEN J. CANNELL PRODUCTION

                    All rights reserved


        Copyright 1984 by Stephen J. Cannell Productions


              No portion of this script may be performed
              or used by any means, or quoted or published
              in any medium without the prior written
              consent of Stephen J. Cannell Productions,
              7083 Hollywood Blvd., Hollywood, CA 90028


                                  August 13, 1984 (F.R.)
                                  October 8, 1984 (F.R.)
                                  October 9, 1984 (F.R.)
                                  October 12, 1984 (F.R.)
                                  October 15 1984 (F.R.
                                  October 16, 1984 (F.R.)
```

Figure 4.1
Source: Courtesy of Stephen J. Cannell Productions.

```
#4209                                          Rev. 10/9/84


                         "PRISONER OF WAR"

                               CAST


          CODY
          NICK
          BOZ

          QUINLAN

          LIFEGUARD #1


          PEGGY
          DRIVER
          DYING (NON-SPEAKING) SOLDIER

          COP #1
          TYRONE DIAMOND
          BLADEMAN
          THE REVEREND
          HOOKER
          STONE


          IRENE WILCOX, R.N.
          MR. HSU
          MR. WRIGHT
```

Figure 4.1 (Continued)

```
                 #4209

                              "PRISONER OF WAR"

                                    SETS

            INTERIORS

            RIPTIDE
            POLICE HQ
            WHITE CADDY LIMO
            BAR
            THE JIMMY
            HOSPITAL TREATMENT ROOM
            PEGGY'S HOUSE
               BEDROOM
            VA HOSPITAL
               OFFICE
            FISHMARKET RESTAURANT
            DIAMOND'S APARTMENT
            LEXINGTON ARMS
            TENEMENT BUILDING




            EXTERIORS

            KING HARBOR BEACH
            ANOTHER BEACH
            BEACH STREET
            RIPTIDE
            LEXINGTON & HOTEL STREETS
               (REDLIGHT DISTRICT)/ALLEY
            BAR
            KING HARBOR HOSPITAL
            APARTMENT BUILDING
            PEGGY'S HOUSE
            PIER 56 MERCHANTS' DISTRICT
            DIAMOND'S APARTMENT BUILDING
            LEXINGTON ARMS
            TENEMENT BUILDING
```

Figure 4.1 (Continued)

#4200   Rev. 10/9/84

RIPTIDE

"PRISONER OF WAR"

ACT ONE

FADE IN

1   EXT.   BEACH AREA IN KING HARBOR - DAY - ESTABLISHING   1

Kids with surfboards, tourists with cameras and the
residents going about their usual business populate
this recreational portion of King Harbor. Play titles
over these shots of weekend fun at the beach until
camera finds:

2   2
through OMITTED   *thro
    10   10

11   NICK

In the middle of a pretty passionate kiss with a pretty
nice looking lady by the name of PEGGY BURKE. After a
few beats, they separate and Peggy snuggles her head against
Nick's shoulder as they lie on their beach towel. The
remains of a picnic lunch sit before them. Both of them
sigh contentedly. Then:

                                                     CONTINUED

Figure 4.1 (Continued)

#4209   2.   *Rev. 10/9/84

11   CONTINUED   11

                              PEGGY
                    So go on.

                              NICK
                    Hmmm?

                              PEGGY
                    You were telling me about yourself.

                              NICK
                    I was?

                              PEGGY
                    Yean. Right before you found
                    yourself totally swept away by my
                    presence, you were disclosing some
                    very personal things.

                              NICK
                    What was I saying?

                              PEGGY
                    Well... you were starting to talk
                    about your feelings, your emotions.
                    You were even alluding to some of
                    your...
                              (whisper)
                    ...flaws.

                              NICK
                    That's impossible. I don't have
                    any flaws.

                              PEGGY
                              (zings him)
                    That you'd believe that proves you
                    have at least one...

          Nick grabs Peggy around the waist playfully.

                              NICK
                    Why do you give me such a hard
                    time? No, better yet -- why
                    do I <u>let</u> you give me such a hard
                    time?

                                        CONTINUED

Figure 4.1 (Continued)

#4209   3.   *Rev. 10/9/84

11   CONTINUED - 2
                              PEGGY
                           (laughs)
                    Oh, now you're just mad because
                    your manly rap doesn't work on me.

                              NICK
                    What manly rap?

                              PEGGY
                    You know, that garbage all guys
                    try to con women with that I saw
                    through immediately.

                              NICK
                    No way! No way, ma'am. Because I
                    happen to have excellent manly rap.
                    Ask Cody. It's excellent.

Peggy waves her hand back and forth to indicate a mediocre
evaluation.

                              NICK
                           (pretending to
                           be hurt)
                    Come on, I used some pretty creative
                    lines on you. It wasn't the same
                    old "Haven't-I-seen-you-somewhere-
                    before?" routine.

                              PEGGY
                    True. Instead, you hung out in my
                    office for five weeks pretending to
                    book a vacation.

                              NICK
                    What's wrong with that? It makes
                    sense -- you're a travel agent, I'm
                    a traveller. It gave me a chance to
                    ask things like, "Is this a good
                    time of year to see Paris?" or
                    "How's the dollar in Italy?" I sounded
                    well-bred, sophisticated, worldly --

                              PEGGY
                    --phony...

Nick laughs because he knows it's true.

                                              CONTINUED

Figure 4.1 (Continued)

#4209   4.   *Rev. 10/9/84

11   CONTINUED - 3

                              NICK
                         (needling her)
                    Yeah, but you had dinner with me
                    anyway.

                              PEGGY
                    You better believe it. After work-
                    ing a month on a vacation you never
                    planned to take, I was at least
                    gonna get a free meal out of it.

Peggy and Nick are both laughing now, enjoying their
romantic jousting. Nick knows he's not going to con
this woman and that seems to make the interaction all
the more exciting for him.

                              NICK
                         (eyeing her)
                    There is no fooling you, is there?

                              PEGGY
                    It's hard to fool anyone who isn't
                    into playing games.
                         (beat, seriously)
                    And I'm not.

Nick takes her hand and becomes more serious.

                              NICK
                    No... you're not.
                         (beat)
                    I think that's what makes you so
                    special.

Peggy gives him an appreciative smile and they both lean
over and kiss each other gently.

                              NICK
                    The way you kiss probably has some-
                    thing to do with it, too.

Peggy smiles and sits up, followed by Nick.

12   ANGLE - PEGGY AND NICK

     sitting on the beach as the tide comes washing in just
     inches away from them. They stare dubiously at the
     close proximity of the ocean. Another wave washes

                                        CONTINUED

Figure 4.1 (Continued)

#4209   5.   * Rev. 10/9/84

12   CONTINUED

in and takes a glass with it this time. Peggy and Nick
look at each other.

                         PEGGY
               A few more minutes and I think
               this is gonna turn into that scene
               in "From Here to Eternity."

                         NICK
               I think you're right. Better grab
               the stuff fast before we have to
               swim away from this picnic.

Peggy and Nick laugh as they hurriedly scoop up the
blanket and plates, etc., and pile it all into the
picnic basket. Arm in arm, they head up the beach
toward the road.

                                      CUT TO

13   EXT. BEACH STREET - DAY - ON VETTE

parked along a curb. Across the street a bus is stopped
at the corner letting off and taking on passengers.
As Nick and Peggy approach the car, one of the bus
passengers, a young serviceman, steps down and
crosses in front of the bus to go across the street.
He seems unaware of a car that is headed in that
direction.

14   CLOSE ON PEGGY

as her face registers what is about to happen in a
split second. A yell gets caught in her throat as:

15   ON SERVICEMAN

as he walks right out from behind the bus into the
path of an oncoming car. The car screeches to a stop,
but not before it hits the serviceman.

16   CLOSE ON NICK AND PEGGY

as they react to the accident. As all other traffic
comes to a screeching halt, Peggy runs across the
street toward the serviceman, followed by Nick.

Figure 4.1 (Continued)

#4209   6.   * Rev. 10 /84

17   ON SOLDIER

lying on the street, unconscious, as Peggy and Nick
reach him. By now, the driver is out of the car and
other people have gathered around.

                    DRIVER
                (distressed)
        I never even saw him! He just
        came running out of nowhere!

Peggy immediately feels for a pulse on his neck and
wrist.

                    PEGGY
        Call an ambulance.

When the soldier chokes for air, Peggy responds with a
degree of efficiency that is far more advanced than
the average person's first-aid knowledge.

                    PEGGY
        He's choking. He could have internal
        hemorrhaging or a crushed trachea.
        There's blood in his esophagus. Help
        me get him flat on his back.

Nick, concerned about the soldier and at the same time
intrigued by Peggy's control of the situation, helps her.
By now, people are pushing in as accident-watchers
usually do. As Peggy starts giving mouth-to-mouth
resuscitation:

                    DRIVER
        I swear I never saw him! Is he
        gonna be okay? What's the matter
        with people?

                    NICK
                (to the crowd)
        Okay, everybody, stay back! Don't
        push into us, please! We've got
        a seriously injured man. Please --
        stay back.

Figure 4.1 (Continued)

5. Scene descriptions, stage directions, and camera directions, if they are given by the writer, are typed across the page within the scene numbers. LOCATION OF THE SCENE, indication of NIGHT or DAY, and CAMERA DIRECTIONS are typed in CAPITALS. Scene descriptions, mood, characters, actions, sound and music effects are typed in lowercase. Single spacing is used within each paragraph of description.

6. Dialogue is typed within a narrower column (about 3 inches) centered on the page. The name of the character who speaks is centered (in CAPS) just above his or her lines. The lines themselves are typed in lowercase, single-spaced. Directions on how the lines are to be spoken are placed between the character's name and the lines, in a column slightly narrower than the lines themselves, and set off by parentheses.

7. Double spacing is used to separate one scene from the next; also to set off methods of transition between two scenes (such as DISSOLVE, or CUT TO). It is also used to separate the lines of two characters, or lines from various types of directions. Paper is cheap, and the script may be more easily followed by performers and crew if it is not jammed up. When in doubt, space it out!

8. For further guidelines we recommend the *Professional Writer's Teleplay/Screenplay Format*. This pamphlet is available from the Writers Guild of America, East, 555 West 57th Street, New York, New York 10079. Price: $2.50.

The Television Storyboard

The *storyboard* is a specialized form of television copy. It is used primarily for the presentation, in draft form, of concepts for commercials, and for the development of sound-slide audiovisual presentations. A storyboard will be developed, for example, by the copywriter at an advertising agency to show a commercial idea to a client for approval. Revisions and modifications are much more quickly and cheaply made on the storyboard before the final script is written and actual production begun. Often, if a good storyboard has been laid out and the production is not complicated, no further script will be needed.

The 30-second announcement (Figure 4.2, pp. 79–81) was produced on film using live action. The cameraman and talent used only the storyboard as their script.

A variation on the storyboard layout form is that used in the preparation of scripts for sound-slide presentations. Here are two examples. The first (Figure 4.3, p. 82) is reproduced from a pamphlet, *How to Design and Produce Individualized Instruction Programs*, by the 3M Company.

The second example of a sound-slide script (Figure 4.4, pp. 83–90) uses a two-part approach. The storyboard provides space for the development of the sequence, the visual content of each slide frame, and instructions to be followed by the photographer (or person researching a photo file). A separate script (see p. 90) does not repeat these complex visual directions. It merely aligns the slides (by number and brief description) with the sound track—music and narration.

Many variations exist in storyboard layout forms, and that is quite permissible because usually they are not used to prepare programs or announcements which will be aired live, so there is little danger of mistakes being shown to an audience.

The number of "cells" or individual pictures in a storyboard will vary, depending on the complexity of the content, but usually a new "cell" will be

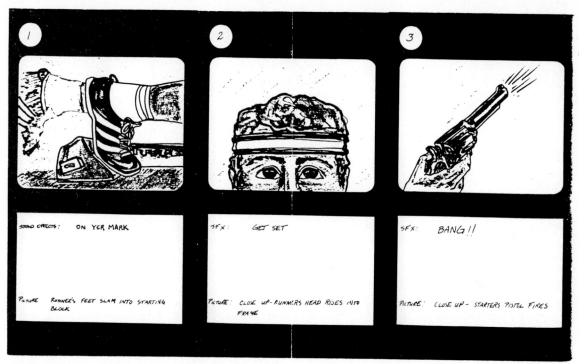

Figure 4.2
Source: Courtesy of Western Water Education Foundation, Sacramento, CA.

used for each important visual change—each new camera shot, or new character, or the addition of the product logo, or printed material. Accompanying the picture cells, in written, script form will be the sound portion of the script and descriptive instructions about camera angles or camera movement, if those are important to the sequence.

Other Aspects of Script Mechanics

In the preceding sections we skipped several aspects of scriptwriting that can present problems both to the writer and to the other members of the production team—namely, how to handle punctuation, numbers, and abbreviations. Recall our admonition that the writer should prepare the script to be as clear as possible and to be quickly understood by talent and production personnel. Our guidelines regarding these mechanics are designed with that goal in mind.

Punctuation   In broadcast copy, punctuation is intended only to help the reader of the copy deliver its meaning to the listener or viewer with maximum clarity. Most basic rules of punctuation still apply, but the single most important rule is that punctuation marks should be used to help the oral reader of the copy deliver that

Figure 4.2 (Continued)

copy clearly, without stumbling and without ambiguity. Careful punctuation is particularly important if the reader will be working without rehearsal and therefore without any chance to mark the copy to suit his or her own style.

Punctuation marks in oral copy, then, generally serve one of two functions—to indicate *pauses* or to indicate *emphasis*.

Indicating Pauses

The comma, the period, the dash, the ellipsis, and occasionally the semi-colon are the punctuation marks used to indicate pauses in broadcast copy.

The comma is used more frequently in broadcast writing than in writing for print. It is used whenever a small pause is needed to establish the meaning of the copy, and not just where required by grammatical rules, such as setting off items in a series, separating dependent clauses, and so on.

The period is used in broadcast copy, as it is in print, to denote the end of a thought, the end of a sentence.

The dash (—) and the ellipsis (. . . .) represent somewhat longer, more obvious pauses than does the comma. The use of these two varies somewhat with the preference of the writer or style manual being followed.

The *United Press International Broadcast Stylebook* says: Use an ellipsis to indicate a pause . . . a dash to indicate a longer pause—. This author prefers to use dashes within a sentence—denoting a pause only slightly more important

Figure 4.2 (Continued)

than a comma—and to use ellipses to indicate longer pauses, especially those denoting hesitation or indecision, or at the end of an incomplete speech, or when one person's speech is to be interrupted by another. (Note how ellipses are used in the Perry Boys radio ad earlier in the chapter.)

The semi-colon can be used as it is in print and to further set off series of phrases that already contain commas, but most writers prefer to use the dash in places where a semi-colon might be grammatically correct.

Indicating Emphasis

The most common punctuation marks used to provide emphasis in print material are the exclamation point and the question mark. The problem with the use of these two marks in broadcast copy is that they come at the end of the sentence. If the reader has not been able to read through the copy in advance, he or she may not realize until well into the sentence that special emphasis was intended by the writer. The outcome, which you probably have heard on radio or television at one time or another, is that a question may be read as if it were a statement; then the reader will discover the line was intended to be a question, fumble, pause, consider rereading the line, become confused, and sound unsure on the air.

Rather than relying on the exclamation mark and the question mark, it is better to *underline* those words or phrases that are to receive special emphasis

SOUND/SLIDE—Story Board Pad

SAMPLE
F-3

LINE DRAWING

ILLUSTRATION SHOWING COMMON BATTERY DEFECTS— LOW ELECTROLYTE, FRAYED CABLES, CRACKED CASING, OVERFILLED CELLS, CORROSION ON TERMINALS, ETC.

FRAME_____

Batteries, like other parts of the car, require periodic servicing. Whenever the hood is raised, you will want to inspect the electrolyte level, exterior condition and cable connections...and service the battery if necessary. The inspection takes very little time...and can help your customers avoid serious problems. You will learn about common battery defects and how to correct them in this unit of instruction. Go on to the next slide.

SLIDE

TOP VIEW OF BATTERY (CLOSE UP) WITH TWO CELLS OPEN. INTERIOR OF CELLS SHOULD BE VISIBLE SHOWING "C-RINGS."

FRAME_____

Begin your inspection by removing the cell caps and checking the electrolyte or fluid level against the manufacturer's specifications. Normally, the electrolyte should cover the plates and reach the C-rings in the cell neck. You will find specifications for most batteries in the ATLAS SERVICE GUIDE.

SLIDE

ATTENDANT ADDING DISTILLED WATER TO BATTERY CELLS.

FRAME_____

If the electrolyte is below the specified level, fill the cell to the correct level with DISTILLED WATER. Insert the funnel-like spout of the refill bottle into the cell opening and press down until the cell is correctly filled. BE CAREFUL NOT TO OVERFILL THE CELL.

Visual Products Division 3M

© COPYRIGHT 1969 BY 3M COMPANY

Printed in U.S.A

Figure 4.3

Source: *How to Design and Produce Individualized Instructional Programs*, Visual Products Division, 3M Company, 1969. Used by permission.

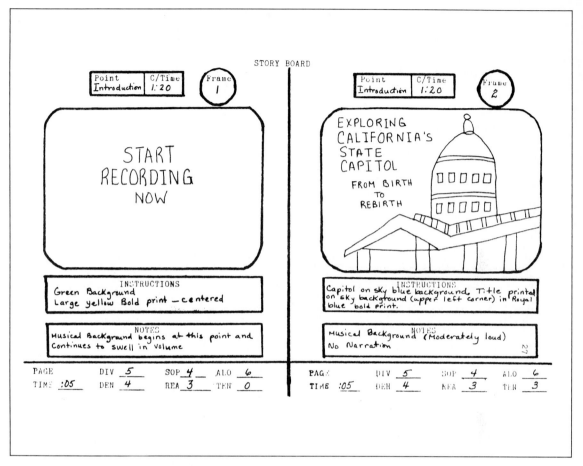

Figure 4.4
Source: Courtesy of the author, Maude Spencer.

and to reword questions so that they sound like questions from the very beginning of the sentence. Go ahead and include the marks at the end of the sentence, for they are grammatically correct there, but don't depend on the punctuation mark alone to signify your intent.

Be careful that you do not overdo exclamations or words and phrases to be emphasized. Many beginning writers are so concerned that the emphasis be in the right place that they underline words in every sentence of the copy. In most cases, the normal structure of the copy indicates to any experienced reader where the emphasis should be placed, and no extra marking is necessary.

Recall the two examples of inflection used in Chapter 2, "Where have all the flowers gone?" and "The President insisted that the American forces would be used for peace-keeping purposes only." As explained there, different emphases can change the meaning of such statements. Underlining would be necessary in

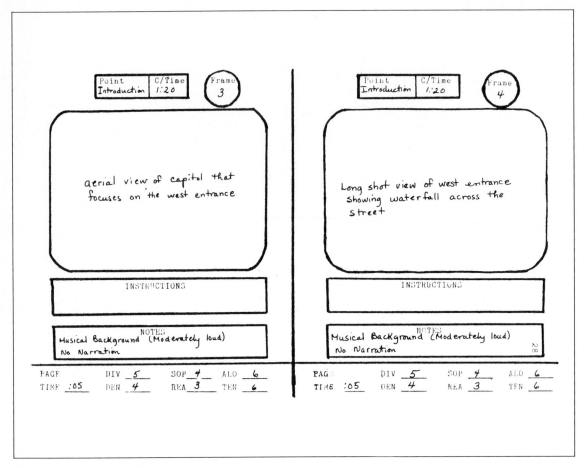

Figure 4.4 (Continued)

those examples to be sure the oral reader provided the emphasis intended by the writer. Underline if special or unusual emphasis is wanted.

Useless Punctuation

Several punctuation marks have little or no value in spoken copy. One of these is the colon, a mark used to separate material. In spoken copy the separation is probably better done by a dash, which is much easier to see. Avoid colons.

Another mark that has no value in spoken copy is parentheses, used in printed copy to set off "interjected explanatory or qualifying remarks." In print the parentheses tell the reader that the material may be of some interest, but that it can be skipped without harm to the main sequence of ideas. In spoken copy, the material must either be delivered aloud or left out. It can't be partially set aside. So if the writer wants an idea to be spoken, it should be written into the text of the copy. If the idea is not to be used, delete it.

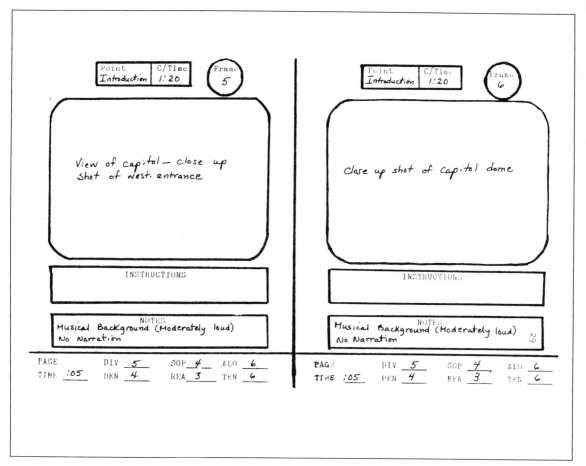

Figure 4.4 (Continued)

Parentheses are used, however, to separate nonspoken material, such as directions to a performer, from spoken copy, as we have shown in several examples.

Quotation marks are another punctuation symbol that presents a considerable challenge to the writer and the oral reader of broadcast copy. It is a very awkward punctuation mark to use, since again the listener cannot see the words that have been set off by the marks. And the reader of the copy may not be certain of the method he or she should use to set the word or phrase in quotations apart from the rest of the copy. How should a news announcer handle the quotations in the following story excerpt, for example?

Pravda said recent comments by President Reagan and other American officials **made** it necessary for the Soviet Union to offer its appraisal of the situation. On Wednesday,

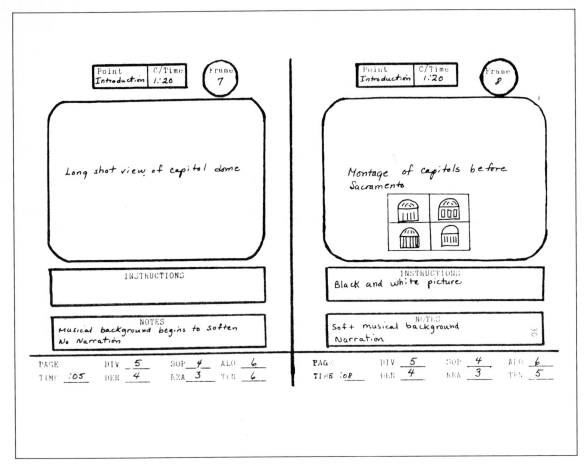

Figure 4.4 (Continued)

Mr. Reagan said that he was "a little optimistic" that some agreement could be reached on strategic arms reduction. He said his arms negotiators "feel the Soviets really are negotiating in good earnest."

The *Pravda* editorial said the Geneva talks on reducing strategic arms, meaning long-range missiles and bombers, had become deadlocked because of United States efforts "to insure by hook or by crook a unilateral weakening of the U.S.S.R.'s defense potential."[2]

One approach would be for the announcer simply to change the tone of delivery—in effect reading through quotation marks. A more accurate rendition of the content would be to voice the marks—to say "quote" and "unquote" each time quoted material appears. But these words are jarring to the ear; they are abrupt and they interrupt the flow of the story. Rather than clarifying, they may well confuse the listener. Even more stiff and formal are the phrases: "and I quote" and "end of quote."

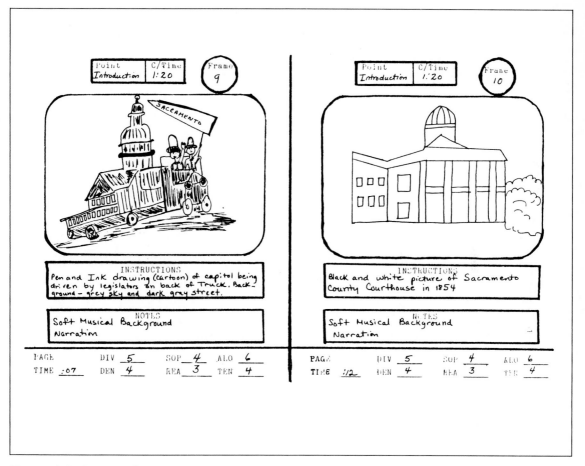

Figure 4.4 (Continued)

In Chapter 12 we will discuss the use of actualities, which are quotations in the source's own voice as well as words. When available, the actuality provides one way to avoid the problem of quotations. But often the best way out of the problem is not to quote at all; instead, use a paraphrase. Usually the exact words of a source are not as important as transmitting the sense of the story clearly to the audience. A paraphrase, which conveys the meaning but without the necessity to set apart the precise words of the source, becomes the preferred approach.

However, if a direct quote seems important or necessary, then alert the announcer and the listener to the quotation in a manner similar to this example from the *United Press International Broadcast Stylebook:*

The senator attacks what he calls—needless and irresponsible use of federal powers. He says he believes this is our most serious problem. Then he adds—in these words— The tentacles of the state are closing around the individual.[3]

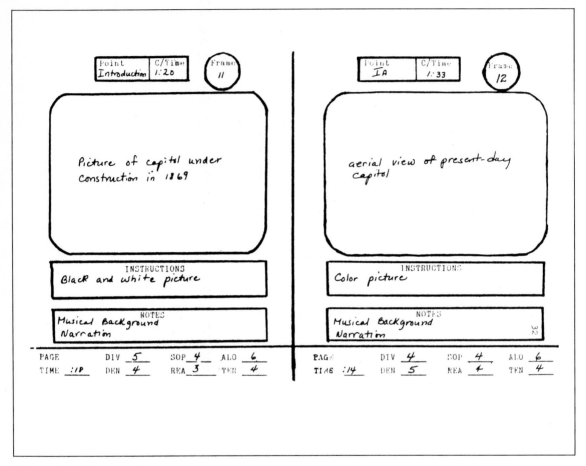

Figure 4.4 (Continued)

Quotation marks can be used to suggest emphasis on individual words or brief phrases. Like underlining, they call to the announcer's attention that the material in quotes should be given special emphasis or inflection to set it apart from the rest of the copy:

Americans have a "thing" about labels, it seems. In the 1960s we labeled people with unusual life styles as "hippies" and "beatniks.". . .

As with underlining, don't overdo this form of emphasis, and make sure the announcer understands that the quotation marks are in the script only to call his or her attention to the designated words, and not to identify a quotation.

Writing Numerals

One matter of mechanics on which there is much difference of opinion is the proper way to present numerals in copy. Some style manuals say that all numbers

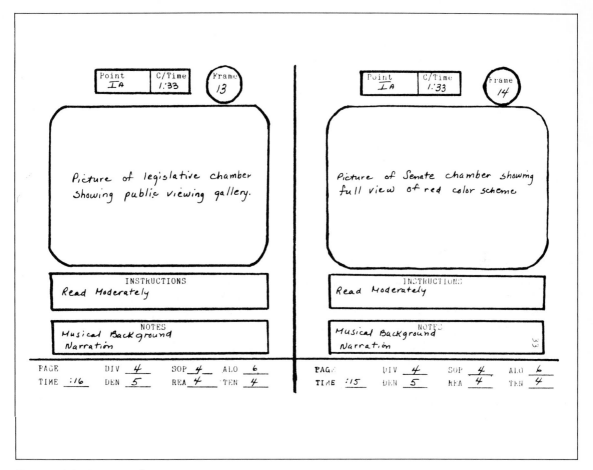

Figure 4.4 (Continued)

should be written out, so that the announcer will not have to make a mental translation from numerals to words that may result in hesitation or error. But most writers feel that writing out all numbers as words is terribly cumbersome and suggest that complex combinations be written as numerals. The overriding considerations are that the writing should be clear and in a conversational style. In the absence of a specific guideline from your station or agency, here are our suggestions for writing numbers:

1. Write out all numbers from one through twenty: seven, ten, sixteen.

2. From 21 through 999 use numerals, unless there is a specific reason to use words: 47, 583.

3. Write out hundred, thousand, million, billion: thirteen hundred (which sounds better than one thousand three hundred), five billion, 69 million.

```
                          PROGRAM SCRIPT


         VISUAL                    AUDIO

     1. Cue Frame             1. Silent

     2. Title Frame           2. Musical Background

     3 through 7. Views       3 - 7. Musical Background
        of capitol

     8. Montage of early      8. Beginning in 1849, California has
        capitols                had more capitals than any state
                                in the union.

     9. Capitol on wheels     9. In the early days, the capital be-
        (Political cartoon)      came known as the "Capitol on
                                Wheels."

    10. First Sacramento     10. After a long, political struggle,
        County Courthouse        Sacramento won the capital! The
                                County Courthouse became the first
                                capitol.  It was eventually de-
                                stroyed by fire and flood.

    11. First capitol un-    11. The Capitol's birth was long and
        der construction         complicated.  It took many years,
                                from 1860 to 1874, to complete the
                                Roman Corinthian-style structure.
                                In 1869, it was occupied as the
                                permanent home for state government.

    12. Aerial view of       12. Today, there are two separate struc-
        capitol                  tures that link together as the Ca-
                                pitol--the "old" or historic build-
                                ing and the modern style annex,
                                which was completed in 1952.

    13. Viewing gallery      13. The Capitol is the public workplace
                                for the legislators.  Viewing gal-
                                leries from the third floor allow
                                citizens and visitors to observe
                                .that portion of the legislative pro-
                                cess that unfolds in the senate and
                                assembly chambers.

    14. Senate chamber       14. Both chambers are located on the se-
                                cond floor of the old building.  They
                                are now gracefully decorated to re-
                                semble the early 20th century.  Red
                                is the dominant color of the senate
                                chamber.
```

Figure 4.4 (Continued)

4. For large numbers, use a combination system that provides the greatest clarity: 4,329,733 would be four million, 329 thousand, 733. Other examples: one thousand, 49; five thousand, three; one thousand, three hundred, 22; 3 thousand, fourteen; eight million, three hundred thousand.

5. Write out fractions; one-third, five-eighths, six and one-half.

Note these problem areas in dealing with numbers:

1. The number 1954 may be read as one thousand, nine hundred, fifty-four, but the year 1954 is commonly read nineteen, fifty-four.

2. A business establishment with its address at 3850 Elm Street may want the number read as thirty-eight fifty. If that's the way they want it, write it that way.

3. A phone number—333-8800—can be read several ways. The client may prefer three, thirty-three, eighty-eight hundred. Or he or she may wish each digit to be read individually. The preferred method then would be to write it out in words: three-three-three-eight-eight-zero-zero. Some stylists, however, use digits with hyphens between: 3-3-3-8-8-0-0.

4. Rounded-off numbers, especially in the case of large numbers, are usually better than a long series of numerals. ''A budget deficit of about four and a half million dollars'' is more easily understood by the listener than ''a budget deficit of four million, 433 thousand, 692 dollars,'' and most of the time the precise amount is not that important in the story.

Writing Abbreviations

Do not use abbreviations in script copy, with the following exceptions:

1. These very common abbreviations may be used: Mr., Mrs., Ms., St. (when used for saint): Mr. George Brown, Mrs. Louise Smith, Ms. Penelope Jones, St. Louis.

2. Well-known acronyms may be given as initials. They are probably more easily recognized by their initials than by the full name anyway; A-M, P-M, U-N, Y-M-C-A. (The *United Press International Broadcast Stylebook* recommends using hyphens rather than periods between the letters in acronyms; we have followed that practice here.)

    Some acronyms are commonly pronounced as names. These do not take hyphens: OPEC, NATO, UNESCO.

3. Do not abbreviate fort, mount, names of cities, countries, states, or address identifications: *Fort* Hood, *Texas; Mount* Vernon, *New York;* the *United Kingdom; New Zealand; East Elm Street;* Sepulveda *Boulevard;* Orange *Avenue.*

4. Do not abbreviate days of the week or months of the year: Wednesday, September.

5. Do not abbreviate junior or senior after a person's name; company, corporation, or incorporated; or titles of officials: *Professor* James Edwards, *Junior;* the Xerox *Corporation.*

Conclusion

The preparation of material for broadcast via television and radio almost always is a group activity that involves some combination of writers, actors, or other presenters, directors, equipment operators, and other personnel. In order for each of these people to contribute to the production, in order for rehearsals to be completed efficiently, and in order for materials to be presented without error, there must be an accurate blueprint for the program. That blueprint is the script. Errors that appear on the air usually can be traced to an incomplete, illegible, or inaccurate script, or to a person who did not have a script, did not follow a script, or did not make necessary corrections or notations on a script.

Regardless of what specifics are used, the goal remains the same. The copy and the instructions you write must make it possible for the presenters of the script to deliver the content easily and without error. The most important instructions to accomplish that goal are these: Be neat. Be accurate. Be consistent.

Exercises

1. In the remaining chapters of this book there are exercises to write particular styles or types of copy—radio commercials, TV news, drama, documentary, slide-tape instructional presentations, and so on. The most appropriate exercise for this chapter is to write those scripts using a format that meets the guidelines presented here.

2. Select a news story from your local newspaper. Rewrite it in the following versions, paying particular attention to aural style (Chapter 2) and layout.

   a. As a 45-second story for radio, single announcer.

   b. As a 60-second story for radio, with one actuality approximately 15 seconds long.

   c. As a 30-second story for TV, no visuals, single announcer.

   d. As a 60-second story for TV, but with visuals. Assume your camera crew was able to get whatever visuals were important.

   e. Same as (d), but including one actuality from a participant in the story.

3. Similarly, choose newspaper stories with these characteristics and rewrite as indicated. Again, consider primarily aural style and layout.

   a. A financial story with a lot of statistical detail. Rewrite for radio. Write the numbers to ensure clarity.

   b. A story that depends heavily on the descriptive accounts of witnesses or participants. Rewrite for television, with particular attention to the handling of quotations.

   c. Rewrite and *punctuate* any story you find to be particularly complex and confusing in its printed version.

Key Terms and Concepts

actualities	out cue
BIZ	raw sound
ellipses	SFX
FONT (CHIRON)	slug
format	split-page layout
LIVE—SOT—SOF	storyboard
master-scene script	SUPER
MORE	voice-over (off-camera)

Notes

1. The Associated Press, *AP Broadcast News Handbook* (New York: The Associated Press, 1982), p. 230.

2. *New York Times,* January 2, 1983.

3. *United Press International Broadcast Stylebook* (New York: UPI, 1979), p. 14.

Chapter 5

Program Structure

People usually watch television or listen to radio as a matter of choice. Except in unusual circumstances, viewing or listening is not a forced activity; it takes place because each individual person decides to watch or to listen.

From that premise, three corollaries can be stated:

1. Viewing and listening are in competition with many other possible activities in which each individual might engage at any particular time.

2. Each program is in competition with all other programs being presented at the same time.

3. If the program does not provide something of interest to each individual viewer or listener, that individual will turn to some other activity.

Successful programs will have some combination of content and structure that will capture and hold the interest of audience members. In this chapter, we will look at the principles that pertain to structure—how to organize program materials to attract and hold audience attention. We will present these ideas using examples from programs currently on the air, but you will be able to understand the concepts best and use them most effectively if you (1) do your own analysis of programs you watch or listen to, and (2) write scripts that consciously include these principles of program structure.

Attention

Although radio listening and television viewing are usually free-choice, unforced activities, we don't mean to suggest that people always watch out of conscious choice. Individuals may watch programs that do not have strong attraction for them simply as a matter of habit, or to escape the boredom that comes from having nothing else to do. Or they may watch programs chosen by other members of the family.

This pattern of behavior on the part of audience members has led to the formulation of an interesting proposal regarding television programming known as the "least objectionable program" theory. This viewpoint suggests that habitual viewers of television are prepared to watch something at a particular time period, and in the absence of a program with positive appeal, will choose the program that is least objectionable.[1]

We prefer to cast viewer or listener choices in a more positive fashion, and suggest that there must be some positive attraction for each individual. If not, that person will find some way to dissociate him or herself from the program. He or she may ignore the program and turn to other activities in the same room, leave the room, change the channel, or turn the set off altogether. The outcome of all these behaviors, in which the message from the TV or radio is no longer being received, is negative, at least from the point of view of the program's producers and sponsors. They want the audience to stay tuned and to pay attention to the program and its commercial content.

Intensity of Attention

Even when an individual has a program turned on, the intensity of his or her attention will vary. If the program contains content the individual perceives as being important, that person's attention will be focused on the program, and other activities competing for attention will be excluded. At the other extreme, if the content is uninteresting or unimportant, the individual will place attention elsewhere, and the broadcast program simply becomes background noise.

Between the two extremes is a whole range of other behaviors, including those of the person who watches the program most of the time but picks up a paper or magazine, or starts a conversation whenever low-interest material appears; or the person who divides attention between the program and routine tasks such as knitting or ironing; or the person who habitually turns on the set and then goes about other activities around the house, to be drawn back to the receiver only if there is a major change in the content of the program—such as the sudden breaking into the program with a news bulletin.

Attention Span

Not only does the intensity of a person's attention vary, but so does the length or span of attention. No person is able to give undivided attention to any one stimulus for very long; competing stimuli will draw off attention after a period of time. Some means must be provided in the program to recapture that attention, and to draw it back to the television or radio set.

The length of attention span will vary in relation to several factors: the extent to which the content of the program is of interest or value to that individual, and the ease with which the materials can be processed by the individual. Complex, difficult material will mean a shortened attention span. And attention will vary by demographic characteristics as well—children as a rule have shorter attention spans than adults.

In general, after a minute or so of attention to one idea or element in a program, an individual's attention tends to diminish. That person can continue to focus on the sound coming from the radio or the picture from the television

Figure 5.1
Source: Reproduced by permission of
Universal Press Syndicate.

screen only by exerting some degree of effort. And the longer the same kind of material appears, the greater the effort becomes.

As a rule, audience members do not want to exert much effort to follow a television or radio program. We have become conditioned to look upon these media primarily as sources of entertainment. Therefore, the expenditure of mental effort, of "working" to pay attention to the program when the limit of attention has been reached, is at odds with the idea of relaxing, enjoying, and being entertained by the program. We will not and do not force ourselves to pay attention. It must be the program, and not the viewer or listener, that provides the impetus to return one's attention to the screen.

Program Elements

To deal with this problem of holding attention, radio and television programs must—at very frequent intervals—give the listener something new to hear or to watch. Some sort of change is needed in some aspect of the program which will be sufficient to reattract the attention of the viewer or listener.

Each time there is such a change, some new element of program content has been introduced. We will use that term—*program element*—to describe segments of a program separated by some definite type of change. The program element will become our basic building block for analyzing and constructing broadcast programs.

The content of a half-hour television program, for example, may be made up of twenty to thirty, or even more, program elements. If too few elements are used to construct a program, each element, or some of them, will be long, and the limit of audience members' attention span will be reached before a new element is introduced. The program will seem slow and boring. If, on the other hand, a great many elements are used in a program, the program will be perceived as having a rapid pace, perhaps even too rapid for the comfort of the audience.

Types of Program Elements

A number of different types of change are possible in any program; new elements may be constructed in a wide variety of ways. The following list is suggestive of some of the more obvious ways in which changes can take place and new elements can be introduced. We are likely to think of these changes in relation to television, since that is where we find more structured programs. But the concept is equally valid for all types of radio programming as well.

- By making a change in the scene, or the setting before the cameras or microphones
- By changing the type of material presented, from talk to music, music to dance, action to talk, and so on
- By starting a new musical number after completing an earlier one
- By making a definite change in the topic or subject matter of a talk program—introducing a new idea
- By using a different method of presenting material, as in changing from a one-person talk to a two-person dialogue or to an interview
- By bringing a new important character into a dramatic scene or taking one away, thereby creating a change in the relationships of characters in the drama
- By changing the mood, or tempo, or a scene; for example, from calm conversation to excitement and action

These descriptions represent the separation points of one element from another. The elements themselves may be further explained by these descriptions of types that commonly appear in broadcast programs.

A Scene in a Dramatic Show

Any segment in which there is no change in main characters, in place, in time, or in subject discussed or amount of action is a single element. The same characters are involved and subject matter, mood, and action remain the same. If another major character enters the scene, there is invariably a change in emphasis and frequently in subject matter as well, and therefore the start of a new element. Change also would take place and a new element be introduced if during the scene one character sings a song, or if after a long "all talk" segment, there is a quick change to violent physical action.

A Musical Number by a Vocalist or an Orchestra

Any self-contained musical selection of reasonable length would be a program element. If a longer number, begun by an orchestra, is followed by a substantial vocal section, you might be justified in separating into two elements. Similarly, if the selection is begun by the orchestra or vocalist but contains a dance routine in the middle and the camera focuses on the dancers, even though the vocalist continues to sing, the focus of attention changes, and a new element has been started.

A Commercial or Public Service Announcement

Obviously, the insertion of an announcement into a program marks a change from the type of material both preceding and following. Commercials and PSAs usually are not integrated into the content of programs, and from the audience's point of view they frequently are seen as interruptions. But in considering program structure, they must be considered along with the other elements that make up the total program. (By the way, each announcement is considered a single element, regardless of the number of changes which may appear within it.)

A Major Item in a News Broadcast

It's difficult here to differentiate major and minor items; arbitrarily any news item of about 30 seconds or longer can probably be considered a separate element. Several short items presented by the same anchorperson probably represent only a single element.

A Round of Questions in a Game Show

The description of a round will differ, depending on the structure of the game, but usually it will involve a series of similar questions to one contestant, or the responses of several contestants to one question. In "Family Feud," for example, the starter "tossup" question/response is one element, the continuation of that question line with one family is a second, and if they miss, the completion of the group of questions is yet a third.

Remember that the key to the identification of elements is change *that will recapture attention*. A lot of minor changes take place within all types of programs which are too brief or too inconsequential to be used to separate elements. For example, applause or laughter following a segment of entertainment material should not be classified as a separate element, but as part of the element it follows. A very short introduction of an entertainer or a musical number is combined with the element it introduces. Bridge music in a dramatic program and entrance music are too short to be elements.

Note that program elements in television are not the same as camera shots. Elements are portions of the content of a program; if the same essential materials remain "on stage" in a television show, changing the angle of the shot by shifting from one camera to another does not produce a new element, but having a variety of camera shots within an element may prolong the viewer's span of attention. Often several camera shots will appear within a single element, but what makes a new element as we have defined it is the change in the content being treated, not in the technique of presentation.

Most well-structured programs will have elements usually between 40 seconds to 2 minutes in length, but there is no set length. In most programs not many elements will be shorter than 15 to 20 seconds. In TV, the possibility of having varying camera shots within an element makes it possible to have somewhat longer elements than normally would be used in radio.

Using Program Elements

The concept of elements provides a useful and universal way to analyze the sequence and relationship of the various individual pieces that together make up a broadcast program. It should be understood, however, that this is not a precision tool. Two people analyzing the same program are not likely to agree completely on the number of elements in the program, nor on the precise points at which changes occur between elements. But it takes only a little practice to become familiar with the concept and to be able to identify the major types and locations of change within a program.

Here we show in a standardized format the element analyses for two television programs. We have chosen two half-hour programs, but the approach can be used with programs of any length, or at least with all programs in which attention span might be a problem, and that means everything but very short materials. After these analyses we will continue an examination of the principles of program structure, and then return to the examples to see how well they meet the criteria for a well-structured program. Much more important, however, than reading these analyses is for you to analyze current programs using the same method— locating the points that represent the refocusing of audience attention through changing program elements, counting the number of elements in a program, and timing each element. (A blank analysis form you can use for this practice is included in the exercises at the end of this chapter.)

Even doing an analysis of existing programs represents only an intermediate stage in your progress toward writing scripts organized to ensure maximum audience attention. Regardless of what type of program you may be called upon to write, be it news, documentary, drama, a game show, a religious or political program, you will have to consider how you are going to maintain and recapture audience attention. Using the principle of program elements, and recognizing how these elements are provided in various types of existing programs, will help you to determine the most appropriate ways to structure your own scripts to hold audience attention.

The layout form used for our sample programs describes both the content and structure of the program. The five columns used for the first analysis, "Newhart," provide:

1. A count of the number of elements in the program

2. A description of the content of each element

3. A word or two which identifies what in the program caused the change from one element to the next.

4. The starting time of each element given in minutes and seconds from the beginning of the program

5. The length of each element

Newhart   This program series was first aired as a network prime-time situation comedy series, but it is now in syndication. It is the second series in which Newhart has starred. The writers and producers of the series seem to be relying on Newhart's star value, and strong comic talents in the cast, to pull through a program that is not strong structurally.

Element #	Content/Description	Type of Change	Start Time	Length
1	Signature: panoramic scenes of New England countryside; program and cast identifications	material	0:00	1:00
2	Commercial: ACT Flouride toothpaste	material	1:00	0:30
3	Commercial: Dodge Trucks	material	1:30	0:30
4	Conversation among three teenagers explains program premise—mother is being interviewed by local newspaper	location, characters	2:00	1:15
5	Conversation: Newhart, wife Joanna, reporter in another part of lodge	location, time, characters	3:15	4:15
6	Conversation: Newhart and handyman George at breakfast next morning	characters	7:30	1:00
7	Joanna enters, leaves, enters again	characters	8:30	3:40
8	Joanna leaves; Newhart and George tag line	material	12:10	0:20
9	Commercial: Mary Kay Cosmetics	material	12:30	0:30
10	Commercial: Agree Shampoo	material	13:00	0:30
11	Promo: Archie Bunker's Place	material	13:30	0:30

Element #	Content/Description	Type of Change	Start Time	Length
12	Joanna at travel agency for a job interview with male head of agency (Herzog)		14:00	3:45
13	Move to outer office, introduce Joanna to other workers	characters, location	17:45	0:40
14	At inn; George and teenagers playing Monopoly	characters, location	18:25	0:50
15	Joanna enters, tag line	character	19:15	0:15
16	Conversation: Newhart and Joanna in office	character, location	19:30	3:45
17	Newhart and Joanna next morning at travel agency; introduce Newhart to Herzog	time, location	23:15	1:00
18	Conversation, Joanna and Herzog in inner office	characters, location	24:15	1:05
19	Conversation: Newhart and secretary in outer office	characters, location	25:20	0:20
20	Return to Joanna and Herzog	character, location	25:40	0:20
21	Joanna and Newhart in outer office	character, location	26:00	0:20
22	Herzog comes out: Newhart, Joanna, Herzog	character	26:20	0:15
23	Visual closing credit over conversation	material	26:35	0:10
24	Commercial: Wendy's	material	26:45	0:30
25	Commercial: Ocean Spray Cranberry Juice	material	27:15	0:30

Element #	Content/Description	Type of Change	Start Time	Length
		material		
26	Promo: Tucker's Witch		27:45	0:15
		material		
27	Credits: music in background and voice over promo for following program—"Trapper John"		28:00	0:20
	END		28:20	

Source: Analysis from "Newhart," Sunday, March 27, 1983, on the CBS network.

Entertainment Tonight   This program is a five-day-a-week syndicated series which most stations carry in the prime-time-access slot between local news and prime-time entertainment programming. Its focus on entertainment news and features provides an effective way to hold over an audience from news into entertainment programming.

The analysis follows the same layout form as before, except that we have eliminated the "Type of Change" column. In this program, almost every change is in the content or material.

Element #	Content/Description	Start Time	Length
1	Opening: Title—tease stories to be on show—quick clips w/voices over	0:00	0:40
2	Opening: Signature-theme music and video montage	0:40	0:25
3	Male anchor—Erin Fleming/Groucho Marx story (on camera-no tape)	1:05	0:30
4	Female anchor—lead to reporter story on videocassette award show	1:35	0:55
5	Female anchor on camera—four short news items	2:30	0:30
6	Male anchor, lead to reporter story on Carole Burnett's appearance in soap opera, with actuality insert	3:00	1:20
7	Female anchor, lead to reporter story on "nostalgic review" retrospective of movie *The Day the Earth Stood Still*	4:20	2:00
8	Signature—Trivia Q & A (visual only)—tease for upcoming story—bumper	6:20	0:35
9	Commercial: Oil of Olay	6:55	0:30
10	Commercial: Atra Razor	7:25	0:30
11	Commercial: KGNR Radio	7:55	0:30

Element #	Content/Description	Start Time	Length
12	Commercial: Stockton Auto Dealers	8:25	0:30
13	Title: style section; female anchor lead to—	8:55	0:20
14	Reporter story-interview with Martin Scorcese—intercut with clips of *King of Comedy*	9:15	2:55
15	Male anchor, bridge to—	12:10	0:10
16	Movie reviewer, on camera and clip from film,	12:20	0:55
17	Movie reviewer, mini reviews of four additional films	13:15	0:30
18	Female anchor, lead to reporter story on new magazine, *TV Cable Week*, and reaction from *TV Guide*	13:45	1:30
19	Commercial: Cousins Furniture	15:15	0:30
20	Commercial: AVCO Thrift	15:45	0:30
21	Commercial: Datsun	16:15	0:30
22	Commercial: KRAK Radio	16:45	0:30
23	Title: Male anchor, lead to reporter story on Ferrante and Teicher, pianists—intercut performance and interview	17:15	2:45
24	Female anchor, lead to reporter story on Cab Calloway, including historical film clip	20:00	1:30
25	Male anchor, lead to reporter story on Tom Petty and the Heartbreakers—intercut performance and interview	21:30	3:10
26	Signature—Trivia Q and A (visual only)—tease for tomorrow's show	24:40	0:35
27	Commercial: Kuppenheimer Clothes	25:15	0:30
28	Commercial: Eppies Restaurant	25:45	0:30
29	Commercial: Pepsi Light	26:15	0:30
30	Closing: Anchors, tease tomorrow's show	26:45	0:15
31	Credits: Visual crawl over Ferrante and Teicher	27:00	0:45
	END	27:45	

Source: Analysis from ''Entertainment Tonight,'' Thursday, March 24, 1983, as broadcast by KCRA-TV, Sacramento, CA.

These examples will give you an idea of how to approach the analysis of an existing program—that is, what information to observe and a useful form in which to collect that information. We'll return to these examples, and use these analyses in an evaluation of program structure, after we have presented some additional principles.

Three-Part Structure

Some types of program elements are self-contained—individual announcements, for example, and news feature stories which may be written and produced in such a way that they can be inserted randomly in a magazine-type program. But most of the time individual program elements do not stand alone. They are just as the name implies—elements or portions of programs. They must be organized and sequenced in various ways to meet the structural requirements of longer programs.

Almost all TV programs and a substantial number of radio programs are of predetermined, fixed length and have an identifiable three-part structure. They have an opening, a body or central part which contains the bulk of the content, and a closing. Each of these parts has a contribution to make to the overall structural strength of the program, and to maintaining audience interest in it.*

Program Openings

Functions of Program Openings

The opening of a broadcast program should accomplish two purposes: It should attract the attention of potential audience members, and it should identify the program and the series, if it is part of a series. The program opening may also be expected to accomplish some additional useful, but not critical or universal, purposes. It may set a mood or explain the nature of the program, or provide for the insertion of commercials or other types of announcements.

Attracting Attention

We've already discussed in some detail the importance of attracting audience attention. This is a particularly important consideration at the beginning of a program. For the person who is already watching television or listening to the radio, the end of one program and the beginning of another represents a break in that individual's commitment—an opportunity to change easily to another activity or another station. The person just tuning in will quickly determine if the program is one that is worth time and attention.

---

* One major category of exception we are not considering here are music radio stations. These stations play their particular style or format of music more or less continuously. Their programming does not have a formal structure.

Note also that under the system of programming used by most United States broadcasting stations, programs usually are separated by a "station break," a period of time (from 30 seconds or so up to a couple of minutes) which is used to provide station identification and to insert additional announcements into the station's schedule. The IDs and announcements that appear in these breaks are not part of the structure of programs as such.

If the program is one episode of a continuing series which is very popular, then some audience members will make their commitment based in part on past pleasant experiences with the program. These individuals may be willing to wait a little longer before making a decision to change activity. The opening for "All in the Family" did not have strong attention-getting material; nevertheless, the program was a popular series for a number of years. But even in this situation, the writer cannot afford to have an opening that is too casual or too slow.

**Providing
Identification**

At the beginning of a time period audiences who have tuned to reach a particular program want to be assured that they have reached the program they were looking for. Other individuals, who may be tuning randomly just to see what they can find, will also want to know what program they have reached. Programs therefore provide identification to the audience through such standard materials as program and series titles and the names of featured performers and guest artists.

Setting a Mood

In addition to the two primary requirements, a program opening may also be used to establish overall tone or mood. If the program is a lighthearted situation comedy, it should have a lively, friendly, humorous opening. A police drama which features a lot of on-location, exterior activity should set that tone in the opening with fast-moving action sequences and quick-cut camera action. In the former category would be the openings for "Three's Company" and "Cheers;" in the latter, "Spencer for Hire" and "Hill Street Blues."

**Providing
Explanations**

Series that are familiar to the audience will not require much in the way of explanation, but new series and one-time special programs will usually require at least some brief description of the premise or purpose of the program.

Dramatic programs, particularly comedy series, often require an explanation of the premise or "gimmick" on which the series is based. One of the first program series to use this approach, "Beverly Hillbillies," placed a family of backwoods hillbillies into a mansion in Beverly Hills. The plots were based on their coping with the strange new environment. Some explanation of how they came to be in that situation needed to be given. It was built into the opening of each program in that series. Similarly, a number of comedy dramatic series have been based on supernatural "gimmicks." An explanation of the "gimmick"— the witch who can change people by twitching her nose in "Bewitched," or the genie who can transport people by a similar action in "I Dream of Jeannie," or the similar plot devices in "Mork and Mindy" and "Bionic Woman" and other series are typical of the explanations needed for audiences to understand and follow what happens within the program.

Other forms of explanation needed in program openings are the "rules" that govern the actions of contestants in game or audience participation programs and descriptions of the topic and its importance for public affairs programs.

**Providing
Place for
Announcements**

You are already aware of the need to place commercial announcements within the structure of most programs. When commercial breaks are required in a program, some of those breaks will appear in the opening. Their placement must be considered along with the other elements and requirements of the opening.

How these various purposes are best accomplished depends a great deal on the type of program being presented and on which of these purposes is considered by the producers and writers as being most important. Will commercials need to be inserted? How much explanation will be necessary? How easily will the audience be able to identify the program?

Provide a Strong Start

At first glance it may seem that this instruction, to provide a strong start, is the same as the requirement to attract attention at the beginning of the program. Although they are related, they are not the same. An element included in the program opening and specifically designed to attract attention is only one of the types of material which may be included in that opening. Providing a strong start, on the other hand, considers all of the materials which are included in the opening portion of a program.

Minimize Low-Interest Material

Some of the elements which go into the opening are likely to be low in audience interest. Their presence in the opening, although necessary, is in conflict with the requirement to attract audience attention. It becomes a challenge to the writer's creativity to include low-interest elements in such a way that their negative or weakening impact is minimized and the overall opening is kept as strong as possible, given the various elements that must be accommodated.

For example, audiences frequently view the placement of commercials in a program as an interruption of the entertainment, since they are not integrated into the program content. On the other hand, the advertiser who has paid to have an announcement inserted in the program does not see the commercial as unimportant. That advertiser wants the best possible placement for the ad and wants all the audience members to be paying attention when the announcement comes on.

The writer, in order to balance these conflicting views, must provide strong attention-getting materials to "hook" the audience before presenting announcements at the beginning of a program. If too many announcements appear in the opening moments of a program, or if they appear too early in the opening, before strong attention-getting materials have been presented, their presence will have a seriously negative effect.

Avoid Lengthy Explanations

A well-constructed game show has very simple rules that can be explained very quickly, or that don't have to be explained at all for the audience to enjoy the program. The writer of a public affairs program will have to be very careful, when introducing background information on the topic of the program, to point out quickly its importance to the audience.

In new programs—the first program of a new series, or a one-time special— explanations and identifications may be more necessary than in a continuing series. Names of the cast may not be known, and a "gimmick" will have to be explained in more detail on the first broadcast. In those situations the writer is faced with the important and difficult task of incorporating the necessary explanations and identifications without becoming too detailed, and while maintaining audience attention. In all too many new or one-time programs, this problem has not been recognized by the writer and is not satisfactorily solved.

The audience's reaction is one of impatience, waiting for the program to get going. They will not wait long.

Limit Credits

Credits too may be low-interest materials. The problem of presenting credits in television may be contrasted with that of the motion picture. Traditionally movie credits are given at the beginning of the film (although even that has changed and frequently credits are presented at the end). But in the theater the audience has paid an admission price to see the film and is not likely to walk out even if weak opening credits take several minutes. In television, the audience will leave if the credits badly weaken the opening of the program.

One effective technique for television drama is to present the credits graphically over scenes that establish the program's location, when there is no dialogue to conflict with the visual credits, and where there is strong visual attraction to the audience.

Types of Openings

The creative challenge to satisfy the requirements set down for a program opening, and to do so while attracting and holding attention, has resulted in two basic types of openings and then many variations and combinations which have developed from them.

The Signature Opening

This form of opening started in the early days of radio, when tuning into a program was a rather complicated task. There were no receivers with push-button tuning. People had to scan the dial to find the correct frequency position for the stations that carried their favorite programs. It was therefore important that programs have readily identifiable openings—a pattern of music, sound effects, and/or voices that was the same for each broadcast in the series and that the audience could quickly and easily identify. This standardized opening is known as a *program signature*.

Among the well-known program signatures of network radio programs were a theme from ''The William Tell Overture'' used on ''The Lone Ranger''; a montage of marching feet, whistles, sirens, clanging doors, and machine-gun fire, intended to be representative of crime and of prison, used on ''Gangbusters.''

Even when radio tuning became much easier, program signatures continued and the form is now used in television as well. Well-known television programs using standardized signature openings include ''M*A*S*H,'' ''Star Trek,'' ''Happy Days,'' and ''Barney Miller.''

In addition to providing identification, one other function easily accomplished with a signature is that of mood setting. In early radio, a very well-known mood-setting signature was the sound effect of the squeaky door opening and the eerie, echoing voice of the narrator on ''Inner Sanctum.'' Most well-constructed signature openings in television also contribute to the mood of the show, or at least match the tone of the program in both style and approach.

The signature also can be an effective and efficient way to provide explanations, especially in dramatic programs where there is a gimmick to be explained. The program series given as examples in our earlier discussion of gimmicks—

"Beverly Hillbillies," "Bewitched," "I Dream of Jeannie," "Mork and Mindy," "Bionic Woman" all use signature openings.

The most serious deficiency of a signature opening is that it does not satisfy the other major requirement of a program opening; its very familiarity weakens the signature as an attention-getting device. Since the audience may have seen or heard the signature many times previously, attention is not particularly drawn by that material.

The Cold Opening

This type of opening originated on dramatic programs, but is now used with other types of content as well. With this opening, the program begins immediately with content material. The content starts "cold" without identification and may continue for up to several minutes before being interrupted by any other type of material. If material of high dramatic value—conflict, action—is chosen for the cold open, then the audience's attention will be strongly attracted.

Two substantially different variations of the cold opening exist. One form, which was the first to be used extensively in television but is seldom seen any more, takes a "chunk" of high-interest material out of the body of the program and opens with that material. That same "chunk" is then shown again in the program in its proper location. The value of this type of cold open is that the material can be taken from near the climax of the program, where the intensity of the material and audience interest would be high. The section lifted out also will involve the main stars in the program.

Both major purposes are accomplished. High-interest material is presented at the beginning of the program, and the program is identified for regular members of its audience through its performers. This opening sequence may last for a minute or so and then be followed by a more formal identification—titles, performer credits, and other opening materials, including announcements. The plot of the drama begins after all opening elements are completed.

A weakness of this form of opening is that it "gives away" some of the climax and lessens the impact of the material when it is shown the second time in its proper place in the plot. Probably for that reason, this approach is no longer used very frequently.

The second type of cold open also begins the program with content material, but in this case the content is in its proper sequence—the introductory section is the beginning of the plot. Then identification of the program is given, and commercials or other materials are presented. Finally after the other opening elements are completed, the plot resumes from the point at which it had been interrupted.

One producing organization, Quinn-Martin, made this approach quite formal. The writers on some of its series, for example "The FBI," actually scripted a three- to four-minute "prologue" which was given that label on the screen.

Other types of programs may also use this type of opening. A talk-interview program may begin "cold" with conversation between host and guest, or a news program may open with headlines or one major story before the program is identified and other opening elements presented.

This form of opening does not give away any plot secrets, and if properly constructed can strongly attract and hold audience attention. But there are also some problems that need to be recognized and overcome in order to use this approach successfully. Traditionally, the opening of a dramatic plot includes material that sets the locale of the drama, introduces the characters, and introduces the conflict. Often this expository material, though necessary, does not contain high-interest content. If used as an opening it would be slow and weak, without much attention-getting force.

If we reverse the situation, another problem emerges. Providing dramatic, high-interest, important material early will attract attention, but if important material is included too early in the cold open, late tuners will miss that content and will be behind in trying to understand the plot as it unfolds.

Finally, if the cold open does not contain the main characters—that is, those who are the readily recognizable stars of the series—audience members will have no way to identify the program and to confirm whether they have tuned to the right channel. They may tune away, or go searching for a TV log to see if perhaps the program they were expecting to see has been preempted, or changed to another time, or whatever. They have no clue that this is in fact the program they tuned in to see.

The solution to these three possible problems—taking advantage of the strong attention-getting characteristic of a cold open while at the same time starting the program at a logical beginning, accommodating late tuners, and identifying the program—requires a delicate balancing act on the part of the writer. So a well-constructed cold opening will:

- Contain high-interest material, even if that material is not directly related to the main content which will be developed later

- Not include important facts or events too early which might be missed by late tuners

- Have some easily recognizable element appear early, either the appearance of the featured performer or performers in the series, or the keying in of titles over program action, or something similar

Hybrid Openings

In practice, creative writers are constantly developing variations that find ways to combine the strengths of both signatures and cold opens. A typical hybrid form found on quite a few program series uses a sequence of quick (3- to 4-second) scenes lifted from various places in the body of the program and formed into an audio/visual montage. These scenes are then intercut with titles and identifications of the featured performers, as in "Hotel." Or the montage may be formed from scenes lifted from preceding episodes, if the program is one with a continuing plot line, like "soap opera" dramas. The result is a form of signature, a standardized pattern identifiable very quickly by the audience, but with enough variation from program to program to provide interest.

In summary, the program opening should attract attention and identify. It may also set a mood, explain some feature of the program, or provide a place for inserting commercials or other announcements. How the writer accomplishes and balances these various requirements will depend on the type of program, the demands of sponsors and producers, and the writer's own creativity.

The Body of the Program

In the main portion of the program it is necessary, first, to maintain or reattract audience attention, to provide changes of sufficient intensity and frequency to keep the audience tuned and interested in the program. Second, in most programs it will also be necessary to organize the content so that there are breaks for the insertion of announcements.

The type of content being presented dictates the structure and method of presentation. Dramatic programs are by definition different from news broadcasts, talk shows, musical variety programs, and so on. But the writer of a successful program will need to consider several structural requirements independent of the type of content. It is the writer's job to be sure the program provides unity, variety, good pacing, and a climax.

Unity

This requirement refers to those characteristics in a program which make the audience feel the program "hangs together"—that it is a single, logical unit into which no extraneous elements have been introduced. A program that consists of elements apparently thrown together at random, without rhyme or reason, leaves the listener bewildered and uncomfortable, because it will require effort to follow the idea of the program.

Unity does not mean that only a single kind of material can be used—a musical program should not be made up entirely of vocal solos by a single entertainer. But the music used, no matter of what type or by what means it is presented, must harmonize with the general spirit or "mood" of the program. To use extreme examples, you wouldn't insert a rock and roll piece in a program of symphony music, nor would you put a prayer in the middle of a comedy monologue.

Unity in a program may be ensured or heightened by:

1. Dealing with a single idea in the program. If it is a news program, it should deal with current news; if it is a forum, it should be a discussion of one topic.

2. Using a "theme" or "situation" that runs throughout the program. In a variety program, every episode or "act" might be related in some way to a program theme—in one program the theme might be based around a holiday, or a location, or some occupation or hobby.

3. Using a central "featured personality"—with the entire program revolving around that featured person or persons. This is one of the most common approaches to unity. The performer may be a featured entertainer, a master of ceremonies, the anchor in a news broadcast, or the "lead" in a dramatic program—but that person or persons has the duty of carrying the show.

4. Eliminating materials that obviously do not belong—scenes in dramatic programs which do not advance the plot and which seem to be dragged in; materials which do not fit the "mood" of the program, such as comedy routines in a serious program.

5. Making effective use of transitions. In a variety program, each "act" should be introduced. In a forum, a change in the subtopic discussed should be clearly identified

by the moderator, so the listener knows that the material which follows is not intended to apply to the previous subtopic.

6. Handling middle commercial announcements in such a way that they provide the least possible interruption and listener annoyance.

In most programs, the most serious violations of unity result from the indiscriminate insertion of commercial announcements. Commercials are necessary in most programs, but they *can* be handled in a sensible manner. They can be inserted at natural breaks in program continuity—at the conclusion of the performance of an "act" in a variety show, or following the completion of a section devoted to some one type of news in a news broadcast, or at the end of a complete scene in a dramatic program. Dramatic programs written for the commercial broadcast media, if well written, will be structured into "acts" that provide logical breaks to accommodate commercial inserts. In contrast, a motion picture originally produced for theatrical release, where it is shown without interruption, will seem choppy when shown on television because the commercial breaks seem to be—and are—especially disruptive.

Commercials can be separated from program content by some type of *bumper*—a visual or aural midprogram signature, a gong ringing, a strain of music, a "freeze frame" of the last shot in the content, or some similar transition. Even "and now, a word from our sponsor," which is pretty crude, is better than nothing.

Another aspect of unity that is important in a program series is series unity. The viewer has a right to expect that all programs in a series will be similar. If he or she enjoyed the first broadcast, the expectation is that subsequent programs in the series will provide the same enjoyment. Any program titled "Dallas" should be of the same general pattern as any other program in that series. Series unity is provided by consistent use of the same general kind of content, by the use in each broadcast of the same featured personalities, by the use of the same general sort of locale, and by the use of essentially the same format.

Variety

The idea of *variety* has already been introduced under a different name—change—in the discussion of program elements. On first examination, the requirements for variety and for unity may seem to be at odds, but a well-structured program will have variety within a unified theme or approach. Some of the methods that may be used to provide variety include these:

Variety in Kinds of Materials

Many different kinds of materials can be used in a broadcast program. In music alone, there is new wave, disco, country, folk, religious, jazz, Latin, and several styles of rock, just for starters. A variety program may offer comedy in the form of sketches and monologues, dance routines, musical numbers, and so on.

Dramatic programs may have several parallel plots and subplots progressing through the program. The presence of these several plots does not violate the principle of unity so long as the various plots are connected in some fashion—using interlocking character relationships, or the same locale, for example—and so long as all the plots move forward toward climax and resolution. "Love Boat" and "Fantasy Island" both use multiple plots, connected by locale and the interactions of the continuing performers with the guests in each sketch.

"Hill Street Blues" has received considerable acclaim for its ability to keep several plot lines developing simultaneously, all connected through the police precinct and the major characters. But during its first season "Hill Street Blues" was nearly taken off the air because of poor audience response, probably because this approach was different from anything previously presented on television. Even now, a new viewer who has never seen that program before will have to commit a fair amount of time and effort in order to understand the various character relationships and to get used to the multiple-plot concept.

Variety in Methods of Presentation

A musical number might be presented as a vocal solo, as a number by a trio, quartet, or other small vocal group, as a vocal solo with backing by a large chorus, as an instrumental solo, as a presentation by a small instrumental group, or as a full orchestra performance. Talk materials might be presented as "straight" talk by a single speaker, as dialogue between two speakers, as regular narration by two speakers alternating, as a question and answer segment, by a single speaker in the form of reading a section of a letter or part of a book, and so on.

A farm broadcaster may talk in general about farming and farm problems, but one portion of the program may be spent discussing market trends, another reading market forecasts from the U.S. Department of Agriculture, and another in discussing the need for spraying fruit trees—there are a lot of different subjects included under the general heading of "farming and farm problems."

The announcer can use actualities—the actual voices of farmers or agricultural experts—either live in the studio, by phone, or in pretaped segments. A secondary personality may be used on the program to permit back-and-forth talk, to present certain items in a semi-comedy "heckling" role, or to represent the "typical listener" and interrupt with questions.

Variety in Types of Performers

This form is well illustrated by the types of characters ordinarily found in a dramatic program. Usually there will be a male lead and a corresponding female lead; possibly a comedy-type who is a friend of the hero's; sometimes a juvenile character—a teenage boy or girl; occasionally a younger child, frequently one or two older people. In a well-structured play, hardly ever are there two important characters who are of the same sex and of approximately the same age unless variety is provided by making the characters quite different in other respects.

In a talk or discussion program, variety might be introduced by having both male and female and older and younger people appearing. But more important would be to have people with differing points of view regarding the topic. A discussion program in which all the participants agree is going to lose audience interest very quickly.

Other Forms of Variety

Some additional ways of achieving variety include these:

1. The use of "feature spots"—material deliberately different in content and/or method of presentation from the surrounding materials in the program.

2. The use of music or sound effects for background, transition, or punctuation.

3. The use of different types of "stunts" for participants to perform and a variety of types of people as participants. For a quiz program, the subject matter of the questions can be changed. Prizes are usually given in audience participation shows; here too there is opportunity for the introduction of variety and novelty.

4. The use of "characters" or entertainers who look different or who wear costumes of different types. Change also can be introduced in settings or backgrounds and by the use of lighting effects.

5. The use of "visuals"—slides, films, rear projection, charts or diagrams included in the set or with the format of the program. These graphic devices are frequently used in news and talk programs to provide visual variety.

Pace

In every type of entertainment, pace is a requirement. *Pace* is not a synonym for speed; it refers primarily to an impression, the impression of "going somewhere" and not "dragging." In part, the effect of good pace comes from the avoidance of materials that themselves move slowly. In part too, the effect comes from avoiding the stretching out of materials. Otherwise listeners get the impression that the program lacked enough material to fill the time—and that interferes with listener attention and interest.

The impression of pace is provided by:

1. Seeing that participants do not include speakers who are needlessly and intolerably slow in their speech patterns—or if such speakers must be used, that they are held to short appearances.

2. Making use of entertainers or speakers who are vigorous and lively in their manner of speaking—obviously allowing for the use of some other types to satisfy requirements of variety.

3. Eliminating or shortening any materials or types of materials that tend to slow up the program—long explanations, or overlong, very slow musical numbers, or long talk scenes—exposition with no action—in a drama.

We have emphasized the *impression* or the *sense* of good pace provided in a well-structured program. But the most effective way to determine whether or not a program has good pace is to check on the number and consequently the length of the elements that make up the program. If the elements are regularly long, pace is necessarily slow and the program suffers. Even if just a few of the elements are unusually long, the listener will have the impression of the program being "draggy." You have undoubtedly seen programs that seemed slow. If you had numbered and timed the program elements, you would have found comparatively longer and fewer program units than in a program in which each element is ended, and replaced by another, before the listener has a chance to get tired of the material in that element.

At the other extreme, programs such as "Laugh-In" have an extremely rapid pace, with program element changes an average of every 30 seconds or so. (The rapid pace was made possible by videotape editing. The program could not have maintained that pace with live sequences, and therefore could not have been developed and produced until tape editing was perfected. The "Laugh-In" style of fast-paced comedy and frequent element changes can still be seen on the syndicated country/comedy program "Hee-Haw.")

Climax

The requirement for climax is most easily recognized in dramatic programs. Throughout the body of the program, as the plot situations develop, the problems facing the central characters become more and more complex and reach what seem to be an unsolvable peak. The moment of greatest tension is the climax. It is followed quickly by the solution and the end of the program.

But this sense of building to climax, of raising audience interest to higher levels as the program progresses, is not and should not be limited to dramatic programs. In a variety or musical program, it can be the big closing production number in which all the featured performers and guests appear, along with the dancers, orchestra, and so on. It can also be accomplished by holding back some of the important guest performers until near the end of the program. In a quiz program or game show, it may be the awarding of the biggest prize at the end of the show. In an interview program, some of the more important questions to be asked of the interviewee may be held back and developed near the end of the program, in order to provide some strong material at the close which the audience perceives as climax and remembers after the program is over.

In addition to the use of tension or "bigness," climax may be achieved through emotional stimulation. A featured musical performer might, for example, appear alone and perform a song that has strong emotional associations for the audience. Some years ago the Tennessee Ernie Ford television program did just that, using a religious hymn as its final number each week. For the target audience, the emotional appeal of that powerfully and simply sung hymn provided a strong climax which they waited for each week with real anticipation.

News broadcasts would seem to be an exception to the climax rule. These broadcasts do place the most important news stories at the beginning of the newscast. Audiences cannot be expected to wait through an entire broadcast to find out the major stories. But frequently news programs will close with a human interest story, one that has strong emotional pull and that does provide a form of climax.

In addition to the "final" climax in a program, longer programs and programs which have breaks for identification and/or commercial insertions will need to have subclimaxes—one to precede each break in the continuity and to heighten audience interest enough to bridge the gap until the program is resumed.

This requirement for climax refers to the organization of the content materials in the program. But the content closing and the program closing are not usually the same, as we will see.

Program Closings

In a dramatic program, the content close comes with the climax and the denouement, which is the final resolution of the plot. However, several minutes of other materials—credits, commercials—may still have to be presented before the program can end. In other types of programs, the time between the end of the content and the closing of the program may be somewhat shorter, but in all programs there are materials that come after the content of the show has been completed.

Functions of Program Closings

A program closing has several important functions. The particular ones required will vary with the type of program and some of them are similar to those performed by openings.

Providing Identification

Most of the members of the audience will have watched a program from its beginning and will know what program they have tuned to, but some late tuners may not know the name of the program. They should be given at least a brief identification somewhere in the close.

For that purpose, some programs use a closing signature, frequently the same signature used in the opening, or a shortened version of it, or the same sound track. Here, as in the opening, the familiar signature aids in identification and is also useful in providing a sense of finality to the program.

Closing credits are another type of identification. Usually the credits for the major performers are given in the opening, but those for production personnel and secondary performers are usually provided at the end. Audiences don't find this listing particularly interesting, but the contract for the broadcast of the program usually requires that these people be given credits, even if the listing is low-interest material.

When the movie *Superman* was first shown on television, it was split into two parts and shown on two successive nights. The contract stipulated that the full credits be shown on both nights—*eleven minutes of credits each time!* Certainly there was very little audience left at the end of that time to watch the following commercials and programs. But imagine how much worse the problem would have been in maintaining audience attention if those credits had been required at the beginning rather than at the end.

Providing Place for Announcements

The closing for most programs must also contain positions to place announcements—commercials or PSAs—just as there is a need for such positions in the program opening and the body. However, the problem of holding audience attention, so that audience members can be exposed to those messages, must be approached slightly differently in the closing. In the opening and the body, if the attention-getting material has been effective and if the program is well structured and written, the audience will stay through commercials to watch the remaining content. In the closing, after the content of the program has been presented and completed, the plot climax has been reached and resolved, the major news stories have been given, or the major guests have appeared it is much more difficult to keep the audience's attention for the closing commercials.

One device commonly used for this purpose is the *epilogue*. The epilogue in a dramatic program follows the closing commercials with some final bit of conversation among the major characters. It may be the denouement, or an explanation, such as how the detective figured out the murder, or a final laugh. If the epilogue for each episode of a series is well written, each week the audience will stay tuned through the closing commercials to see what "twist" the writer has put in for this episode.

Epilogues can appear in programs other than dramatic shows. In a news broadcast, the final "human interest" story may be held until after closing commercials for the same reason. The term *epilogue* is commonly used in the industry to describe this type of closing material, but the only major producers to identify it formally as such on the screen are the same ones who labeled the openings of their programs prologues, Quinn-Martin.

Promoting Subsequent Programs

Frequently there will be material in the closing of a program used to attract the attention of the audience to a subsequent program. This material is called a *teaser*, and it can take several forms. It may be used to "tease" the audience into watching the next program of the same series, the next day or the next week, whenever that program series next appears. The producers and writers who decide to include this form of tease assume the people watching will then have a sufficiently strong mental image to remember and will tune in to the next broadcast.

A teaser may also be used to hold the audience over for the immediately following program. People are prone to stay with a channel or station anyway. However, this audience flow, which is an important strategy of programmers, may be strengthened by a teaser for the program to follow.

Or the programmers may use the teaser to promote some other program in the schedule appearing later in the day, or even on a subsequent day. This teaser may be for a new program that needs additional promotion, or a special, one-time program, or a program that has been reassigned to a new day or time, or one that is doing poorly in the ratings and the programmers feel needs a boost.

For television, if the tease is for the next program in the same series, it will probably take the form of some brief scenes lifted from that episode, very much like the montage of scenes used in many openings. But most often the teaser in television is an audio-only message—essentially a radio promotion delivered by an announcer over the visual closing credits. Seldom do audience members actually read the closing credits, and those few seconds can be used effectively, at least in the opinion of the producers, for a teaser.

Providing a Sense of Finality

This function is that of "rounding out" or providing to the audience a feeling that the program has concluded. For most programs, again especially those that have been prerecorded and pretimed, there is no question as to when the program is over. Even live programs such as news broadcasts end with a closing statement by the anchor and a closing credit. But occasionally a program that has been badly timed and poorly prepared, or that has had to be put together at the last moment, will just end without the sense of finality it should have. If you have been in the audience for such a program, you can recall the momentary sense of frustration and bewilderment you felt when the program suddenly disappeared.

Adjustments for Timing

One function of a program closing that merits special attention is timing. Broadcast programs, with rare exceptions, have precise time requirements. They must end exactly at the time scheduled, and can be neither short nor long. Most programs are prerecorded, and the final timing is done in the editing process before the programs are broadcast. Live programs, however, must contain provisions for timing adjustments.

Major adjustments will be made during the body of the show. A game show may not reach its final round in time for the contest to be completed in one episode, so the contestants will be asked to come back and complete the contest on the next program. In a news broadcast, the director will have preselected one story to be dropped if the program begins to run long.

Final, short, "fine-timing" adjustments will be made in the closing. The materials that will be used or dropped in the closing to make the final adjustments are known as the *pad*. These are items that can be expanded or contracted, run more slowly or faster, or omitted. On television, the closing credits are frequently used as the pad. They may be "rolled" across the screen at a faster or slower rate, as needed. For radio, a common pad is the theme music used for a signature, which may be played for varying lengths of time.

The following is a typical timing pad for a local live public affairs program. It uses only the moderator's voice to provide the necessary adjustments to get the program out on time:

MODERATOR:

Thank you, Martha and Joe.

1. Today's guests on "Community Viewpoint" have been Martha Jones, founder of the Concerned Parents' Patrol and Joe Smith, Community Services Director for the Sheriff's Office of Sacramento County. (0:15)

2. On our next program we will have as our guests Bill Wright, area representative of the California Taxpayers' Association and Ken Irwin, County Supervisor from the Fourth District of Sacramento County (0:15)

3. They will discuss recent changes in the state property tax laws and their effect on county taxpayers and on county revenues. (0:10)

4. Please join us next week at this same time for a lively discussion of a topic which is important to every householder in our community. (0:10)

5. I'm Mary Hammer, thank you for being with us on Community Viewpoint. (0:05)

6. This program is a presentation of the Community Services Department of KXXX (0:05)

MUSIC:

SIGNATURE UP TO CLOSE.

There are six separate segments in this close, not counting the signature theme. The six individually range in length from 5 to 15 seconds. They can be put together in varying combinations, depending on the time to be filled. Any 5-second length from 5 to 60 seconds can be accommodated by using an appropriate combination of segments.

Use	#5	for a :05 second pad
	#5, 6	:10
	#4, 5	:15
	#1, 5	:20
	#1, 5, 6	:25
	#1, 4, 5	:30
	#1, 2, 5	:35
	#1, 2, 5, 6	:40
	#1, 2, 3, 5	:45
	#1, 2, 3, 4	:50
	#1, 2, 3, 4, 5	:55
	#1, 2, 3, 4, 5, 6	:60

The closing elements of a program, then, should be chosen and arranged in such a way as to accommodate as many of these purposes as may be required and at the same time to close the program as quickly as possible after the climax has been reached. As we have noted, audience interest drops quickly after the resolution of the plot or the presentation of some form of climax. If the audience is going to be held for the following program, the closing materials must continue to hold attention, or at least be brief enough that anticipation of the upcoming program will provide the lure.

Analysis of Program Structure

Having now established criteria for the evaluation of program structure, we can return to the two programs, "Newhart" and "Entertainment Tonight," for which analyses were prepared, and see how well they measure up structurally. However, as we said earlier, it's a more meaningful exercise if you apply these criteria to programs you personally see and analyze.

Newhart

1. The program *opening* consists of three elements, a signature and two commercials. The signature identifies the program and main performers by title, but the performers are not seen. The visual sequence is strictly pastoral; it sets the scene in a small New England village. It does not establish any of the mood of comic interplay expected in a situation comedy. The audience will have to rely on prior recognition of Newhart's name and comic approach in order to have any idea of what the program is to be about.

   The two opening commercials come very early. The audience has not yet been very strongly attracted by just the signature. Fortunately both signature and commercials are short, so the content does begin only 2:00 into the program.

2. *Unity* is strong. There is one dramatic theme, and all the elements in the drama relate to the story of Joanna's feeling that she is not appreciated by her husband for her work at the inn, her consequent decision to find an outside job, and the final reconciliation between husband and wife.

3. *Variety,* as in most situation comedies, is provided primarily by character changes. There are four major characters—Newhart, Joanna, Herzog, and George, who appear in varying combinations. There are some additional minor characters. Each character differs from the other in age, sex, role, acting style, and so on. Location changes, another common way of obtaining variety in a dramatic program, are fewer here (possibly a reflection of cost; the fewer locations, the less it costs to produce a program). There are two main locations—the inn and the travel agency—but several sublocations are used within the inn and there is both an inner and outer office at the travel agency.

4. The *pace* of the show is somewhat uneven, but rather slow overall. There are 27 elements, which is not a bad average, but there are several very long conversations early in the program that slow the pace considerably, and the total of 27 is reached only by adding 9 elements in the final three minutes of the program, including the final 5 elements, which are not dramatic content.

   Two of the long conversation sequences are worth special comment. The scene at the breakfast table (elements 6–8) begins with the two men talking. Joanna enters, making a new group of characters and a new element; she then leaves, but returns almost immediately. We chose not to use her intermediate exit and entrance to establish new elements. When she leaves the second time, with finality in her action, we created a new unit. The unit (8) is the typical situation comedy tag line—a brief subclimax before the midprogram commercial.

   Another lengthy conversational sequence takes up the entire time block between 23:15 and the end of the plot at 26:35. This sequence is broken into a number of shorter elements which gives the audience the impression of faster pace and stronger build to *climax*. The elements are separated by different combinations of characters and different locations (the inner and outer offices). Note particularly element 19, which is inserted as a cutaway between 18 and 20 to break up what would otherwise be a very long element.

5. The program *closing* is also structurally weak. Element 23 closes the drama and also in practical terms, the entire program. The final credits do end the program on time, re-identify, and provide the sense of closing. But the audience members know, when they see the visual credit in element 23, that the program is over. Nothing remains to hold their interest through the two final commercials and the promo.

Entertainment Tonight

1. The program *opening* does a good job of meeting the requirements of an effective opening. The program opens immediately with news content; element 1 is a quick cold open that immediately attracts attention. Then, for identification, there is a signature element. These two elements, which make up the opening, last only 1:15 total. There are no low-interest, long, slow elements in the opening. The first commercials do not appear until nearly 7:00 into the program.

2. The program producers chose to provide only three blocks for the insertion of

commercials. That decision means that the blocks are fairly long, two of 2:00 (elements 9–12 and 19–22) and one of 1:30 (elements 27–29). Shorter interruptions could have been provided, but there would have to be more of them to provide the total amount of time needed for commercial insertions. Both the first and last commercial blocks are separated from the main content of the program by a brief element consisting of signature music and a visual question and answer which serves as a buffer (elements 8 and 26).

3. *Unity* in the program is kept strong by using similar material throughout. All the news stories and features are about events and performers in the entertainment industry. All the stories are delivered, or at least introduced, by one of the two "anchor" personalities. *Variety* is provided by using two anchors, one male and one female; using other reporters to cover many of the stories; providing "news" in the first program segment and human interest, feature material later, and by providing special feature spots such as the movie reviews. Several of the stories include a segment that shows a performer actually performing, which contrasts with the reporter's narration and with interview segments. In element 24 a piece of historical black and white film adds variety to the contemporary story, which is of course in color.

4. From the "element" column we can see that there were a total of 31 elements for the 27:45 long program. That total number suggests an overall brisk *pace*. But there are four elements which are two minutes or more in length (7, 14, 23, and 25). Normally these would be expected to slow the pace of the show, especially during the portion of the program between the 17:15 and 24:40 marks. (What the analysis doesn't show, however, is that these longer elements were in each case made up of a series of quick scenes of the performers intercut with brief interviews, a technique which helps maintain the feeling of rapid pace.)

5. The sense of *climax* isn't strong. The position for the strongest climax (element 25), just before the closing commercials, is filled by the story on Tom Petty and the Heartbreakers, which is a well-known musical group for at least some of the target audience, and thus may provide some climax for them. During the program that story was promoted several times to heighten audience anticipation.

6. Neither is there much material to hold the audience through the closing commercials. Only a brief tease for the following day's program, and closing credits rolled over additional musical material from one of the featured performers follow the closing commercials. But there is an attempt, at least, to provide that hold by having new material in the close.

7. The program is of course prerecorded, and so it is pretimed. But since it airs the same day it is produced, there is not much time available to edit precisely. The closing element (31) provides a quick way to adjust for timing. The performers are introduced and they begin to play a selection. This time it was duo pianos; on other broadcasts it will be some other type of musical performance. Credits are rolled visually over that performance, and the whole thing is faded out at the correct time. It's easily done, but the fadeout in midperformance does not give a strong feeling of finality to the program.

In these examples, and throughout most of this chapter, we have been emphasizing television program structure. But these concepts are equally applicable to radio. Most radio programming provides frequent change, even if that change is just from one record to the next. Unity and variety are also present. Unity is known by the terms *sound, image,* or *format,* referring to that general type of music (or talk) which provides the consistent sound of that station. Variety is the changes—of music recordings, or of voices and other material—within that format. Climax is not present on most radio stations, because programs of specific length are not provided. Audiences flow in and out throughout the day. But whenever there are programs of determinate length, all the structural requirements for opening, body, and closing should be considered.

Conclusion

In this chapter we have shown how the behavior of audiences and the structure of programs are related. Programs must be structured to take into account the various levels of attention and the limited attention span of audiences. Only if audiences find the content of a program extremely interesting or important will they expend the effort to continue to watch or listen to a poorly structured program.

One universal tool that can be used to analyze existing programs and as a building block for writing new programs is the *program element*—a segment of a program separated from preceding or following segments by change of sufficient strength to reattract audience attention. All programs are made up of program elements of different kinds and lengths. Well-structured programs will have frequent new elements.

Generally programs have a three-part structure consisting of an opening, body, and closing. All three parts have important functions to perform within the program. The opening should attract attention to the program and identify it for its audience. It may also be used to set a mood, to provide explanations, and to provide a place for announcements to be inserted. Whatever functions are expected of the opening, the elements should be arranged so that the program gets off to the strongest start possible.

The structure of the body will depend in large part on the type of content being presented, but all programs should be organized to provide unity, variety, good pace, and a sense of climax, regardless of the specific content.

The closing may provide further identification, including credits. It may also be expected to provide a place for announcements, promote subsequent programs, and give a sense of finality to the show. Particularly important for live programs is the requirement to bring the program to a close on time.

If a program has been structured well, that structure will add to the inherent interest of the content and the two together—structure and content—will make the program attractive to its target audience and successful in accomplishing its purpose.

Exercises

1. Complete an element analysis of a television program, filling in the form here with data obtained from the program. The program may be any "made for TV" program—don't use sporting events, feature movies, or other material

not produced for TV. You may view a program of any length (30 minutes or more), but whatever length you choose, *analyze the entire program.*

In the first column, number the elements. The total number of elements contained in a program provides some indication of pace.

In the second column, give a brief description of the *content* of the element—an automobile chase scene, a conversation between which major characters, a song and dance routine by the program host. In a few words describe *what* is happening, *who* is doing it, and possibly *where* it is taking place. If the element is a commercial, what is the product?

The next column is deliberately set off one-half space to emphasize that it represents change *between* elements. In it you should indicate the type of *change* that takes place between the preceding and following elements. If element 1 is a title sequence and element 2 is a commercial, the change between them is in the type of content or *material.* Other changes might be in *character*—a major character enters or leaves a dramatic scene; in *time*—a lapse between scenes; or *location*—change of location between scenes; or combinations of these. Other types of changes are possible—name and describe them briefly in this space.

The column labeled "Start" is for the start time of each element *from the beginning of the program.* The first element of the program starts at 0:00. To calculate the start time of an element, add the length of the preceding element to its own start time. The start time for element 4 would be the start time of element 3 plus the length of element 3.

The column labeled "Length" is for the *length* of each element. You should try to be accurate to within about 5 seconds for each element.

Use the "Newhart" and "Entertainment Tonight" examples as models.

2. Using the element analysis from exercise 1, analyze that program for its structural strengths and weaknesses. Describe specifically what was done to satisfy each criterion and *evaluate* what was structurally good or bad on each point.

   a. The program opening
      _____ Attention getting?
      _____ Identification?
      _____ Strong start?
      _____ Place for announcements?
      _____ Other goals in the opening (e.g., mood setting)?

   b. The body of the program
      _____ Unity?
      _____ Variety?
      _____ Pace?
      _____ Climax?

   c. The program closing
      _____ Identification?
      _____ Place for announcements?

<u>ELEMENT ANALYSIS</u>   Name _____

Program _____   Length _____

Station _____   Date/Day _____   Hour _____

Description of Material	Type of Change	Start	Length
1. _____		_____	
2. _____	_____	_____	
3. _____	_____	_____	
4. _____	_____	_____	
5. _____	_____	_____	
6. _____	_____	_____	
7. _____	_____	_____	
8. _____	_____	_____	
9. _____	_____	_____	
10. _____	_____	_____	
11. _____	_____	_____	
12. _____	_____	_____	
13. _____	_____	_____	
14. _____	_____	_____	
15. _____	_____	_____	
16. _____	_____	_____	
17. _____	_____	_____	
18. _____	_____	_____	
19. _____	_____	_____	
20. _____	_____	_____	

_____ Sense of finality?

_____ Other?

   d. What is your overall evaluation of the program's structure? What specific structural changes would you make to strengthen the program?

Key Terms and Concepts	attention span	pad
	bumper	program element
	climax	program identification
	cold open	prologue
	credits	signature
	epilogue	station break
	feature spot	teaser
	gimmick	unity
	pace	variety

Note

1. The least objectionable program theory was originally presented in Pat Paul Klein, "The Men Who Run TV Aren't All That Stupid," *New York Magazine*, January 25, 1971, pp. 20–29.

Chapter 6

Handling Sound

The broadcast writer deals with two uses of sound—with the meaning language conveys and with sound as such. In most of the other chapters of this book we are concerned with language and meaning. In this chapter we will examine the second use of sound, which includes music, all the varied sound effects (to use the term in its technical application), and voices when used for their sound value.

The emphasis will be on radio, because that medium must rely on sound exclusively for communication of its ideas. But sound is used in television (and other audiovisual media) for practically all the same purposes and in the same ways as it is used in radio.

As the writer of the script, it is your responsibility to describe what sounds are to be used and how they are to be used to achieve the desired effect. This you will have to accomplish through careful, detailed description, for seldom will you, the writer, also be involved in the actual creation of the sounds and voices used in the final production. The insertion of music, sound effects, and voices takes place on location, in the studio, or in the control room and is done by actors, announcers, and technicians.

We consider first, the basic characteristics of sound. Then we examine techniques for using each of the three components of sound—sound effects, music, and voices—to strengthen the structure of programs and announcements.

Characteristics of Sound

We are concerned here not only with the actual characteristics of sound, but also with the perceptions sounds generate in the ears of listeners. The writer needs to understand the psychological effects the various characteristics of sound produce in listeners, so our comments will be directed toward that end rather than to the physics of sound.

The characteristics we will examine are: (1) pitch, (2) quality, (3) volume, (4) distance, (5) acoustical setting, (6) rhythm, and (7) juxtaposition. Although we will describe each characteristic individually, in practice they cannot be separated and will be difficult to illustrate independently.

Pitch

This is the term commonly used to describe the frequency of a sound, or the wavelength of the vibration of an object. Examine a piano keyboard. The long strings at the left end of the keyboard have a longer wavelength and the lower frequency or pitch than the shorter strings at the other end.

In general, low pitches are more pleasing to the ear; they become more disturbing and irritating as they get closer to the upper end of the range of human hearing. Pitch may be exciting, disturbing, or merely irritating as it goes upward, depending on the other characteristics of sound that accompany it.

The writer can use several methods to control pitch, depending on the kind of program and the specific circumstances of the script:

1. Choose music that will use a predominance of instruments in the desired pitch range. A bright, cheery pastoral musical bridge might be written this way:

   MUSIC: FLUTE SOLO
   or
   MUSIC: LIGHT, AIRY

   The music to *Peter and the Wolf*, in which each character in the story is represented by an instrument with a different pitch and quality, is a perfect example of using music to help define character.

2. Describe the voice of the person who should be chosen to read the lines. Assume we have a leprechaun as a character in a commercial. We don't know what leprechauns sound like, but the character could have a high-pitched, almost falsetto voice. This vocal pitch might be found naturally, but more likely it would be artificially assumed by the actor playing the role, or filtered electronically to give it an unnatural pitch range.

3. Write a stage direction to indicate how the line is to be read:

   ANNCR: (LOW, QUIET) One of the good things in life is being able to afford the luxury. . . .

   JIM: (FRANTIC, TENSE, HIGH-PITCHED) My God, Pete, we aren't going to make it! We'll crash. . . .

   These directions indicate to the person voicing the copy what tone and especially what pitch is required to convey an intended message.

4. Write in a sound effect in which a particular pitch will predominate:

   SOUND: HIGH-PITCHED WHINE OF JET ENGINE IN BG

   This effect will help create tension in the scene. It would be appropriate behind dialogue in which two characters argue.

5. Choose words for the script that will help control pitch. You might write:

   ANNCR: Tonight, in the quiet of the evening, when long shadows fill the corner of the room and memories drift in like the smoke of an autumn mist. . . .

Notice how the word choice makes it easy to use a low pitch. The words *long, corners, room, smoke, autumn* all use vowel and consonant combinations that encourage low pitches. It would be hard to read the copy in a tight, high-pitched voice; the word choice discourages it. By way of contrast, suppose the announcer were given this to read:

ANNCR: Settle back in your chair. Fill up your pipe. Put out the lamp. Look at the fire dance in the grate.

This piece of copy is an attempt to capture a mood of reminiscence, but it certainly does not encourage low pitch. The choice of vowels and consonants makes low, smooth reading difficult. Even though the ideas may be appropriate, the word choice is wrong if the writer wishes low pitches to predominate. The words *settle, back, look, dance,* and *grate* all have short vowels followed by consonants that cut them off sharply and discourage the use of low pitches. By choosing music, voices, and effects that have appropriate pitch ranges, the writer can manipulate and control this aspect of sound within a script.

Quality   Also called timbre, this characteristic, described in terms of the physics of sound, represents the complexity of the wave form. A pure tone or frequency is an unpleasant sound if heard for very long. Most sounds are complex wave forms created by the interaction of several frequencies all present at the same time. For example, the presence of overtones, which are multiples of a fundamental pitch, distinguish a musical note played on a violin from the same note played on a clarinet.

The actual measurement of these complex wave forms can be done only by special instruments, but we recognize different timbres or qualities when we hear them and we use descriptive terms to indicate different qualities. We may talk about the *harsh* whine of a saw, and the *mellow* sound of a French horn; the *strident* call of a bluejay and the *soft* whisper of a breeze; the *brassy* fanfare from a trumpet and the *liquid* voice of a flute. We may describe the sound of an orchestra as *full,* or the simulated voice of a robot as *mechanical.*

The writer controls the quality of sound by the same methods used to control pitch. Since we tend to describe the quality of sound in terms that indicate its effect on us, the writer need only indicate the quality desired in any given spot, using standard descriptive words:

MUSIC: TO SIMULATE A BABBLING BROOK

SOUND: DISSONANT AUTO HORNS IN A TRAFFIC JAM

Consider again for a moment one of the problems posed in the discussion of pitch, the choice of words. In the two examples above, there is a marked difference in the quality of the sounds, quite aside from pitch and the ideas expressed. The words *long, room,* and *autumn* all use a long vowel in conjunction with a consonant that can also be prolonged. This helps create a soft, pleasant quality of sound. In the other example, *settle, pipe, look,* and *grate* all contain short sounds. The combination of vowels and consonants sounds abrupt. These are crisp, unmusical words, and the whole passage is affected by their quality.

Volume

Audience reactions to various volume levels tend to be similar to those for pitch. Low volume tends to be soothing, comforting, and reassuring. As volume increases, sounds become more disturbing and more irritating until they reach the level of actual pain.

The writer controls volume through directions written in the script and through the selection of the music or sound effects to be used. Some music has to be loud to be right, and so do some sounds. There is no such thing as the quiet sound of an iron foundry or assembly line. The volume of the announcer's or actor's voice can be controlled by directions in the script. In the absence of directions to the contrary, such as LOUDLY or IN A WHISPER, script continuity is spoken at a normal speaking level.

One of the conventions established in the early days of radio drama was that background sound effects used to identify a location be introduced at normal volume, and then the volume be reduced behind the voices of the actors in the scene. Sometimes the sound was even removed after it had been established, even though in "reality" it would have remained in the location.

Suppose you are writing a scene that takes place in an automobile. By the very nature of the scene, if the car is running we should expect to hear the motor. To establish the scene, the sound of the car would be introduced at a normal volume. Then, as the scene progresses, it can be gradually reduced in volume until it is at a lower background level. It is still there enough to maintain awareness of the locale, but it is considerably faded down in volume and does not interfere with or distract the audience from the action. This process parallels what happens in real life when the human ear is exposed to continuous sound. The ear tends to get used to sounds, even fairly loud ones, and ceases to hear them in the foreground of attention. In conformity with this psychological fact, a good writer, having introduced a sound to indicate a continuing background effect, will submerge it gradually after the locale has been accepted.

The radio drama series "Dragnet," when it was first broadcast, broke with that tradition. A unique characteristic of "Dragnet" was that background sound in a scene continued at a level more closely approximating the real situation. If the scene was in a factory and the actors would have to shout to be heard, then the script called for them to shout. Because it modified the convention, "Dragnet" became known as the first "realistic" radio drama. Now, the "realistic" use of sound is common practice in both radio and television. However, high-level sound should not continue unmodified throughout a scene. It can be very annoying if the audience is forced to fight the sound in order to hear dialogue.

Sound volume is also important to the aural perception of distance, which we consider next.

Distance

In television, the positions of the various persons in a scene can be seen, so there should be no problem for the audience in that regard. But for radio, the relative positions of actors in a scene, and movement taking place within that scene, must be established in terms of perceived distance—the perception being in the ear of the listener.

One of the conventions of radio/audio writing is that the listener is always perceived to be with the microphone. If, for example, two voices are carrying on a conversation and both are at full, normal volume, then both are perceived to be in the same location and the listener, mentally, places him or herself as an observer at the same location. If, on the other hand, the writer wants to place some distance between the two voices and tell the audience that one of these voices is some distance from the scene, that actor will be backed away from the microphone. If both voices are off-mike, the listener would perceive both actors to be at a distance from the location established as the center of action. If both voices then took on a shouting, projected tone, they would be perceived as being some distance from each other as well. Here are three brief examples of on-mike and off-mike dialogue.

SOUND:	GUNSHOTS IN DISTANCE; IMMEDIATELY FOLLOWED BY RICOCHET SOUND OF BULLETS OFF ROCKS IN FORE-GROUND
ONE:	Well, it looks like they found where we are, boys. We may be pinned down here for some time.
TWO:	I don't know about you, but I don't want to sit here like a clay pigeon in a shooting gallery. There's got to be a back way out of this rockpile.
THREE:	Well, why don't you just go find it then, and we'll try to keep as hidden as possible.
TWO:	Ok, I will, (FADE) but you keep that posse occupied while I'm climbing around out there, y'hear.
SOUND:	MORE SHOTS—OCCASIONALLY THROUGH THE FOLLOW-ING:
THREE:	I didn't want to give him much encouragement, but I really do hope he can find a way out back there.
ONE:	Yep, me too. And I hope that if he finds a way he tells us about it.
THREE:	You don't suppose he'd just take off by himself, do you?
ONE:	Stranger things have been known to happen, y'know.
THREE:	Well, I'll be . . . I never thought . . . (SHOUTS) Hey, Pete. Are you still there? Have you found a way out? (PAUSE) He doesn't answer . . . Maybe you're right . . . Why that dirty, sneaky, no account . . . .
ONE:	I wasn't sure about that guy from the very beginning. Well, now it looks like we're going to have . . . .

TWO: (OFF MIKE SHOUTING) Hey, there is a way out, but you've really got to crawl to keep from being seen.

JOHN: (PANTING—OUT OF BREATH) I've got to stop for a minute, Tim. I'm just exhausted.

TIM: (A LITTLE BREATHLESS) Ok, I'm kinda tired, too, but we can't stop long. We've got to get out of this river bottom before dark comes.

JOHN: I know, but I don't know if we're going the right way. Maybe we ought to split up and look for a trail.

TIM: I don't want to, but maybe you're right, John. Why don't you try that canyon over there, and I'll go down stream some more.

JOHN: Ok, (FADE) I'm on my way. Keep yelling so we can find each other.

TIM: (OFF MIKE, FADING) I will, you just watch your step . . . don't fall and hurt . . .

JOHN: (OFF MIKE) Yeah, and the same thing goes for you . . . .

NANCY: Is there anything in that trunk that will give us a clue to Mrs. Jones' disappearance, Mike?

MIKE: It doesn't look like it, Nancy. Nothing in here but old clothes.

RAY: But we've got to keep looking. Something up here in this attic really scared Mr. Hoffer when he came up here yesterday, and there hasn't been a chance for anybody to take anything away since.

NANCY: Well, you fellows keep looking in here. I'm going to go look in that room over there. (FADE) It looks appropriately spooky—all full of cobwebs and all.

RAY: I just wish we had some clue as to what we were looking for.

MIKE: I know, but Nancy's right, Mrs. Jones wouldn't just get up and leave town without telling anyone. Something's wrong. (SHOUTS) Anything in there, Nancy?

NANCY: (SHOUTS OFF-MIKE) No, I can hardly see anything: the window's so dirty that . . . wait a minute, maybe there is something. Hey, come here. I've found the answer.

SOUND:	HURRIED FOOTSTEPS
NANCY:	(ON-MIKE) This is it fellows, this is what we've been looking for.
RAY:	You're right, Nancy, you've solved the mystery.

In the first example actor 2 leaves the scene, which remains with voices 1 and 3. Actor 2 is heard later from a distance. In example 2 both John and Tim leave in different directions; the listener remains at the location from which they left. In example 3, Nancy leaves the scene to go into another room; then the scene shifts, as Ray, Mike, and the listener move to join her in the new location.

Unless otherwise indicated in the script, the production staff will assume that all sounds take place on-mike. If the writer visualizes the broadcast any other way, those lines which are to be faded on or faded off, or which take place at a distance from the microphone will have to be indicated in the script.

Two-channel stereo sound adds another dimension to the spatial relationship; it makes possible left-right shifts in the positions of characters as well as close–far away. In example 2 above, where John and Tim start in opposite directions, they would begin in the center (both channels); then Tim's microphone would be panned to the left channel as he fades, and John's microphone would be panned to the right channel. The use of stereo would give a clear indication to the audience that the characters were going in different directions.

As we noted, for television the viewer has no problem with perception; spatial relationships are easily seen. But the control of aural distance in television is the same as for radio; it should match the visual distance. For example, the voice of a character who is seen at a great distance should be faint and far away. If he calls to another actor from that distance, he will have to shout to be heard. That sound should have a distinct, forced quality. Similarly, the voice of a character leaving a scene should fade.

Acoustical Setting

This characteristic refers to the changes or alterations made to a sound by the surroundings in which that sound is emitted. It might also be viewed as one means by which the quality of sound is changed, because the different spaces that enclose a sound affect its quality. A given sound will have one quality in the open air and quite another at the bottom of a well. In the first case, where there is no surrounding enclosure, the original sound is unaltered; in the other, where a very solid, close enclosure surrounds the sound, an echoing, boomy quality is given the sound by its reverberation within the enclosure. The yell "Help! Save me!" would sound much different in the two situations. The writer should be sure that the appropriate acoustical setting for the script has been written in.

Acoustical relationships are very important in the establishment of location in a radio broadcast because the listener cannot "see" the location of a scene, except as that scene is built up as a mental image in the listener's mind by the sounds presented in the script. Suppose you are writing a script and wish to establish the fact that the scene is taking place in a large, empty cathedral. The acoustical quality of that location can be approximated by adding a considerable amount of echo to the lines spoken by the characters in the script. The audience would assume from the echo that the scene was taking place in some fairly large, hard-walled enclosure. A simple statement in the script would be enough to let the audience know that it was a church.

Another example: A radio commercial calls for the announcer to be in the client's store during a sale, with large, excited crowds milling around in the background. The commercial will be prerecorded. There are no large crowds available at the moment, and better control (at less cost) can be obtained by working in the studio anyway. The writer calls for a sound effect:

SOUND: CROWD NOISE IN BACKGROUND

ANNCR: (SLIGHTLY OFF-MIKE: LOUD, WITH ENTHUSIASM). Good after-
            noon, this is Joe Jones, and I'm here at the biggest sale ever at
            Smith Brothers Furniture. The crowds are tremendous. . . .

A little experimentation in the control room will find the proper balance between the recorded sound effect and the announcer's voice and provide the acoustical setting required. This same principle is applied to any scene where there would be an abnormal acoustical condition. The acoustic setting cannot just be suggested in the dialogue; it must be specified by the writer, with directions or production notes in the script.

Rhythm

We are accustomed to thinking of rhythm as patterns of sounds or of music. Almost all music has some sort of rhythmic pattern, or beat. And many sound effects contain repetitive, rhythmic elements. In general we know that long, slow, steady patterns are reassuring; short, staccato, or irregular patterns are disturbing, upsetting, and exciting. The beat of jungle drums is a cliché with which everyone should be familiar. Other patterns of rhythm and sound quality are used to suggest space travel, electronic communication, factories, computers, and so on.

Another aspect of rhythm we don't frequently recognize is vocal rhythm—distinctive patterns of speech. Some announcers and newscasters have individual patterns that are highly distinctive, such as Paul Harvey and, from an earlier time, Walter Winchell and Gabriel Heatter. Most announcers and actors are adaptable enough that if a particular rhythm—slow and smooth, or rushed and breathless, or whatever—is wanted, they can provide it.

Finally, the writer controls rhythm with the kind of words and sentences he or she writes. The style of the copy can control the rhythmic flow of the language to a greater extent than it can either pitch or quality, because the natural rhythm of the lines is completely under the control of the writer. Turn back again to the two brief examples used to demonstrate low-pitched words and notice how rhythm works. The first example flows smoothly. Each phrase can be read easily and smoothly, as a unit, and all the phrases flow together naturally with very little interruption in thought. The second example, on the other hand, is jerky. It stops and starts abruptly with each phrase. There is no smooth connection between phrases. Each comes to a full stop. They are written as commands, which encourages staccato reading. If the object was to create a piece of smooth, soothing copy, that would be impossible with the rhythm of the second example.

Juxtaposition By the *juxtaposition* of sound, we mean having several sounds introduced simultaneously, relying upon the ear's ability to determine the distance of each from the listener and from the other sounds and to distinguish differences in the quality, direction, volume, and pitch of the sounds.

The radio writer can use one sound juxtaposed against another to help tell a story and establish a scene. Suppose you are writing a scene at a football game. You may have an actor simulate an announcer working directly at the microphone. Behind this you might place in the script shouts of a crowd, some of them at fairly close range. Still farther away you might call for a band playing. The three sounds, occurring in juxtaposition to one another, would be sufficient to create a complete scene. The audience, hearing those simultaneous sounds and perceiving distance relationships among them, would recognize the situation. The writer would be using juxtaposition to help establish the locale.

As with the perception of distances, the juxtaposition of sounds is made more obvious by stereophonic broadcasting (or by other forms of audio presentation that feature more than one independent sound track). The human hearing system, which is a binaural system, readily perceives even small differences between two sound tracks being received simultaneously, and the brain translates those differences into perceptions of different positions and distances.

In the following example, several of the characteristics of sound are used simultaneously to develop a sense of excitement and tension in the scene.

SOUND:	PLANES APPROACHING AND LANDING . . . GETS LOUDER AS THEY ARE LANDING.
BING:	See, Joyce—they top over there.
JOYCE:	I see. When does Wallie's plane come in?
BING:	His is in the next three to—Holy!—
JOYCE:	What's wrong?
BING:	Nan, you were right. Something must have happened.
NAN:	I told you I saw something fall off when they were way up.
JOYCE:	(GETTING EXCITED AND NERVOUS): What is it? What's wrong?
BING:	I don't know—but his landing gear has come off.
NAN:	What can he do?

BING:	Bail out. He can't bring that plane in.
JOYCE:	Oh no. Nan—I . . .
NAN:	Hold on, Joyce, don't let yourself go.
SOUND:	PLANE SOUNDS LOUDER
BING:	Why he's crazy—he's going to try to do it anyway.
NAN:	He can't land that way, can he?
BING:	(TENSE) It's a crackup for sure! Why doesn't he bail out?
JOYCE:	Oh, Nan, I can't stand this!—Wallie—please don't try to land.
BING:	He's bringing her in now. There's a chance in a million that he can do it.
NAN:	He's slowing down.
SOUND:	MOTOR CUTS
BING:	He has to.
JOYCE	(FRANTICALLY) He's getting so low—
BING:	He's going to try to slide it in—a pancake!
NAN:	Bing, he's going to . . .
SOUND:	LONG SCREECH OF SLIDING PLANE . . . THEN SUDDEN QUIET
BING:	(PAUSE—RELEASES OF HELD BREATH) He did it.

Source: Adapted from Albert Crews, *Professional Radio Writing* (Boston: Houghton Mifflin, 1946), pp. 64–65.

To begin with, there was a natural aid in the sound effect. The noise of a plane coming in to land increases in volume, which is in itself exciting. The pitch also increases as the plane comes closer. Both pitch and volume come to a crescendo as the plane skids to a stop on the runway. The actors' voices will build the tempo, volume, and pitch of the scene just as the sound builds. In fact, the increasing sound forces them to shout over it. Their tension also increases as the crisis comes to a peak. Notice how short and jerky the speeches are, how many of them are incomplete sentences. Toward the end they are little more than fragments, mounting in emotional intensity to match the scene. At the end, the sudden silence after the plane skids to a stop will be all the more effective after the climax of sound. One simple line releases the tension of the scene. All the basic factors of pitch, volume, quality, and rhythm go into the building of this climactic scene.[1]

These seven characteristics of sound—pitch, quality, volume, distance, acoustical setting, rhythm, and juxtaposition—are universal. They apply to sound effects, to music, and to the voice when it is used as a sound instrument.

Sound Effects

A *sound effect* may be defined as any sound occurring in a program that is not classifiable as speech or music. In an audience participation program, the laughter elicited from the audience is a sound effect. The cheering of a crowd picked up by the broadcasting of a football game is also a sound effect. Sound effects are not restricted to the dramatic programs with which they are most often associated.

Sound effects may be considered in two categories. In a realistic or nondramatic program, managing the sound pattern consists chiefly of deciding which of the natural sounds actually being produced at the locale are desirable and should be picked up. For example, suppose the writer is designing an audience participation game show. Should the microphone be arranged so that the sounds made by the audience in the studio will be picked up? What sounds created by the mechanics of the program should be heard or enhanced? These are decisions the writers and producers of the program must make, though there is no problem in creating the sound. The sound is inherent in the situation; the only question is whether it should be picked up and broadcast or eliminated by technical means.

The second category are sound effects introduced by the writer to help create an illusion. These effects are employed mostly in dramatic programs or in dramatic vignettes in commercials. They must be artificially produced to simulate the sounds they represent.

Uses of Sound

There are a number of different ways in which sound can be used to strengthen the structure of a program:

1. Establish a locale

2. Create a mood

3. Project action and support climax

4. Establish time

5. Indicate entrances and exits

6. Serve as a transition device between scenes

7. Contribute to a montage effect

Some of these are exclusively dramatic uses of sound, but most of them have equal application to nondramatic programs and may be either realistic or created sounds. Frequently a sound effect or group of effects will serve several of these uses simultaneously, so it is difficult to provide examples that illustrate just a single use.

Establish a Locale

When a speech is to be broadcast from a banquet hall, the pickup of the rustle of the audience, the clatter of dishes, and the clink of glassware will help to establish the locale in which the speech is going to take place. If establishing that locale is important and the production director feels the audience should get the flavor of the meeting, arrangements are made to pick up some of these sounds just to help set the scene. In a dramatic program, if a similar locale were called for in the script, a similar pattern of sound would be produced artificially to establish that location in the play.

Create a Mood

During the broadcast of national political conventions, pickups are frequently broadcast direct from the floor. The shouting, the talk on the floor, the confusion, the bands playing—all these are let into broadcast microphones and sent out over the air to give the audience the general mood, the atmosphere, the "feel" of the convention.

In a dramatic program too, the writer may wish to create a mood. Perhaps the scene is to take place along the waterfront on a dark, foggy night. An actor in the preceding scene can preview the scene with a line of dialogue; then a combination of sound effects both establishes the scene and creates a mood. Finally, dialogue confirms and completes the new locale.

BILL:	OK, now listen. We've got to get that stuff off the boat tonight. I'll meet you down at the dock at 10:30. You be there (FADE) and bring the big truck.
SOUND:	<u>FOGHORN IN DISTANCE: SEAGULL CRIES: OCEAN WAVES, CONTINUES BEHIND</u>
FRED:	(LOUD WHISPER) Hey Bill?—Where are you? (PAUSE) Bill?
BILL:	(OFF MIKE) Over here. (FADING ON) Did you bring the truck?
FRED:	Yeah. It's on the other side of the dock.

Project Action and Support Climax

When a boxing match is being broadcast, a microphone will be strung over the ring so that the actual sound of the blows landing may be heard over the air. This is an example of the projection of real action. In a dramatic representation, where pickup of sound from an actual event is impossible, the sound effects department fills in the appropriate sound, as indicated in the script. Even the "impossible" events of purely imaginary tales—for example, Superman's flight through the air—can be projected by the accompaniment of sounds which simulate a perception of what the real sounds might be.

The broadcast of a football game is a good example of the buildup of climax through sound. A good broadcaster will let us hear the cheers of the crowd, which burst out spontaneously as the ball is pushed over the goal line. This natural sound effect creates the climax of the touchdown better than anything the broadcaster might say. At the end of the game, when the gun goes off to mark the final climax, the broadcast extends and intensifies that climax by including the crowd's shouts and cheers.

Establish Time
This use of sound effects should be familiar to everyone. In dramatic programs the use of striking clocks and crowing roosters has become so much of a convention that it is almost cliché.

Sound is also used to reinforce the passing of time. During the 20 seconds the contestant has in which to answer the question and win the big prize, a ticking clock (or another effect that simulates the rhythm of a clock) adds intensity to the passage of time.

Indicate Entrances and Exits
This use too is very familiar to audiences. In dramatic programs, the dialogue usually indicates when an actor enters or leaves a scene and that dialogue may be supported by fades—a fade-in when the character enters the scene and a fade-out as the character leaves. But the use of sound reinforces those transitions; it makes them much more positive. If an actor leaves the scene angrily or hastily, he slams the door behind him. The impending appearance of a new character is signaled by a car driving up, a car door slamming, steps on the porch, a squeaky screen door opening, and finally, the actor's speech.

Transition
Although music is a much more common transition device, especially in drama, sound effects can be used to accomplish the same purpose. The picking up of the bell and buzzer between rounds of a prize fight makes a transition from one scene to the next. The use of applause between numbers in a variety show is a conventional effect familiar to every listener.

Montage
In a montage, a number of disconnected scenes are blended together by a unifying device. Music is sometimes used, but often some sound effect serves as the fusing agent that welds these successive fragmentary scenes together to produce an impressionistic effect. For example, suppose you want to tell the audience that revolt is breaking out all over the country. The device of a high-pitched radio code key might be used as a sound effect to knit the scenes together; between those quick, staccato dots and dashes might be heard the voices of various announcers with one or two lines each, giving us a fact here, a situation there, something breaking out somewhere else. All these reports, coming in quick succession with the sound tying them together, constitute the montage effect.

Properly used, sound effects add believability and realism to a scene and contribute important structural strength. There are, however, unforeseen pitfalls for the novice, and before leaving the subject we should add a few cautions.

Unneeded Sound
Beginning writers have a tendency to overwrite sound effects. In an attempt to set up a realistic situation, the novice may write sound effects into a script that are meaningless in the scene. If the drama calls for a mob scene, the writer

should realize that the scratching of a pencil as a reporter takes notes would be inaudible in the noise and confusion. Obviously, then, a quiet action sound should not be delivered in the midst of high-volume sounds that would drown it.

A scene taking place in a kitchen, with dialogue between two housewives, can be begun this way:

MARY: Have another cup of coffee, Ruth?

RUTH: Well, just a little; I really have to get back home.

MARY: Please don't rush—I want to talk to you.

No sound effects are used to establish the scene. Various "kitchen" sounds—a whistling teakettle, dishes, pouring coffee—could have been added, but the few words of dialogue set the scene quite adequately and much more efficiently. Effects are frequently needed for all the reasons we have discussed, but they should never be included in a script just for the sake of having them there. A sound effect has no value unless it accomplishes a dramatic or an expositional purpose.

Identifying Sound

In television, sound effects usually are reinforced for viewers by their being able to see the source of the sound. A repetitive click-click sound can easily be associated with a view of a train traveling down a track. But in radio the listener has only his or her ear to identify the effect. For the writer, this means that where sound is used, it must in most cases be anticipated or supported by dialogue or narration.

Only a few effects are "self-identifying." These include train whistles, fire sirens, door and telephone bells, and foghorns. Most effects require some sort of support in the script. Suppose the script calls for two people to be engaged in spirited conversation, and suddenly one of them slaps the other. If that sound effect is given without any warning, the listeners will not recognize what has happened. They will hear the sound, but will not be able to interpret it. On the other hand, if the lines clearly indicate that the two are quarreling and that physical violence is imminent, the audience will be prepared for the sound and will be able to identify it. Do not use a sound to project physical action unless the intention to act or the possibility of action has already been hinted at in the dialogue.

In a preceding section we described the use of sound to set a scene on a waterfront on a dark night. The sounds used to establish that scene—foghorn, waves lapping at pilings on a pier—can be recognized and accepted by the listener because the final lines of dialogue in the preceding scene anticipated the location—on the waterfront.

Similarly, the rattling of a pan on a stove or the whistling of a teakettle will be recognizable if it has been established that the scene is in a kitchen; various clankings and motor noises will be accepted as factory sounds if that location has been previously established. The sound of galloping horses needs to have been established by previously indicating that horses are part of the scene.

Some sounds are so easily confused with other sounds or so unrecognizable that they require immediate dialogue or other identification. This category includes the crackling of fire, rain and water effects, and footsteps and other physical activity sounds. But any sound that is not easy to identify, or for which the audience might be unprepared, should have verbal reinforcement.

Forty to fifty years ago, during the heyday of live radio drama, major stations and networks employed technicians to do nothing but create sound effects. Now, although some mechanical effects still exist in the closets of older stations (such as coconut shells to make the sound of horses' hooves), most effects come from recordings. Several companies sell collections of sound effects records. Here is the list of the effects available on just one disc from the *Major Records* catalog:[2]

Volume 19
Monaural 1034

Side A:		*Side B:*	
1. Drill (hand held)	:14	1. Touch tone phone dialing	:06
2. Moped (two)	:13	2. Galactic breathing	1:18
3. Electronic chimes	:35	3. Police sirens (3 different types)	:20
4. Flying saucer	:36	4. Shack collapse	:14
5. Robot transmission	:20	5. Buckshot gun blast (3 shots)	:05
6. Faulty computer	:17	6. Two cars making a fast stop with screeching	:10
7. Asteroid passing by	:08		
8. Outer space effects	:20	7. Polaroid land camera shutter clicks	:30
9. Laser beam (various frequencies)	:26		
10. Divers working underwater	1:25	8. Polaroid timer buzzer	1:30
11. Underwater explosion with avalanche	:23	9. 35mm camera with electronic film advance	:22
12. Explosion of house with falling debris	:25	10. 35mm camera with manual shutter	:16
13. Spear gun shot	:01	11. Laser gun shots	1:40
14. Underwater explosion with splash and avalanche	:40	12. Descending UFO	:16
		13. Swooping sounds (various)	:45
15. Outer space noise	:58	14. Dog howling	:26
16. Ghost effect	:23	15. Bottle cap pop with pouring	:08
17. Ghost effect	:41	16. Bottle cap pop with pouring and fizz	:17
18. Ghost effect	:18		
19. Space monster	1:02	17. Belch	:02

Writing Sound Cues

In Chapter 4 we showed the correct way to lay out sound cues within a script, but a few additional comments should be said about the writing of sound cues. Each cue should describe as exactly as possible the effect desired. A cue saying only "footsteps" is not enough. The program producer needs to know what kind of footsteps—hurried or slow or walking at a normal pace; walking on what kind of surface and in what kind of shoes; footsteps of a man or a woman, of one person or many. "The closing of a door" does not tell enough to the production personnel who will have to execute the instructions in the script. Different kinds of doors have different sound qualities. Do you want the closing of a closet door, a screen door, a car door, or a bank vault door? Be specific.

Music as Sound

Music has several possible uses within broadcast programs:

1. To act as a signature

2. To establish a mood or background

3. To serve as a transition device between scenes or between sections of a program

4. To serve as a sound effect

Keep in mind that here we are considering only the uses of music as sound. A great deal of programming consists of music, especially in radio. But we are not concerned here with music as a content form, only with its uses to strengthen or support the structure of other types of program content.

Musical Signatures

If a signature is chosen to open a program, it usually contains music. That music should be easily identifiable, distinctive enough to be remembered, and immediately associated with the program it introduces. Its instrumentation and arrangement should set the mood for the program to follow.

Beginning writers often start their scripts by simply writing "theme music" and letting it go at that. If the writer is to be a composer in sound, he or she cannot dismiss so important a part of the total sound of the program by simply indicating "theme." (Of course, once a theme has been established for a program, the use of "theme" is sufficient to describe to the production staff where that music is to be used in the script. But for assignments or for new programs, the writer must describe the music to be used.)

Decide on the effect you want from the music, then describe it accurately, including the length of the cue:

MUSIC: FAST TEMPO MARIACHI BAND UP FOR 8 SEC, THEN FADE
                                    UNDER AND OUT

ANNCR: Welcome to Down Mexico Way. Today's program features the
                                    Latin stylings of. . . .

Mood Setting and Background

One common use of music for background is to provide a music "bed" behind a commercial announcement. Usually this is done when the announcement is straight narration read by an announcer. A music bed can be useful when it really contributes to the ad, by adding emotional strength or setting a mood for the spot. Martial music behind an ad for a big weekend sale would add excitement; a dreamy, romantic tune would provide a mood appropriate to an ad for perfume. Christmas music, of course, contributes to the mood of that holiday season, as in this example:

MUSIC BED:	"SLEIGH RIDE" UP FULL FOR 5 SEC THEN UNDER

ANNCR: Out of money . . . time . . . and creative ideas? There is still time to create your own "Christmas with Love" for family and friends. Attend the Holiday demonstration workshops at the Woodlake Inn. One and a half hour classes. Quick delightful ideas. Holiday foods and entertaining. Toys and clothes for kids. Stitcheries, ornaments and decorative gifts. 15 ideas each class plus recipes and patterns from home economists and designers . . . advance reservation only $15 per class; day of show $20. Workshops are Saturday, December 11; Monday December 13 and Tuesday, December 14. To enroll call 325-4770 or 325-4771. That's 325-4770 or 325-4771. Make it a Christmas with love by you.

MUSIC BED: CONTINUES UNDER FOR TAG

Source: Courtesy of KGMS, Sacramento, CA.

Some radio stations put a "bed" behind practically every commercial, under the assumption that the announcement will be less jarring to an audience if it is backed by music. But that can have a negative result; if the bed sounds too much like the regular content of the station, the audience may not pay attention to the commercial. It will seem to fade into the background, just like the musical content of the station.

Music may also be used in radio and in television as a background for other types of broadcast material. Some dramatic programs are almost completely scored for music, which supports most of the dialogue and narration in addition to providing transitions. Background music occupies a secondary level of attention behind the primary action. It is used to underline and highlight the emotional content of whatever is being broadcast over it and also, in many cases, to induce emotional reactions in the audience. This use of music demands very skillful planning and execution, but when it is handled well, it is extremely effective.

This interweaving of music with drama is obviously expensive and is generally available only to the networks, but it is perhaps the most challenging and exciting use of music in broadcasting.

Musical Transitions   Transition music is usually used for two simultaneous purposes. First, it may separate scenes or other portions of a broadcast, or tie off the end of a scene. Second, it may resolve the mood or emotional key of a scene it follows and set the mood for the scene it precedes. Here are some examples:

BILL: . . . . you can go ahead and try to get a divorce if you want, but I assure it won't be easy!

MUSIC: ORGAN STINGER, 4 SECS, SEGUE TO SOFT ROMANTIC THEME ON GUITAR, FADE OUT BEHIND

TOM:	Was he angry?
BETTY:	Oh, Tom, he was furious. He won't let me go without a terrible battle. . . .

BILL:	. . . . you can go ahead and try to get a divorce if you want, but I assure you it won't be easy!
MUSIC:	ORGAN STINGER, 4 SECS, THEN CROSS-FADE TO RINGING OF TELEPHONE (3 RINGS)
TOM:	Hello.
BETTY:	(ON FILTER) Tom?
TOM:	Yes . . . Betty? Is that you? How did it go?

The transition function is not limited to dramatic programs. It is a standard technique for any program where a division point is wanted—between two sections of a game show, between two acts of a variety program, and so on. Because of the high cost of having a live orchestra, recorded music is used for most transitions, and is added to the program during postproduction editing, but live musical transitions are still provided by the studio orchestra on "The Tonight Show."

If you are not familiar with a range of musical styles, it will take some time to get a feel for the uses of music in broadcast. But time spent familiarizing yourself with different types of music will be worth the effort in becoming more creative and more effective in your writing. One crutch available to writers in many stations and advertising agencies is a recorded library of production music. We have reproduced here a typical page from the catalog of one supplier, *Major Records*. Each selection in the catalog is described by the style of music and/or the effect that selection is intended to suggest to an audience. Written descriptions like these can help the writer choose music for a particular purpose, but the final decision on whether a particular selection is right for a transition, or whatever use, can be made only after listening to it.[3]

62 B1. DAMASCUS	George Chase	BMI	:3:08
The teeming multitudes of the East—oriental splendor in the land of the Caliphs.			
2. RENDEZVOUS	Roger Roger	BMI	:51
Suggestive of furtive meeting in the dark, with romantic color.			
3. ROMANTIC INTERLUDE			:33
Warm bridge or background for short romantic scenes.			
4. REVERIE			1:41
Nocturnal soliloquy in the romantic flavor for quiet sequences.			
5. SERENATA	George Chase	BMI	3:08
A rhythmic number in romantic feeling for most neutral applications descriptive of mild activity.			
6. CHAMPAGNE TIME	Roger Roger	BMI	3:02
Bright bustling city life at night, suggesting traffic motion or holiday crowds celebrating.			

Music as   Music is seldom used as a realistic sound effect, except when a dramatic scene
Sound Effect calls for an orchestra playing in the background or something of the sort. Then,
technically, the music would be fulfilling the function of sound. But in a nonrealistic
program, music is quite often used as a sound effect. Suppose you are writing a
children's program with a pseudoscientific script in which a comic inventor is
getting ready to take off on a rocket trip to outer space. The launching of the
rocket and the takeoff into the stratosphere could be done as a realistic sound
effect. Those effects are available. But to maintain the mood of the show, the
effect might very well be assigned to music, so that the audience, instead of
feeling it was actually hearing the sound of a rocket ship taking off, would
experience musically an impression of the same thing.

As with the writing of sound effects cues, music cues should indicate the
nature of the music as precisely as possible to the production personnel who will
assemble the final sound track. Indicate the artist and selection if recorded music
is to be used, or at least the style and instrumentation desired. Also show in the
script how long the music cue is to last, whether it fades behind dialogue or
narration, and when it is to be removed.

The most common terms used to manipulate music and sound cues are not
difficult to understand:

UP (or FULL).   At full volume

FADE-IN.   Turn the mixer pot for the sound in the control room from zero up
                  to normal volume

FADE-OUT.   The reverse, from normal or whatever the present setting is down
                  to zero

FADE-DOWN.   Lower the volume, but not out completely; often used like FADE-
                  UNDER

FADE-UNDER.   When other material is to be given prominence

CROSS-FADE.   Two different sounds or musical passages are manipulated simulta-
                  neously, one being faded in, the other out

SEGUE.   One effect or passage is immediately followed by another, without
                  any change in volume

Voices as Sound

Voices can contribute to the overall sound of a program in ways quite different
from their use to convey the meanings of words and sentences. They can
contribute to the structural strength of a program, particularly to variety.
Variations in vocal delivery can aid in providing clarity to the content, make it
easier for audiences to follow a sequence of ideas and events, and provide the
changes that help to maintain audience attention.

In the sections that follow we will examine several ways in which voices
can be used to strengthen a program.

Single-Voice   Maintaining audience interest in a straight speech, monologue, or narration is
Narration   particularly difficult in any medium in which sound is the only form of commu-
                     nication, because in those situations there is practically no way to achieve change
                     and variety. It is somewhat easier to maintain audience interest when the talk or
                     narration is on television; in that medium at least there is a visual component
                     which can be manipulated to provide some form of change.

                          To illustrate the problem, here are the opening paragraphs of a radio talk—
                     not the entire script. It is a well-written script; it follows good aural style and it
                     is full of descriptive phrases that evoke mental images of the country described,
                     Switzerland, even though many people in the audience would never have been
                     there. When broadcast, it was delivered well by a competent narrator. But it
                     expects a lot of its audience, asking them to maintain interest in a single voice
                     for what was a full fifteen-minute program.

NARR: You, like the rest of us, may know something about Switzerland.
                                               We know it's a federation, a land of high mountains and some
                                               of the most spectacular scenery in the world. During the war,
                                               some Europeans found, like myself, that it was one place
                                               where you could escape from the restraints of Nazi Germany
                                               and feel able to breathe fully once again. You were able to
                                               look relaxed on Lake Zurich as you strolled down its banks
                                               and watched swans, wild ducks, steamers, sailboats and
                                               rowboats glide by. You thrilled at the sight once again of
                                               American cigarettes, French liqueurs, American whiskey, and
                                               Scotch in the bars. The more simple system of a coupon for a
                                               restaurant meal, instead of each item, and a choice of coffee,
                                               tea, or chocolate was unbelievable luxury. Wandering, after
                                               a dinner that was a feast, smoking a Corona, you blinked at
                                               a city not blacked out until ten o'clock. The lights in signs and
                                               store windows seemed glaring. The posters outside the cinemas
                                               advertised American pictures, not just Nazi propaganda ones.
                                               You bought a newspaper and were able, in adjoining columns,
                                               to read side by side the communiques from Britain, Greece,
                                               Italy, and Germany, stories sent out by the Britain's Reuters,
                                               Germany's DNB, and America's UP and AP. In any case, it
                                               was the background of freedom that had taken me to Swit-
                                               zerland in 1941 so that I could telephone to Columbia's office
                                               in New York without being overheard by Nazis.

                                               Tomorrow is the day the Swiss people set aside each year
                                               to celebrate their independence and freedom, and character-
                                               istically the day is not so much one of riotous festivity as it is
                                               of prayer. Switzerland's Independence Day is her Thanksgiving
                                               Day, with her people going to church and kneeling down
                                               tomorrow to thank God that they have been able to preserve
                                               their way of life.

                                               They've been independent for a long time, too—longer
                                               than most of us realize. it was 656 years ago, back in the
                                               thirteenth century, that three mountain clans, the Schwyz, the
                                               Uri, and the Unterwald signed the famous Pact of Brunnen.

> The Schwyz, the Uri and the Unterwald were three humble clans who lived on the shores of Lake Lucerne, free-born subjects of the Holy Empire, which gave them its protection to secure better control of the Saint-Gotthard, over which led a road connecting Italy and Germany. But the Dukes of Austria, the Hapsburgs, sought to gain control of these passes and planned to enslave the Swiss tribes. To meet that threat, the three tribes sent representatives to a secret meeting in the Grutli, an Alpine meadow overhanging the Lake of Lucerne, and there in 1291 they signed a treaty of alliance, the Pact of Brunnen, the document that began the federation of Switzerland. . . .

Source: Harry Flannery, broadcast on the Columbia Broadcasting System, September 20, 1957. Reprinted by permission of CBS, Inc.

At this point you may be tempted to ask, if the problem of maintaining audience attention to single-voice talk material is really as severe as we claim, why are there still so many programs on both radio and television that use a single voice throughout? One answer is that it costs less. Using a single voice is usually much less expensive than using multiple voices. Not only does it cost less to hire only one talent, but there is less time and money spent in production and editing. The cheapest form of commercial, and probably the only form many small businesses can afford, is straight announcer copy. In these cases, and in other small-scale productions such as locally produced and unsponsored public affairs programs, or the narration in small budget corporate/instructional presentations, the cost of talent can be an important limitation. Another answer is that it provides greater efficiency. The amount of information that can be presented in a given length of time is greater using a single voice, so it is a more efficient way to impart information when only a limited amount of time is available.

But regardless of the savings in cost or the greater efficiency, if a lack of variety in a script causes the attention of the audience to be lost, then the communication has been ineffective. The writer should work to provide vocal variety in a script whenever it seems that attention will be hard to maintain by other means, using techniques that employ multiple and different-sounding voices.

Split Narration

We are not considering at this point talk programs that involve more than one person in conversation, such as interviews, panel discussions, phone-in programs, or studio audience participations. Those programs are structured from the outset to use multiple voices and automatically provide vocal variety. Rather, we are suggesting means by which multiple voices can be introduced specifically to provide an alternative to single-voice narration.

One technique is simply to split the narration between two voices. The approach is more effective and less obvious if some logical reason can be found for the split. The technique was used effectively in the early TV series "Winston Churchill: The Valiant Years." Gary Merrill was the narrator. Churchill's own words, taken from his speeches and writings, provided the contrast, and were delivered by Richard Burton.

Another well-known series using two-voice narration is "The Cousteau Odyssey." A narrator is used for the main commentary, but that is broken up by frequent use of Cousteau's own voice, explaining his thoughts and opinions on the subject, or amplifying the main narration, as in Figure 6.1 (pp. 147–150).

The Cousteau program actually uses two different narrative techniques. At the beginning of the example, both the narrator and Cousteau are heard off-camera, narrating while the audience watches some marine activity. Later in the excerpt Cousteau is seen on-camera, in conversation with Barnes, in lip-sync sound. He then becomes part of the action, which is a different vocal technique.

Another easily recognized use of dual narration is in sports announcing, where one announcer is designated as the "play-by-play" voice and the other as the "color" voice.

In a commercial the same approach—dividing up the copy for more than one voice—is frequently used. The simplest way is to split the copy, but the use of more than one voice also permits the message to be presented in more attention-getting ways. Here are two examples:

ANNCR: Butte County Supervisor, Bernie Richter, knows the value of a dollar and he knows how hard you work for it . . .

BERNIE: I was raised in my father's house to believe in thrift, frugality, and hard work . . . I learned that you don't get something for nothing . . . Those are things I learned as a youngster, and I've tried to bring those things into government.

ANNCR: Richter doesn't spend public money just because it's there . . .

BERNIE: I should like to think that I spend public money just as if it were my own . . . consequently, I abhor waste . . . and I abhor the use of funds for frivolous purposes . . . .

ANNCR: Richter supported proposition 13 and knows what you wanted when you passed it . . . .

BERNIE: The people wanted us to go after those wasteful kinds of things that government does for itself . . . we have no deficit spent in our county . . . we don't operate that way . . . we are a frugal county . . . and I and my colleagues on the Board of Supervisors have tried very hard to spend county money wisely . . .

ANNCR: Bernie Richter gets things done . . . and it doesn't cost you a lot of money . . .
re-elect Supervisor Richter . . . .
Paid for by Citizens for Richter

Source: Courtesy of the author, Frank LaRosa.

VIDEO	AUDIO

THE COUSTEAU SOCIETY

CALYPSO

THE COUSTEAU ODYSSEY

THE WARM-BLOODED SEA: Mammals of the Deep

VIDEO	AUDIO
	ACT I
	COUSTEAU
ROCKET ASCENDS	Infinity beckons humanity. We who hunger for companionship reach to distant planets, searching for liquid water, the cosmic sign of life.
MOON SURFACE/ MOON SURAFACE CU	Our expeditions end in dryness, desolation, dust.
EARTH RISING WATER PLANET	Obsessed with lifelessness in space, we have disinherited ourselves from life on earth.
SLOW MOTION WAVE	There is a water planet.
EPISODE TITLE	THE WARM-BLOODED SEA Mammals of the Deep
	NARRATOR
CELL-LIKE MATTER IN WATER	The sea, indeed, is the womb of life. Here the first cell took shape, with DNA, and its genetic codes, implanted like a seed within. Creatures adapted to meet the menace of their environment. And eon after eon, they endowed their improvements to the future.

Figure 6.1
Source: Copyright 1984 The Cousteau Society, Inc., a nonprofit, membership-supported organization located at 930 W. 21st Street, Norfolk, VA 23517. Annual dues are $20 for an Individual Membership and $28 for a Family Membership.

THE COUSTEAU ODYSSEY

THE WARM-BLOODED SEA: Mammals of the Deep

VIDEO	AUDIO
	COUSTEAU
GORGONIA, SHELL CRAB, NAUTILUS, OCTOPUS	The miracle of life defies the universal law of degradation, continually becoming ever more intricate. This phenomenon inspired the French philosopher, Teilhard de Chardin, to envision three infinities. There is the infinitely big, of course, and the infinitely small. To them, Teilhard added the infinitely complex: life itself.
	NARRATOR
TUNA	Landmarks of time: nerves, jaws, vertebrates. Finally the cold sea embraced the model of cold blood --the shark.
SHARK TURNS	
IGUANA CLIMBS TO ROCK	After billions of years in its liquid cradle, life came to land. Creatures now developed a new trait to help them master the onerous pull of terrestrial gravity.
BIRD-RHINO-LION	Warm blood. With high central temperatures the body's inner combustion engine could be even more powerful. The mammal appeared, quivering with energy, endurance, and formidable strength.

Figure 6.1 (Continued)

THE COUSTEAU SOCIETY

Page 4

T H E   C O U S T E A U   O D Y S S E Y

THE WARM-BLOODED SEA: Mammals of the Deep

VIDEO	AUDIO
	(Sound of motor boat in the clear)
JYC AND CHRIS BARNES ON MOTORBOAT	Ancient bones have just been found in Southern California. Cousteau visits the remote site with the son of paleontologist Lawrence Barnes, who is directing a dig for the Los Angeles County Natural History Museum.
	COUSTEAU
JYC AND CB WALK AMONG DIGGERS; C/U BONES IN SAND	These hills were once submerged in primal sea. The bones here are scattered pieces to a prehistoric puzzle. After millions of years spent adapting to land, some mammals returned to water. No one knows why. Motivations are not buried in clay; only broken skeletons, fragmented answers.
	(Sound of hammer in the clear)
	BARNES (SYNC)
BARNES POINTS OUT PARTS OF SKULL	We've got the skull here, and the front end of the skull is up here, the brain case back here. The blow holes are between these...and the lower jaw lies to the side.
	COUSTEAU (SYNC)
KNEELING NEXT TO SKULL	How far back, uh, were fossils of whales found?

Figure 6.1 (Continued)

THE COUSTEAU ODYSSEY

THE WARM-BLOODED SEA: Mammals of the Deep

VIDEO	AUDIO
	McCLOUD (SYNC)
	Fossil whales are known from at least 45 million
	years ago.
	COUSTEAU (SYNC)
	Forty-five million years! And is that about the
	time when those, some mammals came back to the, to
	the ocean?
	BARNES (SYNC)
	Yeah.
	COUSTEAU (SYNC)
	Or is it still further back?
	McCLOUD (SYNC)
	Well, it was at least at that time, perhaps a little
	older, when they came in the sea.
	BARNES (SYNC)
	This ... this is what the lower jaw of one of
	the earliest whales ever found looks like.
	COUSTEAU (SYNC)
CHRIS BARNES HANDS	Where's your shark tooth? To me these teeth look
JYC SHARK TOOTH	a little like shark teeth. Triangular...

Figure 6.1 (Continued)

VOICE #1	Introducing the new, exciting miracle Linville Bros. . . .
VOICE #2	No, no, please stop. We're not new. We've been around for years, and hey, we don't create miracles, just honest business . . .
VOICE #1	OhhhhhKay, how about, if you really want to improve your social life get a front end alignment from Linville Bros. and a great set of tires at the same time . . .
VOICE #2	Oh please, we don't promise anything we can't deliver, (FADE) Great social life, Geez.
VOICE #1	How's this . . . if you want to keep pace with your neighbors . . .
VOICE #2	Come on, most of our business comes from referrals from friends and neighbors.
VOICE #3	If all you want is honest price and honest work for your tire and front end needs, Call Linville Bros. at 929-63-82. We're on El Camino between I-80 and Ethan Way. We'll work while you wait. Be sure to check our specially priced clearance items. Just call us at 929-63-82. Linville Bros. will give you the best work at the best price we can. You can ride on your reputation, we do.
VOICE #2	Ahhhhhhhh, that's more like it . . .

Source: Courtesy of KRAK Radio, Sacramento, CA.

Drama and Narration

Another means for breaking up single-voice narration is to mix dramatic dialogue with that narration. The combination of narration and drama can be mixed in various proportions from mostly narration to mostly drama. Many radio dramatic programs require at least a little narration at the beginning of the plot, to establish the locale and the premise of the story. They may also use narration to bridge different scenes, and possibly even to provide a wrapup at the end of the plot. Some television dramas use narration in the same way, even though the presence of the visual element makes it much easier to establish locale and begin the action without narration.

An inexpensive and effective device for radio, but one that is no longer used very frequently, is to write a script which is largely narration, but which is broken up by dramatic inserts. In the first of the two excerpts that follow, the primarily dramatic plot is introduced by a narrator. In the second example, the plot line is advanced mostly through narration, but the narrator, Ray, also becomes an actor and interacts with other characters in brief dramatic scenes.

MUSIC:	DESCRIPTIVE, FADING TO BACKGROUND UNDER
NARR:	The year 1915. The red soil of Georgia yields its rich rows of cotton. The hills of the Carolinas are lush and green, and the land is peaceful and good. The Gulf Coast is a blue curve against the high surf; and the rich sun slants through the canebrakes of the valley of the Mississippi. But stalking the Carolina hills, striding sure-footed across the copper earth of Georgia, through the black-belt to the banks of the great river and beyond, is Death—a red, ravaging phantom—choosing his victims without mercy, without design. No man sees him; no man knows the times of his coming, but all see where he has been, and all wonder and fear. For the cropper's hoe will fall to the earth, and the men bend double with the agony inside him, his face scarlet with the marks where the plantom has touched him—the raw, red mark of the Red Death—a mark shaped like a butterfly moth—and the sign of a man's doom is branded upon him—the moth-mark—the mockery of the Death that is red and moves invisibly among the poor folk, the cabin folk, of the hills and fields of America's Southland.
MUSIC:	UP TO A QUICK ENDING
VOICE:	1915. Five thousand lie sick unto death of pellagra, the disease of the Red Death.
MUSIC:	UP FULL . . . FADE INTO
SOUND:	DOG HOWL IN DISTANCE
DR. HORNE:	Well Granny, I guess there's nothing I can do now.
GRANNY:	Dead. Sam's dead. They're all gone now. All my boys.
DR. HORNE:	I did all I could. I'm sorry, Granny.
GRANNY:	Cotton's going to rot this year—same as down to the Bennett's last month when Red Death took the old man away. What'll I do?
DR. HORNE:	Granny, things are going to be different now, maybe. The government's going to help us get rid of this plague. They say there's a big scientist coming down here.
GRANNY:	Humph! Government! What they know about Red Death any how?

Source: Ruth Barth, "Red Death," in A. H. Lass, Earle L. McGill, Donald Axelrod, eds., *Plays from Radio* (Cambridge, MA: Houghton Mifflin, 1948), pp. 195–196. Reprinted by permission of E. I. duPont de Nemours & Co.

ANNCR: Ladies and gentlemen, RKO Radio Pictures present an original
                                radio play. . . .

SOUND: DRUMS HAVE SNEAKED IN

RAY: . . . Tabu. (PAUSE) Have you ever returned home from the
                                dead? It's not as pleasant as you might think it would be.
                                Neither for you or for the women you love, because the point
                                of it is . . . You're dead. And she may love you yet, too late
                                and too much, just as you love her. That's my story. The story
                                of Tabu!

MUSIC: OMINOUS FINAL AND OUT

                                (INSERT COMMERCIAL)

MUSIC: IN AND DOWN IN BACKGROUND

ANNCR: And now, an original radio play written and directed for RKO
                                Radio Pictures by Dave Drummond—with Ray Lewis as its
                                narrator. Tabu!

MUSIC: UP TO A BUTTON AND OUT

RAY: How it is on the Tongans right now I just wouldn't know. No
                                more of that South Seas stuff for me. I've got a cigar store on
                                Fillmore Street and I'm doing all right—if making a living is
                                doing all right. As for the Tongans, themselves, I'n not going
                                back. Never heard of them? You haven't missed much. Just a
                                handful of islands a long way from here. The friendly Islands
                                is what it says on the charts but I think somebody was kidding.
                                The trouble is, you see, the Tongans are too close to Malay-
                                anasia—to the Marquesas. And that's where the cannibals
                                live—or did in my time. Nice chaps. With a taste for long pig,
                                meaning somebody like you or like me. Boiled or roasted or
                                raw. They're not fussy that way. Not good neighbors. But that's
                                how it was when I took my bride out to Waka-Nui, that was
                                the first mistake. The second mistake was taking young Watson
                                along to help run the trading post. That was the worst mistake.
                                I sent for him a week after we got there. (TURN AWAY FADE)

SOUND: FOOTSTEPS FADE IN TO MIKE ON WHARF AND STOP AT
                                MIKE

WATSON: (SHORT FADE IN) . . . . One of the boys came to my hut and
                                said you wanted me, down here at the wharf.

RAY:	Yes.
WATSON:	Yes sir?
RAY:	I'm taking the schooner out, I'll be gone two months. I'm leaving this place in your charge.
WATSON:	Yes sir.
RAY:	You won't have any problems or trouble. Take care of the place and . . . of my wife.
WATSON:	Ruby?
RAY:	. . . Ruby?
WATSON:	I meant . . . your wife.
RAY:	Yes, my wife.
WATSON:	She's not going with you?
RAY:	She's down with a touch of fever. I'm leaving her here.
WATSON:	. . . Oh.
RAY:	Just keep one thing in mind . . . I'll be back!
<u>MUSIC:</u>	<u>DANGER</u>
RAY:	That was the third mistake. But I learn the hard way. Two weeks later, knocking around in strange waters, I put the schooner on a reef that didn't show on the charts and knocked a hole in her hull. Made it to shore all right in one of the boats and the natives there didn't like my looks. They knocked a hole in my head. That and fever and a lot of hard luck made a lot of time go past. It was a year before I saw my island again and when I put foot on Waka-Nui the place was deserted, the trading post looted, my bungalow burned down. No one left on the island but a Kanaka boy who thought I was a ghost because they'd heard I was dead. All he would say was: "Him fella long time go. Long go!" And he pointed toward the west— toward the Marquesas—where the cannibals were.

Source: Dave Drummond, *Tabu*, an original radio play.

A similar mixture of dramatic dialogue and narration can be used in a commercial. One common approach is to use the dialogue to set the scene, attract attention, and possibly establish a problem. The announcer/narrator then delivers the "pitch" for the product. Variations are endless; here is one:

ANNCR:	PERRY BOYS' Smorgy presents another "Perry Tale"
MUSIC:	HARP
ANNCR:	Once upon a time . . . there lived a boy and a girl named Jack and Jewel . . . Jack loved Jewel . . .
JACK	I love you Jewel . . .
ANNCR:	And Jewel loved Jack . . .
JEWEL:	I love you Jack . . .
ANNCR:	Jack wanted so much to take Jewel to dinner . . . But alas, couldn't afford it . . . even now, he moonlighted counting sheep, Baaa Baaa, at the Mother Goose Amusement Park and Window Shade Company. One night . . . as Jack dreamily counted his sheep, there appeared his perry godfather . . . dressed in a chicken suit . . .
GODFATHER:	My other things are at the cleaners . . .
JACK:	What ho . . .
ANNCR:	Said Jack . . .
GODFATHER:	Ho, nuthin, you turkey . . .
ANNCR:	Said the godfather . . .
GODFATHER:	What have you already in your poke???
JACK:	A pig.
ANNCR:	Said Jack, Oink . . . Oink . . .
JACK:	And only 7 dollars . . .
GODFATHER:	That is more than enough for dinner for you and Jewel at Perry Boys' Smorgy . . . they have over 40 good things to eat . . . and beer and wine are only a quarter . . .
JACK:	And we'll live happily ever after, right???
GODFATHER:	Jack . . . you're a real Jewel!

SOUND: HARP

ANNCR: You'll live happily ever after . . . when you eat at Perry Boys'
                                Smorgy restaurants . . . $1.99 for lunch and $2.89 for dinner
                                . . . in Santa Cruz . . . Salinas . . . and Monterey at 2066
                                Fremont Blvd.

Source: Courtesy of the author, Frank LaRosa.

Actualities   Two techniques used by news writers and producers to relieve the monotony of
and Anchors   single narration within the newscast are the actuality and the anchor.
                       If the information in a news story comes from an authoritative source, the
                       actual voice of that source can be used. The expert's voice is obtained by the
                       reporter, in person or by phone, in the form of an interview. The complete
                       interview is likely to be far longer than the small section which is finally chosen,
                       edited, and inserted into the story.*
                       The other technique is the use of news anchors. Most television stations use
                       this approach, as do those radio stations that specialize in large blocks of news.
                       In contrast to a single-person newscast, the anchor serves primarily to lead into
                       and out of stories reported, on tape, by other reporters and other voices. To add
                       even more vocal variety, most stations now use dual anchors on major newscasts.

Different   In the preceding section we have been making one critical assumption. We have
Voices   assumed that the use of more than one voice provides variety *because the two
                       or more voices sound different*. It would be of no value to the audience to have
                       multiple voices if the listener couldn't tell them apart. Two voices that are similar
                       in pitch, quality, or other vocal characteristics may actually make it more difficult
                       for the audience members to follow, as they may have to concentrate on
                       differentiating the voices rather than on the content of the program. The various
                       voices must sound sufficiently different for the audience to be able to distinguish
                       easily between them.
                       In a dramatic program, for example, the characters portrayed in a scene will
                       usually be quite different—male and female, young and old, and possibly from
                       ethnic groups with distinctive vocal patterns. Some dramatic scenes, however,
                       will call for characters who are very similar—three Caucasian male teenagers,
                       for example. In television, the characters would be chosen to be physically,
                       visually, different; in a radio drama, where only sound will distinguish among
                       the characters, the vocal pattern and voice quality of each character must be
                       easily distinguished by the audience.
                       Different vocal patterns not only help to set each voice in a scene apart from

---

* There is some disagreement in the industry of the terms used to describe this practice. Some
persons use *actuality* to describe only real events recorded on location; such as at a fire, or a parade;
for them, interviews recorded over the phone or in a studio are not actualities. Others use either the
term *actuality* or *sound bite* to describe all inserts into a narrative newscast.

the others, but also aid in character delineating. When a script employing these variations is translated into sound, there is added to the meaning of the language the particular sound of each speaker. Contrast, for example, these two passages, which indicate two quite different characters, even though the speakers are really saying the same thing.

"Perhaps you'd better tell me. I'll find out under any circumstance. You can save time for both of us by telling me now what Mr. Davis did with those papers."

"C'mon, kid, spill it. It won't do you any good to dummy up. I got my sources. Y'better give now before I get sore. Where'd Douglas put them papers?"

The flavor of individual speech can be achieved by word choice, by distinctive sentence rhythms and by a characteristic sentence length. Staccato speech is full of short, quick vowels and short words that incorporate them. Slow, deliberate speech uses longer words, more sonorous, open vowel sounds, and longer sentences and sentence rhythms.

Distinctive speech patterns most often are the result of national, regional, or ethnic background. Recognizably different vocal characteristics exist in different countries and areas of the world, in different regions of the country, and among different ethnic groups. If the geographic, ethnic, or social background of the speaker is important to the development of the script, and if that background includes a speech pattern—pronunciation, intonation, or syntax—which is distinctive, then the writer must indicate that fact in the script.

For the writer, scripting to indicate a foreign origin of the speaker can be a difficult, laborious job. One simple technique that can be quite effective, however, is to use in English the grammatical structure of the foreign language to be suggested. Then allow the actor who is creating the part to make whatever dialect and pronunciation patterns are needed. For example, the expression of the same idea by different speakers might be indicated in a script as follows:

FRENCH: "Is that not so, M'sieur?"

GERMAN: "That is true, no?"

AMERICAN: "Isn't that right?"

These three renderings, each idiomatically different but all in English, manage to give some flavor of the different background languages by means of word choice and word order alone. Here is another; similar situation:

ANNCR: At ABW Foreign Auto Parts our clientele is very international.

SWEDE: I need some valves for my Volvo.

BRITISH:	Old Chap, I need a muffler for the M.G.
ITALIAN:	I want-a-plugs for my Peugeot.
SOUTHERN:	I need one of them things that fits on the whatchamijigger for my Toyota Land Cruiser.
ANNCR:	Foreign auto parts—that's our business. Make sure that only original quality foreign parts are used on your car. . . .

Source: Courtesy of KRAK, Sacramento, CA.

Regional and ethnic patterns can be handled similarly. In this country, there is a wide sectional variation in the English of ordinary speech. Some of these regional differences are actual differences in pronunciation. Others are local peculiarities in the stress or value given to certain sounds. In still others, the difference is largely a matter of voice quality and intonation. These differences in speech should be known and taken into account by the writer, but he or she need not actually indicate all of them in the script.

There is also a characteristic idiom indigenous to some regions, which is richly connotative and picturesque and which should be used by the writer. Obviously, it should not be assumed that every Texan greets friends by saying, "Howdy, pardner." Circumstances of the individual situation must determine the amount and kind of regional idiom to be used. Nevertheless, there are certain expressions in regional speech which are widely used and which are as valuable as pronunciation in giving the flavor of local speech.

In the following example, the writer used both spelling variations to indicate regional pronunciations of certain words and idiomatic expressions characteristic of the rural South to provide distinctive vocal patterns for each character and to set the scene in its geographic location.

MUSIC:	OPENING MELODY, SUGGESTING MORNING IN COUNTRY, FADING INTO:
SOUND:	THE SUBDUED SOUNDS OF DAYBREAK IN THE FLORIDA SCRUB. NOW A DISTANT COCK CROWS. PRESENTLY THE FAR OFF HOWLING OF A DOG. CLOSE AT HAND, THE SAD CALL OF MOURNING DOVES, DRAWN OUT, REPEATED, SUBSIDING RELUCTANTLY. (PAUSE) THEN THE SOUND OF WEARY FOOTFALLS MOUNTING STEEP STAIRS.
MAMA:	(A HINT OF PITY IN HER VOICE): Sleepin' and dreamin' . . . still full of their baby concerns. Hit ain't in my heart to waken 'em. Hit ain't in my heart to—Oh Lord, I'm fearful. I don't know iffen I'm actin' right or not, Lord.

SOUND:	THE MOURNING DOVES CALL SOFTLY AT THE WINDOW
MAMA:	Our father which art in heaven, Hallowed be they name. They kingdom come. They will be done on earth as it is in heaven (BREAKS OFF SOBBING)
JIM:	(STARTLED FROM SLEEP): Mamma! Mamma!
MAMA:	(REASSURINGLY): Nothin's wrong, Jim. Don't be scairt.
JIM:	Mamma, you ain't crying?
MAMA:	No, Jim.
JIM:	You're a-prayin'?
MAMA:	Yes, I were prayin. Hit'll be day soon. You better be risin' up. Your Uncle Holly'll be along directly.
JIM:	(WITH GROWING EXCITEMENT): Hit's really come. The day. The day we're going to Czardis in the wagon to see papa.
MAMA:	(DULLY) Hit's come, all right.
JIM	Seems like I jest cain't believe yet we're goin' . . .
MAMA:	(CUTTING IN) There ain't time fur talk now, Jim. You best bestir yourself. And waken up Dan'l too.
SOUND:	RECEDING FOOTSTEPS ON FLOOR BOARDS.
MAMA:	(VOICE MORE DISTANT—OFF MIKE): Put on the clean things I washed fur you so you'll look decent and be a credit to your raisin'.
SOUND:	FOOTSTEPS DESCENDING STAIRS, THEN FADE-OUT
JIM:	Wake up, Dan'l Wake up!
DAN'L:	(WHIMPERING IN HIS SLEEP): Leave me be. Make 'em leave me be. Jim! . . . Jim!
JIM:	(PATIENT, KIND): Don't be feared, Dan'l. Ain't nobody a botherin' you.

Source: Edwin Granberry, ''A Trip to Czardis,'' in Lass, McGill, and Axelrod, *Plays from Radio*, pp. 157–158. Reprinted by permission of CBS, Inc.

The writer must be cautious, however, not to allow the presence of distinctive vocal patterns to be construed as derogatory stereotyping of minority groups. Broadcasting depends upon the use of stereotypes. In most dramatic programs, very little time can be devoted to the development of characterization, particularly of secondary characters. The action of the plot must begin quickly to maintain audience attention. Lengthy character development interferes with that requirement, so characters are sketched quickly, using standardized stereotypes.

The practice is not inherently degrading to minorities, but in practice some stereotypical characterizations of members of minority groups have developed which are derogatory. We simply want to call attention to those differences that do exist in speech patterns because of geography or ethnicity and that are important, especially in radio, to the audience's understanding of characters, to the setting of a scene, and to vocal variety.

Conclusion

There are times when the absence of a visual image can be a distinct advantage in broadcast communication. A few words, music, and sound effects can suggest a myriad of impressions, a whole world of make-believe. But the absence of the companion visual sense also puts a burden on the writer to provide frequent change in the sound patterns being transmitted.

This chapter discusses the special characteristics of sound that shape every aural communication—pitch, quality, volume, distance, acoustical setting, rhythm, and juxtaposition. The broadcast writer finds special problems and opportunities in sound using the three components of sound—effects, music, and voice.

Not only may sound be used as a medium by itself, but it also is half of any audiovisual presentation. We have concentrated here on the uses of sound when it is used alone, but these principles apply with little modification to audiovisual media as well.

Exercises

1. Listen to a radio dramatic program, with particular attention to its uses of sound effects. For each effect you hear:

   a. Name and describe what that effect is—fire crackling, siren, foghorn, teakettle whistling, machinery, and so on.

   b. What indication (clue) was given as to what the effect was; in other words, *how* do you know that the effect is what you named it?

   c. What purpose did that effect have? Did it heighten action, set a mood, set time or place, or what?

2. Similarly, in the same or a different program, listen for music cues.

   a. List all music cues; describe the kind of music.

   b. Note how long each cue lasted; indicate whether it was faded in, faded out or under, and so on; describe how it fit into the dialogue or narration.

   c. What purpose did each music cue serve?

For both exercises 1 and 2, radio dramatic programs are most frequently found now on public radio stations, although some commercial stations play recordings of old programs. A lot of old programs are also available on records and tape. If you are listening off-the-air, you may find it helpful to make your own recording, so that you can go back over the material as you complete these exercises.

3. Choose a favorite short story and write for radio the first two scenes (or more if you wish). For this exercise, it is important that you:

   a. Choose the locations of your scenes, and decide how you will describe those scenes to your audience.

   b. Set time.

   c. Identify and describe the characters appearing in the scenes.

   d. Decide how to open the play; will you use narration to introduce the story? If so, how much?

   e. Determine how to provide the transition between the two scenes; will you use the preceding scenes to set up the following scene (as in the example in this chapter on the waterfront), or sound effects, or music, or narration, or a combination?

   Ideally, this assignment would combine considerations of the use of sound from this chapter with concepts of dramatic structure covered in Chapter 16. If you have the opportunity, read that chapter as well before beginning this exercise.

Key Terms and Concepts

acoustical setting	narration
dialogue	split narration
distance	pitch
fades: in, out, under, cross	quality (of sound)
juxtaposition (of sounds)	rhythm
montage	segue
music bed	timbre
on-mike and off-mike	volume

Notes

1. Albert Crews, *Professional Radio Writing* (Boston: Houghton Mifflin, 1946), pp. 64–65.
2. From the *Major Records Sound Effects* catalog (New York: Thomas J. Valentino, Inc.). Reprinted by permission.
3. From the *Major Records Production Music* catalog (New York: Thomas J. Valentino, Inc.). Reprinted by permission.

Chapter 7

Handling Visuals

In the forty-plus years since television became a major medium of communication, modern audiences have developed a quite sophisticated understanding of the rules and conventions of visualization. We are probably more aware of the visual conventions held by members of our culture than we are of literary ones. As a writer, you will need to recognize, understand, and appreciate these fundamentals of visual structure. With that familiarity, you will be able to write more precise and effective scripts for television and other audiovisual media.

We do not mean to suggest that the writer always controls the visualization of a program. In dramatic programs, for example, the director and editor usually will choose the precise camera angles, the sequences of shots, the frequency with which shots are changed, the type of change, and so on. In live programs also, the director will place the cameras, move them, and select the shots that will be seen on the air. In these kinds of programs writers are not required, or expected, or even encouraged to include visual directions.

On the other hand, in television journalism the writer is often also the reporter, the director (on location for a story), and the editor, and in smaller stations quite possibly the cameraperson as well. During the two to three stories a writer/reporter may put together in a normal day, it will be necessary to at least direct the camera operator to get the kind of shots necessary and then also direct the editor on how those shots should be put together to provide visual continuity that supports and parallels the verbal story. Under those circumstances, understanding visual structure is critical.

Writers of television commercials similarly need a good basic knowledge in this area. Frequently the commercial will be written as a storyboard. Visual composition of the various shots that make up the sequence, if not the precise camera angle and distance, is important if the final product is to have the impact you intended when you began the assignment.

You will find as you read this chapter that you are already familiar with many of the ideas it contains. Over the years you have watched thousands of hours of television and film, looked at countless photos in newspapers, magazines, and books, and read comic strips. The principles presented in this chapter apply to all these media, and many of them you have already unconsciously absorbed. So read on and discover what you already know.

Visual Point of View

One fundamental principle of visualization is the relationship between audience and camera position. Simply put, there is a direct correlation between what the camera sees and what the viewer sees when watching the screen—the camera becomes the viewer's eyes.

The television viewer sits still, often in a semi-darkened room, and stares passively at what is on the screen. After a while, the person actually will lose some awareness of his or her own body, especially if the surrounding environment is sufficiently comfortable. The senses of smell, touch, and balance diminish in importance. At the same time, the senses of sight and sound become more acute and directed toward the screen. There is very little eye movement. In that somewhat trancelike state, the viewer is able to move freely with the camera and experience the sensation of occupying the same space the camera occupies, seeing things from the camera's point of view and absorbing the emotional impact of each camera position.

People who have grown up in the age of movies and television often find it difficult to become interested in a live theater performance. The live play is likely to seem boring and slow to develop. In part that impression is due to the construction of a play. A theatrical drama, usually two to three hours long, can take longer to develop characters, mood, and plot nuances than does a 30- to 60-minute TV drama.

But in large part the feeling of frustration and boredom you may feel in the theater is because when you watch the theater presentation you have only one point of view—that from your own seat. What you are seeing will be a somewhat different angle or viewpoint from what the couple down in the front row is seeing and different again from the person in a seat in the balcony. For each of you, the point of view is slightly different, but most important, for each of you there is only one point of view.

Television and film, on the other hand, provide the viewer with multiple viewpoints. Each time the camera shot changes (or even within a single camera shot, if there is camera movement) the viewer is transported to a new viewpoint. This phenomenon is what gives these media their expressive power. By letting the camera be our eyes, we can move anywhere in relation to a subject. We can float above a football stadium filled with cheering fans, crawl below a science fiction monster, or meet a commercial announcer eye-to-eye. We can be at the side of the road as the cops and robbers go rushing by, zoom toward an opera singer in mid-aria, or pull away from the earth in a rocket ship.

We might mention at this point, to avoid confusion later, one particular type of camera shot, known as the *point-of-view shot*. This shot, inserted into a sequence, looks at the scene from the point of view of one of the characters involved in the action—that is, as if the camera were the eyes of that person. We, the audience, become that person for the length of that shot and experience the scene as he or she would experience it.

For example, assume we are following a search party as it seeks a missing child who has wandered away from a campsite. We see a series of objective shots that show members of the party beating through the brush, walking up a stream bed, and so on. Then, suddenly, someone off-camera yells "I found her!" and we see the searchers all run toward that voice. The next shot, a point-of-view shot, has the camera looking up at the rescuers from the bottom of a pit into which the child has fallen. We look up through the child's point of view.

In the correct format for a television script, the shot might be written this way:

16. AMY'S POV: LOOKING UP FROM BOTTOM OF PIT   16
     Tom is looking down, happy and excited. One by one the rest of the
     searchers come to the edge, similarly elated.

As we move from one camera position to the next, we experience the emotional and psychological payload each viewpoint gives us, and move on to the next. We absorb the story being told us by allowing the camera to be our eyes, and letting the rest of our being react to what the camera sees.

What are the effects of these manueverings? How do camera positions affect us? In this chapter we will consider five aspects of visual storytelling: vertical camera angles, camera to subject distances, camera movement, the juxtaposition and sequencing of shots, and transitions. These five provide a basic grammar sufficient for the beginning broadcast writer. When you need to go beyond these basics, you should turn to the literature of cinematography and television production.

Vertical Camera Angles

The position of the camera in relation to the subject on the vertical axis is very important because it will determine to a large degree the emotional or psychological effect of the shot. There are three basic positions: the camera above the subject, below the subject, or at eye level with it.

Low Angle   People understood the power of low angles long before there were cameras. Architects built cathedrals as tall as possible and put the stained glass windows well above eye level for one purpose: to get people to look up at them. Sculptors, when designing statues of national heroes, put them on large pedestals for the same reason. The people who have been responsible for depicting our religious, political, and cultural heritage have understood that in our culture we associate height and size with power. The taller something is, the more powerful it is. Conversely, the smaller, the less powerful.

Camera angles affect us the same way. When we put the camera below the subject, we say the shot is a low angle shot. The camera will make whatever it

Figure 7.1 Low Angle Shots

is looking at seem big. If the camera is looking at a person, the person will look taller and larger than in real life—more powerful, possibly more dangerous. Since the camera's point of view becomes the audience's point of view, from this low angle the audience feels small and perhaps helpless. Objects too look very large, even overwhelming from this angle.

A low camera angle also gives a general sense of dramatic intensity—an impression that momentous events are taking place. It could convey, for example, the importance of the signing of the Declaration of Independence, the power of a marching army, or the intensity of a man's mind. A low angle can also make a subject seem threatening; it is often used to build the stature of a villain or monster or to give a general sense of danger.

High Angle   High angle shots are those where the camera is above the subject, looking down on it. The psychology behind the high angle shot is the reverse of the low angle shot. From the lofty heights of a cathedral window or a military hero placed high on his pedestal, we humans look small indeed. In the same way, when the camera is above the subject, it makes the subject look smaller. The high camera diminishes the subject in size. It takes a dominant position over the subject.

When we want to show weakness or vulnerability, therefore, a high angle is appropriate. During a dialogue between two leads in a drama, we would give the high camera angle to the weaker character, so we are looking down on that person, and the low angle to the stronger person, so we are looking up at that one. By visually reinforcing the psychological relationship between the two, we add depth to the meaning of the scene in a subtle but powerful way.

Of course, there are varying degrees of height we can take with a high angle

Figure 7.2 High Angle Shots

shot. And each different height will change the meaning of the shot. Shots just slightly above eye level have more subtle effects. A slightly high angle is used in standard portrait photography because it is flattering to the subject, both physically and psychologically. It will make the subject look safe, nonthreatening, and friendly.

As we raise the camera higher above the subject, we increase the drama and intensity of the effect. We are now looking down on the subject at a stronger angle. The subject will begin to look more vulnerable, even victimized. We can continue to raise the angle of the shot so that because of our extreme height in relation to the subject, the subject can look trapped.

A high angle does not always have that effect, however. Such an angle can also support a mood of compassion, of divine goodness looking down, say, on a young mother and her newborn child. The point is that this visual power we gain by being above our subject can be any kind of power we choose, a benevolent power, a menacing power, or perhaps even a detached, abstract power. But being above a subject *does* give the camera/viewer power.

Eye-Level Angle

The eye-level angle may serve either of two functions: It may provide a neutral narrative position, or it may support a high-impact, confrontation function.

The narrative function is used more. Think of the millions of shots you have seen which have had no dramatic impact—the pictures you have looked at without emotion, just to get visual information. In most cases, these were eye-level shots. The camera position at eye level invites the viewer to "read" the shot, rather than to respond to it emotionally, as would be the case with either a high or low angle shot. It is the proper choice to deliver factual, nondramatic content.

Because the camera is at "normal" height, this angle feels the most comfortable and is the easiest for audience members to relate to. There is an equality between the viewer and the subject being viewed. We are literally "on the same level" with the subject, and it is thus appropriate to use this angle to convey an impression of honesty and frankness. The eye-level shot, for this reason, is often used for political advertising, in news broadcasts, and in commercials where the announcer needs to appear as honest and frank as possible.

Take, for example, the sequence of shots in the Amtrak commercial in Chapter 4. The opening shot is a high angle of the announcer quite a distance away from the camera. He is very small in the frame, but as he walks toward us he gets larger. The camera moves toward him too, and gradually drops down in height. Finally the camera reaches eye level, and the announcer begins to speak. This opening, moving from a high angle far away to an eye-level close shot of the announcer, adds drama and intensity (as well as a mood of distance and nostalgia) to a shot which without the dramatic camera angle would be merely matter of fact and not as interesting.

But with just a little emphasis in the lighting, or a slight change in composition or in the subject's expression, the eye-level shot can take on a quite different emotional meaning. It can create an impression of intensity and tenseness that goes beyond honesty and frankness. This is the visual representation of confrontation, of the cliché phrase "eyeball-to-eyeball." In this context, the eye-level

Figure 7.3 Eye-Level Shots

shot can convey dramatic intensity without distorting the visual information as much as an angled shot of the same subject.

Note too that being eye level to a person is very different from being eye level to an object like a telephone. And in that difference is a key to understanding the whole theory of camera angles. It is easy to understand the effect of the eye-level shot when the subject is a person because when people are all standing, or sitting, they are naturally at eye-to-eye level. But telephones are not normally found at that level. Usually they are below us, on tables or desks. Our normal frame of reference is that we are looking down at them. Our minds are used to seeing phones as below us, so if you look at a telephone at eye level (straight across at it), the camera angle will not depict objectivity or honesty, as with a normal eye-level shot. Instead, it will show power and weight, characteristics of a low angle shot (Figure 7.3, right).

Even though we are on eye level with the phone, in our minds we have lowered ourselves from our normal frame of reference in relation to the phone and have come down to its normal plane. The mental effect is that we have gotten smaller, the phone has gotten bigger. As a consequence, all the impact of a low angle shot applies to this shot even though it is, strictly speaking, an eye-level shot.

Therefore, when we talk about the eye-level shot as being able to convey honesty, frankness, and objectivity, we can't say that this is true in all cases. It applies only to people and subjects that are eye level in terms of our *normal frame of reference,* from roughly 4 to 6 feet in height.

To sum up, the camera angles on the vertical axis are of three basic types. The low angle shot, in general, confers power on the subject, the high angle shot conveys vulnerability, and the eye-level shot may convey either objectivity and honesty, or confrontation.

But as we shall repeat frequently throughout this chapter, it would be a mistake to oversimplify. Camera angles alone do not give a shot its entire meaning.

Figure 7.4 Long Shot

Medium Shot   *Closeup*

Camera Distance

Another powerful, expressive device is the choice of camera distance—that is, the *apparent* distance between the camera (audience) and the subject. We emphasize the word *apparent*, because in reality what appears to be a closeup shot, of a football player in a game, for example, may be taken from a camera using a telephoto lens that is quite some distance away.

The designations for camera distance in scripts are probably familiar to you. They include such basic terms as *long shot (LS), medium shot (MS),* and *closeup (CU),* and combinations—*extreme long shot (ELS), medium long shot (MLS), medium closeup (MCU),* and *extreme closeup (ECU).* But in practice it is difficult to set clear rules about the use of these terms to describe shots, because they are all relative.

For example, assume we have this series of three shots, which we label as a long shot, medium shot, and closeup, respectively (Figure 7.4). We decide to add another shot to the opening, which will be an even wider panorama. The new series is shown in Figure 7.5. In describing this new series, how shall we label the shots? Is the second shot still a long shot, even though it is not the longest shot? If so, what label do we give the first shot? We can call it an extreme long shot. The labels are arbitrary, but useful when production personnel must discuss the scene. Labels have meaning only in the context of the particular group of shots being considered.

Figure 7.5
Extreme Long Shot   *Long Shot*

Medium Shot   *Closeup*

Figure 7.6 A Long, Wide, or Establishing Shot

Now, within one particular framework, the room pictured in Figure 7.6, let's examine the different types of shots commonly used in writing for visual media.

Long Shots

The overall picture will be called a long shot. It's also known as a *wide shot,* and sometimes an *establishing shot.* When it is referred to as an establishing shot, that means it is being used at the beginning of a scene to establish the scene and its location. The shot establishes the parameters within which the action of the scene will take place. It's an introduction.

When you see this long shot, you know immediately that there are two main characters in the scene. They are inside a room (where the decor, easily seen in an establishing shot, can make a significant expressive statement), and they are waiting for a phone call. The long shot can also establish the mood of the scene, by means of the lighting, the composition, and the blocking that is built into the shot. In short, when used as an establishing shot, a long shot will establish basic visual facts and relationships on which the rest of the scene is built.

But long shots can do more than establish. When they are used within a scene, not just at the beginning, they convey moods like loneliness, estrangement, and isolation. The farther away we are from someone or something, the less direct involvement we feel. We can reflect upon the subject matter and think about it without being asked to be involved with it. We are a safe distance away. These shots, in most contexts, are long shots.

Long shots frequently are also used to end scenes. Just as we draw away from something when our interest in it diminishes, the long shot pulls us away from the action of a scene when it is over, or nearly over. By doing so, the shot is telling us that we have seen all we are going to see of that situation. The long shot releases the visual tension of the scene and gives it a feeling of closure.

Long shots can, of course, be shot from high, low, or eye-level angles, and their meaning will change accordingly.

Medium Shots

In our photo, a medium shot would be a shot of the two characters (a two shot), a shot of either character with the phone, or even a loose single shot of either of the characters. In general, medium shots of people are head and shoulder or waist-up shots (Figure 7.8).

Medium shots are used to deliver the bulk of the factual information that moves the story along. The emotional value of a medium shot is minimal, simply because the shot is neither very far away nor close to the subject. The camera is close enough to see significant details, but not so close as to produce emotional reactions from the viewer. This is the range at which we become aware of the subject's presence without becoming dramatically involved. Please note, as part of this discussion, that there is a range of medium shots—medium long, medium close—not just one length.

When the medium shot follows the long shot, it has the effect of narrowing the field of interest, focusing and heightening our attention to the subject on which the shot has narrowed.

Figure 7.7 Long Shots

When no other shot has been specifically indicated in a script, directors usually will choose medium shots.

Closeups   Closeups are the most penetrating, the most scrutinizing, and the most emphatic types of shot in visual stories. They get us the closest and most intimate looks at the subject matter.

Figure 7.8 Medium Shots

In real life, getting close to something or someone can provoke intense reactions, from extreme pleasure to fascination to revulsion. There is something about being very near that heightens our reactions. Perhaps it is the involvement. As we move in close, we eliminate options; we eliminate chances for escape. Psychologically this puts us in a position of heightened awareness. Whatever we confront at this close range, we see and react to in a more intense way.

The closeup (sometimes also called a *tight shot*) creates this same reaction visually. The camera sees less of its surroundings than it does in a medium or long shot. The shot focuses on one subject. When it does that, its primary emotional effect is to convey intensity. As such, it becomes a very powerful tool in visual storytelling.

Possible closeups in our scene would be shots of the faces of either character, in which emotions might easily be read, or a shot of the phone, a character's hand picking up the phone or getting something out of a drawer in the table, some detail of the decor in the room—a portrait on the wall or a clock, emphasizing time. The specific closeups chosen from among these possibilities, of course, would be the ones that further the plot of the story (Figure 7.9).

Closeups of people are commonly used to convey emotions and interior conflicts. Here is a situation frequently found in television news reporting which uses a common pattern of shots:

Figure 7.9 Closeups

A reporter and cameraperson are covering a story in which a family's home has just been destroyed by fire. The camera opens with a wide shot showing the family with the charred remains of the house in the background, while the reporter asks the family: ''What happened to your house?'' The shot stays wide or medium while the basic facts of the story are presented. But when the reporter turns to questions that elicit the emotional responses of the victims—''What are you going to do now? How are you going to recover from the loss? What are your feelings?''—the camera shifts to closeups—the faces of the victims, a doll clutched in the arms of a small child, and so on.

Soap operas use closeups a lot. Of course, since this program form deals with emotions, the use of closeups is certainly appropriate. But when closeups are used often, as they are in a soap opera, they serve another function. They set up a motif.

A *motif* is the repeated use of a formal structural element such as the repeated use of the color red or the repeated use of a certain shape making a pattern, or in the case of a soap opera, the repeated use of closeups.

When a structural element is repeated frequently, that repetition takes on a second meaning. In this case, each closeup still has its primary function; it still provides intensity of emotion. But the frequent use of closeups also sets up the motif, which in this case is to give the story an overall feeling of intimacy. The audience gets the impression that the story is a very intimate, personal one, even when closeups are not on the screen. The audience responds to the residual effect of seeing repeated closeups. It is responding to the motif. Of course, an audience cannot take a long series of closeups. The emotional impact of the shots will diminish if they are used too frequently, and will quite likely be replaced by a feeling of discomfort.

Closeups may also be used for other purposes. By focusing on a small part taken from a larger scene, the closeup channels attention to particular details that might otherwise be missed in a longer shot which contains many different visual cues. This application, directing attention through the use of closeups, is used in all types of productions, but it is particularly important in commercials and instructional scripts.

Camera Movement

Our comments earlier regarding multiple points of view in a visual story referred primarily to the ability of film and video to provide rapid transitions from one camera position to another, an effect that is achieved in the editing process. But it is possible to change the viewing perspective *within* a single shot by moving the camera or zooming the lens. Several types of movement can be used. The most common are zooms and pans. Others include the dolly, the truck, and the boom.

Zooms

A *zoom* movement is accomplished by a special lens on a camera that permits changing the field of view continuously (either in, closer, or out, farther away) without losing focus during the movement.

A zoom-in has the effect of a change from a wide shot to a closeup, increasing the level of involvement and intensity. It literally pulls the audience into the scene. In addition, as the movement narrows the field of view, it directs the attention of the audience to those items which remain in view. There are now fewer items in the scene with which to deal, and these are seen in more detail; closer scrutiny is possible. And this focusing of attention is accomplished without losing the relationship between the larger scene and the detailed closeup, which might happen if, instead of a zoom, the sequence were to cut from long shot to closeup—that is, with a cut the audience might not be able to recall how the detail fits into the larger scene, but with a zoom the eye is drawn in a continuous motion from broader to narrower perspective.

A zoom-out provides the reverse. It establishes the detail first, then begins to reveal how that detail fits into a larger picture. And it pulls the audience away, psychologically, from the action, begins to disengage them emotionally, and sets the stage for the conclusion of the scene.

Pans

A *pan* is accomplished by swinging the camera in an arc from its fixed position. The term is used for a horizontal sweep. A pan-type movement in the vertical plane is called a *tilt*.

A pan across an auditorium quickly establishes the size of the hall, the number of people present, and the level of movement or excitement involved. A pan may also follow a character across a room, or a car negotiating the twists of a mountain road. In the latter case the speed of the pan, which should match the speed of the car, imparts a sense of movement to the scene. If it's a fast-moving car, the need to hurry and the feeling of excitement are enhanced. In contrast, a slow-moving vehicle, and a slow pan, may suggest calm, deliberate, even reluctant movement.

Tilts can heighten the emotional impacts provided by the various vertical camera angles. From a neutral wide, eye-level shot, for example, a combination zoom in and tilt up would dramatically increase the emotional level and the threat suggested by the subject of the shot.

Very rapid pans, called *swish pans,* which are so fast as to blur the action, accomplish a different purpose. They are transition devices, intended to separate two scenes or shots, yet at the same time maintain a relationship between them.

Other Camera Movements

Several other types of camera movement can be used. We'll mention only three, which are reasonably common.

Dolly

With this movement, the entire camera is moved closer to (*dolly in*) or back from (*dolly back*) the action. The word comes from the wheeled platform—a dolly—on which cameras are frequently mounted, but a hand-held camera walked into or back from a scene would provide the same effect. That is, it would provided it were held steady. The bobbing and jiggling of the hand-held camera, which originated with cinema vérité and early television news photography, now is used as a deliberate technique even when the camera can easily be kept steady. Audiences perceive a wobbly camera as adding "reality" or "immediacy" to a shot, but that's a stylistic consideration beyond the scope of this discussion.

A dolly has somewhat the same effect as a zoom, and has largely been replaced by the zoom, but they differ somewhat. The zoom makes a scene appear to move closer to the viewer. The dolly appears to move the viewer into the scene.

Truck

This movement also involves the physical movement of the camera, horizontally and usually parallel to the action. It may, for example, be following a group of runners down a road, keeping a set distance and frame size by moving at the same speed as the runners. There is movement to the scene—action taking place—but a stable emotional relationship is maintained between the audience and that action.

Boom

This is also called a *crane movement*. Many high angle shots are accomplished by placing the camera in a crane. When the crane is operated *during* the shot, the camera is physically moved in the vertical plane. As with the tilt, but even more emphatically, the emotional payload of the vertical camera angle may be manipulated by this movement.

Sequences of Shots

So far we have discussed only individual shots. They are, of course, the essential building blocks of the video story, serving very much the same function that sentences do within a written essay or story. Each shot conveys a particular meaning and makes a specific, single statement. But a written story needs more than just a random series of sentences to be called a story. It needs organization. And so does a visual story. Individual shots must be put together in sequences that group the individual ideas into more complex patterns.

Here are eight shots. Each has an individual meaning, and yet when they are placed together in order, each reinforces and adds meaning to the shot that comes next.

A sequence of shots is very much like a paragraph—it presents a series of

Figure 7.10 Sequence of Shots
(1) Establishing shot: man looking out window of apartment; gun on table in foreground.
(2) Medium shot, low angle: two men burst into apartment.
(3) Closeup, low angle: man turns, shows surprise and fear.
(4) Closeup, high angle: gun on table; focuses attention, establishes gun as key element in scene.

(5) Medium shot, low angle: men move toward camera.
(6) Medium shot, low angle: gun in foreground, man behind; he jumps forward.
(7) Closeup, low angle: man has gun, pointing.
(8) Medium shot: men are surprised, scared, move suddenly backward.

statements which together make up a complete thought. The analogy between written paragraphs and visual scenes cannot be extended very far, however, because when you tell a story with pictures, the nuances, overtones, and implications of the actions you show are much more powerful, much deeper than they are with the written word. In our example, the first man might strike us as a drug addict, just by the way he acts, and yet no direct statement was made to that effect. This perception is part of the rich visual subtext. The two people who enter the room might be there by accident. The gun on the table could be broken and not capable of firing. The room might remind us of another room we'd seen earlier in the story in which a person was killed, and so on.

The point is that with visual storytelling, the associations the members of the audience make as they follow the story are made quickly and cover a broad spectrum. Even visual information that is not consciously perceived by the viewer has an impact. The human eye makes hundreds of associations instantly each time a new image is shown. It picks up so much subtle information that if you were to try to use words to describe everything that *could* be happening in a sequence, it would take pages and pages.

Of course, as the writer of the script and the originator of its ideas, if you *need* to have some of these subsidiary ideas in your presentation, you will have to include them in the script, in character and setting descriptions.

Juxtaposition of Shots

As an introduction to the grammar of visual sequences, you should understand two basic characteristics that affect the selection of shots to be placed next to each other.

First, everything in visual storytelling is relative. That is, the shot just before the one we are seeing has determined, to a great degree, our point of view for the one we are now seeing. And the shot we are now seeing will establish our point of view for the next one we see. We have already had one example of relativity regarding the distance of a camera shot. If we begin a scene with a long shot, then change our minds and precede that shot with an even longer one, the first long shot is not made any shorter in absolute terms, but it is shorter *relative* to the new, longer opening shot. So it is perceived as shorter.

Second, visual storytelling makes extensive use of comparisons. Because one shot can quickly be cut next to another, the subject matter of the shots is quickly and easily compared. It is in that comparison that much of the meaning of the scene is derived.

One of the first persons to recognize these visual truths was the Russian filmmaker Lev Kuleshov. In a now classic demonstration, he created three film sequences. In the first, a shot of an actor's face preceded a shot of a plate of soup on a table; in the second, a shot of the actor was followed by a shot of a coffin in which lay a dead woman; and in the third, the face was juxtaposed to a shot of a little girl playing with a toy. The results were described by Kuleshov's associate, Vsevolod Pudovkin:

> When we showed the three combinations to an audience which had not been let into the secret the result was terrific. The public raved about the acting of the artist. They pointed out the heavy pensiveness of his mood over the forgotten soup, were touched and moved by the deep sorrow with which he looked on the dead woman, and admired the light, happy smile with which he surveyed the girl at play. But we knew that in all three cases the face was exactly the same.[1]

Kuleshov's demonstration established the fundamental principle of visual sequencing: The order in which you display pictures will directly affect the meaning those pictures will have for an audience.

The implications of Kuleshov's demonstration and other principles of filmmaking that evolved from the early films by Pudovkin, Griffith, Eisenstein, and others were set down in several books by Sergei Eisenstein. He developed a language that still forms the theoretical foundation for cinematic and video production. We recommend that you study his books if you intend to write extensively for visual media.

Controlling Tension

Another consideration in the sequencing of shots is the control of the tension within the scene. Any good story, written or visual, builds and releases tension several times during the course of its telling. And the writers of expressive media which take place over a fixed time, such as a symphony, a ballet, a play, a movie, or a television drama, are particularly concerned with tension.

As a general rule, the writer tries to make the flow of images reflect the natural tension points in the story. For example, a dramatic story about a celebrated jewel thief might have as its highest tension point his incredible break-in and theft of a highly guarded gem. The visual sequence should build to that point. If, on the other hand, the story is a news item about a convicted jewel thief, and the focus of the story is his release from jail, then that would be the point to which to build the tension. In either case, we look to the message of the story to suggest the proper point or points toward which to build the tension.

Once we determine these points, we can begin organizing the visual sequence. Our object will be to try to design sequences that follow the basic shape of the story, and to change direction when the story changes direction.

Generally speaking, closeups contain more tension than longer shots, and low angle shots contain more tension than high angle shots. Consequently it would seem that whenever you wanted to create tension, you would include closeups and lower angles, and when you wanted to release tension, you would change to longer and more neutral eye-level shots. That is generally correct, but with experience you will learn to sequence shots so that the energy associated with tension buildup and tension release will be transferred to specific ideas, regardless of the angles and distances of the shots.

Building a Scene

Just as in a sentence, where the choice and order of words will determine the final character of the thought, the choice and sequence of the shots will determine the visual statement of the scene. There is no single right way to express an idea visually; there are many ways, each with its own subtle differences. For the sake of brevity, however, the following exercise explains some of the more obvious.

In this scene (Figure 7.11, p. 180), the first idea we want to express is confrontation, the confrontation between the house and the man. The simplest form this scene can take is shown in the first three shots of this sequence.

Shot 1

As a general rule, the opening shot in a scene will be an establishing long shot. It orients the viewer to the area in which the action will take place during that scene. In this case, we have chosen a very high angle. Why? It works with the long shot in establishing an opening position. Recall the feeling you got when you sat at the top of a children's slide at a playground, then slid down. That movement is similar to the relationship between the opening shot and the second shot in this sequence. We are propelled from a high, long shot (dissociation) into a low closeup (involvement in the action).

Shot 2

The second shot is a low angle closeup. It is the opposite of the opening shot, and it maximizes the contrast between the idea of dissociation (shot 1) and the idea of involvement (shot 2). It is an emphasis shot. It doesn't further the action; the character doesn't do anything new. Instead, it emphasizes the personality of the main character and how he is reacting to the situation he is in. Since the main idea we want to express in this sequence is that of confrontation, even though the second shot doesn't further the action, its characteristics—the low angle, and being in so close—support the idea of confrontation.

Figure 7.11 Shots in a Scene
(1) Long shot, high angle: man in foreground, house on hill in background.
(2) Low angle: man looking at house.
(3) Medium shot, medium angle: house.

Shot 3   The third shot follows logically from the second. It is a natural response to several issues the second shot raises. For example, the second shot asks the question, "What is this man looking at?" The third shot answers that question, and shows us that he is looking at the house. We have chosen an eye-level medium shot of the house to "describe" it for the audience. We might have used a low angle shot to present the house in a more dramatic, malevolent way. If the house were haunted, we would clearly emphasize the house by giving it the low angle. But in this situation such a shot would perhaps be excessive, overstated, too exaggerated.

Also, by giving our hero the "dramatic" shot in the sequence, we shift the emphasis slightly toward him and away from the house. As this shot flashes on the screen, the audience should feel a sense of resolution and of completion. With the introduction of the third shot, we have answered all the questions the first two shots asked and completed our first idea, that of confrontation. We have finished our first sequence. And we did it in a way that is formally correct.

What have we learned? We can say that it is acceptable to open a scene with a long shot, that generally each shot should offer a new bit of information, but that the information it offers does not have to further the action. It can instead be about a character's personality, the setting, or anything else that will enhance the story.

When a relationship is set up between two subjects, in this case the man and the house, cross-cutting between them will strengthen the relationship. It will also keep the relationship balanced.

Now, look at a different ordering of these same three shots:

Shot 1   The opening shot of a scene does not *have* to be a long shot. When we use a tight shot as the opening shot, the emphasis changes. The original sequence was organized to stress the idea of confrontation. This ordering, however, stresses suspense and mystery, and the opening shot is primarily responsible for this. By opening with the tight shot, we are immediately thrust into the action and our curiosity is high. Since we are deprived of the orienting, establishing shot, we immediately want to know, "What is this man looking at?" The longer the shot is held, the more the suspense mounts.

Figure 7.12 Shots in a Different Order
(1) Low angle: man looking at house.
(2) Long shot, high angle: man in foreground, house on hill in background.
(3) Medium shot, medium angle: house.

Shot 2   This shot answers the question by showing us what he's looking at, and in so doing, breaks the initial suspense. But by showing us new information—he's standing by a car parked some distance from the house—new questions are raised—not so much about him, but about his purpose. We have shifted the suspense away from the man to the situation. So far this arrangement of shots is presenting the information in an interesting, balanced way.

Shot 3   In this ordering, this shot does not fit well. Each shot should offer some new bit of information, and this shot does not do so. The sequence could end after the second shot. Not only has the information of the sequence been completed with the second shot, but by pulling out to a wide shot, we have signaled the end of the scene by reducing the tension.

**Changing
Scenes**   When a change of direction or a new idea is introduced in a story, that is a transitional point. It is the appropriate place to start a new scene. That change of direction will be preceded by the release of tension. In the story we have been developing, the first scene contains the three shots of the man's confrontation with the house. Another scene begins with shot 4.

     The number of shots in a scene can vary from two or three to at least ten, to possibly as many as twenty. There is no ideal number of shots, just as there is no ideal melody or ideal poem. Each sequence has to be tailormade to express its particular message. What might take four or five pages to write might easily be said in a three-shot sequence. What might strike you as a particularly rich though brief written idea can be expanded into quite a long visual scene. However, if a scene runs fifteen or sixteen shots, say, without releasing tension, it probably has run too long.* Without the frequent building and releasing of tension, the audience will become bored. For a story to have life, it has to have pace (a concept we discussed at length in Chapter 5), and its pace is to a large degree created by the manipulation of tension and tension release. To control pace, control the speed and frequency of the changes in scenes.

---

* We are using the terms *scene* and *sequence* somewhat interchangeably, but in a filmmaker's vocabulary a *scene* is a series of shots which the viewer perceives as taking place in the same location during a brief period of time, and a *sequence* is a larger unit consisting of a number of related scenes.

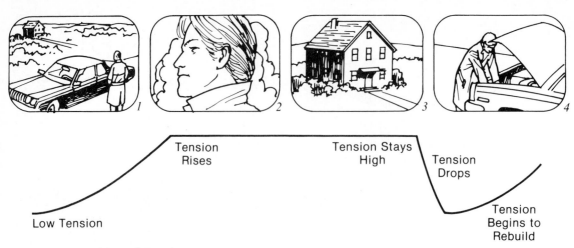

Figure 7.13 Buildup of Tension

      The following group of scenes illustrates the use of the concepts we have been discussing. It also introduces some new ones. We'll continue with the story we have begun; picking up the analysis with the fourth shot, which begins a new scene. This sequence of shots presents a new piece of information in the story—namely, ''The man has a bomb in the trunk of his car.'' The scene will have to express the idea visually. It starts with a wide shot. Although it is really a medium shot, it is the widest shot in this scene and as such it helps separate this scene from shot 3, which concluded scene 1. Even more important in separating the scenes, however, is the camera angle. In 3, we are looking straight on to the house, and in 4 we're clearly looking down. Even though both shots are medium shots, they are completely different in point of view, and this shift signals the beginning of a new sequence.

      Shot 5 is a tight shot. We are developing the second sequence as we did the first, by moving the camera closer, a standard approach. Shot 6 shows us what the man is working on—a time bomb. It's a tight shot, again from a high angle, and it simply extends the development started in 5 by moving the camera in even more. It focuses the attention of the audience on the bomb.

      The scene ends here. The most important reason for ending at this point is that finally seeing the bomb—what the man was looking at—completes what the scene set out to say. In addition, it is the third shot in the series, and three-shot patterns form natural, complete groups.

      Shot 7 introduces a new idea, and confirms that shot 6 ended the previous sequence. It also heightens the suspense which this story is building by the sudden cut to a closeup (without an introductory wide shot) of the man's wristwatch. Although shot 7 introduces a new idea, it does not begin a new scene. Notice that shots 7 and 8 represent completely different ideas, each of which is expressed in a single shot. We call these *passing shots*—that is, they get us quickly through steps in the story we don't want to spend much time with. If we wanted to spend more time here and develop shots 7 and 8 into full scenes,

Figure 7.14
(1) Long shot, high angle: man in foreground, house on hill in background.
(2) Low angle: man looking at house.
(3) Medium shot, medium angle: house.

(4) High angle, medium shot: man is getting something from back of car.
(5) Closeup, low angle: spy's face from trunk's point of view.
(6) Closeup, high angle: time bomb.

(7) Closeup, high angle: man sets his watch.
(8) Rear shot, long lens, low angle: man is framed by house in background; he walks toward house.
(9) Low shot, low angle, wide-angle lens: man is silhouetted in doorway; he enters house.

we could. On the other hand, we could eliminate these shots and go directly to shot 9.

Shot 9 begins the third scene. As we have said, when there are distinct differences between the last shot of a scene and the first shot of the new scene, it will be easy for the audience to follow the story. Compare shot 9 to shot 8. They are different, opposite in almost every way. Shot 8 calls for a telephoto lens, with its flattened perspective; shot 9 calls for a wide angle lens that deepens perspective. In shot 8, the man is in the foreground, with the house in the background; in shot 9, the opposite is true. Shot 8 is outside the house; shot 9 is inside.

Pointing out obvious differences like these and suggesting you use the same

  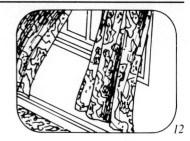

Figure 7.15 Further Continuation of Scene
(10) Low angle, closeup: man looks around
(11) Medium shot, high angle: chair
(12) Medium shot, high angle: window with drapes blowing in the wind.

(13) Closeup, low angle: man spots something and is looking at it closely.
(14) Closeup, high angle: man holds book.
(15) High angle, over-the-shoulder shot: someone is watching our spy.

(16) Low angle closeup: He's watching intently.
(17) Medium shot, high angle: our spy continues to work.
(18) Extreme closeup, low angle: He's getting madder.

techniques may seem to overstate the case, possibly even overstate the story. But when you consider that each of these images will be seen by the audience for only a very short time, their effect is much more subtle.

Shot 9, a wide shot, also orients the viewer to the new surroundings. Shot 10 then directs the attention to the man, who by now we may perceive as being a spy. We see that he is looking around. Notice that we have chosen a low angle shot rather than an eye-level shot. It makes our spy look formidable and dangerous. However, there is an additional reason for this which we will deal with in a moment.

Shots 11 and 12 show us what he's looking at (the same relationship we had between shots 2 and 3, and shots 5 and 6). But we've included two shots here and not just one to get across the idea that he's looking around the whole room rather just at one thing.

Shot 13 is an extremely tight shot, and now it shows the spy looking at something in particular, no longer just "looking around." What makes us feel that he is looking at something in particular, that somehow his situation has changed since we saw him in shot 10? Two things contribute to the change. First, his screen direction has changed. Originally he was looking off screen left; now he's looking off screen right. Second, he's looking down, like he's seen something, rather than looking up as in shot 10. We've taken the basic idea of shot 10, and by changing both screen direction and camera distance, totally changed its meaning. Notice also that shot 13 is from an extremely low angle.

Shot 14 shows us what he's looking at. By now, you should have noticed the association that says if you use a shot showing someone looking at something, then you should include an accompanying shot showing what is being looked at. Shot 14 is also an extremely tight shot, so you can read the label "Top Secret" on the book. It also increases the tension.

Shot 15 begins the fourth scene, and introduces a new character. Once again, as the transition between scenes we have scene 3 ending with a tight shot, and scene 4 beginning with a wide shot, a standard transition. Notice that in the first shot of this scene, we immediately set up a visual relationship between the new character and the spy; the new character is larger than the spy, and thus more powerful and dangerous.

Up to this point in the story, we have reinforced the idea of the spy's powerful stature by using low angle shots to describe him. But now we are going to switch the audience's associations of power from the spy to the new character by showing the new character with low angle shots and by making him bigger in the frame than the spy. The spy, on the other hand, we show from a high angle and from behind to make him look weak. This shift may seem obvious to us, as we discuss it here, but during the actual viewing of these shots in the context of a story, the audience would feel the shift in power without consciously recognizing why. During this scene, we build the tension by constantly moving in, cutting to progressively tighter shots of each character until we reach shot 18, where a climactic series of shots is now inevitable.

We will leave it to you to finish the storyboard of this story.

Horizontal Camera Angles

You may have wondered earlier why we did not discuss horizontal camera angles when we discussed vertical angles. The reason is that horizontal angles are important only as they are arranged in sequence. The horizontal position of individual shots does not carry any of the emotional implications of vertical angles. It serves only to show relationships—relative positions—of the persons and objects in a scene.

Seldom are writers concerned with specific horizontal sequences, but you may be if you also work as a reporter-director in TV news. There you should be aware of these uses and cautions regarding horizontal shot combinations.

Reverse Angle

This technique is most often seen in interviews. The main focus of attention is on the interviewee, while he or she answers a question. Then, when the reporter asks the next question, the camera angle shifts to the reverse angle, showing the

Figure 7.16 Reverse Angles

reporter full-face. (Usually these shots also show the second person in the scene, with the camera looking over the person's shoulder; consequently these shots are frequently called *over-the shoulder shots*. See Figure 7.16.)

The reverse angle is also used to give some feeling of size and shape to an event. At a political convention, the main focus would be on the speakers at the rostrum, but reverse angles shot from the rostrum toward the crowd would show the reactions of the audience to the speakers. Similarily, in a parade, shots of the spectators would be reverse angles.

Line of Action   (Other terminology used to describe this rule is the *180° rule* or *principal action axis*.) Generally speaking, all shots in a single scene should be taken from one side of a line drawn through the middle of the scene. Figure 7.6, seen from above, is diagrammed in Figure 7.17. The camera (or cameras, depending on whether this program is shot "live-style" with multiple cameras, or shot by one camera, recorded and the shots edited into a sequence) can be moved about to get a variety of angles, so long as it (they) stay on the same side of the line of action. Even reverse angles will have to be slightly less than 180° apart, so they don't cross this line. A direct cut to a shot taken from the opposite side of the line would confuse the audience, as the characters will suddenly seem to have reversed their positions in the scene.

Sometimes this rule can be broken. Professional football telecasts now use occasional shots taken from the opposite side of the field, but so far at least the announcers have been careful to explain that it is an opposite angle shot, so the audience will understand why the player who moments ago was running from right to left is now seen running from left to right. Also, as performers move about in a scene, the line shifts; camera shots can now move with the new line. Cutaways—to a picture on the wall, for example—also break the continuity of the scene and permit further shots to be taken from a different axis.

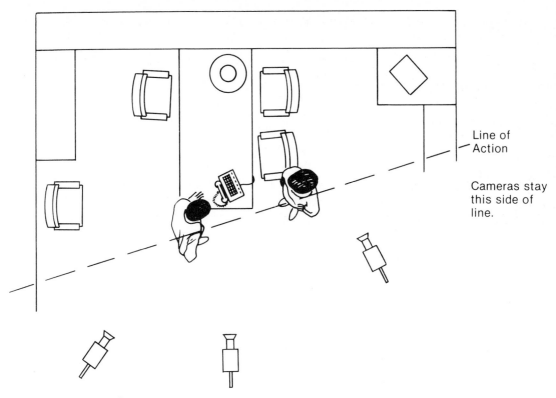

Figure 7.17 Line of Action

Transitions

Another part of visual grammar is the means used to provide transitions between camera shots. In recent years the increasing sophistication of the switcher/fader units used in television have added all sorts of image splitting, wipes, page turning, spinning, and other tricks for the manipulation of transitions. We couldn't attempt to catalogue all of them here even if we wished to. But there are several standard transitions audiences have come to associate with certain meanings.

Cut

This is the simplest, most used transition; a direct, immediate change from one camera position to another. Many films and video programs are put together using nothing but cuts. They are the simplest and least expensive transitions and are readily understood by audiences.

Most cuts are unobtrusive, natural transitions. They blend the two adjoining shots. These are *match cuts*. Another type of cut is the *jump cut*. Depending upon the circumstances, and on how careful directors are in using the terminology, you may receive instructions that say either: Don't use a jump cut under any circumstances, or: Use jump cuts to provide deliberately jarring transitions that throw the two shots into sharp contrast. For example, in recording a speech by a public official, and then editing that speech for broadcast, you have two quotes you wish to place back to back. If the two camera shots have been taken from the same distance and angle, and you splice them next to each other, you will have a jump cut. The speaker's head and face will not be in precise alignment in the two shots and will seem to jump unexplainedly between the two shots. You will need to insert some other material, at least briefly, between the two shots.

In a different situation, however, you may want to cut without explanation from one scene to something quite different. The unanticipated shift, although momentarily confusing to the audience, heightens curiosity.

Dissolve

The *dissolve* is a slower, softer transition. It gradually blends two images by showing both shots simultaneously for a brief moment. While the first shot is fading out, the second one is getting stronger, until the first shot fades out completely. Dissolves allow more time for the audience to adjust and react to the transition, and they carry more significance to the audience than a cut. They also suggest that a relationship does exist between the two scenes. One common relationship might be that the two scenes are taking place simultaneously. Other relationships might be that a character remembers a former event, and the dissolve then is the "flashback" to the earlier time; or it may be a means of going into a person's mind for a "stream of consciousness" sequence.

Fade

The *fade,* or *fade to black,* is an even more dramatic, stronger transition than a dissolve. During a fade, the scene gradually disappears into blackness, usually with an accompanying fading of the sound track. A fade-out or fade to black is used at the end of a scene to give a particularly "final" feeling. For a brief second, that audience is staring at a blank screen, hearing no sound, and feeling a definite sense of the story being stopped.

Because fade-outs produce this reaction, they are extraordinarily strong means of transition. They are most appropriately used to break the flow in a narrative or to string together several scenes that are to be seen as separate incidents. Often fades are used to indicate a major passage of time, change of place, or psychological shift in a character. Fades can vary in length, from one second or shorter to several seconds. In dramatic programs, they are often accompanied by music. Usually a fade to black in one scene is accompanied by a fade up from black to begin the next scene, but it is also permissible to cut to the next scene from black.

Other Transitions

Of the many transition devices available, three more deserve brief mention.

Defocusing

The deliberate racking of a camera lens out of focus provides another way to change shots. Frequently the flashback and stream of consciousness transitions use a combination of dissolve and defocusing (or some other technique for blurring the image, such as smearing grease on the camera lens).

Defocus-refocus transitions can also be used for time or time and place changes. Defocus a scene on a street in a frontier village at noon, then refocus on the same scene with the lighting—the sun—at a different angle. It's now sunset; six hours have passed. Or defocus on the clock face of Big Ben with the hands at 10:30; refocus on a closeup of the hero's wristwatch at 5:00—a change in time and place.

Swish Pan

We mentioned this camera technique earlier, in the discussion of camera movement. In order to prepare the audience for future action, the camera may at the end of a shot rapidly swish across the scene, so rapidly in fact that the movement is blurred. At the beginning of the next scene (say, for example, that an actor is leaving scene 1 and will next be seen entering a different location), a swish pan will end with the camera focused on the door through which the actor will now enter. In the editing, the two swish movements will be placed together to give a continuous blur. The emotional effect of the transition is that the actor has left scene 1 and arrived at scene 2 with the same sense of urgency, intensity, and purpose. If that is not the effect wanted, then use some other transition device.

Wipe

A *wipe* is a transitional effect used often in television. It uses electronic techniques to accomplish the effects of either a cut or a dissolve, depending on the circumstances. When used within a scene, for example as a change of camera angle shot within a musical number, the wipe helps maintain the continuity wanted in that situation. It functions much like a cut, but not quite as abruptly. When used to conclude a scene, the wipe acts like a dissolve—one scene replaces another without any break in the continuity. There is an impression created that one scene has pushed the other off the screen, that the first scene may actually be continuing, even though we, the audience, cannot see it any longer. A wipe may move from left to right, right to left, top to bottom, or from the center out like the ripples on water caused by a thrown stone. The shapes of wipes are virtually endless, limited only by the complexity of the electronic switcher used to create them.

Very sophisticated electronic devices now available in most television stations and certainly at the networks and major production studios permit all sorts of split-screen and multiple-image effects, electronic focusing, color manipulation, and wipes of many types. These techniques can be employed simply for their visual attention-getting capability, as in many commercials, or they can further the action of or add emotional force to a story. They function, however, only as variations on the basic transitional techniques we have discussed.

Writing Visual Cues

As we have said, in real life most often the writer will not be expected to provide detailed camera directions, except perhaps in writing commercials (and drawing storyboards), and in preparing news stories in the field. But in the writing of assignments for critique in a class, you will have to give sufficient detail so that your instructor can visualize what you have in mind. To the extent that you will need detailed cues, you should use the terminology we have introduced in this chapter—high angle, long shot, dissolve, and so on—along with sufficient descriptive language to make your instructions clear. Here is a sampling of typical directions, some from scripts reproduced elsewhere in this text:

Medium shot—Bernie on levee (river in background) dissolve to shots of:
    Farmer on tractor in field
    Downtown shoppers

Fade in LS of room dark with shadows. Baby's crib in foreground. Back of rocking rocker in front of fireplace in BG. Dolly in slowly for MCU of back of rocker

Dissolve. Forest scene. Snowing, snow on ground and on trees. LS of unbroken path through trees. Camera walks along path. At times branches brush past screen.

WS of vacant train station while camera booms down to eye level. Throughout the boom a single figure walks toward the camera from some distance. . . .

CU man as he walks head on toward camera, as he walks the camera trucks back to keep him from coming too close and to give a feeling of movement

---

    MS: Diamond cutter's hands holding diamond in the dop.

    CU: Diamond in the dop

    ECU: Same

    Insert ECU: Diamond cutter's eyes looking down

    Insert CU: Hands marking line

    MCU: Diamond cutter

Exterior: Close-up on gate: Zoom out as gate begins to open; camera starts down driveway past saddle rock sign

CU: Sign

Long shot of mountain (6 sec); pull back as truck passes by (4 sec)

Conclusion

Visual grammar is not a science; it is rather a codification of principles surrounding an art form. There are people who try to define the phenomena of visual communication in specific terms (part of the study of signs and symbols called *semiotics*). Our purpose has been much more general. We have presented some principles you can use to make simple visual statements. We have suggested how camera angles, camera distance, and camera movements can convey and reinforce certain emotional and intellectual messages. Audiences respond not only to the words and the aural tone of a message, they are deeply influenced by relationships, settings, needs, and behaviors they perceive visually.

Not only are audiences affected by single visual images or shots, but as we have also shown, they gather meaning from the juxtaposition of shots, the sequence in which shots are presented, and from the types of transitions used to separate scenes and sequences.

Using all these principles, you will have a basis on which to make artistic choices. These principles will help you intensify and sustain audience interest in your script when it finally makes it to the video screen. Understanding visual grammar and writing your requirements carefully and accurately into the script will also give you better control over the visual side of your script when it goes into production.

Exercises

1. Complete the story used to explain visual sequencing. Make up any ending you want, and take as many frames and scenes as you like to finish it, with each frame representing one camera shot. Describe each shot, as we did in the analysis, by writing under each storyboard frame the specific camera angle, camera distance, action taking place in the shot, and anything else you feel is necessary to explain what is happening. Also, explain *why* you have made the selection of shots as you have. Justify in the same way that we did the remaining shots in your story.

2. Write (draw) a television commercial in storyboard form, again with attention to visual shots and the development of the series of shots. For a commercial to be effective as well as visually interesting, you should incorporate into the commercial other principles from other chapters, if possible, such as persuasive motivation (Chapter 10), and suggestions on the structure of commercial messages (Chapter 11). But the main thrust of this exercise should be the choice of camera angle, distance, and possibly movement, the juxtaposition of shots and transitions—the primary emphases of this chapter.

Key Terms and Concepts

boom
cut: match cut, jump cut
defocus
dissolve
dolly
fade
juxtaposition (of shots)
long shot, medium shot, closeup
pan
passing shot
point of view

point-of-view shot
reverse angle
scene and sequence
swish pan
tension
tilt
truck
vertical angle: low, high, eye-level
wipe
zoom

Note

1. From V. I. Pudovkin, *Film Technique*, 1929. Quoted in Karel Reisz, *The Technique of Film Making*, 2d ed. (London: Focal Press, 1954), p. 31.

Chapter 8

Sponsors and Their Purposes

Two aspects of the communication process deserve more attention than we are able to provide in our overview in Chapter 1. The first of these is the relationship of program originators to the overall process of broadcasting. The second, which we consider in the next chapter, is the expectations held by the individuals who make up the audiences for programs.

The business side of broadcasting is a complex topic, all the details of which might be more appropriately discussed in a management text rather than in one for writers. But writers cannot afford to be wholly ignorant of management and programming, because the content, sequence, form, and style of their scripts are directly shaped by the commercial decisions made by advertisers, managers, and programmers. To write effective, successful scripts, writers must understand why some individuals and corporations invest in broadcast stations, and why other corporations are willing to pay to sponsor programs on those stations. In short, our chapter is an examination of the purposes that dictate the actions of broadcasting's "originators."

Making a Profit

In the United States, the broadcasting system is primarily commercial. Although public television and radio stations, and cable access channels, are operated on a noncommercial basis, they are the exceptions. For the most part profit making, or at least the potential to make a profit, is what drives the system. We can begin with an analysis, very much simplified, of how that works.

When the owner-licensees of stations invest in those properties, they do so with the intent of making a profit. For the most part, their intentions are realized. Nearly all TV stations have shown profits in recent years, some as high as the 20 to 30 percent range, an excellent margin of profit for any investment. Radio stations on the whole are not quite so successful. Only about two-thirds are profitable, and the margins of profitability are generally lower than for TV. But here too there are individual examples of highly profitable operations. In any event, the expectation of making a profit is sufficiently strong that there are willing buyers for most stations that come on the market and numerous applications for new channels when those are available.

The primary source of income and of profit is the sale of time to advertisers for the broadcast of commercial messages. (A second source of profit may come from selling a station to a new owner. That can be very profitable, but it is a one-time gain.) *Profitability* can be simply stated as the ability to sell enough time to advertisers, at high enough rates, to have income greater than the costs of operation.

The amount of time a station will be able to sell, and the rates it can charge to advertisers, depends on a number of factors, but in the simplest terms we can say that advertising rates depend on the number of listeners or viewers who are attracted to the programming offered. At the one extreme would be a small-market radio station with a very small audience. This station can charge only a few dollars for each commercial aired because the size of the audience is so small. At the other extreme would be the more than half a million dollars charged for a 30-second spot in a Superbowl telecast. But many millions of viewers will view that spot—enough to make that price competitive with other announcements in other programs.

Consider the situations of two hypothetical radio stations. One station has recently changed its programming and has hit upon a very successful format. Audience sizes, as reported by an audience measurement firm, have increased substantially, and advertisers, recognizing a good buy for their advertising dollars, have bought up much of the available time. The managers of this station will raise the rates they charge for advertising time. By doing so they will increase income, and increased income coupled with constant cost equals increased profit.

In contrast, the second station is not doing so well. For some reason—tough competition, poor promotion, poor programming, or whatever—audiences have been declining, and the number of advertisers and amount of time they have been buying have also been declining. The management of this station may do several things. It may cut costs to maintain profitability on reduced income. It may modify the format in an attempt to recapture lost audiences, or change format altogether and try to draw a totally different audience group. It will almost certainly have to reduce the rates charged for advertising.

The point at which a station reaches a balance among competing stations (and with other media, which also compete for advertising revenue) is roughly determined by a ratio known as the *cost-per-thousand (CPM)*. That is the cost to the advertiser to broadcast a commercial message to 1,000 individuals.*

The first of our two hypothetical radio stations will take advantage of its success—increased thousands of audience—and raise its rates, which were too

---

* Since our example is of radio stations, the CPM is based on the estimated number of *individuals* exposed to the advertiser's message. In television, CPM is based on the number of *homes* in which that commercial is estimated to have been seen. Later we will refine this generalized statement to consider the targeting of commercials to specific audience groups. Advertisers will pay higher CPMs to reach specific groups that are important to the sale of particular products.

low on a CPM basis, to the market average. The second station, to remain competitive, must do the reverse. As a consequence of its dwindling audience, it must lower rates to a CPM that also is competitive in the market.

The analysis is further complicated by the fact that most stations will have different sizes of audiences at different times of the day or week. These differences will be reflected in the rates. Radio stations that show only small variations in audience size may have only a single rate, but many stations have three or four rates for different day and time periods. A television station may change its rates hourly, or for each different program in its schedule, charging different rates for even small variations in audience size.

In summary, in order to sell time for commercials in a program, and in the breaks between programs, a station must be able to show potential advertisers that their announcements will be heard or seen by an audience. The more popular the program, which is the same thing as saying the more people in the audience, the more the station can charge advertisers for the spots they purchase. When income exceeds the cost of operation the station is profitable, and that's the name of the game.

Sponsorship of Broadcast Programs

Up to this point we have used the term *originator* to refer to people and agencies involved in the preparation and distribution of messages. As we have noted, origination involves both the creative roles of writing, directing, producing, and so on, and the financial support for these creative efforts.

We want now to discuss the advertising-programming aspect of origination separately from the creative, and to do so we introduce a new term, or rather we redefine an old term that has become badly misused. We will use the word *sponsor* to refer to individuals and more commonly, organizations that have a financial interest in the content of broadcasting. Using this definition, stations, networks, and cable system operators are included as sponsors, because they are required to invest in some way in every program they distribute. Also included will be those agencies which supply public service announcements and, in some circumstances, even audiences themselves.

Someone must pay, in some form—money, time, effort—for every bit of content that appears. Who, then, are the agencies who make these payments? And why are they willing to incur the costs of programming? What do they hope to gain from having invested in programs and announcements?

Here are the more common situations, but as the industry continues to change additional types of sponsorship, and additional purposes, may appear.

The Advertiser as Sponsor

Broadcasters tend to use the terms *sponsor* and *advertiser* interchangeably. We are attempting, however, to differentiate between the two. We want to use *advertiser* in its limited, but correct, definition to refer to that situation when a person or firm purchases time for placement of an advertising message. The advertiser is, of course, a sponsor, but advertisers are by no means the only sponsors.

The advertiser's financial stake is, first, the cost of air time purchased for the presentation of a commercial. That purchase might be for only a single announcement, or for an extended campaign of spots on a number of different stations and programs, or the purchase of a block of time to present an entire program. In most cases, the advertiser also pays for the production (prerecording) of the commercial message (although often radio stations will produce simple commercials without additional charge). And the advertiser may pay an advertising agency to design the commercial and determine its best placement on the air. For a major advertiser, this combination of costs—air time, production, and research and media buying—can run to many millions of dollars a year.

The costs of advertising can be justified if the audience members who are exposed to that advertising can be persuaded to do what the advertiser wants done, which is usually the purchase of a product or service. So we might generalize that an advertiser's purpose is to increase, or maintain, sales. However, most commercials do not attempt to sell merchandise directly. Rather, they are intended to accomplish other, more indirect, purposes related to sales, such as getting the customer into the store, or reminding him or her of the brand name of the product to be purchased at the grocery. So we might more accurately say that broadcast advertising is intended to *help* in the sales of products or services. We'll have more on this point in later chapters.

Advertisers can have other purposes as well. For example, an electric power utility company that operates as a regulated monopoly in its community really does not have to sell its product. But it may wish to persuade its customers to modify their behavior in other ways. It may want to use its advertising to conduct a campaign on energy conservation, or it may want to improve its public image in the community so that when it next asks for a rate increase, its customers will be sympathetic to that request. This type of advertising is known in the industry as *institutional advertising*.

Yet another slightly different purpose for paid advertising is represented by political campaigns. Their purposes will be to obtain votes for a candidate, or for or against a political proposition.

These purposes all have a common thread. They intend to influence the behavior of the audience members who are exposed to the advertising messages— that is, to *persuade* in some fashion.

Program Advertising

Two quite different approaches to the placement of advertising have evolved within the industry. During the heyday of network radio in the 1930s and the 1940s, and the early period of television in the 1950s, the standard advertising practice was for a single advertiser to purchase a block of time from a local station or from a network for the presentation of a program, and to include within that program commercial messages advertising the product or products of that company. This practice is known as *program advertising*.

The implications of this practice are, first, that it is possible to integrate program and commercial content. The advertiser's name usually appears in the program's title, and the program talent frequently deliver the commercials. Second, when one advertiser purchases the advertising rights for an entire program, that advertiser may also expect to make decisions on program content and to control production. Under this pattern the client is all important. Audience attraction, although important in exposing the commercial messages to large numbers of people, is secondary to satisfying the client. In early radio, instances existed where a program stayed on the air even with a very small audience simply because the program's content satisfied the whims of its supporter, the client-advertiser.

On network television only a few program sponsors remain. One of them is Hallmark Cards, which still occasionally sponsors the "Hallmark Hall of Fame." But at the local level program sponsorship is common, particularly the sponsorship of religious programs. Overall the practice is returning to broadcasting, and full program sponsorship is now frequently found on advertiser-supporter cable channels. In a later chapter we will describe a program called "Celebrity Chefs," produced and sponsored by the Campbell Soup Company, and distributed through cable systems.

**Participation
Advertising**

When television took over from radio as the dominant medium of home entertainment, and as the cost of producing programs increased substantially in the 1960s, advertisers became very nervous about spending large sums to sponsor program series, some of which turned out to be failures. They moved away from program advertising and toward what is now the most common practice on both television and radio—*participation advertising*.

With participation advertising, programs are not designed by advertisers, but by the stations or networks themselves (or by independent producers who sell their programs to the stations or networks). These programs contain short, blank periods of time that can be sold to advertisers for the insertion of commercial messages. These holes in the program's structure are known as *availabilities*. Other availabilities may be sold during periods between programs. The announcements that appear in the availabilities are called *spots* or *participations*. If an availability is not sold to an advertiser, the station will place a public service announcement (PSA) or a promotional announcement in that location. Individual participations are most commonly 30 seconds or 1 minute in length, sometimes less, but usually participations are clustered so that the total time block available may be up to 2 or 3 minutes.

Under this system an advertiser has no direct connection with the program in which its ad appears; it has purchased only the right to participate—only the length of time necessary to run the announcement. The emphasis for the writers of a new program, for example, which will be sold on a participating basis therefore must be on making that program as attractive as possible to audiences. If the station (or syndicator or network) believes the program can be successful in drawing audiences the managers will place that program in the schedule. If the program draws audiences its availabilities can then be sold to participating advertisers. But if, after a trial run, the program does not draw an audience of some size, advertisers will not "buy in," and soon the series will be cancelled.

The writers of the commercials that appear in and adjacent to participating programs usually have no way of knowing which programs will surround their ads. They will write to attract and motivate a particular target audience group, but the placement of their ads will be made by others—advertising agency media buyers and station or network managers. Most times the target audience for the program—that is, the people attracted by its content—and the target audience for the commercial—that is, the people needed by the client in order to sell the product—will be the same, or close at least. But sometimes wild mismatches between program and advertiser target groups do occur.

Barter Advertising

One additional practice that has become quite common in recent years in both broadcast and cable is that of *barter,* also known as *barter syndication,* because it is also a form of program syndication. A barter program is made available to a station by an outside producer, with commercial messages already inserted in about half of the available spots, advertising the product(s) of the barter advertiser.

For example, one of the first and most familiar barter programs is ''Mutual of Omaha's Wild Kingdom.'' The insurance company, Mutual of Omaha, is the owner-producer of the program (although the program actually is produced for it by an independent production company). Mutual of Omaha's name is associated with the program as part of its title, and it has commercials totaling about 90 seconds that are built into the program package. When a station contracts to broadcast the series, it pays nothing to Mutual of Omaha to get the programs; they are free to the station. But the station also receives no advertising income from the insurance company. The built-in commercials are broadcast free by the station. That's the barter—program free to station in exchange for free advertising for the company. The station makes its profit, if any, by selling the remaining 90 seconds of availabilities to other clients.

Barter has become a very large part of the broadcasting industry in the past few years. Some independent UHF television stations are programmed nearly 50 percent of the time with barter shows, and barter is also common on advertiser-supported cable channels.

The Station or Network as Sponsor

Each commercial broadcasting station and each programming network has a financial investment in almost every program they broadcast. They have to pay, in some way, for that content, with only a few exceptions. One exception, just described, is full program sponsorship. In that case the advertiser pays a fee which covers both the costs of program production and the overhead charged by the station or network for its air-time.

Most of the time, however, the station or network must cover both the cost of production or other acquisition for each program as well as their general overhead—the costs of operating the transmitter, paying personnel, building rent, taxes, and all the other costs of doing business. In return, of course, the station or network expects to recover those costs and add a measure of profit as well, by selling participations in and adjacent to its participating programs.

As we noted earlier in this chapter, the larger the audience for a program, the more the station or network may be able to charge for the insertion of commercials. In most instances, then, the purpose of the commercial station or network can be easily described: It is attempting to attract as large an audience as possible for each program, so that availabilities can be sold for the highest price.*

There can be other purposes, however. One might be that of obtaining good-will in the community. The station can accomplish that by showing programs that receive critical acclaim and are recognized by community leaders as having a socially significant impact. The station management can use these programs to strengthen the image of the station in the community. And having a strong image may lead indirectly to increased sales and profit.

Yet another purpose for the station might be to meet legal obligations imposed by the Federal Communications Commission. Recent changes in FCC rules have relaxed many of the requirements formerly imposed on stations. However, it is unlikely that the commission will eliminate all expectations for public service programming.

Sustaining Programs

Some programs carried by commercial stations and networks do not contain advertising matter. These are called *sustaining programs*. There are several reasons why programs may be sustaining. First, the station may simply have been unsuccessful in obtaining participating advertisers. The program may be too new to have attracted an audience yet, and for the sales staff to have interested advertisers. Or the program may be in the wrong time slot to attract a sufficiently large audience to interest advertisers. Or the advertising rates and therefore the cost for reaching the audience may be too high, or some combination of these reasons.

A program may also be sustaining because it contains controversial material. Potential advertisers may be afraid that association with the program will result in negative publicity which would outweigh any positive exposure of their advertisement to an audience.

Finally, a program may be sustaining because the station or network feels that advertising would not be in keeping with the content of the program. Many public affairs programs are in this category, as are editorials, some commentary and cultural programs, and some religious programs.

Even for sustaining programs, the station's primary purpose usually is to attract the largest possible audience. Commercial stations and networks are generally reluctant to accept programs, either sustaining or commercial, that reach too small and narrow an audience, if for no other reason than that small audiences for one program will reduce the ratings for surrounding programs and for the overall schedule.

Public Broadcasting

Thus far we have been discussing the programming and advertising practices of commercial stations. Programming on public stations presents a different situation because of their different regulatory status. Unlike their commercial counterparts, public stations are by definition noncommercial and nonprofit. They may not

---

* We have used the terms "station" and/or "network" throughout this discussion with the understanding that this process operates in parallel fashion at the local level, where individual stations produce or purchase programming, and at the national level, where networks also produce or purchase programs that they then distribute to their affiliate stations.

accept revenue from advertisers, and are therefore forced to get the funds to cover their programming and operating costs from other sources.

Most of their income comes from various levels of government—national, state, and local—and from private and corporate donations, including the funds solicited from individuals during auctions and pledge drives on the air. Public stations are also permitted to accept *underwriting,* in which commercial firms and individuals donate funds to cover the costs (only costs, not profit) of producing or acquiring programs. In return, the public station is permitted to acknowledge the underwriting gift on the air, but not to broadcast direct advertising messages from the underwriter.

Since the underwriter cannot present direct advertising on behalf of a product, we must conclude that the purpose in underwriting a program on a public station is that of collecting a measure of goodwill and improving public attitudes toward the company. It might be only coincidental, but during the late 1970s, when gasoline prices shot up very rapidly and the major petroleum companies were subject to a good deal of negative publicity, these companies began to underwrite quite a few public television series. In fact, so many programs were being underwritten by oil companies that one humorist suggested that the Public Broadcast Service (PBS) be renamed the Petroleum Broadcast Service.

Managers of public stations, like their commercial counterparts, may also look to maximum audience size as a possible purpose for choosing particular programs to broadcast. However, most of the managers (and governing boards) of public stations believe that their primary purpose is to provide alternatives to commercial programming. These alternatives, which include presentations for a wide range of minority audience groups, and instructional, educational, and cultural programming, are likely to draw more specialized and smaller audiences than most commercial programs.

The Public Service Agency as Sponsor

Some programs and announcements are broadcast on behalf of public service agencies, organizations like the Red Cross, the Boy Scouts, the Blood Bank, the local Council of Churches, and so on. In these situations, the station broadcasts the message without any charge to the agency. The station pays the costs of the air time involved, and may absorb production costs as well. As with sustaining programs, the station's purpose is that of building goodwill in its community.

On other occasions the public service agency will produce an announcement, which it then delivers to the station for broadcast, or it will commit staff time and effort to the production of a program. The agency's purpose is similar to that of a commercial advertiser—to persuade audience members. That persuasion may take the form of an appeal for donations, or to encourage people to attend an event, or to support a cause in some other way. Public service organizations may also sponsor programs to inform or enlighten the public or to raise cultural standards, although these are not common purposes.

The Audience as Sponsor

Under the traditional system of broadcasting which has operated in the United States for the past fifty years, programs are brought to the audience "free of charge." There is no direct payment by the audience for the programming received. The audiences of commercial stations do, of course, pay for programming, but only indirectly, through purchases of products advertised. Most audience members are not even consciously aware of the fact that every time they buy soap, or a new car, or nearly any product, they are also paying for their radio and TV programming.

The practice of "free" broadcasting is being eroded, however, by various situations in which audiences pay directly for the privilege of obtaining programs they wish to have. Pay services can be distributed in several ways, the most common of which are the pay-TV channels on cable systems.

When the holder of a cable TV franchise in a community markets cable services to potential customers, the manager of that franchise will select from among all of the available services those which he or she believes will be the most attractive to subscribers. These programming services (also called channels) will then be arranged in various packages for the subscribers. Subscribers will first be offered a *basic service,* which will contain mostly off-the-air, along with local origination channels, and possibly some specialty channels such as education or Spanish-language programming. National services which are in part advertiser supported, such as the Cable News Network, may be included in this basic service, or they may be placed as part of a second-level offering, known as a second *tier,* available for an additional monthly fee.

Premium-pay channels, which do not contain advertising, like Home Box Office, make their income and profit on fees they charge to each cable system operator that carries their channel, so much per subscriber per month. Almost universally these fees are passed along by the operators to subscribers by placing access to these services in upper tiers, for which additional subscription fees must be paid.

In addition to channels which are paid for through monthly subscription, there is a trend toward cable marketing on a pay-per-view basis. Under this approach, subscribers pay only for individual programs they want to watch.

Yet another form of direct payment for programming takes place whenever you rent a movie or other program from your neighborhood video store. While that's not a broadcasting function as such, this form of audience involvement with programming has had a marked impact on the sizes of audiences available to watch traditional broadcast offerings.

In these cases, the audience members are, in a very real sense, the sponsors, since they pay directly to receive programming they want. And if, for example, a substantial number of people were to drop their subscriptions to Home Box Office, the producers and writers employed by that channel would quickly react to change its programming.

Conclusion

There are several different reasons why organizations may be willing to incur costs for production and transmission to an audience of radio, television, or other electronic messages. There is a similarity among these purposes: All intend to influence the program's audience in some way.

We can summarize the topics covered by phrasing them in the form of questions. These are the first questions in a longer series we will consider in the next two chapters. They tie together the concepts of origination, purpose, content, and reception. They are questions writers need to be able to answer in order to write effective copy.

1. Who is the sponsor (or are the sponsors) for the particular program or announcement?

2. What is (are) the sponsor's purpose(s) in presenting this program or announcement?

In the next chapter we will consider answers to the next question in the series: What audience group or groups must the sponsor reach in order to accomplish that purpose? And in Chapter 10 we will consider the fourth question in the series: What persuasive appeals would be most effective in convincing the members of that target audience to do what is wanted?

We will apply the first two questions to three typical situations:

● An independent TV station has purchased rights to the "Barney Miller" syndicated series and decides to air the programs at 11 P.M. Monday through Friday. Although a number of participations probably will be sold in the program, the advertisers will not be the sponsors. The station is the sponsor; it made the commitment to buy the series and the decision where to place it in the schedule. The station's purpose is obviously to draw an audience for that series so it can sell participations.

● A local radio station, in conjunction with a little theater group, agrees to air a series of 15-minute programs that will feature scenes from dramatic works. Some will be from plays the group will present during the coming season; others will just be good, strong dramatic material. There will be no commercial advertising involved. Both the station and the theater group may be considered as sponsors; both have made substantial commitments to the effort. The station's purpose is goodwill. The theater group's purpose may be partly goodwill, but it probably hopes to attract audiences to productions with this promotion.

● The final example involves the purchase of an entire program by a single advertiser. This is program sponsorship. The program is the play-by-play broadcast of a local high school basketball championship game. The sponsor is a local pizza restaurant. Here advertiser and sponsor are the same. The purpose will be to increase sales in the restaurant, and possibly gather some goodwill in the community that could indirectly increase sales as well.

We will return to these questions and these examples after we look in more detail at the role which audiences play in the broadcast process.

Exercise

1. View an assortment of television programs at different times and days and on different stations to get a variety of program types and sponsorships. For each program, attempt to determine:

    a. Who was the sponsor for the program?

    b. What seems to be the sponsor's purpose?

c. How did you arrive at the answers for (a) and (b)?

Remember, the "creative" originator-producer is not necessarily the same as the sponsor. Remember too that in programs with participating advertising, which are the ones you will find most frequently, the advertisers are *not* the sponsors. Just from viewing, without any additional information it is not always easy to make these judgments accurately, but the practice is valuable even if you are not correct in every instance. (This exercise may also be done with radio, but not as much variety exists in sponsorship patterns on most radio stations.)

Key Terms and Concepts

advertisers
availabilities
barter
basic cable service
CPM
originator
participation advertising

premium-pay cable service
program advertising
public broadcasting
sponsor
sustaining program
tiering
underwriting

Chapter 9

Audiences and Their Expectations

In two chapters thus far we have discussed aspects of the relationship between sponsors, the messages they sponsor, and the audiences who are the recipients of those messages. Obviously, we feel it is important that you understand the implications of the relationship.

Our perspective has been primarily that of the sponsor. In this chapter we will consider the sponsor-program-audience relationship from a different perspective—from the audience's point of view. Why do people choose television or radio in preference to other activities available to them, and how do they choose among competing offerings?

Remember, television viewing and radio listening are usually free-choice activities. Seldom are audience members forced to spend their time viewing or listening. Audiences must want to tune to programs. The writer who hopes to attract and to hold audience attention must give audiences what they want.

The two main considerations in this chapter are target audiences and audience gratifications. But before presenting those, there are some additional concepts and definitions with which you should be familiar.

Potential, Available, and Actual Audiences

These three concepts of audience—potential, available, and actual—help define the size, the composition, and the behavior of television and radio audiences.

Potential Audience

For all practical purposes, the total population of the country may be considered to be the potential audience for American broadcasting. Only 1 to 2 percent of the people do not have access to receiving sets, but that group is so small in absolute terms as to be insignificant.

On the other hand, the potential audience for each individual station—that is, the audience which is able to pick up that station's signal—is different from that of every other station. Similarly, the potential audiences for each broadcast program are different. Here are just a few examples of these widespread differences:

- In general, stations with coverage patterns covering a large area will have a greater potential audience than stations which are more restricted. Wide variations exist in the coverage area for radio stations, especially AM. Some AM stations operate with as few as 500 watts of power and reach out only a few miles from their transmitters. Others, which broadcast with maximum power (50,000 watts), can cover large regions, especially at night, when their skywaves are reflected off the ionosphere and are received hundreds of miles away. FM stations, on the other hand, are limited to line of sight between the transmitter and receivers, and that usually restricts these stations to a roughly circular coverage area of between 20 and 60 miles from the transmitter—depending upon the height of the antenna. Terrain features, such as mountain ranges and even large buildings in the path of the signal, also affect FM coverage.

   Television signals, like FM radio, are also line of sight between transmitter and receivers, and antenna height is the major factor in television coverage. Both propagation factors such as power and frequency, and geography, give each station a different coverage pattern, and thus at least a slightly different potential audience from every other station.

- Stations in large metropolitan areas have a much larger potential audience than stations in rural areas, even if their facilities are identical. There are simply more people within reach of the signal. The difference is recognized in the higher charges for advertising in metropolitan areas, the larger budget and larger staffs for most such stations, the generally larger margins of profit, and the higher prices paid to purchase urban stations.

- For cable services the concept of potential audience involves several levels of concern. First, only those homes that are passed by the cable system can be counted as potential audience for that system. Some communities are still without cable service; in others only the more densely populated, or more affluent, areas are wired.

   Then, the management of the system will decide which services to offer to subscribers. Those choices will be made based partly on the number of channels available on the system. Older systems tend to have fewer channels, thereby limiting the number of services that can be offered.

   Finally, each subscriber will decide which services (beyond the basic tier) he or she wishes to subscribe to and pay for. Only when a service is actually available at the TV set can that home legitimately be counted as part of the potential audience for that service.

- As with cable services, the potential audience for a network distributed or syndicated program series depends on the number of stations that choose to offer it. Sometimes network affiliates choose not to air a controversial network offering, thereby reducing its potential audience. A large audience cannot be attracted to a program, no matter how well it is written or how important it may be, if it is not widely offered in the first place.

Available and Actual Audiences

These audience groupings are smaller groups within the potential audience. The available audience are those who have ready access to the medium (TV or radio) at any particular time. The actual audience is, or course, those who are in fact listening or watching. While the potential audience is static, not changing significantly in size or composition, both the available and the actual audiences are dynamic. They change with time. Again, a few examples are sufficient to explain:

- *Prime-time* television hours are those evening hours when the largest numbers of people are available to watch television, and in which the largest number do watch. The term prime time indicates just that. These are the most valuable hours. The most expensive programs are placed in this time period, and the highest rates are charged for advertising.

- Radio has similar prime-time periods, known as *drive time,* when the largest number of people are in automobiles driving to or from work, and therefore somewhat of a captive audience for radio. At least that's true in most metropolitan areas. Drive time doesn't have much meaning in a rural community, where there is no commuter traffic.

- Weekend programming reflects the fact that most men are not available during the day on weekdays. When they are home on the weekend, and available, they can be pulled into the actual audience with programs they find attractive, as, for example, sports programs. Before television the baseball leagues used to schedule World Series games for daytime on weekdays. Now all World Series games are scheduled on weekends or at night, when more men, the group most interested, are available to watch.

- Programs aimed at children must be scheduled when they are available, not when they are at school. And preferably not when there is heavy competition from other members of the family for access to the TV set. Children's programming, therefore, shows up in the later afternoons on weekdays and early morning on weekends.

- In the summertime, TV programming reflects the fact that the available audiences are smaller. Many people have other activities—vacations, weekends at the beach or mountains, long evenings at the park—which take them out of the available, and thus also out of the actual, audience. Programming therefore is largely reruns or summer replacement series that are inexpensive to produce.

Remember too that the total actual audience in a market must be divided among all the stations in that market. There are millions of people in the potential audience in Los Angeles, for instance, but by the time the actual audience at any given hour is divided among a dozen or so television stations, 50 to 70 radio stations, plus cable, subscription TV, and home VCRs, the actual audience for any one individual station may be quite small. Nevertheless, station owners, cable operators, and other entrepreneurs look at the potential audience in that market and are convinced they can capture at least their fair share of that potential.

Target Audiences

Target audiences are those groups which are identified *by the sponsor* of either a program or announcement as being the most important *in order to accomplish that sponsor's purpose.*

In the early years of broadcasting, programmers could schedule almost any program at any time and be assured of sufficient audience to satisfy commercial demands. Now that the novelty of radio and television have worn off, and especially with the tremendous increase in the number of channels of programming and other media available to individuals, it has become very important for advertisers and programmers alike to identify target audiences carefully.

Most of the time, target audiences are described in *demographic* terms—by age, sex, race, education, income, place of residence, or other characteristics. Certain demographic groups will watch or listen to certain types of programs more than will others, or they will be the primary buyers of certain types of products. Occasionally, however, target audience groups are better described using nondemographic, behavior-oriented "life-style" characteristics.* The distinguishing characteristics of the potential buyers for small sailboats, for instance, might be more accurately set forth in life style terms—amount of leisure time, discretionary income, love of adventure—rather than in the more conventional demographic indicators.

We will present a few examples here in order to show the process used in defining target audiences. These are, however, generalized examples. In practice, both broadcasters and advertisers spend considerable sums on detailed focused research aimed at identifying target groups.

Target Audiences for Products

Advertisers were the first to recognize the importance of aiming messages at special groups. They aim for those target groups that are either most likely to purchase the product or service, or who will purchase the largest quantities of it.

Washing Detergents

The makers of washing detergents want their commercials to be seen by and to influence the purchases of those people who buy the largest amounts of detergent. Who are they? Women, primarily between the ages of 20 and 35, who have families that include small children (who get dirty). You might go so far as to say those women who are least likely to send out their laundry. But those three demographic indicators—sex, age, and family size—are the most important.

To be sure, other groups of people also buy washing detergents—single people, older people, and so on—but they are likely to purchase smaller amounts as a group. The primary target is the group described, and the advertiser who wants to be successful in marketing a detergent must sell a large portion of it to that target. Secondary campaigns directed at smaller target groups can also be conducted if the budget permits.

Auto Stereo

Similarly, let us assume that the makers of an aftermarket stereo radio/tape player for automobiles are preparing to introduce a new model that will sell for approximately $200. What group forms the largest potential buying group for this product? If there is any doubt, the manufacturer could—and very well might—

---

* Some years ago, the term *psychographics* was used to label this method of describing audiences and to contrast with demographics, but that term is no longer much used. *Life style* is now more common.

conduct a preliminary study on potential target audiences before spending the money for a major advertising campaign. But a good guess for this product would be young men between the ages, say, of 17 and 30 who have enough money saved or borrowed to make this fairly significant purchase, who have a car, and who like music.

Next, the advertiser and media buyer will have to consider how best to reach this target group—that is, they will have to find a program targeted for the same group. Marketing research will show them that these young men are heavy listeners of radio, and even more specifically of certain rock music radio formats. From those data, the writer can develop a successful ad campaign for the client.

Target Audiences for Programs

As we have just seen, program producers also design programs, or whole formats, for specific audiences. The radio station with the rock format chose that programming specifically to draw the young male audience. Here are three more examples, these from television, of programs with specific targets.

Meet the Press

The audience for this NBC network series is determined by the content and the style of the program. The content is purposely limited to important issues in politics, economics, and foreign affairs. The style is a straightforward interview with an expert in the subject matter. The target audience is men and women who have a serious interest in those topics, either as individuals or as managers and owners of businesses that might be affected. The target audience, then, might be described as both men and women with above-average education and income, therefore somewhat older, say 30 to 50 or even older. Equally important as the demographic description is the recognition that the audience is interested in the content and has the ability to follow the usually quite abstract interviews.

Star Trek

Producers and programmers do not always accurately assess the target audiences for their programs in advance of presentation. One example is "Star Trek." It was originally broadcast by the network in a 10 P.M. time slot, with only reasonable success in drawing the adult audience available at that hour. After the network run, the program was released into syndication, where it has had phenomenal success in attracting young teen and preteen audiences in late afternoon time slots. What has turned out to be a primary audience for that series is not the same group originally targeted.

Cheers

For our final example, we'll look at a situation comedy broadcast by a network in prime time. It could be "Cheers," but if that series is no longer around, there undoubtedly will be something similar.

The term *prime time,* describing the evening time period in which these programs are shown, is itself an indicator of the nature of the target audience. The reason the time period is designated "prime" is because the largest and most diverse audience group possible is available to watch television during those hours. And the producers of this comedy series want to capture as much of that very large and demographically diverse group as possible.

For the writer, the requirement to reach a large and diverse audience means that the level of language, the concepts of the plot, and the structure of the program must be understood by many different types of people—young and old, educated and uneducated. Under these circumstances, the appropriate writing style is to use simple language, plots, and characterization in order to ensure clarity and understanding for as many viewers as possible.

Please understand, however, that although prime-time network programs still are the most important group of programs from an economic standpoint, they represent a comparatively small portion of all programming. In general, the broadcasting industry is moving away from such broad-based programming and toward increased specificity in content and in audiences.

The trend toward specificity, or *narrow-casting* as it is called, can be seen in public broadcasting, in radio, and in cable. Public radio and television stations produce and broadcast a wide selection of programs intended for different minority audiences. Most commercial radio stations air a distinctive format of talk or music intended to reach a narrow segment of the total listening audience. As cable television and other new technologies of communication, satellite transmission, videotape, and so on expand throughout the country, the choices for audiences are becoming greater. Greater choice leads to more specific programming for increasingly narrow target groups. The writer who has a clear understanding of the target audience for whom a script is to be written, and of why that target has been chosen, is then in a position to make decisions on how to influence that audience's behavior.

Quantitative and Qualitative Measurement

The entire economic structure of commercial broadcasting depends on quantitative audience measurement. Stations and networks set their advertising rates and make programming decisions based on the size and composition of their audiences as estimated by the rating surveys taken by measurement companies.

The data obtained from these surveys are voluminous, and are organized and analyzed in many ways. For each market and for each station in the market, information on the size and demographic composition of audiences is available. Trends can be shown by following similar data over the time span of several surveys. The viewing (or listening) habits of any particular age or sex group can be identified. The demographic breakdown of the audience attracted to a program, or to all programs of a particular type, can be charted and compared over time or in various sections of the country.

Individual broadcast stations and networks collect this information for their own sales and programming purposes. A writer working for a station, network, or ad agency would have access to these data and should use them in designing programs and announcements to reach audiences of known composition.

Occasionally large collections of quantitative data are analyzed by independent researchers, and the results of these studies are generalized to provide broad conclusions on audience behavior. One such study, published under the

PORTIONS OF THE FOLLOWING PROGRAM MAY OFFEND SOME INTELLECTUALS, BUT THE REST OF YOU FOLKS ARE IN FOR A REAL TREAT!

Figure 9.1
Source: Reproduced by permission of NEA Newspaper Syndicate.

title *Television and Human Behavior,* has provided numerous insights into program-audience relationships.

Children watch about the same amount of television per week as adults, although at different times. Children from 2 to 5 years watch somewhat more than those 6 to 11 years old. . . .

Teenagers watch the fewest hours of television . . . almost 7 hours less than average.

Men from 18 to 49 watch less television than the other adult groups. . . .

Men over 50 years old watch more then men under so . . . about 7 hours more than younger men.

Women from 18 to 49 watch more hours than men the same age. These younger adult women viewed almost 7 hours per week more than younger adult men. They are above the overall average for individual viewing, with over 31 hours a week.

Women over 50 watch far more television than any of the other groups . . . nearly 35 hours per week [which] is 3.4 hours a week more than younger adult women and 3 hours a week more than men over 50.

Viewing declines between elementary school and high school, rises in adulthood, and rises again quite markedly after age 50, particularly for men. . . . Both men and women over 50 watched several hours a week more than younger adults.

Viewing patterns, arranged by program types, showed the following characteristics:

GENERAL DRAMA. General drama programs have higher ratings among women—both younger and older—than among men. The ratings between younger men and older men are about the same.

SUSPENSE AND MYSTERY. Suspense and mystery dramas conform more closely to the general viewing patterns. Older adults watch slightly more than younger adults.

SITUATION COMEDY AND VARIETY. Females are more frequent viewers than males; however, the average rating for situation comedies among older adults is more than 10 percent higher than it is among younger adults, and for variety programs more than 30 percent higher.

FEATURE FILMS. Feature films have the highest rating among younger adults of any category of prime-time programs and are the only category that has higher ratings among younger than among older adults. The journalist Les Brown, in *Television: The Business Behind the Box* (1971), astutely notes that network programmers are not in the business of selling products to viewers. Their business is the selling of viewers to advertisers. Feature films have become prominent on television because their ratings profile indicates that they are the best vehicle for reaching that principal consumer population—younger adults of both sexes. For this purpose, variety programs are least attractive. General drama, situation comedy and suspense and mystery all attract substantial portions of the younger adult audience, but in each case the rating is lower than for feature films and markedly so for men.

EVENING NEWS. Commercials for pills, tonics, and denture adhesives dominate the advertising for network evening news. Where are the soft drink and sporty car ads? [The answer is that] although network evening news achieves respectable "household" ratings . . . only about 7 percent of younger adults view the average minute, compared to a figure more than double that for older adults. In fact, ratings among older adults are about the same for the average minute of the evening news as they are for the various prime-time program types.

SOAP OPERAS. It is not surprising to find that daytime viewing of soap operas and quiz and game shows is highest among women. Younger and older women have about the same likelihood of watching soap operas while the older women are much more likely to be interested in the daytime quiz and game programs. . . .

Differences between younger and older adults in the early evening period can be better understood in light of the finding that older viewers are far more likely to watch evening news programs. Viewing by more older than younger adults in early prime time and a narrower difference in late prime time is associated with the scheduling of situation comedies and variety programs earlier than suspense and mystery dramas and feature films. Similarly, the greater proportion viewing early in the day and the earlier peak in viewing among older women is associated with the generally earlier scheduling of game shows than soap operas, which draw a much larger proportion of younger women.

PREFERENCES. The various segments obviously have different preferences. Children are most likely to watch the children's weekend schedule. However, the proportions of 2 to 11 year olds watching situation comedies, general drama, and variety programs are also relatively high. Children are less likely to be watching suspense and mystery programs, feature films, news, and sports. . . .

Children do a considerable amount of viewing between the end of school and the start of the evening news. During this period they are watching locally originated materials primarily—situation comedy and action drama and cartoon reruns.

Among the program types for which we have data, the trend seems to be a leveling of children's ratings across program types. Children's viewing of situation comedy is still the highest rated among prime-time programs, with about 13 percent of the potential audience viewing. General drama and variety programs are second with about 11 percent.

Teenagers have highest prime-time rating figures for situation comedy and feature films and lowest viewing for the average minute for variety programs, with the other three types of programs falling between these.

Younger women are more likely to be watching feature films and dramas than variety programs. Older women are most frequently found watching situation comedies and dramas. They are also frequent viewers of feature films, evening news, and suspense and mystery. Variety programs attract the lowest prime-time proportion of women 50 and over.

Feature films, suspense and mystery programs, and sports are seen by a higher proportion of younger men than any other types of program. There has been an increase in younger male audience for feature films. Sports and suspense and mystery viewing have remained about the same. Highest ratings for older men are for feature films; then come situation comedy, suspense and mystery, evening news, weekend sports, and general drama. Lowest ratings are for variety programs.[1]

Quantitative information is critical to programmers and sales managers, and it can be helpful to writers in knowing what the general relationships are between certain types of programs and audiences. But it doesn't help writers very much with the specific task of preparing a script for a new dramatic series, or a public affairs program, or in developing any kind of a new program idea, because it doesn't give any indications of why individuals choose television or radio in general or why they choose particular programs and stations in preference to others.

To get that information, we turn to qualitative research, and specifically to that branch of qualitative research known as *uses and gratifications* (or, often, just *gratification*) studies. Communication researchers in this field attempt to learn how people meet their basic psychological needs through use of media and what gratifications they derive from those uses.

Audience Gratifications

Although gratification studies have been conducted for twenty years or more, until recently their conclusions were too scattered to have much impact on broadcasters. That situation seems now to be changing. The accumulated data from many studies do begin to show patterns in the uses audiences make of media. And at least one major commercial company has been formed to conduct gratification research for clients in the industry. That company, Television Audience Assessment, rates programs on their entertainment appeal and their intellectual and emotional stimulation. The company president, Elizabeth Roberts, describes the need for qualitative evaluation of programs:

> Shows that do well in both appeal and impact are likely to be good buys for advertisers. . . . We consistently found that just knowing the size of an audience didn't necessarily say anything about the appeal or impact of a show. . . . With an increasing multitude of channels . . . with remote control devices making channel-switching so easy . . . television programmers and advertisers want to know if they indeed are reaching their intended audiences.[2]

One of the leading researchers on audience gratifications is Professor Jay G. Blumler, currently at the University of Maryland. He has identified three major orientations audiences take toward program content:

First of all a *cognitive* orientation, whereby the audience member looks primarily for information about some feature of society and the wider world around him—as in "surveillance" sought from the news, information about party policies and other issues of the day from election broadcasts, or perhaps "reality exploration" as a use of many fictional series and serials scheduled on television and radio.

Second, people want *diversion* of many kinds, including, for example, the relief from boredom and constraints of daily routines derived from chat shows, music, comedy, and other forms of light entertainment, as well as the excitement generated by adventure serials, quizzes, sports and competitive games, and even the horse-race appeal of following an election campaign.

Third, uses and gratifications studies have often highlighted a separate *personal identity* function, standing for ways of using media materials to give added salience to something important in the audience member's own life or situation.[3]

By analyzing the conclusions of a number of qualitative studies, and by modifying some previously devised lists, we have arrived at a list containing eleven categories of gratification. It is our belief that the presence in a program of any of these characteristics represents an attraction, at least to some audience groups. A popular program might have several gratifications, each with moderate attraction strength for its target audience, or it might have only one or two gratifications, but ones that are very strong in attracting that group. These categories are:

1. *Tension.* The development of unresolved issues leading to a climax; various forms of conflict, both mental and physical.

2. *Action.* The presence of physical action and movement, including violence.

3. *Sex appeal.* Physical attractiveness; sexually suggestive situations and dialogue, plots using love as a theme; music, especially with love or sex in the lyrics.

4. *Comedy.* Humor, in a range of categories from very broad to sophisticated.

5. *Information.* The need or usefulness of knowing.

6. *Importance.* The relevance of information; the presence of authority, or of important personalities with recognized names; "bigness."

7. *Value.* Worthwhileness; ethical or moral values presented in program content and situations.

8. *Personalism.* The extent to which the audience can identify with characters, events, situations; includes empathy, sympathy, and nostalgia.

9. *Curiosity.* Our interest in other human beings particularly, but also curiosity about places, events, and so on.

10. *Realism.* The plausibility, believability, and reality of characters or situations.

11. *Novelty.* The presence of unusual characters, situations, presentations; freshness.

The sequence into which these gratifications have been organized is a reflection of the three basic audience orientations identified by Blumler. The first four—tension, action, sex appeal, and comedy—are most strongly found in programs that provide diversion for audiences. Information, importance, and value cluster together readily; programs in which they are found satisfy the cognitive orientation. Personalism, curiosity, and realism are related to the personal identity orientation, or at least more strongly related there than to the other orientations, in our view.

We make no claim that these are discrete categories. To the contrary, items on this list interact to a considerable degree. Some of these gratifications frequently cluster together and reinforce one another. You should also be aware of these further cautions.

1. Don't become bound to the labels given these categories. Each is identified by a single word or phrase with which we have tried to express the essential nature of the appeal to audiences, but each gratification can be presented in a variety of ways and in most cases is actually a cluster of related behaviors.

2. Please understand that the concept of gratifications is separate from that of content or program types. Quantitative studies, such as those referred to earlier in this chapter, show very easily the relationships between audiences and content (for example, females watch situation comedies more than males). But in examining gratifications, we are attempting to find factors that cut across program types, and that may also separate popular from less popular programs within the same type.

3. The list may not be complete. As qualitative research continues, different factors emerge from studies which use different methodologies, different audiences, and different content. Future research may discover new categories of gratifications. But based on presently known findings, this list, we believe, provides a reasonable explanation of the media choices audiences make.

4. You will also recognize some similarities between this list and the list of persuasive appeals presented in the next chapter. Sex appeal, for example, appears on both lists. There is a similarity in that both approaches deal with the relationships between content and audiences. However, it is important for you to understand that two quite different perspectives are involved. Persuasive appeals are used by sponsors to influence audiences, to motivate and direct their behavior. Gratifications, on the other hand, are descriptions of the results of freely made selections from among choices offered to audiences.

5. There is also a relationship between program structure and gratifications. We believe that an individual's choice to tune to a particular program can be explained primarily by the gratifications he or she will receive, but a well-structured program will support those gratifications, whereas a poorly structured program will work against audience enjoyment. A program structured to provide above-average variety and fast pace will also be perceived as having tension and action, for example.

Tension

The dictionary definitions of *tension* use such terms as mental or emotional strain, anxiety, suspense, and excitement. Another description would be "uncertainty about the outcome."

In dramatic programs, tension is present in the uncertainty over how the plot or plots are to be resolved. The well-written play is structured to provide climax, the heightening of uncertainty as the play progresses, until the final resolution at the end of the drama. Subsidiary climaxes are also provided at the end of each act, and in continuing series programs such as soap operas, a climax of uncertainty is reached at the end of each episode and not resolved until the following episode. We have discussed climax as a component of program structure; tension is highly related.

Danger

One very powerful form of tension is found in physical danger. In dramatic thriller programs such as westerns, police or detective programs, or science fiction dramas, the uncertainty may be over the life or physical safety of the hero or some other characters, who may be in danger of being killed or of suffering some other terrible fate at the hands of a villain, or by the forces of nature—wild animals, a sudden blizzard.

A less physical but still very powerful form of danger is the fear of loss— loss of a job, loss of one's reputation, loss of a marriage, or loss of a girl or boy friend. Love plots are rooted in the uncertainty of the outcome, or at least uncertainty as to *how* the outcome will be resolved. Viewers of television soap operas will certainly recognize these forms of tension as prime appeals in those programs.

Danger can be present in nondramatic programs as well—for example, in adventure documentaries such as mountain climbing expeditions, and even in news broadcasts, as in the live, on-the-spot coverage of a hostage situation.

Problem-Solving Tension

In dramatic programs this may involve "battles with one's conscience," in which the hero or heroine is forced to make an uncomfortable decision—either way he or she decides will hurt someone he or she loves, or force an unpleasant outcome.

This form of tension also exists in game programs and quiz shows. Audiences are attracted at least in part because of their interest in finding out who will "win" the game. The gratification is further heightened if the program is structured so that the audience can play along. The tension is no longer just vicarious observation of the contest; now it is real. "Can I win the game before the on-screen contestant does, or before the solution is announced?"

Recall the short-lived dramatic series "Ellery Queen," in which at a point most of the way through the program Ellery turned directly to the viewing audience, announced that he had sufficient clues to solve the crime, that the same clues had been presented to the viewers, and could they identify the criminal? Although this program was unique in making its statement directly to the audience, many programs provide indirect invitations to audiences to solve the problems presented on the screen. By so doing the audience replaces tension with personal involvement, which is a different gratification, with strength for different audiences.

Other Tensions

A panel discussion program in which the participants hold different, conflicting points of view provides tension through the conflict of ideas. Individuals in the audience will be interested in knowing which opinion will prevail: Will one participant be able to convince others to change or modify their opinions? Audience members can also test their own opinions against those held by the panel.

Uncertainty over the outcome is also one of the strongest gratifications for audiences of athletic contests. In most such broadcasts, uncertainty over which participant will win holds the audience to the end of the contest. But whenever the contest becomes lopsided, when one contestant is sufficiently far ahead that the outcome is no longer in doubt, tension is removed and the size of the watching audience declines sharply. Audience members find other programs to watch or other things to do.

By using a variety of examples to describe various forms of tension, we have tried to suggest that this gratification is present in many types of programs. It seems, also, that it is a gratification which can have strength for all types of audience groups—that it is not strongly differentiated by sex, or age, or other demographic characteristics. Quite probably tension is heightened by its interaction with realism (discussed separately below)—that is, the more realistically presented the program, the stronger will be the tension perceived by the viewer.

However, it seems to be possible to have too much tension and realism in a program. Probably you have watched programs in which the tension was so intense, in which you feared for the hero or heroine so much, that you were forced to leave the room until the scene was resolved. Even though audiences know intellectually that what they are watching is not real, the emotional tension can become so great that many people do have to remove themselves from the program until that tension is released.

The key to this gratification is that whatever the type of program or situation, if there is uncertainty, then there is tension, and for many audience groups at least, a positive attraction.

Action

This gratification can be most quickly and easily described as a sense of movement or activity. Adventure programs are frequently listed in program logs as "action-adventure." Along with the uncertainty of the outcome, there is a great deal of movement—automobile chases, fights between cowboys and Indians, between police and criminals, between space warriors and robots, and so on.

Action can also be seen in variety programs in the movement of individual dancers or dance troupes on a stage; in news and documentary programs that report "real life" activities involving movement, and in game shows in which the contestants are involved with stunts.

The different types of action present in different types of athletic contests provide a clue to the strength of this gratification for different audiences. "Contact" sports, such as football, boxing, and ice hockey, attract a different type of audience from noncontact sports such as tennis, baseball, and golf. The difference does not seem to be team or nonteam sports, but solely the amount of physical contact among the participants, which we will consider to be a form of action.

To some extent, the amount of action, or movement, that can be included in a program is a function of the budget and the production approach. Action-adventure programs are filmed or taped on location, where a large variety of different settings can be used. This variety of backgrounds in itself contributes to the feeling of movement in the program, in addition to the actual movement that takes place. In contrast, situation comedies are filmed or taped in a studio, frequently in front of a live audience. These programs must be contained within a few static sets. There is little opportunity for movement or action other than characters entering or leaving the scene. Consequently, action is minimal in such programs.

Action can be a gratification on radio as well as television; there it is the description or suggestion of movement in actors' lines or in narration which provides the appeal, as in the play-by-play account of a football game, for example.

Many programs—all types of adventure programs, both dramatic and documentary, and sporting events are examples—present both tension and action. But some programs present tension without much action—soap operas, for example—and other programs present action, or movement, without the necessary accompaniment of tension. We've seen an example in the athletic contest when the outcome is no longer in doubt. Tension is reduced, although not necessarily removed, but the same level of action continues until the game is over.

The only discernible relationship between this gratification and audience groups is a stronger positive attraction of men than women to physical activity. This tendency may be the result of conditioning and stereotyping—"Boys can climb trees, but girls can't"—but whatever its antecedents, it is an identifiable difference. The difference appears in early childhood. Boys watch action cartoons more frequently than girls. Action stays strong through early and middle adulthood, then falls off somewhat in older age, but remains stronger for men than for women throughout life.

The difference in the strength of gratification of the different types of sporting events—contact vs. noncontact sports—is at least in part due to other categories of gratification, but to the extent that there are differences in the type of action, it seems that contact sports appeal more strongly to lower education and income groups, and that noncontact sports have greater appeal for a more educated, higher income audience—again primarily men in both cases.

There may be an opposite pole to this gratification—quiet and calm. Certainly many programs do not contain action to any important degree, but whether the lack of action represents also a lack of gratification, or whether calm is in itself a positive gratification to some audience groups, there is no research to determine.

Sex Appeal   This gratification should be familiar, and recognized, in one form or another by practically everyone except small children. It is presented in radio and television programs in a variety of ways, of which these are a few examples.

Physical   The most obvious manifestation is the presence of "sexy" or physically attractive
Attractiveness   people on programs. The attribute does not have to be limited to physical features, however. Sex appeal may also be found in the personality of a performer who is not necessarily physically handsome. The important consideration is the degree of attractiveness and/or warmth of personality the person possesses.

Note also that sex appeal is not just a visual characteristic. It may be present in a person's voice, which if it is warm, pleasant, friendly, and inviting, will contribute to the appeal.

The gratification is strong for both sexes; the individual providing the appeal may be either male or female. For every "Charlie's Angels," there's also a "Magnum, P.I."

Blatantly obvious use of physical sex appeal, such as the costumes worn by female performers on "Battle of the Network Stars" or on "Dukes of Hazzard," have led to strong criticism from feminist and religious groups and a consequent toning down of the more flagrant uses, or abuses, of this gratification at the network level. But costumes displaying skin (or muscle) continue to be a mainstay on some programs and commercials, and the success of cable channels showing R- and even X-rated films indicates that this is indeed a powerful attraction.

It's interesting to note the rationale used by the producers of sex appeal productions. A considerable group of "women warrior" shows have appeared in recent years, including "Wonder Woman" (on TV) and *Beastmaker, She, Conan the Barbarian, Hundra* and others in movie theaters. The producers of these fantasy adventures have justified the roles played by their scantily clad heroines as having appeals to both sexes. The visual attractiveness to men, they argue, is balanced by the "take charge" attitude of the heroines, who appeal to female viewers by their ability to keep male marauders at sword's distance.[4]

Love Stories

Here we have the programs which dramatize "boy-meets-girl" situations, the love triangles common in soap-opera-type programs, and other romantic plots. Love stories are most commonly found in dramatic programs, but they can be found in other types of programs, such as game shows—a contestant is asked to tell how she first became acquainted with her husband, or he is asked to tell how she proposed.

Talking about Sex

Included in this category are the sexually based conversations on "The Dating Game" and "The Love Connection" and the whole genre of radio call-in programs involving discussion of sexual attitudes and problems and the making of dates that fostered the name of "topless radio."

Music as Sex Appeal

Many popular music selections, both current and older standards, have vocals that express love or deal with unrequited love. Even if the music is presented without vocals, listeners will fill in the lyrics in their own minds if they are familiar with the song. Old familiar music having a love theme has strong sex appeal value (along with nostalgia) for audiences of the age group who were in high school or college and "falling in love" at the time when the music was first popular. Some radio stations draw large audiences with these "oldies" formats.

Even without a direct love theme or lyrics, music has some sex appeal value; rhythms have a sexual connotation. Recall the movie *10* and its use of "Bolero."

This gratification, as the examples suggest, is dependent upon both sex and age. It is practically nonexistent for young children (although even in children there is curiosity about sex without sexual drive). It is very strong for teenagers and young adults, then falls off in intensity slowly but steadily into old age.

Sex appeal is highly related to the gratification of personalism—that is, to the ability of audience members to identify with characters. This does not mean that performers need be of the same age as the audience to be attractive; many mature men are strongly drawn to programs featuring attractive younger women, for example. But in general the attraction is strongest for individuals to whom the audience can relate most easily.

The romantic story form of this gratification, as opposed to physical attractiveness or use of music, seems to be stronger for women generally than for men. However, the strength of soap-opera-type programs for women comes only partly from the sex appeal in the plots, and partly from other gratifications in these programs which also are strong for women.

In analyzing this gratification within a program, you should be aware that it can be present in a variety of forms, and have attraction for a variety of different audience groups. This brief overview barely scratches the surface of the possible manifestations of this powerful gratification.

Comedy

One very effective force in attracting many audience groups is humor. Some programs offer comedy as their strongest gratification. In other programs the use of comedy is secondary, as in a serious dramatic program, when comic relief is used to relieve the tension of the drama.

Comedy can be a gratification only if it is recognized or perceived as such by the individual. We've all experienced situations at a party, or in reading the comic strips, where one person will find a joke outrageously funny and another one will say: "What's funny about that?" Even after an explanation, he or she may not appreciate the humor because that person's experience does not extend to the type of situation being made fun of. Political cartoons are especially susceptible to this problem. They cater to a minority audience that must be quite politically aware in order to see humor in the usually abstract illustrations.

The wide variety of comedy styles can be organized into several subcategories with the aid of another gratification—action—but in reality each use of humor in a program series is different from all others. These are but the broadest of categories.

Broad Slapstick Comedy

This type is highly dependent on action and movement, and strongly visual. Dialogue does not even have to be present, but when it is, it often involves the exchange of insults between characters. Characterizations are very broadly drawn. Most contemporary comedians work in several styles, but names that come readily to mind for this type of comedy are Steve Martin, John Belushi, and Soupy Sales. Older practitioners were the Keystone Cops, Abbott and Costello, and the Three Stooges.

Situation Comedy

This of course, is one of the major programming forms of television, and in itself it exhibits a wide range of styles. The broader comedies—less realistic, with characterizations very broadly drawn and with lots of movement and visual humor—have appeal almost identical to slapstick comedy. Other scripts are more realistically drawn; the humor is more subtle and is more likely to be combined with human interest, tension, and personalism, as opposed to action and possible sex appeal. In the broader, more exaggerated category we might include "Mork and Mindy" and "Gilligan's Island." On the more realistic side would be

"Newhart," "One Day at a Time," and "All in the Family." Many other program series range somewhere between these two poles.

Gag Comedy Standup comedy or gag comedy uses even less action and movement; no situations or locations are used. This is the style of comedy used in the monologues of Bob Hope and Johnny Carson, among others. Gag comedy can involve characterizations—Minny Pearl in "Grand Ol' Opry" and Grandpa Jones on "Hee Haw" play country hayseed roles. But most often the comic delivers the monologue "straight." The emphasis is on the use of clever, laugh-provoking lines and the poking of fun at people, situations, events. The humor may be topical, aimed at politics and politicians, for example, and may involve a quite sophisticated satire; that is, it may require that the audience have a good background in the topic in order to recognize the people and situations being satirized. Then we have a situation similar to that of the political cartoon: The gratification will be limited to those people in the audience who understand.

We've already suggested the prime way that audiences relate to humor: It is funny only if you understand what's being made fun of. That means, for example, that children are likely to find humor primarily in the more visual, action-oriented, slapstick style and in broad situation comedy. Less sophisticated, lower socioeconomic, and less educated groups also respond more strongly to broader styles of comedy. Older audiences do not find any form to be strong, as a rule.

Although comedy is an important gratification in many programs, its presence is not always a strength. There are serious programs—news, documentary, religious, and others—in which the presence of comedy would be a serious breach of structural unity, and would weaken the other intended gratifications.

Information Information may be both content and gratification. Many programs—news broadcasts, public affairs programs, documentaries, and the like—provide content that is largely if not totally informative, and the popularity of these types of programs attests to the strength of information as a gratification. But other programs can also provide content which is perceived as informative, and which is gratifying to audiences.

Recall Blumler's cognitive orientation, which identifies two aspects of cognition as presented by programs: (1) surveillance, as in news broadcasts and other obviously "informative" programs, and (2) reality explorations, in which audiences may draw information from fictional programs as well.

Surveillance It is this gratification which we see most clearly when audiences tune in to news broadcasts, public affairs programs, and documentaries. Statements made by the respondents in one study showed that audiences tune to news programs for these purposes:

1. To follow what is going on in the world generally. "Watching the news keeps me in touch with the world." "I like to see how big issues are finally sorted out." "It tells me about the main events of the day."

2. To see the relationship between such events and the viewer's own personal circumstances. "I follow the news so I won't be caught unawares by price increases and that sort of thing."

3. To see the relationship between such events and the forming of judgments about the performance of powerholders in society. "Watching the news helps me to keep an eye on the mistakes people in authority make."

4. To help them make up their minds on current issues: "Television news helps me to make up my mind about things." "Television news provides food for thought."[5]

Reality Exploration

Information is also present in many programs where we might overlook its presence, particularly in dramatic programs. These statements are responses to questions about listening to a radio serial drama:

"It sometimes helps me to understand what is happening in my own life."

"The people in [the program] sometimes have problems that are like my own."

"It deals with realistic problems without offending me."[6]

There is a strong relationship between the gratification of information in whatever form it is presented and that of importance (to be discussed next). In fact, we may say that information has strength as a gratification only to the extent that it is perceived to be important to and by each individual audience member. In a news broadcast, for example, for an item to have strong appeal it should deal with issues that may affect the audience members, or with persons or situations known to them.

A program about wheat farming may be of considerable interest to a person engaged in agriculture, but it offers no information of importance to the average city dweller, and consequently provides no degree of appeal for the urban listener. Similarly, we are likely to be interested in local news, which may contain names and places with which we are familiar, but will be less interested in happenings in other places unless we have been there or the newscaster points out at the beginning of the story how it may affect us.

As we have suggested, information is a highly selective gratification, but in general it is stronger for older audience groups, for males, and for the more highly educated. One study of program-audience relationships identified a number of different categories of viewers, one category of which was the "news and information" viewer. These people had an average age of 47, an average income (in 1977) slightly over $14,000, and were largely white-collar workers. They were heavy users of television generally, but especially of news, news commentary, talk shows, and documentaries and also of variety shows, movies, and sports.[7]

Broadcast programmers, aware that audiences for news programs skew toward older, male, and more educated groups, began a few years ago to take steps to attract younger and more female audiences because the younger, female group is a much more important target audience for many products advertised on television. They have done so successfully with so-called soft news programs which present more human interest and "good news" stories, and fewer of the negative, unhappy stories likely to be found in the major events taking place each day.

Importance

Like the situation with information, it is the individual's perception of importance that is critical to this gratification. In a public affairs discussion, the topic, say, of tax increases may have a very direct bearing on all the residents of a community, but unless each individual viewer understands how that topic may affect him or her, it has no strength. Importance can take several forms:

Subject Matter Importance

This is the form of importance we have already linked with information. The link is strong and obvious in newscasts, in public affairs programs, and in religious programs. Audience members choose to tune to informative programming if they believe that the content of the program will be important to them in some way. That importance may be only that the person will be able to converse knowledgeably with co-workers about news events on the following day, but the gratification can be sufficient for individuals to tune in to certain programs.

Authority or Star Quality

A second form of importance is the presence of authority or of a person who has "name value." Television and radio depend heavily on "stars" to attract audiences, a phenomenon that is also obvious in the motion picture industry. A script for a dramatic program might be extremely well acted by unknown performers, but audiences are not as likely to turn to it as they will to the same script with one or more well-known performers. New programs that feature unknown performers will use "guest stars" to attract audiences until the series is established, or if the program is a special, to help in the promotion for the show.

Using persons who are known and respected to endorse products is also an effective advertising technique. Sometimes the person presented as an authority on a topic or issue is legitimately qualified on that subject, but that is not a necessary qualification. Movie stars often are used to endorse political candidates or to speak on behalf of political propositions. They may have no qualifications to speak on the topic, but their name value is an important gratification.

Bigness

Finally, the mere presence of "bigness"—of programs done a large scale—can add some measure of gratification, especially for younger, less sophisticated and therefore more impressionable audiences. We include that as a form of importance. After all, if the producers are willing to spend all that money on the program, it must be important, right? Anyway, producers seem more than willing to include the cost of production in publicity releases about new programs, and their purpose in doing so is to impress the potential audience.

Importance will rarely be able to "carry" a program unaided. As a rule, it serves as a secondary gratification, reinforcing one or more other gratifications.

Value

We have to be particularly cautious in defining and describing this gratification, and differentiating it from others. In one sense, all gratifications may be considered to be aspects of value. After all, what we have been saying all along is that people tune in to programs because they get some gratification from that activity. We might just replace the word *gratification* with *value*—saying that programs are chosen because audiences get value from so doing.

However, our definition is more narrow. *Value* in our view represents the "worthwhileness" audiences place on a program and its contents, especially when that quality has ethical, moral, or religious overtones.

This gratification is highly related to both information and importance. But value contains an emotional component that is not present in information or importance. It can be seen in audience responses to patriotism, to religion, or to the introduction in a program of babies, young children, elderly people or animals, all of which are representative of valuable attributes to some audience group.

A common comment made by individuals who view religious programs or who watch a Fourth of July special is that the program "makes them feel better" or makes them "proud." These comments indicate that the emotional stimulation provided by that program has been converted into a value by the individual. And that behavior points out a crucial aspect of this gratification. Even more than for information or importance, the strength of value as a gratification to an individual will be dependent on that person's perception of the program's content as providing value.

There are demographic relationships between certain groups and value, such as that between religion and older people, particularly women, and even more particularly older women who reside in certain geographic regions, or between older male war veterans and patriotism, or between women and the appeal of babies and small children, or between retired blue-collar workers and Democratic politics. But even more important than demographic generalization is each individual's perception of value. If audience members do not recognize that a program has value for them, then it does not (regardless of what the program's writer and producer may say in the publicity release).

Personalism   We have chosen this term (used in several gratification studies) to label a broad-ranging gratification tied strongly to Blumler's description of the *personal identity orientation*. Other words used to describe the gratification are intimacy, or involvement, or identification or participation between audience and program content. In the theater yet another term is used—*empathy*—defined as the intellectual identification with or vicarious experiencing of the feelings, thoughts, or attitudes of another.

The gratification is present in many types of programs and is frequently found in conjunction with other appeals. Some of the forms in which it can be recognized include these:

Personal   This is evident in any program in which the audience can identify with the
Identification   characters or plot situations, finding them believable, sympathetic, and, most important, real. A common comment that describes this appeal is: "I know how they feel: I've been through a similar situation myself."

Although identification is particularly strong in dramatic programs, the programs do not have to be fictional for this involvement to take place. One elderly lady we knew watched only one television program each, but she watched "Lawrence Welk" faithfully. And she felt that she knew every performer on the program as if they were nextdoor neighbors. In her mind, these were friends who visited each week in her home. Television fan magazines, and the articles about television stars that appear in other publications as well, feed off this gratification, along with those of importance and curiosity.

One may identify with locations as well as with persons. If you have been to a foreign city, and that city appears on the screen as the locale for a play, you are more likely to stay tuned to try to recognize the scenes, and vicariously, to relive memories of having been there. For athletic contests, having played the sport in high school or in college, or at least being familiar with the rules and therefore able to follow the progress of the contest more easily, makes enjoyment stronger. The networks have spent considerable effort and money to explain the rules and techniques of professional football to women in pregame and half-time shows. Their purpose, of course, is to get more women to watch, or at least to make them more sympathetic to their husbands' watching.

A more direct form of involvement is possible in programs that have audience feedback, such as telephone call-in talk programs, and two-way interactive cable TV channels.

Under the heading of tension we mentioned that it may be possible to have too much tension, that the appeal may be so strong that individuals leave the room because of anxiety over the fate of a character. When that situation exists, it's a reflection of strong personalism as well. Of course we know the program is make-believe and prerecorded on a tape or film, but the empathy with the character has become so strong as to suspend disbelief.

Fantasy

By this term we do not mean the use of supernatural or fantastic gimmicks as plot devices; we don't believe such devices have any particular appeal in themselves. But fantasy whereby individuals in an audience can imagine themselves in a role as depicted in a program can be a very strong gratification. We see it as an intense form of personal identification.

Children and teens are more likely to become caught up in this projection into media roles than are more mature adults. But who wouldn't like to have their fantasies come true, with no harm done?

Nostalgia

This aspect of personalism carries the connotation of favorable recollection of past events—situations in which audience members are reminded of their childhood, early school days, old friends, and so on. These elements may appear in a television program that re-creates a past period in time. They also appear in radio on stations that feature "golden oldies"—music from past periods which will be recalled by audiences as pleasurable experiences from their youth.

Sympathy

There is a strong tie between personalism and human interest, as shown by the concept of sympathy. In addition to our interest in or curiosity about other people (or animals), there can be an emotional, sympathetic, feeling sorry for persons with troubles or who are less fortunate than ourselves. This combination of personal involvement and human interest can be a very strong gratification.

There are few obvious relationships between demographic audience groups and personalism. We have already mentioned the possibility that younger or less sophisticated groups may be more likely to fantasize their involvement with characters or situations. On the other hand, younger audiences do not have as many or as broad personal experiences to relate to their viewing or listening, and are not likely to find strength in nostalgia or sympathy.

Ethnicity may provide a strong tie to this gratification. Black audiences, for example, will watch programs that feature *believable* black performers, and so on.

Curiosity

In some gratification studies, curiosity has been identified as a major audience orientation, given equal ranking with cognition, diversion, and personal identity. There is no question but that it is a very strong gratification in some program types, and reasonably strong in many others. To a large extent the gratification arises from our curiosity about and interest in people—in the way they behave, in their problems, and in the things that interest them. Therefore we have made human interest a major subcategory of curiosity.[8]

Human Interest

This gratification is strongly tied to those of personalism and realism. We are especially interested in the activities and problems of people with whom we can identify. They don't have to be people like us—interest in celebrities, royalty, the wealthy negates such an assumption—but they do have to be "real," genuine people or if in a fictional program, they must be believable characterizations. "Ordinariness" is another good term to further describe human interest—ordinary people doing ordinary things in ordinary situations, and coping with ordinary problems. The script writer may strengthen human interest by:

- Avoiding stiffness and formality in the style of presentation of an entertainer.

- Providing "stage business" for performers that is ordinary and normal routine. It makes the dramatic role human and believable if the leading character can't find a match to light his cigarette, or can't make his cigarette lighter work, or has difficulty tying his necktie, or bumps into a piece of furniture.

- Providing situations that are recognizable and commonplace. For example, in a comedy dramatic program, the plot may revolve around very common family situations—such as the problems arising when Junior brings home a report card showing a low grade in English, or the family turmoil created when the teenage daughter goes to her first formal dance, or the husband-wife differences with respect to plans for a family vacation. Situation comedies depend heavily on this aspect of human interest.

- Emphasizing the problems ordinary people face. We're not interested just in the fact that they have problems—all of us have problems—but in the way in which people react to problem situations. We like to know what things bother them, how they feel about things, and what they think. One early television (and before that, radio) series, "Queen for a Day," awarded its daily prize to the contestant with the "worst" hard-luck story. More recent programs, like "The Dating Game," also award prizes on the basis of "problems."

Human interest is obviously a strong appeal in continuing serial drama programs, although some of these programs now tend to present characters and situations with more glamour than would be the case if human interest were the only appeal.

Television and radio news broadcasts have for years used the "human interest story" as a break from the straightforward, factual news story. Frequently this type of story is placed at the end of the newscast to conclude on an optimistic, lighthearted note and provide a bit of an emotional climax. In the last few years, whole programs devoted to this type of story have evolved, such as "PM Magazine." Although information is still present both as content and as a gratification in that type of program or story, its strength as an appeal is diluted by the lack of immediacy and importance of the stories. That lack is compensated for by human interest, and possibly personalism and value. And, as we have noted, since different gratifications are present, the audiences for these "soft news" programs are also different from those for traditional or "hard news" broadcasts.

Intellectual Curiosity

Although human interest forms a large portion of curiosity, it is not the only aspect that can be identified. We can be curious about places, about past or future time, about the operations of the world around us, and so on. The programs that most obviously cater to these forms of curiosity are travelogs; science information programs like "Cosmos," "Nova," "The Undersea World of Jacques Cousteau;" historical dramas like many of the series in "Masterpiece Theater;" and of course programs of formal education.

The kinds of programs we are describing contain large amounts of information, which is also a gratification, but they differ from other informative programs such as news and news commentary in that the information provided is not timely. They also differ in the sizes of the audiences they draw. The comparatively small audiences for programs which have intellectual curiosity as their primary gratification indicate that this gratification is not strong for most people.

Curiosity can be built into almost any form of broadcast message simply by withholding information the audience wants or expects to hear. In a drama, curiosity takes the form of building for climax; we stay tuned and watch to see how the plot is going to be resolved. In a commercial, a briefly stated problem is presented at the beginning of the ad, and then the product is introduced as the means of solving the problem. We become "hooked" by the problem and curious to find out how it will be resolved.

One well-known radio program series that very effectively uses curiosity as a primary appeal is "The Rest of the Story," a series developed and presented by news personality Paul Harvey. Each broadcast in that series tells a little-known but interesting story about a famous person. The person's name is deliberately withheld until the end of the vignette. Audiences, with their curiosity aroused, stay tuned just to find out who the story is about. News headlines and "teasers" which hint at stories coming up later in the broadcast serve the same purpose.

Realism   Of necessity we have mentioned realism several times already in connection with other gratifications. Realism, or the lack of it, is a consideration in every program. The gratification, however, does not mean reality in a literal sense. Literal reality would deny appeal to any program that contains elements of fantasy—cartoon programs for children, broad farce situation comedies, and the long series of programs with supernatural gimmicks, such as "Superman," "I Dream of Jeannie," "Wonder-Woman," "Mork and Mindy," "Bewitched," "Six-Million Dollar Man," "Gemini Man," "Manimal."

Rather, reality means that characters, events, behaviors must be believable or plausible in the perception of the individual audience member. We know that radio and television dramatic programs are fiction, and that the amount of literal reality, or fantasy, in a particular program can range over a wide scale. But in general we expect that the things that take place are things that reasonably "could happen," and that the characters who appear conform to our ideas of what those characters should be like in "real life."

If there is some sort of gimmick, it must be explained; for example, Buck Rogers is back in the twenty-fifth century because of a time warp, and so is Mork; the Bionic Woman can do superhuman stunts because of surgery that replaced human parts with mechanisms. We will accept these fictional explanations so long as the remainder of the situations are realistic, and so long as the behaviors of the characters are plausible.

Possibly the most frequent problem with the appeal of believability results from actions on the part of an actor that "don't fit" the character portrayed. Actions in any way out of the norm must be given sufficient motivation, in advance—and some actions simply "couldn't happen," regardless of the motivation. If the characters, the situations, and the actions of characters fall short of being plausible and believable, the overall attraction of the program will be damaged.

Our discussion has focused on realism (or its lack) in dramatic, fictional programs. We have assumed throughout that "real" programs, all types other than fiction, have this characteristic automatically, and that its presence is expected and normal. If for some reason implausible, unrealistic material should appear in a news documentary, for example, the combined effect of whatever other gratifications are present will be seriously weakened.

Novelty   The effectiveness of a program is affected by the degree of freshness, newness, originality, and novelty it provides. This concept of "freshness" is one about which it is difficult to draw hard-and-fast conclusions. We all know of programs and program personalities that have been continually successful in attracting listeners over periods of many years. At the same time, every program has a tendency to wear out after a time—after the newness and freshness and novelty have worn off. Some highly successful programs have fallen off rapidly in listener attractiveness by the end of their third or fourth season of broadcasting. Further, some programs have skyrocketed into popularity within a period of a few months or even a few weeks, largely because they offered something new and quite different from other programs available to listeners.

In the sections on realism and curiosity we have been tempted to call attention to "Real People" and "That's Incredible." These two programs contained an interesting mixture of gratifications. Both emphasized "odds and ends" information, unusual people and their activities (human interest/curiosity), and the fact that the activities are real. There can be tension and action in the stunts performed, but probably the strongest gratification in these programs was the unusualness of the items chosen for presentation. The programs became immensely popular very quickly after their introduction into network schedules. They combined a number of gratifications effectively, and they made use of two aspects of novelty—unusual content in the program, and a fresh form of presentation.

In general, it seems fairly safe to conclude that as the newness or freshness of a program wears off, the program will decline in attractiveness to listeners even though other gratifications remain unchanged. Further, in comparing two programs that offer gratifications of equal strength, the program which has a higher degree of "differentness" or uses the fresher or more original treatment is likely to have stronger overall attractiveness. "Different quality" is a decided asset to a program in making that program attractive to listeners. Major new types of programs do not appear very often, but when they do, and if they contain other strong gratifications as well, they are very likely to be successful.

Other Considerations

Over time, we can expect to have to modify this list of gratifications. Programs will change; the tastes of audiences will also change; and new research will become available. Even now there are some appeal-audience relationships about which we have come to no firm conclusion.

For example, there seems to be a dimension of simplicity-complexity in viewing decisions. We discussed simplicity in the chapter on aural style, noting at that time that in order to capture large, broad audiences, prime-time television programs have to be kept simple in language and plot. We also noted that the trend toward narrow-casting—more channels with more programs for more specialized audiences—will permit more complex programs. But this simplicity-complexity factor is not only structural; it behaves like a gratification as well. Some audience groups seem to be positively attracted to programs that are more complex and require more intellectual effort. Not surprisingly, these are groups with higher levels of education and socioeconomic status. The failure of "educational" television to live up to its promise of raising educational and cultural standards may very well lie in that program-audience relationship, the fact that those groups which watch educational programs are, generally, those who are already educated. They are the groups who are best able to organize and to appreciate receiving new knowledge. The less educated seek simpler fare that is more entertaining and requires less effort to process.

Fantasy is another area frequently identified by gratification researchers. It can be both a program type and a form of gratification. We considered adding it as a separate gratification, but we do not understand how it relates to realism. Are they canceling gratifications? Can a realistic program also contain an appeal to fantasy? We weren't sure what to do, so we included it as part of the discussion of personalism, on the ground that fantasy is merely a very intense form of identification.

The examples given for each gratification are programs that, in our opinion, show the appeal strongly, but obviously not exclusively. Other programs, and new programs which will come on the air after this analysis has been written, may also exhibit certain gratifications to equal or greater degree. Two programs may seem to be very similar, but each will have its own unique mixture of gratifications. They will differ if ever so slightly in the gratifications presented, or in the forms in which they are presented, and therefore in the strengths of their overall appeal for different audiences.

That's the whole point of this analysis. We know that different groups respond differently to the various programs available to them, and this process of analysis gives a means for identifying, at least in part, why those differences exist.

The writer who chooses certain gratifications for inclusion in a program will not automatically be successful in gathering an audience for that program. There are too many variables, both in the writing of the script and in external programming factors to even suggest that. Every season many programs on every station and every network fail to maintain audience interest and are removed from the air. If this analytical approach were a foolproof tool, that failure rate would be greatly reduced.

But a list of gratifications does have value for the writer. It is a method of approach the writer can employ to make programs more attractive to audiences. It is a particularly useful tool because it considers the consumer's interests. Writers who have been successful over a long period of time may not consciously go to a list and pick gratifications they want to use in a program. They have learned by trial and error what approaches are successful with various types of audiences. For the beginning writer, we have provided a substitute for that trial and error experience. An important question you should ask yourself when preparing a script for a program is this: What will there be in this program that will provide an attraction to my target audience? And you should be able to provide an answer.

Conclusion

The two most important concepts which relate to the audiences of broadcast messages from a writer's perspective are those of targeting and gratifications.

Audience targeting was the topic of the third question in the series we introduced at the conclusion of the preceding chapter. There we encouraged writers to apply a series of questions in analyzing any writing task before them:

1. Who is the sponsor (or the sponsors) for a particular program or announcement?

2. What is (are) the sponsor's purpose(s) in presenting that program or announcement?

3. What audience group or groups must the sponsor reach in order to accomplish that purpose?

In the next chapter, we'll add a fourth: What persuasive appeals would be most effective in convincing the members of the target audience to do what is wanted?

In Chapter 8 we also introduced three final examples, as tests of this sequence of questions. We can now consider our question about targeting as part of those analyses:

- The local TV station had purchased the syndicated series "Barney Miller" and placed it in an 11 P.M. strip. The target group might be any of several possible audiences, but from published information based on past experience with that series, the station's managers know that "Barney Miller" has very broad appeals for both women and men and holds up well across adult age ranges. The proportions of its audience in late-night time periods are approximately:

| Women 18–49 26% | Men 18–49 25% | Teens   4% |
| 49+   24% | 49+   18% | Children 2% |

In contrast, "M*A*S*H," another syndicated series frequently scheduled in this late-evening period, does not hold up as well across adult ranges. It skews more strongly toward younger audiences, as shown by its proportions:

| Women 18–49 31% | Men 18–49 31% | Teens   7% |
| 49+   16% | 49+   13% | Children 2%[9] |

Programmers look at these kinds of comparisons in making decisions on which program series to put in particular time periods. This program manager has selected "Barney Miller" for this period on the assumption that it will be a good counter to the news programs usually found on network affiliated stations at that hour.

- Our second example was of short radio programs prepared by a local little theater group, using excerpts from plays to attract attention to that group's performances. For this program, the target audience will be more difficult to identify precisely. From the station's standpoint, it would be desirable to keep the audience it already has, which has been attracted by its regular programming, so we might say that the station wants to avoid alienating its already determined target. By accepting this program series idea in the first place, the station's managers have implicitly assumed they will not materially damage their audience size or demographics. For the theater group, the target would be people who do not currently attend little theater presentations, but who probably have had some prior experience with dramatic productions. The station's audience and the theater group's target must be pretty much the same; otherwise it will be hard to reconcile the two purposes. That is, if the station appeals to teenagers and the theater group wants to reach mature adults, the differences are too great for the program to be successful, regardless of how well written it is.

- The final example we posed in Chapter 8 was program sponsorship by a local restaurant of a play-by-play account of a high school basketball game. The target groups, and in this case we can identify two groups, would be first people who eat pizza or who might be induced to try it. Second would be those who have an interest in high school sports—students, their families, and so on. Again, for the sponsor's campaign to be successful, the audience that is most likely to be interested in the program content needs to be similar in composition to the target for the product. In this case, that seems likely. The commercials, when written, can emphasize the goodness of the product, or the sponsor's contribution to the community by bringing this significant event to the audience, or both.

To summarize our discussion of audience gratifications, we can turn to one of the early researchers on that topic, Professor Harrison Summers, who taught at Ohio State University. He did not use the term *gratifications,* but he effectively stated the essential premise:

> Some programs are far more effective than others in attracting listeners and in holding the attention of the listeners they attract. Obviously, this is a result of differences in programs; those programs which are unusually attractive to listeners, and unusually effective in holding listener attention, contain in higher degree than other programs' elements which have compelling values for listeners—elements which make the individual listener want to listen.[10]

Writers faced with the tasks of preparing copy for a program can use this approach in developing ideas, in choosing participants, in creating plot situations, in scripting dialogue—all part of the creative process of scriptwriting.

And please note that throughout this chapter we have been generalizing about the behavior of audience groups. It is appropriate to do that when one is attempting to attract and communicate with large numbers of people. In the aggregate, audiences do behave as both quantitative and qualitative research describes them. But the writer should also remember that listening or viewing takes place usually in locations where only one person or at best a small group is present. Prepare your copy using a style in which you speak conversationally to individuals, not to mass audiences.

Exercises

1. Choose several different consumer products or services—a chain of fast food outlets, a savings and loan association, a brand of automobile tires—or any item or organization with which you are familiar. Then analyze that item in terms of its target audience.

   a. What is the primary target group that *must* be reached in order for that product to be marketed successfully? How narrowly can you define the target? Is the target best defined using demographics or life style characteristics, or some of each?

   b. Are there secondary groups of sufficient size that might be the targets of different campaigns? How would a company change its advertising approach to aim at these groups?

c. How do you arrive at these judgments? For example, for a shaving cream, you would need to consider among many other questions: What groups use blade razors as opposed to electric shavers? Younger or older? Other differences? What are the differences between this shaving cream and its competitors? Price? Feel? Smell? Packaging?

You may not know the answers to some of the questions you raise; some form of research would be needed to answer them definitively. But if you are doing this exercise as a class activity, which we strongly recommend, any consensus arrived at by the members of the class is likely to be pretty close to the truth.

2. Proceed through the same process of analysis as in the preceding exercise, but for a *new* product—something you invent or something just coming on the market. At what audience would you aim your advertising? Why?

3. Look at a selection of television programs and/or listen to a variety of radio station formats. For each program, describe in detail and with as narrow a focus as possible the audience targeted. Then, if possible, verify your impressions. Talk to the programming staff at the station which broadcasts each program you chose, and find out how they describe the target. Again, be careful in making this analysis for programs with participating advertising. It is the sponsor's target audience with which you are concerned, and that group may or may not be the same as the advertiser's target. Mismatches do occur. Sometimes advertisements are inserted in programs that have drawn a different group from that which the advertiser needs to reach.

4. Obviously the most important application of gratifications for writers is being able to write programs which contain the ones you choose to include, and which attract and hold the attention of your target audiences. But before you can do that, you need to develop some ability to recognize the existence and strengths of gratifications in existing programs. The following exercises are directed toward that skill.

a. Select and view several different types of television programs—for example, a news broadcast, a drama, a game show. For each program, (1) Identify the primary target audience. Be as specific as possible; focus quite carefully on just the one audience group which is most important to the sponsor. (2) List the gratifications you recognize as being present in the program. Describe for each the form of the gratification—that is, for comedy, what type of comedy—and the way in which it was presented in the program. (3) Do you believe that the gratifications present were strong *for the target audience?* Explain why this program should be successful in capturing the target group, or why not.

b. Select two TV programs that are very similar in content and form—for example, two network evening news programs, or two soap operas, or two situation comedies. (1) View both programs and, as in Exercise 4a; list and describe the gratifications you recognize as being present. (2) Particularly important, attempt to discern any *differences* in the types and strengths of gratifications between the two programs. (3) How do you think those differences might affect the audiences drawn to each program? What differences would you expect to find in the audience groups that choose each program?

Key Terms and Concepts

actual audience
audience gratifications
available audience
coverage
demographics

drive time
empathy
potential audience
prime time
target audience

Notes

1. Adapted from George Comstock and others, *Television and Human Behavior* (New York: Columbia University Press, 1978), pp. 91–93 and 114–116. Copyright© 1978 by The Rand Corporation. Used by permission.

2. Elizabeth Roberts, President Television Audience Assessment, Inc. (Cambridge, MA), quoted in the Sacramento (CA) *Bee,* April 26, 1983, p. B8.

3. Jay G. Blumler, "The Role of Theory in Uses and Gratifications Studies," *Communication Research,* 6 (January 1979), p. 17.

4. From Pat H. Broeske, "Women Warriors, Sexy and Brave," *Datebook: San Francisco Sunday Examiner and Chronicle,* July 31, 1983, p. 17.

5. Adapted from Jay G. Blumler, J. R. Brown, and Denis McQuail, "The Social Origins of the Gratifications Associated with Television Viewing" (Mimeographed: Leeds, Eng.: Centre for Television Research, University of Leeds, November 1970), p. 52.

6. Ibid., p. 14.

7. From Ronald E. Frank and Marshall G. Greenberg, "Zooming in on TV Audiences," *Psychology Today,* October 1979, p. 102.

8. See particularly Mervin D. Lynch, Brian D. Kent, and Richard P. Carlson, "The Meaning of Human Interest: Four Dimensions of Judgment," *Journalism Quarterly,* Winter 1967.

9. Arbitron Ratings Syndicated Program Analysis, May 1985.

10. Harrison Summers, "Audience Appeals" (Mimeographed course materials, Ohio State University, 1958).

Chapter 10

Persuasion in Broadcast Messages

In several previous chapters we argued that all broadcast programming has some form of persuasion as its central purpose. Not everyone agrees with that point of view; many in the industry feel we are being unnecessarily harsh in ignoring entertainment and information as basic purposes. We will not belabor the point; you can make your own judgments, ultimately, on the matter. We will continue to point out, however, that information and entertainment are used as means to attract audiences, so that those audiences can be persuaded by the program's advertisements and/or its content.

We also argued that the writer who hopes to prepare successful programs and announcements must look at success from the sponsor's point of view and, as a corollary, must have a clear understanding of who is paying for each program or announcement and what they hope to accomplish by their sponsorship. In the conclusions to Chapters 8 and 9 we used several questions to summarize sequence of decisions that must be made before actual writing begins:

1. *Who is the sponsor for the program or announcement?* In most cases this question is easily answered, but remember, for example, that in a program which contains participation advertising, those advertisers are not the sponsors of the program. The program was selected *and paid for* by the individual station or network, which makes that station or network its sponsor. In that case, advertisers are the second step in the process. They will buy participations only if that program is demonstrated to be a successful vehicle for reaching the target groups they need to accomplish their purposes.

2. *What is the sponsor's purpose?* The discussion in Chapter 8 includes most, but probably not all, of the reasons why programs and announcements are sponsored. Conspicuously absent from that discussion are information and entertainment as purposes. Those are, in our opinion, merely means to another goal. Most often that

other goal is attracting a sufficiently sized audience so that participations may be sold at a profit.

3. *What target audience group (or possibly groups) must be reached in order to accomplish the sponsor's purpose?* Sometimes this question is posed in reverse. First, a producer will create and air a program, then see what audience is drawn to it. But it is a very risky and expensive approach. A station or an advertiser, and the writers who work for them, will be better off in most cases by carefully delineating target groups in advance—that is by identifying those people who are most important in accomplishing the sponsor's purpose.

4. *How can the individuals in the target audience be convinced that they should act in the manner desired by the sponsor?* What techniques can the writer employ to persuade audiences? What persuasive appeals can be worked into the script copy to accomplish the sponsor's purpose?

In Chapter 9, when we discussed audience gratifications, we were looking at one aspect of this problem. Audiences do select specific programs because something in the program attracts them, so to the extent that writers and programmers choose content, performers, and so on with gratifications in mind, they are accomplishing part of the sponsor's purpose. They are attracting the individuals who make up the audience.

Persuasive appeals are similar to audience gratifications in that both affect audience behavior, and you will notice the same terms used to describe some appeals as we used for some gratifications. But these persuasive appeals, or motivational appeals as they are sometimes called, are more deliberately manipulative. These are the means by which audience members are encouraged to act in accordance with the sponsor's goals. Most often that persuasion is exercised on behalf of commercial clients, inducing persons to purchase products or services, but it can also be employed to persuade on behalf of public service campaigns, to accept and act on an editorial opinion expressed by station management, to contribute to a religious organization or accept that organization's doctrine, to vote for a political candidate—any situation in which the sponsor's purpose is to elicit action from audience members.

Persuasive Appeals

A great deal of research has been done and a number of volumes written on persuasive theory and on the application of that theory to communication. From that research we have constructed a list of persuasive appeals that can be applied to broadcast messages. The typology we will use, listed alphabetically, contains the following headings:

1. Acquisition and saving

2. Adventure and excitement

3. Argument

4. Companionship

5. Creation

6. Curiosity

7. Destruction

8. Fear

9. Guilt

10. Health and safety

11. Imitation

12. Independence

13. Loyalty

    a. To family . . . love
    b. To friends
    c. To social groups
    d. To nation

14. Personal enjoyment

    a. Of comfort and luxury
    b. Of beauty and order
    c. Of pleasant sensations
    d. Of recreation

15. Power

16. Pride and vanity

17. Reverence or worship

    a. Of leaders
    b. Of traditions or institutions
    c. Of the deity

18. Revulsion

19. Sexual attraction

20. Sympathy and compassion

Before examining the application of each of these appeals to persuasive writing, however, there are a few cautions on the use of this or any similar list.

Appeals can be described in different terms—don't get stuck on the terminology. For example, appeals to health and safety and to fear are based on a primary motive of self-preservation. One, health and safety, approaches the idea positively; fear is a negative derivative.

Usually appeals do not operate individually, in isolation; instead, they are to be found in clusters. It is useful and almost unavoidable to use natural clusters of appeals in a persuasive campaign. But be careful; while two or three appeals may be mutually supporting and add strength to the overall persuasive message, more than that number are likely to scatter the emphasis and weaken the effect.

Occasionally, two appeals will operate against one another. Adventure and fear, for example, may be self-canceling; our desire for adventure is overridden by fear of failure or of the unknown. Companionship and independence also may be seen as mutually contradictory; some people have a much greater need for one and others for the other.

Some appeals are more or less universal, but many of them have different strengths for different target audience groups. Those strengths are the result of previous experiences common to members of those groups. To take an obvious example, sexual attraction is not an appeal with strength for young children, because they simply have no experience with or understanding of sexual urges.

Similarly, there are obvious and easy connections between certain appeals and certain categories of advertised products. Writers frequently use these connections, often to excess. An advertising campaign which finds a new but legitimate connection between audience, appeal, and product will not only be successful; it will draw praise and awards for its creators.

Finally, most of our examples in the pages that follow are taken from advertising campaigns because those are the most obvious and the greatest users of persuasion. Keep in mind, however, that some programs have direct persuasive purposes as well, and that all broadcast content is persuasive at least to the extent that it attempts to keep audiences tuned in.

Acquisition and Saving

The most obvious application of this appeal is connected with money and property—getting it, keeping it, and spending as little of it as possible to get the things we want. Every ad that says:

> On sale for this week only. . . .
> Twenty percent off the manufacturer's price. . . .

or that in any way implies that the customer will make money or save money is aiming for this appeal.

Not only can one save by spending less, but also by putting money aside. Banks and savings and loans use this appeal in almost all their ads:

> Save with the highest money market rates and insured safety at. . . .

The appeal may also take the form of collecting. People like to collect a variety of things, from stamps, theater programs, and postcards to rare books and expensive art objects.

> You'll want to have the entire set of these valuable collector plates, so act now while they are still available. . . .

This appeal is widespread among adults, and may be particularly strong for individuals or groups who have suffered financial setbacks at some point, but financial saving will have almost no value to children or others who have not had experience in managing money. On the other hand, children seem to be born collectors of all sorts of things, so acquisition in a nonmonetary sense can be a strong appeal for them.

Adventure and Excitement

The thrill of excitement and the sense of the unusual and the unknown are present to at least a small degree in most people. But in general this appeal is likely to be stronger for younger groups than for older ones; for most people the appeal of adventure diminishes with age. It also takes different forms for males and females. The traditional outdoor adventure in the wilderness is still more male-oriented, probably due simply to childhood conditioning which perpetuates that stereotype, while the more glamorous, romantic adventure is more female-oriented.

In commercials, adventure can be inserted in the form of the setting—a glamorous resort, an ocean liner, an expensive restaurant, and/or in the activity—scuba diving, skiing, hang gliding, or so on. The product, whatever it may be, that is displayed in connection with that setting or activity takes on the aura of the adventure.

The appeals to both acquisition and adventure can be combined in various forms of gambling or risk-taking activity, like playing blackjack in Las Vegas or plunging on the stock market.

Argument

Competition, fighting, and argument are nearly universal appeals. Small children fight over possession of a toy; adults take legal action when they feel wronged in some fashion; at the extreme, nations go to war. The appeal can be evident in intellectual forms—such as debate and verbal argument—or be more emotional and physical, involving anger and fighting.

A common application of this appeal is that of fighting back against forces which threaten us in some way. This appeal is easily combined with savings.

Fight back against high prices . . . buy our product on sale. . . .

This appeal is also the basis for most consumerism campaigns. A very successful syndicated television program series has been developed using both the appeal and the title: "Fight Back."

Argument, again combined with savings, is also present in "comparison" ads in which the sponsor's product is compared with the competition.

Our product is better than. . . .
Our remedy contains 25% more of the miracle ingredient. . . .

Companionship

Most of us prefer company in our activities, either with family or friends. We go to parties, join clubs, and do many other things to avoid loneliness. In our beliefs and opinions we also prefer to do what is socially or politically acceptable, what other people are doing, rather than chart an independent, and uncomfortable, course.

This appeal is present, at least in some moderate sense, whenever a group of people are placed together in an ad. It can be made stronger if the group is obviously enjoying each other's presence: two couples in a mountain cabin around a warm fireplace drinking the sponsor's coffee, or a group of boisterous, active ex-professional athletes engaging in horseplay and drinking Lite beer from

Miller. Companionship is frequently used in beverage ads, because more beverages are consumed in groups than by people alone.

This appeal also can be used effectively in political campaigns by referring to what other people presumably are doing or thinking and then suggesting that the listener should do the same to be among the majority.

Creation

This appeal may take various forms involving organizing or building and may include both physical creation—artwork or structures—and social creation—the organizing of people into athletic teams, political parties, business firms, and so on.

Creation can be especially effective in public service campaigns. For example, a public service announcement on the formation of a new knitting club for senior citizens could apply the appeal in both senses: Join the club and help create a new social organization, and at the same time create articles by knitting them. That approach would also appeal to companionship; one can knit alone, of course, but by doing it as part of a club, companionship is added to the overall appeal.

Curiosity

We have already discussed curiosity as one type of gratification. Those comments can be applied here as well. This appeal is nearly universal, but its form can vary widely depending on the individual or group of people involved. Children will tear apart toys to see what's inside. Adults will watch a parade to see a celebrity go by. Scientists and explorers are people who combine the appeals to curiosity and adventure.

In general we can say that people will be curious about topics, people, and situations of which they already have some prior knowledge, or where the writer of the program or announcement is able quickly, at the beginning of the broadcast, to make a connection in the audience's mind to the topic. If the listener's attention is caught, if he or she thinks: "This broadcast may be something I need to know about," then curiosity has been used effectively.

Destruction

You may remember the TV commercial for the Jack-in-the-Box restaurant chain which featured blowing up the clown. That destruction served two purposes. It was an effective attention-getting device, and it dramatically described the change the owners were making in the food and in the image of their restaurants. It also caused some unexpected and unwanted reaction in small children who were very upset by the violence of the act and the loss of a friendly character for whom they had developed a loyalty. Destruction is not a common appeal, but as the Jack-in-the-Box example shows, it can be quite effective. It can be used to precede the appeal to creation—destroy, then rebuild. And it can be used, possibly in connection with argument, to demonstrate our ability to control the events in our lives and to show our superiority over the things we can destroy.

Fear

This appeal has both positive and negative attributes. It may prevent us from doing things that bring danger, and it may also cause us to take actions to protect ourselves from that danger. Many ads for health care products and services appeal to fear. We will get sick, even die, if we don't take care of ourselves by using the sponsor's product or service. Or when we are sick, we should take the product in order to recover.

Similarly, products that emphasize personal protection—deadbolt locks on our doors or automobile tires which lessen the risks of skids and accidents in a storm—are using this appeal.

Physical injury or illness is not the only thing we fear. We may fear loss of a job, or property, or friends:

> Use our deodorant (or mouthwash) or you will lose the companionship and affection of friends. . . .
> Buy our insurance to protect your loved ones from the fear of losing their home. . . .

This last example points up another strong fear—fear of the unknown, of what we cannot anticipate or control in the future.

Fear would seem to be an almost universal appeal, but highly related to the action feared. Children who have not experienced ill health are not likely to respond to that form of the appeal, but children do have a strong fear of the dark and of the unknown. Coupling those fears with the appeals of adventure and curiosity can be a very effective way to capture children's attention to, say, an ad for a horror movie.

Guilt

One of the most powerful social conditioners, at least in American society, is guilt. From early childhood our behavior is modified by parents, other relatives, friends, teachers and others who use guilt as their tool.

Advertisers also use this emotion for persuasive purposes. Guilt can be seen, along with sympathy, in appeals for charitable causes. It is used by life insurance companies in campaigns which suggest one has responsibility to loved ones even after death. The telephone company has used guilt to remind us to call our parents long distance, and so on.

If the writer should choose to use guilt in a campaign to reach a particular target audience, it would be necessary to know what forms of guilt are likely to have been instilled into the members of that group. Different kinds have been implanted in each sex and in different social, racial and ethnic groups.

Health and Safety

This appeal may be viewed as the opposite of fear, at least as far as fear relates to physical danger. Just as many health care products appeal to the fear of illness, they can also appeal to the positive attributes of well-being. Vitamin products and exercise clinics would be two obvious examples. So would a public service announcement urging participation in a marathon race. Companionship, health, and pride would be three appeals easily clustered together in that spot.

The health appeal can be made to most adults, but for older adults the negative approach, fear, may be more effective, as they are more likely to have experienced ill health and to be fearful of its consequences. It is difficult to make this appeal to young people who, if they think about it at all, seem to expect to live safely forever. Try, for example, to build a safety appeal into a public service campaign for bicycle safety for, say, sixth-grade children. It will be very difficult to find a way to use this appeal in such a campaign. If you should find a way to get those twelve-year-olds to practice bicycle safety, quite likely the appeals used are different and much more indirect, involving, perhaps, imitation, or pride, or companionship.

Imitation

People tend to imitate others both consciously and unconsciously, and the appeal is evident in many types of persuasive copy. It can be seen in all the "keeping up with the Joneses" or "getting ahead of the Joneses," campaigns (along with the appeal to pride). It can also be seen in the latest fashions, styles, or fads in clothing, or activities in the social group to which the target audience belongs or aspires.

The appeal is often presented by a television personality or radio voice who is similar to the member of the target audience group. That person uses, enjoys, or gets some benefit from the advertised product and then, by direct statement or by implication, says to the audience: "You too can get the same benefit I am getting by using this product."

Imitation is used with many categories of products. Among the most obvious and frequent are cosmetic products—shampoos, shave cream, perfumes. All audience groups can be reached with this appeal, but one of the most susceptible groups is teenagers, who can rather easily be induced to participate in new fads and to purchase products that identify them as part of the crowd.

We also tend to imitate the actions, beliefs, attitudes, and opinions of people we admire and respect. This attribute can be very effective in political campaigns; an endorsement of a candidate or proposition by a respected figure can influence a good many votes from otherwise undecided persons. The endorsement of a product also can result in increased sales, especially if that product and its competitors are very similar in other ways. Examples abound, but change frequently. You'll probably recall the series of people with well-known names but less well-known faces who endorse the American Express Card, and all the exprofessional athletes who appear in the Miller Lite beer ads (also mentioned under companionship, because they invariably appear in group activities).

Of course for the appeal of imitation to be effective, the audience must respond to the people shown on the screen or heard on the radio. For an endorsement to be effective, the person giving the endorsement must be known to and respected by the audience.

Independence

In one sense, this appeal may be seen as an opposite to companionship. For example, when students are asked to recall commercials that use independence as an appeal, they frequently describe motorcycle ads in which a lone rider on a sleek, powerful machine rides off into the mountains, or the desert, or a futuristic landscape—a combination of independence and adventure as appeals. The same sense of individualism may be seen in an ad which features a lone mountain climber who drinks a thirst-quenching soda when he reaches the top of the peak. Independence, adventure, and imitation are all present in that situation.

Generalizing on the basis of these examples, the audiences to which independence is an appeal are more easily described in terms of their life style than in demographic terms. The independent, individualistic, loner attitude is more psychological than demographic.

We should also point out the contrast between independence and imitation. They are not completely contradictory appeals, but they tend to operate as opposites. We will imitate others we admire, or are in our social group, but we do not want to be *forced* to imitate. Clothing, for example, must be in style, but also individual.

Loyalty

This broad term is a general heading for several more specific and more readily identifiable subappeals.

Loyalty to Family: Love

Obviously, this appeal is present in situations in which various family members are shown together in pleasant circumstances. It is extremely evident in all the commercial campaigns presented by life insurance companies; people buy life insurance to protect their families.

It also has been effectively used by the telephone company to encourage people to contact other family members through long distance. "Reach out and touch someone . . ."

Loyalty to Friends

This appeal is very similar to companionship. We are more willing to take action to help a friend than we will a stranger. Radio station disc jockey personalities frequently are seen as friends by the regular members of their audiences. They arouse a strong sense of loyalty in their listeners; then, when a product is "personally" recommended by that announcer, the audience responds favorably out of loyalty and possibly imitation as well.

Loyalty to Social Groups

Such terms as "school spirit," "civic pride," and "club morale" indicate the types of loyalty included here. The appeal is frequently used for public service campaigns to support nonprofit civic organizations in their charitable efforts. The alumni organizations of schools and colleges appeal to this loyalty.

Loyalty to Nation: Patriotism

This appeal may have slipped a bit in its strength over the past twenty or thirty years, but it can be very powerful, especially to older audiences, to war veterans, and the like. In the mid-1980s we see the appeal in campaigns to "buy American," and to support institutions and traditions at all levels of government.

Personal Enjoyment

In varying forms this appeal is present in a great deal of persuasive material. It is a universal appeal and a very strong one. Some of the forms in which it can be recognized are these:

Enjoyment of Comfort and Luxury

This form is used in commercials for automobiles and furniture; used by airlines to push their service as being more comfortable than the smaller seats in the competitor's plane; used by hotels and resorts. Target audiences include both those groups who already are used to these comforts and those who may not yet have had opportunity to experience the luxury, but who may reasonably be expected to have the opportunity later. The appeal can build an expectation:

"When I'm able to do so I'm going to buy a Mercedes, or fly first class, or stay at the Ritz. . . ."

Enjoyment of Beauty and Order

The term *aesthetics* is particularly appropriate here; it describes the enjoyment derived from the fine arts, from music, or from a drive through the beautiful foliage of a New England autumn. A commercial for a wine, with classical music playing in the background, makes use of this appeal, as does the classic Budweiser Beer commercial which shows the Clydesdale team prancing through a pastoral winter snowscape.

The appeal does not have to be snobbish, as these examples might suggest. The design (beauty) of an automobile, along with its luxury, are as important in selling that car as are the appeals to economy and price.

Household cleansers, floor polishes, toilet bowl cleaners, and the like also make heavy use of this appeal in the form of cleanliness and sparkle.

Enjoyment of Pleasant Sensations

This appeal is very similar to the other subcategories of personal enjoyment; all involve sensory gratification of some sort. But this category is related more emotionally to the senses—things that taste or smell good, or that are pleasant to the touch. Of course it is not possible to present these sensations in a broadcast, except for sounds and visual images. But it is possible to describe them, using forceful, descriptive words, and to cause audiences to recall similar sensory experiences they may have had.

Food products use this appeal extensively, as do other products that appeal to the senses—perfumes, deodorizers, pipe tobacco.

Enjoyment of Recreation

We all enjoy the opportunity to engage in activities which are different from those assigned to us, either at work or school. Any product which is directly associated with recreation and fun will have the advantage of being seen from that pleasurable point of view. Recall the ad campaign by AMF products which showed their line of sporting goods coupled with the statement: "AMF makes weekends." Other products may not be directly associated with leisure, but if the writer can find a tie between them, the appeal can be used.

Power

It is more difficult to recognize this appeal than most of the others we have listed. Usually individuals will not admit to seeking power over other persons, but they do. Why do men and women give up lucrative positions and spend millions of dollars to be elected to public office? At least part of the reason is because they will have power over others, and their principles and beliefs can be more easily made into policies and laws affecting others.

Because of the unwillingness of individuals to admit to seeking power, this appeal must be very carefully employed in persuasive copy. But it can be seen, along with loyalty and other appeals, in recruiting ads for the military services and in ads for various types of educational or self-advancement programs.

Pride and Vanity

The appeal to pride can be extremely powerful. It can take several different forms: reputation, the estimate others give to an individual's worth; self-respect, the opinion one has (or wishes to have) of oneself; prestige, defined as reputation based on brilliance of achievement or character; and vanity, excessive pride or self-satisfaction. The differences are partly semantic; some of these terms are more positive in connotation than others.

People will put an incredible amount of effort into a job, or a volunteer activity, or into maintaining a home or other tasks if they perceive that the effort expended will raise their reputation. They may put in even more energy if the task is connected with their estimate of their own self-worth. The writer who wishes to persuade an audience on behalf of a product, or service, or a cause, and who finds a means of connecting the audience's pride to that persuasive message, will be successful.

Earlier, in discussing the appeal of imitation, we referred to the cliché of "keeping up with the Joneses." That cliché is also tied very heavily to the appeal to pride and vanity.

> If you want your lawn to look better than others on the block, buy our lawnmower. . . .
> Be the first in your neighborhood to have this all-new edition of our encyclopedia. . . .

Many luxury products are sold on the basis of the vanity associated with the product (or self-esteem, or prestige; the term used depends a lot on one's attitude toward that appeal). Remember the ads for L'Oreal Hair Color which featured a young woman saying: "L'Oreal is a little more expensive, but then I'm worth it."

Reverence or Worship

This appeal has at least three distinct forms:

Hero Worship

Commercially the endorsement of products or positions by well-known personalities, which we discussed under imitation, might also be considered an application of hero worship or the personal awe important figures command. Frequently, well-known Hollywood or Broadway stars endorse political candidates or issues, even though they have no expert knowledge of the issue or candidate.

Reverence for Traditions and Institutions

This form may be dramatically illustrated by the: "Hot dogs, baseball, apple pie, and Chevrolet" commercials of the late 1970s. In these ads the product, Chevrolet, was equated with three other American traditions. Hero worship and reverence for traditions are very similar to the appeal of loyalty and are frequently blended together.

Reverence of the Deity

This form is not likely to be found in persuasive campaigns for commercial products, probably because of the danger of a backlash from the audience; that is, the audience might react negatively to an attempt to relate a product to the deity. But it is obviously the strongest appeal in all the persuasive religious programming that is broadcast.

Revulsion

Like fear, revulsion is a negative appeal. It can be used most effectively to get the audience to react against an activity or situation. Showing on television the slaughter of the cute, helpless baby harp seals in the Arctic led to a tremendous public outcry to stop that slaughter.

A public service announcement shown on television in New York City had as its purpose convincing people to clean up their household garbage and put it in metal garbage cans. The PSA showed closeup pictures of rats—crawling along telephone lines and down poles, and rummaging in garbage. The audience's revulsion at seeing the rats would then, presumably, motivate them to purchase garbage cans.

Sexual Attraction

You were probably wondering when we were going to get to this one, because it is such an obvious and widely used appeal. It is also used in broadcasting for at least two somewhat different purposes. It can serve a structural purpose, that of attracting and holding audience attention in programs and commercials. Or, as a persuasive appeal, it can take the form of purchasing products because we believe that doing so will provide us with some sexual attraction to others. The distinction is a subtle one, and in practice both uses of sex attraction are often merged.

For example, a local boat dealer produces a TV spot featuring a boat with a bikini-clad local beauty contest winner reclining on the deck. Her presence visually catches the attention of males in the audiences. The persuasive appeal added by her presence is indirect; it is the suggestion that if one buys the boat, girls who look like that (and who are clothed like that) will be available to the purchaser. That appeal can be made even more obvious if the girl is given a vocal part in the spot which says something with the effect of: ''I really go for men who enjoy their pleasures . . . like this beautiful boat.''

That example describes one obvious form of sexual attraction, that of physical appeal, but this is by no means the only form. The appeal may also be presented by any suggestion of romance and through music, most forms of which have sexual, romantic connotations. You should be aware, however, that in recent years there has been a good deal of negative criticism on the use of sex attraction in advertising. A number of campaigns have been criticized for what are seen to be exploitive uses of sex. Sex has also become a more sensitive topic since homosexuality has become more open; it is no longer safe to assume that sexual attraction always means heterosexual relationships.

Sympathy and Compassion

These terms describe the emotional reactions of most people when they are confronted by situations, such as disasters or disease, which place other people in less fortunate circumstances.

This appeal is quite likely to be used in public service campaigns—for example, those which appeal for donations to support research and treatment for diseases, or for homeless and starving children, or for saving the whales, or dogs and cats, or for aid to the victims of floods, fires, and earthquakes.

It may also be used in ads for commercial products that are themselves connected with unfortunate events—florists, funeral parlors, and the like.

Sympathy and compassion are frequently found in connection with the appeals to fear, guilt, and imitation. In order to evoke this appeal effectively in a target audience, the writer will need to make it possible for the members of the audience to see themselves in the situation of the less fortunate.

Conclusion

With this chapter we have concluded our examination of the relationship between the business of broadcasting and writing which we began in Chapter 1 and continued in Chapters 8, 9, and here. We have also concluded our presentation of the principles we feel are important to successful writing. In the next seven chapters we will apply those principles to forms of announcements and programs that make up the bulk of radio and TV schedules.

To set forth our approach to the writing-programming-management relationship, we used a sequence of four questions which we believe writers can and should use to clarify their understanding of what may be expected of them whenever a piece of copy is to be written. Those questions delineate a sequential process writers need to learn in order to prepare effective copy.

It is necessary, first, to be able to identify correctly the sponsors of programs and announcements and to understand precisely why sponsors are willing to finance the production and broadcast of each particular program. They do so because they hope to influence the behavior of audiences. Thus the second requirement, that the writer must have a clear perception of the audience for which these materials are produced. Third, audiences may be influenced by choosing persuasive appeals which are strong for the targeted group.

The word *process* is important to this discussion, because none of the three areas discussed here—program purposes, target audience, or persuasive appeals—can be completely delineated. There are no absolute, final lists that can be developed. The reader should use this outline, as well as those developed in the preceding two chapters, and the examples given as guides in sharpening his or her own ability to make judgments on the other, similar, situations that will be encountered every time there is a program or an advertisement to be written.

One final thought: In this chapter we have tried to explain the process of persuasion as it takes place in broadcasting; we have avoided judgmental or critical comments. There are critics who argue that the entire process of creating or stimulating wants and desires on the part of audiences and then showing how specific products can satisfy those wants—thereby leading to the purchase of those products—is somehow unfair. Other critics object to the process as being manipulative or underhanded. Advertisers should be more open; advertising messages should be straightforward and informational, they argue.

We want to avoid being drawn into these criticisms, either to attack or defend the process as it currently operates. Each individual writer is entitled to determine whether or not he or she can survive or is willing to be a part of "the system," or to what extent he or she wants to expend the effort and energy to attack, modify, or subvert the system. What we have done is to explain how that system works.

Exercises
1. Assume you are writing an ad for a product aimed at each of several different target audiences. First, select several fairly narrowly described target audiences (such as white, middle-class male teenagers). Then, for each target group, consider:

   a. What *authority figures* would you include in your ad to reach that target?

   b. What *specialized vocabulary* (slang) would you use?

   c. What *level* of *intensity* (hard sell, use and style of music) is likely to be most effective?

   d. What persuasive appeals (and what forms of those appeals) would you place in your campaign?

2. View a selection of television commercials and public service announcements (and/or radio spots). What persuasive appeals do you detect in each ad? Which ads contain appeals that provide strong motivation to you personally? If the announcement does not contain strong appeals to you, do you think it has strong appeals for some other target audience?

Key Terms and Concepts

aesthetics
audience gratifications
demographics
participation advertising

persuasive appeals
program purpose
sponsors and sponsorship
targeting

Part 3

Practice

In this part we will examine in some detail the writing of broadcast announcements and the broad categories of programs that make up the bulk of most station schedules. One additional chapter considers writing for corporate and instructional programs, most of which are not actually broadcast, but which follow the same writing principles. A final chapter presents a number of other program categories in somewhat less detail. These are program types that do not usually require detailed scripts in advance of broadcast.

Not only do these genres represent the bulk of the content on station and network schedules, they are also the types beginning writers are most likely to encounter.

Before we consider the various types of programs, we do want to caution you about the use of generalized labels to describe television programs and radio formats. While it is useful to have shorthand labels to communicate within the industry, writers must be careful not to let labels obscure the basic principles of good writing. We now have, for example, the recently coined term *soft news* to describe news programs and stories that cover feature, nontimely items. The difference between soft news and traditional hard news, however, is not so much in the writing; it is in the different gratifications derived by audiences who watch the stories, and therefore in the different audience groups that will be attracted.

Similarly, *docudramas* are a cross between documentaries and dramas. They are based on real events and people, but they are fictionalized, re-created dramatizations, and their preparation follows the principles of dramatic writing.

Another new term is *infomercial,* used to describe a long, presumably factual and informational pitch for a product or company. It is a commercial, but long enough to require attention to structural principles, with information as a primary appeal, and quite possibly using documentary techniques for its preparation.

Another problem with program labels is that they don't all describe the same things; there is an "apples and oranges" problem. Some program labels describe the content of the program. News, music, and public affairs programs are labeled this way. Other categories use terms descriptive of the structure or form in which the content is presented, such as drama, variety, or interview programs. Others may be labeled on the basis of their appeal—an adventure program, for example. Still others are described on the basis of their intended audience; children's programs or women's programs are examples of this practice.

Beware of program labels that inadequately describe the writing task. You should learn to examine each task on the basis of all four descriptors—content, form, appeal, and intended audience.

Now, having provided those warnings, we will proceed to use typical and readily understood labels to title the chapters of Part 3.

Chapter 11

Announcements

In broadcasting, persuasion is accomplished primarily through the use of short materials—announcements. There are three basic types—the *commercial advertising announcement*, usually called a *commercial* or an *ad;* the *public service announcement*, or *PSA*, and the *promotional announcement*, or *promo*. The word *spot* is also used as a synonym for announcement—usually, but not always, to refer to commercials.

Another form of material we will consider is the editorial. Editorials are not really a form of announcement, as most people in the industry categorize content, but they are usually of announcement length, and their intent is basically persuasive, so they can be fitted within the approach of this chapter. In most of the chapter we will use the commercial announcement as our focus; separate sections will consider problems unique to PSAs, to promos, and to editorials.

Preliminary Considerations

To be successful at writing announcements, you will need to do a great deal of planning prior to the actual writing. Before attempting to put words on paper, you must have a clear understanding of the answers to these questions, some of which were raised in earlier chapters.

Purpose

(1) What is the sponsor's long-range goal? (2) What is the specific purpose of this announcement? Does it differ from the long-range goal? How? (3) What other supporting materials are to be used in the campaign—other media, salespersons, point-of-purchase displays, special promotions?

Target Audiences

(4) What audience group must the sponsor reach in order to accomplish the purpose intended? (5) Can that group be reached using the station/channel on which this ad is to be placed and at the time/day when it is to appear?

**Persuasive
Appeals**

(6) What appeals will be used to motivate the audience toward the action needed to accomplish the sponsor's purpose? (7) Are those appeals appropriate for the target audience? Do they relate directly to the specific purpose of the ad?

Structure

(8) What device will be used to attract the attention of the audience to the spot? (9) Are a limited number of concepts used so that the spot has a unified approach? (10) Will any form of structural variety be used? (11) What specialized pacing, or mood, if any, should be given to the spot? (12) Is any form of climax to be included?

At this point we encourage you to go back into the chapters of Part 2 and review the sections on sponsors and their purposes (Chapter 8), on target audiences (Chapter 9), persuasive appeals (Chapter 10), and program structure (Chapter 5). In the next few pages we'll examine how those principles are applied to the process of announcement writing.

Purpose

The intent of the originators of all types of announcements is basically persuasive. For commercials, that's obvious. But the intent behind PSAs and promos is also persuasive, although in those cases it may not be so obvious. Many PSAs and promos are written in a factual style, rather than in persuasive language. For example, a PSA may say: "St. Michael's church will hold its annual bazaar and street dance next Sunday. . . ." A promo may announce: "The John Smith program is now heard at a new time on KXXX—Saturday mornings at ten o'clock."

The intent of both messages, although it is expressed in very low-key terms, is to persuade audience members, in the first instance to attend the function, in the second to tune in to the program. Varying degrees of intensity and styles of presentation may be used, but the sponsor's purpose remains the same—get some form of action from the members of the audience.

Very early in the development of an ad campaign the writer must distinguish between the sponsor's long-range need, which we will call the *goal*, and the immediate and specific intent of the particular ad to be written, for which we will use the term *purpose*. For most commercial campaigns, the ultimate persuasive goal will be to sell a product or service, to create goodwill in the audience for the company, to get votes for a political candidate, or something similar that will benefit the advertiser. However, that goal may be quite different from the specific purpose of a particular commercial.

Here are some examples which show the process of analysis used to distinguish long-range goals from specific purposes.

**Selling
Automobiles**

Accomplishing the sponsor's goal for this product requires that the buyer come to the auto dealer's lot or showroom. Sales are completed by a salesperson at the dealership. Radio and TV ads, therefore, have as their specific purpose getting the potential buyer to the agency. The writer must use appeals that will motivate the listener or viewer to do that. Frequently used approaches include the appeal to curiosity: "New model, just arrived—come and see it and drive it." or to savings: "Special price this weekend only, save hundreds of dollars." Or perhaps a mixture of curiosity, adventure, excitement, and sexual attraction: "Come to the big Ford carnival this weekend. See the flagpole sitter; ride the elephant; talk with Hollywood stars Jane Smith and Randy Brown; free soft drinks; see the show. . . ." Note that this approach doesn't even mention the product to be sold; it concentrates solely on getting the audience to the dealership using appeals that have nothing to do with automobiles.

National ads placed by the manufacturers of cars cannot use the same localized approach as those of individual dealers, but the goal remains the same—sell cars—and the purpose also is the same—get people to stop at the dealer's showroom where a salesperson can then attempt to make a sale.

Of course we are oversimplifying the complex persuasive process that leads a person to buy an automobile, and ignoring the many preconditions that must be present before individuals purchase autos or other major items, like having enough money or having an existing car that one is dissatisfied with. The critical point for the broadcast writer is that for this type of product, the broadcast ad cannot by itself close the sale and should not attempt to do so.

Selling Collections of Phonograph Records

In direct contrast to the preceding example, this is one type of product that is sold successfully by direct appeal to audiences.

> For your collection of the 100 greatest hits by all-time favorite country singers, a collection that you cannot get in the stores, send $19.95 plus $1.50 postage and handling to Post Office Box. . . .

You probably recognize the style of that announcement. Other products are sold by the same approach.

In this case, the general goal of the advertiser and the specific purpose of the announcement are identical—to sell the merchandise. All the appeals and motivations necessary to accomplish that sale must be present within the announcement itself. No other support or secondary action will take place.

Not only must the motivations be strong in the ad, but the action required must be easy to take and clearly stated. By the way, this type of selling has become much more successful now that credit cards are widely distributed and direct dial long distance telephoning using "800" numbers is common. The purchaser doesn't have to find a checkbook and then an envelope and a stamp. All he or she needs is to write down a phone number, call, and charge the purchase to a credit card.

Selling Toothpaste

Grocery and drug items are sold using yet another marketing approach. Seldom does an individual make a special trip to a store to buy these items as a direct result of having seen or heard ads for them. (An exception might be something like a new cold remedy. A person really suffering from a cold might be persuaded to make a special trip for a new product that promised relief!)

Another factor that complicates the sale of grocery and drug items is brand awareness and brand loyalty. Advertisers are aware that some buyers change brands of common products for a variety of reasons—price, availability, competition from new brands, improved quality. At the same time, there are buyers who are loyal to brands they know and trust. Advertisers, therefore, are faced with a multifaceted task—continuing to remind loyal or previous customers about the product in the face of advertising by competitors, and at the same time trying to obtain new customers from those who have not yet established brand loyalty, or who might be pulled away from competing brands.

As with the automobile purchase, the final decision on which brand to purchase is made at the store, and that decision will be made some time after exposure to the broadcast ad, a time period that may range from a few minutes to days or even weeks after the exposure. But contrary to the automobile situation, there usually is no salesperson present to "close" the sale in the grocery store. The customer alone will make the final decision on which brand of toothpaste to buy. In making that decision, the appeals of radio or television spots may be diluted or reinforced by a number of other factors such as price, or special displays at the point of purchase, or coupon offers, or competition. The advertiser, however, counts on at least some purchasing decisions being made as a result of the customer's having been recently exposed to broadcast ads for the product.

Public Utility Company

In most communities, public utilities such as the local gas or power company are regulated monopolies. They do not have to advertise to sell their product. Any customer who wants electricity, for example, must deal with the local power company and pay the regulated rate. But these companies do advertise for purposes not related to direct sales. The goal may be to maintain (or improve) the image that company has among its customers, to negate or minimize the ill will that might otherwise be generated by the next rate increase. To accomplish that goal, the specific purpose of an ad campaign might be to show what a good neighbor the company is and how it contributes to and involves itself in community affairs.

Another purpose for utility companies which has become especially important in recent years is to encourage conservation, thereby reducing the amount of costly new construction needed to keep up with demand. Here the goal and the specific purpose are more directly related. (Interestingly, one of the companies that used to provide an excellent example of "goodwill" sponsorship was the Bell Telephone System, which sponsored broadcasts of symphony orchestras and dramatic programs with little persuasive advertising. Now that the telephone industry has been deregulated, the Bell system and its competitors are engaged in persuasive selling just like companies in other consumer industries.)

Yet another purpose for a utility company would be public safety, as in this announcement:

ANNCR: (ECHO) Ben Franklin's historic kite flight . . . and you are there. . . .

SOUND: THUNDER

BEN: (SINGING TO HIMSELF) I'm singing in the rain . . . just singing . . .

ANNCR:	Ben, this doesn't look very safe . . . I mean here you are flying that kite in a thunderstorm. . . .
BEN:	Not to worry . . . not to worry.
ANNCR:	Shouldn't you also be in a wide open space . . . Away from trees and power poles. . . .
BEN:	What's a power pole???
SOUND:	THUNDER—CRASHING ETC. . .
BEN:	Yeow. . . .
ANNCR:	If only Ben had a copy of kite flight. . . . SMUD has copies to help kite flyers have more fun . . . They're free . . . call or drop in . . . SMUD wants to keep the fun in kite flight. . . .

Source: Courtesy of Sacramento Municipal Utility District, Sacramento, CA.

Political Advertising

The goals of political ads are easily stated—to elect candidates or to pass (or defeat) ballot propositions. That goal is accomplished only at the ballot box on election day. Ads leading up to that point will try to influence the decisions of individual voters using indirect persuasive techniques. Detailed discussion of the types of persuasive manipulation used in political campaigns is beyond our capacity to cover in a few paragraphs, however.

Often, at the beginning of a campaign extensive polling of potential voters will be done to find out their positions and their preconceptions regarding a candidate or an issue. Working from that knowledge, political sponsors will use persuasive appeals important to the various voting groups who are not yet committed on the race or proposition, in an attempt to convince those voters that their own values are best preserved by voting in a particular way.

The political ad on the following page uses people typical of the area in which the campaign was being conducted—two farmers and a senior citizen housewife; many voters in the district would be able to identify easily with these people. The ad touches on four issues important to those voters—stopping urban development, water, government waste, and government interference in individual activities. Finally, the appeals used—independence, authority, fear—are strong appeals in this predominantly rural agricultural area.

These examples have been chosen to suggest, first, that there is a common approach or method of analysis that can be used to determine both the general goal behind any sponsor's use of the broadcast media and the specific purpose to be accomplished by a particular ad or campaign, and second, that these goals/ purpose combinations can vary widely with different products and situations.

BERNIE RICHTER
TV Spot #2
"Testimonial"

VIDEO	AUDIO
SLIDE—BERNIE IN FIELD W/FARMER	ANNCR: Bernie Richter <u>stopped</u> urban development of our agricultural land. . . .
FARMER ON TRACTOR SUPER: BOB WALLACE FARMER DURHAM	WALLACE: Since he's been our supervisor, none of our land zoned for farming's been subdivided. . . .
SLIDE—BERNIE TALKING TO GROUP	ANNCR: Richter's <u>leadership</u> removed one million dollars in waste disposal from property taxes. . . .
SENIOR LADY TAKING OUT GARBAGE SUPER: JEANNE L. WHITE HOUSEWIFE BUTTE COUNTY	WHITE: I'm not paying for the disposal of someone else's garbage. . . . I'm only paying for my own . . . and that makes sense. . . .
SLIDE—BERNIE IN FIELD WITH WATER	ANNCR: Richter <u>prevented</u> the export of our ground waters. . . .
YOUNG FARMER W/WIFE SUPER: JIM AND JOYCE MEAD ALMOND GROWERS CHICO	JIM: Hundreds of wells would be pumping our water south if he hadn't stopped it during the drought. . . .
SLIDE—RICHTER FAMILY SUPER: RE-ELECT RICHTER SUPER: PAID BY CITIZENS FOR RICHTER	ANNCR: Bernie Richter gets things done . . . re-elect Supervisor Richter.

Source: Courtesy of the writer, Frank LaRosa, and of Bernie Richter.

Using this approach, you can make a similar analysis for each advertising campaign on which you work.

Target Audience

In the general discussion of target audiences (Chapter 9), we used two examples of targets for commercial products—washing detergents and car stereos. Here are some additional examples that further describe the kind of analysis needed to match product and audience.

Acne Medicine

Acne medicines are used almost exclusively by teenagers. An effective campaign for a brand of acne medicine is quite likely to use a radio station (as opposed to TV, because teens listen much more to radio than they watch TV) and a station that plays rock music (the first choice of most teens). The cost per exposure to teens will be much less on a rock radio station than it would be on a prime-time television program, where the majority of the audience would have no interest in that product. The high price of the TV ad would be largely wasted on unwanted audiences.

This is an example of a product which has a quite narrowly defined audience. In such situations, both the writing and the placement of the announcement is made somewhat easier because the relationship between the product, the audience, and the persuasive appeals which would be effective in the announcement are fairly obvious.

Geritol

This vitamin product is an example of a product/client that made a deliberate decision to get away from a narrow target audience. Some years ago, Geritol had a reputation as an "old-folks" vitamin. The ads carried that image and were placed in programs that appealed primarily to older people. One such program on which Geritol advertised heavily was the Lawrence Welk program.

Then the advertising agency for Geritol decided that image was too narrow; it restricted the sale of the product. Recent Geritol ads feature younger women (and men) and use different persuasive appeals. And the ads are being run in prime-time programs with broader audiences. (Please note that since prime-time television programs have very large and very diverse demographic audiences, products/clients that can use such a broad audience efficiently must themselves be very broadly based—that is they must be products which can be and are sold to widely different groups of people.)

PSA for a Local Amateur Theater Company

The purpose of the campaign is to increase the size of the audiences attending performances by the company. We can assume that there is a small but loyal group of regular theater goers who are familiar with this company, who know through nonbroadcast promotional means what plays are being presented and when. This group does not need PSAs to be induced to attend. A second group may be people who have had previous positive experiences when attending the theater and who might easily be motivated to attend, but who have gotten out of the habit for one reason or another, perhaps simply because they haven't been kept informed of what is available. For them, the approach used could be mostly informational, and this is the style usually employed by PSAs in campaigns of this sort.

But to increase theater attendance significantly in a community, new audience groups must be persuaded. The campaign is likely to require a considerable period of time to break down prejudices against attending live theater and to build up positive images in audience groups who have not had experience with the theater. Broadcast messages may not be able to accomplish this goal, or at least not alone.

Campaign for a Candidate for a State Assembly Seat

Voter analysis in political campaigns has become a very sophisticated business, well beyond the few considerations we can suggest here. But here is a quick sketch of how a political analysis might be approached. We have chosen an assembly race, which is a partisan campaign, but one in which the election takes place within a reasonably confined geographic area. Since the voting group is defined geographically, one basic consideration would be to use media which match that geographic area. But most important would be to understand the existing political climate in the district, and to identify those groups of voters who might be persuaded to vote for the candidate.

Let's assume the district is balanced, with approximately equal numbers of Republican and Democrat voters, and that past elections have gone both ways. Our candidate in this election is the Republican.

One of the groups in the electorate will be strongly partisan Republicans. We should not take them totally for granted, but in all probability they will vote for our candidate, and it certainly will require very little effort to capture them. At the other extreme will be strongly partisan Democrats. Even if we campaign extensively (and expensively) to reach this group, there is little possibility of converting them to our cause. Better not waste a lot of effort and money on them.

The groups on which to concentrate, then, are voters who are not strongly partisan. In very general terms, these are likely to be younger voters and those who have recently moved into the area who do not have strong ties in the community. Our precampaign research should attempt to identify what issues and qualities in a candidate these groups find important, and then build the ad campaign around those concepts.

As with all our examples, this one is highly simplified, but it pictures the process of analysis that must be done before actual writing can begin on a successful ad. The writer needs to know what audience must be reached in order to accomplish the purpose intended. That audience should be defined as accurately as possible.

Persuasive Appeals

We have already emphasized the importance of motivational appeals in persuasive copy. Briefly summarized, the target audience for any sponsor can be motivated to take action when it can be demonstrated to those individuals that taking that action will be in their own best interests. The copywriter's job is to provide these incentives, to motivate, to point out to the audience what the advantages are of doing what is suggested in the announcement.

Be careful not to dilute and weaken the effectiveness of the ad by using too many appeals. It does not follow that if one appeal is effective, six will be better. Concentrate on the one, two, possibly three appeals which are most appropriate to the target audience and the product, and which relate to each other as well.

The generalizations we made in Chapter 10 on the applicability of appeals to various demographic groups can be usefully applied to commercials, PSAs, and promos. However, in most campaigns those generalizations will need to be made much more specific. Survey research using samples from the targeted audience will attempt to determine attitudes and perceptions of the audience in detail, and how those attitudes and perceptions can be changed to meet the needs of the client.

Here are two examples of how purpose, audience, and appeals are considered in actual campaigns.

A Public Service Campaign for Blood Pressure Testing

This campaign was directed specifically at the Mexican-American population in the Houston area. It was designed to make this population aware of the problem of high blood pressure and to encourage specific behavioral responses to that problem.

The analysis began with the findings of a community health survey which showed that only 15 percent of the Mexican-American population recognized high blood pressure as a primary risk factor in coronary artery disease. It also showed that only 35 percent of this group considered the physician the primary source of health care information. For 46 percent the primary source is the mass media—television, radio, newspapers, and magazines—and over 24 percent turn to television for health care information.

In the creation of the three television PSAs used in the campaign, two types of consultant groups were used—representatives from the target population and representatives of the mass media. In-depth discussions in Spanish were held with two different groups of Mexican-Americans to discover what appeals would be relevant and involving and what kind of language should be used. From this input, a concept of the kinds of PSAs to use was formed.

The producers then consulted with two different groups involved in mass media. The first group included the public service directors of the five Houston television stations. The second was composed of Mexican-Americans who worked in the mass media in any capacity. The expertise and insights of these consultants provided focus to the PSAs and also resulted in approval of and sympathy with the goals of the project.

Three different presentations were chosen: A street scene, a clinic, and a softball game. Scripts and storyboards for the spots were created, and the consultant groups reviewed them before the spots were actually produced. All the 30-second PSAs were in Spanish and used local Spanish-speaking actors and actresses.

The street scene was a night sequence, and high blood pressure was presented as the silent killer lurking in the shadows. The camera took the role of the "killer" that stalked unsuspecting victims on the street. The spot's audio explained why one should be concerned with high blood pressure and what effects coronary artery disease could have on the family. The tone was mysterious and somewhat alarming. At the end of the spot—as in all of them—viewers were given a phone number to call for further information and were urged to have their blood pressure checked.

The clinic spot emphasized that high blood pressure often has no symptoms, and opened with a visit of a woman to a fortuneteller to see what the future held for her. That visit resulted in another, this time a visit to a local clinic for a blood pressure checkup. The sequence was designed to familiarize viewers with the medical procedure and allay any apprehensions they might have. This particular PSA was designed to appeal to the women in the target audiences.

The softball spot was designed to appeal to the men. Softball is an extremely popular sport with Mexican-Americans in the Houston area. There are organized leagues, team uniforms, and all the color of a major sport. Entire families make it a habit to attend the games. The softball spot was very action-oriented and got right to the message that anyone—even youthful athletes—may be a victim of high blood pressure.[1]

Olympia Beer and the "Artesians"

After a series of not very successful advertising approaches had resulted in a "fuzzy perception" of Olympia in the Northwest, proposals from new advertising agencies were solicited. The Chiat/Day agency won the competition with this campaign, which took a radically different approach to the marketing of beer.

The other breweries were essentially saying, "Big hairy guys getting together after work, after a special exertion to reward themselves with our beer." They had all defined beer as a reward and were grouped together in that definition. That gave Olympia the chance for an end run with something entirely different that said, in essence, "Our beer is a lot of fun."

The account executive for the account, Bill Kelley, described the campaign:

> We had an equity in the water. Everyone knows it's the water that makes Olympia famous. So what we have here is a campaign built around the water . . . artesian well water. And the Artesians of course, the benevolent, fun-loving, subterranean critters who own the water. They demanded we expand our tag line to "It's *their* water."
>
> The Chiat/Day creative team realized they could not compete head-to-head with the large national breweries, who could afford to pump many more millions of dollars into their campaigns, so they opted for a low-key approach. The "It's the water" slogan stemmed from the beginning of the beer company.
>
> The Artesian campaign said something directly about the water. Brewery representatives had been so close to it for so long that nobody ever thought maybe there could be an "Artesian" behind it all.
>
> Though we are buying media aimed at men 18-to-34, we feel the campaign itself is very broad. We certainly had no desire to tune out anyone; in fact, we believe our efforts deal with one common factor. It's not the age or sex, but a sense of humor. That's pretty common to most beer drinkers.
>
> And from all indications, the campaign caught on in record time. Beer drinkers in one Washington town could not wait for the supply of company-produced T-shirts to arrive. So they made their own. The front of one such effort reads, "I know an Artesian well."

One of the ads in the campaign is described this way:

> The camera moves slowly, methodically through a dark, dank, secluded rain forest. The audience sees various creatures of the night. An owl peers blankly. The feeling generated is that a gnomelike character might pop out from hiding at any moment.
>
> Instead, the camera circles in on a heavily moss-covered wall, no doubt leading to water from the Glacial Age. The announcer begins as the audience sees a squirrel busily at work on top of the well. "Pick up a six-pack of Olympia and celebrate Artesian New Year . . ."
>
> Suddenly, the well erupts with confetti, streamers, party blowers, horns and other hoopla. The squirrel, unconcerned, continues his task.
>
> The scene dissolves to a shot of a cold foamy mug of the product as an animated title changes from "It's the water" to "It's *their* water."[2]

Another ad, in the same vein, is called "The Skeptic" (Figure 11.1).

GUY No.1: Okay . . . okay . . . the Artesians are
the ones . . .
GUY No.2: . . . that make the artesian brewing
water . . .
GUY No.3: . . . that makes Olympia Beer taste so
good.
GUY No.1: (STARTS TO LEAVE) Nice talkin'
to you . . .

GUY No. 2: (STOPS HIM) No . . . really!
GUY No. 1: You ever see one?
GUY No. 4: See what?
GUY No. 3: An Artesian.

BARTENDER: Well, my brother knows a guy whose
uncle saw one once.
GUY No. 5: Oh yeah . . . short, right?
GUY No. 2: No . . . tall.

GUY No. 1: All right . . . let's go over to the
Olympia Brewery and you can **show** me an Artesian.
GUY No. 4: Can't do that.
GUY No. 1: Why not?

GUY No. 2: Tuesday's their bowling night.
GUY No. 1: Oh . . . (TO HIMSELF) Bowling?

Chiat/Day Inc., Advertising

DISSOLVE TO ANIMATED TITLE WHICH
CHANGES FROM "IT'S THE WATER" TO "IT'S
THEIR WATER".

Figure 11.1   Source: Courtesy of Chiat/Day, Los Angeles.

One point we have tried to make in each of the examples is that for an announcement to be successful in the eyes of its sponsor, a substantial number of the audience members individually must take some specific action—and the announcement must at least assist in motivating them to that action.

However, we do not want to overemphasize this motivational step and leave you with the inaccurate impression that every successful commercial must contain an expressed direct action on the part of the audience. Many ads, especially those for widely advertised national products, are quite indirect in their use of appeals to motivate. They often concentrate on a strong, frequently humorous, attention-getting device. There may be only one brief mention of the product, just to remind the audience of the name.

There will, however, be an association of that product with the people, activities, mood, or style presented in the ad, however brief, and that association ties together product and appeals. The physically attractive young men and women playing on the beach may not be seen drinking diet cola, and the sound track consisting of rock music may not even mention the product's name, but when the product logo appears at the conclusion of the spot, the product has been associated with sex appeal, companionship, and personal pleasure.

The success of having made that association will come when individuals who have seen the ad next decide to purchase soft drinks. They will choose this diet cola (or so the client and the ad agency hope) because its presence on the grocery shelf recalls in the memories of the individuals in the target group appeals that have some strength for them.

Structure

Structurally, announcements differ somewhat from other forms of broadcast content. They are the one short form of content that stands alone. Other short pieces of copy, such as individual news stories, are used as elements within longer programs, but announcements, even though they are usually placed within the structure of a program, are prepared and manipulated independently. The considerations of program structure discussed in Chapter 5 are important in the announcement, but not all of those considerations are as important as they are for longer materials.

Attracting Attention

This is a crucial structural requirement for announcements. Audiences tend to look upon announcements as interruptions placed within or between the programs they have chosen to view (or listen to) and enjoy. The announcements, in their view, are the price they know they must pay for enjoyment of the programs. They will tolerate the interruptions, but they don't have to pay attention to the announcements.

On the other hand, as we have seen, sponsors provide programs to attract audiences who will be exposed to the announcements. In the sponsor's view, the announcements are the more (commercially) important material. The commercial writer must recognize this difference in the expectations of audience and sponsor. Although the program material preceding an announcement will bring the audience to the moment at which the ad is aired, the writer of the announcement still must attract attention to the announcement itself.

We might digress for a moment here to contrast this typical American pattern with two other approaches.

In some European broadcast systems, commercial announcements are separated from program content. After a program has been completed, there may be several minutes devoted to a series of commercial messages before programming resumes. In that situation, even more than in the U.S. model, announcements must stand on their own. Structure, appeals, and content—all must contribute toward attracting audience attention, because there is no support from surrounding program materials.

Note also, as a second example, the recent success of pay cable channels and subscription television systems. These programming channels, which do not show commercials and which rely solely on revenues from subscribers, are an indication that substantial numbers of the potential audience will choose to pay a considerable monthly fee for commercial-free programming.

Unity

In an announcement, the structural requirement for unity may be interpreted to mean that all the data appearing in the spot should relate directly to the specific purpose. Hence our insistence earlier that the writer must clearly understand that purpose. Unity is provided by limiting the number of ideas presented and the number of appeals. All the individual statements within the spot should develop and support, with variations and repetition, the specific persuasive purpose of the announcement.

Frequently a salesperson will come back to a broadcast station with an order from a client which includes a lengthy data sheet on the product or store. The beginning writer will be tempted to include all that information in the spot and in the process will seriously weaken the impact of the announcement, because there is simply too much for the audience to handle.

For example, assume a new store has just opened in town. An obvious purpose of the inaugural ad campaign will be to get the audience familiar with the name of the store. Some other material will have to be present, of course, such as the nature of the business (is it a furniture store or a restaurant?) and why the audience should be interested in the store (good values, beautiful merchandise, spectacular view). But if name recognition is more important—and it is certainly important for a new store—then the name should be repeated frequently in the ad, as in this radio spot.

ANNCR: Are you tired of that same old pizza? Do they all taste alike, and look alike? Do your taste buds need an overhaul? Now . . . your problems are solved!

MUSIC: FANFARE

ANNCR: Now . . . there's Luigi's Pizza.
Only the freshest, all natural ingredients are used at Luigi's Pizza.

MORE   MORE   MORE

Three kinds of cheese on every pizza . . . at Luigi's Pizza.
Dough made fresh, every day . . . at Luigi's Pizza.
And three convenient locations . . . Franklin and Fruitridge
in the South area, Folsom and Watt in the North area, and
Eighteenth and K streets downtown.
Luigi's Pizza. Give your taste buds a treat today!

Variety   This can be provided in announcements in the same ways it is provided in longer program forms. (Review those portions of Chapters 5, 6, and 7 which discuss variety as a general structural principle, aural variety, and visual sequencing.) But when more variety and consequently complexity are added to a spot, cost in time and money is also added. Therefore many ads, especially low-cost ads prepared for local clients, and ads that must be produced quickly, use simple techniques with little variety.

Fortunately, providing variety is not a critical consideration in most spots, because they seldom exceed 60 seconds in length, which is within most people's attention span. Some longer ads are beginning to appear, especially on cable channels, and in them aural and pictoral variety do have to be considered. The announcements used as examples in this chapter demonstrate several ways of providing variety.

Pacing   In longer forms of copy, this requirement is primarily a function of the number and length of program elements. In announcements, the term has a different meaning. It refers to the sense of speed or urgency (or lack of it) in the ad, and as such it becomes a contributor to the mood intended for the announcement.

An ad for a used car dealer for example, may use a hurried, forcing style with a rapid breathless pace: "Hurry down today, while this fantastic sale is still on, and before all these terrific bargains are gone. . . ." In contrast, an ad for an expensive wine may want to set a much more leisurely, relaxed, slower-paced mood:

VIDEO	AUDIO
RUSTIC CABIN, FIRE IN FIRE-PLACE; SNOWING OUTSIDE SEEN THROUGH WINDOW; LATE AFTERNOON, DIM LIGHT	<u>MUSIC:</u> <u>SOFT IN BG</u> MAN: Our tenth anniversary. I want everything to be special this weekend, including the wine. WOMAN: (HOLDING GLASS) This is a wonderful choice, John . . . so fruity and mellow. It's delicious. MAN: It's a new Chardonnay, from. . . .

For each ad, the writer needs to make a decision about the pace and mood which are appropriate, and choose settings, voice, vocabulary, and style which establish and maintain that mood.

Climax   The sense of climax in program-length materials is satisfied by a feeling of building up heightened interest and anticipation as the program proceeds. It's part of the solution to the problem of maintaining audience interest over a period of time. In shorter announcements, that consideration is not as important. But climax serves another function in the announcement—that of leaving the audience with a bit of material to recall at the time and place where the product might be purchased. Recall our discussion about the lag between exposure to the advertising message and opportunity to purchase most products.

Climax, in this sense, takes the form of a tag or punchline to the announcement. Frequently it's some unanticipated or humorous twist to the situation. For example:

VIDEO	AUDIO
WIDE SHOT—LIVING ROOM WALL—FOOTPRINTS WALK UP WALL TO CEILING	SOUND: FOOTSTEPS MOM: (YELLS) Oh, Tommy!
CAMERA TILTS BACK TO RE-VEAL FOOTPRINTS ALL OVER CEILING	ANNCR: No matter *what* happens to your decorative ceiling, Sears can respray it and restore its original beauty. Sears authorized installers will carefully protect your rooms and furnish-ings. . . .
WORKMEN MASKING WALLS AND FURNITURE SUPER: Contractors' Lic. #25455	
CEILING BEING SPRAYED FOOTPRINTS BEING COVERED SUPER: $139.00 up to 44 sq. ft.	And Sears can spray the average living room, dining and hall for 139 dollars. . . .
FINISHED ROOM & CEILING SUPER: Sears logo	Call Sears Home Improvement Center today, for a free estimate in your home. . . .
GO THROUGH TO LOGO	
FOOTPRINTS BEGIN TO WALK UP LOGO	SOUND: FOOTSTEPS
STOP	MOM: (YELLS) Tommy!
TURN AND HURRY BACK	SOUND: FOOTSTEPS, FADE OUT

Reprinted by permission.

Now, after having answered the twelve questions asked at the beginning of the chapter, or having had them answered for you by a client, salesperson, or account executive, you are ready to write the copy for the announcement.

Organization/Sequence

All the questions asked earlier are important in the development of announcements, but two are also critical in the writing process itself. At the beginning of the announcement there must be some device to attract attention, and the action wanted from the audience must be specified and motivated.

**Attracting
Attention**

We've already discussed the structural importance of this step. The audience's attention must be attracted before there can be any hope of accomplishing the sponsor's purpose. If the audience members turn their attention to other matters—pick up newspapers, start talking with others in the room, run to the kitchen or bathroom, or whatever—the persuasive impact is lost.

A number of devices can be used to attract attention.

1. A humorous statement or situation may be introduced, and possibly continued, to provide a consistent mood throughout the spot. The Sears A-Spray and the kite flying spot used as examples earlier in this chapter both contain humor.

2. The interaction of different characters in a dramatic situation or vignette will attract attention. Frequently that device is used to set up a problem facing the characters in the vignette. The remainder of the announcement is used to solve the problem, with the aid of the sponsor's product, of course. The Perry Boys smorgy ad used as an example of layout form (Chapter 4) uses both humor and a dramatic situation to attract attention.

3. Unusual settings can attract attention. Place the announcer and the product up in a hot air balloon, at the whale tank at Marineland or, for radio, simulate a similar setting using narration, music, and/or sound effects. Doing the ad from the client's store provides an unusual setting, but this device is used so frequently that it may not attract the level of attention wanted.

4. Unusual or startling statements also will draw the attention of audience members to the message: "Eight hundred American travelers will be killed on the nation's highways this holiday weekend. Don't you be one of them. . . ."

5. Music and sound can be attention-getting devices in themselves (apart from their use in establishing a mood and/or location). For television, these aural devices must of course be paralleled with an appropriate visual image, but for radio, a bugle, or an auctioneer's patter, or the cacophony of automobile horns will attract attention. (Don't use sirens, however, such as a fire siren for a fire sale. Too much confusion and even panic can be caused by this sound effect.)

   A musical introduction to an announcement frequently is continued behind the narration of an announcement. When it is used this way, it is called a *musical bed,* and its function is primarily to maintain a mood for the ad. Some stations as a matter of policy put a bed behind every spot, but too frequent use of music as background weakens the effectiveness of music for attention getting and mood setting. Use background music only when it provides a positive contribution to the spot and not just to "be there."

**Motivating
Action**

The second necessary element in the successful announcement is to motivate action, and we've already discussed the persuasive tools which can be used to do that. At its simplest, the process of persuasion is one of convincing an individual listener or viewer that it is in his or her best interest to do what is proposed.

Note that we are now emphasizing individuals, whereas in the discussion of target audiences we were talking about demographic groups of people. While it is necessary sometimes to generalize about people, using demographic averages and the generalized and predictable behaviors of groups, in the final analysis it is individuals who buy (contribute, vote), and it is individuals who listen to radio and watch television. In writing announcements, talk to the individual.

The action step itself involves an important writing sequence, which can be explained as follows: First, make the persuasive appeals—show the audience members *why* they should take the action requested; show them the value in that action. Then, tell them *what* to do, specifically, to achieve that gain (and, of course, the sponsor's purpose as well): Go to the store, pick up the phone, mail a letter, go to the blood bank. Finally, tell them *how* to do it. Give the phone numbers, the addresses, the directions, the hours that the store is open; repeat the client's name; or provide whatever procedural information is important. Again, be specific.

Frequently the novice writer will get these steps out of sequence—for example putting the information on *how* to order tickets to the play ahead of the material that provides the persuasive clincher to the audience. In that case, the listener will not pay attention to the what and how of accomplishing the sponsor's purpose, because he or she has not yet been convinced of the value of so doing. Later in the sequence, he or she may become convinced: "Hey that sounds like a great idea for something to do this weekend." But now it's too late to recall the details on how to take the action, because that information was not perceived as important moments earlier when it was presented out of sequence. That listener is now left with a frustration. There is something he or she has become convinced he or she would like to do, but now without the necessary information on where, when, how to do it.

Schemes for Organizing Announcements

There are many techniques you can use to organize the announcement to present the attention-getting material, the persuasive appeals, and other information in a coherent manner. Of course, the overall length of the spot will determine how much time is available for intermediate steps and secondary development. In a 10-second promo, for example, there isn't much time for any embellishment.

Here are some ways in which announcements are frequently organized. These suggestions are not mutually exclusive. Many combinations are used, such as testimonial and demonstration, or a dramatic, problem-solving commercial.

Problem-Solution

This method of sequencing is very common.

1. Set up a problem. Often the problem situation is developed in connection with the attention-getting device. An opening dramatic vignette for example, sets up a conflict between two characters or expresses a problem that seems to be without solution.

2. Create the impression that the problem can be solved by the use of the sponsor's product. Sometimes the relationship between the problem and solution is very direct and obvious: "Do you have dandruff? Then use (NAME) dandruff shampoo." In other situations, the relationship is more subtle: "Do you have a problem getting girls to pay attention to you? It may be your hair. Use (NAME) shampoo."
   And in the final frame for television, the young man is shown with a gorgeous head of hair and several attractive girls hanging around him. The implication is that the product does indeed solve the problem.

FOOTE, CONE & BELDING/HONIG

P.O. BOX 3183 SAN FRANCISCO, CALIF.

(415) 398-5200

Client:	THE CLOROX COMPANY
Product:	TILEX
Title:	"CURTAIN, 2"
Commercial No.:	CXTX 3303
Date Approved:	4/18/83

1. (MUSIC UP)
    (SFX: FOOTSTEPS)
    ANNCR: (VO) Behind this
    curtain is something awful.

2. Something ugly.

3. Something that may be in
    your home right now.

4. (SFX: SHOWER
    CURTAIN THROWN
    BACK)

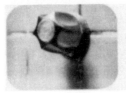   

5. Creepy, black mildew
    stains

6. right there in your shower.

7. It's time you get them—

8. before they get to you.

9. With Tilex Instant Mildew
    Stain Remover.

10. (SFX: SPRAY) With Tilex,
    there is no scrubbing. You
    just spray

11. and leave.

12. Mildew stains begin to
    disappear on contact.

13, In minutes,

14. they're gone.

15. Tilex.

16. It gets mildew stains before
    they get to you.
    (MUSIC OUT)

Figure 11.2
Source: Courtesy of Foote, Cone & Belding/Honig, San Francisco.

Demonstration   This approach to organizing a spot, showing an advertised product in use, is primarily a television technique. It is possible for the creative writer to develop a radio situation in which, for example, two characters talk about and describe a product being used, but that's a difficult task. On television, however, audiences have come to expect demonstration. We watch the announcer/actor actually shampooing his or her hair. We see the coffee being brewed, poured, and drunk, and so on. The Tilex spot (Figure 11.2) combines both the problem-solution approach and that of demonstration.

Telling a Story   The development of a simple story line in which the product is involved is another logical method of providing sequence to a spot. It's very similar to the problem-solution approach and to demonstration, and it usually involves dramatic development. Figure 11.3 (p. 268) is another ad from the Olympia Beer "Artesians" campaign; it uses this approach.

The ad for Pacific Telephone (Figure 11.4, p. 269) is one of a series of spots that uses the same storytelling approach, varying the participants and the situations.

Testimonial   Many variations exist within the testimonial-type commercial, but most fall into one of three types:

1. The sales pitch is given by an expert. A person qualified as a wine expert or a restaurant owner, for example, talks about a wine, or an auto racing driver describes the handling and comfort of a new car.

2. The pitch is given by a celebrity. In this case there is no obvious connection between the person providing the testimony and the product, but the implication is that the product must have value and importance because it is associated with a person who has these qualities. Of course the celebrity must be recognized as such by the target audience to whom the ad is pitched.

3. The pitch is given by an "ordinary person." In this case the persuasive appeal is that of identification rather than importance. The members of the target audience identify with the person giving the testimony, who is "just an ordinary homemaker," or something similar. This form of testimonial is easily combined with the problem-solution approach. The "ordinary homemaker" is confronted with a problem, tries the product that solves the problem, and then testifies to that fact to the audience.

The testimonial for Twice as Fresh (Figure 11.5, p. 270) is one of this last type.

Other Spokespersons   Other types of spokespersons can be recruited or created to make a pitch for a product. The most obvious and frequently used, of course, is to have an announcer deliver the client's message. Well-known personalities may also be used. This approach is almost identical to the celebrity testimonial, differing only in that the personality does not (in this case) "endorse" the product, but merely delivers the client's message. The owner or manager of the company may also appear as his or her own spokesperson. When one person is used to deliver commercials for a company or product over a period of time, then he or she becomes the "image" of that client in the minds of the audience.

"NIGHT VATMASTER"

VATMASTER: Evenin'. I'm Night Vatmaster here at the Olympia Brewery.

I expect you've heard about the artesian brewing water we use.

Well . . . I seen 'em . . . the Artesians. They come up late at night . . . leave little wet footprints all around.

I let 'em be though. I figure, what those Artesians do for the taste of Oly . . .

. . . don't want to make 'em mad.

DISSOLVE TO ANIMATED TITLE WHICH CHANGES FROM "IT'S THE WATER" TO "IT'S THEIR WATER".

Figure 11.3
Source: Courtesy, Chiat/Day, Inc., Advertising.

"MONSIGNOR, SR."

AXPT 3618

CLIENT: PACIFIC TELEPHONE
RESIDENCE USAGE

AGENCY: FOOTE , CONE & BELDING/HONIG
LENGTH: 60 SECONDS

MUSIC UP.

SFX: FOOTSTEPS.

SFX: BIRDS, OUTDOOR SOUNDS.

PRIEST: Monsignor? There's a phone call for you. A Will McDonough?

MONSIGNOR: Will. . . .
PRIEST: . . . . says you played football together. . . .
MONSIGNOR: That we did, that we did. . . .

SINGER(VO): Drift away, drift away,

How the time disappears

Just the blink of an eye

And the days turn into years

Drift away, drift away. . . .

MONSIGNOR: Will!

ANN(VO): Think of all the times you thought about calling old friends and haven't done it.

Then think about how good it would make them feel.

Old friends are only as far away as you let them be.

SINGER(VO): There's so much left to say. . .
WILL(VO): Can you still catch a pass, Patrick?

MONSIGNOR: If you can still throw it, Will.
SINGER(VO): Don't drift away.
MUSIC OUT.

Figure 11.4
Source: Courtesy of Foote, Cone & Belding/Honig, San Francisco.

FOOTE, CONE & BELDING/HONIG

P.O. BOX 3183 SAN FRANCISCO, CALIF.

(415) 398-5200

Client: THE CLOROX CO.
Product: TWICE AS FRESH
Title: "TEST, CAROLE"
Commercial No.: CXAF 1304
Date Approved: 4/9/81

1. CAROLE KALMAN: Garlic.

2. I smell garlic.

3. MAN: (VO) Is Twice As Fresh clearly better than solid air fresheners

4. at eliminating odors?

5. First we tried a leading solid.

6. CAROLE: Well, it's still garlic.

7. MAN: (VO) Later, we tried Twice As Fresh.

8. CAROLE: (SNIFFING) I don't smell any garlic.

9. It's like fresh.

10. ANNCR: Twice As Fresh

11. has an exclusive flow through system

12. with twice the freshening area of leading solids.

13. So it eliminates odors better.

14. You can even wave it for sudden smells.

15. Twice As Fresh. It's clearly better.

16. CAROLE: I would definitely buy Twice As Fresh.

Figure 11.5
Source: Courtesy of Foote, Cone & Belding/Honig, San Francisco.

Spokespersons can also be developed from cartoon or fantasy characters or animals, such as the Jolly Green Giant, or Morris the Cat.

Comparisons This approach compares the sponsor's product with competing brands. Not too many years ago it was considered bad practice to compare brands, or even to mention competitors. Then some products began to compare themselves to "Brand X," a thinly veiled reference to the major competing brand. Finally, direct references to competing brands began to be made and are now quite common. The writer using this approach needs to be careful. Don't just run down the competition; the audience may react negatively and begin to purchase the "underdog" competitor's product. Instead, emphasize the better qualities—ingredients, size, price—of your brand.

Special Effects Up until now, when describing TV commercials we have assumed that if announcers or dramatic characters were to be seen, they would be "live" persons. That doesn't have to be the case. Various forms of special effects provide visual impressions—movement and color particularly—that can be very effective in reinforcing emotional appeals.

To provide all the details necessary to produce a special effects spot, you will need much more background in those techniques than we would be able to provide in an introductory text. Should you choose, at this early stage in your learning, to do an effects spot, you will just have to describe the effects wanted as best you can. Later, if the occasion demands, you can work out the details for a particular spot with producers who specialize in these techniques. Keep in mind, however, that special effects also mean added cost.

The Sears A-Spray ad shown earlier in this chapter requires special effects. The Levis ad (Figure 11.6, p. 272) uses elaborate animation, which is one form of special effect, to get the pants moving across the landscape.

Using Multiple Voices Announcements that use a single voice are by far the most common on both radio and television. They are fast and inexpensive to prepare. Even when recorded, they can be ready in a few minutes. When the voice used is that of a recognized personality, whatever personal credibility that person has is carried over into the spot, and the announcement becomes a form of testimonial.

But single-voice spots are structurally weak, especially with regard to variety, and in attracting attention. The use of multiple voices strengthens these structural elements. At the same time, however, multiple voices create some problems for the writer. Here are some techniques, and some cautions, on using multiple voices in announcements.

The Dialogue Announcement Dramatic dialogue can provide high-interest material quickly. It is also effective in setting up a problem (in a problem-solution approach). However, it is much more difficult to deliver the solution or to motivate action believably using dialogue. What would be considered by the audience as normal or believable dialogue doesn't usually have sufficient persuasive strength. On the other hand,

LEVI'S® "ROUNDUP"

(Music) Yessir, this drive started over a hundred years ago, back in California.

Just a few head of Levi's Blue Jeans, and a lot of hard miles.

Across country that would've killed ordinary pants.

But Levi's? They _thrived_ on it! If anything, the herd got stronger —and bigger.

First there was _kid's_ Levi's. Ornery little critters...seems like nothing stops 'em.

Then there was _gal's_ pants, and tops, and skirts. Purtiest things you ever set eyes on.

And just to prove they could make it in the big city, the herd bred a new strain called Levi's Sportswear.

Jackets, shirts, slacks... a bit fancy for this job, I reckon, but I do admire the way they're made.

Fact is, pride is why we put our name on everything in this herd.

Tells folks, "This here's _ours!_" If you like what you got, then c'mon back!

We'll be here. You see, fashions may change...

...but quality _never_ goes out of style!

Levi Strauss & Co.   Two Embarcadero Center, San Francisco, California 94106

Figure 11.6
Source: Reprinted by permission of Levi Strauss & Co., Two Embarcadero Center, San Francisco, California 94106.

lines of copy that do carry persuasive punch and deliver the sponsor's message effectively won't sound ''right'' coming from the characters in the sketch.

This student commercial for a mythical furniture store demonstrates the problem. When John begins to act as the salesman for the company, he loses his believability as a character.

CATHY: Oh, John! I'm so happy that we've moved here for your new job and I can hardly wait to see our brand new apartment.

JOHN: (WORRIED) Cathy, I think there's something that you should know!

CATHY: What John? Don't tell me you gave the cat away!

JOHN: No, the cat's staying with Harold! Do you remember our old furniture?

CATHY: Of course, John.

JOHN: Well, Cathy, I sold every last piece of it last Saturday at our very own garage sale.

CATHY: You mean that while I was visiting my mother . . . you were selling all of our furniture! I thought you were having a "wonderful" time at the neighbor's garage sale! John, what will we do?

JOHN: We're going to buy all new furniture for our new apartment at Sun City Furniture, Cathy! Sun City Furniture has great looking furniture for every room in our apartment at prices we can afford. I've checked into it Cathy, and we can all have new, modern furniture at a low monthly price at Sun City Furniture. We can get a 10-piece bedroom set—frame, box springs, mattress, 2 end tables, 2 lamps, bedspread, dresser and mirror on sale this weekend for $199.99.

CATHY: I think we've hit the jackpot John! Sun City Furniture, here we come!

ANNCR: That's right folks. Come into Sun City Furniture located at 1000 Morse Avenue. Open 10 to 10 every day. Lots of free parking. You, too, can hit the jackpot!! At Sun City Furniture!

The solution to this problem of believability or unnatural-sounding dialogue is to use the dramatic scene to attract attention and set up the problem, then use an announcer to deliver the persuasive, motivating pitch. Here is a well-constructed example in which a writer with the same assignment included the announcer as a participant in the drama.

YOUNG MAN:	Our first night in our own apartment! Here I come honey.
SOUND:	RUNNING ON FLOOR
YOUNG WOMAN:	No honey. Don't!
SOUND:	CRASH
YOUNG WOMAN:	Well you did it this time. What do we do now about a bed?
SOUND:	CLICK, SCREECH ON RADIO TUNING TO STATION
YOUNG MAN:	How'd the radio come on?
ANNCR:	(ON RADIO FILTER) We know that when you're starting out furniture can be a problem.
YOUNG WOMAN:	You got that right.
ANNCR:	Come to the Sacramento grand opening of Sun City Furniture on Arden Way near Morse Avenue where overhead is low and the savings are passed on to you. Sun City Furniture where you get more for your furniture dollar. We will help you establish and keep a good credit rating. Need to get a good bed?
YOUNG WOMAN:	Yes.
YOUNG MAN:	I'm going to the kitchen, honey.
ANNCR.:	We've got a 10-piece bedroom set including frame, springs, mattress, 2 end tables, 2 table lamps, bedspread, dresser and mirror on sale for only $199 and this 5-piece breakfast room set with 4 chairs and table on sale for just $119.
SOUND:	CRASH OF HEAVY OBJECT & GLASS BREAKING
YOUNG WOMAN:	Honey, what happened?
YOUNG MAN:	The table broke.
YOUNG WOMAN:	Sun City, you're just in time.
ANNCR:	That's Sun City Furniture on Arden near Morse. Plenty of free parking, open 10 to 10 every day.
YOUNG WOMAN:	Honey, we're going to Sun City Furniture before. . . .
SOUND:	CRASH
ANNCR:	That's Sun City Furniture on Arden Way near Morse Avenue. Where your credit is the least of your worries.

Multiple Announcers

Multivoice announcements do not have to include dialogue, however. Having two or more voices simply splits up the narration and also provides structural variety.

This political spot uses the candidate to provide the main voice, with an announcer to add emphasis.

VIDEO	AUDIO
FULL SCREEN ART: Cherie Albusche Certified Public Accountant	ANNCR. VO: Cherie Albusche . . . Certified Public Accountant . . .
CHERIE AT DESK TALKING TO SOMEBODY OFF CAMERA	It's important to understand budgets and finance in education . . . especially after Prop. 13! . . .
FULL SCREEN ART: Cherie Albusche Teacher	ANNCR. VO: Cherie Albusche . . . Teacher . . .
CHERIE AT DESK	Being an instructor at Los Rios College keeps me in touch with the concerns on campus.
FULL SCREEN ART: Cherie Albusche Candidate for Los Rios Community College Board	ANNCR. VO: Cherie Albusche . . . Candidate for Los Rios Community College Board . . .
CHERIE AT DESK	There are practical . . . not costly . . . solutions to our problems . . . I want to make sure we taxpayers get our money's worth.
FULL SCREEN ART: Cherie Albusche Los Rios Trustee LS FONT: Paid for by the Committee to elect Cherie Albusche	ANNCR. VO: Get your money's worth on November 6th . . . vote Cherie Albusche, Los Rios Trustee

Source: Courtesy of KGMS, Sacramento, CA.

Public Service Announcements (PSAs)

Throughout this chapter we've attempted to emphasize the similarities between paid commercial announcements and PSAs. The sponsor's purposes are in both cases persuasive, although perhaps less obviously so with PSAs. Some action by the audience is wanted. Writers should approach PSAs with the same series of analytical questions described for commercials. The only difference that *should* exist, if PSAs are to be effective, is that the PSA is not paid for, whereas commercials are.

In practice, however, and precisely because they do not produce revenue, PSAs are the poor stepchildren of announcements. Usually they do not receive the same care in preparation or placement that commercials receive. Since they present a cost rather than income, they are likely to be written by inexperienced volunteers or interns. Usually only limited funds are available for production. The result often is a "noncompetitive" spot, without the structural or persuasive impact of commercial announcements.

Another problem arises in selecting those public service campaigns which will be aired. Stations receive far more requests to place PSAs than they have time available, and even when a campaign has been selected for presentation, the spots will not be aired as frequently as the organizers of the campaign might like. Some criteria have to be established. Most likely, they will include these considerations.

1. Preference will be given to those campaigns which can be made to appeal to broad audience groups and particularly to the audiences which regularly listen to or watch that station.

2. Balance will be sought between national and local campaigns.

3. Preference will be given to campaigns which are well prepared, for which good scripts have been written and presented to the station (so time will not have to be taken by station personnel to write copy from press releases or rewrite badly prepared announcements).

4. Preference is often given to completely preproduced announcements, although some stations prefer to record their own announcements and use local talent. In order to handle the volume of requests, many stations produce "community bulletin-board" programs. These programs use the same materials—flyers, press releases, and other announcements sent in by organizations—but their preparation differs from that of a persuasive announcement. All the principles of program structure apply.

Yet another problem with PSAs lies in the difficulty in finding persuasive appeals that will result in audience action. We all know we should contribute to charitable campaigns, give our time to the Boy Scouts, give blood at the blood bank. But it's also very easy to find excuses and to postpone taking these actions. In order to contribute to the Cancer Society we have to find the checkbook, get an envelope and stamp, look up the address, and so on. Both the agency for which the PSA is written and the writer will need to work to make the action expected from the audience as clear and simple to execute as possible.

PSAs suffer from problems of ineffective placement as well as from poor preparation. Since no revenue is received from these announcements, they usually are placed within or adjacent to less desirable programs, in the poorer time periods, and with no regard as to whether the target audience for the PSA may be present in the station's audience at that time. (To be fair, some stations do reserve a share of their prime-time availabilities for PSAs even though those spots could be sold, and some do consciously match up PSAs with appropriate audiences.)

Here are some examples with which we can point up some of these problems and their solutions. The first is a flyer that includes storyboards for two spots produced by the National School Safety Center. The spots were prerecorded and sent to stations along with this documentation, so that local public affairs directors

"What's wrong with this picture?"

Sadly, many of our schools are plagued with serious crime, violence, attendance, drug and discipline problems. And until these issues are effectively resolved, our nation cannot attain excellence in education.

The National School Safety Center, a partnership of the U.S. Department of Justice, the U.S. Department of Education and Pepperdine University, has prepared these public service messages to help make your viewers aware of this tragedy and to encourage them to get involved in making sure our children have safe, secure and peaceful places to learn.

You can help by airing these spots often.

Figure 11.7
Source: Courtesy of National School Safety Center.

ANNOUNCER (VOICE-OVER): This is Linda. She's bright, pretty and thirteen — but something's wrong. Linda is afraid for the school bell to ring.

LINDA (VOICE-OVER): These girls . . . it's just like they take over the school . . . Sometimes, during a test, it would just come back to me . . . the whole scene, I wouldn't be able to do any good on it. They're gonna be out there when I go out, and they're gonna be waiting for me . . .

ANNOUNCER (VOICE-OVER): Linda was the victim of violence. Now she's the victim of fear.

To find out how you can help reduce crime and violence in your neighborhood schools, call your principal.

Linda isn't just somebody else's kid. She could be yours.

A message from the National School Safety Center.

ANNOUNCER (VOICE-OVER): Ever wonder why your kids sometimes don't like school?

Maybe they're scared.

You wouldn't believe what's happening in many of our schools. But you better believe something needs to be done . . . now. Call your principal and get involved. These aren't just somebody else's kids. They could be yours.

A message from the National School Safety Center.

Figure 11.7 (Continued)

FAIRYTALE TOWN

1501 Sutterville Road   Sacramento, CA. 95822

(916) 449-5233

RECEIVED

JAN 14 1986

Ans'd..............

FOR IMMEDIATE RELEASE

PUBLIC SERVICE ANNOUNCEMENT

WANTED: Talented Children (12 years and under) to perform in FAIRYTALE TOWN'S Children's Talent Show on Sunday February 9. Call 449-5233 by January 26 for information.

# # #

CONTACT PERSON: Janet Farrar
                  Recreation Program Coordinator

Starting Date: January 13, 1986
Ending Date: January 26, 1986
Length of Spot: 10 seconds

CITY OF SACRAMENTO
DEPARTMENT OF PARKS AND
COMMUNITY SERVICES

Figure 11.8
Source: Courtesy of City of Sacramento, Department of Parks and Community Services, and KTXL, Sacramento.

PROGRAM: COMMUNITY CALENDAR   PAGE   1

SEGMENT: P.M.   TAPING: 1/23/86

TOTAL TIME: :20   TBA: 1/23/86

VIDEO   **AUDIO**

TAKE: SLIDE #108 | GOOD AFTERNOON. THIS IS
                              | TV-40'S COMMUNITY CALENDAR.
                              | ----------------------------
                              | LIVING A FAIRYTALE IS EVERY
                              | CHILD'S DREAM. THAT'S WHY
                              | FAIRYTALE TOWN IS INVITING ALL
                              | CHILDREN, 12 YEARS AND YOUNGER,
                              | TO SHARE THEIR TALENTS IN A
                              | CHILDREN'S TALENT SHOW, SUNDAY,
                              | FEBRUARY 8. FOR MORE
                              | INFORMATION, CALL 449-5233.
                              | ----------------------------
                              | THIS IS KTXL TV-40, SACRAMENTO,
                              | STOCKTON.

Figure 11.8 (Continued)

news release

4600 Winding Way ● Sacramento, CA 95841
For further information contact director:
Gordon Botting Dr. H. Sc., M.P.H.
PHONE 487·HELP

PUBLIC SERVICE ANNOUNCEMENTS FOR
WEIGHT CONTROL PROGRAM

TO BE AIRED   Frebruary 2 - 7

<u>30 second</u> Overweight - a Problem? Then be a winner with
THE WEIGHT MANAGEMENT program offered by Health
Unlimited beginning February 10th at 7:00 p.m. This sensible
program will help you lose unwanted pounds and keep them
off permanently thru Personalized Exercise Techniques,
Diet History Evaluation, Sound Nutrition, Cooking
Demonstrations, Practical Motivational tools and much
more. For further information call 487-4357.

<u>10 second</u> Overweight a Problem? Then be a winner with the
Weight Management class at Health Unlimited. Call 487-
4357 for information.

<u>FACT SHEET</u>

<u>WHO</u>   Health Unlimited (non-profit health enhancement
community service)

<u>WHAT</u>   "WINNING WEIGH" comprehensive programming includes
* Personal Diet Evaluation
* Body Composition Impedance Test
* Blood panel including cholesterol, triglycerides,
glucose, thyroid, etc.
* Exercise Techniques to fit individual needs
* Sound Nutrition - Cooking Demonstrations
* Practical Motivational Tools
* Social, Emotional, Spiritual Support

<u>WHEN</u>   Begins Feb. 10th (8 consecutive Monday evening
sessions).

<u>WHERE</u> Health Unlimited (corner Pasadena & Winding Way,
Carmichael)

<u>COST</u> $89.00 Total Package (includes Body Fat and
personal Diet Evaluation, 24 Blood Chemistry Panel
and Workshop Materials. $79.00 pre-registration.

PREVENTING ILLNESS — PROMOTING WELLNESS

Figure 11.9
Source: Courtesy of Health Unlimited.

KWOD 106
777 Campus Commons Dr.
Sacramento, CA 95825

Attn: Alex

Dear Alex:

Please run the following community service announcement. I would
like to have it run as often as you can so that we can reach the
greatest number of children.

     SUNRISE LITTLE LEAGUE IS HAVING THEIR TRY-OUTS
ON SATURDAY, FEBRUARY 1, 1986 AND SATURDAY,
FEBRUARY 8, 1986 AT C BAR C ON OAK AVENUE
(BEHIND WOODSIDE ELEMENTARY SCHOOL). THE TIMES
ARE AS FOLLOWS:

  9:00 - 12 YEAR OLDS
        15 YEAR OLDS

10:00 - 11 YEAR OLDS
        14 YEAR OLDS

11:00 - 10 YEAR OLDS
        13 YEAR OLDS

12:00 - 8 YEAR OLDS
         9 YEAR OLDS

IN THE EVENT OF RAIN ON EITHER OF THESE DATES,
TRY-OUTS WILL BE HELD AT THE SAME LOCATION ON
SATURDAY, FEBRUARY 15.

ANY QUESTIONS OR FOR ADDITIONAL INFORMATION,
PLEASE CALL STEVE LEE AT 726-8333 OR JACKIE
BURNETT AT 726-0149.

Thank you for your cooperation.

Sincerely,

Gail Wilson
Publicity, Sunrise Little League

Figure 11.10
Source: Letter courtesy of KWOD, Sacramento, CA.

could quickly assess the content without having to preview the actual recordings. The spots are well done; they meet the criteria for a strong, persuasive announcement.

As an example of a locally produced PSA for television, the approach used in Figure 11.8 is typical. The press release from the Department of Parks and Community Services was rewritten at the station as a voice-over. The video is a standard slide which the station uses to accompany many different voice-overs. Production is simple and inexpensive. The spot is not likely, however, to have much impact on audience members.

Figure 11.9 is a well-organized page, a combination news release and fact sheet, including both a 30-second and a 10-second PSA for radios, already prepared. It came with a cover letter emphasizing the social importance of this campaign and urging the station's cooperation.

Figure 11.10 is an announcement of Little League tryouts. Countering the fact that the writer obviously knew the station's public affairs director on a first-name basis are the probability that the station's audience is not likely to be interested in the topic, the awkward way in which the information is organized, and its detail. Writing an effective PSA on this topic would be a formidable task.

Promos

The comments made in the preceding section about the writing and placement of PSAs are also applicable to promotional announcements. A special problem exists with television promos which are run as "audio only" messages at the end of programs. The visual material being displayed during the promo is usually the closing credit for that program. The audio promo is a competing stimulus; it is not related to the video, and that situation causes the announcement to lose some of its impact.

Some stations, however, now recognize that their own air time is a valuable resource to be used in attracting larger audiences for programs, and these stations are placing more emphasis on the writing of effective promos and on putting them where they will be seen or heard by appropriate target audiences. This promo does a particularly good job by using clips from the program to support the narration.

VIDEO	AUDIO
OCEAN; GENTLE WAVES	MUSIC: RELAXED MUTED
	ANNOUNCER:
	The open sea. (PAUSE) Free. (PAUSE) Boundless. (PAUSE) Its vast richness nurtures an amazing diversity of sea creatures whose very existence depends upon the delicate balance of nature . . . a balance which, more than once, has been threatened by mankind in its race to plunder the ocean's treasure.
	MORE MORE MORE

WHALING SCENES; SLAUGHTER	From the days of the great whaling fleets that sailed off the coasts of North America and bloodied the waters from California to Hawaii with their slaugh-ter . . . (PAUSE)
OIL SUPERTANKERS; DRILLING RIGS; PRUDHOE BAY	To the multinational oil conglomerates with their super-tankers and pipelines and floating production platforms that dot our coastlines and extend even to the stormy reaches of the North Sea . . .
DEAD FISH ON SHORE; SLAUGHTER OF SEALS; NOTICES OF POLLUTED BEACHES, ETC.	The touch of man has more often than not been a blight rather than a blessing upon the oceans of the world and the creatures who dwell in them.
ACTION PICS: COUSTEAU AND DOLPHINS	This Sunday, join us as we look at the plight of our world's oceans . . . and see how the work of one ex-traordinary man, Jacques Cousteau, may help to save those waters from devastation.
KEY: Our Fragile Seas (3) Sunday—8:00 p.m.	Watch "Our Fragile Seas" Sunday night at 8, here on channel 3.

Source: Courtesy of the writer, Joan Merriam.

One major problem that faces the promo writer is length. Often these announcements are no more than 10 or 20 seconds long, which provides little time to attract attention and to persuade.

Editorials

Editorials are the opinion statements of a station's owners and managers. We have placed them within this chapter because they share two characteristics with announcements. They are approximately the same length, in most cases about a minute or so, and they have a persuasive intent, although as with PSAs and promos sometimes that persuasive thrust is rather low-key. Nevertheless, both structural considerations and persuasive appeals may, and should, be applied to editorials, just as they are to the various forms of announcements.

Editorials also differ from announcements in one very important respect. They come under a provision of the FCC regulations known as the Fairness Doctrine, the background of which deserves brief comment. For a number of years editorials were prohibited as a result of Federal Communications Commission action in a very famous case, the Mayflower decision. The commission's position, in part, was that:

Under the American system of broadcasting it is clear that responsibility for the conduct of a broadcast station must rest initially with the broadcaster. It is equally clear that with the limitations in frequencies inherent in the nature of radio, the public interest can never be served by a dedication of any broadcast facility to the support of his own partisan ends. . . . A truly free radio cannot be used to advocate the causes of the licensee . . . In brief, the broadcaster cannot be an advocate. Freedom of speech on the radio must be broad enough to provide full and equal opportunity for the presentation to the public of all sides of public issues . . . fairly, objectively, and without bias. The public interest—not the private—is paramount.[3]

In 1949, after extensive public hearings, that position was changed, and stations were permitted to broadcast editorial statements, but with the proviso that they would have to be "fair" in the treatment of persons and groups holding different views on the topics discussed. The new position was stated this way:

> . . . the Commission believes that under the American system of broadcasting the individual licensees of radio stations have the responsibility for determining the specific program material to be broadcast over their stations. This choice, however, must be exercised in a manner consistent with the basic policy of the Congress that radio be maintained as a medium of free speech for the general public as a whole, rather than as an outlet for the purely personal or private interests of the licensee. This requires that the licensees devote a reasonable percentage of their broadcasting time to the discussion of public issues of interest in the community served by their stations and that such programs be designed so that the public has a reasonable opportunity to hear different opposing positions on public issues of interest and importance in the community.
>
> Such presentations may include the identified expression of the licensee's personal viewpoint as part of the more general presentation of views or comments on the various issues, but the opportunity of the licensees to present such views as they may have on matter of controversy may not be utilized to achieve a partisan or one-sided presentation of issues. Licensee editorialization is but one aspect of freedom of expression by means of radio. Only insofar as it is exercised in conformity with the paramount right of the public to hear a reasonably balanced presentation of all responsible viewpoints on particular issues can such editorialization be considered to be consistent with the licensee's duty to operate in the public interest. For the licensee is a trustee impressed with the duty of preserving for the public generally radio as a medium of free expression and fair presentation.[4]

Briefly stated, the Fairness Doctrine requires that licensees seek out and provide opportunity for statements to be heard in opposition to those broadcast by the licensee.*

There is no requirement that stations air editorials, and some licensees choose not to. They may feel that to do so only angers and alienates audiences and/or commercial clients, or they may not want to spend staff time researching the issues to be discussed, or they may not want to provide the rebuttal time that the Fairness Doctrine demands. Other licensees air so-called happiness editorials, commenting only on noncontroversial topics. Still others take the

---

* Although the Fairness Doctrine itself is not complicated, the guidelines and body of judicial actions based on the doctrine are lengthy. If you are faced with the task of writing and scheduling editorials, you should review these materials thoroughly.

opportunity to comment on important issues seriously, do their research carefully, and treat their obligations to air opposing opinions with the same dedication.

Usually editorials are voiced by a senior member of the station's management, or by a spokesperson hired specifically to present editorials. And usually, even on television, they are delivered on-camera and without accompanying visuals.

We have selected three examples, all from the same television station, but on three different levels of issue—one national, one statewide, and one local. They are typical; each provides a brief background on the topic, and each states a position. Only one, however, that on gun control, asks for a specific action on the part of the audience members. The others intend to affect government by weight of the station's prestige and whatever other indirect persuasive pressure might come from individuals who hear and agree with the opinion. Note also the nice play on words used in the editorial on the symphony musicians' controversy, using musical terminology in the statement about a musical problem (Figure 11.11).

Editorials should be clearly distinguished from commentary. Commentaries are the opinions of individuals other than the licensee, and can appear as statements by guests in a program, as carefully scripted news commentary regularly presented by a reporter or anchor, or perhaps by different individuals, each with a self-contained brief program of comment. While the legal requirements for handling commentary and editorials are somewhat different, audiences do not always recognize the distinctions. We'll consider news commentary in the next chapter.

Final Considerations

Length and Timing

Traditionally, broadcast announcements are timed to precise lengths in order to fit openings between network programs, or within prerecorded programs. The nominal lengths for the bulk of these announcements will be either 30 or 60 seconds; in practice, the actual recorded length of television announcements will usually be about two seconds less than the nominal length. An increasing number of 20- and 10-second spots are being created; the greater variety of lengths allows for more flexibility in selling and placing spots into the 90-, 120-, or 150-second openings between and within prerecorded programs.

These prerecorded, precisely timed lengths are supplemented by other, more relaxed practices. Many radio stations operate with casual formats, including ad lib commercials from disc jockey personalities that differ from standard lengths. Also, with the demise of the NAB codes of good practice which had established guidelines for maximum amounts of commercial time, more flexible announcement schedules and longer announcements are appearing. Finally, some stations and TV cable systems are beginning to air *infomercials*, a new term used to describe what are essentially program-length commercials, a combination of information and persuasive appeals about a company or product that may run for a considerable length of time.

The only totally accurate way to ensure precise timing is, of course, to time the spot when it is recorded. But for those announcements which are not recorded

EDITORIAL
KTXL • TV-40 _____ SACRAMENTO • STOCKTON

MC CLURE-VOLKMER BILL
M. MESSMER NOV. 85
(AIRS 18-21 Nov.)

THE NATIONAL RIFLE ASSOCIATION, ONE OF THE MOST POWERFUL LOBBYING GROUPS IN THE COUNTRY, IS PUSHING A BILL THROUGH CONGRESS THAT WILL MAKE IT EASIER TO BUY GUNS ACROSS THE COUNTRY...INCLUDING THE CRIMINAL'S WEAPON OF CHOICE, THE HANDGUN.

THIS BILL, CALLED THE MC CLURE-VOLKMER GUN DECONTROL ACT, WOULD MAKE IT SO MUCH EASIER FOR CRIMINALS TO GET GUNS, THAT EVERY MAJOR LAW ENFORCEMENT GROUP IN THE COUNTRY IS STRONGLY OPPOSED TO IT. ORDINARILY SUCH A DANGEROUS PIECE OF LEGISLATION WOULD DIE FROM PUBLIC EXPOSURE.

BUT THE NRA IS TRYING TO AVOID PUBLIC DISCUSSION OF THIS BILL. THEY USED SENATE RULES TO PUSH IT THROUGH THE SENATE WITHOUT ANY PUBLIC HEARINGS. MANY SENATORS WHO VOTED FOR THE BILL DIDN'T KNOW IT WAS OPPOSED BY LAW ENFORCEMENT PEOPLE. NOW THE NRA IS TRYING THE SAME TRICK WITH THE HOUSE OF REPRESENTATIVES.

IT IS IMPERATIVE THAT THIS BILL BE EXPOSED FOR WHAT IT IS... A DANGEROUS PIECE OF LEGISLATION THAT MUST BE STOPPED. LET YOUR REPRESEVATIVE KNOW NOW THAT YOU THINK THE MC CLURE- VOLKMER BILL OR ANY LEGISLATION THAT MAKES IT EASIER FOR CRIMINALS TO GET GUNS...IS A BAD IDEA.

-END-

KTXL TV-40 PRESENTS EDITORIALS TO ENCOURAGE PUBLIC DISCUSSION OF IMPORTANT ISSUES. REPLIES BY REPRESENTATIVES OF RESPONSIBLE ORGANIZATIONS ARE WELCOME. CONTACT THE EDITORIAL DIRECTOR FOR DETAILS.

KTXL TV-40 / POST OFFICE BOX 40 / 4655 FRUITRIDGE RD., SACRAMENTO, CA. 95820 / (916) 454-4422

Figure 11.11
Source: Courtesy of KTXL, Sacramento, CA.

EDITORIAL

KTXL • TV-40 _____ SACRAMENTO • STOCKTON

BI-LINGUAL EDUCATION
M.MESSMER OCT. 85
(AIRS Nov. 8-11)

THE PRESENT SYSTEM OF EDUCATING NON-ENGLISH-SPEAKING
STUDENTS IN OUR PUBLIC SCHOOLS IS NOT THE ONLY OR EVEN THE
BEST WAY TO GIVE THEM FLUENCY IN ENGLISH.

UNDER THE PRESENT SYSTEM, STUDENTS CONTINUE RECEIVING
EDUCATION IN REQUIRED SUBJECTS PRIMARILY IN THEIR NATIVE
LANGUAGE WHILE BEING GRADUALLY EXPOSED TO ENGLISH. THIS CAN
WORK WELL IF TEACHERS ARE NOT ONLY QUALIFIED IN BI-LINGUAL
EDUCATION, BUT ALSO IN THE REQUIRED SUBJECTS.

UNFORTUNATELY, MANY SCHOOL DISTRICTS CANNOT FIND ENOUGH
TEACHERS WITH THIS DUAL QUALIFICATION. SO THEY COMPROMISE
BY USING TEACHERS WHO ARE EITHER NOT FULLY QUALIFIED IN
BI-LINGUAL EDUCATION OR FULLY QUALIFIED IN THE REQUIRED
SUBJECTS. IN EITHER CASE, THE STUDENT SUFFERS.

ONE PROVEN ALTERNATIVE IS THE IMMERSION METHOD. WITH THIS
METHOD, THE STUDENT CONCENTRATES ON GAINING FLUENCY FROM
A TEACHER SKILLED IN TEACHING ENGLISH AS A SECOND LANGUAGE.
THE STUDENT CAN THEN MOVE MORE EASILY INTO REGULAR CLASSROOMS.

BUT THIS ALTERNATIVE IS PROHIBITED UNDER PRESENT LAW. THE
PRESENT SYSTEM OFTEN FAILS TO ACHIEVE THE PRIMARY OBJECTIVE
OF GIVING STUDENTS FLUENCY IN ENGLISH QUICKLY. TO IMPROVE
THE PRESENT SYSTEM, SCHOOLS MUST HAVE MORE ALTERNATIVES.
FINANCING MUST BE BASED ON MEASURABLE RESULTS RATHER THAN
METHODS.   -END-

Figure 11.11 (Continued)

MAYOR'S SYMPHONY OFFER

M. MESSMER NOV.85

(AIRS 15-18 Nov.)

IN AN ATTEMPT TO RESOLVE THE CONTINUING PAY DISPUTE
BETWEEN THE SACRAMENTO SYMPHONY ASSOCIATION AND THE
SYMPHONY MUSICIANS, SACRAMENTO'S MAYOR RUDIN OFFERED THE
ASSOCIATION TWENTY FIVE THOUSAND DOLLARS FROM THE CITY
TREASURY. WE APPLAUD THE MAYOR'S OFFER BUT CAN ONLY
CONSIDER IT AN OVERTURE.

FOR ONE THING, TWENTY-FIVE THOUSAND DOLLARS REPRESENTS LESS
THAN A DIME OF SUPPORT FROM EACH CITY RESIDENT. AND ITS A
ONE TIME OFFER. EVEN CITIES SMALLER THAN SACRAMENTO PROVIDE
MORE SUPPORT FOR THEIR SYMPHONIES THAN THAT. EVEN IF THE
COUNTY MATCHED THAT AMOUNT...AND IT SHOULD...WE'RE STILL
TALKING CHEAP.

SECONDLY, THE MAYOR'S OFFER HAD SOME STRINGS ATTACHED...SHE
WANTS TO PUT SOME POLITICIANS ON THE ASSOCIATION BOARD.
POLITICIANS AREN'T FAMOUS FOR THEIR HARMONY, SO WE DON'T
SEE HOW THIS SET OF STRINGS WILL CREATE BEAUTIFUL MUSIC.

SO, COME ON MAYOR. YOUR OFFER WAS A GOOD START...BUT WE'RE
NOT TALKING ABOUT DROPPING A DIME IN THE JUKEBOX. WE'RE
TALKING ABOUT GETTING THE SYMPHONY PLAYING AGAIN. PUT SOME
MORE MONEY ON THE TABLE...AND LETS START THE MUSIC.

-END-

KTXL TV-40 PRESENTS EDITORIALS TO ENCOURAGE PUBLIC DISCUSSION OF IMPORTANT ISSUES. REPLIES BY REPRESENTATIVES
OF RESPONSIBLE ORGANIZATIONS ARE WELCOME. CONTACT THE EDITORIAL DIRECTOR FOR DETAILS.

KTXL TV-40 / POST OFFICE BOX 40 / 4655 FRUITRIDGE RD., SACRAMENTO, CA. 95820 / (916) 454-4422

Figure 11.11 (Continued)

in advance, or for approximate timing during production, these estimates may be used. Remember, that delivery speed and production techniques can effect the final timing; and for television, a continuous verbal narration may not be needed or appropriate:

10 seconds—25 words

20 seconds—45 words

30 seconds—65 words

60 seconds—125 words

Product Identification

Names are important in announcements. The product name (or, if no product is involved, the sponsor's name) needs to be clearly and forcefully stated and tied in strongly with the product category it represents. It's not unusual, when asking students to describe favorite commercials, for them to be able to describe in detail an attractively produced mood piece or one which uses an unusual attention-getting device, but for which they cannot identify the product or sponsor. Winning awards for attractive commercial production may be great for the ego of the writer, but to the client, a more important consideration is selling the product.

If the product is already known to the target audience and the purpose of the ad is simply to remind the audience of the product, then only occasional mention of the name may be sufficient. Usually, however, the product or sponsor name should appear several times in the ad. And if the product or sponsor is new in the community or to the target audience, then quite likely a major purpose of the ad will be name reinforcement, and frequent repetition of the name is called for.

Repetition

We have mentioned repetition of product names, but other forms of repetition are also important in broadcast announcements. One of these is the repeated broadcast of the message. Once in a while a single exposure to a commercial will result in action by audience members; for example, you might know that you need a new set of tires for your car, you have the money to buy them and you know what brand you want. A single ad which says these tires are on sale at a 30 percent saving at your neighborhood tire store may be sufficient to get you to act.

But for most clients and products, frequent repetition is necessary, so that when customers are motivated to act there will be recognition and acceptance of that brand in their minds. Usually the writer has no direct control over this aspect of merchandising, but what the writer may be able to do is persuade the client to produce not just one ad, but a series—several ads which use similar themes and approaches, but with distinctive differences as well, so that the repeated broadcast of the sponsor's message will not be perceived as monotonous.

Another form of repetition within an announcement is that of idea repetition. We have cautioned against including too many different concepts within an ad and thereby weakening its impact. When the ideas have been chosen, and limited, the writer should strive to reinforce those ideas through repetition. If, for example, an ad is emphasizing a special preholiday sale with storewide reductions in prices, then the key words *sale, saving, price reduction,* and similar repetitions of the idea—not necessarily repetition of the same words, however—should be used throughout the announcement.

Conclusion

The broadcast writer who is just beginning a career in the industry is quite likely to begin by writing promos and PSAs, perhaps also some commercials. Writing these kinds of copy may not seem to be a glamorous and exciting profession, but it is important writing. The industry depends on effective announcement writing for its economic success. The individual can look upon every new assignment as a creative challenge upon which to practice and improve his or her writing skills, for every assignment will be different.

The approach to writing announcements outlined in this chapter—analyzing purpose, target audience, persuasive appeals and structure and organizing the content of the announcement—provide a method by which the beginning writer can approach any assignment with confidence.

Exercises

1. Write a radio commercial. Since it is possible to write an announcement about almost anything and in almost any style, we have provided some restrictions to make the task more realistic. Choose a *product* from category I, a *presentational style* from category II, an *organizational scheme* from category III, and a *length* from category IV.

   I. Product

      a. A special Memorial Day holiday promotion for selected Stanley (brand) garden tools—shovels, hoes, pruning shears, garden sprayers, etc.—all are 30% off regular prices at "participating hardware stores."

      b. Another special holiday promotion, this one for Mother's Day, for Avon cosmetics. Selected fragrances of colognes for women in specially designed collector bottles are 30% off regular prices. Remember, Avon cosmetics are sold only by door-to-door salespersons—"Avon Calling."

      c. This company, called CONTEMPS, provides temporary help for businesses—secretaries, other clericals, accountants, security guards, custodians, etc. They've been around for a while and have a good reputation, but they are not well known. They seek to increase business by getting their name and what they do more widely known.

      d. This company is a high-volume discount stereo/TV/VCR/etc. store chain; the name is Rosenthal's. They have several outlets in your metropolitan area. They advertise regularly and heavily, with loss leaders and last year's models offered at ridiculously low prices. These are the ones they're pushing this week: Hitachi linear-track turntable—$188; Sony compact-disc player—$328; Sharp 19″ color TV—$298; Sanyo wired-remote VCR—$288.

II. Presentational style

    a. Straight one-voice announcer (male or female)

    b. Two announcer voices (male *and* female)

    c. Dramatic dialogue—at least in part

    d. Use music bed, with either (a) or (b)

III. Organizational scheme

    a. Problem-solution

    b. Testimonial

    c. Storytelling

    d. Comparison

IV. Length

    a. 20 seconds

    b. 30 seconds

    c. 60 seconds

If this a class assignment, your instructor may select from each category; if not, you might draw the choices at random. If you draw, for example, D/C/A/B, you would write a 30-second spot using dramatic material in a problem-solution approach for the discount stereo store.

2. Write (draw) a storyboard for a 30-second TV spot. You could use an approach similar to the exercise above for radio, using either the same or different products and approaches, but we like to use as our product for this exercise a brand and blend of herbal tea, such as Celestial Seasonings' Red Zinger blend.

3. Write a one-minute radio public service announcement. The subject may be any actual (not fictitious) topic related to your university—which is your client. In choosing your topic, keep in mind that it should be an activity or event of sufficiently widespread community interest that it could legitimately reach its target audience on one or more radio stations in your community. (For example, an announcement aimed only at student interns in communication, or at students interested in a library orientation tour, or a dormitory dance would be too narrow to get radio coverage. On the other hand, a concert or concert series, an athletic event, guest speakers, or extension courses are appropriate topics for radio promotion.)

4. This exercise can be attached to any of the above as an additional part. For the announcement you have just written, write a paragraph of explanation on how you approached the task. Include at least:

    a. Description of your target audience,

    b. Why that target; the relationship that you see between the target and the product,

    c. What persuasive appeals you have attempted to work into the ad, and how you have worked them in.

    d. Why you think these are appropriate appeals for the target.

5. From a local newspaper or other sources choose a topic for an editorial. If your source does not have enough background on the topic, do additional research on the issue until you can: (1) decide on the position you want to take, (2) choose a target audience, (3) select the arguments and the persuasive appeals appropriate to influence that TA, and (4) write the editorial.

6. Listen to (and, if possible, record) an editorial broadcast by a station in your community. Research and prepare a rebuttal opinion. (If you find this to be a topic on which you really do disagree with the station's statement, you might proceed to place your statement on the air in opposition.)

Key Terms and Concepts

commentary	problem-solution
commercial	promo
comparison ads	PSA
demonstration	punchline (tag)
editorial	purpose and goal
Fairness Doctrine	spokespersons
multiple-voice ads	target audience
pacing	telling a story
persuasive appeals	testimonial

Notes

1. K. Lee Herrick, Frank J. Weaver, and Amolie G. Ramirez, "A Successful Health Education Campaign Done with PSAs," *E&ITV*, June 1978, pp. 62–63.

2. Bruce Bond, "Anatomy of a Campaign: It's *Their* Water," *Video Systems*, April 1981, pp. 6–15. Reprinted by permission.

3. Federal Communications Commission, Mayflower decision, 1941 (Dockets 5618 and 5640).

4. Federal Communications Commission, *In the Matter of Editorializing by Licensees*, Report of the Commission, 1 R.R. 91:201,211 (1949).

Chapter 12

News Programs

It must be obvious to even the most casual observer that news broadcasts are an important part of the schedules of almost all television stations and of many radio stations. This category of programming in turn represents a wide range of subforms; many styles of presentation and types of content are involved. In addition, our perceptions of what is news change over time and are different for different audience groups.

In just one chapter we can hardly hope to present all the considerations which are involved in the preparation of news stories. We will concentrate instead on the general process by which news personnel, including writers, select the stories to be included in a newscast and then on the techniques they employ to ready those stories for the air, with emphasis on four types of content—the breaking disaster story, the investigative report, the soft news feature story, and the news commentary.

News Judgments

The process of preparing news programs for broadcast requires that several levels of decisions be made before the actual writing of individual stories can begin. These include, first, the decision on whether or not to present news in the station's schedule. Then, determinations of what kinds and how much, and whether to originate one's own newscasts or purchase news material from networks and/or syndicators. Finally, news personnel are faced with the task, on a daily or even hourly basis, of selecting stories from among all those which might be aired at that time.

Why News?   The most fundamental of these questions is whether stations (or networks) should schedule news programs in the first place. Why should they?

Television stations and networks find, for the most part, that audiences for news are large and advertisers plentiful. Despite the high costs of maintaining a news department and production facilities for news, this form of programming is easily marketable and highly profitable.

A popular news program will also contribute to the perceived prestige of a station. In addition, individuals who tune in for news are more likely to stay tuned to the same station for other programs. Consequently, almost all TV stations include some news in their schedule.

In radio, the importance of news is not as widespread. Some stations broadcast little or no news because the audiences to which they are targeted have no interest in it. If, for example, a station emphasizes some style of music as its basic format, the programming of news may be seen by its audience as an interruption of that format. If the station's managers decide, however, that news is nevertheless desirable, the job of the writer under those circumstances will be to structure newscasts and to write individual stories in such a way as not to drive away the target audience.

Other radio stations view news as a positive programming feature, and some have built their entire formats around news and talk programming.

News and Gratifications

The primary audience gratifications associated with news on either television or radio are those we previously identified (in Chapter 9) as information (particularly its surveillance function), importance, and value. But other gratifications can be present as well.

Frequently news exhibits some of the gratifications normally associated with entertainment programming. In fact a number of critics have argued that news (especially on television) is simply another form of entertainment. They have used as their arguments the facts that some stations: (1) choose attractive reporters and anchors in preference to seeking the best journalist for the job (sex appeal gratification): (2) select stories with strong visual content, and stress the involvement of the reporter in each story, as in the "Eyewitness" news style (action gratification): (3) look for stories with strong elements of controversy (tension gratification): and (4) choose stories with sensational, often sexual themes (sex appeal gratification again). To the extent that a station deliberately makes those choices, it legitimately may be accused of choosing entertainment-oriented gratifications over information-oriented gratifications in its attempt to attract different and possibly larger audience groups to the newscast.

Similarly, the gratifications of personalism, curiosity (especially human interest), and novelty may be found in so-called soft news or life style stories. In fact, it is the very presence of these appeals which distinguishes these types of stories from the traditional hard news story.

What and How Much News?

The obvious answer to the question what news is that the news broadcast, like other types of programs, is structured and the stories are chosen to attract particular audience groups, or to hold a group already attracted to the station by other programming. For many years stations and networks concentrated on the traditional all-inclusive newscast, which included along with the breaking hard news stories a few "human interest" features. Then, a few years ago, new programs that deal exclusively with soft news or life style stories began to appear—programs like "PM Magazine," "Entertainment Tonight," Charles Kuralt's "On the Road" (on CBS), and local programs with similar content in almost every market.

Why the change? Simply because these stories, with their different gratifications, reach different audiences from the more traditional news program which emphasizes major events and, often, more negative news. These programs attract younger and less educated groups and more females.

The answer to the question how much news is essentially the same. The length of each broadcast, and the number of broadcasts presented each day, will be a reflection of the uses the station's audience makes of news.

Scheduling News

Television stations, as a rule, have fixed time periods set aside for news broadcasts. Radio stations can be somewhat more flexible, but most of them also program news in predetermined amounts at predetermined times. Only extremely important news events—the outbreak of war, the assassination of a president, or something of that significance—will interrupt a station's fixed schedule or change the established format of a news program. (The most extreme case on record was the period following the assassination of President John Kennedy in 1963. The only programming on the national networks during the four days between his death and funeral was coverage of that tragedy.)

The writer must realize that under these generally inflexible schedules, even the most complex stories must be handled within a fixed time. On busy news days, when there are many important, complex stories, some major items may be left out or treated as mere headlines. On a slow news day, the news producer will have the option of treating major stories in greater depth or of adding less important stories, ones that on busier days would not even be considered. Usually the latter approach is taken.

Contrast, if you will, this inflexibility with the editing of a newspaper. In theory at least, on a busy news day the paper can add extra pages to treat every story with the detail it deserves, and on a slow day it can cut back the number of pages rather than fill them with trivia.

Another comparison might be made with Cable News Network. Most of the time CNN follows a traditional broadcast format with headlines at certain fixed times; weather, sports, and other features at regular intervals. The fact that it is a full-time news service, however, does permit greater flexibility, and on occasion it has taken advantage of that fact. For example, in early 1984 CNN chose to use large blocks of time for the live coverage of the "pool table gang rape" trial from Fall River, Massachusetts. CNN received considerable criticism for that broadcast, being accused of pandering to sensationalism in order to increase ratings and for airing the explicit language heard in the courtroom. Its counter argument, which we find credible, was that the trial was an important news story, that audiences had a right to see how the trial was conducted, and that only CNN, with its programming flexibility, could afford to cover the story at length.

Other examples of flexibility exist. Public television stations carried lengthy portions of the Watergate investigation and the congressional debate on possible impeachment of President Nixon. Public radio stations have done the same thing by carrying live hearings on a variety of public issues. And the ABC network's late-night news program "Nightline" limits its half-hour to one topic considered in depth, and even occasionally will extend that program beyond its normal length.

It may be premature to generalize from those few examples, but they seem to suggest that the changes in the electronic media which will increase the number of options available to audiences, such as the increased penetration of cable and the likely coming of direct broadcast satellite systems, are also changing the previously inflexible news practices of regular broadcast stations. The important next question will be whether or not the additional time will be put to good use—covering appropriate stories and covering them well.

Originate or Purchase?

This question does not have a direct bearing on the writing of stories, but is certainly a part of the process by which news decisions are made. Obviously if a station is going to program local news, it will have to make a commitment to local origination, including a financial commitment to hiring personnel and purchasing equipment for gathering and editing news stories.

A station may also decide to purchase news, in one form or another, from outside sources, of which there are many. One source is through network affiliation. In television there are three major networks—ABC, NBC, CBS—and for independent stations, Independent Network News (a satellite service). We've already mentioned Cable News Network, a service primarily distributed to cable systems. It may also be purchased by regular broadcast stations in noncable areas. In radio there is an even wider range of networks that provide regularly scheduled programs for subscribers.

The news wire services, such as Associated Press, United Press International, and Reuters, distribute news to subscribers in a variety of forms, including voice feeds for radio stations, voice and picture for TV, the traditional teletype service, and a newer service that appears directly on computer screens. These last two, of course, require that the content be voiced by a local announcer.

Finally, a wide variety of news features and stories on specialized topics are distributed through syndication by tape or by satellite, available to any station that finds the materials appropriate to the scope of its news programming, and that wishes to pay the price.

Many stations use all forms of news gathering—their own local origination, a network, news wire, and syndicated features. This decision is made, once again, on the basis of which materials will best fit the station's attempt to reach its audience.

Criteria for Selecting Stories

After all the management and programming decisions have been made which establish the style and quantity of news a station will present come the daily decisions as to which and how many stories will be presented on each newscast, from among those available at the time. On any given day there will be more stories available than there is time in the newscast. This is the gatekeeping function; not all stories will get through the gate. News directors and assignment editors use the following criteria to select among the stories available at any one time. You will recognize similarities between this list and our generalized descriptions of audience gratifications in Chapter 9.

Audience   We have emphasized the concept of target audience at numerous points throughout this book; its importance cannot be overemphasized. A story needs to have relevance to its audience. A story involving a rock music star should get heavier attention on a radio station which plays rock music than on a TV newscast which attracts a broader, more general audience. A story on possible cutbacks in social security programs should be prominent on stations in Sunbelt cities where many retired persons live, but it would merit less attention in a small college town where the bulk of the population is much younger.

Timeliness   How important is this story *now?* A story is never as important later as it is when it first breaks. Tomorrow different events will capture the audience's attention, and today's events will no longer be as timely.

Some stories do not have an obvious time element. This is particularly true of investigative pieces. On a particular day the story is ready, and the assignment editor decides to present it in the newscast. The writer should try to find an angle that gives the story some timeliness—some explanation in the lead as to why this story should be of interest to the audience at this time. If no time element can be found, it may not have been a good piece to work on in the first place.

For a major story, a broadcast station will revise and update the content for each newscast, and will place the newest material in the lead each time, to emphasize the timeliness of the story.

On other stories which are likely to continue over a period of several days, the writer may also prepare a background story, a longer, more analytical piece that places the details of the story in context and explains their significance to the target audience.

Impact   The impact of the story depends on how much of the audience is affected, how direct that effect is, and how immediate that effect is.

A change in the income tax laws reducing the allowable deductions for dependents will have immediate effects on many people, but a change in the oil and gas depletion allowance will have a direct affect on only a few investors— that is, until it is pointed out that a longer-range result of that change may increase the price all of us have to pay for gasoline. The writer working on that story would improve its impact by emphasizing the price aspect.

Similarly, a story on a cold spell in November would not have much impact on people in northern and eastern states where such weather is common at that time of year, but a story describing cold weather in Florida in November would have impact not only in Florida itself, but also upon those residents of colder states who come to Florida to escape cold winters. And the story could be given national impact if that cold weather were to destroy the Florida citrus crop and thereby lead to increased prices for orange juice throughout the country.

Prominence   Names are important in news. Of course the names must be those which are recognizable, prominent, or important to the audience. The activities and the name of a rock music or movie star will be more important in a story for broadcast on a rock music radio station than on a station which has a beautiful music format (and attracts an older audience), because the person will be more recognized there.

Impact and prominence are related criteria. Assume that the secretary of the interior makes a statement on the leasing of public lands for oil drilling. That's news because of the impact this prominent person has regarding that subject matter. But if the secretary of interior makes a statement on the quality of the music provided by a famous singing group, is that news? It certainly turned out to be news early in 1983 when Interior Secretary James Watt refused to allow the Beach Boys to perform on Department of Interior controlled land in Washington, D.C. Watt's name had become far more prominent than that of most cabinet secretaries because of previous controversial statements. This was just one more. And the Beach Boys were one of the best-known names in popular music. The combination was too good for reporters to pass up. In general, we can say that the prominence of an individual adds news value simply because of our strong curiosity about other people, particularly public figures.

Proximity   People are interested in stories that take place close at hand, or in which some local angle can be developed. This criterion ties in closely with impact, because local stories are more likely to have an effect on local audiences.

A classic example involves two train wrecks. One is a local wreck in which a single car is struck by a train, killing two local youths. The second wreck is in India. A train trestle collapses, and several hundred persons are killed in the disaster. If you have time for only one story, which would you use? Of course there is no right answer, because all the criteria need to be weighed in making the choice. Were the teenagers well-known local personalities, high school football stars, for example? That would give added prominence to the local story.

Personalization   Strictly speaking, the personalization of stories is not a criterion to be used in selecting stories. It is, rather, an approach to the writing of a story. Some stories are more easily written in personal terms than others, and to the extent that a story can be personalized for the target audience, it will be more interesting for that audience. Editors look for stories with this in mind.

A story may be personalized for an audience by describing a location that is well known to area residents, or highlighting local people who are involved in the story (even though it may take place elsewhere), or through emotional ties such as religion or economic interests. Personalization also includes telling a story in terms of individual persons who are involved, rather than in the abstract.

For example, a story on farm price supports originating with the Department of Agriculture in Washington can be presented by highlighting its effect on an individual dairy farmer in your own town. Similarly, a story on changes in state benefits for the elderly and handicapped might feature brief interviews with the resident of a local nursing home. The story on U.S.–Soviet relations presented later in this chapter shows how one station made an international story personal for its viewing area.

Personalization may also be considered an aspect of impact. What will be the impact on *individual persons* in the audience?

Conflict

In Chapter 9 we considered various conflicts under the gratification heading called tension. We do not want to imply that people get pleasure from the forms of conflict that appear in many news stories, such as war or political conflict or social upheaval. But audiences will stay tuned to stories about such topics so long as the outcome is in doubt.

Conflict is a component of most news. It may be person against person, nation against nation, persons against nature, persons against a political, or economic, or social system, or many other confrontations.

Novelty

This characteristic we also considered as an audience gratification. The obvious manifestation of this criterion is the classic cliché "if a dog bites a man, that is not news, but if a man bites a dog, that's news." The unusual, the unexpected, and the bizarre increase the news value of a story. In soft news stories some of the other criteria for news value may be missing or weak, such as a lack of timeliness. The compensating criterion in many such situations is novelty.

In each station, whoever makes the broadcast-by-broadcast judgments on which stories to include, and how much coverage to give each story, will make those judgments by assigning some relative weight to each of these criteria. The experienced newsperson does so without formal evaluation of each story, but nevertheless uses this process.

We should caution you again, as we did in the opening paragraph in this chapter, that the relative importance of these criteria will change over time. We've already mentioned the rise in the last few years of soft news and life style programs. Broadcasters found that certain audience groups that were not heavily attracted to traditionally organized news programs could be attracted to these feature-oriented programs. For these audiences timeliness is not an important criterion, but impact and personalization are. They want stories that can be immediately and directly useful in their daily lives.

Writing the News Story

Recall for a moment the basic differences between print and broadcast (discussed at length in Chapter 2). The reader of a newspaper story can stop reading at any point at which a sufficient amount of detail has been obtained, can pick up at midstory later, can review at any point, can go at any speed, and generally is in control of the way in which the story is received and processed.

In contrast, the broadcast story is totally organized at its source. The audience member must be able to process the story through his or her ear, eye, and brain as presented by the newscast. There is no opportunity to ask for a repeat or clarification. The story must be understood the first time through, and the sequence and speed with which the facts and ideas in the story are presented must be such that the audience can process them as they come. Too many facts, names, or numbers presented too fast, or an abrupt shift in ideas without warning

BLOOM COUNTY
by Berke Breathed

Figure 12.1
Source: Reproduced by permission of the Washington Post Company. © 1983, Washington Post
Writers Group.

will cause the audience to fall behind, and once that happens it's impossible to
catch up on that story.

Traditionally the print news story has been written using what is known as
inverted pyramid organization. The lead is followed by the remaining facts in the
descending order of their importance as determined by the reporter and editor.
This sequence permits the reader to stop at any point in the story whenever she
or he feels enough detail has been read. It also permits the compositor of the
newspaper to delete paragraphs in reverse order, from the end of the story, if
necessary, to fit the space available.

This basic organizing principle of providing facts in descending order of
importance also creates a tendency to skip back and forth among the various
aspects of the story, as in this newspaper example:

> Manila
> Thousands of Filipinos, chanting their opposition to President Ferdinand E. Marcos,
> marched on the eve of today's national elections, and police vowed to break up any
> boycott activities.
>
> The government's nearly 300,000 soldiers and police were placed on special alert
> after officials said there were communist rebel plans to disrupt the voting, for 183
> National Assembly seats.
>
> Opposition candidates prayed for peaceful elections at a downtown Manila church
> and filled the air with yellow balloons and white doves.
>
> "God is on our side. That is why we will win," candidate Jose Lina told a crowd
> of 1000 people who chanted, "Fight! Fight! Fight!"
>
> Police threatened to break up an anti-Marcos, anti-American, anti-election rally
> by 10,000 people at Rizal Park yesterday, but it ended peacefully.
>
> General Narciso Cabrera, Manila police chief, said the rally and other demon-
> strations violated an Election Commission ruling that banned campaigning or pro-
> boycott activity after midnight Saturday.
>
> He said he would stop other pro-boycott activities planned for today, including a
> plan to poll voters on whether Marcos should stay in power.

There are 25 million registered voters in this nation of 51 million people. Advocates of a boycott urged their supporters not to register.

Marcos has predicted a 90 percent victory for his governing party. In videotaped newscast appearances, he promised a clean and honest election.

Members of an independent watchdog group said they had reports of vote-buying, missing election forms and other forms of cheating.

Agapito (Butz) Aquino, brother of assassinated opposition leader Benigno Aquino, urged a boycott of the election to protest Marcos and U.S. support for Marcos' 18-year authoritarian rule. His brother's widow, Corazon, has taken a different position and campaigned for Marcos' foes.

Voting is mandatory, and penalties for failure to vote include six months in jail, disqualification for public office and loss of voting privileges.

Two candidates were killed during campaigning for the Assembly, and at least 32 other people were killed in other election-related violence during the seven-week campaign.

Communist rebel activity, also blamed partly on the election, has killed 300 others since the campaign started.[1]

A reader can see the several transition points marked by paragraphs, but the listener would have trouble with this structure at the points where the topic shifts. For that reason, this print style is not usually a successful approach to the broadcast story. In broadcast the story's structure cannot be seen; the audience must be guided through the sequence. Also, in broadcast it is assumed that the audience will stay with the story from beginning to end (if it has a good lead and is well written), so the writer can present the important facts spaced at appropriate places throughout the story. The preceding story might be rewritten this way to fit a 90-second slot:

Thousands of Filipinos marched through the streets of Manila yesterday shouting their opposition to President Ferdinand Marcos. The action on the eve of today's national elections is the latest in a series of election-related incidents in which two candidates campaigning for the National Assembly and at least 32 other people have been killed.

Nearly 300,000 government soldiers and police have been placed on special alert after officials said there were Communist rebel plans to disrupt today's voting for 183 National Assembly seats. Police threatened to break up an anti-Marcos, anti-government rally at Rizal Park, but it ended peacefully. Manila's police chief, General Narciso Cobrera, said the rally violated a ruling that banned campaigning after midnight last Saturday.

Agapito Aquino, the brother of assassinated opposition leader Benigno Aquino, has urged a boycott of the election to protest against Marcos and U.S. support for his campaign even though voting is mandatory and penalties for failure to vote include six months in jail, disqualification from public office and loss of voting privileges.

Benigno Aquino's widow, Corazon, has taken a different position and campaigned for Marcos' foes.

Marcos has predicted a 90 percent victory for his governing party. In videotaped newscast appearances he promised a clean and honest election. However, members of an independent watchdog group said they had reports of voter buying, missing election forms, and other signs of cheating.

The News Lead

The broadcast news story will have two parts. It will begin with a *lead,* which is the attention-getting device. That will be followed by the body of the story.

Ǝ The lead is the first sentence, or possibly two sentences, of the story. It gives the audience a reason to listen. It explains why that story will be important or interesting to them. Obviously, as we have been saying throughout the previous discussion of gratifications and of the criteria for selecting news stories, the writer will need to know something about the audience for whom the story is intended in order to determine what those most important or interesting facts may be.

Ǝ Textbooks used for courses in print journalism have traditionally emphasized the *comprehensive* lead—that is, a lead which contains the who, what, where, when, why, and how of a story, or at least most of those six elements. But for broadcasting, including all these elements in the lead would overwhelm the listener. Individual listeners simply cannot process so much information that fast by ear, especially at the beginning of the story when the person hasn't yet come to understand what the story is about or decided if it is sufficiently important to warrant attention. Instead the writer should determine which two or three elements are the most important in each individual story. That decision will depend in turn on the content of the story and the style in which it is to be developed.

Who

If the story features prominent names, the "who" should be in the lead, but an unknown name in the lead does not attract sufficient audience interest.

What

Usually what happened will be included in the lead, but if the "what" is complex and cannot be simplified without distortion or confusion, another approach should be used.

When

Since broadcast media are immediate, it is assumed that stories are current, and the precise time of a story is not often significant in the lead. It may be significant, however, if the story has an unusual time frame or if it is a major story that is just breaking. Only a word or two is needed to express time—today, this morning, last night—so this element usually can be included without cluttering.

Ǝ Feature stories, which are not timely, can often ignore this element almost entirely, except that you probably wouldn't do a Christmas story in the middle of summer, and, if you did, it would only be because there was a twist in the "when" of the story.

Where

The location where the story takes place may or may not be important in attracting audience attention. If the president makes a major statement about the state of the economy, most people won't care (in the lead) whether he spoke from an Iowa farming convention or from Washington. Residents of Iowa, however, who would be familiar with the location of the speech, would be an exception. In Iowa, put the location in the lead because it adds proximity and personalization for those listeners.

Ǝ On the other hand, the location of a major plane crash would be important to everyone, if for no other reason than to allow them to determine that it happened, or did not happen, where they have family or friends.

Why and How   These elements of a story usually require a more lengthy explanation than can be accomplished in a lead sentence, and therefore they should not be included in the lead.

Leads and Lead-Ins   There is an important difference in broadcast practice between the *lead* and the *lead-in*. It is common practice, especially in television, to use one or two *anchor* announcers who provide continuity to the broadcast. Many of the stories in the newscast will be introduced by the anchor, with the rest of the story delivered by a reporter. The anchor's introduction is a lead-in. It is generally longer than a lead, two to three sentences perhaps. It may set the background of story, especially a continuing story, or provide transition between two stories, or simply provide an attention-getting tease to hold the audience for the story:

> It could be a late night on Capitol Hill. At this hour the House is debating a budget package tentatively approved today by a joint conference committee. Mary Jones has the story.

> People Express Airlines is flying away with new customers from the South. Mark Brown reports the carrier picked up its first passengers today on the new forty-nine-dollar route from Atlanta to Newark.

> How'd you like to buy your own business? Something that's well established . . . well known . . . and more than a little out of the ordinary? Well . . . if your answer is "Yes," Pete Fuentes reports there's a unique opportunity waiting for you in Nevada.

The practice works well when the respective jobs performed by anchor and reporter are understood by the writers involved, but remember that the reporter will also begin the recorded story with a lead sentence. Be sure that the same information is not merely repeated in both lead-in and lead.

Types of Leads   There are many ways to approach a lead sentence, but in general they can be grouped under four basic types—the straight lead, the throwaway lead, the feature lead, and the umbrella lead.

The Straight Lead   The straight, or direct, lead is a straightforward statement of fact, using those facts most likely to catch the attention of the listener. It is the most common form of lead:

> Fire swept through the gambling casino of a luxury hotel in San Juan, Puerto Rico, earlier today, killing at least fifty people, most of them Americans.

> The Miami Dolphins made it five wins in a row earlier today with a 36 to 28 victory over the Cardinals in St. Louis.

> The Reagan administration has unveiled a twelve billion dollar plan to clean up the nation's waterways, but it has drawn immediate criticism by Democratic leaders in Congress.

The Throwaway Lead

Sometimes also called a *delayed* lead, or a *set-up* lead, this form is a pure tease for the audience. It tells little about the facts of the story, but introduces a provocative statement or question, to which the audience responds: "I wonder what that's all about?" and stays tuned.

The throwaway lead is effective if the story is complex and a straight lead would be confusing, or might misrepresent the facts of the story, or would have to be too long in order to introduce the story correctly.

Things continue to be a bit shaky along the coast of Northern California. [Lead for a *minor* earthquake story, one which did no damage.]

There's bad news and good news from the Magic Kingdom tonight. [Lead for a story on an employees' strike at Disneyland, but the park was staying open anyway.]

In the long continuing state college professors' strike, both sides have agreed to disagree. [The story was that an impasse had been reached, had been formally declared, and that under the rules for negotiation a neutral mediator would now be brought in—all much too complicated to include in a straight lead!]

The throwaway lead is a good change of pace in the newscast, but be careful not to overdo its use.

The Feature Lead

This form of lead is very similar to the throwaway lead; its primary purpose is to attract attention rather than deliver information. It is, as the name suggests, used with soft news, feature stories. It is also called a *soft* lead.

Can you imagine a baby horse that lives in a house, sleeps in a playpen, and watches television?

Whoever said children should be seen and not heard didn't work in television.

The Umbrella Lead

This lead is used to tie together multiple stories, where the stories have something in common.

Tornadoes touched down in three mid-Western states this afternoon. Damage was extensive, but no injuries were reported.

The connection between drugs and the movie industry appeared in two locations yesterday, London and Hollywood.

The economy sent a series of confusing signals out yesterday as to the direction it may be heading. The stock market had its biggest advance in more than two months. Gold and silver prices plummeted. And overseas the dollar dropped against most foreign currencies. We have three reports, beginning with Bill Smith on Wall Street. [This is actually an umbrella lead-in.]

This type of lead may also be used to tie together multiple aspects of a story—say two reactions—pro and con—to a Supreme Court decision, or a national story followed by a local follow-up. From the audience's standpoint the umbrella lead effectively makes the multiple stories into one.

Leads of whatever type must be kept brief and uncluttered. Don't include in the lead such things as these:

- Addresses. The general "where" can be amplified with a more specific address in the body of the story, if it is useful to the story.
- Ages. The precise ages of persons involved in the story are not that important; if age is important, a general term—"elderly man," "two small children,"—will keep the lead from sounding like an obituary.
- Statements that don't actually lead into the story: "The City Council held its regular weekly meeting last night at City Hall." There has to be a reason why you are going to talk about the meeting; tell us, in the lead, what it is.

Organizing the Body of the Story

The lead will be followed by the *body* of the story. The writer will have to look at the total collection of facts and opinions that make up the story, decide which will be used in the broadcast, and then find some sequential pattern in which to present these items. Any logical arrangement that will present the story clearly and accurately, within the time allotted, will do. There are some commonly used approaches, and we've provided examples of three, but many stories cannot just be fitted into any one pattern.

Chronological Sequence This structure is the easiest and best for stories in which there is a sequence of events. It is especially common for crime, disaster, accident, and similar stories. The following story has a long lead, which brings the continuing story up to date. Otherwise it follows a chronological approach.

ANCHOR KEY: SNIPER PIC

> A little less than a day after the terror began . . . San Francisco police today burst into a room at the top of a 16 story skyscraper and captured a sniper who fired more than 40 bullets into the Market Street area and held a secretary hostage.
> The 55 year old woman was released unhurt.

SNIPER MINI
SUPER:
SAN FRANCISCO

> This was the scene yesterday afternoon, when the unidentified gunman began spraying gunfire into the business district.
> One man was wounded.
> After that, police cordoned off a 20 block area and the stalemate began.
> The sniper identified himself as Chief Cherokee of the Sla Woo, what he claims is a terrorist group, and he demanded money for rehabilitation of San Francisco ghettos.

MORE   MORE   MORE

BACK TO PIC	Then, just after 4 this afternoon, police decided to rush into his barricaded room and found him asleep. He was captured with no struggle. Tentatively, the gunman has been identified as Chico Cochran. A police investigation of the incident is continuing.

Source: Courtesy of KCRA, Sacramento, CA.

The audience will be helped through a complicated series of chronological events by frequent use of time-oriented transition words. In the story above, *then*, *after that*, *today*, *yesterday*, and *less than a day after* are all used. Other similar words—*next, while, first, finally, last night, now, meanwhile*—also help. (Reread the news story in Chapter 2, which was also written to emphasize time transitions and chronological sequence.)

Effect and Cause Sequence We are used to hearing that phrase in the opposite order—cause and effect—but the news story is most likely an effect, a happening, whatever gives the story its timeliness, and so that comes first in the sequence. Then the writer can go back to explain the cause, what led up to the action, and give meaning to the effect. Frequently used transition words are *since*, *because*, and *for*.

In this story the *effect* is the results of a study, just released.

ANCHOR	The results are in from a nationwide study on people working with video display terminals. A group of clerical workers calling itself "Nine to Five Working Women" studied three thousand people, some of them here in San Francisco. Michael Brown reports that the study found that spending long hours in front of a VDT may be bad for your health.
BROWN (VTR) IN OFFICE w/VDTs	The three year study has some video terminal workers wondering, wondering if the stress, headaches, blurred vision, even psoriasis some of them suffer isn't caused by the machine. It questions whether radiation levels are too high, if the cautions like shields and screen filters too few. But a disturbing find concerns pregnant women who work at display terminals. They found companies around the country where as many as half the pregnant women working at terminals seemed to have miscarriages or malformed children. And one of those companies was here in San Francisco. It's the airlines reservations office where Carol Blank works. In the survey, half the pregnant women there suffered adverse outcomes. Carol says she has had a miscarriage and a prematurely born child who died, and thinks it's because she works at a display terminal.

CAROL BLANK SOUND BITE	We don't know if its radiation or if its pulses or if it's the fact that we're so heavily monitored because our computer equipment is so sophisticated. We're constantly under stress because of the monitoring type situation with our productivity.
BROWN	Carol said the airlines modified her work space to make it safer. Mildred Jones with the Berkeley labor group called the VDT coalition says cases like Carol's are a warning to industry.
MILDRED JONES SOUND BITE	What that tells us is that there is a problem there, and we don't know what's causing it. We don't know if it's the VDT or if it's unrelated to the VDT, but we know research is needed.
BROWN V/O	Pete Peterson represents an electronics industry group.
PETE PETERSON SOUND BITE	No, working with the equipment isn't going to cause that, that incident, in our opinion and in the opinion of research scientists.
BROWN	Meanwhile studies go on, suspicions go on, but everyone agrees that it's time to find out for sure.

Source: Script reconstituted from broadcast, KPIX, San Francisco, August 1, 1985.

**Action-
Reaction
Sequence**

This approach is similar to effect-cause. It is often used with issue-oriented stories in which there is more than one point of view. One person or agency takes an action, which is reported in the story, and then followed by the reactions—comments, responses, counteractions—of other persons or agencies. This story has an action-reaction component in the statements from the two attorneys. It also has a complicated time frame that stretches back several years. The reporter/writer had to work a number of elements together carefully.

ANCHOR	Back in 1982 a boy and a girl were hit by a car in Oakland. Both were badly injured. One is now permanently disabled. The driver who hit them had no insurance so a lawsuit was filed against the city. Tonight Ben Williams reports on how that case was settled and why some city officials are not happy about it.
BEN W/SUSAN in YARD	Susan xxxxx is eleven now. The accident that left her paralyzed from the waist down happened when she was five. She and her eighteen year old cousin were both struck by an uninsured driver while crossing an Oakland street. This month she was awarded two million dollars put into an annuity to last her lifetime. Her mother says the accident is so far behind her now she's no longer bitter.

SOUND BITE MOTHER	
	OUTCUE: ". . . live with it so long."
BEN AT SITE OF ACCIDENT	The case is unusual because the driver that hit Susan and her cousin was uninsured and so poor that the family lawyer went after the city of Oakland. The little girl and her companion were in this crosswalk. It was ten o'clock at night and dark. When they got about here they were both struck by a speeding truck. The little girl was knocked sixty feet. The attorney contended that the intersection was improperly lighted and that three streets intersecting with an 84 foot long crosswalk without proper traffic controls, he said, is a danger trap for pedestrians.
SOUND BITE ATTORNEY	
	OUTCUE: ". . . far more responsible than the truck driver."
BEN	Oakland's attorney says the city should be only partially to blame for the layout of the street and the ruling that forces the city to pay big settlements simply because it has a lot of taxpayers' money, is wrong.
SOUND BITE CITY ATTY	
	OUTCUE: ". . . when it is in fact only one or two percent liable."
BEN W/SUSAN	Susan is a straight A student who already has plans for her life.
SOUND BITE SUSAN	
	OUTCUE: ". . . when I grow up."
BEN: STANDUP	I'm Ben Williams for Channel 5 Eyewitness News.

Source: Script reconstituted from broadcast, KPIX, San Francisco, August 1, 1985.

When using an action-reaction approach to a story, you can help guide the audience through the transitions with words and phrases like *however, on the other hand, in contrast, but.* But be careful not to bounce back and forth between the various sides of the controversy, as newspapers will do when they use the inverted pyramid approach. Instead, cover the statements, arguments, positions of one side with as much detail as the story requires (or time permits); then use a transition to move to the other side.

Rewrites

We have concentrated so far on the original or first-time writing of news stories, but the broadcast writer will spend a great deal of his or her time in rewriting. Frequently the rewrite will be from an earlier version of the story, now being rewritten for a later newscast. If new information has been received on a continuing story, that new material should go into the lead of the story and be emphasized in the rewrite.

Here are the first and later versions of a story:

ANCHOR KEY: JETLINER	Officials in Greece say a Swissair DC-8 jetliner with 154 people aboard caught fire after skidding to a halt on a rainswept runway at Athens International Airport. Preliminary reports indicate at least seven people are dead. A number of others were hurt as flames engulfed the plane within seconds of touchdown. Witnesses say flames shot from the plane's undercarriage as it attempted to brake to a stop, finally halting at the end of the runway. Most of the 142 passengers and twelve crew members managed to escape by sliding down emergency chutes. The DC-8 was on a flight from Switzerland to the Far East with a stop in Athens. The airport has now been closed and flights diverted elsewhere.
ANCHOR KEY: JETLINER	Authorities in Greece now say at least eight people died when fire gutted a Swissair DC-8 just moments after it landed in a rainstorm at Athens International Airport. Two other passengers are in serious condition and not expected to live. Many others were hurt and at least twenty people are unaccounted for. However, officials believe they may have wandered away on their own accord. Witnesses say the plane's undercarriage burst into flames as it tried to brake on the slippery runway, and once it stopped smoke and fire swept into the plane. Fortunately, most of the 154 passengers and crew, including one hundred doctors headed for a medical meeting in China, managed to flee down emergency chutes.

Source: Courtesy of KCRA, Sacramento, CA.

You must be careful, however, when rewriting for updates of a story, to include some of the basic information that made it a story in the first place. You cannot automatically assume that all the persons in the audience will have heard an earlier version and are familiar with the story. On the other hand, you probably will not have time for a complete recap, and those in the audience who have heard the story will not want all the details over again. There's a delicate balance between too little and too much recapitulation.

Another source of rewrite material may be a newspaper story. By the time the newspaper reaches the broadcast station, it will already have been read by its subscribers and in a sense be "old" news. But many people do not read a paper, so the fact that a story has been in print should not be reason in itself to reject it for broadcast. However, the time lapse means that new material, if available, should be incorporated and emphasized, and the writer should be especially careful to rewrite into good aural style.

A third and very common source of rewrite material are those stories which originate with the news wire services. Until just a few years ago, these services provided all their news material to clients in print form via teletype, to be voiced by the local announcer at each subscribing station. The standard teletype service is still available and used by many small-market radio stations. But it is being supplemented or replaced in many stations by newer delivery technologies emphasizing voice and voice-picture feeds sent by satellite.

The availability of these already prepared stories changes the job of the local news staff. First, someone must be responsible for recording the feed on tape, and logging each story, with its content and length. Then a selection is made of those stories that will be used. In some cases, the feed stories will be edited to shorten them, or to fit their actualities into stories delivered by local announcers. In this type of situation, the process is no longer rewrite as such, but a combination of writing and tape editing.

Caution: Don't Crowd

Often beginning writers feel a compulsion to cram as many facts as possible into the story, especially when they realize that they have only 20, or 30, or 60 seconds to tell the story. But be careful. Too many facts, presented too fast, will simply overwhelm the listener. The most important or most interesting material must be selected and spaced throughout the story using some repetition—not of the same words, but of major ideas. On the other hand, don't waste precious seconds with material that has little importance or relevance to the story, or especially to the audience's interest in the story. With practice you will soon get a feel for the middle ground between too much compression and needless repetition.

Broadcast news stories do not usually have closings, at least not in the same way that programs have formal closings, but the last sentence in the story should give a sense of closure. Don't end with new material or an incomplete explanation.

Types of Stories

At this point we can no longer continue to generalize about the structure of individual stories. We will now consider four kinds of stories—the "breaking" disaster story, the investigative report, the "soft news" feature story, and the news commentary. These four provide a reasonable range among the many possible types.

The Disaster Story   Accidents and disasters of various kinds make up a large share of "breaking" stories—auto, bus, truck, plane and train crashes, fires, earthquakes, hurricanes. Most are unforeseen events, and all too frequently they involve the loss of human lives. The reporter-writer cannot even begin to prepare this type of story in advance, and with the possible exception of fires and storms, won't usually get to the scene until the event has concluded.* The story will have to be reconstructed from the accounts of survivors, witnesses, and professional persons—doctors, police, fire personnel, others—who are at the scene.

The most important information to be gathered and worked into the story can be grouped under the traditional six categories:

Who: Number of people involved? Anyone important or prominent? Other identifications; names and roles of people who are providing information.

What: Nature and magnitude of event, subsequent events, extent of death and injury, and so on.

When: The chronology of events and following activities.

Where: Get the exact location, but repeat the location using landmarks familiar to your audience, if possible.

Why: If there is a cause that can be verified, state it—but be cautious, for example, in attributing cause in an auto accident until the appropriate authorities so state.

How: In this type of story, how is mostly a description of the progress of the event. The hotel fire started in a conference room and spread between floors and walls undetected, then shot up a stairwell and erupted on several floors simultaneously, and so on.

If the story is a major one, there will be numerous chances for followups—the continuing condition of injured survivors, statements by authorities including condolences to victims, relief to the stricken area, promises of future aid to prevent similar catastrophes, and so on. In revising the story for future broadcasts, the newest material should appear in each new lead and the first sentences of the rewrite. Older information which you believe your audience might already know can be eliminated to make time for the newer facts and statements.

We've included the full script of a disaster story later in the chapter as part of the discussion of visualization and visual cues.

We have used the term *breaking* story to contrast this type of story with other types that can be prepared on a schedule determined by the journalist. Accidents and disasters, which come without warning, make up one major category of breaking stories, but many breaking stories are developed out of scheduled events. The governor may schedule a press conference, for example, and the station can assign a reporter to cover it, but the story can't be written

---

* A dramatic exception that has become a classic example of on-the-spot disaster reporting is the 1937 radio account of the explosion and crash of the dirigible *Hindenburg,* which we reproduced in part in Chapter 3. Also read the account by Dan Rather in *The Camera Never Blinks* of his experience covering hurricane Carla from Galveston, Texas, in 1961.

until after the meeting is over. It's still a breaking story, the result of an event, and it may have to be written in a hurry to meet a deadline. Parades, conventions, sporting events, and demonstrations are other scheduled events that lead to breaking stories.

The Investigative Report

These stories may appear under various labels: investigative report, special report, or minidocumentary. Although there is a great deal of similarity between investigative news reports and documentaries, and frequently the same topics and even the same raw camera footage may be used for both, we prefer to use documentary to describe a different approach to story development, which we discuss in Chapter 14.

Investigative reports are prepared on a scheduled basis. They do not depend on an event or outside trigger mechanism except that, for example, the death of a group of destitute transients in a flophouse hotel fire might call the attention of an assignment editor to the possibility of doing a series of reports on the plight of the elderly poor.

Suggestions for investigative reports can come from almost anywhere. The ascertainment interviews TV stations conduct with community leaders will lead to a list of local problem areas that may be investigated. There are always government issues to be explored, including those which involve the interaction between "ordinary" citizens and government. Health and economic issues are possibilities, although these, given different treatment, might be soft news features as well.

A problem with the investigative report, which we have already touched upon, is its possible lack of timeliness. If the report can be timed to correspond to a breaking story, then the problem is solved. A series of reports on the rezoning of residential and agricultural land might be timed to coincide with the release of a major study on urban planning, for example. Or the story can be prepared and released when some aspect can be highlighted that gives it timeliness, such as a story on Individual Retirement Accounts released shortly before April 15, the income tax deadline, or a story on water control projects that coincides with the annual runoff from snow melt.

Sometimes other criteria will have to substitute for timeliness. A series of reports on breast cancer may use impact and possibly personalization as its raison d'être. Properly approached, that subject can be very important, especially to a female audience.

Once the topic has been chosen, the research begins. Quite possibly both library research and interviews with experts will be used. Some of the interview material may later appear in the report as actualities. The research will help determine the scope of the topic, identify the most important material, and locate the best "experts." If the topic concerns an issue, about which there are different opinions, the question of how to present those viewpoints fairly also will have to be dealt with.

Point of View

The actual writing begins by identifying a point of view for the story. By point of view, we do not mean that the writer should take an editorial position, such as espousing one side in a controversy, or making evaluative comments on a statement made by a source. Quite the contrary. It is an important responsibility to maintain as much objectivity as possible as the story is being developed.*

Nevertheless, a story, especially one developed "from scratch," like an investigative piece, needs to be constructed with an *angle,* a *peg,* a *hook,* a *point of view*—all terms used by newspersons to describe the approach used to organize the story. Here, using the topics we've already mentioned, are examples of point of view.

The reports on residential rezoning might be organized to emphasize the *process* of zoning and rezoning, focusing on the roles of the various government bodies involved—planning commission, board of supervisors, citizens' advisory groups. The argument on rezoning a particular piece of land can then be treated as a case study of how the process works. Or the same topic might be approached as a controversy, viewed in the form of the opposing forces—status quo v. development—with the governmental bodies caught in the middle trying to find a compromise acceptable to both sides.

The IRA story might be covered as a straight informative piece, listing the various types of investment plans which can be used for an individual retirement account, the rates of interest currently offered, and the risks involved. Interviews with bankers, brokers, and other experts would make up most of the story. But a more interesting story might result if it were approached from the point of view of the consumer. Choose two or three widely different "clients"—a young single career woman, a couple nearing retirement, a manual laborer who works by the job; ask several different experts to plan IRAs for these people; then focus in the story on the similarities or differences in the proposals made by each expert for each different situation.

If there is serious concern that water control projects have been neglected and that neglect poses a threat to public safety through possible breaks in levees, then that's probably the point of view to take on that story. Point up the dangers, seek out the ways danger can be reduced, tell people how to protect themselves from the floods that may come with the spring runoff. If the danger is not acute (but you decide to do the program anyway), the focus might be on possible squabbling between various government agencies over who has the responsibility for water control, cutbacks in government programs that have lessened preventive maintenance, and so on.

The breast cancer series might take a clinical, medical approach. What are the most recent research findings and newly accepted medical techniques for prevention, detection, and control? Or it might concentrate on how women who have had breast cancer have coped with surgery, chemotherapy, and so on.

If the report is to be organized into a series—three- and five-part series are common—then there will need to be an overall point of view for the series as well as one for each individual program. The zoning story, for example, could

---

* We considered editorials in the previous chapter and will discuss commentary later in this one. In our final chapter we will raise some of the ethical concerns journalists face, but an extended discussion of news bias is not within our scope.

easily be structured into three parts—one concentrating on the developers' position, one on a citizens' group trying to slow or stop development, and one on the planning commission as the battleground.

The Soft News Feature Story

There is nothing inherently different in the construction of this type of story. As we have suggested, the difference is primarily in those gratifications which are emphasized. Personalization, curiosity, and novelty are likely to be stronger in this type of story, which would give it a broader audience.

The subject matter of soft news features may also aim at specific groups. A story on a new type of shoe to be worn by joggers that cuts down on sore feet would be of interest really only to joggers; it would be very difficult to find an angle to that story which would give it a broader audience. (Such a story would likely be available as part of a syndicated package of similar features which local stations could put into a locally produced physical fitness series, or nationally it might be shown, on cable, on the Health Care Network.)

As we have also noted, timeliness is not often a feature of soft news stories, although there is no necessary requirement that they not be timely. A story on a man who carves statues with a chain saw will be just as interesting to an audience one week as the next. Of course if the statues he makes are all depictions of Santa Claus, then there would be an appropriate time for the story.

We have used three terms to describe this type of story—*soft news, life style,* and *feature.* All three are used essentially interchangeably, although *feature* seems to be more common in radio, and the others in television.

These stories contain a number of variations, including the "how to cope" story. Most of us spend a lot of our time trying to cope with co-workers and bosses, with spouses and children, with doctors and plumbers, with buying insurance and furniture and groceries, even with selecting a videotape to rent or a place to eat. All these decisions provide stress, and "how to cope" stories deal with handling these problems. They offer advice on any and all of these topics, usually by interviewing an expert in the particular area—a restaurant reviewer, a stock broker, a tax consultant. Other consumer-oriented stories include topics on health care, changes in laws that affect us and stories on the quality and safety of products. Many stations have reporters who specialize in consumer issues.

Also within this genre are stories about interesting but not famous people. Audiences find personalism to be a very strong gratification; tension and action need not be the leading gratifications in every story.

As with the investigative report, begin your research with a point of view in mind. What is there about this person, this event, or this object that will be interesting to my audience?

News Commentaries

The most obvious difference between news commentary and other types of news writing is the shift from objectivity (or at least from the attempt to remain objective in presenting a story) to a subjective and more personal point of view. This two-part commentary exemplifies that difference. It was written and presented by newsman Dick Cable on KXTV, Sacramento, California. It is part of a regular feature called "Cable's Comments."

CROSS TO CABLE

TAKE CABLE

Key: Comment

Key: Comment

(BOB)

Tomorrow is one of those "Theme Days" and Dick Cable is ready to get on the backwagon.

* * * * * * * * * * * * * * * * *

Tomorrow is the "Great American Smokeout" . . . promoted by the American Cancer Society and its local units all across the country.

The object is to motivate and support smokers to quit for the day and consider the dangers involved in smoking . . . and if the motivation and the message is strong enough . . . to get you to stop smoking forever.

I'm impressed that each year the smokeout has been conducted . . . many smokers have tried to quit . . . and a few of them have been able to kick the habit.

The day will mean little or nothing to you if you don't quit . . . It may only aggravate you that that bunch of holier-than-thou goodie-two-shoes are bugging you again.

I've bugged you before . . . and I intend to do it again.

A friend of my teenage daughter smokes . . . and my daughter expressed concern that her friend was smoking more and more. Why does she smoke? I asked. "She says it calms her nerves," came my daughter's reply.

I understand that process well . . . as a one-time three-pack-a-day smoker, I know all about smokers' nerves. An addicted smoker gets nervous for the same reason a heroin addict gets nervous . . . because his body is craving a fix. A shot of heroin calms the heroin addict . . . a cigarette calms the smoker. It is not the nerves being soothed . . . it is the addiction.

When I gave up cigarettes . . . my skin turned a sickish green, I broke out in cold sweats, my hands shook, my voice trembled and I suffered from stomach cramps. Those were cigarette nerves . . . and somehow I finally had found the guts to <u>cure</u> them rather than appease them by lighting up again.

We're all going to die. I'm not trying to prevent death . . . but I hope to <u>live</u> until I die.

The leading risks from smoking are heart disease, stroke, emphysema, and lung cancer. With the exception of a massive fatal heart attack . . . death from these causes is a slow and ever-worsening torture.

The emphysemic slowly strangles . . . it can take years. Lung cancer is shorter . . . perhaps six months, but a year or more is possible . . . and the pain beggars description.

MORE   MORE   MORE

Key: Comment	Only 9 percent of lung cancer patients live five or more years after diagnosis. 83 percent of lung cancers in men are caused by smoking. Give the American cancer society a call . . . they've got lots of help and ideas and support for you if you want to finally kick the habit. That's Cable's comment.

CROSS TO CABLE	Speaking of the great American smokeout . . . some viewers have taken umbrage over an analogy made by Dick Cable in his comment last night.
TAKE CABLE	* * * * * * * * * * * * * * * * Yes . . . but rather than apologizing, I'm going to turn the screw a little tighter. Talk about smoker's nerves. I must have rubbed quite a few of them raw. The switchboard logged a good number of calls from viewers who said . . . "How dare he equate cigarette smoking with heroin addiction?" We don't go out robbing and killing to feed our habit."
Key: Comment	Actually, I didn't equate cigarette smokers with heroin addicts . . . but I did make a statement about addiction. When a smoker's nicotine blood-level begins to decline in the interval between cigarettes . . . he or she begins to feel fidgety, nervous . . . and reaches for another smoke. The cigarette relieves that nervousness . . . and reinforces the habit. That is very <u>much</u> like heroin addiction. When the level of morphine in the body declines . . . the addict becomes increasingly agitated and is only relieved by another dose. The important thing to understand is that almost all smokers are . . . in a true medical sense . . . addicted to nicotine in much the same way that heroin addicts are to their drug.
Key: Comment	Some of the callers who said "How dare you" to me noted that unlike heroin addicts, they do not rob or kill others nor prostitute themselves to feed their nicotine habit. I suggest to you there's only one reason why that might be true. Cigarettes are <u>cheap</u>. If heroin was 50 cents a hit, heroin addicts wouldn't be a crime problem either. Conversely, if cigarettes were $100 a pack, thousands of you would be transformed into thieves and prostitutes. Let me tell you something else too. Cigarettes, in and of themselves, are more dangerous to your health than heroin, in and of itself. Heroin addicts die only rarely from the drug itself. It is <u>not</u> poisonous! MORE MORE MORE

They usually die from inpurities used to cut the street heroin . . . from dirty needles, malnutrition or from being killed during a holdup or by a pusher who didn't get his money on time.

Key: Comment

A lit cigarette, on the other hand, is loaded with poisons, poisonous gases and carcinogenic agents. Nicotine itself is one of the most potent poisons on earth. I've heard it said that a single drop in a bucket of water is enough to kill a horse.

Besides tar and nicotine, cigarette smoke contains hydrogen cyanide, volatile hydrocarbons and carbon monoxide.

Smoking is not only addictive . . . it also poisons its addicts.

That's Cable's comment.

Source: Courtesy of KXTV, Sacramento, CA.

Analysis of that commentary shows both similarities with and differences from other types of stories. It has impact, timeliness, personalization, conflict—all strong criteria for any news story. It is also personal—involves the pronoun *I* and makes personal references to the reporter's own family and friends. An objective story on the same topic might give information on the success of similar smokeout days in past years, how many people might be expected to quit this year, and what arrangements were being made by the local Cancer Society chapter. This commentary goes much beyond that; it has a strong and subjective point of view.

We said early in the chapter that we would not attempt to cover all types of stories. There is no way we could. But most stories will fit reasonably well into these basic patterns. Sports stories, for example, represent a change in content, but not in approach. The most common sports story is a breaking story after a scheduled game. Other sports stories will be investigative, feature, or commentary.

The one major category that does differ is the reporting of weather. To be successful as a weather reporter or writer requires some expert knowledge of meteorology. It also seems to require a heightened sense of showmanship, as this is the one type of news story most often presented ad lib, without script, and which attracts the more outrageous presentational styles.

Television News: Writing with Pictures

The language of television news—that is, the basic principles of aural style—is the same as it is for radio. So, essentially, are the structural concerns of organizing stories and newscasts. But there are differences that need to be addressed.

One difference that pictures make is in the selection of stories. Often a story of minor news value will get heavier emphasis than may really be justified because it is highly visual and the news crew was able to get "good footage." The opposite is also true. A major story that has little pictorial content may be dropped from the TV newscast or given very brief treatment by the anchor just because it is not visual.

Visualizing Stories

A few stories in any TV newscast will be delivered by the anchor without any form of visual support. These will be the less important, shorter stories and perhaps late-breaking items for which no visual material has yet been collected. For all purposes these are radio stories—read by a "talking head."

Graphics

Increasingly, however, some form of graphics will be used on even these simple, short stories. Most common is the use of a single drawing or picture, often with a caption, placed in the background, over the shoulder of the announcer (Figure 12.2). For longer stories, if no other form of visual is available, several pictures might be displayed in sequence. When a new story is started, a new graphic is put up to help signal the transition.

Graphics can also be used full-screen or, using the visual effects unit available at most stations, moved from one position to another, enlarged or reduced, and so on, electronically. This use represents the next step up in visualizing a news story. The graphic is an integral part of the story and helps to communicate the content of the message (Figure 12.3).

Here is how the preceding graphics might be written into the news script, but remember that different stations use different terminology and practices which they have found suit their own operations.

ANCHOR	Headline News, I'm Bob Loeser. Israeli officials say they
KEY: LEBANON	are willing to talk with kidnappers in Lebanon, but
HOSTAGES	Jerusalem says it will not knuckle under to any ultima-
	tums. . . .

In the absence of directions to the contrary the single word KEY or similar term means an insert key in the background.

Figure 12.2

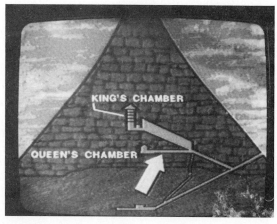

Figure 12.3

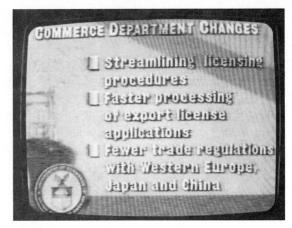

Figure 12.4   *Figure 12.5*

| ANCHOR (V/O) | . . . Their discovery, a hidden cavity filled with sand, possibly an architectural feature to prevent earthquake damage. The Japanese followed with more advanced equipment. . . . |
| FULL-SCREEN DIAGRAM | |

If you want something other than an insert key, that will have to be explained; here—FULL-SCREEN. Don't forget to indicate when the map is to be removed, most likely by using ANCHOR to return the scene to the anchor reporter.

A third form of graphic is the use of titles or other words printed on the screen (Figure 12.4). Often these identify people by name and sometimes title, or they identify locations. Usually they are placed at the bottom of the screen, but titles can be full-screen, top, center, corner, angled, or whatever you want. And they too can contribute to the content of a story.

| CITY HALL | It was yesterday, when the Mayor reported on how city agencies were doing, that the subject of drug testing among municipal workers came up. . . . |
| FONT: (4) JANE HANSON | |

These instructions show that the report is coming live from a camera shooting a standup of the reporter at city hall. The reporter's name is to be identified by a lower screen graphic, as that is standard practice in the absence of other instructions. This station uses FONT as the key word for that graphic; others may use SUPER or CHYRON or other words.

| ANCHOR | The changes include streamlining licensing procedures, faster processing of export license applications, and fewer trade regulations with Western Europe, Japan, and China—steps U.S. manufacturers have been urging for some years. But, the Commerce Department proposals may not resolve all of the problems. . . . |
| OUTLINE: FULL-SCREEN | |

This graphic is definitely part of the story. It helps organize and sequence complex material, so that the audience can see the structure of the story, which is given in much more detail verbally (Figure 12.5).

Standups and Voice-overs   If a story does not have strong visual content, or if there isn't time to get the visuals together on a late-breaking or continuing story, one technique to consider is the *standup*. The reporter will stand in front of a building—the state capitol or a courthouse—while delivering the story on the deliberations taking place inside. Standups may be used for a full story, in which case they are only slightly more visual than the "talking head" in the studio. More often they are used only for the open and/or close of a story, which also contains videotape footage, or as a bridge between two parts of a story.

Seeing the reporter on location where the story is taking place provides another benefit that has nothing to do with the actual delivery of information to audiences. It increases *reporter involvement*. News directors and consultants believe that having the audience see the reporter involved in the process of gathering the story adds credibility to the report.

Several techniques can be used. On a story about a drought and the effect on farmland, the reporter would stand in the middle of a field and dribble the parched earth through his or her fingers. If the story involves a press conference, the camera will cut away from the speaker to show a quick shot of the reporter in the audience taking notes on the speech or asking a question. Or the reporter will deliver a standup from a location associated with the story.

Another variation on reporter involvement is the "Eyewitness" news approach. Not only is the reporter seen at the location of the story, but he or she is also in the studio to introduce the prepared story. The sequence may go something like this:

ANCHOR	This afternoon violence erupted for the first time on the picket lines outside the Greyhound bus terminal in downtown Chicago. Our John Jones was there and he's here now to give this report.
JONES IN STUDIO	That's right, Stan. What had been a peaceful demonstration by striking Greyhound workers turned violent today when a group of nonstriking supervisors attempted to cross the picket lines.
TAKE VCR w/ NAT SD	Several minor injuries were reported, but no one was hurt severely enough to require. . . .

The reporter will continue to deliver the narration live from the studio over the videotape taken on location with the natural sound of the story in the background. When the reporter is heard but not seen, another technique is being used. It is the *voice-over*.

The bulk of most television stories will be narrated using this technique. The pictures may be still photos or graphics. More likely they will be videotape footage shot on location, then returned to the station and edited into a "package."

Depending on the station's preference, the voice-over narration may be delivered live in the studio, as in the Eyewitness format described above, or prerecorded. The live approach permits some spontaneity, an opportunity for a question and response between the anchor and reporter, perhaps. It also leads to risks; since it is live, a mistake will be seen and heard on the air. And it ties up the reporter at the station, preventing him or her from going home or out on another story.

Location Tape   Using tape footage in a story involves, first of all, sending a crew out to shoot the footage. Most stations make this commitment willingly as part of their news programming budget, but only major stories will justify the cost in time and money. An assignment editor earns his or her salary by making these judgments daily.

Two steps are involved in preparing a tape story—collecting the footage and then editing that footage and writing an accompanying narration.

When collecting footage on location, keep these guidelines in mind.

1. Get enough material. Beginning reporters and writers often make this mistake and find, when it comes time to edit the package, that they don't have enough good footage to cover the narration, or the right kind. They find they have to jam the facts together or leave out important material in order to keep up with the visuals.

   One news producer suggests at least 20 seconds on each single shot, to allow for selection in editing. Most stations expect you to shoot about three to four times as much material as you expect to use in the final story.

2. Look for visuals that will tell the story without a lot of narration. In some stories, that's easy. Rushing flood water, raging fires, the pomp of a military parade, a somber funeral—all can carry a story for a substantial period without explanation. At other times it's more difficult. Look for movement, conflict, personalization, and the visual representation of the other criteria we gave for good stories.

3. Get the transitory material first. Your editing job will be easier if you can shoot the story in roughly the same order as it will be presented on the screen, but more important, shoot events *as they happen,* because you cannot recapture those visuals.

4. You will need a variety of shots—establishing, cover shots, "people" shots that add human focus to the story, and cutaways and closeups which will add drama and variety to the final story. Selecting footage to fill these requirements will be much easier if you have decided, at least tentatively, on an organizing scheme for the story before you arrive on location, and have discussed that approach with your cameraperson.

5. In addition to the visual footage, get natural sound if possible.

Then, when assembling the final story, use these additional guidelines:

1. Whenever visual materials are *not* on the screen, during a "talking head" or "standup" segment, the narration can be written as a radio story, in whatever language and verbal pattern seems most logical.

2. When visuals are present, the narration and the pictures must "fit." The narration must relate to what the audience is seeing. It should introduce, explain, amplify,

and provide transitions—in short, provide the viewer with facts that cannot be seen. But it should not repeat what the viewer can see.

For example, assume a story about President Reagan's leaving Washington for a vacation in California. We have footage of his getting in the helicopter, waving to the people on the White House lawn, and flying off. The narration should *not* say: "... and the President and Mrs. Reagan got in the helicopter and took off for California" because we see that, and it's clear visually. The narration also should *not* say: "... in his remarks to the group assembled on the White House lawn the President stated his firm. ..." You don't have footage of his remarks. *Showing* him climbing in the helicopter and waving, and at the same time *saying* that he spoke to the group does not fit.

You might, however, use this narration over the same footage: "The President will be in California for ten days on what he describes as a working vacation. During that time he will have to decide on whether or not to veto the farm bill which Congress. ..." That commentary amplifies and projects the story forward, just as the helicopter is moving off and forward.

3. Select a strong visual sequence, using the principles of visual continuity and juxtaposition described in Chapter 7. Usually that means beginning with an establishing shot, using medium shots for most of the factual presentation, with closeups to show emotional responses where appropriate. Your visual sequence must, of course, support the basic organizational scheme you have chosen—chronological, action-reaction, or whatever.

Sound Bites   At several places in the text we have mentioned the use and value of *actualities*. Although terminology differs from place to place and between radio and television, most TV newspersons refer to any footage shot on location as an actuality and label interviews or other commentary by persons other than the reporter as a *sound bite*. (Other sounds gathered on location, such as the gunfire of a battle, a band in a parade, or sirens are *natural* or *raw* sound.)

The advantages of sound bites are obvious. They add credibility, impact, and personalization to a story. These are the real people who are involved in some fashion with the story. An eyewitness can describe what it was like to see the bank robbery unfold and to be threatened with a gun. An expert can provide information on the cause of a fire, or speculate knowledgeably on the impact of a new government economic policy—information and opinions beyond the level of expertise of the reporter. And the proponents and opponents of a new garbage dump site can themselves make the most effective statements on their beliefs as they argue for their positions.

Structurally too, the sound bite adds variety to the story. In a short story that may not be an important consideration, but in a longer piece the use of other voices and pictures helps maintain audience attention.

The sound bite should be between about 10 and 25 seconds in length. Shorter than 10 seconds is probably not worth the effort, unless it's very dramatic; the quote must be long enough for the audience to grasp that someone other than the reporter is speaking, what is being said, and how it ties to the rest of the story. Anything briefer can be more efficiently summarized by the reporter.

An exception would be a *series* of brief reactions to a situation by several different persons—responses, for example, to the question: "What did you think of the Supreme Court's action?" or: "When the engine fell off the wing of the plane, how did you react?" This technique assembles several short responses into a montage. It can show the variety of reactions in a situation, or it might show a unanimity of response, depending on what you get in the responses and how the tape is edited.

A long sound bite, on the other hand, takes control of the story away from the reporter, and is likely to be an inefficient use of the time involved. Eyewitnesses or experts who are not used to speaking for broadcast media are likely to express themselves in fragmented or convoluted statements that are hard for an audience to follow, and to take considerable time to make a point. If aired in their entirety, these statements will slow the story unnecessarily. Better use two or three separate short quotes than one long, rambling statement. Choose those bites which add information and credibility to the story, and put them in logical places in the development where they can also provide variety.

A fully written out, word-for-word sound bite seldom appears in a script as it did in the VDT story and does in the examples here. It's unnecessary because the writer-reporter and the story editor have already selected the bite in the editing room, extracted it from the raw tape, and put it on the story tape that will roll during the newscast. What is needed is some cue that tells the program's director, and whoever will be voicing the material that follows the bite, when the bite will end. Usually that is done with an *outcue*, the last few words of the bite, and we've shown that in most of our script samples.

The video display story and the story on the lawsuit award to the injured child both show good use of sound bites. Here are some other examples.

REPORTER	A ticket from Atlanta to Newark for this month costs only forty-nine dollars and that compares with a price of some $275 normally charged by the Atlanta-based Delta and other major airlines on the same route. Atlanta mayor Andrew Young says People Express is welcome to challenge the big boys in the South.
YOUNG (S/B)	What we see is additional competition and we see that making all of the airlines respond more creatively and competitively, but we also see a lot more people flying as we make the price of flying more accessible to more of the citizens of our city.
REPORTER	. . . Either way it is not enough to satisfy Senate Budget Committee chairman Pete Domenici, but it is, according to Domenici, the best <u>this</u> Congress can do <u>this</u> year.
DOMENICI (S/B)	Considering where we started, clearly more could have been done and there are many who say more should be done. I join with those. The problem is, we can't do more with this. So for those who want to do more I beg you not to impose on this system more than it can conceivably do at this moment in history.

| REPORTER | For House Budget Committee Chairman Bill Ray, this is his first year in the job, this is a major political win. . . . |

Source: Scripts reconstituted from broadcast, Cable News Network, August 1, 1985.

In both examples the source for the sound bite was identified verbally by the reporter in the lead to the bite, and both were well done. They avoided saying directly: "This is what Joe Brown had to say," but in both cases there's no question who the speaker is. In this next example the name of the source is not important, only his association with the story, and verbalizing a name would interrupt the flow of the story. He is identified visually by the font graphic during the quote.

REPORTER	Since the days of the Shah in Iran, the Iranian military arsenal has deteriorated steadily. Iran's military was once a spiffy force, equipped with some of the latest American fighting equipment, including US fighter planes such as F-4s, F-5s, and F-14s. Since the Iranian revolution and the Iranian hostage episode, the United States has refused to allow any weaponry to be sold to Iran and those fighter planes and smaller hardware have in effect gone to seed.

SOUND/BITE FONT:
  CHARLES REDMAN
  STATE DEPARTMENT
	It's a fact of course that the Iranian military is largely equipped with United States military hardware from a previous era, and that as a consequence it would be advantageous for them to have access to supplies and spare parts for that sort of equipment.

REPORTER	Today the Iranian army. . . .

Source: Script reconstituted from broadcast, Cable News Network, August 1, 1985.

In leading into a sound bite, avoid the scripting error of a "parroted" or "echo chamber" repetition, where both the reporter and the bite repeat the same facts.

| REPORTER | He said he would avoid calling out the National Guard until all other solutions had been exhausted. |
| GOVERNOR
  (SOUND BITE) | I will avoid calling out the National Guard until all other solutions are exhausted. . . . |

Assembling Stories

To sum up, a typical TV news story "package," if there is such a thing as a typical story, consists of:

1. A lead-in, usually from a studio anchor, followed by:

2. The reporter's lead. This might be delivered in

   a. The studio, if the "eyewitness" or a similar format is followed; or

   b. As a standup from the story location, live or on tape; or

   c. Voice-over, if the story goes directly to location tape; or

   d. Occasionally a news story can open "cold." The first shot, for example, is an emotionally charged one of demonstrators climbing a barricade, with raw sound and no narration for a few seconds.

3. An organizational scheme for the sequence that forms the body of the story, with mutually supportive narration and visuals.

4. Sound bites, if possible, and if the story is long enough, to give the story human focus and variety, and to present information or opinion through the voices and faces of actual participants.

5. A tag, some form of close, possibly a standup which puts the story into perspective and, if it is a continuing story, looks to the future.

This story exhibits at least some of these characteristics:

ANCHOR LIVE	President Reagan and Soviet Foreign Minister Andrei Gromyko are expected to have several hours of talks on relations between our two countries this Friday. Many observers are optimistic the meeting will help ease rising tensions between the superpowers. Others are skeptical it may be a preelection ploy. Channel 3's Alice Scott talked with some Northern Californians on the subject and is live in our newsroom with their opinion on how the talks are significant to us.
LIVE NEWSROOM FONT: ALICE S	People in Northern California who have been keeping an eye on Soviet-U.S. relations view this week's meeting between the President and the Soviet leader with cautious optimism. The sentiment is that any dialogue is better than not talking at all.
TAKE SONY :29	SOT—ENDS: Gromyko is the highest-ranking Soviet official the President has met since taking office.
LIVE NEWSROOM	Michael Lokteff produces "Word to Russia" from Bryte. It's a religious radio program broadcast in the Soviet Union. Lokteff is cautiously optimistic about the talks.
TAKE SONY :36	SOT—LOKTEFF
LIVE NEWSROOM	Bruce Rigdon chairs the Committee on Relations with Christians in the Soviet Union. He's touring California to promote peace between the two countries. As a frequent visitor to Russia, Dr. Rigdon says people there want peace as much as Americans.
TAKE SONY :52	SOT—RIGDON

LIVE NEWSROOM	The hope is that with the President's U.N. speech today and in his White House talks with Gromyko, there will be a push for a resumption of nuclear arms talks in the near future. I'm Alice Scott for Channel 3 News.

Source: Courtesy of KCRA, Sacramento, CA.

The story begins with an anchor lead-in, then cuts to the reporter, Alice Scott, live in the newsroom—a variation on the live-reporter-in-studio technique. The first videotape excerpt (TAKE SONY :29) is lifted from an NBC network feed. It gives the national background on the story. The end cue is shown in the script, and the director cuts back to the reporter for a "standup" bridge.

The second and third inserts are sound bites with two local personalities. For some reason end cues were not shown for these excerpts; only timings are given. In normal practice, end cues should be in the script. The story closes back with the reporter.

Finally, this disaster story that follows, which is actually several stories wrapped together, contains a good deal of live reporting. There is an opening summary delivered by the news anchor; the background, including interviews with eyewitnesses (delivered by the reporter from the helicopter for added impact); the sidebar story from the second reporter in San Francisco; and last, an overview of the status of statewide rescue efforts, which itself contains both a live report and a tape insert.

ANCHOR: STAN	Topping our news tonight at five . . . Twelve people have been hospitalized in the town of Gilroy just South of San Francisco after a major earthquake rocked the area. The tremor . . . which registered six point two on the Richter scale . . . was centered just East of San Jose. It was felt as far away as Carson City, Nevada. The quake jarred houses from their foundations . . . and sent skyscrapers in San Francisco swaying.
WIPE TO SONY RUNS :21 FONT: SAN JOSE (3)	In San Jose . . . a shopping center there sustained major damage. Elsewhere in the city . . . flames broke out sporadically after the tremor was reported. Residents also report damage to buildings in Morgan Hill . . . which is about twelve miles Southeast of San Jose. Channel 3's Roy Stearns has been on the scene for us. . . .
LIVECOPTER IN MON	. . . He's aboard livecopter three right now . . . Roy, what can you tell us . . .

LIVECOPTER FULL

   FONT: LIVECOPTER

   FONT: ROY STEARNS

TAKE VTR   2

   RUNS: :46

   FONT: SAN JOSE (3)

   FONT: LEE SUESS
         Dep. Fire Chief

FONT: LEE KING
       Pet Store Owner

ANCHOR: SUSAN

TAKE VTR   1

   RUNS: 120

   TOP FONT: (3) SAN
       FRANCISCO

   FONT: JOHN GIBSON

ANCHOR: STAN

2 SHOT

LIVECAM IN MON

TAKE SACRAMENTO LIVECAM

   FONT: LIVECAM

   FONT: MIKE BOYD

TAKE VTR   2

   RUNS: 60

   TOP FONT: (3) SACRAMENTO
       DEPT. OF WATER RE-
       SOURCES

   FONT: (3)
       OFFICE   OF   EMER-
       GENCY SERVICES

SOUND FULL

   OUTCUE: damage was much less than it could have
       been.

SOT FULL

SOT ENDS: little bit saved.

Not too far away in the San Francisco Bay area . . . the
quake was felt as a rolling motion that lasted about 25
seconds.
Thousands of people were in high rise offices at the time
. . . and they got quite a scare.
Channel 3's John Gibson was among those shaken by
the big tremor.

SOT FULL

TAPE ENDS ON CUE: for Channel 3 Reports.

It's miraculous with an earthquake of this size . . . that
there have been no deaths and no serious injuries.
But several people have sustained minor injuries . . .
and there has been damage.

Channel 3's Mike Boyd is standing by live at the Office
of Emergency Services in Sacramento with an overview.

SOUND FULL

OUTCUE: the quake struck at 1:15 this afternoon.

BOYD: VOICEOVER

TAKE LIVECAM FULL

   FONT: MIKE BOYD

   FONT: LIVECAM

   FONT: AL LOCKHART
      OES Asst. Director

2 SHOT

LIVECAM IN MON

Boyd introduces OES spokesman.

Boyd wraps up . . . tosses to studio.

Source: Courtesy of KCRA, Sacramento, CA.

The story begins with the anchor. The first videotape insert was edited from footage obtained in San Jose. The writer called for the effect of wiping that segment onto the screen, followed by the visual identification on lower screen of the location and the station's channel number/logo (SAN JOSE 3). The anchor continues narrating for the 21 seconds that the tape runs.

The next segment is live aboard the KCRA helicopter. The transition is accomplished by first showing the helicopter shot in a video monitor on the set with the anchor, who turns and talks to the monitor. When the reporter answers, the director takes directly to the helicopter feed full-screen (FULL). Full-level sound is also taken. Two lower screen titles are inserted—LIVECOPTER and the reporter's name. A prearranged outcue is included in the script, to know when to return from the helicopter shot.

The third segment, also on videotape, begins directly—no bridge from the anchor. It runs 46 seconds, comes from San Jose again (identified by another lower-screen title), and includes two sound bites, both of whom are also identified by name and position with lower-screen titles. The sound for the entire segment is on the tape and the outcue is shown—"little bit saved."

Now the co-anchor picks up the story and leads into the next segment, on videotape from San Francisco, 120 seconds long. A variation on titles is used; now the station logo and location are identified in a top-screen title, the reporter with lower-screen. Again, an outcue is given.

Back to the first anchor. He provides a bridge, and then the same transition is used as for the helicopter. He turns to the on-set monitor, which shows a LIVECAM shot from the Office of Emergency Services.

The LIVECAM and its sound come up. Two lower-screen titles identify it and the reporter, who delivers a report and an outcue. This same reporter had earlier recorded a 60-second report, which is now run while he continues to narrate over it. The two locations at which the report was recorded are identified. Then back to LIVECAM, back to the lower-screen ID of the reporter and LIVECAM, while he introduces the OES spokesman and does a brief live interview. The spokesman is identified visually during the interview.

Finally, the LIVECAM reporter wraps up and tosses the story back to the anchors (2 SHOT) in studio. There may be a final question-response with the reporter still seen in the monitor on the set, a thank-you, and the story closes.

Structuring the Newscast

The tremendous range of content and style of news programs prevents our being very specific about any best single way to organize them, but for all types of newscasts the basic structural requirements apply. Get the program off to a strong, attention-getting start and identify it appropriately in the opening. Provide unity, variety, pace, and climax within its overall organization. Then close cleanly and get out on time.

Get Audience Attention

This requirement may be met more easily in news programs than with some other types of programs, because audiences tune to news for a different reason than to entertainment—they want to know what has happened recently that is newsworthy; they want to be informed. The news producer-writer responds to this need by beginning the newscast with the most important story, which automatically serves to attract attention.

Provide Identification

Elaborate program titles and credits to the reporters and anchors are generally not needed in news programs. They tend to slow down the opening and to work against the attention-getting requirement. For radio, a brief identification device in the form of a sound effect which simulates a radio code transmission or an electronic musical signature is often used. Television stations in recent years have begun to use elaborate signature openings that resemble promotional announcements—shots of the newsroom, the mobile news production vans, and the news helicopter (if the station has one). These signatures definitely slow the opening, but they have a positive function as well. They provide time for the audience to get into the room from some other part of the house, tune into the program, and otherwise get settled and therefore not miss the most important opening story.

Frequently, in order to serve both functions—to get attention and yet allow late tuners to catch the opening story—the news opening will begin with headlines, then shift to the signature opening (and commercials), and then present the lead story.

Maintain Unity

This structural requirement is closely tied to the purpose and target audience of the program as determined by management. As audiences have increasingly fragmented and as producers have become more sophisticated in their tailoring of specific programs for narrower target groups, many news broadcasts have become more focused in content and approach. Several times we have referred to soft news programs as being the most obvious examples of that trend, but there are other examples—financial news programs, specialty sports shows, health programs, and so on. All the content should relate in some fashion to the predetermined purpose of the program.

Provide Variety   Within the framework of unity, variety should be provided from story to story. For a general newscast, the choice of stories will not be completely within the control of the news staff. Some stories are not scheduled; others which are scheduled may turn out not to be worth the time. On the other hand, a feature program that does not deal with timely stories can maintain much closer control over the selection of its stories and can choose with variety in mind. Generally this requirement is easily met, for each story is unique in some way.

Since news programs are produced on a regular basis, it is much easier for the news staff to use a standard format. Following a pattern also allows the audience to find the types of stories in which they may have particular interest. Our example, Figure 12.6, is from a UHF independent station, for its 10 P.M. newscast:

Provide Pacing   Our general discussion of pace (Chapter 5) was tied to the problem of maintaining audience attention. Obviously the intensity of the attention of an individual audience member to any particular news story will depend on the importance of that story to that person. Many stories, however, are not of direct personal concern to most people, and radio and television newscasters, who understand the problem of maintaining attention, have developed a pattern that usually limits individual stories to a maximum of about 90 seconds.

Earlier in this chapter we talked about the opportunities for extended coverage, which seem to be increasing. But these "in-depth" broadcasts must also consider pace. For example, even National Public Radio's "All Things Considered," which takes some pride in providing extended coverage of news events, contains brief, 90 second or so, stories in its top-of-the hour summaries. Then, when the program goes back to the major stories in depth for a treatment that may last several minutes, each story is carefully structured as if it were a complete miniprogram, with its own internal variety, pacing, and climax.

Provide Climax   The newscast is one program type where this structural requirement is largely ignored. Audiences would be rightly upset if a newscast were to start with the least important stories and hold the most important to the end. News should be presented in as timely a fashion as possible; the big story comes up front, and with as recent information in it as it is possible to provide.

However, news producers do want to hold the audience to the end of the program, and they attempt to do that in two ways: by providing frequent teases for stories yet to come and by holding to the end a story that has strong audience appeals. Stories with human interest values are very effective in providing an emotional climax for the audience.

Closing the Program   The closing of a newscast is not substantially different from any other type of program. Identification is usually brief; it may only be an announcement of the station's call letters and, for TV, a quick video crawl listing major production personnel. Commercials frequently are inserted prior to the final "climax" story; holding back that story keeps the audience tuned through the commercials. Program promotion often takes the form of a brief announcement by the news anchor, such as "stay tuned for————which follows."

KTXL MEMORANDUM
SACRAMENTO • STOCKTON
KTXL-TV40

TO _News Staff_   FROM _Don Ross_

_____   DATE _____

SUBJECT _Revised Format for NewsPlus effective 7/5/83 (TFN)_

AIR TIME	CONTENT	TOTAL TIME
10:00:00 – 10:00:30	OPEN	:30
10:00:30 – 10:08:30	1st SEGMENT, PRIMARY NEWS LOCAL , NATIONAL AND INTERNATIONAL........	8:00
10:08:30 – 10:08:50	TEASE/BUMP	:20
10:08:50 – 10:10:50	1st COMMERCIAL BREAK	2:00
10:10:50 – 10:16:30	2nd SEGMENT, SECONDARY NEWS LOCAL , NATIONAL AND INTERNATIONAL...	5:40
10:16:30 – 10:16:50	TEASE/BUMP	:20
10:16:50 – 10:18:50	2nd COMMERCIAL BREAK	2:00
10:18:50 – 10:24:00	3rd SEGMENT, NEWSPLUS SPECIAL REPORT.....	5:10
10:24:00 – 10:24:20	TEASE/BUMP	:20
10:24:20 – 10:26:20	3rd COMMERCIAL BREAK	2:00
10:26:20 – 10:30:30	4th SEGMENT, WEATHER	4:10

KTXL TV40/POST OFFICE BOX 40/4655 FRUITRIDGE ROAD/SACRAMENTO, CALIFORNIA 95820//(916) 454-4422

Figure 12.6   Source: Courtesy of KTXL, Sacramento, CA.

KTXL MEMORANDUM
SACRAMENTO • STOCKTON

KTXL-TV40

TO _____   FROM _____

_____   DATE _____

SUBJECT _____

AIR TIME	CONTENT	TOTAL TIME
10:30:30 – 10:30:50	TEASE/BUMP	:20
10:30:50 – 10:32:50	4th COMMERCIAL BREAK	2:00
10:32:50 – 10:38:00	5th SEGMENT, SPORTS	5:10
10:38:00 – 10:38:20	TEASE/BUMP	:20
10:38:20 – 10:40:20	5th COMMERCIAL BREAK	2:00
10:40:20 – 10:44:30	6th SEGMENT, NEWSWHEEL READERS AND VO'S WITH HEAVY USE OF VIDEO, LOCAL STATE, NATIONAL AND INTERNATIO AL	4:10
10:44:30 – 10:44:50	TEASE/BUMP	:20
10:44:50 – 10:46:50	6th COMMERCIAL BREAK	2:00
10:46:50 – 10:50:20	7th SEGMENT, FEATURES, DR. EDELL & MOVIE REVIEWS	3:30
10:50:20 – 10:50:40	TEASE/BUMP	:20
10:50:40 – 10:52:40	7th COMMERCIAL BREAK	2:00

KTXL TV40/POST OFFICE BOX 40/4655 FRUITRIDGE ROAD/SACRAMENTO, CALIFORNIA 95820//(916) 454-4422

Figure 12.6 (Continued)

KTXL MEMORANDUM

SACRAMENTO • STOCKTON

KTXL-TV40

TO _____   FROM _____

_____   DATE _____

SUBJECT _____

AIR TIME	CONTENT	TOTAL TIME
10:52:40 − 10:58:20	8th SEGMENT, SERIES REPORTS, SPECIAL ANCHOR FEATURES, WX UPDATE, NEWS UPDATE, TOMORROW AND CLOSE....	5:40

KTXL TV40/POST OFFICE BOX 40/4655 FRUITRIDGE ROAD/SACRAMENTO, CALIFORNIA, 95820/(916) 454-4400

Figure 12.6 (Continued)

News broadcasts are at least partially live. Individual stories may be prerecorded and therefore accurately timed in advance of the broadcast, but the newscast as a whole is presently without prior recording. Some timing adjustments will have to be made during the course of the broadcast. Frequently these adjustments are left to the news anchors—an extra bit of ad lib conversation if the program is running short; the dropping of one or two brief pad stories if the program is long. The timing adjustments should be managed so that some form of closure is provided, either a verbal close by the anchor or a closing signature.

Conclusion

It would be superficial in the extreme to summarize what is already a very brief summary of the process of gathering, organizing, and writing news for broadcast. Several excellent texts delineate the various steps in much greater detail, and we have listed them in the bibliography. We will, however, leave you with these three questions, which you can use as a test of your ability to write a good news story:

1. Is the story *clear?*

2. Is the story *concise?*

We have seen that under most circumstances broadcast stories will not exceed 90 seconds, and may be considerably shorter. In order to be both clear and concise, the writer must understand the details of the story and be able to identify those which are most significant to the target audience.

3. Is the story *correct?*

There is an expectation on the part of the audience, one shared by any professional journalist, that a story *is* correct. There have been occasions when news has been deliberately slanted by a reporter or by a manager or station owner, but fortunately these have been rare. What is no longer rare is the accusation, or a perception of slanting or bias. Any conscientious professional journalist will try to present every story in an impartial, balanced fashion, although he or she may not succeed to everyone's satisfaction in every case.

Judge your stories by these catchwords: clear? concise? correct?

Exercises

1. This exercise is similar to Exercise 3 in Chapter 2. Choose a major news story from a current newspaper and rewrite it as a 90-second radio story. Observe these cautions:

   a. Avoid feature or unusual material. Choose a timely story with enough material to fill your time without padding.

   b. Write with a clear lead, either a straight lead or a throwaway. Then organize the body into a logical sequence, possibly using one of the patterns suggested.

   c. Concentrate on principles of aural style.

2. Using a newspaper as your first source, *plus at least one other non-newspaper source,* write a 60- to 90-second news story for radio. The story should be "hard" timely news, *not* a feature. It may help to think of the relationship of the two sources in one of three ways: (1) The newspaper had the original story; your second source will *update* it for later broadcast. (2) The newspaper story was based on state or national material, originating elsewhere; your second source will give the story a *local slant.* (3) The newspaper left unanswered some questions which your target audience would want to know; your second source will *clarify* or *expand* on those points.

3. Write a 90-second news story for television, based on original research. The story should be a true news story, not a feature, which means that it should have significance *now*. However, that significance can come in either of two ways: you can cover a breaking story—event, press conference—or you can develop the timeliness into the story. You are encouraged to consider, but not required, to use sound bites. Of course, since this is a TV story, you will have to indicate what visual material is to be seen throughout. (You may assume your camera crew was able to shoot whatever you want.)

4. Do Exercise 2 for television, and/or 3 for radio.

5. Write a soft news story for an evening magazine show on a local TV station, on one of the following:

   a. An out-of-the-way place to spend an unusual weekend or vacation without leaving town

   b. An unusual department (or person's job) in the city government; a part of government most people wouldn't even know existed

   c. A new arrival at the local zoo

   d. The most unusual (but legitimate) business you can find

6. Write a news commentary for radio on one of the following (but make the general topic specific to your area):

   a. Giving blood to the blood bank

   b. The importance of voting in the upcoming municipal election

   c. Remembering the significance of Memorial Day

   d. Drinking and driving don't mix.

Key Terms and Concepts

breaking stories	conflict
graphics	impact
lead-in	leads: straight, throwaway,
natural (raw) sound	feature, umbrella
personalization	novelty
proximity	prominence
rewrite	reporter involvement

sound bites   soft news/hard news
timeliness   standups
voiceovers   video package

Note   1. From the Associated Press, as printed in the San Francisco *Chronicle,* May 14, 1984.

Chapter 13

Talk, Interview, and Discussion Programs

Talk programs are a mainstay of the formats of many radio stations, and they are an important form of television content as well. They are inexpensive and easy to produce in comparison with other types of programs. No wonder so many variations have been developed by creative writers and producers.

We will concentrate on three basic forms: the straight talk, the interview, and the discussion program. There are, of course, many other forms of programs that make use of talk materials, such as news broadcasts, documentaries, and instructional programs, but in most of these the talk or narration does not provide the primary content of the program. It is merely supportive. These types of programs are considered in other chapters.

The preparation of talk programs may be divided into four sequential tasks:

1. Research. The determination of the proper topic and guests to appear on the program; collection of the background material on topic and guests

2. Writing. The organization of that background material into a series of questions or other notes to be used by the interviewers or moderators on the program

3. Presentation. The actual conduct of the talk interview or discussion

4. Editing. Depending upon the use which is to be made of the material, there may be no editing done at all or; at the other extreme, the materials recorded on tape may be highly edited and compressed.

Although we list writing as only one of the four tasks, in practice the writer of talk programs is frequently involved in all four areas of preparation. Research and writing are related. It is quite common for interviewers and moderators to be expected to prepare their own questions for guests. And finally, when edited interviews are used in other types of programs, additional written continuity is necessary to integrate the interview segments into the remainder of the story, as in using a sound bite within a news story.

Research

Some form of research is required as a preliminary step in writing any kind of copy. For talk, interview, and discussion programs, the research process involves three distinct steps:

1. Determining the purpose of the program

2. Analyzing the target audience

3. Choosing the topic and guests

Determining Purpose

You should by now be familiar with the reasons why sponsors choose to produce and broadcast any type of program. That general discussion was covered in Chapter 8, and we will not repeat those considerations here. But we will examine how all three basic purposes of communication—persuasion, entertainment, and information—are used in talk programs.

Persuasive Talks

Persuasion as the purpose behind talk programs is most obvious in religious sermons and in talks by political candidates or by advocates on behalf of ballot propositions. Persuasion may also be the reason behind the appearance on an interview program of the local chapter president of the Red Cross, who wants to encourage participation in Red Cross activities and stimulate donations to the organization, or of a school superintendent, who might use a weekly talk show to convince parents that closing a local school really was necessary to save money, or for many similar situations. Frequently people who hold strong opinions on an issue will agree to appear in a discussion or interview program in the hope of persuading the audience to that point of view, even though the program itself does not have persuasion as its purpose.

A few years ago, political talks were quite common on both television and radio, but producers have come to realize that the straight talk is structurally very weak. About the only audience who would stay tuned through a political talk were those people who were already persuaded to the position being espoused, and who enjoyed hearing a reinforcement of that position.

The political talk has therefore almost disappeared in favor of the political announcement. Commercial political programs—that is, any broadcasts longer than an announcement—are likely to be in the form of press conferences, or call-in programs with some form of audience participation. Those political programs which are arranged by broadcasters themselves or by nonpartisan groups such as the League of Women Voters usually take the form of panel discussions or of formal debates.

The religious sermon is one form of persuasive talk that continues to appear on broadcast media. It can be successful while other types of talks are not because:

1. The target audience consists of people already persuaded to the preacher's point of view; reinforcement *is* the intended purpose.

2. The successful broadcast sermon uses every trick of aural style.

3. Strong emotional gratifications are provided for the target audience.

4. The sermon is usually kept short.

Entertaining Talks

Entertainment is at least partly the purpose behind many interview and talk programs (and we'll ignore here the comedy monologue, which is an entertaining talk, but which is more appropriately considered as part of the discussion of variety programs). Well-known talk programs with entertainment as a purpose include the "David Letterman Show" or the "Tonight Show," programs that conduct interviews with celebrities. The entertainment is provided to the audience by the interplay of conversation between the host and the guest or guests.

Most often celebrity interview programs emphasize the personal characteristics of the guests who appear, because it is the audience's curiosity about famous people that provides the major gratification for the audience. Some programs, however, emphasize the role of the host of the program as much or more than that of the guest. Ratings of the "Tonight Show" vary widely depending on whether Johnny Carson is hosting or a substitute is sitting in. That fact shows that the host, Carson, plays a very important role.

"Firing Line," produced and hosted by William Buckley, is an even more striking example. Mr. Buckley is the best-known practitioner of an interview style in which the focus of attention is maintained much more strongly on the interviewer than on the interviewee. Usually interviews should focus on the opinions and information imparted by the guest, but with Buckley's approach the guests are secondary, and are chosen because they will provide a foil for the host, who has the more important role in the interview and whose opinions are given the greater exposure.

Informative Talks

The imparting of information is by far the most common purpose for presenting talk programs of all types. Even those which have persuasion or entertainment as their primary purpose usually have information as a secondary purpose.

The following list gives descriptions of talk program types that are primarily informative, but the list is by no means comprehensive.

The Opinion Interview. This is the most common form of interview. The topics can range from politics and foreign affairs as in "Meet the Press," to the strategy used in winning a baseball game asked in a postgame interview with the batting hero of the game. The person being interviewed is an expert in some area. The intent of the interview is to draw out information and opinion related to that expertise and transmit it to the audience.

The opinion interview may also take the form of a "person in the street" interview. This is a familiar form in which a cross section of "ordinary people" are interviewed regarding their opinions on a topic that may range from something humorous to a serious question of community or world affairs.

The Feature Interview. This type of interview is common in soft news programs. The person being interviewed is not famous, but has done something or been somewhere unusual or interesting. Perhaps he has just returned from a world trouble spot, or maybe she rents out the wild animals used in making jungle films. The feature should be organized so it gets quickly to the unusual characteristic which makes that person interesting. The audience will not be particularly attracted to the interview until this factor of novelty is introduced.

The Informative Interview. Whereas in the opinion interview information is transmitted by means of the expert testimony of the guest, in this type of interview the program producers want to transmit specific factual information, and choose the interview technique rather than a straight talk or lecture because it is more likely to hold the attention of the audience. Appropriate topics for this approach are publicity for charity drives, in which a representative is interviewed on the purpose and method of the campaign, and direct instruction, in which the interviewer may take on the role of a student, asking questions to draw out the information from the instructor/authority.

The Panel Discussion Program. Although interviews and panels have a great deal in common, they also differ in some significant ways. The panel program is almost always topic-oriented, whereas the interview may emphasize topic or the personality of the guest. The panel program also, by definition, involves several participants, usually chosen because they have different points of view regarding the topic. The interchange provides the audience with high-interest material.

The Audience-Participation Talk Program. This type of program, with many variations, has become a mainstay of news–talk radio stations. It is also found on television, but less frequently. Often it is oriented to a specific type of subject matter, such as finance, or medicine, or even sexual topics, and the host or hostess is chosen because of expertise in that area. Sometimes these programs are totally free of topic restrictions, and callers may phone in to talk on any topic they wish; in other versions, the host will pick a "topic of the day" from the current news.

In some variations the host will not be the content expert, but will have an expert on the topic as a studio guest. In those cases the program begins as a more structured interview program, then opens out to include the phone-in questions and comments from the listening audience. Another variation has been the "dating emporium," in which persons calling in describe themselves and try to link up with other callers for a date.

Most of these programs are done almost completely ad lib, with very little formal script preparation. To be successful, the hosts have to be very well prepared in the content of the program, practiced in listening and in conversational technique, and able to think and respond quickly.

From this overview it should be evident that talk programs can take many different forms and involve the presentation of persuasion, entertainment, information, or combinations of these. Therefore the researcher-writer who is preparing one of these programs for the air must understand clearly the specific intent of that particular program.*

---

* In addition to its function as a program type, the interview serves two other functions in broadcasting. It is the means by which actuality material—quotes using the actual voices of participants in a news or documentary story—is obtained. And even if no quoted material appears directly on the air, the bulk of the data obtained in most news stories are obtained by interviewing sources. Interviewing is the most efficient method of gathering background on a story; it is the reporter's prime tool.

Analyzing the Target Audience

Analysis of the target audience for talk programs is not substantially different from analysis for any other type of program or announcement. The researcher should be able to answer these four questions regarding the audiences for the program being prepared:

1. What is the sponsor's target audience?
2. How can the target audience be attracted to the program?
3. What does the target audience already know about the topic and guest?
4. What does the audience want to learn from the experts who are appearing on the program?

What Is the Sponsor's Target Audience?

As part of the general discussion of target audiences (Chapter 9), we looked at the target audience for "Meet the Press." A similar analysis can be made for any talk program. In general, the more serious topics appeal to more highly educated and probably older audiences. Lighter topics—celebrity and feature interviews, for example—are more successful in attracting younger and less educated groups. Carefully defining the targeted group for the program, and therefore being able to recognize gratifications which are strong for that group, will make it much easier for the writer to answer the next question.

How Can the Target Audience Be Attracted to the Program?

What gratifications can be built into the program that appeal strongly to the target group? If this question is not specifically considered and answered carefully, if the topic and guests are chosen without this analysis, then whatever audience, if any, the program receives will be determined by chance—that is, by those gratifications which just happen to evolve in the program. The program content and form will determine the audience, when it should be just the reverse.

The targeted audience will stay tuned only if it is explained quickly and effectively in the opening material why the topic (and the guest's opinions) will be of interest and value to them. The gratifications for the audience must be quickly apparent, or that audience will tune elsewhere.

What Does the Target Audience Already Know About the Topic and Guest?

It may be difficult to get a precise answer to this question, but general knowledge of the target group will help, and whatever assumptions have to be made can be refined over the span of time during which the program series is broadcast, and by independent research if necessary. On "Meet the Press," for example, the questions asked of the guests reflect the assumption that the audience has a good general knowledge of national and international political and economic issues. Knowledge of basic geography, the fundamental differences among various political ideologies, and the forms of government currently operating in major countries are assumed, and questions which cover those points are not asked.

By way of contrast, assume that a typical "Meet the Press" guest, the administrative head of the European Economic Community, were to be the guest on a similarly structured interview program, but one for which the target audience is high school students. The questions would have to be quite different, starting at a more fundamental level and covering such items as geography and the forms of government in the EEC countries.

Also part of this question is the audience's knowledge of the guest(s) and their understanding of how the guest's expertise and background relate to the topic. An interview with the president of the United States will require little if any explanation. Neither would an interview with the chairman of the Joint Chiefs of Staff—so long as the topic of the interview was military matters on which he is an immediately recognized expert. But if the chairman of the Joint Chiefs of Staff were to be interviewed on, say, the growing of orchids, the program would have to provide some explanation to the audience as to why this person was being interviewed as an expert on that topic, because the relationship is not likely to be one of which people are aware.

A similar approach will be necessary for all topics and guests. The program writer should determine in advance how likely it is that the guest is known and recognized by the audience, and how much prior knowledge of the topic the audience may be assumed to have.

What Does the Audience Want to Learn from the Expert(s) Who Are Appearing on the Program?

This question comes back to fundamental considerations of purpose and gratifications, and the very first question audiences continue to ask—Why should I watch (or listen); what's in it for me? A great many programs, particularly local public affairs programs, fail to attract or hold any substantial audience simply because they fail to make any connection early in the broadcast between the topic and the audience.

We use the word *learn* in this question in a very broad sense. In most informative interviews we do assume that some learning—or at least the transmission of information to the audience—takes place. More formal instructional programs, such as an interview with the head of the company or with an academic expert, have as a purpose learning in a more strict sense; if not, the program may be considered a failure. In persuasive political or religious talk programs, the learning would be acceptance of the point being made by the program.

Recall that ''Meet the Press'' contains two purposes. The sponsor's purpose will be to attract a target audience of some size and demographic composition in order to expose them to advertising messages. But the structure, form, and content of the show is a genuine attempt to convey opinions and information on topics about which the audience has concerns.

We can summarize by emphasizing that the writers and interviewers or moderators of talk programs are acting as surrogate for the audience. Their jobs are to prepare and to ask the questions that elicit the information which audience members would themselves ask if they were in a position to do so. And in order to be an effective surrogate, writers need a clear picture of who the audience members are, what their background and prior knowledge are, and what they might want to learn from the program. Hence our insistence on the careful analysis of audience.

Choosing the Topic and Guests

This might seem to be the place to begin preparation of a talk program rather than being the third step in the research task, but what we have tried to suggest by the preceding discussion is that good choices of topic and guests, and a good sequence of interview questions or discussion topics, cannot be made until the preliminary questions of purpose and audience have been determined. (Of course on many programs, especially those that are episodes of continuing series, the purpose and audience decisions for the series have long since been made, and the researcher-writer does begin at this point—choosing topics and guests for each individual broadcast.)

The questions here are very straightforward. *Why* this topic (at this time)? And *why* this guest or guests? The answers should be easy to state. If there is any difficulty in answering them, the topic or guest is probably not appropriate for this program at this time. If a lengthy introduction must be given to explain the topic to the audience, probably the wrong topic was chosen. If long biographies of the guests have to be delivered to show their relationship to the topic, probably the wrong guests were chosen.

Let's follow these research steps through with an example fairly typical of a local public affairs discussion program. (We'll carry this example throughout the chapter, and build an entire program around this situation.)

The program you research/write/produce is a weekly series, half-hour in length, broadcast late Sunday afternoon. The topics are chosen by the station's programming staff, and usually involve local issues. Frequently the topics arise from discussion with civic officials. This week the city council voted to place before the local voters at an upcoming election a bond issue to build a new centralized sewer system. The program director has decided that the sewer topic would be appropriate for your program.

Your purpose? The accepted purpose of this program series, and of all individual programs in the series, is strictly informative. No editorial positions are taken. Advocates for or against various issues do appear regularly, but the station carefully chooses its participants to obtain balance in every program.

Your target audience? Since the program has been on for a while (and, we will assume, has been reasonably successful in attracting a regular following), you should have no difficulty describing the audience you regularly reach. We will assume these people are a high education/income group and politically aware. They vote regularly, and they influence others. They are opinion leaders. If the city hopes to pass the sewer bond, these are the individuals who will have to be convinced to vote for the bond, and to persuade friends and associates to do so as well. But remember, this program is not intended to be politically persuasive.

How can the target audience be attracted to the program? What are the gratifications for them? Since this is an ongoing series, the attractions and gratifications for your regular audience have been built up over a period of time. They will include importance, information, value, possibly human interest, maybe tension. (It is at this point that you should speak out if you feel this topic is inappropriate to the overall concept of the program. We'll assume the general topic—the sewer bond—is acceptable to you.) Your regular audience may be expected to at least tune in at the start, and so long as this program does not deviate too far from the regular pattern, you can expect to hold them through the broadcast because the gratifications they generally obtain will stay consistent in this program.

If you should want to try to attract additional audience, other than the regular target group, it will require additional promotional efforts—announcements on your station, a press release, word-of-mouth, and so on. You would do that only if the topic was of such importance that you wanted to make the extra effort (or if the station had made a decision to provide extra promotion for this series).

What does the target audience already know about the topic? Well, since the city council just voted to place the bond issue on the ballot, we can assume the audience doesn't know much about the ramifications. But there must have been something in the past that caused the council to act. Maybe the old sewer system is inadequate in size and is restricting future development in the community, or perhaps it has broken down frequently, causing unpleasant smells and potential health hazards. Rarely does an issue of sufficient importance to become a topic of a program appear suddenly. There's usually some background, and this particular target audience may be assumed to have some background on most community issues.

What do the audience members want to know? As we have said repeatedly, they want to know how the topic will affect them. In this case, what the implications are for them of passing or defeating the bond issue. They will want to know what the project will cost in fees or taxes, what the benefits would be, what will happen to the community if the issue doesn't pass, and so on. We'll develop this point when we look at the sequencing of the specific subtopics into the program.

What is the topic and who are the guests? The general topic has already been chosen, but the specific subtopics to be covered and the proper people to cover them must now be determined. One choice would be to assemble a group of engineers who could speak knowledgeably about capacity, flow rates, direction and size of connectors, and so on. But it should be obvious from the decisions already made that that approach is neither consistent with our purpose nor appropriate to the target audience. (Amazingly, however, a good many producers of local public affairs programs fall into precisely this trap when they do not adequately analyze purpose and audience.)

We may want the city engineer as one guest on the program, but not to discuss technical matters. She or he can discuss how badly the city streets will be disrupted, and for how long—issues of vital importance to the target audience. And the engineer can talk in general terms about the size and complexity of the proposed new sewer plant—again not from a technical standpoint, but only to satisfy a general curiosity in the audience.

Another possible guest panelist would be a member of the city council, who could give background to the issue and explain why the council voted as it did. If the council vote was split and there was considerable dissension, then both positions on the council's action probably should be covered by inviting an advocate on the opposing side as well. And even if the council was unanimous in its position, there may be other opposition in the community that should be heard if you want to maintain balance on a controversial issue. You are not forced to air opposing positions on the same program, but doing so provides tension, which is a gratification for some audiences, and you should at least recognize the ethical question of providing balance on a controversial issue.

(There may be legal considerations as well, because your program may fall under Fairness Doctrine regulations.)

A local businessperson, speaking on behalf of the Chamber of Commerce, could be another panelist. He or she could speak to the implications of the sewer for future community growth. Any number of possible panelists might be chosen, but each choice should be tested for his or her value to the program, using the question: What information does this person have that the audience would want to know?

We'll choose these four for the program:

> Mary Smith, city councilperson. She voted for the bond issue, but with some reluctance. She is known to be very fair, quite articulate, and capable of seeing both sides of an issue.

> Paul Jones, vice-president of the Chamber of Commerce. Strongly in favor personally, and represents the Chamber, which has pushed for a new sewer.

> Fred White, long-time resident and major landowner in the city. Well-respected, conservative, opposed to the bond issue.

> Joe Brown, city engineer. Knowledgeable on technical matters, and on why the project will cost what the bond issue is being asked to cover. A possible problem may exist here: He might feel intimidated by the more political types on the panel, but people who know him are certain that won't be the case. However, that's the kind of caution producer-writers must take into account in putting a panel together.

The choice of four panelists is arbitrary, but that seems a sufficient number to get the major points of view. Having any more people would cut down the amount of time each would have to articulate their concerns, and increase the risk that someone might be squeezed out of the discussion.

We've used a panel discussion program for this example, but the process applies to any talk-type program—just substitute the word *interviewee* or *speaker* for *panelist* and recognize that there would be fewer people involved as participants in an interview or a straight talk program.

Edited or Live?

We'll continue this example later; now we are ready to consider the second major task in the preparation of talk programs. In the sequence which would normally take place, that is the writing of questions and other continuity. Here, however, we will discuss editing, even though in actual practice editing comes after both writing and production, as the last step in the creative process. We are taking editing out of the normal order because the decision as to whether a program will be produced live, or edited—rearranged, compressed—does affect the approach to the writing and sequencing of questions and to the conduct of the program.

Live, unedited programs require that particularly careful attention be paid to the sequence of questions or topics discussed, to make sure that the audience (and, for that matter, the participants) can follow the flow of the content. The producers of some interview programs take pride in announcing that the program is "spontaneous and unrehearsed." By so doing they are assuming that the live approach increases the excitement, the immediacy, and the credibility of the program. It's also cheaper and faster to produce a live show. On the other hand, editing of one form or another is frequently done either to conserve broadcast time or to tighten the structure of the program.

For the researcher-writer, the significant difference between edited and live programs is the development of the *sequence* of material in the program, and the phrasing of the questions to be asked. If the raw material of an interview is to be lifted out, edited, and placed back into a news or documentary program, the sequence in which the original questions are asked is not critical, or if questions are not clearly stated or understood by an interviewee upon first being asked, they can be rephrased and asked again. These options are not possible in the live broadcast. The sequence and wording of the questions must be clear to both the interviewee and the audience the first time.

That is not to say that sequence and wording are not important when the program is to be edited. The less time spent conducting any interview—live or edited—and the less time spent in searching for the right questions and answers in the editing room, the less costly the project will be and the earlier the program can get on the air. An experienced writer-interviewer will conduct an interview as if it were live whenever possible, just to cut down on the amount of editing needed later. A few extra minutes spent in research and preparation may save several extra hours in editing.

Scripting Talk Programs

Very seldom will a completely scripted interview or panel program be presented, and then only if the material is so complex and the explanations so important that even a slight miswording would have serious consequences. One possible example might be an interview with a government official who may be quoted, and who might insist on a complete script for absolute accuracy in phrasing. Sermons, political talks, lectures, and other "straight" talks are usually scripted, but because these programs are structurally very weak, the writer must pay particular attention to aural style to maintain audience interest.

In general, however, the disadvantages of completely scripting an interview far outweigh any possible advantages. Many nonprofessionals cannot read well from a script. The result will sound forced, artificial, and lacking in spontaneity. On television, the use of a script is almost always a disadvantage (except possibly when written out on a prompting device), because it is difficult to hide a script from the audience, and the lack of contact with the audience will be resented.

At the other extreme from the completely scripted talk program are interview and discussion programs done completely ad lib, without any form of script. Conducting successful ad lib interviews or panels requires a very experienced interviewer or moderator with considerable poise and the ability to organize material on the spot. Most hosts are not able to do this for an entire program, and expect to have at least an outline to follow.

The middle ground, then, between the completely scripted and the completely ad lib program is the *semi-scripted,* or *outlined,* interview or discussion. This approach provides written questions for the interviewer or moderator, but leaves the answers or comments to be given ad lib by the interviewee or panelists. This approach controls the organization and progress of the program while still preserving a degree of spontaneity. The semi-script is the most common way of preparing and organizing panel and interview programs. The written continuity for such a program will include:

1. A completely scripted opening.

2. A sequence of questions to be asked of the guest or guests. If the program is live, there will be both major questions and some less important throwaway or *pad* questions. These pad questions will be used if the guest(s) answers are short and they are needed to make the program come out on time, but if the guest(s) responses to the questions are more lengthy, and the program is in danger of running over its allotted time, these pad questions can be discarded without destroying the continuity of the topic.

3. A completely scripted close. For a live program, this close will have some final adjustments for timing that can be made in order to end precisely on time.

The Program Opening

As for all types of programs, the critical functions are attracting attention and identifying the program and its participants. Another necessary function for a talk program is to establish the scope of the program.

Attracting Attention

This task can be difficult. The strongest material generally available is a statement which provides information to the audience members on the importance of the topic to them and gives the unique qualifications of the guests to speak on that topic. For television, if the budget permits, some unusual video material shot on location will be stronger than just graphics (the printed titles) and the faces of participants. Sometimes programs begin with a "cold opening"—some startling statement or area of controversy or pictorial material with strong movement or action at the very beginning to catch attention.

Identification

The program should be identified—both the series title (if it is part of a series) and the specific topic of the broadcast. The host-moderator should be identified and, of course, the guests. Not only are the guests identified, but they are also *qualified*—that is, there is some statement of the reason why they have been chosen to be there.

The extent to which the guests will have to be qualified will depend upon several things, including the topic, the audience's familiarity with the topic, and how closely the guests may be connected with the topic in the minds of the audience. The president of the United States, to take an extreme example, would not need to be qualified on any topic. The only introductory statement necessary would be: "Our guest is ———, President of the United States."

In contrast, not many people would recognize the U.S. ambassador to Poland.

A program on current unrest in Poland would require something like this: "Our guest today is ———, current ambassador to Poland, Mr. ——— was appointed to the post two years ago, after having served twenty years in the diplomatic corps. He has served in Poland twice previously and is fluent in the Polish language." That brief statement gives the audience enough information to realize that he really is an expert on the topic, without going into unnecessary detail. Additional information on his current job as ambassador or his previous tours of duty in Poland and his job at those times can be brought out during the program, if important.

Setting the Scope of the Program

In previous sections we've emphasized how important it is for the researcher-writer to understand the intent and scope of the program. It's also important that the audience know early in the program what is going to take place. (In an ongoing series with a loyal, continuing audience this can be accomplished very quickly; in a one-time or less familiar program series, it may take longer.)

We can make the point by using an extreme example again. The guest is the president of the United States. Talking to him about almost any topic would be of interest to some audience, but an interview on his personal life as president—what it's like to have that job, what the responsibilities are, what he misses from the time before he became president—is much different in scope from an interview on foreign policy decisions, or on economic matters, or on his decision to run (or not run) for a second term. The audience has a right to know what topic is to be covered, and the approach to that topic, and it has a right to expect that the questioning will stay within that framework.

The opening for a talk program should be completely scripted, even if the body of the program will be in semi-script form. Here is an opening for the sewer bond public affairs program we began to develop earlier in the chapter:

SIGNATURE	MUSIC: SIGNATURE
GRAPHIC: TITLE	V/O: This is "City Scene," a weekly examination of the problems and issues faced by the citizens and the government of Fair River. Here is your host: Janet Williams.
MS: HOST KEY: Janet Williams	Good afternoon, and thank you for joining me on "City Scene." Each week we try to bring to your attention a topic which will affect all of us who live here in Fair River, and this week's topic will certainly do that for many months, even years, to come. Earlier this week our city council voted to place on November's election ballot a bond issue in the amount of five million dollars for the replacement and improvement of the city sewer system. If that bond issue is passed by the voters, practically every street in the city will be torn up at some time in the next five years, and every property taxpayer will see an increase in taxes to pay for the new system. In return, we will have a

sewer which will permit, perhaps even encourage, new residential and industrial growth, and which should not break down—as did the present sewer line on Power Station Road last month.

But the immediate controversy surrounds the bond issue. Already people are choosing sides—supporting or arguing against passage of that ballot measure. Our guests today will discuss both the implications of the bond issue and of the system which would be installed should the revenue measure be approved by the voters. They are:

MS: GUEST #1
KEY: Mary Smith

Mary Smith, member of the city council. Mary was elected to the council last year from the South district. Her campaign argued for fiscal restraint and a go-slow attitude on new city growth. Tuesday night she voted for the sewer bond issue, but only after considerable hesitation. We'll ask her to explain the nature of her hesitation, and her decision.

MS: GUEST #2
KEY: Fred White

Fred White. Mr. White's family have been residents of Fair River since before the turn of the century. He was born here and has lived in his present home on East Third Street since the 1920s. Fred owns property in the business district and throughout the community. He is opposed to the council's action and the bond issue.

MS: GUEST #3
KEY: Paul Jones

Paul Jones. Paul is the owner of Jones Hardware on Main Street. He is also vice-president of the Chamber of Commerce. The Chamber took a position in favor of a new sewer system more than a year ago, arguing that civic growth was being stifled by the present inadequate system. Paul chaired the Chamber's committee on the sewer problem, and will head another Chamber committee to support the bond issue.

MS: GUEST #4
KEY: Joe Brown

Joe Brown. City Engineer. It has been Joe's responsibility to determine the overall scope and size of a new system, to estimate its cost, and therefore the size of the bond issue required to finance it. Joe has been the city engineer for just about five years, having come to Fair River from Albany.

This opening is simple and inexpensive. Its strength is solely in the topic and guests, as there is very little other attention-getting material. If time and money permitted, other devices could be used, such as these:

Open with the videotape of a news story tied to the topic—tape of the sewer break last month, and the cleanup work done by city crews with a voiceover narration tying that to the topic.

Show tape of the city council meeting, a condensed montage of the arguments and the vote of the council members.

Begin the program with the discussion already in progress, after a couple of minutes the moderator interrupts to introduce the program title, the participants, and tie down the topic, which by that time should be evident. This approach is tricky; it requires a lot of skill on the part of the moderator, and even with the best planning the "cold" opening may not contain high-interest material.

If you can prerecord and have at least a little time to edit, take one strong statement from each guest out of the body of the program which typifies that person's position and repeat those statements back-to-back in a short cold open.

If any of these openings or similar attention-getting devices are used, they should be used regularly and made part of the format of the program series. If the program is not part of a series, then use whatever opening device seems most appropriate to the topic, and that time and money will permit.

Structural Requirements

The four structural requirements to be met by any program are unity, variety, pacing, and climax. Talk programs are difficult programs in which to meet the requirements of strong structure, and for this reason alone these programs as a rule do not attract large audiences.

Unity

We just discussed this concept, but under a different name—setting the scope of the topic of the program. If the program's researcher-writer has carefully considered the topic and the audience's interest in it, then unity should follow. But if the topic has not been clearly defined, and the guests have not been carefully chosen on the basis of what they can contribute to the topic, the likelihood of having a wandering, disjointed interview or discussion is increased. If an interview with the president, for example, contains random questions on foreign policy, economics, politics, and family matters, it lacks unity. The problem could have been avoided easily simply by defining the topic and the target audience's interests before beginning to prepare questions.

Variety

This is one of the most difficult requirements to satisfy in any type of talk program. In the straight talk, with just one person's voice (and face, if TV) it's almost impossible. An interview provides two persons—an interviewer and an interviewee—which helps a little. "Meet the Press" and similarly structured programs use only a single guest, but employ multiple interviewers to provide variety. For television, visual inserts in the program—film or tape shot on location outside the studio—may provide variety, something other than just the faces and voices of the guests. But these inserts must fit comfortably and logically within the topic of the program, and they do add significantly to cost.

Pacing

With an unstructured and unedited live talk show, it's very difficult to control pace. Whatever control exists depends on the talents of the interviewer or moderator, who must know when and how to break into long, monotonous speeches in order to keep the program moving. Some programs use audience participation (live, studio audiences, or telephone call-in) to provide pace and variety.

Climax

This requirement also is difficult in a live, uncontrolled program. It is best managed by the structure and sequence of the questions and subtopics asked by the interviewer or moderator. To attract audience attention at the beginning of the program, some high-interest questions should be asked early. But additional important or provocative material should be held toward the end of the program so that the audience will leave with a feeling of climax.

Preparing Questions

If all of the preceding sections about choosing the topic and relating it to the audience have been carefully considered, then the preparation of the actual questions to be used for the interview or discussion will be easier. Each question should meet these simple tests:

Does the question fit the topic and scope of the program?

Does it provide material the audience wants to know?

Does it follow logically from the preceding question (or has adequate transition been provided so that both audience and guest(s) realize a change in subtopic has taken place)?

Sequencing Questions

The important considerations in sequencing or ordering questions are these:

1. Begin with the known; that is, begin with questions that are the direct, logical result of matters which are (or what you can assume, should be) known by the target audience.

2. Continue with questions in logical progression. Each new question should *seem* at least to flow out of the preceding response. In order to do this well, you will need to research the topic and the guest's likely responses carefully in advance, and possibly ask the guest some key questions before the actual interview or discussion begins in order to know where he or she stands on specific points.

3. When you must change a topic—the previous one has been covered to the extent you feel it warrants—then use adequate warning in the way of transition words and phrases so that both guest and audience are aware of the change which is coming.

4. Use strong, important questions early—to attract and hold attention—and at the end—for climax and to leave the audience members with something to remember after the program is over.

Phrasing Questions

Although it is usually possible to find exceptions to almost any rule, here are some guidelines to use in the phrasing of individual questions.

1. Keep questions short, simple, and conversational. The focus of attention should be the guest, not the host. Long, involved questions place that attention in the wrong place, and make it more difficult for both guest and audience to follow the sequence.

Poor: What is your response to the allegations made by some practicing defense lawyers that the administration's position on this case is a disregard of personal rights?

The qualifying phrases are intended to restrict the question to a narrow response, but instead they only confuse.

Better: How will the outcome of this case affect personal rights?

A frequent phrase used as a crutch by beginners is the line: "Can you tell us . . ." as in this question for Lee Iacocca, president of Chrysler Corporation:

Poor: Can you tell us about some of the new innovations you see in future Chrysler automobiles?

Ask the question directly:

Better: What are some of the innovations planned for future Chrysler automobiles?

2. Avoid double questions. They are confusing to both guest and audience. If the point to be made is sufficiently important, ask both questions, but separately.

Poor: (Question for the secretary of defense): The president seems to have caught the civilian press by surprise with his latest defense proposals. Are his ideas that new, or have they been discussed by the military community for some time?

Better: Are the president's defense proposals really new ideas?

Poor: (Question for an unsuccessful candidate for a local government appointment): Do you feel all the candidates were being evaluated on their qualifications alone, or that there was an ethnic factor involved?

Better: Do you think race was involved in the decision?

3. Another variation on this weakness is the compound question, a form frequently heard at press conferences. It may be appropriate in that setting because the particular questioner may never get another chance to ask another question; in a broadcast sequence it's not a good approach because it's very hard for both audience and respondent to remember all the parts of the question.

Poor: What are your opinions regarding this proposal and if you are in favor of it, why, or if not, what should be done?

4. As a general rule (even though we have broken the rule above) avoid asking closed-end questions—that is, questions which can be answered with just a "yes" or "no." Experienced interviewees, such as political figures, won't respond with "yes-no" answers to questions, but less experienced persons who might be nervous in the interview situation may answer just "yes" or "no" if the question permits them to do so. A good habit to develop is to ask questions using *why*, *what*, or *how* as the operative words, rather than *do*, *will*, or *are*.

Poor: One member of the City Council said she hopes you apply again to serve in some capacity. Do you see this as a possibility?

Better: What is the possibility that you will apply again to serve in some capacity?

Poor: Have there been any changes in production or management practices?

Better: What changes have there been in production or management practices?

Poor: (Questions for the secretary of defense): Is there much support in Congress for the president's proposals?
Wouldn't a bilateral nuclear freeze accomplish the same thing for less money?
Won't this system upset the current arms balance?

Better: What support is there in Congress for the president's proposals?
How do these proposals differ in effect from a bilateral nuclear freeze?
What effect would this system have on the current arms balance?

Exceptions to the closed-end rule would be these: (1) if you want only a quick response, so that you can get the program to come out on time, or (2) when you want quickly to introduce a topic and establish the guest's position, so that you can move on to more important questions.

5. Don't ask questions that assume an answer. The last two questions above, as originally worded, also suffer from that fault. If you have done your research well, you will have a good idea of what the guest's response will be. But don't assume that answer; let the guest present his or her own point of view.

6. Similarly, don't word questions that force a guest to agree. Loaded questions can be embarrassing, and they do nothing to move the interview forward.

7. Don't take an accusatory approach in your questions. There are some situations, for example in recorded, edited documentary programs like "Sixty Minutes," where an accomplished interviewer like Mike Wallace can ask some pretty strong questions. In these cases, if he gets a refusal to answer, the program will be restructured and new material added to fill up the time, something you cannot do in a live show if the guest refuses to continue the conversation.
In all cases, the interviewee has the option of not answering the question if he or she feels it is unfair or misleading, so if you really want information, and if you really want your audience to learn something from the answers provided by the guest, you must be sufficiently neutral so that the interviewee doesn't refuse to respond.
You may think that forcing the interviewee into a statement of "No comment" shows your toughness as an investigative reporter, and that you finally found something the interviewee is trying to hide. In fact, you have just terminated the audience's opportunity to gain any information from the interview.

8. Make sure your questions actually are questions, not statements.

Poor: (Asked of a candidate): Critics would charge that by spending this much in the campaign, if you win you'll have a lot of political debts to pay.

Better: By borrowing this much money to finance your campaign, what political debts will you then have to pay?

9. Finally, ask questions that are within the scope of the knowledge or expertise of the guest; don't ask him or her to speculate on matters outside that area. For example, this question asked of Harold Washington during his campaign for mayor of Chicago:

Poor: Why did Jane Byrne cancel her write-in campaign?

He won't know, and it's unfair to ask why another candidate canceled. If you want an answer to that question, you'll have to ask Jane Byrne. But it would be appropriate to ask this:

Better: What effect will the cancellation of Jane Byrne's campaign have on your candidacy?

In the continuing preparation of our sewer bond program we're now ready to construct some questions for the body of the program. We'll begin with one question directed toward each guest, then work the remainder of the program from a list.

1. (For Mary Smith): Despite the rather serious sewer break last month, it seems that this issue hit the City Council without much warning, and that the Council made a hasty decision to go for a bond issue. How much prior consideration of the issue did you have? (This isn't a major question, but it's a good warmup and establishes the process by which the Council acted.)

2. (For Joe Brown): What process led to this particular choice of system, in terms of size and cost? (Follow up, if he doesn't cover it.) What are the major features of the proposed new system?

3. (For Paul Jones): You personally, and the Chamber of Commerce, have been vocal in support of a new sewer system. Why do you feel we can't just maintain or make minimum improvements on the present system and save millions of taxpayer dollars?

4. (For Fred White): It seems, from these statements, that we really do need a new sewer system. Why are you opposed? (We'll assume, for the remainder of the sequence of questions in the program, that his opposition is not to a new sewer system as such, but only to the bond issue as a means of financing it. His position is that property owners will have to pay all the costs, and that a better way would be to charge actual sewer users, including tenants.)

Additional questions (not necessarily to be asked in this sequence):

5. What other methods of financing the project were considered by the Council?
   Why were these other methods rejected?
   What is it that makes the Council think this is the best system?

6. Why is it necessary to have a project this large? Couldn't a less expensive approach be taken that is smaller in scope? Why not?

7. The Council's action only placed the issue on the ballot. The people of Fair River will make the final decision on whether or not to go ahead. What seems to be the present public attitude?
   What plans are underway to convince people to vote for the issue?
   Is there any organized opposition? If so, what form will the opposition take?
   What arguments will they make?

8. If the bond issues passes, what happens then?
   When does construction begin?
   How long will it last?
   How will the construction affect the citizens of Fair River?

9. What will be the financial impact on the average citizen if the bond issue passes?
   Will it have a greater impact on certain groups or individuals? Which ones?
   Why? Is that fair?

10. What happens if the citizens reject the bond issue?

The moderator will hope that after the opening round of questions addressed to each individual there will be a continuing interchange of opinions and conversation among all the parties. But if that interchange does not develop, these follow-up questions can be directed as well:

#5	Primarily for Councilwoman Smith, but possibly for Mr. Jones
#6	For Mr. Brown and Mr. Jones
#7	For Mr. Jones on the favorable side; Mr. White for the opposition
#8	For Mr. Brown
#9, #10	For anyone

The Program Closing

The closing of interview and discussion programs will include most of the following:

Timing Adjustments

If the program were to be prerecorded and then edited, the final timing would be done as part of the editing. For a live show, some adjustments for timing will have to be built into the closing—material that can be left out or included as necessary. Most of the remaining functions can also be manipulated to assist the program's timing.

Sense of Finality

You've probably encountered programs in which the host says: "Well, I see we've run out of time. Goodbye." The audience is left without a sense of closure, which is an uncomfortable feeling. The program should have a solid closing, including thank-yous to the guest and possibly a summary of the topic discussed and the major points made.

Identification   Some audience members will have tuned in during the show. They need identification of the program title, and of the guest(s), which they did not get from the opening.

Promotion   Subsequent broadcasts in the series may be promoted as part of the closing. Usually the topic and guests for the next broadcast can be announced:

> Tune in next week when our guest will be Ethel Watkins. She will discuss what effect the current oil glut will have on the prices you pay for gasoline, home heating, and electricity.

Some programs make a point out of not naming guests in advance, but on being flexible to interview whoever is currently in the news. In those cases the promotional announcement has to be more general, but it is also weaker.

Here is the closing for the sewer bond program. Like the opening, it is very simple and very brief. The closing signature can be constructed to provide some time adjustment, and a bit more time can be manipulated in the closing statements themselves. As written it lasts 1:40, and the major timing adjustments will have to be made in the body of the program to leave between 1:30 and 1:45 for the close.

MS: HOST	Thank you. For the next few months, at least until the November election, you're going to hear a great deal about the Fair River sewer project—its scope, its cost, its method of financing, alternatives. This program has provided a beginning for the continuing discussion of that issue. Our thanks to our panelists:
CAMERA PANS PANEL	Mary Smith, Joe Brown, Paul Jones, and Fred White
MS: HOST	for their contribution to the discussion. Next week on "City Scene," another topic of current interest and importance to <u>you</u>—the community of Fair River. I'm Janet Williams. Thank you for joining us. Good afternoon.
CLOSING SIGNATURE: START AT 28:30, UP TO END	<u>MUSIC: SIGNATURE</u>

Presenting Interview and Discussion Programs

The actual presentation of interview or discussion programs is not a writing task as such, and we won't take much space here to discuss this aspect of preparation. But it's not unusual for the roles of writer and host/interviewer or moderator to be combined, and it is helpful for the writer to understand the tasks the host must perform. Here are some guidelines for conducting interviews, and a few additional comments on panel discussions. Again, we are assuming live, nonrecorded, or at least unedited, programs.

Conducting Interviews

1. Have the opening and closing of the program prepared in advance, including whatever materials are to be used for the timing adjustment.

2. Have a sequence of questions worked out in advance. As a general rule, follow that sequence, which should provide a logical approach to the topic. If the guest begins to freeze and to provide stiff, short, unresponsive answers, shift to material with which the guest is more comfortable, or about which he or she is more enthusiastic.

3. Allow some time before going on the air for warmup with the guest. It helps to put the guest at ease, and it gives you some indication of how responsive she or he is going to be to the questions asked. You may be able to avoid the kind of problem suggested above.

4. Keep the focus of attention during the interview on the guest. The reason for talking with that person in the first place is because she or he has some content the audience wants to hear. Your role as the interviewer is to draw out that content. You are the voice of the audience members, acting on their behalf. See that the questions used are short, simple, and conversational.

    You may on occasion be stuck with an interviewee who is not very articulate, and who does not provide much material for you to work with. Some interviewers who face this situation frequently, such as sports interviewers, have developed a habit of asking lengthy questions that are really statements of opinion by the interviewer, followed by the question: "Isn't that true?" This approach places the focus of attention on the interviewer—the wrong place. A better approach is to have a longer list of questions ready than you would normally expect to use. If you have an inarticulate interviewee who provides very short answers, you will still have enough material to cover.

5. Listen to the answers given by the guest, and modify the wording of a following question so that it appears to come spontaneously from the preceding answer. If the sequence was well worked out in advance, this should not be difficult to do. Also, by listening to the answers, you can avoid the embarrassing situation of asking a question that has just been answered. If the answer to a question is given before you get a chance to ask it, then just skip over it. But in order to know that, you must listen to the response being given.

6. Don't repeat, or parrot, a response. The audience heard the answer the first time. This needless repetition indicates only one thing, that the interviewer wasn't ready to ask the next question and was caught without anything to say. If the proper preparation of a sequence of questions has been done in advance, this embarrassing situation won't happen.

Consider also these comments by Michael J. Arlen, television critic for *New Yorker* magazine, condensed from a chapter of his book *The View from Highway 1.*

A few weeks ago, viewers of New York's WCBS regular Saturday-evening news broadcast were shown a fairly long film report of a fire in a Harlem tenement, which early that morning had killed a six-month-old Puerto Rican baby and had destroyed a good part of the building. It was a depressing and grief-stricken scene. The dead child's parents, who had been out at the time of the fire, were very young and very distraught. The child's baby sitter was also on hand: a frightened, tearstained, Puerto Rican girl of sixteen, who unfortunately had left the apartment for a few key minutes in order to buy some diapers for the baby. "This is a story of human lives and tragedy," intoned the WCBS reporter, Lucille Rich. A microphone was thrust at the young babysitter, who muttered wretchedly, "I went to take out the baby and I get to the kitchen, but I can't see nothing, so I can't take out the baby . . ."

Why is it that, time after time, almost as if it were an inevitable—a magical—question, TV reporters at crucial moments must extend their microphones toward a subject and ask, "How do you feel?" Whether the interviewee is an astronaut returned from walking on the moon or a politician who has won or lost an election or someone in the middle of a personal tragedy, the question, or one of its equivalents, is so frequently asked by television reporters as to have become a commonplace. 'Well, Luis, how does it feel?" a microphone-thruster asked the Red Sox pitcher after a recent World Series victory. Another reporter went further: "I bet victory can't feel much better than that now, can it?" Or "Tell me what you felt when you saw your new face," as a local-news reporter asked a patient in a story on plastic surgery.

It seems to me that there are two ways of looking at these TV reporters' questions. On a certain level, they are simply childish and inept, though I think the ineptitude often lies not so much in the triviality of the question as in the unaware hostility behind it . . . [Second] At the back of whatever ails the TV interview seems to be a needlessly confused and conservative approach to what a TV interview can be or can't be . . .

Practically speaking, a TV interview is not there to provide the same "information" as a print interview with pictures added. The audience knows this. The reporters know this. Certainly, when a TV reporter goes into a World Series locker room, he knows that he has not been sent there to find out the score or to get a pitch-by-pitch account of the fifth inning. He knows he is there to capture a moment, to show the "feel" of something . . .

So what goes wrong? Two things, I think. The reporter often distrusts himself, meaning that he is often supposed to evoke feeling about an event that he has no feeling for himself—or about which he feels hostile, perhaps, or scared, or tired, or bored— and so, rather than let the real subjects (politicians or baseball players or whatever) go about their own activities, with him following them, and perhaps connecting finally to genuine feeling, what he does time after time is insistently impose his own authority . . .

The TV interrogator asserts his preconceptions, even offers his answers, in a lengthy question that he unrolls into his microphone and then allows the interviewee to sign. "After the years of oppression and danger in your homeland, and after the incredible danger and difficulty of your escape, which carried you to England ten years ago—well, perhaps you can tell us about the kind of hospitality you've met with here?" I heard a network interviewer ask a perplexed but amiable Soviet scientist a while ago.

The other thing wrong with TV news interviews, I think, is that the form they take often seems dictated by a lack of confidence that television newsmen appear to feel in the special visualness of their own profession . . .

Ironically, a better intuitive grasp of the form of television interviewing can be found in an unlikely area: that of the talk shows. On these strange programs, with their grinning hosts and ingratiating show-business guests, two important TV interviewing principles can be found. One is that it is the interview subject who is supposed to do most of the work; the other is that the conduit for conversation is usually a quite "soft" and aimless question . . .

"Do you feel any animosity . . .?" directed at the younger mother in the Harlem-fire story has a preconception built into it that the woman does feel animosity, which she will now produce, or somehow handle (in the manner of a theatrical exercise) for the benefit of the television audience. It is a manipulative question. But when Merv Griffin asks Lucille Ball, "Are you working now when you feel like?" he doesn't have anything in mind. The question has a remote, vague meaning, but no present meaning. Griffin is merely making celebrity small talk, nudging the show along on its prescribed track . . .

What all this adds up to, I think, is that, though there are individual examples of good interviewing on television, especially in the entertainment and cultural fields, TV news interviewing appears to be in some kind of limbo. Its often inexpert reporters are looking for the "feel" of things, which in many situations is a good way to begin, but they start asking those hard questions in order to get it. Or when they're not asking hard questions, they're letting those politicians or endless spokespeople make speeches into their microphones. Or they're trying so strenuously to control the event—to be proper hard-news authority figures—that the event and the people in it all end up awkwardly choreographed into some lifeless and ritualistic dance.[1]

Moderating Discussion Programs

Moderating a panel discussion program differs from conducting an interview in several significant ways.

1. In the interview there are usually only two participants—interviewer and interviewee (although, as we have seen, some programs assign the role of interviewer to several people asking questions in turn). The panel will have more than one guest. In the interview, the two-person structure results in a fairly direct question and answer pattern, whereas in the panel there may be several answers to the moderator's question, possibly answers to answers, and even possibly questions asked by persons other than the moderator. The pattern of discussion is therefore much more free-flowing in the panel than in the interview.

2. Having more than one respondent in the panel permits the introduction of varying points of view relating to the topic. (It would be a poorly structured panel program if all participants held the same position; there is nothing more boring than to hear one panelist state a position and then have three other panelists all say: "I agree.") Structurally, diversity of opinion provides variety; it also provides tension, which is a strong gratification for some audiences. Diversity of opinion in the interview can be accomplished only if two or more interviews are conducted separately and then intercut in the editing process.

3. Whereas an interviewer is an important participant in the conversation with the interviewee, asking questions as a surrogate for the audience, the moderator of a panel discussion program plays a much less prominent role. If the various participants are interacting as was expected by the program producers when the choice of participants was first made, then the panel moderator can be—and should be—almost invisible. His or her role will be to keep the discussion on the topic, or bring it back if it begins to stray into unimportant details, into

repetition, or into personal bickering between antagonists, or to avoid having the program monopolized by one or two panelists.

An outline should be prepared for the moderator, something like the questions we prepared for the sewer bond program, but as long as the program stays basically on its topic, and as long as all the participants are involved, the moderator should not attempt to force a rigid sequence of questions or topics on the guests. An inexperienced moderator working with a rigid outline sometimes will try too hard to shape the discussion to that outline, and arbitrarily cut off a lively and interesting conversation in which the audience has become intently involved.

4. The panel discussion has the potential at least to be structurally stronger than a straight talk or an interview program. We've already mentioned that a well-chosen group of panelists will provide variety, not only in points of view but also visually and vocally. That variety contributes to pace, and to the possibility that the discussion will build to some sort of climax.

Conclusion

Talk-type programs are efficient ways of attracting audiences and imparting information. That is not to say that they attract large audiences—they don't, but in relation to cost, which is almost always very low, they are efficient ways to fill large quantities of broadcast time. In one form or another you can expect these programs to remain in existence—and the beginning writer may expect to be asked to prepare them.

What particular forms of talk programs will be most prominent in years to come is a matter of speculation. Almost certainly, interviews and panels will continue to be popular. Quite likely the upsurge in audience participation conversations that has begun on radio will become an even more prevalent program type on both broadcast and cable TV. Technical, economic, and regulatory changes in the media all will affect program types.

The approach to the preparation of these programs, however, should remain essentially the same. Preparation begins with research into the interests of the audience, the background of the topic, and the expertise and opinions of the program guests. The information gained from that research is then committed to paper, most often in the form of a semi-script, which controls the organization and structure of the program for the interviewer-moderator-host, but leaves the responses from interviewee-guests ad lib. Next the program is produced, and finally aired, either as an unedited live or live-to-tape program, or in edited form in which the talk materials are woven into a documentary or news program or condensed for a more tightly organized and structured presentation.

Exercises

1. Assume you are a reporter for a local news–talk radio station. Your assignment editor has given you the assignment of interviewing a local person (one who was prominent in a story in the morning newspaper) for a follow-up story that will appear in your afternoon drive-time news today.

a. Choose a story and person who was prominent in that story from today's paper.

b. Then prepare: (1) a lead for the story, which will conclude with this line: "A short while ago we talked with ———, and recorded the following interview" (2) a series of six to eight questions you want to ask in order to bring the story up to date. Often these questions and answers will be edited before they are aired, but some stations do broadcast live "newsmaker" segments using almost exactly the format described here. We will assume this will be live, so you should consider the *sequence* of the questions, as well as the content and phrasing of each individual question.

2. You have been assigned as researcher-writer for a television network interview program, a half-hour in length (similar to "Meet the Press"). The guest each week is a major figure in politics, economics, or other national or international topic of importance.

Your assignment is, first, to select the guest for this week's program, and then to prepare for the program:

a. A *scripted* opening that identifies the program and the participants, introduces the topic, and attracts audience attention.

b. A series of questions to be asked of the guest. This is a *live* program, so the sequence is important, as are the presence of "pad" questions the interviewer can use to adjust the timing. You will need 9 to 10 major questions, plus some secondary or sequencing questions and pads.

c. A *scripted* close that ends the program appropriately, and that also contains material which can be used to make final timing adjustments.

3. Record on audiotape a radio or TV interview of approximately 5 to 8 minutes (from a network program like "Nightline," "Good Morning, America," "The Tonight Show," or a locally produced equivalent). Copy the questions asked in the interview. Analyze the sequence of the questions and their wording using criteria presented in this chapter. Reorganize the sequence if you think it can be improved, and add questions that would improve the flow of the interview. Rephrase any questions that are poorly worded. Explain your changes.

Key Terms and Concepts

ad lib
audience participation
closed-end questions
double and compound questions
editing
interviews: opinion, feature, informative
moderator/host
timing adjustments

panel discussions
program scope
qualification
selecting topics and guests
semi-script
surrogate
talks: persuasive, entertaining informative

Note

1. Michael J. Arlen, *The View from Highway 1* (New York: Farrar, Straus and Giroux, 1976), pp. 37–49. Adapted from ''The Interview'' from *The View from Highway 1* by Michael J. Arlen.

Chapter 14

Documentary Programs

Attempting to define or describe what is or is not a documentary can get one into a lot of difficulty. There are, on the one hand, those who would limit the documentary to an "authoritative, journalistic look at the important public-affairs issues of our time." Others take a broader view; they see the form as encompassing "a more personal and idiosyncratic vision of virtually anything with general significance."[1] Definitions can also be humorous: "A film without a plot, without a love story, and without anticipation of a profit."[2] Or they may be based on historical precedents:

> The word "documentary" to describe a type of film was introduced by John Grierson in the late twenties. It derived from *"documentaire,"* a term used by the French for their travel films. Grierson first applied "documentary" to Robert Flaherty's *Moana,* an account of events in the daily life of a Polynesian boy. Later he defined it as the "creative treatment of actuality."[3]

You don't need to have a precise definition, however, in order to prepare programs that fall at least loosely within this category. Our approach will be to describe a group of characteristics which, taken as a whole, give the documentary its unique character, and to contrast the documentary with other forms of presentation with which it shares some common characteristics.

For example, although documentaries frequently depend on the elaboration of abstract points of view, as in presenting a topic on foreign policy, they are not talk programs. Documentary as a technique requires that the program use locations, not just people talking in a studio.

Neither is the documentary a drama. A recently popular term in the broadcasting industry is *docudrama,* used to label what used to be called historical dramas. Evidently the prefix *docu-* lends some suggestion of historical accuracy the earlier label did not provide. But these programs are not documentaries; they are dramas, and should conform to the requirements for dramatic development.

The documentary is also not an overt expression of an editorial position, although the well-written documentary may lead to the members of the audience taking a position.

Finally, the documentary is not news, although here the difference is often not clear. The distinction, which we will develop in greater detail, is simply one of degree. The documentary relies heavily, even exclusively, on the actual places and people involved in the story. It attempts to involve the audience in the story. The news story, in contrast, depends more on the presence of a reporter to explain the story to the audience.

Characteristics of the Documentary

We can suggest three characteristics which are found in well-written and produced documentaries. None of these is unique to the documentary, but taken together they do set this genre apart from other types of content and forms of presentation.

First, there will be a distinct point of view. Second, the documentary makes a deliberate attempt to involve its audience in its presentation. Third, the true documentary, by definition, documents; it does not re-create or fictionalize its topic.

Point of View We have argued that effective writing of most broadcast materials requires a point of view in order to maintain unity and to shape the content for the target audience. On this ground, the documentary is no exception. Take, for example, this situation: You have been asked to write a television documentary for your station based on the premiere of a new musical work that will be performed by the community symphony. You might take a common journalistic approach—record the performance, get interviews with music critics after the performance on their impressions, possibly even add comments by "ordinary" persons who attended the performance, and then edit that material into a composite, interspersing sections of the music with the previously recorded comments.

Another point of view might be to follow the conductor's involvement with the work. In this case the conductor might become the narrator and the catalyst for the entire presentation. He explains why and how the work was chosen, how he studies the score and prepares himself for the presentation, what he hopes to emphasize in the presentation. Next you record rehearsals, as the conductor molds the orchestra to get the sound he wants. Finally you record the performance itself. The final, edited television presentation follows this chronological approach, concluding with the performance, or a portion of it if time does not permit showing the entire work.

Yet another point of view, if there were enough preparation time available to take this approach, would be to follow the composer through the steps of composition of this new work, then observe his reactions during rehearsals, note the last-minute modifications made in the work as the result of conversations between conductor and composer, and then present the performance, with occasional visual cutaways to the composer to observe his reactions to his own work and to the audience for their reactions as well.

Still other approaches might be considered. There are only two real limitations on the writer when it comes to choosing a point of view—the amount of time available to complete the production, and the budget.

From the above you can infer that point of view means looking at a topic from someone's perspective. That person might be one of the participants—the conductor or the composer in our example above. Or it might be the reporter's point of view. Any good reporter will recognize that he or she invariably takes a point of view on every story. The process of selecting material to be included (or left out), of deciding the relative importance (length of time on the screen) of various parts of the story, and of what comes first and what later—all these decisions are influenced by the point of view the writer-reporter brings to the story.

But our concern here is not with subtle or subconscious decisions in regard to reporting or editing the material; it is rather with the deliberate choice to use the reporter's perspective, which is assumed to be as objective and "neutral" as possible, as the point of view of the presentation.

Multiple points of view are also possible. Some very interesting programs have been developed by examining a topic through the eyes of different persons who are affected in different ways.

Audience Involvement

We first considered audience involvement in Chapter 9. It is part of the broad and powerful gratification we labeled personalization.

Compare, once again, the documentary with news and with drama. Personalization may be present in some degree in a news story, to the extent that audiences can identify with persons, places, and events in the story, but that gratification is not usually emphasized. The strongest gratifications in most news stories are those of information, importance, and value. A well-written drama, in contrast, makes us care about the characters. We expect to become emotionally involved in the outcome, to have empathy for the characters, to cheer or to boo the outcome.

Here the documentary more closely approximates drama than news. The content of the documentary will contain information, and have importance and value for its target audience, but now added to those gratifications, deliberately, is the emotional strength of personalization. The audience should be drawn into the topic, and invited to participate in whatever process or activity is taking place, even though it must be a vicarious participation.

TV Guide magazine once asked several of the best-known producers of television programs what forms of the documentary the American public watched and why. Their answers reveal the importance of audience involvement:

Reuven Frank, at that time executive vice-president of NBC News: "Drama. You cannot interest people unless you tell stories. Usually in a good story there's a protagonist, a conflict, and a resolution."

Burton Benjamin, documentary producer for CBS: "Plot values give you the highest ratings."

Bob Drew, president of Bob Drew and Associates, Inc., an independent documentary production company: "Nothing can compete with dramatic logic. Reality films must have similar ingredients to those in fiction—a protagonist, a dramatic conflict."[4]

Involvement is accomplished by exposing viewers to the real people, places, and events involved in the topic, permitting them to hear the voices of the actual participants and the actual sounds of the location, and to see the actual conditions in which the participants are involved.

Suppose you were given an assignment to cover the plight of the elderly urban poor in your community. These are people who are forced to live in substandard flophouse hotels and who, your research shows, are exploited by the managers of those hotels. It would be possible to cover at least part of the content by means of an interview with a local housing official, who reports that there are x thousands of elderly poor in the community, that there are only y thousand housing units, and that z thousand of those units are substandard.

A different technique would be to follow several of these elderly poor people through some of the activities of a typical day—trying to cash a Social Security check or to find a decent meal at a reasonable price, climbing the stairs to a filthy room because the elevator in the hotel has broken down, lying in bed and seeing the rats crawl up the wall. The interview, with the statistics and the official's presence, is simple to do and authoritative. But it carries none of the dramatic value or emotional weight of experiencing through the camera's eye the struggle of one handicapped person up a stairway or the sight of one rat running up a wall.

A Documentary Documents

At first glance, that heading may seem redundant. But it makes a difference in the preparation whether the material used in the program is real—the actual people, places, and events—or whether the actions of the program have been re-created.

The point is simply that *a true documentary cannot be scripted in advance of its shooting.* In this sense, the documentary is similar to news. The story has to come back from its location, and the tape footage has to be viewed and a selection of shots made before the final sequence can be determined and the final narration written. In many programs, no script, in any formal sense, is ever prepared. Instead, writers and producers will put the completed program together from a variety of shot sheets and other notes.

In contrast, any program content that is to be re-created, or staged, and therefore to some degree fictionalized, can be and should be written *in advance* of shooting. A complete script will be needed to describe to actors and crew what is to be performed for the camera. That is why we have insisted that the re-creation of situations, as in a docudrama, is not truly documentary, and should follow the guidelines for dramatic development. After all, in those situations both picture and sound are under the complete control of the writer and the director. By this assertion we do not mean to suggest that the writer's role is any less important or creative when crafting a documentary than with any other type of program, only that the sequence in which the various production tasks are performed will differ.

Common Documentary Types

We do not have the space, nor is this introductory text the proper place, to consider all the forms a documentary might take. But we can consider, briefly, five types we believe will give the beginning writer a better grasp of the requirements of writing these programs. These are the documentary based on public affairs issues, the documentation of a creative effort, the event or process documentary, the nature documentary, and the "slice of life" documentary. The terms are largely our own; other authors use different labels.

The Public Affairs Issue Documentary

This is perhaps the most well-known type. These programs examine topics of public concern—hunger, poverty, war, and other social and political issues. Issue-oriented documentary programs presented by the television networks are sometimes able to stir up sufficient public concern and pressure to help solve the problems documented.

One of the most famous examples of a public affairs documentary, presented by CBS in 1960, was "Harvest of Shame." It presented the problems of America's migrant workers, and showed in graphic detail the miserable conditions in which many of these workers lived.

> Using the photographic record of environment and the direct interview, the *CBS Reports* unit (led by producer David Lowe and with [Edward R.] Murrow as narrator) followed the path of the migrants as they traveled the harvesting route in ramshackle caravans from their Florida shacks. The cameras recorded their squalor and the deadly and hopeless monotony of their labors. In disturbing interviews we listened to mothers forced to leave children alone in rat-infested hovels because they could not afford the pennies to send them to a day-care center; or parents unable to provide milk for their infants more than once a week. As the film progressed, we were offered a devastating visual contrast between the shacks occupied by migrants and the comfortable, clean stables nearby. We saw scenes of cattle cars stopping at regular four-hour intervals in order to water and exercise the cattle, contiguous with scenes of the pitiful migrants riding buses and overloaded trucks for ten uninterrupted hours at a stretch.[5]

The program triggered tremendous resentment on the part of major agricultural interests. Its producers were accused of being blatantly editorial. But it aroused sufficient public indignation to enact some protections for migrant workers.

At the local level, some individual stations are equally forceful in exposing social ills, but a great many stations are reluctant to present documentaries on major issues. The programs are expensive to produce, tying up news crews and editing facilities which might instead be used for straight news programming. Documentaries do not draw large audiences even when presented in prime time, nor do they easily attract sponsors. And they are controversial, and who wants willingly to antagonize leading members of the community? At least those are the arguments frequently used to excuse the relative paucity of local public affairs documentaries. You may judge for yourself if they are legitimate.

Some stations have found an interesting way to reduce the costs of documentary production and to increase viewership by first producing a series of investigative news reports on a topic and airing them within the local newscast. Then, if the topic does generate viewer interest and public reaction, the story will be reworked as a longer documentary. The revised version can include the reactions of public officials to the original stories, but it will also include repeats of much of the raw material from the original.

With this approach, using the same topic for both a news series and a documentary, and using the same content only slightly repackaged, the distinctions between news and documentary become blurred.

Later in this chapter we have reproduced the scripts from just such a series. They were written and reported by Brad Willis and presented by his station, WFAA, Dallas, in October 1984. The stories were developed out of phone calls received by the station's "Contact 8" unit, a service maintained by the station to assist viewers who have consumer complaints against businesses. The complaints suggested consumer fraud involving a barter organization. The trail led from one victim to another. The fraud seemed to affect a lot of people and involve a good deal of money. All the facts suggested that the story would make a powerful investigative series, and in all likelihood would eventually involve the local Better Business Bureau, the district attorney, and even the state attorney general's office. The responses of these agencies, then, would provide fresh material for the "second round" documentary.

Documenting a Creative Effort

This type of documentary exposes its audience to the process of creation, usually of some sort of artistic work. It might document the making of a sculpture, following the sculptor from the choice of material, through the various steps in designing and executing the work, to its final placement. Or it might follow an orchestra conductor through the steps of preparing a new work—a topic we brought up when considering point of view. Or it might follow the process of the creation of a film.

One recent and very successful such effort was "The Making of Thriller," which documents the production of Michael Jackson's video "Thriller." No script exists for this documentary effort, but the producer's point of view and organizational plan are clear from these comments:

> I didn't just want to come out of the project with a bunch of documentary footage. . . . I wanted to establish just how extraordinary this whole undertaking was, with all the incredible talent and energy involved. To me, "Thriller" is more like an art-film than a music video—it really is a mini-movie, with all the special effects and makeup, right down to the "scary music."
>
> Whereas a normal music video will be shot in one or two days, they were shooting for nine days in the various locations around East Los Angeles, and because we were there all the time, not just during the actual shoot, but also at pre-production meetings, rehearsals, post-production, etc., we were shooting for a total of 14 days straight. . . .
>
> We started off by dividing the entire project into separate chapters, each with its own title like "The Fans" or "Graveyard" or "Metamorphosis." So first you meet some of the fans who've found out about the location shoots and have turned up just to get a glimpse of Michael. And you also see Richard Baker, the special effects wizard, work his magic on Michael and the zombie extras. . . .

Along with the behind-the-scenes views and the actual footage are various intercut references and portions of other clips to help shape it and put it in perspective.[6]

Documenting an Event or Process

This form of documentary may itself be considered on several levels, based on the amount of creativity and artistic freedom allowed its writers and producers.

At its least creative level it represents merely the recording of a process or event, such as a manufacturing sequence—how the doors are bolted onto an automobile—or documentation of the firing of a rocket motor, or observing from a single fixed camera position a parade going by.

Taken a step more creatively, that basic documentation can be edited and provided with a narration, to be used in a training tape for workers or in a promotional piece for a company. This sort of presentation, which is often called a "sponsored" film (or tape), is in part the subject of the following chapter on writing for corporate/instructional productions.

But when writers an producers are allowed the creative freedom to employ all the principles of structure and style, and to emphasize audience gratifications as well, documentation can be turned into a much more interesting sort of program. Documentaries of this sort might present a parade, or a circus, a political convention, or even an entire political campaign. Other topics might be the progress of an athletic team throughout a game, or a season, or the documentation of the preparation and launching of a spacecraft.

The Nature Documentary

This form should require no introduction to anyone who has watched television at all. Historically, the popularization of documentaries about natural phenomena probably dates back to Walt Disney's *Beaver Valley* and several other similar films. Those of you now in college have grown up with "Wild Kingdom," National Geographic specials, "Nova," and of course, the several series featuring Jacques Cousteau. We have reproduced an excerpt from a Cousteau program script later in this chapter.

The Slice of Life Documentary

This variation can easily be combined with other forms. It can also be a very powerful and effective approach in its own right. Here the writer-producer chooses to document a "chunk" of human existence. The content is most often combined with a video style that eliminates the subject's awareness of the camera by using hidden or "candid" cameras. This technique, which in some of its variations is also known as the *verité documentary,* seeks to break down the aesthetic distance between the subject and the viewer and thereby heighten viewer involvement.

Often the central focus will be on a location, a particular site from which it is possible to observe the behaviors of persons who happen to be in or passing through that place. This approach was used in *Terminus,* a documentary film produced for the British Transportation Commission, as described by its producer:

The first germ of the idea came from John Maddison of the Central Office of Information, who said to me one day, "Why don't you make a documentary of a night at King's Cross Station?" It was, of course, an interesting subject but seemed likely to prove depressing on the screen. After all, King's Cross was old, inadequate and due for rebuilding. So I did nothing about it. . . .

Some time later I was looking at some candid-camera material showing the handling of parcels at King's Cross—film taken as a time-and-motion study to help us analyse parcel and luggage handling, in relation to the layout and general efficiency of the station. In these pictures members of the general public were seen, as well as railway staff. We were fascinated by the material. Quite apart from its purpose as a study of procedure, the actions of the people—quite oblivious of being shot—were extraordinarily interesting. . . .

There the idea rested perhaps a couple of years. Then John Schlesinger came to me to make a film. We discussed various ideas and then he said he would like to make a film of a day in the life of a railway station. Someone mentioned Waterloo. Waterloo has two important advantages. It's modern and light enough for unlit candid-camera shooting. . . .

How would it relate to British Transport's policy? Two things, it seemed to me, might be put over in such a film: that British Railways still have a vital national job to do and if you sit at a London terminus throughout a day, you see enough vital things happening to prove it; and secondly the film could show the staff were human, warm-hearted people, trying to do a good job.

Both these things seemed very much worth saying.[7]

Writing Documentaries

We have already explained that in the true documentary, in contrast to programs which are re-creations, the sequences cannot be scripted in detail in advance; they can be only loosely planned. The precise shots will have to be left to the judgment of the director and cameraperson on location. In such a situation, if the final program is to have any similarity to the one originally conceived by its author, the preliminary steps in production must be all the more carefully worked out.

Concept
The task of writing a documentary begins with an idea of your own, or with an assignment from a supervisor. That idea or assignment is the essence of the *concept*. A concept statement serves the same purpose for a documentary that it does for a drama; it allows the originator to communicate the program idea to others who will be involved with the program. The producers' statements for both *Terminus* and "The Making of Thriller" which we quoted earlier are concept statements, although in both cases they were written after the production (and we edited them heavily).

The next steps in the process are the same as those for the development of any other type of program. The purpose will have to be accurately assessed, and the target audience identified. The method of delivery, a step we have not considered in previous chapters, will need to be considered. Broadcast is no longer the only alternative. This production might be, for example, a "sponsored" presentation, prepared on behalf of a corporate client for training or promotional purposes and shown on a closed-circuit video system. Or it might be produced for possible sale in videocassette form, as was "The Making of Thriller." Or it might be aired in the traditional manner, by a station or network.

Treatment   The answers to these considerations, plus the determination of the point of view, lead to the *treatment,* which is very much the same as the treatment for a dramatic program—a narrative description of the proposed program. In addition to describing the subject matter, the treatment should indicate style and method of presentation. How much of the verbal description will be provided by spoken actualities, and how much by commentary? Will music be used; if so, how? Will the approach be journalistic, impressionistic, dramatized, or some combination of these? What will be the mood?

The treatment should be carefully written and agreed to by all the key members of the production team, as well as by the sponsor, to avoid misunderstandings later in the production. Without a detailed treatment, the crew that goes out to shoot the raw footage from which the final program will be edited has no guide to follow. They might shoot thousands of feet, but all the wrong stuff, or at the very least they might shoot much more material than will be needed, thereby complicating and slowing the editing process and costing additional money. A good treatment will prevent those complications.

One way to approach the treatment is to suggest a series of impressions, as in this description from *Terminus.*

> Flying high above London and the Thames. The Houses of Parliament on our left.
> Insistent notes of the harpsichord suggest the time, 8 A.M.
> We are now hovering over Waterloo, featuring the enormous acre of glass that covers it.
> Titles—*Terminus,* etc., etc.
> Various angles on the glass roof under titles.
> From the mount of the station—trains are running both ways.
> Inside, the rush to the city is beginning.
> The signal box—the dots of the indicator run towards the station. Intent old faces. Silence. "Give me 23, George." Levers are pulled. Kettles steam with the Houses of Parliament in the background. Harpsichord.
> The business train from Guildford rattles past the box—swift pan to a cat looking down from the top of the internal telephone exchange in the signal box.
> The men in the business train pack up newspapers, take down their umbrellas, bowlers, brief cases—"See you on the 5.45" etc., and join the march.
> Outside the station, the cars and their executive occupants drive away—The Lion and the insignias of War and Peace over the archway gaze down at them.
> Public gazing at train arrival board. The destinations change like magic. A special notice indicates the arrival of boat train from Southampton. Australian line.
> On 11—the people who are meeting the train gather. Curiosity at whom they are meeting. The Salvation Army man—elderly foreign-looking woman—a young girl with a bunch of flowers.
> Bill, the porter, sits on some scales. He whistles, the pointer on the scales registers the rhythm.
> The officials of Cooks, Dawson's, Poly Tours join the group.
> Black Homburg, and top hat—the insignia of the Station Master. Phone conversation about delay of boat train.
> On 11—they wait. Their voices perhaps tell us whom they are meeting. A married sister, a prodigal son returning after ten years, a comrade from the Salvation Army. An ambulance at the ready on the concourse—Nurse in evidence.[8]

The treatment should not be carved in stone, however. It will evolve and expand as additional research proceeds on the topic, and as the camera crew finds and shoots new and interesting material. You might begin the preparation of a documentary on the elderly urban poor with the assumption based on your early research that all the flophouse hotel managers in the city treat their tenants poorly, charge high rates for poorly furnished and maintained rooms, and so on. And then you discover one hotel which is clean, and where the staff is helpful and supportive of the tenants. To be accurate and fair, this hotel should also be featured in the final production. (It also will make a good contrast, and provide variety in what otherwise might be a pretty depressing exposition.)

Be alert for new and powerful visual opportunities, and be flexible.

Notes and Scripts

Once there is film or tape to work with, the task becomes that of editing. One of the first steps in this part of the process will be to summarize the sequences in some form of *shot sheet*—a listing of each shot in sequence. Here are some of the materials used to prepare the series on the barter scam produced by WFAA. First are two shot sheets (See Figure 14.1 on the following page). Each sheet shows the time (or place on the reel) for each shot, other identification of the shot (such as 2-shot, reversal, closeup, extreme closeup, and an identifying line of the audio, usually the out-cue. The shots starred are those finally chosen for the production.

The next piece of development material is the *SOT (sound on tape)* list, a summary of the sound bites to be used in the series. The numbers at the left are references back to the original tape reels (and shot sheets) for each excerpt.

BARTER SOT LIST:

1. Paul Jacobs: KZEW–Positive Barter
1. Mike Coffman: Servco:–Positive Barter, Stung for $8,000 By EE
2. George Brooks–Neg $10,000 Balance at EE Is False
2. Don Grogan: Gun & Tackle: Bought 20,000 Units for $5,000 Cash from TW
4. BW Standup (Edit Room) . . . "Customers Gave in Good Faith . . ."
6. ███████ Barter Broker W/EE: Won't Talk, Won't Give Name, Intervenes W/BW Attempts to Talk to Victims
6. BW Standup–EE: Bank Analogue
6. Randy Staley: Carpet Work–They Owe $400, Getting Runaround
6. Brian White: Worker for TW:–Is Owed $400 Plus 3,000 Units, Mad.
6. ███████ EE–Grabs Camera, Freaks Out
6. EE–Grabs Camera, Freaks Out
7. Bob Bogen: Europtics–Victim, Had 3,000 Unusable Units
7. Carl Ikard: Dallas Diagnostic: Victims; Thinks Its a Scam, Low-Quality Merchandise, 20,700 Units.
8. Robbie Robinson: Barter Trader: Victim; 23,000 ███ Is Crook, Units Confiscated, Milked It Dry, Selling Off Goods for Cash
8. Jean Quick: Quick Movers: Victim 3,000 Units. Given Gems Allegedly Worth 3,000. We Were Robbed, ███ Lied.
9. Dr. Dan Penick: Optometrist: Victim 6–7,000 Units. You Give Up after Awhile.

STORY SLUG:	*Barter #1*	
DATE:		

TIME	SHOT	DESCRIPTION
110		SOT: PAUL JACOBS KZEW
		" Trading w/ TV stations, restaurants, cut expenses with sales lenders of clients + to cut travel expenses by trading w/ airlines and hotels
128		"It does help us cut our overhead. To have the ability to
141		"It helps us cut our expenses in expensive categories like travel. The ability to stay at a Sheraton for example
158	✦	"People get airtime which would otherwise go unsold.
205		" it allows us to do many more things like adv. on TV that we otherwise couldn't.
225	2 shot	Paul Jacobs
250	CU	records — your 2 shot
305		Paul reversal
340	NATS	music / DJ
345	MS	DJ working / music NATS w/ discs
435	ECU	Record & needle

Figure 14.1 Source: Courtesy of WFAA, Dallas.

STORY SLUG:		ƐƐ Ƶ	✗
DATE:		p.1 Robbie Robinson / Jean Quick	
TIME	SHOT	DESCRIPTION	
:60		SOT: ROBBIE ROBINSON trader	
1:05	✗	" they had stuff in Exchange Office they would not sell for trade units "	
129	✗	" I was told at dif times if I wanted to pay cash, I could buy their merchandise	
153	✗	" They was selling stuff cash when members like me w/ ltsa trade units couldnt buy nothing.	
220		" They turned it into cash to pay personal bills, or & salaries, rent, thats not way supposed to be.	
235	✗✗	" They had great big signs saying "everything in this showroom can be bought thru barter, no cash involved, but yet they had all this stuff in there, but wouldn't let anybody buy it.	
310	✗	" I have lawsuit vs. ƐƐ for $23,000.	
315		" They confiscated 15,000 credit from me, saying I didnt pay membership fee	
400	✗✗	" About ƐƐ, I believe ▮▮▮▮▮▮ is a crook	
438	✗	" I think ▮▮▮ getting all merchandise out he can, milking it dry — comin in rapin system	
458	✓	" he's taking everything	

Figure 14.1 (Continued)

10. James Howell: Foam Crafters: Victim 3,000 Units. Bought Stereo Equip. at Auction, but Never Delivered. Trade Unit. No Relation to Dollar
10. Alberto Cercone: Tailor, Victim 1400 Units, Promised World, Gave Zero. Bad Deal, Big Mistake.
11. Charles Yater: Jeweler: Gem Value Fictitious, Appraisal Worthless.
12. Bill Taylor: Balloonist: Victim, Dollar Worthless, Plundered, Inflationary
12. BW Standup: Stratotech
14. John Smith: Olive Crown: Appraisals a Joke, Fenced, Barter Bought

For this series full scripts were prepared, and we present them here in their entirety. Most of the terminology used should be familiar to you by now, but here is a brief review of the directions and abbreviation used:

DOUBLE BOXES.	A special effects technique used for transition from anchor to reporter in newsroom.
NATS.	Natural sound, here used primarily in background behind the reporter's narration.
SOT.	Sound on tape; the sound track is already included, in sync, on the videotape excerpt. The director will bring up tape and sound together.
TRACK.	These portions of the reporter's narration have been prerecorded on an audio track (tape), in contrast to those portions delivered live.
STANDUP.	The reporter, on location, prerecorded these bridges (audio and video) between SOT segments.
B-ROLL.	In general, B-roll visuals are descriptive pictures that are to be shown paralleling a sound track on a separate tape (the A-roll). Often the two are edited into a composite prior to airing, but sometimes both tapes are run simultaneously during the live newscast. The picture comes from one tape, the sound from another.

```
willis    Mon Oct  8 16:00   page   1

PAGE ANCR STORY              FROM  WRITER  VIDEO          * TAPE TIME VIOLATOR
          BARTER SCAM PT. 1                                      3 31
=====================================================================================
```

ANCHOR LEAD   A DALLAS-BASED BARTER CLUB DOING
                                    MILLIONS OF DOLLARS IN TRADE IS UNDER
                                    FIRE TONIGHT.
                                         MEMBERS CLAIM THE CLUB HAS BEEN
                                    LOOTED BY THE OWNER, AND THEY'VE BEEN
                                    LEFT WITH WORTHLESS TRADE DOLLARS.
DOUBLE BOXES   CONTACT 8'S BRAD WILLIS HAS BEEN
                                    INVESTIGATING, AND TONIGHT BEGINS AN
                                    EXCLUSIVE SERIES OF REPORTS.
LIVE NEWSROOM
                                         IT'S CALLED EXCHANGE ENTERPRISES,
                                    PART OF A NATIONAL BARTER GROUP WITH
                                    SERIOUS PROBLEMS IN CITIES THROUGHOUT
                                    THE COUNTRY.
                                         OUR INVESTIGATION CENTERS ON THE
                                    DALLAS EXCHANGE.
                                         BUT FIRST, A LOOK AT HOW BARTER
                                    WORKS AND WHAT THE BENEFITS CAN BE.

NATS; RECORD MUSIC 1-
                                     (TRACK)
                                         RADIO STATIONS GET THE RECORDS FOR
                                    FREE: PROMOTIONAL COPIES. THE AUDIO
                                    DISCS ARE A TRADE-OUT. SO IS THE
                                    MACHINE THAT PLAYS THEM. WHEN YOU LISTEN
                                    TO THE RADIO, YOU'RE IN TOUCH WITH
                                    BARTER.
SOT; PAUL JACOBS   (B ROLL) 1-   'we do trading with tv stations,
KZEW RADIO SALES   restaurants, to cut expenses with sales
                                    lunches with clients, and to cut travel
                                    expenses by trading with airlines and
                                    hotels. '
                                    'people get airtime which would
                                    otherwise go unsold.
NATS; HOUR MAG 5-
                                     (TRACK)
                                         AND WE BARTER IN THE TELEVISION
                                    BUSINESS ON SYNDICATED SHOWS LIKE 'HOUR
                                    MAGAZINE', AND FOR ADS ON RADIO AND IN
                                    NEWSPAPERS.
                                         BARTER HAS BECOME BIG BUSINESS,
                                    AND SO HAVE BARTER CLUBS. MIKE COFFMAN
                                    BELONGS TO ONE. HE OFFERS PLUMBING AND
                                    AIR CONDITIONING. SINCE NOT EVERYONE
                                    NEEDS THOSE SERVICES, HE PROVIDES THEM
                                    TO THE CLUB'S BARTER POOL AND GETS
                                    TRADE UNITS IN RETURN...UNITS HE CAN
                                    SPEND LATER FOR OFFICE SUPPLIES,
                                    PRINTING AND EQUIPMENT. HE GOT THIS
                                    COMPANY SIGN THROUGH TRADE, AND EVEN
                                    SOME NEW DRESSES FOR HIS WIFE AT TH.
                                    SHOP WHICH ALSO BELONGS TO THE BARTER
                                    CLUB
SOT: MIKE COFFMAN   "it's alot easier for me to trade my

Figure 14.2 Source: Courtesy of WFAA, Dallas.

```
willis    Mon Oct  8 16:00  page  2
```

BARTER CLUB MEMBER   services than pull it out of my
                                                 bankbook."

                                                 (TRACK)
                                                          BUT THERE'S ALSO A DOWN SIDE TO
                                                 BARTER. SOME CLUBS DON'T LIVE UP TO
                                                 THEIR PROMISES, AND SOMEHOW THE BEST
                                                 GOODS AND SERVICES SEEM TO DISAPPEAR.
                                                 MIKE COFFMAN USED TO BELONG TO A CLUB
                                                 LIKE THAT, AND IT COST HIM $8,000 WORTH
NATSIG; 1"   OF BARTER UNITS.
                                                 (TRACK)
                                                          THE CLUB IS CALLED EXCHANGE
                                                 ENTERPRISES A NATIONWIDE BARTER
                                                 NETWORK WITH MANY FRANCHISES THAT HAVE
                                                 COLLAPSED, LEAVING MEMBERS HOLDING
                                                 WORTHLESS TRADE DOLLARS.
                                                          MIKE COFFMAN BELONGED TO THE
                                                 DALLAS EXCHANGE, WHICH IS STILL DOING
                                                 BUSINESS DESPITE THE COMPLAINTS OF
                                                 DOZENS OF MEMBERS WHO FEEL THEY'VE BEEN
                                                 CHEATED OUT OF UPWARDS OF A MILLION
                                                 DOLLARS OR MORE.

SOT. MIKE COFFMAN 1-   "i couldn't deal with them
LOST 8,000 TRADE DOLLARS   because they never had anything when
                                                 you wanted it, and when they did have
                                                 it, the prices were jacked up so high
                                                 you couldn't afford to deal anyhow."

STANDUP: 4-   "LIKE MIKE COFFMAN, PEOPLE WHO
                                                 JOINED THE EXCHANGE GAVE OF THEIR GOODS
                                                 AND SERVICES IN GOOD FAITH. BUT WHEN IT
                                                 CAME TIME TO CASH IN AND SPEND THEIR
                                                 BARTER UNITS, THEY FOUND THE PROMISES
                                                 OF WHAT WAS SUPPOSED TO BE THERE WERE
                                                 FALSE."

SOT: BILL TAYLOR 12-   "i was holding 3,000 barter
LOST $3,000 TRADE DOLLARS   points, and the reason you become
                                                 disillusioned is you can't spend them
                                                 anyplace."

SOT; ROBBIE ROBINSON 8-   "they was selling stuff cash whe
LOST 23,000 BARTER DOLLARS   members like me with lotsa trade units
                                                 couldn't buy nothing."

SOT: JEAN QUICK 8-   "there were many service people
LOST 3,000 BARTER DOLLARS   like us who were just taken advantage
                                                 of and robbed."

                                                 (TRACK)
                                                          AND WHILE THESE MEMBERS AND
                                                 OTHERS, LIKE BOB BOGEN OF EUROPTICS
                                                 PHOTOGRAPHY STUDIO, WERE LEARNING THAT
                                                 THEIR TRADE DOLLARS WERE VIRTUALLY
                                                 WORTHLESS, EXCHANGE ENTERPRISES WAS
                                                 DEMANDING THEY PAY $750 ANNUAL
                                                 MEMBERSHIP RENEWAL FEES. AND

Figure 14.2 (Continued)

```
willis    Mon Oct 8 15 00  page  3
```

CONFISCATING THE TRADE DOLLARS OF THOSE
WHO REFUSED

SOT:BOB BOGEN 4-   "it was ridiculous to throw $350
LOST 3,000 TRADE DOLLARS   after what i had already lost."

(TRACK)
THE OWNER OF THE DALLAS EXCHANGE
ENTERPRISES IS ████████████, WHO
REFUSES TO TALK ABOUT OF ALL THIS BUT
WE HAVE LEARNED DURING OUR
INVESTIGATION THAT ██████ WAS SELLING
BARTER DOLLARS FOR CASH...AS LITTLE AS
TEN CENTS ON THE DOLLAR. THAT HE WAS
LIQUIDATING BARTER MERCHANDISE, AGAIN
FOR CASH, AT FLEA MARKETS LIKE THIS
ONE. AND THAT HE WAS GIVING SOME
MEMBERS, DESPERATE TO REDEEM THEIR
UNITS, GEMS ALLEGEDLY APPRAISED FOR
THOUSANDS OF DOLLARS BUT ACTUALLY
ALMOST WORTHLESS.

LIVE TAG: "more on that tomorrow night, plus
a look at the promises exchange
enterprises uses to entice its members
to join."

Figure 14.2 (Continued)

```
willis     Mon Oct  8 16:00   page  1

PAGE ANCR STORY          FROM   WRITER   VIDEO        + TAPE TIME VIOLATOR
          BARTER SCAM PT 2                              :   3.38
================================================================================
```

ANCHOR LEAD	SOME SERIOUS QUESTIONS TONIGHT CONCERNING A NATIONWIDE NETWORK OF BARTER EXCHANGES. QUESTIONS ABOUT TRADE DOLLARS THAT HAVE LOST THEIR VALUE, PROMISED GOODS AND SERVICES NOT AVAILABLE, SOME EXCHANGES COLLAPSING, LEAVING MEMBERS OUT MILLIONS OF DOLLARS WORTH OF GOODS AND SERVICES.
DOUBLE BOXES	CONTACT 8'S BRAD WILLIS CONTINUES HIS INVESTIGATION NOW INTO EXCHANGE ENTERPRISES.
NEWSROOM LIVE	TONIGHT, WE MEET SOME OF THE MANY VICTIMS WHO GAVE THEIR GOODS AND SERVICES TO THE DALLAS EXCHANGE, ONLY TO FIND THE BARTER DOLLARS THEY RECEIVED IN RETURN WERE VIRTUALLY WORTHLESS. BARTER DOLLARS THE EXCHANGE PROMISED COULD BE USED FOR ANYTHING FROM OFFICE SUPPLIES TO TRIPS AROUND THE WORLD.
	(TRACK) EXCHANGE ENTERPRISES IS A NATIONAL ORGANIZATION, HEADQUARTERS: SALT LAKE CITY, UTAH. AT LEAST 15 OF THESE FRANCHISES HAVE COLLAPSED, LEAVING MEMBERS WITH USELESS BARTER DOLLARS. THE DALLAS FRANCHISE IS STILL IN BUSINESS, BUT IT'S ON THE BRINK OF GOING UNDER AS MANY MEMBERS CLAIM THE EXCHANGE HAS BEEN LOOTED, AND THEIR BARTER DOLLARS ARE VIRTUALLY WORTHLESS
NATSIG 1"	(TRACK) THE LITERATURE PROMISES A STUNNING ARRAY OF SERVICES; FROM BROADCAST AND PRINT ADVERTISING, TO RESORT HOTELS AND TRIPS ABROAD, TO MEDICAL SERVICES, LEGAL COUNSELING, AND MUCH, MUCH MORE
STANDUP: BANK ANALOGY 6-	"A BARTER SYSTEM WORKS SOMETHING LIKE A BANK. MEMBERS PUT IN THEIR DEPOSITS AND MAKE WITHDRAWALS. BUT WITH EXCHANGE ENTERPRISES, THE MEMBERS LOST CONFIDENCE, TRIGGERING A RUN ON THE BANK. THE BARTER UNITS- SUPPOSED TO BE WORTH $1 APIECE- LOST MOST OF THEIR VALUE, AND HARDLY ANYONE WAS WILLING TO TRADE."
SOT: ALBERTO CERCONE 10-	"it's a bad deal, i made a big

Figure 14.2 (Continued)

```
willis    Mon Oct  8 16:00   page  2
```

LOST 1400 BARTER DOLLARS   mistake by joining "

      (TRACK)
          TAILOR ALBERTO CERCONE MADE SUITS
      AND PROVIDED ALTERATIONS FOR BARTER
      CLUB MEMBERS. HE WANTED INTERNATIONAL
      TRAVEL, AS PROMISED IN THE LITERATURE

SOT: CERCONE AGAIN   " they promised the world but they
      had zero. when you try to collect, you
      find nothing. "

      (TRACK)
          DR. DAN PENICK GAVE EYE EXAMS.
      $6-7,000 WORTH.

SOT: DR. DAN PENICK 9-
6-7,000 LOST BARTER DOLLARS   "you give up after awhile and
      finally realize you basically have
      given services to people and might not
      get anything in return for it. "

      (TRACK)
          DALLAS DIAGNOSTIC PROVIDED OVER
      $20,000 WORTH OF MEDICAL SERVICES FOR
      PATIENTS. BUT WHEN IT CAME TIME TO CASH
      IN BARTER DOLLARS FOR OFFICE SUPPLIES,
      THE PROMISES FELL FLAT.

SOT: CARL IKARD 7-6:37
20,700 LOST TRADE DOLLARS   "quite bluntly, i think it's a
      scam. patient care has suffered because
      we have to write it off. we're a going
      concern like any other business. "
      (TRACK)
          COMPANY OWNER ██████████ WON'T
      TALK. BUT THE VICTIMS WILL, AND THE
      LIST SEEMS ENDLESS.

NATS: FOAM CRAFTERS 10-   (TRACK)
          JAMES HOWELL GAVE THE EXCHANGE
      OVER $3,000 WORTH OF HIS FOAM PADDING

SOT: JAMES HOWELL 10-
3,000 LOST TRADE DOLLARS   "they had auctions. i went to one.
      bought $2500 worth of stereo equipment
      that was never delivered. "

      (TRACK)
          THERE WERE FREE BALLOON RIDES FROM
      BILL TAYLOR, WHO ALSO LOST 3,000 TRADE
      DOLLARS.

SOT: BILL TAYLOR 12-
3,000 LOST TRADE DOLLARS   "exchange enterprises had gone
      in, sold the account, then immediately
      plundered the account..... so there was
SOT: ROBBIE ROBINSON 8-   nothing left for exchange members. "
23,000 LOST BARTER DOLLARS
      "they turned it into cash to pay
      personal bills, salaries, rent. that's
      not the way it's supposed to be. "

      (TRACK)
          ROBBIE ROBINSON HAS BEEN IN

Figure 14.2 (Continued)

willis   Mon Oct 8 16 00 page 3

TRADE FOR YEARS, WITH A HOUSEFUL OF
BARTER GOODS. BUT HE SAYS HE LOST BIG
WITH EXCHANGE ENTERPRISES.

SOT: ROBBIE ROBINSON 8-

"they had a great big sign saying
everything in this showroom can be
bought through barter, no cash
involved, but yet they had all this
stuff in there, but wouldn't let
anybody buy it. "

NATS: PICS OF SHOWROOM

(TRACK)
THESE PICTURES BEAR THAT OUT. ON
THE RACKS, INEXPENSIVE, LOW-QUALITY
MERCHANDISE AVAILABLE TO MEMBERS.
IN THE BACK OF THE WAREHOUSE,
STACKS OF MORE EXPENSIVE GOODS THAT
MEMBERS SAY ▮▮▮▮▮▮▮▮▮▮▮ REFUSED TO
GIVE THEM ACCESS TO.

BUT THOSE GOODS WERE APPARENTLY
BEING CONVERTED TO CASH BY ▮▮▮▮
▮▮▮▮▮, WHO WAS ALSO REPORTEDLY SELLING
BARTER DOLLARS TO FRIENDS AND
ASSOCIATES FOR CUT-RATE PRICES. . AS LOW
AS A DIME APIECE.

NATS: ▮▮▮▮▮▮▮▮▮▮   6-

▮▮▮▮▮▮▮▮▮▮▮▮▮▮▮▮▮▮▮▮▮▮▮▮▮▮▮▮

(TRACK)
TOMORROW, THE STORY OF LOCATING
▮▮▮▮▮▮▮▮▮▮▮▮ THROUGH A TRAIL OF
DISCONNECTED PHONE LINES, VACANT
BUSINESS ADDRESSES, AND ANGRY
CREDITORS.

LIVE TAC:

"we'll also hear from people who
bought trade dollars for rock-bottom
prices, and details on how ▮▮▮▮▮▮▮▮
turned barter merchandise into
cash...merchandise the members say
rightfully belonged to them. "

Figure 14.2 (Continued)

```
willis    Mon Oct  8 15 59   page  1

PAGE ANCR STORY              FROM   WRITER  VIDEO          * TAPE TIME VIOLATOR
         BARTER  PT 3                                            3 33
================================================================================
```

```
    ANCHOR LEAD                      EXCHANGE ENTERPRISES  WE'VE BEEN
                            REPORTING THIS WEEK ON ANGRY MEMBERS OF
                            THIS BARTER CLUB WHO SAY THEY GAVE
                            GOODS AND SERVICES IN GOOD FAITH, ONLY
                            TO FIND THE BARTER DOLLARS RECEIVED IN
                            RETURN WERE VIRTUALLY WORTHLESS.
                                     FOR MANY OF THOSE MEMBERS, FINDING
                            THE OWNER OF THE EXCHANGE HAS BEEN AN
                            EXERCISE IN FUTILITY, MAKING IT ALMOST
                            IMPOSSIBLE TO REDEEM THEIR BARTER
                            DOLLARS.
    DOUBLE BOXES                     TONIGHT, CONTACT 8'S BRAD WILLIS
                            TRACES THE OWNER AND HIS ACTIVITIES AS
                            HIS SERIES CONTINUES.
    LIVE NEWSROOM                    HIS NAME IS ████████, AND HE'S
                            LEFT A TRAIL OF UNPAID BILLS, ANGRY
                            CREDITORS, DISCONNECTED TELEPHONES AND
                            VACANT BUSINESS ADDRESSES.
                                     BUT HE CONTINUES TO OPERATE THE
                            BARTER EXCHANGE, NOW AT A NEW DALLAS
                            LOCATION. STILL, CREDITORS ARE HAVING
                            TROUBLE FINDING HIM.


    SOT:BRIAN WHITE 6-               "he owes me $400 and 3,000 trade
    3,000 LOST BARTER DOLLARS   units. "

    SOT:MIKE COFFMAN 1-
    8,000 LOST BARTER DOLLARS        "i've got a bad feeling for 'em
                            i've got $8,000 i've never been able to
                            spend with 'em. "

    SOT:ROBBIE ROBINSON 8-
    23,000 LOST TRADE DOLLARS

                                     "i think ████████ is getting
                            out all the merchandise he can, milking
                            it dry, coming in and raping the
                            system. "

                            (TRACK)
                                     ████████:OWNER OF EXCHANGE
                            ENTERPRISES. AS THE VICTIMS OF HIS
                            BARTER EXCHANGE WERE MOUNTING, ████
                            WAS MOVING FAST...CHANGING LOCATIONS,
                            LEAVING A TRAIL OF UNPAID BILLS,
    NATSIG 1"               DISCONNECTED PHONES, ANGRY CREDITORS


                            (TRACK)
                                     MOST RECENTLY, ████████ AND
                            EXCHANGE ENTERPRISE WERE EVICTED FROM
                            THIS RICHARDSON OFFICE COMPLEX AFTER
                            IT WAS DETERMINED THE BARTER DOLLARS
                            GIVEN FOR RENT WERE VIRTUALLY
                            WORTHLESS. THE LANDLORD  STRATOTECH
```

Figure 14.2 (Continued)

```
willis    Mon Oct  8 15:59  page  2
                                         SAYS ▮▮▮▮▮▮▮▮▮ EVEN RAN UP AN
                                         UNAUTHORIZED $4,000 LONG DISTANCE PHONE
                                         BILL.
     NATS:ANGRY CREDITORS 6

                                                    (TRACK)
                                                WHEN WE FOUND THE NEW LOCATION, IN
                                         DALLAS, WE ALSO FOUND ANGRY CREDITORS
                                         TRYING TO TRACK DOWN ▮▮▮▮▮▮▮▮▮... AND
                                         EXCHANGE ENTERPRISE BARTER AGENT ▮▮▮
     SOT:▮▮▮▮▮▮▮▮▮▮▮▮                     ▮▮▮▮▮ WHO TRIED TO STOP THE CREDITORS
                                         FROM TALKING TO US.


                                                 (yells at creditors in threatening
                                         manner, refuses to talk to us, then
                                         says to one man: "i think you better
                                         watch what you're saying...")

                                         (TRACK)
                                                RANDY STALEY DID CARPET WORK FOR
                                         EXCHANGE ENTERPRISES.
     SOT:RANDY STALEY 6-
     IS OWED $400                                "i'm waiting to get my money, over
                                         $400,i don't like it a bit, i did a
                                         class job, i want my money, he's
                                         supposed to meet me here, now i hear
                                         about this ▮▮▮▮▮▮▮ character, i'm
                                         getting the runaround."


                                         (TRACK)
                                                BRIAN WHITE WORKED SEVERAL MONTHS
                                         FOR ▮▮▮▮▮▮▮▮▮. NOW, HE SAYS, HE
                                         CAN'T COLLECT $400 CASH AND 3,000 TRADE
                                         DOLLARS.

     SOT:BRIAN WHITE 6-
     $400 PLUS 3,000 BARTER DOLLARS              "i don't like it, i want to do
                                         something about it to get my money
                                         back."


                                         (TRACK)
                                         ▮▮▮▮▮▮▮▮▮▮ NEVER SHOWED WHILE
                                         THESE MEN WERE WAITING, BUT DID COME TO
                                         THE OFFICE SEVERAL HOURS LATER.

     NATS:▮▮▮▮▮▮▮▮▮▮
     EXCHANGE ENTERPRISES                     (refuses interview)


                                         (TRACK)
                                                DESPITE HIS REFUSAL TO TALK,
                                         WE'VE LEARNED SEVERAL THINGS ABOUT
                                         ▮▮▮▮▮▮▮▮. HE HAS OWNED TWO OTHER
                                         EXCHANGES IN IDAHO AND CALIFORNIA THAT
                                         RAN INTO SERIOUS PROBLEMS
                                                IN DALLAS ,WHILE MEMBERS WERE
                                         COMPLAINING THAT THERE WERE NO GOODS OR
                                         SERVICES AVAILABLE, ▮▮▮▮▮▮▮▮ WAS
```

Figure 14.2 (Continued)

willis   Mon Oct 8 15:59 page 3

SELLING TRADE DOLLARS FOR CUT-RATE
PRICES TO PEOPLE LIKE DON GROGAN, OWNER
OF A GUN AND TACKLE SHOP, WHO BOUGHT
20,000 TRADE DOLLARS FOR 5,000
CASH....TRADE DOLLARS SUPPOSED TO BE
WORTH A FULL DOLLAR APIECE

SOT:DON GROGAN 2-
PAID CASH FOR TRADE DOLLARS

"well that's something we did some
time ago from ▮▮▮▮▮▮▮▮▮▮ "

(TRACK)
▮▮▮▮▮▮▮▮▮▮ ALSO CONFISCATED
BARTER DOLLARS FROM MEMBERS LIKE ROBBIE
ROBINSON WHO REFUSED TO PAY CASH FOR
MEMBERSHIP RENEWAL.

SOT:ROBBIE ROBINSON 8-
BARTER DOLLARS CONFISCATED

"they confiscated 15,000 credits
from me saying i didnt pay the
membership fee."

(TRACK)
AND ACCORDING TO MIKE COFFMAN,
EXCHANGE ENTERPRISES WAS TELLING NEW
MEMBERS HOW TO AVOID REPORTING THEIR
TRANSACTIONS TO INTERNAL REVENUE, AS
REQUIRED BY LAW.

SOT:MIKE COFFMAN 1-
LOST 8,000 BARTER DOLLARS

"when they come out and make their
little sales pitch, they tell you what
you can and can't do. then they tell
you how to get around what you're not
supposed to do."

(TRACK)
NOW ADD TO ALL OF THIS MERCHANDISE
BEING LIQUIDATED AT FLEA MARKETS, AND
MEMBERS BEING GIVEN GEMS THAT PROVED TO
BE ALMOST WORTHLESS. MORE ON THAT
TOMORROW NIGHT IN OUR FINAL REPORT.

LIVE TAG:

"we'll also talk to perhaps the
biggest trader with exchange
enterprises who claims he was sold
trade units for a dime on the dollar.

Figure 14.2 (Continued)

```
willis      Mon Oct  8 15 58   page  1

PAGE ANCR STORY            FROM  WRITER  VIDEO              4 TAPE TIME VIOLATOR
10/9/84   BARTER PART 4          willi                           3 25   c8
```

ANCHOR LEAD	WHAT WENT WRONG? WHY WERE THE GOODS AND SERVICES PROMISED BY A DALLAS BARTER EXCHANGE NO LONGER AVAILABLE TO ITS MEMBERS?
	MANY OF THOSE MEMBERS FEEL THE MERCHANDISE THEY GAVE THE EXCHANGE HAD TO GO SOMEWHERE.
DOUBLE BOXES	CONTACT 8'S BRAD WILLIS NOW CONCLUDES HIS SERIES ON THE CONTROVERSY SURROUNDING EXCHANGE ENTERPRISES
LIVE NEWSROOM	OUR INVESTIGATION SHOWS THAT EXCHANGE ENTERPRISES OWNER, ███████, WAS SELLING BARTER MERCHANDISE FOR CASH AT FLEA MARKETS. HE WAS SELLING BARTER UNITS FOR AS LITTLE AS A DIME ON THE DOLLAR TO CERTAIN FRIENDS AND ASSOCIATES, AND HE WAS OFFERING SOME ANGRY MEMBERS GEMSTONES THAT PROVED TO BE WORTH VERY LITTLE.
	(TRACK) IT WAS A CASE OF RUNAWAY INFLATION. BARTER DOLLARS WERE BECOMING VIRTUALLY WORTHLESS, AND THE VICTIM LIST WAS GROWING.
SOT:ROBBIE ROBINSON 8- LOST 23,000 TRADE DOLLARS	"i've got a lawsuit against exchange enterprises for $23,000.
	(TRACK) BUT WHILE PEOPLE LIKE ROBBIE ROBINSON WERE LOSING, EXCHANGE ENTERPRISES OWNER ███████, AND A FEW OTHERS WERE MAKING OUT.
NATSIG 1"	(TRACK)
	THIS DOCUMENT IS A LEDGER DETAILING WHO HELD BARTER DOLLARS WITH EXCHANGE ENTERPRISES. HUNDREDS OF MEMBERS HOLDING OVER ONE MILLION DOLLARS WORTH OF BARTER UNITS FAST BECOMING WORTHLESS.
	BUT THERE ARE ALSO A FEW NEGATIVE BALANCES. THAT MEANS GOODS AND SERVICES TAKEN OUT OF THE EXCHANGE AND NOTHING PROVIDED IN RETURN.
	FOR INSTANCE: BOISE EXCHANGE, OVER 70,000 NEGATIVE TRADE DOLLARS. IT'S AN IDAHO TRADE COMPANY ONCE OWNED BY ███████, WHO ALSO SHOWED A NEGATIVE BALANCE OF SEVERAL THOUSAND

Figure 14.2 (Continued)

willis   Mon Oct 8 15 58 page 2

DOLLARS WITH HIS DALLAS EXCHANGE
          MEANWHILE, MEMBERS LIKE JEAN QUICK
WERE DESPERATELY TRYING TO REDEEM THEIR
POSITIVE TRADE BALANCES WITH ████.

SOT:JEAN QUICK 8-
LOST 3,000 BARTER DOLLARS

"he said he could sell us gems for
half the appraisal."

(TRACK)
          ██████████ OFFERED HER GEMS,
SAPPHIRES WITH AN APPRAISED VALUE OF
$3,000. WE TOOK THEM TO FINE JEWELER
CHARLES YATER.

SOT:CHARLES YATER 11-
FINE JEWELER

"i would say in excess of $65 they
were completely taken."

(TRACK) BUT WHAT ABOUT THE APPRAISAL
FROM ████████████ WHO PROVIDED THE
GEMS TO THE EXCHANGE?

SOT:YATER AGAIN 11-

"it's the most fictitious
statement i've ever heard in my life."

(TRACK)
          ██████████████, LOCATED AT THE
WORLD TRADE CENTER, HAS NO COMMENT ON
THE APPRAISALS,,, BUT A COMPANY
OFFICIAL DID ADMIT BELONGING TO THE
EXCHANGE AND TRADING THE GEMS FOR
BARTER DOLLARS.
          THOSE GEMS IN TURN WERE BARTERED
TO A COMPANY CALLED OLIVE CROWN.
IT'S ON THE BOOKS TOO, A NEGATIVE
BALANCE OF OVER $40,000.

STANDUP: 13-

"as it turns out, olive crown has
been in the business of liquidating
merchandise at flea markets. the
company is owned by john smith, the
very same man who at one time had a
negative trade balance with exchange
enterprises of almost half a million
dollars."

          (TRACK)
          SMITH TELLS US HE TURNED HUNDREDS
OF THOUSANDS OF DOLLARS WORTH OF THOSE
GEMS BACK TO ████████████ AFTER
REALIZING THE APPRAISALS WERE PHONY.

SOT:JOHN SMITH 14-
OLIVE CROWN

"i'd say they're false. overdone
20,30,40,50 times."

(TRACK)
          SMITH, WHO SAYS HE ACTUALLY LOST
MONEY IN THE END, OPENLY ADMITS THAT
████████████ SOLD HIM BARTER CREDITS
FOR A DIME ON THE DOLLAR, AND HAD HIM

Figure 14.2 (Continued)

willis   Mon Oct 8 15:58 page 3

                                         LIQUIDATE GOODS AT FLEA MARKETS

SOT:SMITH AGAIN   14-   " i would say at flea markets that
                                         ████ did furnish some items for cash
                                         conversion. "

                                         (TRACK)
                                             THAT MEANS ████████ TOOK
                                         BARTER GOODS THAT SHOULD HAVE BEEN MADE
                                         AVAILABLE TO MEMBERS, AND SOLD THEM FOR
                                         CASH INSTEAD.
                                             THIS WHILE PEOPLE LIKE JEAN QUICK
                                         WERE GETTING CHEAP GEMS WITH INFLATED
                                         APPRAISALS, WHILE PEOPLE LIKE ROBBIE
                                         ROBINSON WERE GIVING THEIR GOODS TO
                                         ████████ IN GOOD FAITH.

SOT:ROBBIE ROBINSON 8-   "he's taking everything people in
23,000 BARTER DOLLARS LOST   the exchange will give, he's giving
                                         very little back. "

SOT:JEAN QUICK 8-   "he lied to us, as i'm sure he lied to
3,000 LOST BARTER DOLLARS   many people and people like that should
                                         not be able to be in business. "

              LIVE TAG'   AGAIN, ████████ HAS REFUSED TO
                                         COMMENT. WE DO KNOW THE ATTORNEY
                                         GENERAL IS NOW INVESTIGATING. WE'LL LET
                                         YOU KNOW WHAT HAPPENS.

Figure 14.2 (Continued)

Beginning on the next page is a portion of another documentary script from the "Cousteau Odyssey" series. It reflects both the different type of documentary, a nature production, shot entirely on location, and the fact that the entire production was completely recorded before airing. The script was also undoubtedly written after the fact—after the recording was completed.

Rod Serling is the primary narrator; in this script, only his voice is heard—(OFF-CAMERA). Cousteau is used both as performer, conversing and interacting with his crew and the dolphins, and as narrator—a technique we discussed in Chapter 6.

Additional Considerations

In preparing the final production the writer should consider all the requirements of an effective presentation—purpose, gratifications, structure, aural style—in short, all the principles of good writing. In particular, however, the writer should use techniques that are the logical extensions of the unique characteristics of the documentary—extensive use of actuality material and a minimal dependence on narration. In addition, the writer should be careful about editorializing and about re-creating material.

Use Actualities and Sound Bites

Audience involvement, which we seek in the documentary, comes from being able to experience as closely as possible the situations in which the participants are found. For the viewers, that vicarious experience is transmitted through the video screen by the use of actualities. Sound bites, which are the actual words of participants, are better than the words of the reporter-announcer in this regard, but they are still not as powerful as the actions and natural sounds of the documented activity.

Here the documentary again contrasts with the writing of news. The most efficient method of news exposition—that is, the method that provides the clearest statement of the news story in the briefest period of time—is through narration. However, in order to provide variety and maintain audience interest, writers and producers will insert brief actualities within the narrated story. (This technique is developed at some length in Chapter 12.)

The documentary, in contrast, uses extended actualities, a much higher proportion of actuality in relation to the amount of description, narration, and commentary. Ideally, a documentary would be constructed totally from actualities. All the visual sequences would be "documentation," the actual scenes at the actual locations. And the sound track would be made up entirely of the actual voices of the people involved and the actual sound effects present at the scene. In practice, however, some supplemental visual material and some narrative commentary are usually required.

The contrast between news and documentary might be summarized this way: In news the actualities support the spoken narrative story, while in the well-written documentary the narrative supports the actualities.

METROMEDIA PRODUCERS CORPORATION
8544 SUNSET BOULEVARD
HOLLYWOOD, CALIFORNIA 90069
TEL: 213-652-7075

DATE   February 9, 1972   PAGE   1.
PRODUCTION   Dolphins
PRODUCTION NO.
PREPARED BY
ROUGH: REVISED: FINAL: XX

V I D E O	A U D I O
	PROLOGUE
DOLPHIN IN LAGOON (DOLLY) SWIMS UNDER DIVING BOARD	JEAN (SYNC) Over here, Dolly. Come on. SERLING Free to join its own kind, this dolphin has chosen human companionship. JEAN (SYNC) Come on, now. Tell me, are you a good girl? DOLPHIN (SYNC) That's right.
CLOSE-JEAN	JEAN (SYNC) Good girl, come on.
CLOSE-DOLLY	DOLPHIN (SYNC) Okay...
INTERCUT JEAN-DOLLY	JEAN (SYNC) Are you a pretty girl? Pretty girl? DOLPHIN (SYNC) Awww.... JEAN (SYNC) (laughs) Well, I don't know what that was for. DIP FOR: SERLING
DOLPHIN MAKES SOUNDS	Between Jean Asbury of Florida and this dolphin that came to visit and out of affection stayed -- there is kinship, and communication.

MPC Form 313 (12-68)

Figure 14.3
Source: Copyright © 1984 The Cousteau Society, Inc., a nonprofit, membership-supported organization located at 930 W. 21st Street, Norfolk, VA 23517. Annual dues are $20 for an Individual Membership and $28 for a Family Membership.

METROMEDIA PRODUCERS CORPORATION
8544 SUNSET BOULEVARD
HOLLYWOOD, CALIFORNIA 90069
TEL: 213·652·7075

DATE
PRODUCTION
PRODUCTION NO.
PREPARED BY
ROUGH: REVISED: FINAL:

PAGE 2

VIDEO	AUDIO
DOLLY KISSES JEAN	JEAN (SYNC) Give me another kiss, Dolly? Give your mommy another kiss? (DOLPHIN KISSES HER) Ohhh, beautiful. Juicy, but beautiful. (Jean applauds) You're a good girl! DOLPHIN (SYNC) Thank you, thank you.
DOLLY PLAYS COY. DUCKS UNDER WATER	
	SERLING
DOLPHIN FOLLOWS ZODIAC, LEAPS IN RESPONSE TO HAND SIGNALS	We are familiar with the trained dolphin -- those put on display -- taught to mimic
DOLPHIN BODY SURFS	the human voice -- and to respond to man's
LAST LEAP	signals, and applause. (BEAT) But there
U/W WILD DOLPHIN SWIM	are great herds of dolphins still living in
U/W OBSERVATION PORT AND SWIMMING DOLPHINS	freedom. (BEAT) Too swift to be easily observed, little is known about the dolphin in the wild. This air-breathing mammal was once
T/S DOLPHIN SWIM	an earth-bound animal -- but sixty million years ago he fled the confines of land for the wide waters of open seas -- and became the legendary friends of Gods, men and children.

MPC Form 313 (12·68)

Figure 14.3 (Continued)

METROMEDIA PRODUCERS CORPORATION	DATE	PAGE 3
8544 SUNSET BOULEVARD	PRODUCTION	
HOLLYWOOD CALIFORNIA 90069	PRODUCTION NO.	
TEL: 213-652-7075	PREPARED BY	
	ROUGH: REVISED: FINAL:	

V I D E O	A U D I O
	SERLING (CONTINUED) Now, in the dolphin's natural domain, Captain Cousteau, and divers of Calypso would explore the continuing relationship between man and dolphin -- a relationship that has inspired philosophers and poets from the beginning of recorded time. END OF PROLOGUE
U/W DOLPHIN SWIM	

MPC Form 313 (12-68)

Figure 14.3 (Continued)

METROMEDIA PRODUCERS CORPORATION
6544 SUNSET BOULEVARD
HOLLYWOOD, CALIFORNIA 90069
TEL: 213-652-7075

DATE   PAGE 4
PRODUCTION
PRODUCTION NO.
PREPARED BY
ROUGH: REVISED: FINAL:

V I D E O	A U D I O
	ACT ONE
	SERLING
CALYPSO-GIBRALTAR	In pursuit of dolphins -- Calypso cruises the waters of the Strait of Gibraltar, off the coast of Spain.
	COUSTEAU (FRENCH SYNC) Bon, vous tournez la? Hein? Bon.
	SIROT (FRENCH SYNC) Oui.
SOUND	COUSTEAU (FRENCH SYNC) Alors, Philippe, nous approchons!
JYC-PILOT HOUSE	DIP FOR: SERLING As they approach a dolphin herd, Captain Cousteau alerts the crew to prepare for filming.
PUSH IN-DISTANT HERD	(MUSIC AND EFFECTS IN THE CLEAR)
JYC AND FALCO	COUSTEAU (FRENCH SYNC) Well, listen, I think it's time to go. FALCO (FRENCH SYNC) Yes.

MPC Form 313 (12-68)

Figure 14.3 (Continued)

METROMEDIA PRODUCERS CORPORATION
8144 SUNSET BOULEVARD
HOLLYWOOD, CALIFORNIA 90069
TEL. 213-652-7075

DATE   PAGE   4A
PRODUCTION
PRODUCTION NO.
PREPARED BY
ROUGH: REVISED: FINAL:

V I D E O	A U D I O
	COUSTEAU (FRENCH SYNC)
	Go to the bow and I shall stay in contact with you.
	DIP FOR:
	SERLING
	Cousteau and diving supervisor, Albert Falco,
	also plan to collect a dolphin, for study
	at sea.
DOLPHINS-JYC LOOKS	
	COUSTEAU
	Filming free dolphins is a challenge. They are too
	swift for divers to approach them. They never
DOLPHINS SWIM -"TALK"	stay behind or alongside a ship -- but they are
	attracted to the bow as to a magnet. To Calypso,
EXTENSION OF CALYPSO	we have attached an extension with an underwater
	camera -- aimed backward -- toward the
	nose of the ship. (BEAT) We hope the extension
	camera will reveal dolphins swimming head on --
PUSH IN ON EXTENSION	never before achieved on film.
	Meanwhile, frolicking hitchhikers come from all
	directions, but the main herd continues to outrun
	the ship, its underwater camera boom, and all othe
CREW OBSERVE DOLPHINS	protruding contraptions.

MPC form 313 (12 68)

Figure 14.3 (Continued)

METROMEDIA PRODUCERS CORPORATION
8544 SUNSET BOULEVARD
HOLLYWOOD. CALIFORNIA 90069
TEL: 213-652-7075

DATE
PRODUCTION
PRODUCTION NO.
PREPARED BY
ROUGH: REVISED: FINAL:

PAGE   5

V I D E O	A U D I O
CU-JYC. REVEAL SIROT JYC MOVES TO TV ROOM	COUSTEAU (FRENCH SYNC) Ah oui, oui les voila qui arrivent je les vois. Ah oui, y en a d'autres qui arrivent je les vois. Vous les apercevez sur l' ecran?
JYC AND OMER VIEW	OMER (FRENCH SYNC) No, not yet Captain. DIP FOR: SERLING As skipper Philippe Sirot pursues them, Cousteau fears that the new extension camera might frighten the dolphins away. (BEAT) COUSTEAU (FRENCH SYNC) Well, I am going to go and see. OMER (FRENCH SYNC) Well, well magnificent. COUSTEAU (FRENCH SYNC) I am coming. DIP FOR: SERLING But the system devised by underwater cameraman Yves Omer works! Now, for the first time, front view shots of dolphins swimming freely toward camera!

MPC Form 313 (12-68)

Figure 14.3 (Continued)

METROMEDIA PRODUCERS CORPORATION
8544 SUNSET BOULEVARD
HOLLYWOOD, CALIFORNIA 90069
TEL: 213-652-7075

DATE   PAGE 5A
PRODUCTION
PRODUCTION NO.
PREPARED BY
ROUGH: REVISED: FINAL:

V I D E O	A U D I O
	OMER (FRENCH SYNC)
	Look!
	COUSTEAU (FRENCH SYNC)
	Yes, here we can see them very well. Your system is working.
	OMER (FRENCH SYNC)
	Yes.
	COUSTEAU (FRENCH SYNC)
	There are many of them.
	OMER (FRENCH SYNC)
	Yes, they are going down on the screen.
	COUSTEAU (FRENCH SYNC)
	Yes.
	SERLING
DOLPHIN SWIM TOWARD EXTENSION CAMERA	Another camera mounted on the hull reveals dolphins venturing between the bow and the extension camera.

MPC Form 313 (12-68)

Figure 14.3 (Continued)

| METROMEDIA PRODUCERS CORPORATION
8544 SUNSET BOULEVARD
HOLLYWOOD, CALIFORNIA 90069
TEL: 213-652-7075 | DATE
PRODUCTION
PRODUCTION NO.
PREPARED BY
ROUGH: REVISED: FINAL: | PAGE 6 |

V I D E O	A U D I O
	COUSTEAU
DOLPHIN SWIM TOWARD CAMERA	Now we can observe that the wise dolphin never swims straight ahead of the boat but cautiously leans from side to side, ready to drop off if
OBSERVATION PORT	threatened. (BEAT) From the observation port, the animals are identified as the saddle-back dolphin, one of 50 dolphin species belonging to the whale family. (BEAT) The dolphin is "the
U/W SHOTS	littlest whale", but unlike its endangered brother, the sperm whale, for the time being, he thrives in the sea. (BEAT) Ever
MEN TAKE PICTURES	since they guided the vessels of the earliest
TOP SHOTS AND UNDERWATER	settlers to Crete more than 3000 years B.C. dolphins have accompanied ships. Are they in quest of man's friendship? Or do they merely come to play...?
T/S DOLPHIN SWIM	(MUSIC AND EFFECTS IN THE CLEAR)
	SERLING
CLOSE, JYC WHEELHOUSE WITH WALKIE TALKIE	There are now enough dolphins off the bow to attempt the next phase of the operation -- isolation of a dolphin from the herd.

MPC Form 313 (12-68)

Figure 14.3 (Continued)

METROMEDIA PRODUCERS CORPORATION
8544 SUNSET BOULEVARD
HOLLYWOOD, CALIFORNIA 90069
TEL: 213-652-7075

DATE   PAGE   6a
PRODUCTION
PRODUCTION NO.
PREPARED BY
ROUGH: REVISED: FINAL:

V I D E O	A U D I O
	JYC (FRENCH SYNC) Oh y en a un paquet! Hein? OMER (FRENCH SYNC) Oh, la la! SIROT (FRENCH SYNC) COUSTEAU (FRENCH SYNC) Allo plage avant! Allo plage avant! Je crois que c'est le moment maintenant. DIP FOR:

MPC Form 313 (12-68)

Figure 14.3 (Continued)

METROMEDIA PRODUCERS CORPORATION
8544 SUNSET BOULEVARD
HOLLYWOOD, CALIFORNIA 90069
TEL 213-652-7075

DATE
PRODUCTION
PRODUCTION NO.
PREPARED BY
ROUGH: REVISED: FINAL:

PAGE 7

V I D E O	A U D I O
	SERLING
FALCO HURRIES TO PLAT-FORM	Falco is to be the captor. He hurries into position on the platform directly above the dolphins riding the bow wave on starboard.
FALCO POV DOLPHIN	(MUSIC AND EFFECTS IN THE CLEAR)
MAN PASSES NET TO FALCO	The plan is to net a dolphin at full speed. Upon contact, the small net will break away from the metal fork that holds it and gently enwrap the dolphin. (BEAT) A buoy with a
DOLPHIN BY SHIP	line attached is tossed to the crew in the ZODIAC. (BEAT) The line is tied to the net,
PAN ZODIAC TO NET	so that the crew will be able to haul the animal into the Zodiac -- out of the way of the propellers of the on-coming Calypso.
INTERCUT-CALYPSO ZODIAC (WALKIE TALKIE)	In the rising sea, the Zodiac has difficulty keeping up with its mother ship. (BEAT)
JYC AND FALCO	Dolphins generally cruise at 8 or 10 knotts --
DOLPHINS SWIM	but are capable of bursts of speed up to 35 miles an hour.
	(cont'd...)

MPC Form 313 (12-6 8)

Figure 14.3 (Continued)

METROMEDIA PRODUCERS CORPORATION
8544 SUNSET BOULEVARD
HOLLYWOOD, CALIFORNIA 90069
TEL: 213-652-7075

DATE   PAGE   7A
PRODUCTION
PRODUCTION NO.
PREPARED BY
ROUGH: REVISED: FINAL:

V I D E O	A U D I O

FALCO (FRENCH SYNC O.S.)
Have the Zodiac come

SIROT (FRENCH SYNC)
Zodiac, Zodiac. From the front, you can go
as soon as you are ready; we are only waiting
for you.

COUSTEAU (FRENCH SYNC)
Is it a big one?

FALCO (FRENCH SYNC)
That's too small

VOICE O.S. (FRENCH SYNC)
Well, Bebert's in position (ready)

MPC Form 313 (12-68)

Figure 14.3 (Continued)

METROMEDIA PRODUCERS CORPORATION
6430 SUNSET BOULEVARD
HOLLYWOOD, CALIFORNIA 90069
TEL: 213-652-7075

DATE
PRODUCTION
PRODUCTION NO.
PREPARED BY
ROUGH: REVISED: FINAL:

PAGE 8.

V I D E O	A U D I O
	SERLING (CONTINUED)
DOLPHINS GLIDE	Continually changing course, they are elusive targets. Falco must carefully pick his dolphin, and throw the net immediately ahead of it so that he does not hit the dolphin with the net's metal fork.
INTERCUT ACTION	(MUSIC AND EFFECTS IN THE CLEAR)
	FALCO (FRENCH SYNC)
PAN-JYC, FALCO TO NET AND DOLPHIN	Under thw bow! (Seus le treave) DIP FOR:
SEVERAL SHOTS- THEN "STRIKE"	(MUSIC AND EFFECTS IN THE CLEAR)
	SERLING
FORK ON LINE	It's a miss! They will have to quickly
CU-JYC, ACTION SHOTS	retrieve the fork and try again before the herd is scattered.
	CHEVLIN (FRENCH SYNC)
MAN RUNS FROM BOW TO CHEVLIN AT WHEEL	They must be over there. CHURCH (FRENCH SYNC) Yes, yes.
	COUSTEAU
T/S HERD SKIPS, FLEES	Alarmed, most of the dolphins fly away like arrows through the sea. It is impossible to pursue them. But luckily a few have chosen to
JYC LOOKS DOWN	remain riding our bow.

MPC Form 313 (12-68)

Figure 14.3 (Continued)

METROMEDIA PRODUCERS CORPORATION
8544 SUNSET BOULEVARD
HOLLYWOOD, CALIFORNIA 90069
TEL: 213-652-7075

DATE   PAGE   9
PRODUCTION
PRODUCTION NO.
PREPARED BY
ROUGH: REVISED: FINAL:

VIDEO	AUDIO
JYC, FALCO AND DOLPHIN BOUNCING ZODIAC	(MUSIC AND EFFECTS IN THE CLEAR) SERLING
FALCO STRIKES-HE AND JYC LOOK	The throw is good!
	CHURCH AND CHEVLIN (FRENCH SYNC)
INT. WHEELHOUSE WHEEL TURNED, ENGINES CUT	Il y a! Il y a!
	SERLING
	Calypso is stopped to avoid hitting the
	entangled dolphin.
PAN ZODIAC TO JYC AND FALCO WHO GIVES ORDERS	(MUSIC AND EFFECTS IN THE CLEAR) SERLING
ZODIAC CREW HAUL IN DOLPHIN	The catch is clean -- and harmless -- to the
	dolphin. It is now up to the men in the
	Zodiac to slowly haul in and calm this highly
	sensitive creature .
TIEUP-ZODIAC AND CALYPSO	(MUSIC AND EFFECTS IN THE CEARL)
	COUSTEAU
U/W DOLPHIN IN NET	Our dolphin is bewildered, and gives up easily
	to man. In ancient times it was believed that
	dolphins were once men. Within their talented
	flippers are all the bones of our human hands.
	(cont'd...)

MPC Form 313 (12-68)

Figure 14.3 (Continued)

METROMEDIA PRODUCERS CORPORATION
8544 SUNSET BOULEVARD
HOLLYWOOD, CALIFORNIA 90069
TEL: 213-652-7075

DATE
PRODUCTION
PRODUCTION NO.
PREPARED BY
ROUGH: REVISED: FINAL:

PAGE 10

VIDEO	AUDIO
	COUSTEAU (CONTINUED)
	And I wonder about her brain, as large as ours, and in some ways superior... We appear to be fundamentally equal, but can we ever communicate?
MEN LOAD DOLPHIN	
	SERLING
ZODIAC MOVES OFF	Treated with care, the dolphin will now be delivered beside Calypso, where experiments will take place.
	COUSTEAU
DOLPHIN WET DOWN IN BOAT	Our highly emotive dolphin has been catapulted from the exuberance of play to captivity. Yet, she seems inclined to trust in us -- a trust we must not betray.
BERNARD "SOOTHES" DOLPHIN	(MUSIC AND EFFECTS IN THE CLEAR)
	END OF ACT ONE

MPC Form 313 (12-68)

Figure 14.3 (Continued)

Minimize Narration

We've already touched on this idea in the preceding section. Whenever possible, use actualities; they are more powerful than the commentary provided by an announcer. But commentary will often be needed *to amplify and clarify the picture*. The requirements of each situation will differ, but here is a generalized rule for using commentary:

> It is bad technique to describe in words exactly what is seen on the screen. . . . On the other hand it is nearly as bad to refer to things that have nothing at all to do with what is on the screen. . . . If the picture is self-evident, no words are needed. But very frequently there are many things that the audience wants to know that are not clear from the visuals alone. *Where* is the scene; *who* are the people in it; *when* is it taking place; *how* does the technical process work? These are questions that commentary should answer, subject to one proviso. Does the audience need to know for the purpose of the film? It is possible to spoil a film by telling the audience too much? If they are likely to *want* to know all these things, well and good—if not, silence is golden.[9]

Silence is not golden, however, in the broadcast documentary. Audiences have come to expect some form of sound almost continuously and become edgy—convinced that the transmission is faulty—if sound disappears for more than just a few seconds. If the actuality sound is not appropriate or available, and if narration is not needed, then consider music, or an "independent" sound track. The latter technique is described by the producer of *Terminus:*

> There are times when the words can be quite independent of the visuals. In *Terminus,* for instance, we made candid recordings in the booking office so that we could hear passengers asking for tickets to various destinations and the ticket clerk's replies. These words we placed over visuals showing quite different station activities—we retained a perfectly free relationship between sound and picture—and of commentary, in the conventional sense, there is none.[10]

Music too can be effective not only in filling gaps in the audio, but in making a positive emotional contribution to the program. The best would be original music, such as the very powerful score by Virgil Thompson for Pere Lorentz's *The Plow That Broke the Plains,* which is now an American classic in its own right. That approach, of course, is very expensive, but an effective musical background can also be culled from recorded music libraries. Or, if the style is appropriate, you may be able to get a local folk music group to perform standard, noncopyright selections which you can use.

When narration is used, the most common approach is that of voiceover narration, in which an off-screen voice reads the commentary. Other techniques are available, however. The narrator might assume the role of a guide or questioner. He or she is then seen on-screen frequently, making comments and asking questions. In that role, the narrator becomes a surrogate for the viewers as they are guided through the content of the presentation.

Another technique uses an on-camera expert who speaks directly to the audience. News documentaries frequently place the reporter in that role. Another variation combines off-camera narration with an on-camera expert to provide a two-voice narration, as in the Cousteau script. It's a technique that is strong in audience involvement.

Yet another variation is that of the overheard conversation. The viewers "listen in" while two experts, or an expert and a subordinate, discuss a process or problem. This approach closely approximates the actuality, and is also good in maintaining audience involvement, if it can be written to appear natural.

Don't Editorialize

We will not have universal agreement from critics, producers, and writing instructors on this point. Many people feel that the public affairs documentary should take an editorial stand on whatever topic it presents.

The point we want to make, however, is that the well-written and presented documentary *need not take an editorial position.* Frequently, in doing the research on a topic and in preparing the treatment for the program, you will find that there is a social injustice involved, and you will want to bring that injustice to light in the program. But don't *tell* the audience what the problem is, and don't *tell* people what they should feel or believe with regard to the issue: *Show* them. *Document* the problem, and *document* proposed solutions. (It is on this ground that we too find fault with programs like "Harvest of Shame," "Hunger in America," and "Selling of the Pentagon." We find them too blatantly editorial because they leave viewers with little opportunity to make up their own minds regarding the issue.)

To return to our program on the elderly poor as an example, you may find that these people really are receiving poor treatment at the hands of their landlords. Don't preach. Don't point out the obvious. And don't tell audience members how terrible the situation is, or what they should be feeling. Frequently there is a backlash in such an approach; audiences resent being talked to in that way. Instead, take advantage of the documentary's ability to involve the audience. Follow some of these elderly people through their activities, as described earlier.

Let the actualities speak for themselves. If the scenes you show have been well chosen, and if the viewers really do have the feeling of being involved in the plight of these unfortunate people, the audience will come willingly to the conclusion you want. Then, in a brief summary to the program, the narrator can channel that emotional reaction and suggest ways in which viewers can make their concerns felt—letters or calls to government agencies, contributions, or whatever is appropriate.

Re-Creation: An Ethical Problem

In shooting and editing the documentation—that is, the raw material for the documentary—we have emphasized the value of using real experiences the audience can respond to in emotional terms. But suppose a particular sequence is not available on film or tape. Perhaps the camera was not there when the event took place, or through an error the footage is unusable. To what extent is it legitimate to re-create a visual sequence?

In the docudrama, or any other historical re-creation by whatever name it is called, the entire program is re-created, dramatized, even though it may be based on carefully researched information. Critics sometimes complain that these programs are not sufficiently accurate historically, but audiences generally understand that these are dramatizations and accept them as such.

On the other hand, the audience watching a documentary will assume that the material is real. To what extent in that situation is re-creation acceptable? In *Terminus,* producer Anstley used a combination of ordinary people and "planted" actors:

> . . . who could be brought in to act the more complex parts, and give point and emphasis to the more difficult sequences. . . .
>
> They each had a part to play, among the ordinary passengers. One was a man who was late and just missed his train—both morning and evening—and retired frustrated to the bar. Then the little lost girl was "planted," although the later tears were genuine enough. The whole thing proved rather much for her. Among the other "planted" actors were, of course, the prisoners on their way to Dartmoor—we shouldn't have been allowed to film real prisoners and reveal their identity.[11]

Another producer was making a program on the blooming of the California desert in the spring, with ". . . flowers blossoming, lizards blinking awake. But the lizards were not cooperative, so [he] stuck them in the refrigerator; when it came time to film, they warmed up appropriately on camera."[12]

Any re-creation involves some dramatization, or perhaps better stated, fictionalization. So what is an acceptable level of fictionalization? When is that level exceeded? When does the staging of an event become distortion? If a simulation or re-creation does take place, is it faithful to the original situation? Or was it staged to support a predetermined editorial position?

We're very good at asking the questions; answering them is another matter. These are ethical judgments. They all touch on the very sensitive issue of editorial discretion. And the answer will have to be: It depends.

In the creative documentary on the musical premiere, there would be little problem in asking the symphony conductor to re-create a scene in which he works out passages of the music on the piano. It is less clear, however, in the public affairs documentary. Is it appropriate to re-create the scene of a handicapped senior citizen struggling up a flophouse stairway? Visually, it's a powerful image, and probably it's faithful to the overall point of view of the documentary. But is it honest?

If the topic of the documentary is controversial, as we have made our program on the elderly poor, then there are likely to be attacks by those holding another opinion on the accuracy and honesty of the presentation. It will do your credibility no good if they are able to prove that you faked even one scene. Be careful.

If the issue is legitimate, and if you approach the documentation with an open mind and not a closed editorial policy, you should be able to document fairly. But if you assume that these hotel managers rent filthy rooms and don't clean up their hotels, and then you can't find the filth and have to scatter a can of garbage down the hall, you have not treated the topic fairly.

A directly parallel situation exists with regard to editing the material to be shown in the documentary. Take care to edit fairly, to show a balanced view of what you saw when you were collecting the visual material in the first place. In recent years, we have seen a number of cases in which documentary producers and the stations and networks that have aired their programs have been sued for libel, or have been the subject of congressional investigation, as a result of charges of biased editing, of taking statements or scenes out of context. It goes beyond the scope of this text to comment on these charges. Nor can we provide any advice that would ensure the writer-producer against similar accusations in the future. If the program investigates a controversial issue, if there is a social wrong to be righted, you may expect attack. Your defense will be the truth, both in the presentation itself and in the process by which you developed the program.*

Radio Documentaries

Thus far our examples have referred exclusively to visual documentation, using film or videotape to collect the images out of which the video documentary is made. The form can be presented on radio as well, but it's not easy to do. If we attempt to apply to radio all the characteristics we set forth as distinguishing the documentary form, then very few radio programs will qualify. Some of these characteristics are very hard to build into a radio program.

It's much more difficult, for example, to get audience involvement in a problem or process when audiences cannot see what's going on. The sounds of an activity without the accompanying visuals do not effectively or accurately place the audience into the situation. Only if audience members have had some prior experience in similar situations will they be able to develop mental images of what is going on, and even then their mental view will be conditioned by their prior experiences and will not likely be accurate in reproducing the image you want to portray in your program.

In describing our program on the elderly urban poor, we have used visual images—struggling up a stairway, rats on the walls. The sounds of these activities are not helpful. The voices of the people who suffer these conditions would help; they can describe their problems and frustrations. But now you're putting together a news interview program, something that is no longer really a documentary.

A radio documentary on the development of a new symphonic work should be possible, since the topic is aural to begin with, but we'll miss those wonderful

---

* One of the disquieting grounds which the Supreme Court now permits claimants in a libel suit to use as part of their suit is to inquire into the "state of mind" of the program's writers and producers, to see if "actual malice" might have been present in the process of writing and editing the program. So we emphasize that the program must be truthful not only in its presentation, but throughout the process of preparation. For a more complete explanation of the background of the Court's actions, and descriptions of the cases involved, a number of reference sources are available. For a concise review, we recommend Sydney Head and Christopher Sterling, *Broadcasting in America,* 5th ed. (Boston: Houghton Mifflin, 1987), pp. 504–506. Two cases that came to trial in 1985, *Westmoreland* v. *CBS,* and *Sharon* v. *Time, Inc.,* are also worth review, although neither provided the definitive statement on libel observers thought might be their outcomes.

images of seeing the composer react to the first performance of his work. We'll have to be content with asking him his reactions afterward. A radio documentary on the preparation of a new ballet, to choose a parallel topic, would be very difficult, and you would probably have to revert to interview and discussion.

Effective radio programs on documentary topics almost always require a considerable amount of narration, another characteristic we tried to avoid in the TV documentary. Narration is necessary to give accurate descriptions, to introduce, and to bridge between whatever sound documentation is to be used.

So although radio programs can be developed in many of the same content areas we have described for the TV documentary, and although they can be equally effective, they must use different techniques in order to be successful. The differences diminish the distinctive qualities of the documentary. Many radio stations that advertise documentaries on local issues are really producing extended news stories or some cross between news and a public affairs interview/discussion program.

The one organization that consistently comes the closest to meeting all the characteristics of the documentary on radio is National Public Radio. The quality of the writing and editing on its "Morning Edition" and "All Things Considered" programs is excellent. The verbal descriptions of locations, events, and people provide strong images for listeners. This script uses an extensive but very descriptive opening narration to set its locale and the topic, and then—to a greater extent than most radio stories—it allows the actual voices of participants to carry the remainder of the story.

MAPLE SUGARING

Noah Adams

At just about the right time, at the time it really needs to, spring begins to come to New England. The snow still falls, but it's softer and wetter. The sun is up earlier and stays later. The frozen ground gets muddy. The nights are still cold and crisp, below freezing, but daytime temperatures climb into the forties and the low fifties. On the snow-covered hillsides, deep inside the sugar maple trees, the sap begins to flow. The sap of a sugar maple contains about 1 or 2 percent sugar. If you drill a hole into the tree, the sap drips out. If you collect the sap and boil it down, you've got maple syrup. Boil it some more, you've got sugar. It takes about thirty-five gallons of sap to make one gallon of syrup. It works out just about like this: Each spring one sugar maple tree will produce enough sap to make one gallon of maple syrup.

In late February, in the Connecticut River valley of Vermont and New Hampshire, the farmers get ready for their first crop of the year. Donald Crane of Washington, New Hampshire, likes to tap a couple of trees early, as a test. Then each day he checks the buckets. A couple of weeks back, in March, Art Silverman stopped by the Crane farm to see how the 1978 season was going to be, to see if the sap was flowing yet.

SFX	(Creaking/groaning/sap dripping beats)
Silverman	Where're the buckets that you have up now?
Crane	They're right here beside the road. You didn't notice them?
Silverman	No.
Crane	You're not very observant.
SFX	(Walking/snow crunching)
Silverman	Let's concentrate on not falling down and not stepping in anything.
Crane	Well, it's a good idea to look down because you have two things in sugarin' that bother your footin'. One's ice. The other's mud.
Silverman	And if you have a few oxen there might be a few other things?
Crane	Well, that's why a farmer never looks up.
SFX	(Bucket sounds/walking)
Crane	I tapped this tree three days ago. See that little icicle right there? That means the tree's willing, but it can't do it. And this one over here is just as dry as can be. You see, this tap is a little more to the west; that one is a little more to the southeast, and it apparently just hasn't got warm enough right here yet. Those trees are froze clear through, you know. So it takes a little time to get 'em loosened up.
SFX	(Tapping sounds/clanking bucket handles)
Adams	For those who are involved in the sugaring, the beginning of spring means about six weeks of hard work for everyone in the family. Someone has to cut the firewood. Someone has to haul the sap buckets. And there's another problem: Almost everyday is laundry day.
First woman	Because maple sap is very sticky, and when it's boiling away it seems like it's a rather nice pretty cloud of white steam coming off the evaporator, and it's very tempting to lean over and kind of smell that steam coming off the evaporator.
Second woman	But, unless you want to look like a candy-coated apple, you don't do it.
First woman	You don't do it. Nope.
Second woman	No.
First woman	No. Because that steam is very sticky. It's pretty and it smells really nice, but it gets on everything—everything! Everything you own smells like maple syrup after a while.
Second woman	Right.
First woman	And it takes so long. The amount of time that they spend preparing the maple syrup doesn't include the hours that those of us who don't tap and collect and boil spend supporting the people that actually do those things. By "supporting" I don't mean just feeding them, but I mean washing their clothes, getting their meals, picking them up, driving them home to sleep for four hours before getting up and driving them back

MORE   MORE   MORE

	up to the sugar house so that they can boil some more. Dealing with meals for lots and lots of people.
Second woman	Hearty meals that are going to be served to all of the people who come help. Instead of pay.
First woman	Regular meals.
Second woman	Regular.
Reporter	That's a lot of work. Is it worth it? Do they make much money?
First woman	Not at all.
Second woman	No.
First woman	They wouldn't do it if they really had to make a living at it, because they wouldn't be able to. Takes too much time. It's a passion, and that's the only reason they're doing it. Something happens when you start tapping a tree and you see little stuff dripping out of it, drip-drip-drip, and then a few days later you pour it out of a can. There's just some magical thing that happens, and they all get addicted.
Second woman	In the springtime, when the trees start to operate, you want to be in on it. You want to watch spring start up right from the beginning. You want to watch the sap starting to run. And during sugaring season, you're just so intimately involved with the coming of spring, it's like you breathe the coming of spring.
Reporter	You forget everything else?
First woman	Yeah. You don't even worry about mud season anymore.
SFX	(Music/tapping/whistling)
Teacher	Can you get maple syrup out of any other tree except a maple tree?
Children	No! No! No!
First child	You can get it out of an oak tree.
Second child	You can only get oak out of oak trees. Eric's being ridiculous.

Conclusion

We began this chapter with two brief quotes that set forth opposing views on what should constitute a documentary. On the one side was the limited "authoritative, journalistic" approach. On the other, the "more personal and idiosyncratic vision of virtually anything with general significance." Those two quotes came from a pertinent and provocative article entitled "The Last, Best Hope for the TV Documentary," by Philip Weiss, which appeared in the November–December 1983 issue of *Channels of Communication* magazine.

The article, and the question it raised as to the proper purpose of the documentary, are based largely on an examination of the work of David Fanning, producer of the acclaimed but controversial series "Frontline," shown on many public television stations. We raise the question again to conclude this chapter because it is a continuing issue that writers for this form will have to face.

At one point in Weiss's article, two of Fanning's programs come under scrutiny. Both were criticized for their irregular content and approach:

Abortion Clinic was an emotionally wrenching verité film about a clinic in Chester, Pennsylvania, featuring graphic shots of two women undergoing abortions. The film contained minimal narration and no authoritative interpretation, but it communicated as a raw experience, in a way that is difficult to put into words, just what an abortion involves and why a woman might choose it. . . . Yet journalists who sought a clear message were disappointed.

Daisy, in turn, seemed almost frothy, with its pop music and the amiable, sometimes flirtatious presence of its distinguished author . . . in intimate range of his subject, a Canadian woman deciding to have a facelift. One critic wondered "what the hell it was doing in this series," although he did marvel at its demonstration of the power of the youth cult. No, *Daisy* was not explicitly about public affairs, but it treated a social question of universal significance in an extraordinarily penetrating and often ironic style.

Moreover, *Daisy* and *Abortion Clinic* apparently played well in the heartland.[13]

You might conclude, as do some of those quoted in Weiss's article, that the documentary form is in decline in spite of, or perhaps because of, such controversial work as Fanning's. At the network level that would seem to be the case, and in the article the words *suffering* and *dying* are used by authoritative sources.

There are other outlets, however, although they are without the financial resources of the national networks. Some local television stations still produce powerful documentaries on local topics. We cite the barter scam series on WFAA as a case in point.

Cable access channels also provide a very available outlet for independent documentary productions. In those cases, production funding usually will have to come from other sources. Corporate production, the topic of our next chapter, is yet another outlet for the documentary writer-producer.

Exercises

1. Prepare a concept statement for one of the following:

   a. A documentary on a creative effort

   b. A nature documentary based on a location (such as a forest or a swamp) or on an animal or plant (unique local butterflies, an endangered plant species, or something similar)

   Choose a real topic with which you are already somewhat familiar or can readily get information, to ease the burden of research.

2. Prepare a three-part minidocumentary series or "special report" on a topic of your choice, but one that might legitimately be found on the 11 P.M. news broadcast of a local TV station. Each segment should be planned for about four minutes of air time. One segment (probably the first, but not necessarily)

is to be completely scripted. The other two should be outlined. For the scripted segment:

a. Follow the appropriate format for television news scriptwriting.

b. Make sure there is ample visual description. What are we supposed to be seeing at all times?

c. If sound bite interviews are used, the questions or the leads to the answer (if the actual question is not to be heard) should be written out completely. (The sound bite itself need not be written word for word, but give a suggestion of what is expected in the answer, and the out-cue. You will have to anticipate much of this, since you wouldn't know for certain what would be said until you actually went on location.)

d. Pay particular attention to the sequential development of the material, and to the use of appropriate and adequate transitions, so the audience will know at all times where the story is leading.

For segments 2 and 3:

a. Write out the open and the close completely.

b. Provide a sequential outline for the remainder of the segment, indicating each major content point to be made, and a general description of the visual material you would try to collect to support each point.

Overall, make sure there is an obvious and logical division of the topic into the three segments; at the same time, each segment will stand on its own. Keep in mind that the less narration, the better. Let the real scenes and people tell the story as much as possible. But be careful to provide sufficient narration so that the audience can follow the progress of the story.

Key Terms and Concepts		
	actualities and sound bites	re-creation (dramatization)
	audience involvement	shot sheet
	concept	slice of life documentary
	docudrama	SOT list
	point of view	treatment

Notes

1. Philip Weiss, "The Last, Best Hope for the TV Documentary," *Channels of Communication,* November–December 1983, p. 86.

2. Dudley Moore, presenting the awards for documentary film production at the 1983 Academy Awards show.

3. W. Hugh Baddeley, *The Technique of Documentary Film Production* (New York: Hastings House, 1963), p. 9. Excerpts reprinted by permission.

4. Edith Efron, "The Great Television Myth," *TV Guide,* May 6, 1967, p. 9.

5. A. William Bluem, *Documentary in American Television* (New York: Hastings House, 1965), p. 104.

6. Iain Blair, "The Making of *Thriller," On Location,* February 1984, pp. 124–125.

7. Baddeley, *The Technique of Documentary Film Production,* p. 24.

8. Ibid., pp. 24–25.

9. Ibid., p. 192.

10. Ibid., p. 197.

11. Ibid., p. 27.

12. Weiss, "The Last, Best Hope for the TV Documentary," p. 85.

13. Weiss, "The Last, Best Hope for the TV Documentary," p. 89.

Chapter 15

Corporate/Instructional Programs

Throughout the earlier chapters of this book, we have emphasized basic principles that underlie all good writing for electronic media. We believe it is both possible and legitimate to generalize on considerations of style, structure, and gratifications, among other things, because there are certain constants in the communication process when radio and television are used as the media for the delivery of the message. Although the content of broadcast messages may change—from news, to drama, to talk, or whatever—the methods of delivery, and the relationship between programs and audiences, remain the same.

In contrast, corporate/instructional programming generally is *not* presented to audiences through broadcast. Instead, the content is most often delivered by some form of closed-circuit system. In that situation, the audience's involvement with the presentation may be changed substantially, and if it is, then so are the writer's concerns. The focus of this chapter, then, differs from previous ones in that we will concentrate on how the writer's approach to the task is affected by differences in the delivery system. You should not forget, however, that for the most part the principles of writing for corporate/instructional presentations and for traditional broadcast are the same.

Before we proceed, we should note that not all those who write and produce these types of programs use the same terms to describe their work. We have combined the two most common descriptive terms, *corporate* and *instructional*, into the heading for this chapter, and from here on we've shortened it to simply C/I. Other labels which are used for this same genre are "institutional," "industrial," or simply "non-broadcast." In general, we are describing scripts for presentations which either are made for corporate clients, and which the corporation may use for employee training, for promotion, or for sales, and, as a second category, scripts for formal instructional presentations in other, non-corporate settings.

We have selected four types of programs from those broad categories upon which to concentrate in this chapter. We have further picked a series of examples, all based on real situations, which we will bring up at appropriate points as we work through the planning and writing of C/I programs.

Types of C/I Programs

The four types of programs we have chosen are the telecourse, sales and promotion programs, training programs, and interactive instruction. Most C/I programming will fall into one or another of these categories.

The Telecourse

College-level telecourses were fairly common on broadcast station schedules in the 1960s, especially in the early mornings when there was very little other programming available for the "ghetto" hours at 6 or 7 A.M. Telecourses were even distributed by the networks; CBS had "Sunrise Semester." Not many such programs remain, although a few are still being produced by educational syndicators like Orange Coast (California) College. These are leased to colleges, who arrange to air them on local stations and cable systems and award credit to students completing the course—viewing and whatever other activities are assigned.

One reason for the slackening of interest in telecourses is that the production costs can be very high. Audiences have come to expect a quite sophisticated level of production, and that means money. To justify substantial costs, the course will have to be widely used, and therefore it will have to appeal to substantial numbers of participating institutions and potential students.

Another reason for the lack of interest is, in our opinion, the inflexibility of the broadcast delivery system. That system forces the course into lessons of absolutely fixed length, uses linear presentation, and provides for little or no feedback. However, we see some changes taking place. Cable channels can play back the lessons more frequently—several times a day or week; copies of the tapes can be made available for individual viewing in public locations—schools or libraries; and individual VCRs are now so widespread that many people can tape their own copies for later viewing and study.

Sales and Promotion Programs

Even within this category, the range of situations in which programs are used is considerable. As examples we'll pick one videotape shown at point-of-purchase within a store, where the tape might assist a salesperson in making a sale. You've undoubtedly seen them—for skis, for kitchen appliances—our example is for a riding-type lawnmower. Other sales videotapes are prepared for use at conventions, to attract attendees on the exhibit floor to a booth and a possible sale. Our example, including the script, is for a computer software program.

Promotional presentations at conventions and sales rallies can be presented to large auditoriums full of people. For this purpose, a multiscreen slide-tape show is often chosen. We'll briefly describe one prepared for Dr. Pepper. At the other end of the scale, in terms of numbers, is our final example. It is a videotape for a horsebreeding farm. Only one copy was ever made, and it was shown to only one potential client at a time, at exclusive horse shows. We include the script here.

Training Programs

This area of C/I production has expanded rapidly in recent years as videotape has become easier and less expensive to use, as more trained professionals enter the field as a career, and as more corporations have come to recognize the value of audiovisual presentations. There are some outstanding examples. We were particularly struck by an approach used by General Foods Corporation for training lift truck operators. Its producers explain the problem they faced:

> The level of training and on-the-job efficiency of more than 600 lift truck operators is of vital importance to General Foods. The company sells over seven billion packages of product in this country each year, and it's the job of the lift truck operators to load and unload that mountain of product onto and off of the fleets of trucks and railroad cars that keep it all moving through the distribution pipeline.

Management wanted a training program for these employees. The solution, which we will talk about at various points in the chapter, was to produce two 30-minute programs that covered "safety, sanitation, preventive maintenance, loading and unloading methodology, and dunnage requirements—in a format that GF management certainly never expected, but was delighted with once it saw the results."

A game show format was chosen for the programs, which were titled "Highstacks I" and "Highstacks II."

> As the familiar game show format unwinds on the screen, [the viewers] become personally involved in the questions and answers that encompass between 60 and 70 instructional points important to lift truck operators. And while the contestants on the screen move through the game show's familiar series of main rounds, lightning rounds, bonus rounds and commercials, the lift truck operator audience moves along with them, laughing at their foibles, exalting in their correct answers, groaning at their apparent shortcomings, and learning all the way.
>
> That, of course, is the point. They're learning. The game show format is functioning as an instructional and motivational device to make learning easier and more attractive— creating an environment in which new employees can acquire needed information in an interesting, nonthreatening way, and experienced operators can learn the errors of their ways without criticism.[1]

Our second example is not exactly a training program, but it does have viewer orientation as its focus. It's a videotape shown to children visiting an orthodontist's office for the first time. It explains the importance of having good, straight teeth, and how an orthodontist can straighten them. It's a contrast to the successful "Highstacks" programs in that, although slickly produced, it was not successful in accomplishing its purpose, at least not as we saw it.

Interactive Instruction

Later in the chapter we'll consider various levels of interaction between the viewer and the material in an instructional setting. Here we want to call your attention to the newest and most exciting subfield in writing and producing C/I materials, individualized interactive instruction. The periodical literature is full of examples of programs (using that term now in both its audiovisual and computer senses) that direct students to a wide variety of devices—videotape, videodisc, slide-tape, audio cassette, and a computer itself—to accomplish self-paced learning.

If you are interested in this area, it will require some expertise in three disciplines—in educational pedagogy, that is, the study of teaching and learning; in the content area to be presented, and in media writing itself. Our assumption is that you are coming to the task from the latter perspective. In that case it would be a good idea to get some background in the other two areas.

As an example of an interactive instructional program, here is the description of an electronics course now available commercially to any school that might want to purchase it.

All the required software, lab equipment, computer, video player and monitor are arranged in the learning station, creating a pleasant work environment . . . . trainees are guided through the course by following the structured student manual. The course is divided into modules. For each module there is a separate box of diskettes and students are referred to the correct corresponding videotapes. Each module can include up to five different types of activities. . . . The five are:

HOMEWORK REVIEW. The trainee . . . loads the review diskette and answers the questions on the previous homework assignment.

PRE/POST TEST. Trainees may feel that their previous knowledge and experience make it unnecessary for them to proceed through a particular module. They are free to test out of the module by passing the Pre Test. If trainees do work through the module, they must pass the Post Test before moving on to the next module. Pre/Post Tests include about 10–12 questions, which are randomly generated from a bank of approximately 125 questions.

THEORY LESSONS. Almost all of the modules include at least one theory lesson, providing the required understanding to complete the laboratory applications. Trainees load the theory videotape and the corresponding diskette and proceed to work through the lesson. The [computer] controls the VCR, showing only 2–3 minute segments of video, which are ended either by computer-generated directives or by a question(s). Trainees cannot advance to the next segment of video before correctly answering the question(s) at the end of the previous segment. Wrong answers automatically activate the system to provide a review segment. Right answers are acknowledged by a friendly computer-generated pat-on-the-back.

SKILL MODULES. The skill modules are usually brief interactive video lessons, which sharpen specific skills needed to complete laboratory applications. For example, one of the skill modules is on the basic operation of an oscilloscope. Trainees are guided through the procedures for setting up and operating an oscilloscope by means of an interactive hands-on experience.

LAB JOBS. The interactive lab jobs are perhaps the most powerful learning tool in the system. Lab experiments are carefully explained on video and trainees are given specific instructions for setting up equipment, making correct connections and setting appropriate dials. Trainees feed readings and measurements into the [computer] at relevant intervals, so that the computer can check progress throughout the experiment. Once again, the computer will not allow the trainee to advance to the next phase of the experiment until all previous procedures have been correctly executed.[2]

Implications of Nonbroadcast Delivery

For the most part, C/I presentations are not delivered to their audiences by broadcast. Most often the delivery system will be some sort of closed-circuit system, and frequently it will be a playback device that is actually present in the same room with the audience. When that situation exists, two of the fundamental characteristics of broadcast communication are no longer operative: (1) *Repetition is possible.* No longer does the content pass by the audience only once, without provision for repetition. (2) It is now possible to have *immediate feedback* from the audience to the source of the message, and therefore also possible to modify the message in some ways during its delivery. This possibility is not always taken advantage of, but often it is there.

Contrast these altered characteristics with those originally postulated for broadcast delivery (Chapter 2), where the presentation must be linear, with speed and sequence totally controlled from the source. Now the audience can interact with the presentation. A videotape can be stopped and started, either at preplanned pauses to allow for group discussion, or just because the audience members decide to stop it.

Control of the flow of the presentation by the recipients also makes it possible to use a combination of "live" presenters along with the mediated material, and/ or to integrate printed materials with the electronic delivery. This presentation can also be designed to branch in different ways to meet the needs and interests of very small groups of people, even of individuals, in the target audience.

The use of a nonbroadcast delivery system also modifies the program-audience relationship in two additional ways that are critical for the writer. It creates the possibility of *forced exposure* of the audience to the program, and that, in turn, may affect the *gratifications* audience members receive from their exposure.*

Forced Exposure

In the early chapters we placed considerable emphasis on the necessity of using style, structure, and gratifications that will attract and hold audiences, because the audience members always had the option of doing something else—changing the channel or finding some other activity—if the program was not interesting. Several of the examples we are developing in this chapter are ones in which the audience members do *not* have that choice. The lift truck operators, for example, must watch "Highstacks" as part of the requirements for the job, and the students in the electronics course must work through the sequence of the content, and

---

* Of course, not all instructional materials are delivered by closed-circuit systems or in interactive formats. Corporate and instructional productions also appear from time to time on broadcast and cable channels, and when broadcast delivery is used these presentations are subject to all the principles and limitations that affect all the other types of content delivered by that means and that we considered in earlier chapters.

then pass exams, in order to complete the course. Their viewing is forced, and at least some pressure exists to watch and learn.

The extent of that pressure will vary with the situation. Even though one may be forced to sit in a room and be exposed to a presentation, it does not necessarily follow that the individual is attentive or actually learns anything. The children watching the videotape in the orthodontist's office have little chance of escaping the viewing, but they won't pay much attention to the screen if they don't find the content interesting. Even when viewing is forced, the presentation will not accomplish its purpose unless there are some gratifications each individual gets from the experience.

Gratifications   The relative strengths of the gratifications received from the reception of corporate/ instructional presentations are likely to differ considerably from those obtained from broadcast presentations. We emphasize the word *relative* because we believe that the overall list of gratifications does in fact remain the same, but the stronger gratifications in free-choice broadcast viewing, such as action, tension, sex appeal, comedy, and personalization, are not likely to be the stronger gratifications in forced-viewing situations. There value, importance, and information are likely to be stronger.

Consider, for example, the gratifications received by two different groups who may watch a broadcast college telecourse. Those students who have enrolled in the course have done so to receive college credit, and they have paid a fee to enroll. Some of those who enrolled will have done so to satisfy requirements and get credits, without any particular interest in the subject matter. For this group the expected gratifications are value and importance, *but those gratifications are achieved externally to the broadcast,* in the form of the credit, the degree, or the boost in salary from an employer as a result of having completed the course. These individuals will do whatever is necessary to get the credit, including watching the presentations if they have to. But if they can find a way to get the credit without watching, say, by reading the text and taking exams, they may choose that option. They have no commitment to the programs themselves.

Others will choose to watch the presentations (for this is a free-choice viewing situation) because they do get gratifications from the content, or possibly from the style of the programs. Information will be the primary gratification for this group. Value and importance may also be present, in the form of valuable or important content. If the script is well written, it might also include person- alization, in the form of an articulate, interesting instructor, and possibly comedy if the instructor presents the content in a witty manner. Curiosity and novelty may be present as well.

The sales tape for the computer program is also presented in a free-choice setting. This short program is designed to be shown over and over, continuously, in the company booth at a convention. Individuals strolling through the exhibit floor would be attracted by the presentation and stop long enough to receive its message. Success in such a situation will depend on a strongly written script and attractive visuals to hold the audience. Curiosity and information will be the strongest gratifications, but others—comedy, action, and novelty are good possibilities—would strengthen the presentation.

The tape on lift truck safety poses yet another problem in gratification. We have already established that this is a forced viewing situation—a requirement of the job. The company wants to increase the level of training and on-the-job efficiency of its employees. But the employees may not be similarly motivated; they may feel that they already know how to do their jobs well enough. Writing and producing a program that contains gratifications for this audience, who may enter the viewing situation a bit hostile to the presentation, or at least unenthusiastic, will be a formidable challenge. Research has shown, however, that a good way to overcome hostility and any implied threat to any employee from the instruction is to use an interactive format in which the audience members are encouraged to respond actively to the presentation. You already know how that was accomplished.

Planning and Writing C/I Programs

We pointed out in other chapters that the broadcast writer is quite likely to leave the creative process before production takes place, having turned over the script to experts in other aspects of the production. The writer who is involved in corporate/instructional production, in contrast, may very well be involved in: (1) planning, including the writing of the script; (2) production, quite possibly as the director; (3) presentation, for the writer might also be the instructor for a course; and (4) two forms of evaluation, both the pretest of the message before it is delivered to its target audience and postpresentation evaluation which assesses whether the program did in fact accomplish its purpose. We'll consider only the first of these four tasks, planning and writing. But you should develop skills in production, presentation, and evaluation as well if you are to work professionally in this area.

The planning function can be further divided into five steps: (1) defining purpose, (2) describing the target audience, (3) selecting the medium to be used for delivery, (4) organizing the content, and (5) selecting techniques for the presentation. The first two we've considered before with other types of content. The third we've not had to take into account previously, since up to now the only medium we've considered has been broadcast. The final two steps also differ from broadcast in part because of the different preconditions that may be set up by the first three steps.

Defining Purpose

In two previous chapters we've worked through the process of identifying purpose. We began in Chapter 8 with a generalized discussion; then in Chapter 11, when considering announcements, we cautioned you to distinguish carefully both the long-range goals and specific purposes of your clients. A similar caution is appropriate here. Make sure your purpose is clearly stated and understood by all parties—client, producer, and, of course, you the writer.

In preparing formal instructional programs, educational planners often further divide this step into the *needs assessment* and the *learning objectives*. Their approach is worth some consideration.

**Needs
Assessment**

As an example, let's go back to the lift truck operators. Assume there have been a number of minor accidents in the company warehouses. Management is concerned about employee safety and the costs to the company of disposing of damaged products. There is pressure to find a solution. From management's point of view, one logical way to attack the problem might be to authorize the preparation of an audiovisual presentation to be shown to employees. One can imagine a manager saying:

> After all, we have the video production folks down there and that's why we set up the unit in the first place—to help solve personnel problems. I'll bet they're just itching to produce a program. Give them the job and let them take care of the problem.

In this case the program worked, and very well, but in other circumstances the problem might not be solvable using an audiovisual presentation. There might be a morale problem. Warehouse supervisors might be treating employees unfairly, keeping them tense and edgy, which leads to a high accident rate. Or perhaps the warehouse is poorly lit, the products poorly stacked, or the aisles too narrow. There could be many possible causes.

We have taken minor liberty with the "Highstacks" story here and extended it far beyond its original scope, but to make a point. It may seem hard to believe that a client corporation would not know precisely the nature of a problem existing within the organization, but sometimes management's perceptions of a situation are not accurate, and the actual causes of a problem are not those the media production team is being asked to correct. If you are confronted with that kind of situation, it will require diplomacy and tact to insist to management that adequate research be done on the causes of the problem before any decision is made to use media to tackle the solution.

**Learning
Objectives**

Lists of learning objectives may be presented in a variety of forms. Frequently they are stated as *behavioral* objectives, in terms like these: "The learner will list from memory the six steps . . ." or "The learner will assemble the parts. . . ."

We prefer instead this list, which was developed by our colleague at CSU, Sacramento, Patrick Marsh. He has identified nine categories of purpose, which he calls *strategies.*

To *inform*. . . . provides the receiver with new information in an effort to enable the receiver *to recognize* it. Recognition implies the ability to discriminate an item from other items in a set. Given several instances or items, an informed person would recognize or identify the appropriate one.

To *stimulate*. . . . attempts to elicit or prompt the receiver to recognize intuitive knowledge which may be fanciful or even false; the effort is *to elevate* implicit thoughts from the experience level to the explicit level.

To *interpret*. . . . attempts to create a context which enables the receiver *to retrieve* tacit knowledge . . . in essence, [tacit] means that we know more than we are able to tell. Interpretation enables the receiver to retrieve and then to communicate what was originally unaccessible and uncommunicable knowledge.

To *instruct*. . . . guides the receiver in the acquisition of knowledge, attitudes, or skills which may be performed by recall or demonstrated at will. Since the tactics of such guidance are differentiated, three sub-types of instruction are defined: To instruct (*details*) involves forming associations; to instruct (*concepts*) involves forming classifications; to instruct (*relationships*) involves forming relationships.

To *solve*. . . . guides the receiver through a selected process in an effort to identify a solution which reduces the gap between the desired state and the actual state of affairs. This strategy seeks to prevent further complaint or search after the "solution" is identified.

To *persuade* (to *promote*). The strategies "to persuade" and "to promote" are similar with only one essential difference. In the strategy "to persuade," the source makes plausible intellectual and/or emotional appeals in an effort *to change* selected attitudes, beliefs, or values already held by the receiver. The change can be in either strength, direction, or both. The best evidence of change is the unsolicited change in behaviors related to the changed beliefs, attitudes, or values. The strategy "to promote" differs only in that it seeks *to mobilize* the changed attitudes, beliefs, or values to achieve a specific, desired action. Evidence of the desired action's performance is the criterion.

To *argue*. In [this strategy] which is defined here more narrowly than in popular usage, the source submits a reasoned case in support or in refutation of a particular proposition in an effort *to test* the case's adequacy against the receiver's most critical response. Successful argument means that the receiver has been unable to debilitate the source's case. The crucial difference between the strategies "to argue" and "to persuade" lie in their differing goals and methods. Persuasion attempts *to change* the receiver; argument attempts *to test* the case. Persuasion uses all available appeals; argument employs only reasoned discourse.

To *entertain*. . . . attempts *to hold* the attention or interest of the receiver in an effort *to divert or amuse*. Literally, to entertain means "to hold between," which connotes tension and suspense. The most general categories of amusement are probably inspiration, portrayal, and down-play. Evidence of having entertained takes various forms depending upon the category involved.

To *transform*. . . . guides the receiver through processes intended to cause the receiver *to reframe* his or her perceptions of the self and the situation or context so that his or her everyday activities in life reflect the reframed perceptions . . . its accomplishment is typically characterized by behavior changes on several dimensions.[3]

Briefly summarized, these objectives, or any other similar list, are used to specify the outcomes intended by the instruction. Which of these does the client wish the instruction to accomplish within the audience members?

This very brief introduction to the complex issues raised in needs assessment and learning objectives is barely enough to begin. If you are to write instructional programs, we urge you to read some of the works on instructional planning cited in the bibliography.

Describing the Target Audience

Any well-written program will have a clearly defined target audience. We've discussed that concept in several previous chapters. The difference between most C/I programs and broadcast programs in this regard will be that the target for the

C/I program will be even more specific than for the most narrowly targeted broadcast. It might be just the nursing staff at one hospital, or a crew that performs only one assembly function on an automobile, or the lift truck operators. In these cases the audience is completely preidentified, and the time and place at which it will be exposed to the message can also be preselected.

The audience for the point-of-purchase sales presentation on the riding lawnmower is somewhat broader, although still not as broad as it would be if the client had decided instead to produce an ad for broadcast or cable TV. In this case, the manufacturer of the lawnmower has decided to produce a videotape extolling the virtues of this machine and to place copies of the tape, along with a player, in the showrooms of major garden supply dealers.

The client would be wise to choose those dealerships where nearby residents are likely to have large pieces of property. Those are the customers who are more likely to want a mower one rides like a small tractor, which is a large and expensive piece of equipment. The audience would be men (probably) who have come into the dealership. They might have been attracted to the showroom to see this product by a broadcast commercial, a newspaper ad, or some other means, or they may have come to buy some other product. But for whatever reason they have come, once inside the store they become the target audience for this presentation.

Narrowly selected target audiences are an advantage for the writer in that they make it much easier to tailor both content and approach to a specific group. However, the cost of a presentation goes up as the audience is narrowed. That is, when the fixed cost of production is divided by smaller audiences and fewer presentations, the cost per viewer is increased. At some point it becomes uneconomical to produce for a very small audience and necessary to generalize the presentation to a wider, less specific group.

The videotape presentation for children in the orthodontist's office provides an example of this problem. The tape this author and his children viewed featured a young actor in his mid-twenties who played the role of a bumbling, comic "tooth fairy." For these children at least, the approach was a condescending putdown. The approach was obviously intended for younger, less sophisticated children. Since children's levels of interest, attention span, and ability to understand complex material change very rapidly, the orthodontist really needed a whole series of presentations, each one geared to a different age, with a different one for about every two years' difference in the children's ages. But for some reason, most likely cost, only one tape was available, and therefore it was impossible to match content and audience as closely as was necessary to be effective. In this particular case, the children involved would have had a more positive view of the experience had no tape been used, rather than a poorly matched one.

A highly specialized audience, but one that is easily identified, is targeted for the videotape for the horsebreeding farm. It was intended to be shown only to the owners of mares who would be willing to pay substantial fees to have those mares bred to the sires owned by the farm. It was shown, by invitation only, at several shows and sales of high-priced thoroughbreds.

What is critical from the writer's standpoint is that a careful assessment be made of the target group. Not only must it be accurately identified, but a determination must be made on what content is relevant to those people (which is the area of gratifications) and how that content can be presented in an authentic manner.

One C/I producer has summarized the point this way:

> The concept on which a program is based and the progressions it employs must be developed with an understanding of the knowledge and perceptions of the intended audience. If a tape attempts to present what is already known, the viewers will be bored. If it presumes knowledge that is not there, they will be lost or confused. If the program's premises and logic do not ring true when tested by the viewers against their experiences and values, they will label that program as artificial or "off-base" and will reject its message. Little learning can be expected from such programs.
>
> It is also important that the rate at which the information is presented and the amount of repetition provided give the viewers a challenge appropriate to their abilities. Accurate assessment of the audience and effective use of pace and repetition in the programs helps prevent the viewers from feeling "talked down to" because their capabilities are more extensive than the program assumes or, conversely, from perceiving the message as "over their heads" and therefore difficult, if not impossible, to assimilate.[4]

If the targeted group are company employees, gathering the information to determine gratifications and to provide for authenticity in the presentation should not be difficult. You can get background information from personnel records, and arrangements can be made to observe the group or even meet with representatives from it if that would be helpful.

In the case of the lift truck operators, the program producers studied the educational levels and at-home TV viewing habits of the target group. They found that these employees frequently watch game shows at home on their own time. They enjoy the fast action, the rapid-fire give and take, and the excitement of tension-building situations in which a lot is riding on fast and accurate decisions.

With that information in hand, the possibility of using a game-show format began to be considered. But the producers found that using such a format had both advantages and problems:

> On the one hand, it meant that a training program presented as a game show would be readily accepted by the target audience. On the other hand, it meant that, to be believable, the show would have to be authentic—not just a simulation of a game show, but as close to the real thing as possible. It would have to look, sound, feel, and above all, play like a real broadcast TV game.[5]

In other situations obtaining a detailed description of the targeted group will be more difficult, and more costly. Assume, for example, that you are preparing a promotional program on a new real estate development which will be shown by salespeople to the managers of small high-tech businesses, for the purpose of persuading them to locate or relocate their companies in your new industrial park. Who are these managers? You may be able to get some information on them by second-hand means, such as examining the periodicals they purchase and the products that advertise in those periodicals, but you also may have to invest some funds in primary research—interviews with a sampling of the people in the group, for example—in order to get an accurate profile of your target.

Selecting the Medium

Frequently the corporate writer/producer, as opposed to the broadcast writer, will have the opportunity to choose the medium of delivery of the message. The writer who works for a radio or television station or an ad agency knows that his or her work will have to conform to the conventions established for those media, such as standard lengths for programs and announcements, the need to leave places in programs to insert announcements, and so on. In contrast, the corporate writer often will have the opportunity to suggest and possibly even to decide what delivery system will be used, and can ignore some of broadcasting's conventions.

The choice of delivery system will depend on at least four factors: the budget available for the production, the amount of time available to complete the production, the complexity and form of the concepts to be presented, and the circumstances under which the program will be shown to its audience.

Budget

In some situations, programs will be produced "in-house" by that department of a corporation that is responsible for training, sales presentations, or whatever types of corporate production are used. An in-house department will probably have a fixed operational budget for all its activities, some fraction of which will be made available for each individual production. The allocation for your project often will be less than you would like to have, but if you approach management with a well-prepared proposal, with clear objectives and a well-thought-out budget, and if management understands that a successful outcome depends on a well-produced program, then you may be able to spend what you need.

Other corporations "contract out" their media presentations to companies that specialize in such production. Contract production involves careful negotiation, so that both parties know precisely what is to be produced, and at what price. That price will include not only all the direct costs of production but also overhead and profit for the contractor.

Time

Allow sufficient time for proper planning and production, and then allow extra time for the inevitable problems that will arise and eat into your timetable. You may have scheduled an interview with the company president, for example, parts of which you intend to use as the basis for the narration of a program. But when the day arrives, the president has to cancel: He must go out of town for an important meeting. Or shooting is completed and you are ready to do the postproduction editing and a critical piece of equipment fails. Those things happen. The well-prepared writer-producer will have built a cushion into the schedule.

When a presentation must be done on a short schedule, then it will have to be done more simply. The result may not be as eye-catching or as effective as you would like, but if you must meet a deadline, meet it with the best presentation you can.

Complexity of Content If the information to be conveyed consists primarily of words, then a sound-only medium (audiotape) may be the most efficient. Even if there is some visual material to be presented, the low cost of preparation and presentation may still suggest audiotape, supplemented with some sort of printed handout.*

If a substantial amount of visual material must be presented, but the use of motion is not important to the learning, then slide-tape has traditionally been the preferred medium. However, there is a trend away from the use of slide-tape presentations. They are being replaced with videotape even in those situations where the visuals are only stills, because videotape eliminates some of the problems commonly associated with slide presentations, such as having slides stick in the projector or difficulties in synchronizing audiotape sound tracks with the slides. The use of videotape also permits the writer-producer to introduce special effects not possible with slides.

It is not our intention to try to sell videotape at the expense of slide-tape, however. Slide-tape will continue to have value and impact, especially when used in large auditoriums with large audiences, when multiple screens and multiple sound tracks are employed and when they are mixed with other media into a multimedia extravaganza. Picture if you will this presentation, made to the bottlers of Dr. Pepper at their annual meeting:

> As bottlers entered the auditorium, the stage was bare except for a large circular sign displaying the ''Pepper Pride'' theme. As the house lights dimmed, an environment was created via sound, lighting and special effects to represent the feeling of being aboard a ship. Music began and a solo performer was spotlighted singing an original song about pride, beginning with the pride of the first Americans arriving in the new world. Four projection screens (one horizontal, one vertical and two circular) were lowered into position, and visuals told the story of pride in America, in sync with the prerecorded sound track.
>
> The emphasis shifted to the pride of being a ''Pepper'' and a Dr. Pepper bottler. On the video screen, eight performers were seen in a choreographed routine, taped in a bottling plant. At the end of the taped sequence, the same performers appeared on stage, jumping through the ''Pepper Pride'' sign, made of paper. The ensemble then concluded this portion with a live dance number.
>
> Executive speakers were introduced via digital video effects and the speeches were supported with pretaped excerpts of interviews conducted with bottlers throughout the country, as well as multi-image slide support, utilizing the various screens. Live skits and dance numbers were performed between speeches and to begin and end meeting segments.[6]

When the content of the presentation requires motion, then the choices are reduced to only two—videotape or film. A few corporate/instructional productions are still shot on motion picture film, and some producers still believe that film provides a final product with higher visual quality, more suitable if the presentation must be projected for large audiences. But for our purposes it makes little

---

* We are not considering corporate or instructional presentations which use no audiovisual support at all, or nonmediated support such as chalkboards, display charts, and overhead projectors. Those types of presentations are not within our scope.

difference to the writer whether the program is shot on film or on video. Both approaches will require that the raw visual material be edited before the final production can be presented. About the only significant difference is that it takes longer to process film for editing, while videotape is ready to edit as soon as the electronic image is put on tape.

Circumstances of Presentation

You will need to consider here how the presentation is best delivered to its audience or audiences. How easy must it be to operate? How many times will the presentation be shown? How frequently? How disastrous will it be if it doesn't come on at the precise time scheduled? What would happen if a slide were to jam in the projector? In short, how bulletproof must the presentation be?

Organizing the Content

Now that you have defined purpose, described the target audience, and chosen the medium of presentation, you can begin to shape the content into specific form. You will be faced with questions like these: Will it be presented in a series of lessons to be broadcast so many a week over an entire semester, as is our telecourse? Will it be a single, one-shot presentation? If not, what sort of segmentation should be used? If the program is to be presented to groups, what activities should be planned to take place during breaks in the presentation? Should the audience be required to answer study questions, participate in group discussions, or take exams?

Audience Interaction

One key consideration in the organization is the amount of interaction wanted or expected from members of the audience. We know from research studies that learners who are required to respond immediately after material has been presented are much better able to understand and retain that material than they are when no response is required. A program that encourages active responses from viewers draws them into a dialogue. It provides them with a chance to check and clarify their understanding of the information. They gain a sense of achievement because of their progress.

In addition, interaction is important for the producer-writer. It provides information on the effectiveness of the program, and points out difficulties learners may have with the content.

One study on video training programs found some additional benefits from programs that emphasize interactive instruction:

> The . . . process is viewed by employees (trainees) to be a less authoritarian or hierarchical form of training and corporate communications than traditional linear means. Some users feel that interactive video is an important step in eradicating the invisible barrier that often hampers information exchange and learning. . . .
>
> No longer must employees wait for classroom training sessions (which are conducted sporadically) to clarify key information. . . .
>
> It was found that the privacy and concentration required in using the video technology produces a worker who is more independent, and "work-involved" in his or her actual work environment.
>
> Because interactive video emphasizes personal involvement, independent problem-

solving, and self-initiated information retrieval, communications managers believe this training technology has cultivated a more mature employee who requires little supervision. It is clear that the technology's capacity to allow user control over the training and communications processes has functioned to nurture such positive employee attitudes as increased confidence and creativity.

What is most surprising . . . is the lack of data to confirm the feelings of depersonalization or other negative reactions because of an automated training process. The concerns that the technological intrusion into the workplace might cause isolation and other undesirable effects are based primarily on opinions and assumptions of those who have considered, yet have not actually used or tested, interactive training. Actual users report increased training satisfaction and improved job effectiveness among employees.[7]

Yet another benefit from an interactive presentation is that individuals can make mistakes without exposing their errors to other students or instructors—without, in effect, showing how "dumb" they are. They are able to work through the material without threat.

In general, the more complex the material to be learned, the more important it is that the audience become involved with the presentation and interact with it. If we were to construct a hierarchy of levels of interaction, at the one extreme would be presentations with no provision for interaction on the part of the audience, such as the early morning telecourse, or any other "broadcast" program that calls for no active feedback from the recipients and proceeds linearly at a speed determined by the source.

The next level of interaction provides opportunity for the audience, either groups or individuals, to start and stop the presentation at will, and to back up for review by starting and stopping a videotape recorder or similar device. This is not a very high level of interaction, but at least it places some control in the hands of the recipients, not solely with the source. (If an individual should happen to have a VCR at home, he or she can easily convert a broadcast program with no built-in interaction, such as the broadcast telecourse, into this next level simply by recording the broadcasts for later review, then starting and stopping as he or she wishes.)

Another level of interaction would be introduced by using printed materials in conjunction with the mediated presentation—discussion guides, outlines, study questions, quizzes.

Yet another form of interaction takes place when an instructor or discussion leader is present along with the audiovisual presentation. Here the question becomes, which is the primary and which the secondary source of the instruction? Is the presentation to be made primarily by a "live" instructor, supplemented by audiovisual demonstration, or is the presentation made primarily by the videotape, and the "live" individual used as a discussion leader or to respond to questions? Either approach may be correct, given the specific circumstances. Primary emphasis on the mediated presentation will provide consistency and uniformity to the presentation, which may be important if that presentation has to be given frequently to different audiences. But a greater degree of flexibility is provided by giving the major instructional role to the "live" instructor.

Finally, at the most sophisticated level of interaction, we have the very recent technological revolution brought about by integrating audiovisual materials, primarily videotape and videodiscs, with computer controls to produce "interactive instructional systems." A state-of-the-art system today can demonstrate processes or techniques using all the complexities of advanced video production, including multiple images, split-screens, instant replay, slow motion, and so on. The access to these demonstrations is controlled by the student's responses to questions posed by the computer. Once the student begins the program, the pace of the presentation is completely under that student's control. But the sequence of ideas, facts, and concepts to which he or she is exposed is selected by the computer, based on his or her responses, as in the electronics course described earlier.

Selecting Techniques for Presentation

When planning has been completed and it is time to begin actual writing on the script, the techniques available to the corporate/instructional writer are basically the same as those used in broadcast, although cost constraints and time considerations often force the use of the simpler forms of presentation. On the audio side, they range from single-voice narration through the use of music, sound effects, and multiple voices to full dramatic presentation. Visual techniques range similarly.

Recall that within each program or segment, the basic principles of program structure still apply. There should be unity, which should not be difficult to accomplish if purpose and objectives are clearly understood. There should be variety, which may be more difficult to achieve. If cost is a consideration, then costly techniques like location shooting, large amounts of postproduction editing, or multiperson casts may not be possible.

Pacing, the idea of having program elements that will change frequently to reattract audience attention, remains an important consideration, especially in linear, noninteractive presentations. But as we have shown, many corporate/instructional presentations are broken up by nonmedia activities, and therefore pacing is somewhat easier to accomplish.

Even climax should be considered. The audience members are more likely to remember or to be persuaded by the material they receive near the end of the program. So build the development of the content to conclude with the most important points.

Talking Heads

"Talking heads" is the simplest and least expensive visual technique, that of having a person narrate, lecture, or explain on-camera. Interviews and panel discussions also fall into this category, except that more than one head is involved. Writers and producers have mixed feelings about the use of heads, as is shown by this comment:

> The face shot, or "big talking head," has been the bane of in-house, closed-circuit television. It smacks of low-budget production, absence of visual material, and a real lack of creativity and imagination. We have all lost sleep over finding cutaways to hide a droning voice—talking away, paragraph after paragraph, in front of the camera.

Admittedly, head shots do not make maximum use of the full potential of the television medium. But even as I hear the echoes of my supervisor's voice saying, "I don't want to see one talking head in this videotape," I still believe that talking heads have a deserved place on the screen. Creative things can be done with them to help them add an important dimension to the videotape program.

We must remember that, for certain professions, there is a great advantage in using well-known, credible authority figures on camera when gathering testimonial footage or presenting lectures. At times, nothing is more important than letting practitioners talk directly to other practitioners.[8]

If you choose to or are forced to use "talking heads" for the bulk of your presentation, consider these suggestions for minimizing the structural weaknesses that technique presents:

1. At the very least, make sure your "talking head" is articulate, or if you must use a poor speaker, pair that person with a second voice who is articulate, and use a two-narrator approach.

2. Get a presenter who is credible, one who is perceived as an authority by the audience. Audience members will be more likely to suffer the talking head if it is an individual who has recognized expertise in the content.

3. Try to place the talent "on location" rather than just in a studio. Use a location in an office, a shop, or outside the plant if appropriate. Or consider an atypical location such as driving to the factory, or at the talent's home doing some task not directly related to the content of the program, but which shows the talent in a comfortable, favorable situation.

4. Shoot silent footage on location, then use a professional voice to do nonsync voiceover commentary. Or use two voices, the expert and the professional narrator, as in the scripts for the "Cousteau Odyssey" programs given in Chapter 6 and 14.

5. Use actuality inserts as in a news broadcast. Select only the most succinct statements using the talking head of the authority, with most of the content paraphrased and delivered by a narrator.

6. Use role-playing by actors; dramatize the situation.

7. Juxtapose different points of view. Intercut between different individuals and locations to avoid long sections of material from one source.

Other powerful techniques appropriate to corporate/instructional presentation, if time and budget permit, are demonstrations, interviews, and documentary. Both the computer software convention videotape and the horsebreeding farm scripts are good examples of the appropriate uses of visual and audio techniques.

As you recall, the convention promotion requires that passersby stop and watch. For that reason, the tape is quite complex visually—lots of changes and variety—but its audio is mostly single-voice narration, a straightforward pitch, except for the opening lines and two "user" sound bites on page 3 of the Script (Figure 15.1).

DOUBLE VISION

DATE_ May 12, 1982_   PAGE_1_ OF_ 4_

CLIENT_ Software Dimensions_   JOB #_____ WRITER_ Benvenuti_____

VIDEO		AUDIO
3 quick shots of talking heads, each with one line	1	IT'S REALLY VERY SIMPLE. HUMANIZES THE HARDWARE·
	2	IT'S EVEN FRIENDLY.
fade to black		
Voice over black	3	THE MYSTERY IS GONE.
Fade up to S.D. logo	4	FOR PEOPLE WHO WANT TO DO ACCOUNTING -- NOT COMPUTER
Multiple Accounting Plus logos (Rolls over S.D. logo.	5	PROCESSING -- SOFTWARE DIMENSIONS PRESENTS ACCOUNTING
	6	PLUS, THE FULLY INTEGRATED, USER-ORIENTED SOFTWARE
quick appearances of programs in package on manual	7	PACKAGE. AND IT WORKS. ACCOUNTING PLUS, AVAILABLE
	8	ON CPM AND APPLE COMPUTER SYSTEMS, AND WITH MORE THAN
multi-image of computer	9	3500 INSTALLATIONS ACROSS THE COUNTRY, INCORPORATES
Hand putting in software disk; fingers typing	10	THE NEWEST IN STATE OF THE ART TECHNOLOGY. IT COMBINES
Xclose up screen word.	11	SYSTEM INTEGRITY WITH USER CONVENIENCE TO HELP SOLVE you
Xclose up screen words	12	ACCOUNTING PROBLEMS.
	13	AND HOW DOES IT WORK?
Box diagram	14	ACCOUNTING PLUS CONTAINS MULTIPLE, FULLY INTEGRATED
highlight as they are named	15	MODULES—GENERAL LEDGER, PAYROLL, ACCOUNTS PAYABLE,
	16	PURCHASE ORDER ENTRY, INVENTORY, SALES ORDER ENTRY,
	17	RETAIL POINT OF SALE, ACCOUNTS RECEIVABLE.

Figure 15.1 Courtesy of the writer, Jeanne Benvenuti.

DOUBLE VISION

DATE May 12, 1982   PAGE 2 OF 4

CLIENT Software Dimensions   JOB #_____ WRITER Benvenuti

VIDEO		AUDIO
rippling across system	1	THE KEY FEATURE OF THE SYSTEM IS THAT A SINGLE
	2	ENTRY TO ANY MODULE AUTOMATICALLY POSTS THE GENERAL
	3	LEDGER, AS WELL AS ANY OTHER INTERACTIVE MODULE
	4	REQUIRING UPDATING.
Close ups of fingers operating key board/ appropriate screen words/printer & hand reaching for printout.	5	ACCOUNTING PLUS PROVIDES INSTANT REPORTS FOR MANAGEMENT
	6	ACTION AND DECISION MAKING.
Same as above	7	PRODUCES MONTH AND YEAR-TO-DATE FINANCIAL REPORTS,
	8	WITH COMPARISONS TO BUDGET AS WELL AS PRIOR YEAR.
Printing/3 angles	9	GENERATES ACCOUNTS PAYABLE AND PAYROLL CHECKS, SALES
	10	ORDERS, INVOICES AND STATEMENTS, AND PURCHASE ORDERS,
MS screen, showing password requirements. Male hand tries to use	11	WHILE PROVIDING PASSWORD PROTECTION AT THE PROGRAM
	12	LEVEL.
Group at staff meeting reviewing reports	13	YES, ACCOUNTING PLUS VIRTUALLY DOES IT ALL. . . PLUS,
	14	IT DOES IT WITH EASE.
	15	IT'S MENU DRIVEN.
	16	

Figure 15.1 (Continued)

DOUBLE VISION

DATE May 12, 1982   PAGE 3 OF 4

CLIENT   Software Dimensions   JOB #_____ WRITER Benvenuti

Cut to user   1   USER:

                         2   I DON'T HAVE TO BE A COMPUTER EXPERT TO RUN IT;

                         3   I ONLY HAVE TO INTERACT WITH THE OPERATING SYSTEM

                         4   ONCE.

                         5   NARRATOR:

                         6   IT'S SCREEN ORIENTED.

Cut to second   7   USER:
user
                         8   I DON'T HAVE TO GUESS AT THE DATA REQUIRED. I

                         9   CAN SEE ALL THE INFORMATION I NEED AT ONE TIME.

                        10   NARRATOR:

                        11   AND, FREE OF THE OPERATING COMPLEXITY TYPICALLY

                        12   ASSOCIATED WITH COMPUTER PROCESSING ···········

Accounting Plus   13   ACCOUNTING PLUS IS USER FRIENDLY.
logo comes back

Wipe up to user   14   IT FEATURES FILL-IN-THE-BLANK DATA ENTRY . . .
at system. Zoom in
to screen, cuts
between close ups   15   USER PROMPTING. ⟋ .. EASY-TO-UNDERSTAND ERROR
of face and close
ups of screen.
SUPER: fill in   16   MESSAGES. IN SIMPLE, NON-TECHNICAL LANGUAGE,
the blank; User
prompting; Simple
Error messages

Figure 15.1 (Continued)

DATE May 12, 1982   DOUBLE VISION   PAGE 4 OF 4

CLIENT Software Dimensions   JOB#_____ WRITER Benvenuti

VIDEO   AUDIO

	1 IT GUIDES THE USER EVERY STEP OF THE WAY.
Wipe to user picking up	2 AS AN ADDITIONAL PLUS, PRODUCT SUPPORT SERVICE
phone. Screen wipes to	
split. User/customer	3 BY SOFTWARE DIMENSIONS IS IMMEDIATE AND
service.	
Super: Dealer toll free	4 PROFESSIONAL. (SNATCH OF CONVERSATION
hot line. Super logo	
over customer service	5 BETWEEN THE TWO) ACCOUNTING PLUS IS CON-
conversation	
	6 TINUALLY UPDATED THROUGH RIGOROUS RESEARCH
Graphic: 3 appear	
and disappear	7 AND DEVELOPMENT IN LANGUAGES AND OPERATING
R & D staff at work	8 SYSTEMS. AS NEW INNOVATIONS APPEAR, SOFT-
Manuals of languages	9 WARE DIMENSIONS BUILDS THEM INTO THE
	10 PRODUCT. STILL ANOTHER REASON IT'S THE
	11 FASTEST GROWING, BEST ACCEPTED PRODUCT
	12 ON THE MARKET.
Logo accounting	13 ACCOUNTING PLUS WILL TRANSFORM COMPUTER
Plus; Super over	
video. Roll over	14 TEDIUM AND INTIMIDATION INTO VITAL
person at computer	
Wide shot of research	15 INTERACTION WITH BUSINESS INFORMATION.
area.	
	16 IF YOU KNOW THE BASICS OF ACCOUNTING,
	17 WE CAN HAVE YOU OPERATING THE SYSTEM
	18 WITHIN MINUTES. ACCOUNTING PLUS BY
Logo, Software	19 SOFTWARE DIMENSIONS--PIONEERING AN ARRAY
Dimensions	
	20 OF PRODUCTS FOR THE 80's.

Figure 15.1 (Continued)

The promotion for the horsebreeding farm will be shown in very selected settings and to a very exclusive clientele. It depends on its strong visual impact—lush scenery, beautiful animals, and a documentary approach. The audio is primarily single-voice narration, supplemented by occasional use of sound effects and ambient sound in the background (Figure 15.2).

We can't leave this chapter without one more look at "Highstacks." The actual scripts are too long to reproduce here (54 pages for each of the two programs), but this further description by the producer gives the flavor of the shows:

> [The programs utilize] the classic elements of the game show format to provide maximum instructional and motivational effectiveness. "Main" rounds were used to disseminate large blocks of general information, e.g., how to load a railroad car. "Lightning" rounds were used to introduce such specific information as the seven steps necessary for the correct opening of the door of a railroad car, and to reinforce other general information. "Bonus" rounds served to weave in such warehouse mottos and instructional concepts as "Work Smarter, Not Harder," and such basic principles of warehouse operation as "Inspect, Correct, or Reject."
>
> Regular game show viewers also expect several commercial breaks in a 30-minute show, so these were included. They provide information on lift truck safety, maintenance, and sanitation. In addition, they also give the show the pacing needed. . . .

> The set is a colorful re-creation of a General Foods warehouse, complete with light-up lift trucks and a background of assorted General Foods product cartons.
>
> Typical warehouse situations, depicted during the main rounds on a giant chromakey pick-up screen, were shot on location at the General Foods distribution center warehouse in Newark, Delaware. . . .
>
> The first contestant in this head-to-head confrontation of lift truck logic is Big Moose Wheeler from Fork Worth, Texas, "a man who can pull-pack 27 cartons of Log Cabin Syrup on a slipsheet of Kleenex"—an impressive accomplishment among warehousemen. His opponent is Gnat Stacker the Third, from Cargo, North Dakota, "a clamp truck operator who can't get a grip on himself.". . .
>
> Moose and Gnat match wits from behind their lift truck podiums while show host Bill O. Lading, "the man with a warehouse of knowledge," quizzes them on categories selected by the show's glamorous hostess, Honeycomb Dunnage.
>
> Throughout the game, Moose and Gnat are challenged to look for mistakes being made by the lift truck operators who appear on the chromakey pickup screen. When he spots one, the contestant is to honk the horn on his podium. He who honks first gets a chance to identify the mistake, describe the proper procedure, and score points to win the game and go on to play the exciting "10,000 bonus" round where he can pick up some really "sweet" prizes—10,000 marshmallows.

According to the manager of General Foods' Video and Graphic Communications Department, William Hoppe, the programs are an overwhelming success:

> What we saw in the game show and what attracted us to use it for this program, is its tremendous potential for conveying a large number of individual pieces of information in a relatively short period of time. The professional game show format has developed the art of pacing into a science to achieve a maximum of audience attention, suspense, entertainment, and involvement. That's what we were after.[9]

Double Vision

READING TIME: 2:55

DATE 12/28/82   *ORiginal*   PAGE 1   OF 5

CLIENT SADDLE ROCK RANCH ___ JOB # _____ WRITER BENVENUTI

① VIDEO	AUDIO
EXT. Up on close up gate; zoom out as gate begins to open, and we start down driveway past SR sign.	1 ① *Music— Ambient sounds*
② *C.U. sign*	2 (sound of horse whinnying)
③ *Full shot of mountain— pull back-* 6 sec *truck passes by.* 4 Sec	3 NARRATOR
	℗ ② 2½ ③ 6
	4 WELCOME TO THE SADDLE ROCK RANCH. / WE'RE LOCATED IN
	5 SONOMA, CALIFORNIA, IN THE HEART OF THE BEAUTIFUL
	6 WINE COUNTRY'S VALLEY OF THE MOON. . . . *4 -* APPROXIMATELY
	7 ONE HOUR'S DRIVE NORTH OF SAN FRANCISCO.
④ *8 secs* shots of Nadom, either in paddock or inside arena.	℗ ④ 8
	8 THE SADDLE ROCK RANCH—HOME OF CHAMPION S.R. NADOM—
	9 IS PRESENTLY OFFERING BREEDING SERVICES FOR A LIMITED
	10 NUMBER OF APPROVED MARES.
Truck unloading a mare. show usual procedure.	⊤ ⑤ 3½ *that*
	11 OUR SERVICES INCLUDE EVERYTHING WE PROVIDE OUR <u>OWN</u>
⑤ *C.U.- on feet or head. Zoom out* ⑥ *Activity*	⑥
	12 MARES—CLEANLINESS, SAFETY, COMFORT, AND PERSONALIZED
	13 CARE BY A HIGHLY QUALIFIED STAFF.
Medium and close ups of groom receiving & leading mare toward barn. ⑦ *Ms Groom & mare*	⑦ 4
	14 WHEN YOUR MARE ARRIVES AT THE RANCH, SHE'LL BE ASSIGNED
⑧ *Leading toward barn*	⑧ 4
	15 TO A GROOM / WHO WILL BE RESPONSIBLE FOR HER WELL BEING
	16 THROUGHOUT HER STAY.

Figure 15.2 Courtesy of the writer, Jeanne Benvenuti.

Double Vision

DATE __12/28/82__   PAGE __2__ OF __5__

CLIENT __SADDLE ROCK RANCH__ ____ JOB # _____ WRITER __BENVENUTI__

VIDEO		AUDIO
① *5½ sec total* INT. Shot from aisle of barn toward door in which groom is entering with mare. On one side of aisle is person rebedding a stall. As groom & mare pass, there is brief exchange. *Then*	1	
	Ⓣ2	SHE'LL BE SURROUNDED BY ALL THE COMFORTS OF HOME.
Narrator speaks. They continue. ②Shot of open stall. groom leading horse in to ~~stall.~~ *picture &* *places in stall*	3	
	Ⓣ4	② A SPACIOUS 12 by 16 STALL, WITH AUTOMATIC WATERING AND
	5	FLY CONTROL./ (THE STALLS ARE CLEANED AND REBEDDED
	6	DAILY.)
③ Cut to another horse feeding ④then to CU of hands stirring grain.	Ⓣ7	③ 6 LIKE ALL THE OTHER HORSES ON THE RANCH, SHE'LL
	8	RECEIVE HER DAILY NUTRITIONAL REQUIREMENTS. NO SHORT
	9	④ 4 *The highest quality alfalfa, and* CUTS./GRAINS SPECIALLY MILLED FOR SADDLE ROCK ~~AND THE~~ *Ranch.*
	10	~~HIGHEST QUALITY ALFALPA.~~
⑤ *Over shoulder from ¾ angle. close enough to see screen. 3 sec zoom. Person walks in Operator looks up & takes sheet.*	Ⓣ11	⑤ 7½ TO ENSURE THAT YOUR MARE'S INDIVIDUAL NEEDS ARE MET,
	12	WE ENTER ALL PERTINENT DATA INTO THE RANCH'S COMPUTER
	13	SYSTEM IMMEDIATELY UPON HER ARRIVAL.
Lab person looking at printout.	Ⓟ14	⑥ 4½ DETAILED PRINTOUTS ARE MADE AVAILABLE TO THOSE INVOLVED
	15	IN ANY ASPECT OF HER CARE.
	16	

Figure 15.2 (Continued)

agency uses to design productions against those described in this chapter. Write a report on your observations, or make a class presentation.

3. Find out if your university (or another in your area) is currently offering a telecourse. If so, observe the presentations for one week. What forms of presentation are used—talking head, interview, discussion, demonstration, documentary, other? For what level audience do the programs seen to be aimed—introductory, advanced, graduate? Are the presentational techniques appropriate for that audience? Will it hold their interest? Are there gratifications in the presentations, or will the students have to seek their rewards outside of the programs? Explain in a written report or class presentation.

Key Terms and Concepts

audience feedback	interaction
closed circuit	learning objectives
delivery medium	needs assessment
forced exposure	talking heads
gratification	telecourse

Notes

1. Bob Shewchuk, "Edutainment Pays Off with Game Show Antics," *Video Systems,* July 1982, p. 60. Reprinted with permission.
2. Condensed from *Electronics Training Via Interactive Computer/Video,* a brochure of the Wisconsin Foundation for Vocational, Technical and Adult Education, Inc., 5402 Mineral Point Road, Madison, WI 53705. Reprinted with permission.
3. Patrick O. Marsh, *Messages That Work: A Guide to Communication Design* (Englewood Cliffs, NJ: Educational Technology Publications, 1983), pp. 9–10. Reprinted with permission.
4. Gerald E. Glassmeyer, "How to Design Programs That Encourage Response," *E&ITV,* August 1979, pp. 52–53.

5. Nat Skyer, "The Training Game: How General Foods Made Two Programs with Help from Production Companies," *E&ITV,* May 1982, p. 38. Copyright 1982 by C.S. Tepfer Publishing Company, Inc. Reprinted by permission.
6. "A Pepper-Upper Rally," *Audio-Visual Communications,* February 1983, p. 21. Reprinted by permission.
7. Linda Hershberger, "How Interactive Training Affects Corporations," *E&ITV,* January 1984, pp. 64–65. Copyright 1984 C.S. Tepfer Publishing Company, Inc. Reprinted by permission.
8. James Onder, "Techniques to Use with the Talking Head," *E&ITV,* February 1980, p. 44.
9. Skyer, "The Training Game," pp. 38–39.

Chapter 16

Dramatic Programs

The historical development of the conventions of Western drama goes back at least to the fifth century B.C., to the early Greek dramatists and to the first recognized dramatic critic, Aristotle. Centuries later, the dramatists and critics of the Italian and French Renaissance revived, then revised, the early theories to form the basis of dramatic construction as we know it today. In the last hundred years those conventions, originally developed for the stage, have been further modified and applied to three new media of communication—to film, then to radio, and most recently to television. The critics, teachers, and writers who have worked in each of these media have in turn added significantly to the body of works and of critical comment available for study.

For film, we have already mentioned the important contributions of such early practitioners as Eisenstein, Pudovkin, and Griffith. Their pioneering techniques form the foundation of film theory, which has carried over largely intact to television. Similarly, the innovations of Norman Corwin, and of Arch Oboler, among others, are important works to study for the radio writer, as are the radio dramas of Orson Welles, who wrote, produced, and performed in the most celebrated radio broadcast ever aired, the 1938 Mercury Theater adaptation of *War of the Worlds*.

The thirty or so years of television drama represent only a tiny fraction of the time span of dramatic history, but there are critics who believe we have already passed the Golden Age of TV drama. These critics remember fondly the period when television drama was presented live, and they point to plays like *Requiem for a Heavyweight* by Rod Serling, *Marty* by Paddy Chayefsky, or *Judgment at Nuremburg* by Abby Mann as the "classics" of the genre.*

---

* Without question, many of these plays from the 1960s are worth studying as models. They have also been collected and published, often with comments from their authors, which provide important insights into the process of writing teleplays. We have listed several of these collections in the bibliography. If you do plan a career that includes dramatic writing for television or radio, we suggest you read the plays in these collections, as well as some of the other books that discuss dramatic construction in much more detail than we can in this single chapter.

It's a matter of opinion as to whether the quality of television drama is as high now as it was in the 1960s. But the quantity remains high—and so does the cost of producing dramatic programs. For that reason TV dramas are produced primarily for the networks or for other methods of distribution, such as national cable channels, which ensures that the program will be shown to very large audiences and therefore keep the cost per viewer within reason.

In turn, that restriction on distribution limits the number of employment opportunities for TV dramatists. Writing for network soap operas is limited to a handful of thoroughly experienced writers under contract to the networks. A similar situation exists with writing for prime-time series programs. The writers are usually chosen from among a small stable known to the show's producers. Only a few TV series will even consider scripts submitted by freelance or unknown authors.*

Despite this depressing outlook for careers in television dramatic writing, we will emphasize that medium. At the present time there is far more writing of dramatic materials for television than for radio. But we have reserved one section of the chapter for the unique challenges radio provides.

If, as a result of these comments, you feel a bit discouraged in hoping to develop a career writing dramatic scripts, please understand that it takes time and experience to "pay your dues" in this field. You can begin by employing dramatic principles, and even short dramatic scenes, in other types of programs— in commercials, in vignettes that might appear in a religious program, in documentaries, in role-playing scenes as part of corporate training tape, and many other places.

Become proficient at other forms of writing, and practice dramatic writing whenever the opportunity arises. When you feel that you are ready to tackle the "big time," and are also ready to accept rejection of your scripts, then you are ready to move to Hollywood. Writers and producers who have "made it" in dramatic production invariably include a move to Hollywood as an important step toward success—you simply have to be where the action is.

Concept

To begin, recognize that the evolution of a dramatic script from the first germ of an idea through to the finished production is a single, ongoing process. There are, nevertheless, two intermediate stages which are generally recognized in the industry as important points in the marketing of scripts—the *concept* and the *treatment*—so we'll divide the process into three steps: concept, treatment, and finished script. Understand too that there are very few absolutes in this business. If you look, you can find exceptions to just about any rule or principle. But in general, it works this way.

The story line for any dramatic situation, be it a lengthy network production or the introduction to a commercial, begins first as an idea, a single thought:

---

* The Writers Guild of America, West, publishes a monthly market list of television series that do accept manuscripts. It is one of the services from WGA available to freelance writers. Additional information on WGA membership and its services is given with the bibliography for this chapter.

A story idea can be derived from a personal experience or observation, any music, poetry, or book that moved you, a newspaper article that intrigued you, any source under the sun that sparked your imagination. However, the selection of the story idea must be more rational. First and foremost, it must have a hook—a unique premise that will grip the audience immediately. If the hook is strong, the story has a much better chance of eventually reaching the screen. . . .[1]

This *idea* will next be expanded into a *premise,* or *concept,* or *approach*—all these terms are used to describe the same thing. Major characters will be identified and described, the point of view will be determined. The central conflict will be sketched out, and the resolution of the story will be decided.

Consider at this point the type of material you wish to present. Although television has presented a tremendous range of material, including big spectacles with "a cast of thousands," the TV screen is best suited for more intimately scaled productions. The medium is also well suited for the dramatic development of "ordinary" stories. One of the best-known television dramatists of the 1960s, Paddy Chayefsky, describes the contrast between writing for the stage, the movies, and television in this way, in an introduction to the published version of his teleplays *Marty* and *The Mother:*

[These teleplays] both deal with the world of the mundane, the ordinary, and the untheatrical. The main characters are typical, rather than exceptional; the situations are easily identifiable by the audience; and the relationships are as common as people. The essence of these two shows lies in their literal reality. I tried to write the dialogue as if it had been wire-tapped. I tried to envision the scenes as if a camera had been focused upon the unsuspecting characters and had caught them in an untouched moment of life.

This sort of meticulous literalness is something that can be done in no other medium. On the stage, reality is a highly synthesized thing. The closest thing to reality I ever saw on the stage was in *Death of a Salesman,* but even this extraordinary play involved a suicide and an incident in which the son discovers his father in a hotel room with a woman other than his mother. These are excellent dramatic incidents, but they are not everyday occurrences in the life of the lower middle class. In writing the stage play, it is necessary to contrive exciting moments of theater. You may write about ordinary people, but the audience sees them in unordinary and untypical circumstances. . . .

In television, however, the same insights into a character or into a social milieu can be made with the most identifiable characters and the most commonplace situations. I set out in *Marty* to write a love story, the most ordinary love story in the world. I didn't want my hero to be handsome, and I didn't want the girl to be pretty. I wanted to write a love story the way it would literally have happened to the kind of people I know. I was, in fact, determined to shatter the shallow and destructive illusions—prospered by cheap fiction and bad movies—that love is simply a matter of physical attraction, that virility is manifested by a throbbing phallus, and that regular orgasms are all that's needed to make a woman happy. These values are dominant in our way of life and need to be examined for what they are.[2]

That description, although written after the production, exemplifies much of what is included in the concept of a teleplay. The following excerpts, which we have condensed from the full proposal, are from another famous television series. The creator of that series, Gene Roddenberry, outlined his concept for "Star Trek" this way. Trekkies will note that some changes had been made by the time the series made it to the TV screen.

STAR TREK
Created by
Gene
Roddenberry

STAR TREK will be a television "first" . . . A one-hour science-fiction series with continuing characters.
Combining the most varied in drama-action-adventure with complete production practicality. And with almost limitless story potential.
STAR TREK keeps all of Science Fiction's variety and excitement, but still stays within a mass audience frame of reference. . . .
By avoiding "way-out" fantasy and cerebral science theorem and instead concentrating on problem and peril met by our very human and very identifiable continuing characters. Fully one-third of the most successful of all Science Fiction is in this "practical" category. Tales of exotic "methane atmosphere worlds with six-head monsters" are rare among the Science Fiction classics. The best and most popular feature highly dramatic variations on recognizable things and themes. But even within these limits, there are myriad stories, both bizarre and shocking, plus a few monsters legitimus. Space is a place of infinite variety and danger.

.   .   .   .

Or to put Star Trek into the language of television . . .
The format is "Wagon Train to the Stars"—built around characters who travel to other worlds and meet the jeopardy and adventure which become our stories.
The time could be 1995 or even 2995—close enough to our times for our continuing cast to be people like us, but far enough into the future for galaxy travel to be fully established.
The Star Trek key is the bold establishing of . . .
GALAXY TRAVEL FULLY PERFECTED. April and his crew, unlike our limited astronauts of today, are in charge of their own destiny, must find their own answers to the jeopardies they meet on far-off worlds. The perfected spaceship concept allows us to move efficiently from story to story, freeing the audience from tiresome details of technology and hardware. Our aim is drama and adventure.
THE USS ENTERPRISE. A permanent set, also provides us with a familiar week-to-week locale. There is even a suggestion of current naval terminology and custom which helps link our own "today" with Star Trek's "tomorrow."
As with "Gunsmoke" 's Dodge City, "Kildare" 's Blair General Hospital, our Cruiser is a complete and highly varied community; we can, at any time, take our camera down a passageway and find a guest star (scientist, specialist, ordinary airman, passenger or stowaway) who can propel us into a new story.
THE SIMILAR WORLDS CONCEPT. Just as the laws of matter and energy make probable the other planets of Earth composition and atmosphere, certain chemical and organic laws make equally probable wide evolution into humanlike creatures and civilizations with points of similarity to our own.
All of which gives extraordinary story latitude—ranging from worlds which parallel our own yesterday, our present, to our breathtaking distant future.
PRINCIPAL CHARACTER. Robert T. April. The "Skipper," about thirty-four, Academy graduate, rank of Captain. Clearly the leading man and central character. This role, built about an unusual combination of colorful strengths and flaws, is

designated for an actor of top repute and ability. A shorthand sketch of Robert April might be: "A space-age Captain Horatio Hornblower," constantly on trial with himself, lean and capable both mentally and physically.

Captain April will be the focus of many stories—in still others he may lead us into the introduction of a guest star around whom that episode centers.

A strong, complex personality, he is capable of action and decision which can verge on the heroic—and at the same time lives a continual battle with the self-doubt and the loneliness of a command.

As with such men in the past (Drake, Cook, Bougainville, and Scott), April's primary weakness is a predilection to action over administration, a temptation to take the greatest risks onto himself. But, unlike most early explorers, he has an almost compulsive compassion for the rights and plights of others, alien as well as human.

Other cast regulars are a variety of excitingly different types: "NUMBER ONE," a glacierlike, efficient female who serves as ship's Executive Officer; JOSE "JOE" TYLER, the brilliant but sometimes immature Navigator; MR. SPOCK, with a red-hued satanic look and surprisingly gentle manners; PHILIP "BONES" BOYCE, M.D., ship's doctor and worldly cynic; and uncomfortably lovely J. M. COLT, the Captain's Yeoman.[3]

Generally, the concept statement will be written in narrative form. Depending upon the length and complexity of the final program or series, it might vary in length from a few sentences to several pages.

Treatment

Sometimes an established author will sell a script on the concept alone. More probably, one more stage of development will be needed to get the idea into sufficient detail for presentation to a buyer. That would be the *treatment*. This is a scene-by-scene description of the drama. Length will be about 3 to 15 pages, in narrative form, as is this first part of a treatment for a one-hour teleplay written by a student.

Script
Treatment for
GAMBLERS
by
Dennis
Rasmussen

Prologue:

A train pulls up to the AMTRAK Train Depot in Sacramento. Out front of the station a car pulls up and stops. A man and wife, Brad and Nancy Millar, get out with their bags. Another woman, the driver, also gets out, helps the couple with their bags and wishes them well—and good luck—on their trip. Says to win big in Reno. She hugs and kisses both man and wife and gets back into her car. She says this little trip will be good for both of them, considering . . . alluding to some problems in their marriage.

The couple goes into the depot. He says he must make a phone call before they board the train; she protests, says it is about to leave; he says he'll hurry. In his absence she goes to the candy counter to buy some gum. She sees someone familiar—a man who politely nods, pats his breast, and, taking care to be private, opens his coat just enough to reveal a gun. He buttons his coat, nods and leaves. She acknowledges the gun with a nod.

Brad is at the phone booth talking to someone in a desperate manner. He explains he will have the money by Monday. He has a system and is sure he'll win. He knows it's his final, desperate chance to save his company from going bankrupt. He has taken all his savings and will bet it all in order to win big. Brad Millar is in a huge financial mess and this is his last hope. He hears the "final boarding" announcement, goes back to his wife, and they hurriedly go out to the train.

We see a sign which reads "Reno Gamblers' Express" as the couple board the train. They are the last ones on and the brakeman signals to the conductor. The train pulls out of the station.

Act One:

Aboard the train the couple is in a coach car. He is full of hope and anticipation and she is too, but for a very different reason. She is sitting by the window looking out. In a brief conversation he suggests they go up to the lounge car for a drink. They get up and go. Transition to exterior of train crossing river.

Inside the lounge car they order drinks and find a seat. They begin playing a two-handed game of poker as the man from the candy counter scene comes in. He says, in mock surprise, he didn't know she was on the train. Nancy, quite uncomfortable, introduces the Stranger to her husband as Mr. Marvin Karr, an associate of her employer, whom she met once before. He explains he is going to Reno on business. Brad invites him to sit down and join their little poker game. Nancy doesn't like it but cannot say anything. They play with nickles and dimes but soon Karr talks them into playing with "real money."

In a series of shots, the game progresses, intercut with scenes of the train moving higher and higher into the Sierras. In time we see it is Nancy who is the big winner in their little three-handed game.

Karr is a poor loser and excuses himself. There's an expression of worry on Nancy's face but Brad can't see it. He says her good luck is an omen; that they are bound to win in Reno. She is pessimistic and says it is HE who must get lucky. In an ironic comment she says, "Reno can kill you." The train winds its way through the mountains—[4]

Developing the Script

To complete the treatment for a teleplay, the author will have to have considered at least these aspects of the development: *plot, characters, settings,* and *structure.* They interact, of course, but we will try to consider each separately.

Plot

The difference between a plot and a story, according to novelist E. M. Forster, is that a story is

> . . . a narrative of events arranged in their time sequence. A plot is also a narrative of events, the emphasis falling on causality.
>
> "The king died and then the queen died" is a story. "The king died and then the queen died of grief" is a plot.
>
> Or again, "The queen died, no one knew why until it was discovered that it was through grief at the death of the king." This is a plot with a mystery in it, a form capable of high development.[5]

Constructing the scenes and actions that are the plot of a play is one of the most difficult tasks for most beginning writers. As you become more experienced, you will find your own best technique for developing sequences, and will intuitively recognize patterns of development that work. But until you reach that point, we suggest you use this series of steps to develop the plot.

First, write the treatment of your *climax.* After all, it was the climactic idea, the outcome, that prompted your script from the very beginning, and that idea should have been stated as part of the concept. Now develop it into a full scene. The climax usually will be the next-to-last scene in the teleplay. For structural reasons, the final scene is usually an *epilogue,* separated from the climax by the closing commercials. Don't worry about that scene yet.

The climax is the scene in which the uncertainty developed in the play is finally resolved. It is the culmination of the plot. If your basic story idea was sound and its expansion into the concept was faithful to that original idea, then the climactic action is already determined. Either the cavalry will arrive and rescue the hero and heroine from the Indians, or it won't. The pursuing suitor will get the girl, or he won't. The money will arrive in time to avert bankruptcy, or it won't. And so on.

Next, move to the other end of the story—the opening scene. This scene, of necessity, will introduce characters and place them in some sort of physical location, or setting. It begins what is called by dramatic theorists the process of *exposition.* It should also establish the dramatic problem that ultimately will have to be resolved by introducing the first *complication.*

One common technique used in drama since the ancient Greeks is to open ''in the middle of things.'' An event is already in progress in which the major characters, or at least some of them, are involved. Establish quickly why this particular point in time, this location, and this action have meaning for these people.

Remember that one of the critical differences between television and radio drama, as opposed to the theater or movies, is that the audience can easily tune away from an uninteresting play. The opening scene must attract attention, so there is likely to be more action and less dialogue and character development in the opening scene of a teleplay than in a staged production or film.

Now, develop the remaining scenes that will connect the opening to the climax, and build the tension and uncertainty over the outcome. Again using the terminology of dramatic theory, there will be further *complications,* forces introduced into the play that will affect the course of the action. These complications will lead to *crises,* clashes of interest that build in intensity toward the final crisis, the *climax.* Complications also result in *reversals,* in which the protagonist is embarked on a course of action that seems to lead to a solution, only to have a sudden change of direction lead instead to possible disaster.

The number of scenes you need will depend on the overall length of the play, but again recall that structurally there will need to be frequent changes to maintain audience attention. Seldom should a scene exceed 3 minutes in length, and on the average they should not exceed 1 ½ minutes. Here the teleplay is much different from the theater, where scenes can be many times that length.

Most plots are presented in linear, chronological order. However, that does not mean the plot must proceed in ''real time,'' as the Greeks believed. Modern audiences are perfectly willing to accept time lapses, even very long ones—years, or even generations—between scenes or acts. Whatever the time lapse between scenes, however, each scene is presumed to take place after the preceding one and somehow to be the result of the actions in that preceding scene.

There are exceptions. *Flashbacks* to an earlier time are a legitimate plotting technique, often used to explain the motivation for a character's behavior. They need to be clearly identified to the audience, however.

A now quite common technique in television is *intercutting* between several separate plots presumed to be taking place simultaneously. In this case, each plot carries its own chronological progression toward a climax. The intercutting is purely an editing technique. In "Loveboat," for example, not only are the three plots being developed simultaneously, but each script has been written by a different author!

One important aspect of plotting is the concept of *foreshadowing,* described by one author this way: "A startling idea must not be sprung upon an audience wholly unprepared to accept it." A further description of foreshadowing is this now classic line: "If you are going to sink the ship in the last act, you must first let the audience know that the vessel is leaky, and then later inform them that a storm is approaching."

Foreshadowing applies not only to the actions of the plot, but equally to the motivations of the characters. Characters must behave in a consistent fashion. If the outcome of the plot is dependent upon a change in behavior on the part of a major character, that change must be forewarned.

Characteri-zation

The plot of a television drama can be moved along from opening scene to climax only through the actions, reactions, and interactions of characters. Contrast this method of development with many works in print that are primarily descriptive or narrative, forms of exposition that are not generally effective on television because they do not provide opportunities for change and for the refocusing of audience attention.

Playwrights do not agree on the best way to approach the development of characters. Some argue:

> . . . the characters are not preconceived. They evolve as the plot evolves, out of the main incidents of the story. They grow and change in accordance with the demands of the plot. At the same time, however, the characters affect and change the plot. . . . There is a constant interaction between the development of the characters and the development of the plot.[6]

Other playwrights counsel the beginning writer to develop each major character thoroughly at the treatment stage, to:

> Know your principal characters as you know yourself. Study your characters as if you were a psychologist—and good writers are, by nature, fairly good psychologists. Know their occupations, motivations, habits, fears, joys, prejudices, vices, how they walk and dress and talk.[7]

This approach is often used by authors who write novels. They will develop elaborate biographies for their characters, describing in detail physical attributes and family history, as well as the characteristics mentioned above. Using this approach of giving your characters a past that suggests their lives will help the beginning writer to make characters seem more lifelike, avoiding the wooden, one-dimensional characters found in poorly written scripts. It will also make it easier for you to provide consistency in the behavior of characters as they evolve during the play.

In television, characters are revealed to the audience through a combination of appearance, behavior, and speech. Appearance includes physical characteristics, clothing, and other physical objects with which a character is associated, such as the car the person drives. Behavior includes the patterns or habits the character displays, and the body language. Speech—including vocabulary and dialect—will be considered in more detail in the final phase of script development, when we talk about dialogue. However, you should remember that what a character does *not* say can be just as revealing as what he or she does say.

A frustration for many playwrights and a topic of considerable criticism is the limited amount of time available in most television dramas for the development of interesting and rounded characters. Successful characters will be those about whom the audience really cares, those the author makes believable. Yet the time constraints of the medium and the necessity to get the program off to a strong start in order to hold audience attention work against detailed character development.

If the program is part of a series, especially a long, ongoing series such as soap operas, or "M*A*S*H," or "Dallas," then there is opportunity for incremental character development. The audience builds its affinity for, or antagonism toward, a character over time. Hawkeye Pierce and J. R. Ewing are fully developed individual characters, but that complexity did not become evident in the first episode of the series. Fortunately for those programs, the characters were sufficiently interesting from the start to attract audiences. Many programs that fail after just a few episodes do so because the characters held no interest for audiences.

Try to avoid the use of stereotypes in establishing character. For secondary characters who appear only briefly, or for other situations in which only limited character development is possible, it is an easy out to resort to recognizable "standard" character types—the absent-minded professor, the jock, the blonde bimbo, and so on. These cliché characters have been so overused that they no longer hold the attention of audiences, if they ever did.

Even more important, don't perpetuate demeaning racial and sexual stereotypes—the female office worker who always has a dominant male boss, the black or Latin domestic servant. Give each character a unique identity even if that identity must be briefly sketched. It takes a bit more work, but it's worth it.

All these suggestions regarding character are part of this critical rule:

. . . audiences must *identify* with the characters, they must *worry* about what's happening to them, they must *love* and *hate* the characters, they must be *entertained* by them. . . .

Your audience must take sides in the conflict raging between your characters. The audience must be partisan. Their sympathies must be roused and sustained. Detachment on a spectator's part must be avoided at all costs. A disinterested audience is an uninterested audience.[8]

A character can be developed only in part through the writer's script. After the part has been written into the script, the casting director will choose a performer to play the role. That choice further defines the character. Then, to a major extent, the character will be brought to life by that performer. Nevertheless, the more accurately the writer describes the character, and the more precisely the written dialogue fits the character, then the more precisely will the portrayal match the intent of the writer's script.

Finally, and we mentioned this once before, the number of characters in the drama should be limited. Television is an intimate medium, most effective presenting small-scale situations involving only a few characters. Of course, over time—as, for example, over many episodes of a continuing series—the total number of different characters can be increased.

Settings

Every dramatic scene has to take place in a setting of some sort. In a well-constructed drama, each location will be chosen to further, or at least support, the action or mood. Even if a location is incidental or has no direct bearing on the plot, there nevertheless must be one. As the writer, you will have better control over your script if you choose your locations carefully and describe them accurately, rather than leaving the choices to the program's director and set director.

The action and dialogue that take place in each setting should be appropriate to the setting, whether it be a restaurant, an apartment, a car, or in the bleachers at a ballpark. Logically two characters at the ballpark might discuss the game, or baseball in general. They might also talk about a third friend who couldn't come to the game with them, because he's henpecked by his wife who wouldn't let him come. They might discuss other things of mutual interest that could as easily take place in other settings. But the ball game has brought them together; it provided the catalyst for any number of changes in the conversation.

On the other hand, it would be less likely that two characters would choose a ballpark in which to get together to plan a bank robbery. They could too easily be overheard.

Sometimes, however, a twist in the setting for a piece of plot action will do just that—use an incongruous location. A ''bad guy'' who is being trailed by the police goes to the ballpark to meet his accomplices, using the crowd as a means of protection and deception. It's difficult to present ''rules'' about dramatic development, for a creative writer can add to the strength of a plot and heighten tension by occasionally doing precisely the opposite of what would be expected.

Our point is simply that there must be a setting. The writer must consider the locale for every scene in the teleplay. And the drama will be stronger if each setting actually contributes to the plot.

The number and types of settings for television dramas will be dictated by the type of program. A fast-action police drama is not likely to be convincing if it doesn't use a lot of different locations, and both interiors and exteriors. The writer of a historical drama will have to be particularly careful to describe scenes that are authentic for the period and the action, and then the set designer will have to ensure accuracy in their reproduction. On the other hand, a soap opera or situation comedy may very well be confined to a series of interior sets in a studio. Audiences have come to accept that limitation in programs in which settings are not usually critical to the development of the plot.

Cost is also a factor. The police drama that requires a good deal of location shooting obviously will be a high-cost program to produce. A situation comedy confined to only a few sets in a single studio will cost much less. Well-known situation comedies such as "All in the Family" and "Three's Company" were set in just that way—one major livingroom set in which probably 75 percent of the action took place, plus one or two secondary sets such as a kitchen, bedroom, or neighborhood bar to provide some visual variety and a logical alternative location for development of parts of the plot.

Most television programs use fully realistic settings, either on location or in a studio. If the setting is the livingroom of a house, all the details of an appropriately decorated living room will be there. A good deal of information about the characters, the plot, and the mood of the drama can be transmitted to the audience by the composition, lighting, and color used in the setting. This information will be subconsciously processed by the viewers, quite apart from and before any action or dialogue takes place.

A few programs use *suggestive* settings. In a suggestive setting, a living-room might be indicated by a table containing a bouquet, a couple of chairs, and a lamp—set in limbo with no walls, doors, or windows to be seen. The decision to use a suggestive set may be dictated by cost, or by time (too little to prepare a realistic set), or by other considerations. Be careful, however. That decision should also consider the audience for whom the drama is targeted. An audience that is not familiar with the use of suggestive settings may not be comfortable viewing a play staged in that manner and may tune away.

Structure

Earlier in the text we devoted an entire chapter (Chapter 5) to program structure. For dramatic programs, those principles should be applied at the treatment stage.

Unity

The concept of dramatic unity has been recognized by successful playwrights, and by critics, for centuries.

From Aristotle:

> The structural unity of the parts [of a play] is such that if any one of them is displaced or removed, the whole will be disjointed and disturbed. For a thing whose presence or absence makes no visible difference is not an organic part of the whole.

From Voltaire:

> Ask anyone who has crowded too many events into his play what the reason for the fault is. If he is honest he will tell you he lacked the inventive genius to fill his play with a single action.

And from veteran Hollywood screenwriter Alfred Brenner:

> A single action means there is one main plot, one protagonist, one central conflict, one central emotional line, and one climax, which is the focal point of both the plot and the struggle of the main character.
>
> Thus each incident the writer selects must move the protagonist a step further toward his goal. All other incidents, no matter how exciting or dramatic, must be dispensed with.
>
> In the same way, each of the characters is there only to advance the main character's story. There should be no others. Moreover, *that story will be told largely from the protagonist's point of view.*[9]

That is not to say that a television drama may not have secondary plots moved forward by secondary characters, but when there are secondary themes, they must be connected back to the main plot at or before the climax. Few television plays, however, use much secondary development, simply because there is not usually enough time to do so.

Variety

Variety must be accomplished *within* the framework of unity. The most common ways to provide variety in broadcast dramas are with characters and settings.

Each individual is unique. In different scenes different combinations of characters are presented, thereby setting up different interactions among the characters. Even if all your characters are male, WASP teenagers, each should be differentiated from the others by appearance, manner, voice, or other readily distinguishing characteristics.

We've already commented on the value of multiple settings. They add excitement, presence, and realism, especially to an action-based program. But multiple settings are costly. When they are not possible, it becomes even more important to move characters in and out of scenes quickly to provide variety and maintain audience attention.

Pace

The number of program elements and the frequency with which they change dictates the pace of any program. (Review the discussion of program elements in Chapter 5 if you have forgotten them.) In a drama especially, the frequency of element change—that is, the pace—also contributes a great deal to the mood of the program. Audiences expect a police drama, for example, to move at a rapid pace (even though in real life police officers report that they seldom encounter the types of situations or act with the urgency suggested by these dramas). On the other hand, even though soap operas have picked up the pace of their action in recent years, the public perception of these programs is still that they move more slowly than life. Long program elements and even longer scenes are the primary cause of that perception.*

---

* Recall, from Chapter 5 also, that a program element is not necessarily the same as a scene. Several characters may move in and out of a single scene. Each time a major character enters or leaves, and causes the audience members' attention to be drawn again to the screen, a new element is begun— within that scene. Neither are program elements and camera shots synonymous. The camera may view a scene, and a program element within the scene, from a number of different angles, all of which help direct the audience's understanding of the action, but do not contribute sufficient attention-getting force to be classified as new elements.

Climax   This is the resolution of the plot and normally the final scene in a theatrical play. In a television play, however, the conclusion of the drama and the conclusion of the program are not the same. If they were, where would the sponsor put those final commercials? And don't forget the closing credits—and the trailer for next week's episode!

The common convention used to accommodate closing program elements is to include an *epilogue*. Final commercials come immediately following the climax, while audience attention is still high. The writer tries to hold the audience by providing one final scene after the commercials. In dramatic theory, the scene or action that follows the climax is the *denouement*, the untying of the knot the complications have formed. It restores order and provides an ending that seems necessary and probable.

For the television drama, this epilogue will be a scene in which the detective explains how he figured out who the murderer was, or in which the major characters express their relief at the outcome of the action. If the epilogues for a series are well written, the audience will hang around just to see what the author has thought up this time. Good epilogues, however, are a real challenge for the writer, and are not done well on many programs. The epilogue, if one is present, is then followed by the program closing—a trailer that previews the next episode, credits, and the production company logo.

One other aspect of climax is providing secondary climaxes at each act. Broadcast dramas, with the possible exception of those appearing on public stations, are written into acts of approximately 10 to 15 minutes each, for the obvious purpose of providing intermediate spots to insert commercials. This structural constraint sets up the additional requirement for the writer to provide high-interest material immediately preceding each of these breaks to carry the audience through the break and back into the drama.

Strong Start   This structural requirement has been brought up in a number of places previously. You must interest viewers as quickly as possible, because they don't have to stay tuned, and if you don't get their attention, they won't. For this reason, many dramatic programs use a *cold opening,* beginning with the opening scene of the play before any titles, credits, or commercials.

But whether the drama opens cold and is followed by the program opening, or the program opening precedes the drama, the drama itself must still capture audience interest in its opening scene. It does that by establishing the premise quickly, by introducing major characters and quickly arousing our curiosity about them and their problem, and by setting the mood of the drama, whether that be comedy or menace.

A Script Development Checklist   At this point your treatment ought to be complete. Many authors believe that at this point the hardest task has been accomplished. The characters and their motivations, the basic actions and settings, the sequence of events, and the structural form are all in place. Before we leave the treatment, however, let's review some of the considerations of its development, using these questions:

1. Is each character an individual, not a stereotype, and has sufficient development been given to each character for the audience to recognize that individuality?

2. Is there proper and adequate motivation for the actions?

3. Is there adequate foreshadowing? Has the audience been forewarned that things may turn out as they do?

4. Do subsequent actions logically follow from previous actions?

5. Do the behaviors and attitudes of characters remain consistent throughout? If there is change, is there explanation of and motivation for the change?

6. Does each scene contribute to the action and move the plot forward toward its climax?

7. Is the setting of every scene adequately described? Is it appropriate to the action? Better yet, does it contribute positively to the pace and the mood of the drama?

8. Does the structure of the drama meet the demands of the program format, and does it support the audience's expectations of unity, variety, pace, strong start, and climax?

Although your play will be well developed at this stage, it is still a treatment. There will still be time to fix details if is is discovered later that they won't work. Be patient in putting together the final script. As one producer put it: "There's nothing worse than having the *structure* of this 'house' (story) we're building creak and crumble as we take up residence." You should try to make your treatment as polished as you can, but don't worry about every detail at this point.

Final Script

Three more steps need to be taken to complete your script. *Dialogue*, the actual spoken lines of the characters, will have to be written. Some aspects of *visualization* will need to be detailed, beyond that of the description of settings. And the final draft will have to be typed in an appropriate format.

Dialogue

Two suggestions are frequently made to beginning writers when it comes to constructing the dialogue of a radio or television play. The first is to listen carefully to the voices of people in all types of conversations, and to use what you hear as the pattern for your dialogue. That advice is good, but only up to a point. Script dialogue should *seem* to sound like actual conversation, but in fact actual conversation rambles a lot and is wasteful of time. The dialogue in a radio or television drama must move along more rapidly. It must further the development of the plot.

You can make constructed dialogue seem natural, however, by using the limited vocabulary most of us use in everyday speech, and using the vocabulary expected from the type of character you have created. You should also make frequent use of sentence fragments, pauses, and interruptions, as these too are common in normal conversation. Review the principles of aural style (Chapter

2) and of voice as a component of sound (Chapter 6) for specific suggestions on developing appropriate dialogue.

The second suggestion made to beginning writers stems from the earlier advice to create for each of your characters a complete biography and environment:

> The more you know the character in your play, the easier it is for the character to help *write his own dialogue.* . . . See him in your mind's eye as he appears in the drama. Know what he looks like, how he moves, what he thinks. Imagine the sound of the character's voice, the timber, the inflection. Now put him into a dramatic situation and *let him talk. Aloud. Through you.*[10]

Visualization

In the completed script, the description of the visual action usually is written in narrative form. Only on rare occasions will the writer be asked to prepare a shooting script, which gives each camera angle, distance, and so on. Much more common is what is known as the *master-scene* script. Here each scene is detailed, the movements of the characters and their interactions are given in narrative fashion, and the dialogue is written in its proper sequence. But the precise camera shots are left to the discretion of the director, to be worked out on the set at the time of production, and in the editing room during postproduction.

Although writers frequently express frustration at having to turn their creation, the script and its characters, over to others at this stage, they can still maintain some control over the final production if they do provide detailed descriptions of the actions expected, and if the behavior and motivations of the characters are consistent and realistic.

To help delineate each character, you should include descriptions of the "business" in the scene. *Business* is the term used to label the behavior of characters, their idiosyncracies, and so on. If a character is expected to show nervousness in a scene, for example, you might write a direction to tap a pencil on the desk, or nervously and continuously flick the ash from a cigarette.

But don't write camera shots. An exception might be an instruction for a *point-of-view* shot, where the camera becomes the eyes of one of the characters, and views the scene from that character's point of view.

The two excerpts of dramatic writing for television in this book, Prisoner of War from "Riptide" (Chapter 4) and "Gamblers," in this chapter, are both good examples of master-scene description.

Format

The examples we just mentioned are both written using the layout form recommended by the Writers Guild of America, which has become the standard of the industry. Review the guidelines on dramatic format in Chapter 4, which are sufficient to get you started. Then, if you begin to write dramatic scripts seriously, obtain the full set of format instructions from WGA.[11]

Here, in WGA format, are the opening scenes of "Gamblers," which we used as an example of a treatment earlier.

GAMBLERS

Prologue

FADE IN:

1. EXTERIOR. SACRAMENTO AMTRAK RAILROAD STATION, DAY   1

A passenger train pulls into the station. A crowd of travellers are waiting on the platform as the train comes to a stop. Crowd and train noises.

2. SAME, BUT IN FRONT OF STATION   2

A car pulls up in front of the depot and quickly a couple jump out. They are Brad and Nancy Millar. Another woman, the driver, also gets out and helps the couple with their bags. This is Jil Raymond, their best friend. Brad Millar is in a mood of high expectation but Nancy, by contrast, is quieter and in a mood which, to Jil, appears to reflect the strain of the Millar's marriage. It is not working well.

> JIL
> (Cheerfully)
> Good Luck, you two. Wish I was going too.
>
> (Motherly aside to Nancy)
> Give it a chance, honey, this should do both of you some good.

> NANCY
> (Sarcastically)
> Well, for one of us anyway.

She looks over to Brad who is closing the trunk.

> JIL
> (Hugging them both)
> Hurry or you'll miss the train.
>
> (Getting back into her car.)
> Win big in Reno, bye.

Nancy and Brad wave thank-yous to their friend as she drives off. Quickly they go into the depot.

3. INTERIOR OF TRAIN DEPOT   3

A crowd of travellers hurry here and there in the busy depot. We hear the announcement: "All passengers Eastbound to Colfax, Truckee and Reno, now boarding at Gate 5." Brad looks at his watch as they stop in the middle of the depot.

> BRAD
> We still have a few minutes. Here . . .
> (Hands her a checkbook)
> You get the tickets. I have to make a phone call.

NANCY
(Protesting)
The train is about to leave!

BRAD
I won't be a minute.

He goes off and leaves her to buy the tickets. She heads for the ticket
counter.

4. AT A PHONE BOOTH IN THE DEPOT   4
   Brad puts in a coin, dials and waits a moment.

5. Nancy is seen buying tickets. When she's finished she gathers up her 5
   bag and purse and starts to walk toward the waiting area. She looks up
   to see someone familiar—someone she expected to see. He is a big,
   muscular, slimy man who gives her a half smile and a nod. He is well
   dressed and gestures to his breast, giving something under his coat a
   careful pat. She returns his half smile and nod, then turns away. We
   hear the announcement: "Passengers Eastbound . . . last call." She
   anxiously looks through the crowd for Brad.

6. AT THE PHONE BOOTH   6
   Brad is finishing up his conversation.

BRAD
If I come up with the money by Monday we won't have to go
bankrupt. . . . I know that, but it's my only chance. . . . What
other options do I have? . . . Yeah, and if I can win, maybe I can
buy myself back into this marriage, too.

He looks across the depot to see Nancy impatiently waiting.

The train is about to leave . . . Bye.

He hangs up the phone, picks up his bag and hurriedly walks over to
his wife. They quickly go out to the train.

7. EXTERIOR, AT THE TRAIN PLATFORM   7
   Brad and Nancy are the last to board the train, which carries a sign:
   "RENO GAMBLER'S EXPRESS." The brakeman makes a signal and the
   train pulls out of the station.
   FADE OUT.

Source: Courtesy of the writer, Dennis Rasmussen.

Radio Drama

Dramatic writing for radio is enjoying a modest rebirth after a considerable decline
in the face of television's competition. Public radio stations now produce and air

some significant dramatic programs; short comedy vignettes are being marketed successfully for use as inserts in station formats; and, of course, even though they are brief, dramatic introductions are used as parts of many radio commercials.

Plot

Full-length radio dramas have essentially the same constraints as those for television. The time frame—30 minutes, an hour, or whatever—limits the number of complications that can be developed. But in contrast to TV, the number of scenes, and the number of characters involved, can easily be increased. It costs very little more to add scenes and locations, just a few words in the dialogue and perhaps a sound effect. New characters are also added easily. The actors already in the studio can change their voices to create a line or two for an added character.

But be careful. Just because location changes and new characters are easy to create, that doesn't mean you should create them. Don't add without purpose; that just adds clutter and reduces the audience's understanding of the plot development. But scenes you might leave out of a TV drama because they would be too costly to set up and shoot for just a few seconds on-screen may be added in radio.

Characteriza-tion

In Chapter 6 we spent some time discussing vocal techniques used to develop radio characters. It goes without saying that the only ways to give a radio character a personality, and to differentiate one character from another, are through words, dialect, inflection, and pauses and hesitations in vocal delivery. Listen to people's speech patterns and copy those patterns you want when writing radio characters.

Settings

The beginning writer preparing a dramatic program for radio sometimes overlooks the fact that the requirement to have a setting for each scene applies to this medium just as much as it does for TV. One of the strengths of radio drama, however, is that the details of a setting will be provided for each member of the audience by his or her own imagination.

One of the great stories of radio is this one about Stan Freberg, who was commissioned by the radio industry to write a "commercial" for radio that could be used to counter the competition from television advertising. Taking the role of a radio newscaster, Freberg announced that he was on location to report the event of the century . . . the creation of the world's largest cup of hot chocolate in Lake Michigan. Freberg explained in exciting detail how this monumental task would be accomplished through the assistance of the Royal Canadian Air Force.

The crews were ready. As Freberg shouted a step-by-step account over the roar of engines and horns, the whipped cream was sprayed from giant hoses with appropriate squishing and whooshing noises. The moment of triumph had come. A squadron of helicopters hovered, ready to drop the jumbo cherry "bomb" dead center on the colossal confection. By now listeners could almost taste it. Amid a great whirring of helicopter blades, and the sound of guide cables whistling from the strain, the gigantic cherry dropped into place with a satisfying plop! Having created a picture only the imagination could create for the eye, Freberg issued a challenge from above the cheering crowd: "Now, you want to try that on television?"[12]

Structure   The structural requirements for radio drama are no different from those for television. Audience responses to both forms are the same. If you succeed in attracting attention with a strong opening; provide unity, variety, and a sense of pace throughout; and build to climaxes before commercial breaks and at the end, you should be able to hold an audience throughout.

Dialogue   Radio dialogue differs from television dialogue in one important way: Television dialogue should not describe what is obvious to the audience visually; radio must use dialogue (or narration, which is often a weaker alternative) to accomplish this.

Here are two brief bits of dialogue used to set up the problem in a problem-solution commercial. In the first example, a few key words and phrases provide all the description of both location and characters that is needed. The target audience, which is the same group as the characters in the dialogue, will be able to supply mental images from their own experience to fill in details from this description:

Mary: Steve, when are we going to get some decent furniture in this apartment? I'm ashamed to invite friends over because all we have are these old broken, hand-me-downs from your parents.

Steve: I'm sorry, honey, but we both know it's hard to afford new furniture when you're newly married. Just as soon as I get a raise at work. . . . (FADE)

In addition to the topic of the conversation, furniture, the keys are *apartment*, which sets location, and *parents* and *newly married*, which establish the age and relationship of the characters. In contrast, this dialogue was another student's attempt to set up the same situation:

Mary: Steve, we need new furniture.

Steve: Why, what's wrong with what we have?

Mary: Well, the sofa and the chairs don't match; the lamp shades are filthy; and the mattress on the bed is all lumpy. . . .

Any dialogue will give the listeners some information, but this one isn't very helpful. The location could be anywhere from a small apartment to a mansion; the characters could be newly married to elderly; and the furniture might be broken hand-me-downs, or expensive items just slightly used by a very fussy couple. Even the relationship between Mary and Steve is not clear.

One additional way in which radio dialogue differs from television is in the frequent use of names. Since characters cannot be seen, the audience needs to be reminded frequently which characters are present, and who is speaking to whom. Don't use names in every bit of dialogue, but do use them more frequently than you would in normal conversation, or for TV.

Format   The correct format for general radio production, including drama, was given in Chapter 4. Review those guidelines and examples in preparation for writing dramatic radio scripts.

Conclusion

If it is your ambition to be rich and famous as a television writer, you will probably have to make your success as a dramatic writer. The odds are not in your favor, however. Only a fraction of the ideas, concepts, treatments, and scripts written with the hope of being sold are in fact accepted. Even fewer are actually produced and broadcast. Cynics would argue that an even smaller fraction of what is broadcast is worth airing, and that the number of worthwhile dramas which appear on television is indeed few. The countering argument is that network television audiences are so large that even an occasional worthwhile production will be seen by millions more than will the best and longest running theatrical productions.

Although the chances of being successful as a dramatic writer for television are slim, the rewards are substantial for those who do succeed in getting an original series onto a network, or who get a contract to write a serial drama, a miniseries, or an original play.

If you are to succeed you should study drama—its history, its theory, and all its forms. Attend the theater, study films, watch television, and if you can find it, listen to radio drama as well. Watch people; make note of interesting characters you may want to use later in your plays. Become a careful observer of the actions of individuals, and of their interactions with others. Catalogue interesting places that would strengthen the action in a drama. Carry a recorder, or take notes when you think of an idea.

And write. It is possible, sometimes, to get a job writing commercials or PSAs without any significant prior experience. And it is even possible to land a position as a newswriter without specific broadcast writing experience, by relying on expert knowledge of a topic area or by having had experience in print journalism. But we have never known of a successful dramatic writer who did not put in considerable time and effort practicing on every opportunity that came along—commercials, corporate scripts, comedy vignettes, whatever.

You might become another Henry Slesar. In the early 1970s, he was the head writer for not just one, but two successful television serial dramas, "The Edge of Night" and "Somerset." He originated 10 new half-hour shows a week, 520 programs a year, and he had a gross annual income estimated at $350,000, out of which he paid an agent, subwriters, a secretary "and a murderous tax bill."

Before he became "the writer with the largest audience in America," he wrote 4 novels, had 700-odd short stories published, wrote screenplays, and contributed articles to *Playboy*. "One of his greatest thrills was discovering at age 8 he could mesmerize the kids on the block with his ghost stories. When he first began selling science-fiction and mystery stories, it was 'like tasting blood—unimaginable that people would pay for doing what I so enjoyed.' ''[13]

Exercises

1. a. Do a structural analysis of a TV dramatic program following the instructions in Exercises 1 and 2, Chapter 6.

   b. Then, comment on the other aspects of dramatic construction by answering the first seven questions of the script development checklist in this chapter.

2. Write a concept statement for one of the following:

   a. A daytime TV soap opera.

   b. A situation comedy that features a supernatural gimmick.

   c. A one-time special historical drama featuring an important person in the history of your community.

3. Using a favorite short story as your plot, rewrite enough of it to get the first two (at least) scenes for a radio drama. Consider especially these matters:

   a. How will you introduce the story, and its characters, and set the first scene?

   b. What characterizations are the performers to give to the roles they play? What dialects, if any, or other vocal techniques should they use?

   c. How is the transition from scene 1 to scene 2 accomplished? How is the second location (and/or time) distinguished for the listener? What transition device is used?

Key Terms and Concepts

business	master-scene scripting
characterization	plot
climax	program element
cold opening	reversal
complication	scene
concept	setting
crisis	soap opera
dialogue	stereotype
epilogue	treatment
exposition	visualization
foreshadowing	

Notes

1. Richard A. Blum, *Television Writing: From Concept to Contract* (New York: Hastings House, 1980), p. 57.

2. Paddy Chayefsky, *Television Plays* (New York: Simon & Schuster, 1955), pp. 173–174. Copyright ©1955 by Paddy Chayefsky, renewed © 1983 by Susan Chayefsky. Reprinted by permission of Simon & Schuster, Inc.

3. Stephen E. Whitfield and Gene Roddenberry, *The Making of Star Trek* (New York: Ballantine Books, 1968), pp. 22–30. Reprinted by permission.

4. Courtesy of the writer, Dennis Rasmussen.

5. Alfred Brenner, *The TV Scriptwriter's Handbook* (Cincinnati: Writer's Digest Books, 1980), pp. 59–60.

6. Ibid., p. 72.

7. Constance Nash and Virginia Oakey, *The Television Writer's Handbook* (New York: Barnes and Noble Books, 1978), p. 7.

8. Coles Trapnell, *Teleplay: An Introduction to Television Writing* (San Francisco: Chandler, 1966), p. 23.

9. Brenner, *The TV Scriptwriter's Handbook*, pp. 80–81.

10. Michelle Cousin, *Writing a Television Play* (Boston: The Writer, Inc. 1975), p. 79.

11. Write to: Writers Guild East, 555 West 57 Street, New York, NY 10019. Ask for *Professional Writer's Teleplay/Screenplay Format*. The cost is $2.50.

12. The Freberg spot was commissioned by the Radio Advertising Bureau.

13. Albert J. Zuckerman, "The Writer with the Largest Audience in America," *TV Guide*, December 11, 1971, pp. 16–19.

Chapter 17

Other Program Types

In the introduction to this part of this text we gave a caution about the use of one- or two-word program labels. That caution is worth repeating here. Although abbreviated labels are handy to use in conversation, they do not adequately or accurately describe the planning, writing, and production tasks to be performed in the preparation of programs. Instead, often they mislead.

For example, many people seem to believe that the label "women's programs" identifies a particular type of program. It does not. If we wished to argue the point, we might infer that the label means programs produced *by* women. Following that line of argument, we could then examine the problems women have had, and still have, in being accepted in the industry as producers, writers, and directors on an equal footing with men.

Or we might choose to read "women's programs" to mean programs *about* women. After all, the activities and concerns of women make up the subject matter of many programs and are mixed into the variety of content that make up many more. The discussion of abortion, to take just one very obvious example, is a topic that focuses on women. It has been the topic of many discussion, interview, and documentary programs, and abortion stories are frequently found in news programs.

But we know that the primary meaning of "women's programs" is programs *for* women. The label refers to women as the intended audience. That label encompasses a wide range of different content and an equally wide range of different forms of presentation. There are dramatic programs intended for women—soap opera serial dramas. There are news programs intended for women—most programs and stories of the soft news type. There are discussion programs similarly targeted—any program that chooses topics of primary concern to women, such as the program on abortion.

We could go on, but the point should be obvious by now. If you intend to write "women's programs," you may choose any of a number of forms; you will select content and gratifications that are strong for women; and you will schedule the program at an hour when that target group is available and not likely to be busy with other activities.

The same argument may be made for any type of "minority" programming—programs for senior citizens, programs for blacks or Hispanics or any other ethnic minority, programs for children. We have discussed in previous chapters most of the major program forms which are used to package content to reach these various target groups, and because we have already done that, we will not repeat those comments here. We will, however, briefly review and reemphasize the gratifications that appear to be strong for these groups, and note some trends that will affect future programming.

We will also consider three program types that do not fall under the "programs for . . ." category—music programs and religious programs, which are types based on content, and variety programs, a label that describes structure.

Programs for Women

Having just made a point by using women's programs as an example of inaccurate labeling, what more can be said about programs for this group? Well, first, that women *in general* represent a very large and very diverse target group. In almost all instances you will have to narrow the target considerably before being able to select content and gratifications that will attract and hold one particular age group or other subcategory of women.

Second, women represent a tremendously important buying group. Not only do women decide on the products they use personally, they decide most household purchases as well. For the types of consumer goods that find TV and radio advertising most effective, women are the decision-making group.

Although it is risky to generalize within such a broad category of audience, we can identify several gratifications that seem to be stronger for women than for other groups. Quite obviously these are gratifications found in programs that most successfully attract women. Keep in mind, however, that given the proper set of circumstances, any gratification can be important.

Sex Appeal

We can see evidence here in soap operas, especially, where love and sexual attraction make up much of the plots. In radio, we note that musical formats which appeal to women have a high proportion of songs with love themes.

Personalism

This gratification can be strong for all audience groups, but it is here that programming *for* women and programming *about* women merge. Our general definition of personalism is "the extent to which the audience can *identify* with characters, events, and situations." Identification with women appearing on the program—as actresses, as news reporters and interviewers, or as the subjects of the program—is an obvious and effective gratification.

Value

A traditional role for women in American society is that of transmitting values to the next generation. Mothers are expected to pass on religious, ethical, and moral standards to their children. So, by indirection, they are the group that will pay more attention to, and be more attracted to, programs which portray those values.

Curiosity

Particularly since we have included human interest as a large part of this gratification, it is strong for women. This is another traditional position. Men are expected to be more interested in work or other *activities;* women to be more concerned with *people*—family, neighbors, friends, and the extended family which is brought to them by television.

We may be accused of perpetuating stereotypes with regard to the gratifications of value and curiosity, but the evidence strongly supports those contentions. Women do watch programs which contain those appeals far more than other groups.

We can summarize this style of programming by reference to an article that recently appeared in the trade press. The article promotes an organization called Creative Programming, and two programs which it has developed for women. There is nothing unique about this particular approach. We have chosen it precisely because it is typical of what is happening in the industry as a result of two factors: (1) increased numbers of delivery channels, especially on cable, and the corresponding audience fragmentation; and (2) increased awareness of how to use the new media to accomplish sponsors' goals.

> By the end of this year [1985], half of all homes in the United States will have been wired for cable. As more TV viewers have cable viewing as an option, networks will feel the continued heat of competition for viewers for both their programs and commercials.
>
> Part of the appeal of cable is its transmission of narrowcast programs; series that are tailor-made to smaller audiences with clearly defined and specified interests and that draw viewers who prefer the more personalized programming to which cable has traditionally lent itself. Recently, another development has surfaced that further enhances the attractiveness of cable programming. However, in this case, it appeals to cable advertisers as well as viewers. Realizing cable's program and commercial potential, a growing number of video production houses are approaching large corporate advertisers and offering to create for them a new hybrid type of programming—advertiser-sponsored TV series specifically designed to match audience profiles, product lineups and the merchandising objectives of the advertiser. In effect, it allows corporations the opportunity to develop, produce and own their own TV series. In the vanguard of these specialized production houses is New York's Creative Programming. . . .
>
> CPI's first challenge came about when Campbell Soup asked a number of independent producers to submit ideas for an ''upbeat and contemporary'' program that would appeal to women from the ages of 18 to 49. CPI was chosen from nearly 10 other competitors with its *WomanWatch.*
>
> *WomanWatch,* entirely conceptualized, written, produced and directed by CPI, is a 30-minute program that each week profiles three contemporary but usually noncelebrity women. Guests have included women who work as private investigators, circus tutors, magicians, state troopers, Army parachutists and astronauts. . . .
>
> [The producer] believes that the program was chosen by Campbell probably because it appealed to the target audience but was not a stereotypical program for women. . . .

The early success of *WomanWatch* prompted Campbell to ask for a second series. CPI responded by creating *Celebrity Chefs,* a different type of cooking show than had previously been seen on both network and cable. Hosted by the British actor Robert Morley, *Celebrity Chefs* each week features two stars preparing their favorite recipe and, more importantly, just having fun in the kitchen.

Guests have included Henny Youngman, who delivered 1-liners while making blintzes; Vic Tayback, who recreated his Mel's Diner chili from *Alice;* and Phyllis Diller, a real-life gourmet cook, who dazzled the set with her salmon in papillote.

The 30-minute show is more concerned with providing the viewer with a unique kitchen view perspective of their favorite celebrity than it is with the precision preparation of food.[1]

As we have argued, there are no "women's programs." Neither is there such a thing as a "typical" program for women. We think these two programs are worth your attention, however, because they typify what writers and producers must consider when aiming for this audience.

Programs for Children

One topic that comes immediately to mind when considering programs for children are the ethical issues raised by both the content and the advertising associated with those programs. Children are different as an audience because of their general lack of experience. That lack of experience leaves them vulnerable to manipulation by both program producers and advertisers, who have used practices frequently seen as unethical by parents and by organized consumer groups.

The list of issues is lengthy. You will probably be able to cite examples based on these general descriptions, and add others of your own.

1. Children are not yet able to distinguish reality from fantasy in many instances. Commercials should not take advantage of that by using camera angles and other video tricks to portray toys, for example, with attributes they do not have.

2. Similarly, children are not able to make reasoned choices between good, healthful food products and junk food. Sugared cereals, candy, and so on should not be advertised in children's programs and thus create demand which parents often are powerless to resist.

3. Cartoon and puppet programs that feature characters also sold as toys and dolls, and that have commercials inserted for those products, take advantage of young children's inability to distinguish between program content and commercials.

4. For the same reason, live performers in a program should not also serve as the "pitch persons" for products.

5. Children are attracted to programs with lots of action and movement, and with frequent change, because of their short attention span. Too often, action is equated with violence.

Consumers groups have from time to time made appeals to the FCC and to Congress asking that regulations be enacted providing changes in children's programming and advertising, but without much success. Other types of protests, including boycotts of firms that advertise on children's programs, have on occasion been successful. Some individual stations have taken programs off the air after they were pointed out as being excessively violent, for example. The networks have established codes to address some of these concerns. But the pressures to attract and hold the attention of children, and to sell products to them, are often at odds with ethical issues. About the best we can say is that programming is better than it used to be, but that continued vigilance will be necessary to hold the gains and make any future improvements.

One bright spot in the picture is the phenomenal success of "Sesame Street" on public television. Another is the Nickelodeon channel on cable. Similarly well-produced network series and specials include the ABC "Afterschool Specials" and NBC's "Special Treats." Their successes are due in part to the fact that because this is nationally distributed programming, networks can pay substantial amounts for writing and production, and these costs can be further justified by frequent repetition of the same materials. From the standpoint of a writer looking for a career, however, not many opportunities are available writing nationally syndicated programs for children.

Locally produced programs are not nearly as innovative as the national ones we mentioned, and for the reason mentioned as well—cost. An expensive-to-produce live origination cannot recover its costs with the limited audience in one market. So stations, if they originate anything at all for children, will purchase syndicated cartoons and other features (a nationally available service again) and meld them into a type of variety show, using a live host, possibly a short segment featuring a live local guest (the zookeeper or such), and maybe a few kids in a studio audience to add personalization as a gratification. Some opportunities will exist in these programs for the writing of at least minimal scripts.

Radio programs for children are now almost totally gone. Where they are found at all, they must be produced on almost no budget and consist largely of readings from children's literature and records—both music and spoken-word recordings. Audiences too are nearly nonexistent.

Programs for Minority Audiences

The quantity and variety of programming for minority audiences will vary tremendously from station to station and market to market, depending obviously on which minorities exist in that market in sufficient numbers to be the legitimate target audiences for programs and ads, and also on which are vocal in demanding air time for programs about their group and of interest to them. We are referring most obviously to ethnic minorities, but there are other groups—the elderly, and minorities identified by other demographic or life style characteristics.

Almost by definition, because they are designed to appeal to minorities, these programs are not common on TV network schedules. Networks are the mass medium. The history of the "Lawrence Welk Show" makes an excellent case study to prove this point.

The program series, which consisted largely of the Welk orchestra playing older popular music, with visual variety provided by different soloists and dancers, originated on the ABC network. Over several years it developed a very loyal audience of senior citizen viewers. Its contents and gratifications were perfectly targeted for that group.

One of the early advertisers on the program was the Dodge division of Chrysler automobiles. That, too, was a good match. Dodges sold very well to that group, in fact so well that Dodge began to get a reputation as the "old-folks" car. To counter that image, and attempt to get back a broader-based clientele, Dodge finally decided to drop its advertising in the program. Other senior-oriented products took over, however, and the program continued to be a commercial success.

Although the program was hugely successful with seniors, and it was almost the only program on the networks which was, it did not draw well from other groups. The narrowness of its audience limited the total size of audience and finally the network cancelled—figuring to replace it with a program with broader appeal, larger audiences and higher advertising rates and revenues. The series was still sufficiently valuable as a marketing device, however, that it immediately moved into syndication, where it remained successful for several additional years on stations which could afford to place it in their schedules. The audiences may have been small by network standards, but they were still as large or larger than those for many other syndicated shows.

Now, as the number and variety of channels and options for audiences continues to grow, there will be more programming for more narrowly focused minority groups of all types—so long as the group remains sufficiently large that the economics of producing for it justifies the expense.

All types of programs can be targeted for minority groups, simply by recognizing the gratifications that are important to them and adjusting the content of programs accordingly. The safest way to do that is to hire representative members of that minority to write and produce the programs—or, if that isn't practical, hire them as consultants to work with staff writers. Be sure, however, that your writers or consultants are indeed representative of the target minority. Individuals who are not members of a minority group tend to assume these groups are homogeneous. In fact, ethnic minorities exhibit the same diversity of interests within the group as are found in the majority.

If you are yourself a member of a minority group in your community, you may have an excellent opportunity to practice your broadcast writing and production skills right away. Often programs for these groups are produced with minimal budget on local radio, television, or cable. Frequently the program staff are volunteers (or some mix of volunteers and station personnel). Turnover among volunteers is high, and if you offer to assist, you are quite likely to have a job. If a program does not exist for your group, you might get together with others and propose one to a local station. If you make a well-organized presentation using the principles we've set forth in this book, you may very well be able to get a program on the air.

Musical Programs

We need to distinguish first between musical *programs* and musical *programming*. The first implies structured programs of determinate length; the latter describes the format of most radio stations and, more recently, of music video cable TV channels.

There is very little that can be said about writing for musical programming. Quite simply, very little writing is done. That is not to say that musical programming is haphazard; it is not, but written continuity in any formal sense is rare.

Music radio stations are very careful to maintain a consistent format in order to hold an audience they may have built up over a considerable time. Individuals are quick to tune away if the "sound" deviates very much from that to which they have become accustomed—that is, if their gratifications are no longer fullly realized.

To maintain consistency, stations do several things. They may conduct quite sophisticated *call-out* research to determine audiences' musical preferences. They often hire consultants who have had experience with similar formats in other markets and a record of success. They will purchase syndicated formats that have been successful elsewhere. And they will hire well-known, experienced air personalities (disc jockeys, or whatever other term is current) to play the records.

Some stations use *rundown sheets* which list the sequence in which records are to be played. Jocks will not be permitted to deviate from that sheet. Other stations take a more relaxed approach, allowing the staff to select at random from music in the station's library. Most common, we think, is a middle-ground approach which uses some form of a *format clock*. The programming staff will have developed a clock that diagrams for each hour the times at which musical selections are to be played, commercials inserted, news read, and so on. Clocks will be modified for different day-parts to match the interests and moods of the audience—peppier music in the morning, no news late at night, and so on. How musical selections are to be chosen and sequenced to provide variety can also be plotted on the clock. The clock here is a bit more sophisticated than some, but still typical.

The categories of music which fit the labels on the clock are as follows:

1. *Power.* Eleven songs are in the power category. Four are played each hour for a turnover rate of 2 hours and 45 minutes—the time elapsing before the eleven-song cycle begins again. These songs are the most important in the system and, consequently, receive more air play than any other music. They attain power status through a combination of high national *chart ranking,* high local *sales ranking,* high *research status* and the unanimous *verdict as winners* by the music selection board.

2. *Yellow.* The yellow category contains nine or ten songs comprising the *lower status records on the current chart.* They are all *up-tempo or fast songs* and

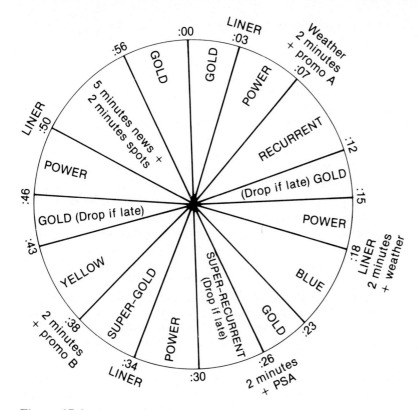

Figure 17.1
Source: From *Broadcast/Cable Programming: Strategies and Practices,* 2d ed., by Susan Tyler
Eastman, Sydney W. Head, and Lewis Klein. © 1985 by Wadsworth, Inc. Used by permission.

are positioned within the music clock to achieve a tempo balance. These records may be either rising in popularity to power status or songs recently withdrawn from the power rotation because research indicates their popularity is declining. The yellow category songs are played at the rate of two per hour and are recycled every 3 hours and 15 minutes.

3. *Blue.* The blue category is exactly the same as the yellow category except they are *down-tempo or slow songs*. In fact, the most important thing about these two categories is that they are tempo categories. They comprise the *bottom 18 to 20 songs on the current playlist,* and two are played in an hour.

Note that the content of the power, blue and yellow categories changes weekly to conform to changes in the current playlists. These three categories comprise what might be called the radio station's "core contemporary music marketing strategy."

4. *Super-recurrent.* The super-recurrent category contains 15 songs recently on the playlist. To qualify as super-recurrent, a song must have had *a number one ranking* in one or more of the trade magazines and be absolutely accepted by the prime target demographic audience as measured by the station's own

research. One super-recurrent song is played every hour for a rotation of 15 hours.

5. *Recurrent*. The recurrent category contains 30 songs *recently in the super-recurrent* rotation. These songs are also played at the rate of one per hour. This category is designed to increase the amount of very recent popular music aired on the station. It creates the impression that the station plays more varied music than it actually does because one current song (power, yellow, or blue) is cut to make room for a recurrent. Listeners get the impression the station airs a broad range of music although only one song is added per hour. The recurrent songs are proven winners and do not harm format attractiveness. The whole list is heard only once in 30 hours.

6. *Super-gold*. The super-gold category contains 53 songs that have climbed the ladder to the *top and moved downward* through the recurrent list. These songs are the "never dies" the target audience will always recognize and immediately identify as *classics*. These 53 *songs change periodically* to make way for newer songs. The age of records in this category may very from three months to two years, but they are the all-time winners and greatly enhance a music format.

7. *Gold*. The gold category completes the formula. Gold songs are played at the rate of four to five per hour depending on the daypart and the availability of audience with the desired demographics within each daypart. For a song to make the gold list, it must be a *proven winner*. A gold stays a gold *forever*.[2]

The format clock is a visual representation of the principles of structure applied to music radio. Throughout this book we have discussed program structure mostly with regard to television programs of fixed length and formal organization. But successful radio programming, even musical formats, also adheres to the same principles. Unity is present in the overall format or sound. Variety exists in the variations found within the clock—in artists, instrumental or vocal, big band or small combo, fast or slow.

Pacing is evident by the frequent change from one record to another and from records to other types of content. You are probably aware that many popular music selections appear in two lengths. The version you buy in the record store may be three to five minutes long. A shorter version, perhaps only one and a half to two minutes, is recorded for air play on radio stations, because the longer version would slow the pace. (There are exceptions. Some stations play longer cuts, even full LP sides. They are deliberately sacrificing pace for gratifications they believe will compensate for this structural weakness.)

Climax is the only structural principle not usually found in music radio programming, but it too may be consciously added on occasion. A disc jockey may promote the fact that a popular new tune will be heard later in the show. Countdown programs that play the "top 20" records in reverse order of popularity are also building climax. And more popular selections will appear just before commercial breaks.

We have been talking of course about recorded music. It's important that you understand the relationship between the recording and broadcasting industries.

Stations depend on a selection of fresh music supplied—free—by recording companies. The record companies, in turn, depend on radio stations to popularize selections that listeners will buy.

Television, until recently, has had only limited success with musical programs. The problem, obviously, is what do you show while you are listening to music. Watching the music being played by an orchestra works only moderately well. This is the approach used by symphony orchestra programs on public television. But regularly scheduled programs of orchestral music on commercial television no longer exist; "The Voice of Firestone" disappeared years ago, and even "Lawrence Welk" is now gone. Television programs of popular music have usually been in the form of musical variety programs featuring a name performer, or the broadcast of concert extravaganzas, or the dance party. In this latter format, the visual interest is supplied largely by dancers, and recorded music is played. If budget permits, there may be a "guest" appearance by a live performer or band. In the past few years, the on-stage antics of live bands have grown increasingly bizarre, we suspect in part because of TV's need for attention-getting visual material.

And then came the music video, which is television's equivalent of the vinyl record. There is the same symbiotic relationship here as with records and radio. The costs of producing the video are justified by the record companies as part of the promotion for the artist and the song. (However, the videos themselves are now finding a separate market, as they are being purchased by the owners of home VCRs.)

Videos originally appeared on cable channels. The MTV channel, for example, is programmed in a format directly comparable to the format of a music radio station. Now regular broadcast stations are also programming videos, but so far in shorter, more structured programs. As might have been expected from the radio precedents, these videos are now carefully selected by program directors so that their style and sound is appropriate for the intended audience.

As we said at the beginning of this section, very little script writing is done for musical programs. The interviews and commentary that fill the intermission periods in symphony concerts are written, and to do that successfully requires a knowledge of music, but that's not writing for a musical program as such. The occasional semi-documentary programs that follow the history of a form of music or the biography of an artist similarly require research and writing of the narration which bridges musical excerpts. The preparation of a music video, on the other hand, usually takes the form of a concept or treatment, a narrative description of the style, mood, and activity that will be recorded (as with the description we reported in Chapter 14 on "The Making of Thriller.")

Variety Programs

We pointed out earlier that the label for this program type is based on its structure, so we will discuss it primarily on the basis of structural concerns, particularly the relationship between unity and variety.

Early in television's history, when audiences were less sophisticated in their viewing choices, so-called general or vaudeville variety programs were popular, especially the long-running "Ed Sullivan Show." But these types of programs, as several producers have since learned to their sorrow, no longer attract large audiences. Now audiences expect a more focused, more unified theme, even within the general description of "variety." Among the many subcategories are the musical variety, the comedy variety, and, for want of a better term, the novelty variety program.

In the 1980s the musical variety program is most likely to be a special; few such programs exist on a regular basis. The program typically will have a musical star as host or hostess. The basic unity is provided by that person and by the type of music he or she represents. The target audience is also defined by that choice as people who enjoy that type of music. Other acts—guest performers who will appear and who may in addition perform with the host—will be chosen to fit the format (and the audience) set by the host.

As its name states, the comedy variety program puts its emphasis on comedy as a gratification, and most of the acts or activities will include something humorous. Some Bob Hope comedy specials have featured awards given to college All-American athletes, an event that is not inherently humorous, but Hope's writers make sure the awards are presented in that vein. The comedy and the star performer provide unity. Having different guests and acts, and doing some routines as "standup" comedy and some as sketches, adds variety within the overall theme.

Novelty variety programs come and go with considerable frequency, simply because the gimmick wears off quickly. Just a few years ago "That's Incredible" and "Real People" were hit programs, with their emphasis on unusual people with unusual hobbies or performing acts. These programs also added an element of adventure and tension by showing (and financing) daredevil stunts like parachuting off bridges. As this is being written, these programs are gone. Instead, we are in the middle of a rash of "TV Bloopers" and "Practical Jokes" shows. The interest in the activities of "regular" people has been modified just a bit to focus more on the foibles of "stars." To the basic gratifications of personalism, curiosity, and novelty has been added that of big name importance.

We have suggested that these types of programs depend heavily on good structure. Pace and climax, the remaining structural principles, are also important. The programs must maintain strong pace—frequent changes of material. And they must build for climax—put the big production number at the end.

The success of variety programs of all subcategories will depend on: (1) the selection of lead performers who can carry off the role of "unifying force" successfully, (2) careful selection of other performers who fit the theme of the program, (3) structure—a sequence which gives a strong sense of pacing and climax because these programs cannot be allowed to lag, and (4) as always, gratifications important to the target group. The gratifications most easily achieved in variety programs are sex appeal, importance (especially "big name" importance), comedy, and novelty.

Religious Programs

An overview of religious programming allows us to review once more matters of purpose, gratifications, program content, and target audience groups.

In radio, religious programming is an important format in its own right, with stations broadcasting this content exclusively, and with subformats to attract different audience groups. Advertisers may be attracted not only from among companies seeking to sell religiously oriented articles, but from those who simply see a good buy for products of interest to the target audience.

Some religious programs are paid for by stations and presented on a sustaining basis, with community goodwill as a purpose. (A second purpose, to present "balanced" programming that will meet with FCC approval at license renewal time, is not much of a consideration any longer with relaxed requirements for renewals and across-the-board changes in government expectations through deregulation.)

A large proportion of religious programming on both radio and television falls into the category of *paid religion*. A block of time is purchased by a religious organization to present its message. In cable, entire channels are programmed by religious groups. The Christian Broadcasting Network (CBN) reaches over 22 million homes on nearly 4,000 systems, more than half of all cable homes. It presents 24 hours a day of religious and family entertainment, including an innovation in the soap opera format—a Christian daytime series emphasizing prosocial and family life values. It also broadcasts college sports and classic movies.

The purposes of the sponsors who provide these programs are not significantly different from the purposes of the sponsors of other programs. They seek audiences. They also seek to persuade to a point of view, or to reinforce already held beliefs and attitudes on religious, political, and social topics. And they seek viewer contributions. In recent years, the amounts of money viewers have contributed to religious organizations as a result of pleas for funds delivered on the air have paid for some very elaborate production studios and provided substantial stipends for video preachers. Broadcast religion is a large and lucrative industry.

The gratifications provided by religious programs are only slightly more limited than those for programming as a whole. Sex appeal and action are not prominent, but even they are found in CBN's soap operas and sports programming. Value and importance, on the other hand, are strong.

Programming that can be labeled as religious represents again a wide range of content and form—music, talk, discussion shows, and many others, all overlaid with spiritual concerns. These are programs, for the most part, which do require scripts, and thus there are opportunities for writers in this area.

Conclusion

Every program is unique in some way (although sometimes it seems that some programs try very hard to be as similar to a successful show as they can). We could in no way include in this chapter or this book all the programs or even all of the fairly large categories that exist, and it would be of little value to you even if we tried. You will have to operate as writer, producer, director, or in whatever capacity you enter the industry, in a climate that is constantly changing.

What we have done is give you a foundation of principles that have endured and should serve for some time to come, and then to select some common types of programs and broadly described situations in which these programs are applied. You can use what you have learned from this text as a guide to the programming and writing decisions you will have to make, and you can come back from time to time to refresh your memory. In time, the processes described here will become second nature to you. You will make your own judgments and write copy based on what has worked well for you, plus what you learn from colleagues. We believe that until you have that professional background, this book will serve.

Exercises

1. Locate "WomanWatch" or "Celebrity Chefs" on cable or TV in your area.

   a. Watch a broadcast of one of them and analyze the program in terms of its structure and gratifications. (Use the materials in Chapters 5 and 9 and their exercises.)

   b. Compare this program with another program for women with which it competes (similar content and/or similar placement in TV schedules). What do you find in "WomanWatch" or "Celebrity Chefs" that would support their producer's contention that they are not stereotypical programs for women?

2. Write a narrative concept/treatment for a music video for an *older* song—something out of the 1940s, 1950s, or 1960s.

3. Investigate the possibilities for students to become involved with the writing and production of minority programs in your community. (As a class assignment, this exercise could be divided among several students. Report back to the class.)

Key Terms and Concepts

call-out research   narrowcasting
format clock   radio (station) format
gratifications   run-down sheet
music video   target audience

Notes

1. Kerry Green, "A New Idea in Corporate Production," *Video Systems,* June 1985, pp. 54–56. Reprinted by permission.
2. Susan Eastman, Sydney Head, and Lewis Klein, *Broadcast/Cable Programming: Strategies and Practices,* 2d ed. (Belmont, CA: Wadsworth, 1985), pp. 345–347. ©1985 by Wadsworth, Inc. Used by permission.

Part 4

The Writer in the Industry

Our book thus far has been designed to sharpen your talents and to provide you with the writing tools to enter the broadcast industry. We would be remiss, however, not to include before we close some discussion of what the industry may expect of you and, conversely, what you may expect from it—in short, what it means to be a professional broadcast writer.

This final chapter provides an overview of some of those considerations.

Chapter 18

Careers in Broadcast Writing

Given the tremendous range of activity that may be part of the broadcast writer's job, it would be impossible to generalize accurately on the working situations which exist in all stations, agencies, and networks. But there are some aspects of the job which are very nearly universally true:

1. Writing is most often a part-time activity, which may be combined with any number of other tasks to make up the total job responsibilities of the individual.

2. The writer usually works as part of a team and is most often an employee. To be successful, you will have to adjust your own creativity to the goals of others, and recognize the authority of supervisors.

3. The job comes with pressure built in—pressure to be creative and original, but even more important, pressure to be on time. There is also the pressure, shared by all individuals in the industry, to be successful—to make a profit, if that's what is called for. And there will be pressure on you as an individual from those newer, younger talents who think they can do a better job than you, and who are anxious to have the chance to prove it.

4. In the employer-employee relationship, questions of ethics may arise. The writer may be forced to choose between personal values and the goals of an employer.

Writing as a Part-time Occupation

Most broadcast writers, especially those just starting their careers, spend only part of their time writing, and part of their time doing something else. It's quite likely, in fact, that the "something else" will be the primary reason why you have been hired and the writing comes along only as a secondary responsibility.

There are many combinations of writing and "something else" jobs, and the proportion of time spent in each different activity will vary considerably even within these combinations. Here are just a few examples.

The Salesperson-Writer

In smaller markets, in smaller stations, and in radio, the station salesperson also will be his or her own writer of commercial copy. In larger markets and in television there is greater likelihood that specialists will be hired to write commercials, or that commercials will come to the station in completed form, having been produced at an advertising agency. Many people who are employed in this combination of roles see themselves as salespeople first and writers a reluctant second.

Another type of salesperson-writer can now be found working in independent instructional media production companies. This person will have been hired to seek out contracts from business, government, and educational agencies for the production of mediated instructional and public information presentations. As part of the process of obtaining a contract, he or she may be called upon to prepare and present a script treatment to the prospective client. Then, after a contract has been signed, a final script will be completed, either by the salesperson or by another writer.

The Account Executive-Writer

In advertising agencies the title "account executive" is used to describe the individual who is in charge of a client's account. In large agencies the account executive's role is largely conceptual and "creative" in a broad sense; specialists will actually write the copy. In a small agency, one person will be not only the account executive for several different accounts but probably will write the commercials for each of those clients.

The Researcher-Writer

Almost all broadcast writing requires some form of research, whether the script be for a dramatic program, a news story, a commercial, or whatever. Some types of programs require that an extensive, organized research effort be undertaken prior to writing the script. Research is especially important in developing instructional, informative, and documentary programs, where the subject matter is likely to be complex and difficult to present understandably to an audience. In those situations, the writer must take the time to be sure that he or she understands the concepts correctly, and that they are placed in the proper order and with appropriate emphasis. Both library research and interviews with experts may be needed before the script can be written.

Formal research may also be necessary before a writer can prepare the questions to be asked in an interview or panel discussion program. The persons assigned this task will discuss the topic with the expert guests who will be appearing on the program and then organize their material into a series of questions that can be asked by the program's host. Student interns and beginning employees are frequently asked to do this form of research.

The Reporter-Writer

Most radio and TV reporters write their own copy, even those who work for large television stations and at the networks. They do so for two reasons. First, the reporter who has been on a story will be more familiar with the content and therefore is in the best position to be able to organize the story to present that content clearly and accurately to the audience. Second, reporters like to write the copy so that it fits their own personal style of delivery.

Larger stations do employ writing specialists to assist reporters, to rewrite copy coming in from outside sources, and to provide the script for news anchors. Although some anchors do write their own copy, most often the anchor's portion of a newscast will be prepared by an assistant in the news department.

The Producer-Writer

Whether or not these roles are combined is largely a function of the size, scale, and budget of the production. In radio, and in corporate audio/visual production, producer's and writer's roles are frequently combined. The individual will function first as a producer, developing the concept of the program from the initial ideas of the client. Then he or she writes the script through however many drafts are needed. Finally, as producer again, he or she supervises actual production from the script.

In larger-scale productions the producer will maintain overall responsibility for the production, but will be able to hire (or have on staff) writing specialists.

The Publicist-Writer

The job of a station's promotion department is that of "selling" the station itself, and promoting its programs and personalities. In order to accomplish that task, the station will use both its own air time and cross-media promotion—that is, advertising its programs on other stations (TV on radio, and vice versa) and in newspapers. Staff members in the promotion department usually write these promotional ads as part of their jobs.

The Instructor-Writer

This combination of roles is found in the preparation of corporate and other instructional materials. Frequently these are low-budget programs, and there are no funds to hire a separate writer or researcher. So the instructor, who is the content expert, is also given the task of preparing the script. Some instructors are able to translate their understanding of content into very good scripts; others never quite master the peculiarities of writing for broadcast, and their programs suffer as a result.

In these examples we've tried to suggest only a few of the situations and combinations in which broadcast writers work. This list could be almost endless, for every situation is unique in some respect. Note, however, this obvious lesson for the person who is starting out and who wants a job as a writer in broadcasting: Become adept at some other skills as well. Learn to be a reporter, or learn public relations and promotion, or sales, because probably you will need at least one of these other skills in addition to your ability to write in order to get that first job.

We do not mean to suggest that all broadcast writing jobs are part-time; there are full-time positions that are exclusively or at least largely devoted to writing. These are more likely to be found in larger markets, at larger stations, at larger agencies handling bigger accounts, and at the radio and television networks, where there is greater opportunity for specialization. These openings are not entry-level positions, but are filled by writers who have learned their craft in combination jobs like those described above.

The Writer as Part of a Team

In the descriptions above, we have emphasized that the broadcast writer is part of a team. The writer's place in the team is somewhere in the middle of the creative process. Before the writer can prepare a script, decisions have to be made by managers and sponsors on purpose, scope, budget, form, and so on. We provided a general review of that process in Chapter 8, when we considered the relationship between programming and advertising in the broadcast industry. We also digressed from the direct discussion of writing principles at other places in order to consider such topics as sponsor's purposes, target audiences, and audience gratifications. We believe that the writer must understand how those preliminary programming and audience decisions establish the parameters within which the script is written.

Another limitation placed on the script writer is budget. One producer put it this way:

> Contrary to general belief, programs are recorded not on magnetic tape, but on adding machine tape. Dollars make the reels go 'round, so—talk to the producer and find out what the program budget is.[1]

It makes no sense to write a script that calls for location shooting if the decision has already been made that the program will be produced in a studio to keep costs down.

Recognize too that the broadcast writer is nearly always an employee or representative. He or she may work for a station or an advertising agency, or a corporate media production department, or in any of the other situations we have described. Writers who are both employees and parts of a creative team must learn to subject their creative individuality to the client's goals and to the control of supervisors.

All professional writers must adjust their inspiration to the realities of the marketplace in which they hope to sell their work, but the writers of novels, short stories, and other print writing, who often work freelance, have somewhat greater control over the final shape of their work than do broadcast writers. After the broadcast writer has completed his or her script, it is unlikely (unless the writer is also the producer) that he or she will have any further influence on the final shape of the program. The actual creation—rehearsal, production, recording, editing—will be done by others. Some individuals become frustrated by having to leave the creative process before the completion of the final product.

Not all broadcast writers are employees. There is some opportunity for the freelance writer, especially in two areas. Some network dramatic programs accept freelance submissions. A substantial amount of the writing of corporate/instructional presentations is also handled by freelancers, who work under contract with the corporate clients or the independent production houses that produce for those clients.

Pressure

Recognize at the outset that in broadcasting there are deadlines—daily, even hourly, in some cases. Broadcasting runs on time. Live broadcasts go on the air at the time they are scheduled, to the second. Prerecorded programs must be of exact length. Usually there will be a fixed schedule of days or hours set aside for production, and a preestablished budget. Extra time for rehearsal, production, or editing means extra money, a commodity sponsors are reluctant to part with.

The implication for the writer is that the script must be ready on time. At some point there no longer is any more time for additional research or for another rewrite to polish the dialogue or narration. When air time or the scheduled production time arrives, the script must be there. Without the writer's contribution—a script—other people cannot do their jobs. The news announcer won't be able to read the news, or the entire cast and crew assembled to record a dramatic program will be idled.

Another aspect of pressure is the constant demand to be original. Not only must the script be written to meet a deadline, it is expected to be a good script—to follow the principles of good broadcast writing and to be different, distinctive, even unique. For commercial copy, it's also a good thing for the script to be successful—that is, to accomplish the advertiser's purpose of selling the product!

Not all scripts meet this criterion of originality. A lot of broadcast writing is ordinary, banal, crass. The industry is regularly criticized for turning out mediocre writing and programming. But when the tremendous quantity of material that has to be written every hour and every day is considered, the lack of consistent creativity may at least be understood. Even the best writers can't write truly creative, distinctive scripts every time. But knowledge of that fact doesn't reduce the pressure from producers, sponsors, and audiences, who expect the writer to create a masterpiece for every broadcast.

Yet another form of pressure is the general pressure felt throughout the industry to be successful—to draw audiences, to sell advertising, to make a profit. Writers participate in this pressure because it is their copy that is expected to accomplish the goals that mean success.

Finally, there are more people seeking careers in broadcasting than there are jobs in the industry. There are new, young talents seeking the job you just won not so long ago. If you falter, if you grow tired or lackadaisical, someone will be there to push you out. Broadcasting is competitive at all levels. Some would say, even, that it is cutthroat.

Ethical Considerations

In the relationship between writer and employer there is potential, at least, for a difference of perception and outlook over what is the most appropriate, or desirable, or necessary approach to a given problem—a program to be developed or a news story to be written, for example. Questions of ethics arise.

We do not mean to suggest that employers are generally or even frequently unethical. Far from it. But there can be, and are, genuine differences of opinion as to how a writer ought to handle the details of given situations.

Ethics and News

In news, for example, very seldom is there a documented case in which management deliberately attempts to control or slant the presentation of news stories. But choices have to be made. Among all the stories in the days' news, which will be placed in the lead position? Which stories in television will be assigned a camera and have visual support, and which will be read by the anchor without supporting video? How much time will each story get? Which facts will be covered and which left out? Stories must be organized so that the audience can follow and understand their content; what "point of view" will best provide that structure? All of these decisions affect the objectivity—or at least the perceptions of objectivity—with which the story is finally presented.

As a writer, you will be faced in every story with this "dilemma of objectivity," a phrase used by Peter Sandman, David Rubin, and David Sachsman in their discussion of journalistic ethics in *Media: An Introductory Analysis of American Mass Communications:*

> . . . it can be argued that objectivity is a false god. All too often, objectivity means writing in such a way that the reader or viewer cannot tell where the reporter's sympathies lie. If the reporter does in fact have sympathies and those sympathies are in fact influencing the story, this simply makes the prejudice less obvious. Reporters who talk to representatives of both sides in a controversy, who quote and attribute every judgment they use, who start the story with who/what/where/when and only then go to why, are protecting themselves from criticism. The story may be no less misleading for all its objectivity, but it is safer. . . .
>
> Suppose a reporter is somehow successful in keeping his or her values from influencing the story. Is this necessarily good? What is the value of having humane and concerned journalists if they hide their humanity and concern when they set out to cover the news? Was objectivity a good thing in the 1950s, when it forced the media to be "fair" to the incredibly unfair allegations of Senator Joseph McCarthy? Ultimately, why should a conservative reporter be "fair" to the scourge of Communism? Why should a radical reporter be "fair" to the capitalist Establishment?
>
> On the other hand, the notion of objectivity does impose a useful discipline on journalists. Even if it is unattainable and sometimes a bit hypocritical, objectivity as a goal reminds reporters that they are paid to tell us about events, not about their own feelings; that they are obliged to talk to all sides in a dispute before writing their story; that they should resort to volatile language sparingly and only where it is justified. Objectivity is journalism's cautious response to its own power. In limiting the reporter's freedom to guide the audience, objectivity also limits the reporter's freedom to misguide the audience.[2]

There are many other ethical concerns reporter-writers must face. Among them:

Deception: [Are] reporters obligated to identify themselves? Doing so naturally puts people on their guard; often you'd get a better story without your press card. Nonetheless, it is generally accepted that sources have a right to know that they are talking to a reporter.

But there are plenty of exceptions. A restaurant critic does not announce his or her identity before sitting down to eat. The temptation to the staff to provide special service and unusual dishes would be too great, and the journalistic goal would be defeated. Similarly, a consumer reporter would have a tough time making an accurate appraisal of an auto repair service if the mechanics knew a story was in the works. Most journalists accept this sort of deception because the reporter is simply doing what ordinary citizens do—eating in a restaurant or getting a car fixed and then evaluating the service received. . . .

Invasion of privacy. The privacy issue comes up most forcefully not in the newsgathering process but in the decision to publish what the reporter has found out. . . . In 1965, for example, a *New York Times* reporter discovered that a prominent member of the American Nazi Party was of Jewish ancestry. The Nazi made it clear to the reporter that his "career" would be finished if this fact were revealed to the public. The *Times* ran the story anyhow, and the Jewish Nazi committed suicide. Was this a valid intrusion on his private life, or was it unethical?

Journalists are aware of their power to damage people's lives. They try to deal with it by not dealing with it. Their job, they say, is to get the facts and tell the public not to worry about the consequences. But journalists are people, too, and in reality they do worry about the effects of what they write. . . .

Withholding information. What about the harm done by refusing to publish information? When journalists withhold a story for reasons that have little to do with the mission of journalism, they are vulnerable to the charge that they have defaulted on the reporter's highest ethical obligation: to inform the public. . . .

Community leaders often argue that publicity makes social problems worse, that the problems might diminish if the media left them alone. The argument sounds reasonable for certain kinds of problems—airline hijackings, for example, tend to feed off the notoriety of previous ones. Assume for a moment that there would be fewer such skyjackings if reporters ignored the ones that did happen. Is that enough reason to justify withholding the story? Is it the reporter's job to prevent skyjackings, or to tell people about them?

Conflict of interest. Reporters are also private individuals, and they are entitled to a personal life and to be involved in community activities. Yet virtually any outside interest on a journalist's part may begin to affect news coverage—or at least raise the suspicion of affecting news coverage. Where do you draw the line? In financial matters, for example, it makes sense to forbid business reporters to take advantage of inside information by cashing in on a tip before reporting it. But to really protect against financial conflicts of interest, we would have to forbid business reporters to own stocks altogether. Is that fair to the reporters?[3]

Even this discussion of journalistic ethics, which we have drastically condensed from the excellent analysis published by Sandman and his colleagues, barely touches the surface of potential issues reporters and writers must face. Yet another concern voiced by many critics is the oversimplification of stories and especially of the issues raised by stories in the news. How can one hope to explain the complexities of arms negotiations with the Russians in a single 60-second story in the evening news?

Ethics and Drama

Parallel issues of ethical judgment affect the writers of dramatic programs. Sexual themes are an important part of the content of network dramas, as are scenes of violence. Both are strong attractors for audiences. Dramatic programs are frequently criticized for excessive sex or violence. Where is the line? Other issues include the oversimplification of characters, resulting in sexual and ethnic stereotyping, and implicit statements made about moral issues in programs—for example, having a soap opera take the position that abortion is a satisfactory solution to an unwanted pregnancy.

Ethics and Advertising

For the advertising copywriter, similar questions arise. Advertising is based on the deliberate attempt to manipulate the behavior of audience members toward the client's goal. Given that foundation, how much use of sex appeal, for example, is a legitimate attention-getting device for a commercial? When does the use of scantily clad women (or men) step over the line and become sexual exploitation?

Ethical Guidelines

For the most part, these ethical and legal issues involve the entire industry, not just the process of script writing. Within the industry, there are numerous policy manuals that provide some guidance on ethical issues. The National Association of Broadcasters has produced two codes (one for radio, the other for television) that describe, in broad terms, appropriate and inappropriate practices for both program content and advertisements.* Each of the major networks has offices which review both program content and advertising, and each has published guidelines for its employees. Professional organizations also assist by publishing guidelines for their membership. We have reproduced here the *Code of Broadcast News Ethics* of the Radio Television News Directors Association.[4]

Code of Broadcast News Ethics

Radio Television News Directors Association

The members of the Radio Television News Directors Association agree that their prime responsibility as journalists—and that of the broadcasting industry as the collective sponsor of news broadcasting—is to provide to the public they

---

* The NAB codes have always been part of the voluntary self-regulation exercised within the industry by responsible broadcasters. Station licensees were not required to subscribe to the provisions of the codes, although many did so. However, in 1983 a federal judge ruled that the codes, even though voluntary, were a restraint in trade and ordered them dismantled. At the present time the only importance they have is that some station owners individually use them as guidelines for their employees.

serve a news service as accurate, full and prompt as human integrity and devotion can devise. To that end, they declare their acceptance of the standards of practice here set forth, and their solemn intent to honor them to the limits of their ability.

Article One

The primary purpose of broadcast journalists—to inform the public of events of importance and appropriate interest in a manner that is accurate and comprehensive—shall override all other purposes.

Article Two

Broadcast news presentations shall be designed not only to offer timely and accurate information but also to present it in the light of relevant circumstances that give it meaning and perspective.

This standard means that news reports, when clarity demands it, will be laid against pertinent factual background; that factors such as race, creed, nationality or prior status will be reported only when they are relevant; that comment or subjective content will be properly identified; and that errors in fact will be promptly acknowledged and corrected.

Article Three

Broadcast journalists shall seek to select material for newscast solely on their evaluation of its merits as news.

This standard means that news will be selected on the criteria of significance, community and regional relevance, appropriate human interest, service to defined audiences. It excludes sensationalism or misleading emphasis in any form; subservience to external or "interested" efforts to influence news selection and presentation, whether from within the broadcasting industry or from without. It requires that such terms as "bulletin" and "flash" be used only when the character of the news justifies them; that bombastic or misleading descriptions of newsroom facilities and personnel be rejected, along with undue use of sound and visual effects; and that promotional or publicity material be sharply scrutinized before use and identified by source or otherwise when broadcast.

Article Four

Broadcast journalists shall at all times display humane respect for the dignity, privacy and the well-being of persons with whom the news deals.

Article Five

Broadcast journalists shall govern their personal lives and such nonprofessional associations as may impinge on their professional activities in a manner that will protect them from conflict of interest, real or apparent.

Article Six

Broadcast journalists shall seek actively to present all news the knowledge of which will serve the public interest no matter what selfish, uninformed or corrupt efforts attempt to color it, withhold it or prevent its presentation. They shall make constant effort to open doors closed to the reporting of public proceedings with tools appropriate to broadcasting (including cameras and recorders), consistent with the public interest. They acknowledge the journalist's ethic of protection of confidential information and sources, and urge unswerving observation of it except in instances in which it would clearly and unmistakably defy the public interest.

Article Seven

Broadcast journalists recognize the responsibility borne by broadcasting for informed analysis, comment and editorial opinion on public events and issues. They accept the obligation of broadcasters, for the presentation of such matters by individuals whose competence, experience and judgment qualify them for it.

Article Eight

In court, broadcast journalists shall conduct themselves with dignity, whether the court is in or out of session. They shall keep broadcast equipment as unobtrusive and silent as possible. Where court facilities are inadequate, pool broadcasts should be arranged.

Article Nine

In reporting matters that are or may be litigated, the journalist shall avoid practices which would tend to interfere with the right of an individual to a fair trial.

Article Ten

Broadcast journalists shall not misrepresent the source of any broadcast news material.

Article Eleven

Broadcast journalists shall actively censure and seek to prevent violations of these standards, and shall actively encourage their observance by all journalists, whether of the Radio Television News Directors Association or not.

Ethics and You

As an individual writer, ethical considerations are limited largely to the single question: Can I work with my principles, within the system?

If you watch television news stories with the suspicion that more has been left out of the story than put in, or that the reporter is telling the story from a biased viewpoint, and if you can't overcome those feelings, then you'd better not plan on becoming a TV newswriter. Similarly, if you have serious misgivings about the role of advertising in society, if you feel that advertising creates false wants and hopes and fuels the American business enterprise at the expense of the consumer, and if you can't overcome those feelings, then you need to recognize now that you won't make a good commercial copywriter.

Some individuals do plan on careers in broadcasting precisely because they want to reform the media—to do the job better, and more honestly, than those who are now doing it. If you are in that category, we don't want to diminish your desire to make broadcasting better. But recognize, please, that reform is a very difficult and often lonely task and that most of the time your result will be frustration—not change. You stand a better chance of personal success as a writer if you don't choose to fight the system.

Fortunately, the hard questions don't come up very often, but when they do each writer will have to decide where his or her values lie and whether they will be compromised in a particular situation. If you are to be a broadcast writer, recognize now that you will have to establish standards, and you will have to live with them throughout your career.

It requires an entire book to discuss ethical issues in detail, and we've noted several which do just that in the bibliography. If we have raised some issues which do, indeed, bother you then please use them to clarify the issue and your position.

Conclusion

If you aspire to a career in broadcast writing, consider these aspects of your job. You are very likely to be hired not as a writer, but to do some other task primarily. You will need to have the skills for that task as well as the ability to write. You will be expected to work as part of a team and to be comfortable—from an ethical standpoint—in creating your scripts and handling the requirements your employer has established for the job. And you will be expected to work under the pressure of deadlines and originality. The successful writer will be able to work, even thrive, under such conditions.

There are a few exceptions. Some free-form radio stations and access TV channels operate under relaxed time schedules, and a few opportunities do exist for independent writers to sell scripts on a freelance basis. But these probably will continue to be the rare case, not the rule.

Exercises

The exercises suggested here do not bear directly on writing per se. They are aimed instead, as has been this entire chapter, at sharpening your perceptions of broadcast writing as a career, and how you might fare in that activity.

1. Arrange an interview with a broadcast writer—someone whose job is like one of those described in this chapter. The focus of your interview should be to verify the assertions we have made, or to modify those statements for your own time and place. Ask your interviewee:

   a. What other tasks are performed besides writing; how is a typical day divided among the various jobs to be performed?

b. What types of research are performed; how important is research to the overall job?

c. How much control does the writer have over the final product, be that program or announcement?

d. What background—experience, college courses, etc.—does the interviewee have for the job? What other skills or knowledge does he or she think are important by way of preparation?

e. What bothers him, or her, most about the job; what ethical problems have had to be faced, and with what results?

Also ask about working conditions, about any problems with sexual or ethnic bias (if appropriate), and other matters we did not discuss in this chapter. Try to get a sense of how, in this interviewee's opinion at least, one should prepare to be a broadcast writer.

2. Investigate professional organizations in your community or nearby that deal with matters of interest to media writers. Among the national organizations which have chapters in many major cities are: International Association of Business Communicators (IABC), International Television Association (ITVA), Radio/Television News Directors Association (RTNDA), Sigma Delta Chi. There may also be local clubs which include advertising and public relations writers among their members. Most such clubs welcome students and sponsor activities that help student members to enter the profession. Specifically, you should:

a. Establish a list of appropriate organizations.

b. Arrange to attend a meeting of each club or invite a representative from each club to speak to your class.

c. Consider joining the club, if its goals are compatible with your own and its members are supportive of the direction in which you wish to take your career.

3. Use the paragraphs in this chapter on ethical questions, and additional readings, to organize a class discussion on one or possibly several related issues. The discussion might be organized as a formal debate between different class members taking different positions on the issue, or as an interview with a guest. Invite someone who writes for a station, agency, or network, or who, as a manager, must make frequent judgments—for example on the content of news stories (an assignment editor), or on the selection of program series to make up a station's schedule (a program director).

Key Terms and Concepts

account executive	exploitation
conflict of interest	invasion of privacy
deception	stereotyping
the dilemma of objectivity	withholding information
ethics	

Notes

1. James A. Gustafson, "Think Before You Write: Avoiding the Pitfalls of Video Scriptwriting," *E&ITV,* November 1980, p. 80.

2. Peter M. Sandman, David M. Rubin, and David B. Sachsman, *Media: An Introductory Analysis of American Mass Communications* 3d ed. (Englewood Cliffs, NJ: Prentice-Hall, 1982), pp. 83–84. © 1982. Reprinted by permission of Prentice-Hall.

3. Ibid., condensed from pp. 87–98.

4. Reprinted by permission of the Radio Television News Directors Association.

Bibliography

In the Preface we made a statement about bibliographies that is worth summarizing here.

We assume you are reading this book because you have an interest in writing as a career, or at least as part of a career in broadcasting. To be successful in that endeavor, you need to have at your fingertips a personal library containing both reference books and specialized texts. The references in this section will help you build such a library, and the comments may help you select from among the substantial number of books suggested.

Chapter 1

Several good references discuss the theoretical process of communication. Among them are:

BERLO, DAVID K. *The Process of Communication.* New York: Holt, Rinehart and Winston, 1960.

BLAKE, REED H., AND EDWIN O. HAROLDSEN. *A Taxonomy of Concepts in Communication.* New York: Hastings House, 1975.

BRYSON, LYMAN, ED. *The Communication of Ideas.* New York: Harper and Row, 1948.

RUBEN, BRENT D. *Communication and Human Behavior.* Riverside, NJ: Macmillan, 1983.

SEVERIN, WERNER J., AND JAMES W. TANKARD, JR. *Communication Theories: Origins, Methods, Uses.* New York: Hastings House, 1979.

A number of popular texts used in introductory courses in mass communication provide good overviews of mediated communication systems. Consider reviewing relevant sections of one or more of these:

DAVISON, W. PHILLIPS, JAMES BOYLAN, AND FREDERICK YU. *Mass Media: Systems and Effects.* New York: Holt, Rinehart and Winston, 1976.

BLACK, MAY, AND FREDERICK WHITNEY. *Introduction to Mass Communication*, Dubuque, IA: Wm. C. Brown, 1983.

BROWN, CHARLENE, TREVOR BROWN, AND WILLIAM RIVERS. *The Media and the People.* New York: Holt, Rinehart and Winston, 1978.

DOMINICK, JOSEPH R. *The Dynamics of Mass Communication.* Reading, MA: Addison-Wesley, 1983.

WELLS, ALAN, ED. *Mass Media and Society*, 3d ed. Palo Alto, CA: Mayfield, 1979.

WOOD, DONALD N. *Mass Media and the Individual.* St. Paul, MN: West, 1983.

Chapter 2

Since the emphasis of this chapter has been on style, the bibliography is limited to manuals and comments regarding style. The standard work on print style and layout is listed first. It should be in every writer's library, even though little of its content applies directly to broadcast.

A Manual of Style, 13th ed. Chicago: The University of Chicago Press, 1984.

Three works that are widely used and highly recommended on the use of language are:

FLESCH, RUDOLF. *The Art of Readable Writing.* New York: Harper, 1949.

PROVOST, GARY. *Make Every Word Count.* Cincinnati: Writers' Digest Books, 1980.

STRUNK, WILLIAM, JR., AND E. B. WHITE. *The Elements of Style.* New York: Macmillan, 1959.

This next reference is one we personally like, and still find useful on occasion, even though it is old and out of print. The section on aural style formed the foundation for this chapter.

CREWS, ALBERT. *Professional Radio Writing*. Boston: Houghton Mifflin, 1946.

For broadcast journalism, these manuals are recommended:

HOOD, JAMES R., AND BRAD KALBFELD, EDS. *The Associated Press Broadcast News Handbook*. New York: The Associated Press, 1982.

KESSLER, LAUREN, AND DUNCAN MCDONALD. *When Words Collide: A Journalist's Guide to Grammar and Style*. Belmont: CA: Wadsworth, 1984.

The UPI Broadcast Stylebook. New York: United Press International, 1979.

And, finally, these entertaining and at the same time very instructive commentaries on style:

NEWMAN, EDWIN. *A Civil Tongue*. Indianapolis: Bobbs-Merrill, 1976.

———. *Strictly Speaking*. Indianapolis: Bobbs-Merrill, 1974.

Chapter 3

The books selected for this chapter are, for the most part, the standard texts used in audio and video production, along with a few more specialized titles, and some production-oriented periodicals.

For audio production:

ALTEN, STANLEY. *Audio in Media*, 2d ed. Belmont, CA: Wadsworth, 1986.

MCLEISH, ROBERT. *The Technique of Radio Production*. Stoneham, MA: Focal Press, 1978.

NISBETT, ALEC. *The Technique of the Sound Studio*. Stoneham, MA: Focal Press, 1979.

THOM, RANDY. *Audiocraft*. Washington, DC: National Federation of Community Broadcasters, 1985.

For video production:

BREYER, RICHARD, AND PETER MOLLER. *Making Television Programs: A Professional Approach*. New York: Longman, 1984.

BURROWS, THOMAS D., AND DONALD N. WOOD. *Television Production: Disciplines and Techniques*, 3d ed. Dubuque, IA: Wm. C. Brown, 1986.

COMPESI, RONALD J., AND RONALD E. SHERRIFFS. *Small Format Television Production*. Boston: Allyn and Bacon, 1985.

MILLERSON, GERALD. *Effective TV Production*, 2d ed. Stoneham, MA: Focal Press, 1984.

ORINGEL, ROBERT. *Television Operations Handbook*. Stoneham, MA: Focal Press, 1984.

PATTERSON, RICHARD, AND DANA WHITE, EDS. *Electronic Production Techniques*. Hollywood: American Cinematographer, 1985.

ZETTL, HERBERT. *Television Production Handbook*, 4th ed. Belmont, CA: Wadsworth, 1984.

Other production references:

The ASC Treasury of Visual Effects. Hollywood: American Cinematographer, 1986.

ENSIGN, LYNNE NAYLOR, AND ROBYN EILEEN KNAPTON. *The Complete Dictionary of Television and Film*. Briarcliff Manor, NY: Stein and Day, 1985.

YOAKEM, RICHARD D., AND CHARLES F. CREMER. *ENG: Television News and the New Technology*. New York: Random House, 1985.

These periodicals are all useful sources for production information.

For commercial and dramatic production activities:

ON LOCATION: THE FILM AND VIDEOTAPE PRODUCTION MAGAZINE, 6777 Hollywood Blvd., Suite 501, Hollywood, CA 90028.

VIDEOGRAPHY, 475 Park Avenue South, New York, NY. 10016.

Aimed more at the local production house or station:

VIDEO SYSTEMS, 9921 Quivera Road, PO Box 12901, Overland Park, KS 66212.

For corporate and instructional producers:

E-ITV, 51 Sugar Hollow Road, Danbury, CT 06810.

AUDIO-VISUAL COMMUNICATIONS, 50 West 23rd Street, New York, NY 10010.

Somewhat more management-oriented, but still useful for production:

BROADCAST MANAGEMENT/ENGINEERING, 295 Madison Avenue, New York, NY 10017.

VIDEO MANAGER, 701 Westchester Avenue, White Plains, NY 10604.

Chapter 4

Many of the books listed for other chapters contain sections on layout and mechanics, and of course have examples that can be followed. For news, both the Associated Press and United Press style manuals (listed for Chapter 2) are very helpful. And for drama, the best reference is:

COOPERSMITH, JEROME. *Professional Writer's Teleplay/Screenplay Format*, rev. ed. New York: Writers Guild of America, East, Inc., 1983.

Chapter 5

We know of no books that cover the topics of this chapter. There is periodical literature on attention span, but we have no ready references to the relationship between that topic and listening and viewing behavior.

Chapter 6

Since the emphasis of this chapter is on sound, the books listed are primarily or exclu-

sively devoted to radio. Very little has been written in recent years on the creative uses of sound; the more recent titles seem to concentrate more on the mechanics of sound production and the manipulation of sound equipment (see titles listed for Chapter 3).

Several of these books are no longer in print, but would be worth buying if you can find them in used book stores. One, already noted in Chapter 2 as being particularly useful in discussing the creative uses of sound, is:

CREWS, ALBERT. *Professional Radio Writing*. Boston: Houghton Mifflin, 1946.

These four are collections of radio scripts, old but worth reading:

BARNOUW, ERIK, ED. *Radio Drama in Action*. New York: Rinehart, 1945.

CORWIN, NORMAN. *Thirteen by Corwin*. New York: Henry Holt, 1942.

LASS, A. H., EARLE L. McGILL, AND DONALD AXELROD, EDS. *Plays from Radio*. Cambridge, MA: Houghton Mifflin, 1948.

MACKAY, DAVID. *Drama on the Air*. New York: Prentice-Hall, 1951.

A newer collection of scripts, this time emphasizing news, documentary, and interviews as presented by National Public Radio, is:

STAMBERG, SUSAN. *Every Night at Five*. New York: Pantheon, 1982.

Chapter 7

From an extensive range of possible sources we have selected the following as providing the best foundation or being the most directly useful in increasing one's knowledge of film and television theory and technique. Among the ''original'' sources of film theory are:

EISENSTEIN, SERGEI. *Film Form*. New York: Harcourt Brace, 1949.

————. *Film Sense*. New York: Harcourt Brace, 1947. (In at least one edition these two titles by Eisenstein are printed together: Meridian Books, 1957.)

PUDOVKIN, V. I. *Film Technique*. 1929.

Other recommended titles on film, television, or visual grammar in general are:

DONDIS, DONIS. *A Primer of Visual Literacy*. Cambridge, MA: MIT Press, 1973.

ENGLANDER, A. ARTHUR, AND PAUL PETZOLD. *Filming for Television*. New York: Hastings House, 1976.

HARRINGTON, JOHN. *The Rhetoric of Film*. New York: Holt, Rinehart and Winston, 1973.

KRACAUER, SIEGFRIED. *Theory of Film*. New York: Oxford University Press, 1965.

LEWIS, COLBY. *The TV Director/Interpreter*. New York: Hastings House, 1968.

REISZ, KAREL. *The Technique of Film Editing,* 2d ed. London: Focal Press, 1954.

ROBERTS, KENNETH H., AND WIN SHARPLES, JR. *A Primer for Film Making*. New York: Bobbs-Merrill, 1971.

ZETTL, HERBERT. *Sight, Sound, Motion: Applied Media Aesthetics*. Belmont, CA: Wadsworth, 1973.

Chapter 8

The emphasis of this chapter is on programming and its relationship with writing. If you are lacking background on the business practices of the broadcasting industry, consider reading portions of these works:

EASTMAN, SUSAN, SYDNEY HEAD, AND LEWIS KLEIN. *Broadcast/Cable Programming: Strategies and Practices,* 2d ed. Belmont, CA: Wadsworth, 1985.

HEAD, SYDNEY, AND CHRISTOPHER STERLING. *Broadcasting in America,* 5th ed. Boston: Houghton Mifflin, 1987.

JOHNSON, JOSEPH S., AND KENNETH K. JONES. *Modern Radio Station Practices,* 2d ed. Belmont CA: Wadsworth, 1978.

QUALL, WARD L., AND JAMES A. BROWN. *Broadcast Management,* 2d ed. New York: Hastings House, 1976.

These critical commentaries on programming, although some years old, are still worth your consideration:

BARNOUW, ERIK. *The Sponsor: Notes on a Modern Potentate*. New York: Oxford University Press, 1978.

BROWN, LES. *Television: The Business Behind the Box*. New York: Harcourt Brace Jovanovich, 1971.

Finally, this is a very useful manual on the conduct and application of programming and audience research:

FLETCHER, JAMES E., ED. *Handbook of Radio and TV Broadcasting: Research Procedures in Audience, Program, and Revenues*. New York: Van Nostrand Reinhold Co., 1981.

Chapter 9

The titles listed for the previous chapter also are useful when studying audience behavior. In addition, consider these:

BLUMLER, JAY. G., AND ELIHU KATZ, EDS. *The Uses of Mass Communication: Current Perspectives on Gratifications Research*. Beverly Hills, CA: Sage Publications, 1974.

COMSTOCK, GEORGE, AND OTHERS. *Television and Human Behavior*. New York: Columbia University Press, 1978.

FRANK, RONALD E., AND MARSHALL G. GREENBERG. *The Public's Use of Television: Who Watches and Why*. Beverly Hills, CA: Sage Publications, 1980.

Both the Arbitron and Nielsen audience measurement research firms publish frequent reports on methodology and current trends in audience behavior. They may be contacted at:

Arbitron Ratings Co.
1350 Avenue of the Americas
New York, New York 10019

A. C. Nielsen Co.
Nielsen Plaza
Northbrook, IL 60062

Chapter 10

One of the major sources on persuasion theory is:

MASLOW, ABRAHAM H. *Toward a Psychology of Being,* 2d ed. New York: Van Nostrand Reinhold, 1968.

These general texts will also be helpful if you have no background in persuasion:

BETTINGHAUS, ERWIN P. *Persuasive Communication.* 3d ed. New York: Holt, Rinehart and Winston, 1980.

BOSTROM, ROBERT. *Persuasion.* Englewood Cliffs, NJ: Prentice-Hall, 1983.

REARDON, KATHLEEN KELLEY. *Persuasion: Theory and Context.* Beverly Hills, CA: Sage Publications, 1981.

ROLOFF, MICHAEL E., AND GERALD R. MILLER, EDS. *Persuasion: New Directions in Theory and Research.* Beverly Hills, CA: Sage Publications, 1980.

A quite different approach to the analysis of persuasive messages from the traditional is presented in:

TOULMIN, STEPHEN. *The Uses of Argument.* Cambridge: At the University Press, 1958.

Finally, these are popularized discussions of persuasion. They were widely read and discussed when first published, are now somewhat dated, but still worth reading:

KEY, WILSON. *Subliminal Seduction.* New York: New American Library, 1974.

PACKARD, VANCE. *The Hidden Persuaders.* New York: Pocket Books, 1957.

Chapter 11

Books that support the topics of this chapter range from broad reviews of advertising and marketing strategies to detailed examinations of commercial production. This is only a small selection:

BALDWIN, HUNTLEY. *Creating Effective TV Commercials.* Chicago: Crain Books, 1982.

BOOK, ALBERT C., NORMAN D. CARY, AND STANLEY I. TANNENBAUM. *The Radio and Television Commercial,* 2d ed. Lincolnwood, IL: National Textbook, 1986.

CONRAD, JON J. *The TV Commercial: How It Is Made.* New York: Van Nostrand Reinhold, 1983.

HEIGHTON, ELIZABETH, AND DON CUNNINGHAM. *Advertising in the Broadcast and Cable Media,* 2d ed. Belmont, CA: Wadsworth, 1984.

MURPHY, JONNE. *Handbook of Radio Advertising.* Radnor, PA: Chilton. 1980.

SEEHAFER, GENE F., AND JACK W. LEAMMAR. *Successful Television and Radio Advertising.* New York: McGraw-Hill, 1959.

WEAVER, J. CLARK. *Broadcast Copywriting as Process.* New York: Longman, 1984.

WHITE, HOOPER. *How to Produce Effective Television Commercials.* Lincolnwood, IL: National Textbook, 1986.

ZEIGLER, SHERILYN KAY, AND HERBERT H. HOWARD. *Broadcast Advertising: A Comprehensive Working Textbook.* Colombus, OH: Grid Publishing, 1978.

Erik Barnouw's book: *The Sponsor,* is also appropriate here (see Chapter 8). Among the many works on advertising, we have chosen a periodical article and a recent and very enjoyable work by the same author:

OGILVY, DAVID, AND JOEL RAPHAELSON. ''Research on Advertising Techniques That Work . . . and Don't Work,'' *Harvard Business Review,* July–August, 1982.

OGILVY, DAVID. *Ogilvy on Advertising.* New York: Crown Publishers, 1983.

Chapter 12

The number of titles in the fields of news writing in general and broadcast news writing in particular must almost equal the number of writers in the field; it seems that every practicing journalist and every journalism instructor must have authored a book. And all of them that we have seen have some worthwhile suggestions, though there is tremendous overlap, of course. We list here a number of titles alphabetically under several subheads.

For broadcast news writing particularly:

BITTNER, JOHN R., AND DENISE A. BITTNER. *Radio Journalism.* Englewood Cliffs, NJ: Prentice-Hall, 1977.

BLISS, EDWARD, JR., AND JOHN M. PATTERSON. *Writing News for Broadcast,* 2d ed. New York: Columbia University Press, 1978.

BROUSSARD, E. JOSEPH, AND JACK F. HOLGATE. *Writing and Reporting Broadcast News.* New York: Macmillan, 1982.

COHLER, DAVID K. *Broadcast Journalism.* Englewood Cliffs, NJ: Prentice-Hall, 1985.

FANG, IRVING E. *Television News, Radio News,* 3d ed. St. Paul, MN: Rada Press, 1980.

SHOOK, FRED. *Process of Electronic News Gathering.* Englewood, CO: Morton, 1982.

SMEYAK, G. PAUL. *Broadcast News Writing.* Columbus, OH: Grid Publishing, 1977.

STEPHENS, MITCHELL. *Broadcast News,* 2d ed. New York: Holt Rinehart and Winston, 1986.

WEAVER, J. CLARK. *Broadcast Newswriting as Process* New York: Longman, 1984.

WHITE, TED, ADRIAN MEPPEN, AND STEVE YOUNG. *Broadcast News Writing, Reporting, and Production.* New York: Macmillan, 1984.

WIMER, ARTHUR, AND DALE BRIX. *Workbook for Radio and TV News Editing and Writing,* 5th ed. Dubuque, IA: Wm. C. Brown, 1980.

WULFEMEYER, K. TIM. *Beginning Broadcast Newswriting,* 2d ed. Ames: Iowa State University Press, 1984.

These titles are mostly oriented to print journalism, but the chapters on reporting—in contrast to those on writing—can be applied by broadcasters as well.

BROOKS, BRIAN S., AND OTHERS. *News Reporting and Writing,* 2d ed. New York: St. Martin's Press, 1985.

MENCHER, MELVIN. *Basic News Writing,* 2d ed. Dubuque, IA: Wm. C. Brown, 1986.

NEWSOM, DOUG, AND JAMES A. WOLLERT. *Media Writing: News for the Mass Media.* Belmont, CA: Wadsworth, 1985.

STEPHENS, MITCHELL, AND GERALD LANSON. *Writing and Reporting the News.* New York: Holt, Rinehart and Winston, 1986.

On matters of mechanics, the Associated Press and United Press International style books listed for Chapter 2 are invaluable, as is this quick reference on legal points:

ASHLEY, PAUL P. *Say It Safely: Legal Limits in Publishing, Radio, and Television,* 5th ed. Seattle: University of Washington Press, 1976.

On news production, this title (also listed for Chapter 3):

YOAKEM, RICHARD D., AND CHARLES F. CREMER. *ENG: Television News and the New Technology.* New York: Random House, 1985.

These next titles speak to other concerns. They include comments by working or former newscasters and critics. (See also the titles on journalistic ethics listed in Chapter 18.)

ABEL, ELIE, ED. *What's News: The Media in American Society.* San Francisco: Institute for Contemporary Studies, 1981.

CHANCELLOR, JOHN, AND WALTER R. MEARS. *The News Business.* New York: Harper and Row, 1983.

GANS, HERBERT J. *Deciding What's News: A Study of CBS Evening News, NBC Nightly News, Newsweek and Time.* New York: Pantheon Books, 1979.

MATUSOW, BARBARA. *The Evening Stars: The Making of the Network News Anchor*. New York: Ballantine Books, 1983.

RATHER, DAN. *The Camera Never Blinks*. New York: Ballantine Books, 1977.

SCHORR, DANIEL. *Clearing the Air*. Boston: Houghton Mifflin, 1977.

SMALL, WILLIAM. *To Kill a Messenger: Television News and the Real World*. New York: Hastings House, 1970.

Finally, this title which although written more than forty years ago is not considered old. It is, rather, a classic in the field:

WHITE, PAUL W. *News on the Air*. New York: Harcourt Brace, 1947.

Chapter 13

For this chapter, we have listed several titles which cover aspects of interviewing. As we noted in the chapter, interviews are used several ways—as the content for interview programs, as the raw material for inserts and actualities, woven among the other materials which make up news stories, documentaries and features, and simply as a means of gathering information, an important reference source. The latter use of interviewing is covered in many of the reporting texts listed for the previous chapter. These titles are aimed more at interviewing as a primary purpose.

BIAGI, SHIRLEY. *Interviews That Work: A Practical Guide for Journalists*. Belmont, CA: Wadsworth, 1986.

BRADY, JOHN. *The Craft of Interviewing*. New York: Random House, 1977.

This next one is very broad, covering many topics in addition to informational interviews, such as employment interviews, counseling, and so on. Still, it contains good ideas:

SINCOFF, MICHAEL Z., AND ROBERT S. GOYER. *Interviewing*. New York: Macmillan, 1984.

An alternative point of view is presented in the following book. It is a compendium of techniques and cautions for persons who are going to be interviewees. For those who want to be interviewed—to promote a book, or a fundraising drive, or whatever—it discusses preparing for the interview. For those who are thrust reluctantly into the interviewee's hot seat, as corporation executives often are, the book presents techniques for turning aside a hostile interviewer. Highly recommended, to see how the other side views the interview process:

HILTON, JACK, AND MARY KNOBLAUCH. *On Television: A Survival Guide for Media Interviews*. New York: Anacom Division of American Management Associations, 1980.

Chapter 14

Although there has been extensive writing about the film documentary, there is no comparable literature on the broadcast documentary. Recommended titles are sparse:

BADDELEY, W. HUGH. *The Techniques of Documentary Film Production,* 4th ed. Stoneham, MA: Focal Press, 1975.

BLUEM, A WILLIAM. *Documentary in American Television*. New York: Hastings House, 1965.

See also Susan Stamberg's *Every Night at Five* (listed for Chapter 6).

Chapter 15

As suggested in this chapter, writing for corporate instructional programs does differ in some respects from writing for regular broadcast programs. It is no surprise, then, that this genre has spawned a number of specialized texts, and that new ones are appearing frequently. Among the ones that we've seen and that are useful are:

MARLOW, EUGENE. *Video and the Corporation.* New York: Knowledge Industry Publications, 1982.

MATRAZZO, DONNA. *The Corporate Scriptwriting Book.* Philadelphia: Media Concepts Press, 1980.

SWAIN, DWIGHT V. *Scripting for Video and A/V Media.* Stoneham, MA: Focal Press 1981.

VAN NOSTRAN, WILLIAM. *The Nonbroadcast Television Writer's Handbook.* New York: Knowledge Industry Publications, 1983.

In this chapter we promised some references to works on instructional design. This first title is particularly useful; all four are good references.

BAIRD, LLOYD S., CRAIG ERIC SCHNEIER, AND DUGAN LAIRD. *The Training and Development Sourcebook.* Amherst, MA: The Human Resource Development Press, 1983.

GAGNÉ, ROBERT M. AND LESLIE J. BRIGGS. *Principles of Instructional Design.* New York: Holt, Rinehart and Winston, 1976.

CRAIG, ROBERT L., ED. *The Training and Development Handbook.* New York: McGraw-Hill, 1976.

KNOWLES, MALCOLM S. *The Modern Practice of Adult Education.* New York, Cambridge: The Adult Education Co., 1980.

Other helpful references include this work by my colleague at CSU, Sacramento:

MARSH, PATRICK O. *Messages That Work: A Guide to Communication Design.* Englewood Cliffs, NJ: Educational Technology Publications, 1983.

and these additional titles:

FLOYD, STEVE, AND BETH FLOYD, EDS. *The Handbook of Interactive Video.* New York: Knowledge Industry Publications, 1982.

SOLOMON, DOUGLAS S. *Message Design: A Manual on Formation Evaluation.* Norwood, NJ: Ablex Publishing Co., 1983.

Chapter 16

Next perhaps to news writing, the category of dramatic script writing has produced the largest number of specialized texts in this field. That may seem surprising, since there is such a limited market for actually selling such scripts, but a lot of people want to try selling their script ideas, and they will buy books they think can help them accomplish that goal.

We made reference to several of the better such texts within the chapter. Those books are again listed here, with some others. Beware, however, of texts whose titles suggest they cover all forms of writing, but really only consider dramatic writing.

BLUM, RICHARD A. *Television Writing: From Concept to Contract,* rev. ed. Stoneham, MA: Focal Press, 1984.

BRENNER, ALFRED. *The TV Scriptwriter's Handbook.* Cincinnati: Writer's Digest Books, 1980.

COE, MICHELLE. *How to Write for Television.* New York: Crown Publishers, 1980.

COUSIN, MICHELLE. *Writing a Television Play.* Boston: The Writer, Inc., 1975.

NASH, CONSTANCE, AND VIRGINIA OAKEY. *The Television Writer's Handbook.* New York: Barnes and Noble, 1978.

TRAPNELL, COLES. *Teleplay: An Introduction to Television Writing.* San Francisco: Chandler Publishing Co., 1966.

We listed several volumes of radio dramatic scripts in Chapter 6. Similar collections of television scripts exist; here are a few worth perusing:

CHAYEFSKY, PADDY. *Television Plays.* New York: Simon and Schuster, 1955.

SERLING, ROD. *Patterns.* New York: Bantam Books, 1957.

VIDAL, GORE, ED. *Best Television Plays.* New York: Ballantine Books, 1956.

A very interesting discussion of the development of a program series, from which we drew in this chapter, is:

WHITFIELD, STEPHEN E., AND GENE RODDENBERRY. *The Making of Star Trek*. New York: Ballantine Books, 1968.

Somewhat similar, this account of the development of a series from idea to broadcast has been fictionalized and made into extremely entertaining reading:

MILLER, MERLE, AND EVAN RHODES. *Only You, Dick Daring!* New York: William Sloane Associates, 1964.

In this chapter we have made reference to the Writers Guild of America and the materials and services offered by this organization. There are two affiliated organizations. WGA, East publishes the *Professional Writer's Teleplay/Screenplay Format* booklet and is the membership organization for writers living east of the Mississippi River. Their address is 555 West 57th Street, New York, NY 10019. WGA, West publishes the "Agency List" of writers' agents, including those who will consider unsolicited material. It also publishes the "TV Market List" of production companies and TV series that purchase scripts from freelance writers. Qualified writers living west of the Mississippi River would join WGA, West. Their address is 8955 Beverly Blvd., Los Angeles, CA 90048.

Chapter 17

A few books exist on speciality programming, but as we stated in the chapter, most of this programming is merely adaptations of principles and program forms to fit the interests of specific target groups. Titles suggested for other chapters can frequently be adapted as well.

Here is one speciality text that may be helpful to radio writers:

*The Method to the Madness: Radio's Morning Show

Manual*. Bridgeport, CT: The American Comedy Network, 1986.

Chapter 18

The book by Sandman, Rubin, and Sachsman quoted in this chapter contains a well-written discussion of ethical concerns. We recommend you study the complete discussion:

SANDMAN, PETER M., DAVID M. RUBIN, AND DAVID B. SACHSMAN. *Media: An Introductory Analysis of American Mass Communications*, 3d ed. Englewood Cliffs, NJ: Prentice-Hall, 1982.

Other primers on mass media raise similar issues; however, each approaches them from a unique point of view. You can get informative contrasts from:

ALTHEIDE, DAVID L. *Creating Reality: How TV News Distorts Events*. Beverly Hills, CA: Sage Publications, 1976.

BRENNER, DANIEL L., AND WILLIAM L. RIVERS. *Free But Regulated: Conflicting Traditions in Media Law*. Ames: Iowa State University Press, 1982.

GOODWIN, H. EUGENE. *Groping for Ethics in Journalism*. Ames: Iowa State University Press, 1983.

HULTENG, JOHN L. *The Messenger's Motives: Ethical Problems of the News Media*, 2d ed. Englewood Cliffs, NJ: Prentice-Hall, 1985.

Next, you might consider these titles, which are reference volumes:

ASHLEY, PAUL P. *Say It Safely: Legal Limits in Publishing, Radio, and Television*, 5th ed. Seattle: University of Washington Press, 1976.

BARRON, JEROME A., AND C. THOMAS DIENES. *Handbook of Free Speech and Free Press*. Boston: Little, Brown, 1979.

NATIONAL ASSOCIATION OF BROADCASTERS. *NAB Legal Guide to FCC Broadcast Rules, Regulations and Policies*. Washington: NAB, 1984.

Finally, look at these titles, which are not

discussions of issues as such, because they take strong, opinionated points of view. They are certainly worth reading, if only to test your own position and understanding against others, on the issues raised:

FRIENDLY, FRED W. *Due to Circumstances Beyond Our Control*. New York: Random House, 1967.

————. *The Good Guys, The Bad Guys, and The First Amendment: Free Speech vs. Fairness in Broadcasting*. New York: Random House, 1975.

Index

About the Author

ROGER WALTERS is Professor of Communication Studies at California State University, Sacramento, where he has been a member of the faculty since 1960. From 1960 to 1973 he was director of the university's instructional television center, and responsible for writing, directing, and producing a wide range of telecourses for both resident students and community viewers. Since 1973 he has taught full-time in the communication studies department. He teaches courses in broadcast writing, programming, management, and mass communications.

Prior to coming to CSU, Sacramento, Mr. Walters taught at the U.S. Army's Artillery School and at Idaho State College. He has BA and MA degrees from Stanford University, and has done additional graduate work at Ohio State University and the University of Southern California.

Mr. Walters is President of the Board of Mendocino County Public Broadcasting, a nonprofit organization that is working to build and operate a public radio station in Mendocino County, where he lives. He is a member of the Broadcast Education Association, the International Radio and Television Society, and the Press Club of San Francisco.